WEBSTER'S NEW WORLD™

WEBSTER'S NEW WORLD™

FINANCE AND INVESTMENT DICTIONARY

By Barbara J. Etzel

Webster's New World® Finance and Investment Dictionary

Copyright © 2003 by Wiley Publishing, Inc., Indianapolis, Indiana

Published by Wiley Publishing, Inc., Indianapolis, Indiana
Published simultaneously in Canada

For general information on our other products and services or to obtain technical support please contact our Customer Care Department within the U.S. at 800-762-2974, outside the U.S. at 317-572-3993 or fax 317-572-4002.

Wiley also publishes its books in a variety of electronic formats. Some content that appears in print may not be available in electronic books.

Library of Congress Cataloging-in-Publication Data is available from the publisher.

ISBN 0-7645-2635-9

Manufactured in the United States of America

5   4   3   2   1

Dedication

To my parents, Robert and Mary Jane, for their encouragement, unfailing belief in me, and for teaching me to finish what I start.

About the author

Barbara Etzel has been reporting on economic and financial markets since 1993 after receiving a Masters of Business Administration degree and a bachelor of science degree in journalism from the University of Kansas. She has written about international financial news coming out of the U.S. Treasury, White House, Federal Reserve, and international agencies such as the International Monetary Fund and World Bank for Futures World News, a news wire now known as Oster Dow Jones Commodity News. Financial market coverage includes writing about the equity, bond, foreign exchange, and commodities markets for news agencies including Oster Dow Jones, Reuters Plc., and Dow Jones. Economic coverage includes reporting on U.S. and U.K. economic data. She also has covered investment banking as a senior editor for Investment Dealers' Digest. Ms. Etzel is the author of another book, *Personal Information Management* (Macmillan Press), which was published in 1996 as a guide to analyzing workflow and managing personal information in order to avoid information overload.

The Technical Editors on this book were George Farra, CFA, and Donald Woodley, CFA.

Introduction

Complexity has increased tenfold in the world of finance and investment as innovative financial planning strategies, tax law changes, and market booms and busts have changed the landscape for investors. Not surprisingly, as complexity heightens, so does the number of new terms that investors must understand.

No doubt investors could benefit from an ally that helps them decipher what the terms mean and supplements their knowledge. That's exactly what *Webster's New World Finance and Investment Dictionary* strives to do. Its goal is to provide a basic definition of investment terms in an easy-to-understand format and then add context so readers comprehend the meaning of the term.

The later half of the 1990s gave investors a wild and profitable ride on the stock-market wave as the value of the Dow Jones Industrial Average doubled from 1995 to its peak in 2000. As the market began its ascent into the clouds, Federal Reserve Chairman Alan Greenspan warned investors in December 1996 about the market's "irrational exuberance." That comment sent the market reeling, momentarily, before it returned to its former trajectory. Greenspan's comment introduced a new, often-cited term into the vernacular and was just the beginning of the wave of new language that investors would need to learn.

As the market continued to rise, the initial public offering (IPO) market took off, bestowing billions of dollars of gains upon investors. Now investors had to grapple with understanding IPOs, which are stock offerings for a company that transforms itself from a private to a public company. Internet companies soon got into the act, and alphabet soup terms, such as *B2B* (business-to-business) became familiar as Internet companies began to sell goods to businesses over the Internet. Telecom companies shared in the exuberance, and soon investors were talking about *ARPU* (average revenue per user), a financial measure that breaks down how much revenue each customer generated.

Adding fuel to the fire were unrealistic earnings and revenues estimates that companies and the analysts that covered them espoused. *Pro-forma* earnings, or earnings "as-if" certain circumstances had existed, made their way onto companies' income statements and pushed GAAP (Generally Accepted Accounting Principles) accounting aside.

The tremendous ride couldn't — and didn't — last, and the market put in its last hurrah in 2000. The next several years erased the historic gains and left billions of dollars of losses in their wake. Not surprisingly, lawsuits commenced and regulators began investigating, which introduced a whole new set of terms.

Many explanations were offered for the tremendous run-up in the share price of IPOs, resulting in a slew of new terms, such as *laddering,* which means allocating shares of hot IPOs to investors only after they promise to buy more stock once it begins trading. Laddering was offered as a possible explanation for the unprecedented triple-digit one-day gains seen in the shares of IPOs.

Soon, regulators were taking aim at research analysts and investors began to hear about the *Chinese wall,* the separation that is supposed to exist between a bank's objective research analysis about a company's prospects and its investment bankers who are pitching the bank's services to lead IPOs and debt offerings.

As companies lost money, accounting scandals emerged. In late 2001, Enron Corporation, which had been a top-rated company, collapsed and ended up in the bankruptcy heap. As the investigations mounted, new terms were introduced, such as *Monthly Income Preferred Shares* (MIPS), which was one of the aggressive accounting tools that Enron used to hide the size of its debt while simultaneously reducing its tax bill. WorldCom Inc. followed shortly behind as facts emerged about its massive accounting fraud.

Accounting practices soon came under fire. Revelations about *smoothing,* an accounting technique that lets companies manipulate when they record various expenses and assets, were made. Smoothing can reduce or increase debt or income levels, depending on companies' needs for the quarter.

Congress soon began passing legislation, which introduced new terminology. The Sarbanes–Oxley Act was passed in 2002 with the intention to improve public companies' disclosure of financial and material information and eliminate conflicts of interest. In the process, the law popularized a whole new set of terms, such as *corporate governance* and *board independence.*

While corporations continued to lose money, terms such as *reverse stock splits* became popular. This financial technique reduces the number of shares each shareholder owns while retaining the proportional ownership in the company. Corporations undertook reverse stock splits in order to increase a company's share price and thus prevent it from being removed from the stock exchange.

Venture capital, which many investors became quite familiar with during the stock market boom, introduced its own words, such as *clawback.* A clawback is a refund that VCs are contractually bound to make if they pocketed more than their 20 percent share of a fund's overall profits based on early profits. In later years, if the fund loses money and the 20 percent threshold has been violated, some of those profits have to be returned to the limited investors.

However, the more everything changes, the more it remains the same. *Bull market* and *bear market* are terms that have existed for several hundred years. While many understand that a bull market is a sharply rising market and a bear market is a falling market, few know the origin of the terms. This history is presented in the book.

For people who like to crunch numbers, the *Rule of 72* may sound familiar. But what is it? Very simply, it is a formula that calculates approximately how many years it takes to double money when compound interest is being paid. Terms such as these also are included.

Similarly, *leading indicators* has a familiar ring. Each month this composite statistical index is released. Less easy to remember is that the leading indicators are ten economic statistics that typically indicate an economy's recovery before the recovery fully occurs. This dictionary explains what the leading indicators are.

Exchange-traded funds, which are open-ended mutual funds that trade on a securities exchange and are designed to mimic the price movements of a specific index, have been around for some time. However, their profile rose with the stock market.

Triple-witching periods, the simultaneous expiration of stock, index, and futures options, have occurred for many years. Now nearly all investors have heard of this quarterly phenomenon, not just professional money managers.

Whether a term is new or old, *Webster's New World Finance and Investment Dictionary* provides an easily understood definition that is presented with a context that encourages learning. With increased understanding, investors can improve their knowledge and thus make better and more profitable investment decisions. My wish is that this book will help your investments produce healthy returns.

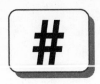

1040 Form The basic form that is used by taxpayers to file their income tax returns. The form is on one double-sided piece of paper. Schedules may be attached to the form. For example, if mortgage interest, medical, and other expenses are itemized and deducted from income, Schedule A is attached to Form 1040. Business expenses for unincorporated business owners are included on Schedule C. Individuals who make a modest amount of money and have uncomplicated tax situations can use Form 1040 EZ.

1040-ES A federal income tax form, used to calculate estimated taxes that must be paid by individuals.

1040EZ A federal income tax form used by individuals who have a simple income tax situation. Single and joint filers with no dependents can use Form 1040EZ.

1098 Form A tax statement prepared by a bank, mortgage lender, or the manager of a coop apartment building that shows how much mortgage interest a taxpayer paid during the previous year. Mortgage interest can be deducted from income, which reduces the amount of income taxes that has to be paid. Individuals use Form 1098 to prepare their income tax returns.

1099 Form A tax statement mailed out to the Internal Revenue Service and the taxpayer by a financial institution that shows how much the taxpayer received in interest, capital gains, and dividends, along with other financial information. The taxpayer uses the form to file income tax returns with the Internal Revenue Service.

10-K The name of the annual report that public companies must file with the Securities and Exchange Commission (SEC). This report includes a thorough explanation of the company's business, along with an income statement and balance sheet for the year. The 10-K report is due 90 days after the end of the company's fiscal year.

10-Q The name of a quarterly report that public companies must file with the Securities and Exchange Commission (SEC). This report includes the income statement and the balance sheet, which are not audited at this point in the company's fiscal year. The 10-Q report must be filed within 45 days of the close of the quarter. It is filed each quarter.

1116 Form A U.S. federal income tax form that is used to calculate foreign tax credits earned by individuals.

12b-1 fees Fees paid by mutual fund investors that are deducted from the fund's assets. These fees pay for marketing and distribution expenses, such as brokers' commissions. They fall under the heading of annual operating expenses. Rule 12b-1 fees are disclosed in a fund's prospectus and typically are less than 1 percent.

1G The first generation of wireless technology, which began in the late 1970s and lasted throughout the 1980s. These wireless communications systems used analog voice technology in comparison to 2G (second generation) digital technology. 3G (third generation) technology is wireless technology that allows for transmission of data images and Internet access.

1Q Shorthand for *first quarter*, often found in analysts' reports. Companies report their financial results in quarterly periods. 1Q03 stands for the first quarter of 2003.

2.5G technology Short for *two-and-a-half generation,* wireless technology that is between second generation (2G) and third generation (3G). The term came into use because of the delay in rolling out 3G technology and products. Instead of making broad advances to 3G technology, wireless companies made incremental improvements in 2G technology.

2106 Form A federal income tax form, used by employees to deduct unreimbursed business expenses.

2441 Form A federal income tax form, used by individual income tax filers to report and deduct child and dependent care expenses.

2G The second generation of wireless communications technology. This phase of wireless technology began in the 1990s and continued into 2003. This technology offers digital voice encoding.

2Q Shorthand for *second quarter,* often found in analysts' reports. 2Q03, for example, is the second quarter of 2003.

30/360 A method of calculating interest that has accrued on a bond which uses 30-day months and a 360-day year.

30-year paper Another way to refer to a 30-year Treasury bond.

3G technology Short for *third-generation technology;* wireless technology on the cusp of innovation, which is expected to come into wider use over the next several years. 3G technology includes devices that can send high-speed data and video using wireless technology, cell phones with e-mail, paging, faxing, and Web browsing capabilities, and phones that can receive calls throughout North America, Europe, and Japan.

3Q Shorthand for *third quarter,* often found in analysts' reports. Companies typically report their financial results in quarters. 3Q03 is the third quarter of fiscal year 2003.

401(k) plan A retirement savings plan, established by an employer, that allows employees to send a percentage of their pre-tax compensation into a retirement account. Employers may match a percentage of the amount that the employee has withheld. If funds are withdrawn from a 401(k) before the owner is age 59½, the proceeds are taxed at the individual's regular rate and a 10 percent penalty is assessed. Many 401(k) plans allow employees to borrow against the money in the plan. Mutual

fund companies often are hired by corporations to manage the 401(k) plan.

403(b) plan An individual retirement account that allows employees of qualifying non-profit organizations to save for retirement on a tax-deferred basis. These plans work the same way as 401(k) plans. See also *401(k) plan.*

4Q Shorthand for *fourth quarter,* often found in analysts' reports. Companies report their financial results in quarterly periods. 4Q03 stands for the fourth quarter of 2003.

501(c)(3) The section in the Internal Revenue Service tax code that describes the criteria an organization has to meet in order to receive tax-exempt status; such an organization is a 501(c)(3) organization. The organization may be charitable or religious, or it may be set up to promote common interests, such as the environment or running. One advantage of being classified as a 501(c)(3) is that donors can deduct their contributions from their income taxes.

504 corporation See *Certified Development Company.*

504 Program A U.S. Small Business Administration program that awards loans to small businesses. Loans made through this program can be used to purchase real estate and heavy equipment, or to build facilities. For fiscal year 2003, up to $4.5 billion was authorized to be lent through the 504 Program.

529 College Savings Plans Named for Section 529 of the Internal Revenue Service Code, College Savings Plans are qualified tuition programs designed to help parents save and invest to pay for their children's college education. 529 plans are created by state or local governments to let parents pre-pay the cost of tuition at an in-state or municipal university. 529 plans are regulated just like municipal securities. A variety of investments can be chosen for 529 plans, with the money growing tax-deferred as long as funds are kept in the plan.

Funds can be withdrawn to pay for qualified education expenses, such as tuition, dormitory fees, books, and supplies. The owner of the account can select the beneficiaries, and benefits can be transferred between one family member and another. The benefits apply regardless of the recipient's age. The funds may be withdrawn if they aren't needed for educational expenses, however, the withdrawn funds are subject to a tax and penalty.

52-week high The highest price that a security, such as a stock or a mutual fund, has traded at during the last year. Typically, the 52-week high and the 52-week low are included in stock tables that list closing prices.

52-week low The lowest price that a security such as a stock or a mutual fund has traded at during the last year. Typically, the 52-week low and the 52-week high are included in stock tables that list closing prices.

8-K The form used by companies to comply with Securities and Exchange Commission requirements to report material developments. Although much case law has been developed to determine exactly what is a *material development,* the term means, in general, something that a reasonable shareholder would likely consider important to making an investment decision. Some material events include a planned merger, an out-of-the-ordinary purchase, the sale of significant assets, the resignation of the chief executive officer, the firing of the company's auditor, or a bankruptcy filing.

A

A shares

1. In a mutual fund with multiple share classes, the mutual fund class that typically comes with a *front-end load*, which is a sales charge that is paid when investing in the fund.

2. In China, the shares of stock that are denominated in local currency and traded on stock exchanges in Shanghai and Shenzhen. These markets have been closed to foreign investment since they were established.

A/B trust   See *bypass trust*.

AAII   See *American Association of Individual Investors*.

AB   Stands for *aktiebolag,* which is a Swedish company designation, similar to *Inc.* Companies with the AB designation can be publicly traded or privately held. The designation also is used in Switzerland.

abatement   The reduction or suspension of payments. For example, a municipality may give a corporation tax abatements to lure the corporation to the city. An abatement also may be used in a contract in the event that some extraordinary situation arises. See also *tax abatement*.

ABC agreement   An agreement that outlines a brokerage firm's rights when it purchases a *seat,* or membership, on the New York Stock Exchange for one of its employees. The membership must be purchased for the employee, and not for the company, because only individuals may own an NYSE membership. The term *ABC agreement* may have gotten its name from the options that the employee who is given the seat has when leaving the brokerage firm. The employee can a) keep the seat but buy another seat for a person named by the company; b) sell the seat and give the sale proceeds to the brokerage firm; or c) transfer the seat to another of the firm's employees.

ABC News/Money Magazine Consumer Comfort Index   A survey, released weekly, that has information from interviews with about 1,000 adults nationwide that took place during the previous four weeks. Telephone survey respondents are asked to rate the national economy, the buying climate, and their personal financial condition, and they are asked if they agree with positive or negative comments about the economy. The most positive score the index can have is +100 and the most negative is −100. The index has a relatively low impact on the financial markets. However, if confidence shows a multi-week decline, it is viewed as an indicator that consumer spending will decline.

The data is not seasonally adjusted. It is broken down into responses by age, employment status, education, income, and gender. It also is calculated for four different U.S. regions.

abeyance

1. A suspension of the title to real estate while the rightful ownership is being discovered.

2. Temporarily setting aside, such as holding a plan in abeyance.

abnormal rate of return   A return on a security that differs from the market's expected rate of return, or the return that a security would normally produce.

ABS

1. See *asset-backed security.*

2. See *automated bond system.*

absolute priority rule   A legal concept used in bankruptcy proceedings that says that creditors' claims are given priority over shareholders' claims if a company is liquidated or reorganized. Shareholders receive a payout if anything is left after debtors have been fully paid off.

absorption rate In the real estate industry, the speed at which vacant properties are able to be sold or leased.

abusive tax shelter An investment that is being used to avoid taxes illegally. The Internal Revenue Service lists abusive shelters and gives people using those shelters a limited time to propose settlement options. Some abusive transactions involve inaccurately setting the price that an asset or business is acquired at in order to decrease the amount of taxes that have to be paid. Abusive tax shelters may involve contingent liabilities.

ACARS See *American Corporate Accrual Receipts.*

acceleration clause A clause in a loan agreement that can be invoked by the lender when the borrower fails to make payments, files bankruptcy, or otherwise breaks a loan agreement. The clause allows the lender to demand that the borrower pay the outstanding loan balance or provide additional collateral.

accommodative monetary policy A policy of having low interest rates; a central bank is attempting to stimulate economic growth by lowering short-term interest rates. If interest rates are lower, more people and businesses may borrow money, thus stimulating growth. The opposite is a *tight monetary policy,* which signifies increasing interest rates. Accommodative monetary policy may also be referred to as *easy monetary policy.*

account executive

1. A person who sells securities and who works for a brokerage firm. In order to be an account executive, a person must pass the Series 7 and Series 63 exams, which are administered by the National Association of Securities Administrators (NASD). Also called *stock broker* or a *registered representative.*

2. In companies other than brokerage firms, salespeople, often salespeople who

work for a professional services organization, such as an advertising agency.

account reconciliation The act of matching a checkbook balance to its bank statement. Charges are subtracted from the checkbook balance; interest earned is added. Checks that haven't been cleared are added back into the checkbook balance. When these steps are completed, the checkbook balance and the balance shown on the bank statement should equal each other.

accountant A highly trained professional who is responsible for reporting financial results for a company or individual in accordance with governmental and professional regulations. A *certified public accountant* is a person who has passed a licensing test, has taken a minimum number of college courses, and has met experience guidelines established by the state of residence. See also *certified public accountant.*

accounting A system that measures, organizes, and communicates financial information about a specific business, government, or other entity.

accounting equation The foundation of the accounting system used in the United States, which states that assets equal liabilities plus owners' equity. The two sides of the equation must always be in balance.

accounting fraud Knowingly falsifying accounting records, such as sales or cost records, in order to boost net income or sales figures. Accounting fraud is illegal and subjects the company and the executives involved to civil lawsuits. Company officials may resort to accounting fraud to reverse a loss or to ensure that they meet Wall Street's earnings expectations.

accounts payable The amount of money that a company owes for goods and services received. The amount of accounts payable is listed on the company's balance sheet as a liability.

accounts receivable Money that is owed to a company by a customer. Accounts receivable are listed on a company's balance sheet under assets. Reserves can be set aside to provide the company with a cushion in the event that the accounts receivable are not paid. In order to obtain quick cash, accounts receivable may be sold to another party that will provide the value of the receivables at a discount from what the company would have received.

accounts receivable financing Obtaining funds by selling a company's accounts receivable. Typically, a company that sells accounts receivable takes less than the full amount for the money owed on the accounts. The advantage is that the funds are obtained now rather than later, which eliminates credit risk. It also allows company management to focus on business issues instead of on collecting payments.

accounts receivable turnover Net sales divided by average net accounts receivable. This financial measure shows the relative size of a company's accounts receivables and how well the company is doing at collecting the money it is owed. In order to be relevant, a company's turnover must be compared with others in the industry.

accredited investor A legal term defined by federal securities law to mean an investor who is financially knowledgeable. An accredited investor is someone who has a net worth over $1 million, or who has a trust with over $5 million in total assets that is managed by a professional. Another measure of an accredited investor is someone who has had an individual annual income in excess of $200,000 for the past 2 years or $300,000 for a married couple with reasonable expectations of achieving the same income in the current year.

accretive A term commonly used to refer to a merger, acquisition, or joint venture that will be *accretive to earnings,* meaning that it is expected to add to earnings per share. When equity markets become bearish and merger, acquisition, and joint venture activity slows in response, a merger, acquisition, or joint venture must be perceived as being accretive to earnings, or shareholders will not be supportive.

accrual accounting A type of accounting system that records income when products or services are sold and recognizes expenses when they are incurred. In contrast, the *cash method of accounting* recognizes expenses and income when the actual money is received.

accrual basis accounting The most frequently used accounting method, it records income when it is earned and expenses when they are incurred, regardless of when the money is actually received or spent. Guidelines govern the timing of when income and expenses must be recognized. This contrasts with *cash-basis accounting,* which reports income and expenses when they are received or paid.

accrual bond See *zero-coupon bond.*

accrued benefit Pension benefits that have been earned by an employee based on years of employment, but not yet paid. The benefits are paid to the employee upon leaving employment.

accrued dividend A regular dividend issued by a company that is anticipated, but hasn't been declared or paid.

accrued interest Interest that is owed on a fixed-income security such as a bond. Interest accrues on bonds between regularly scheduled interest payments, which usually occur every six months. When a bond is sold in the secondary market, the buyer pays the price and the accrued interest and is reimbursed for it when the issuer makes the next interest payment. For corporate and municipal bonds, accrued interest is calculated using a 360-day year; for government bonds, accrued interest is calculated on an actual calendar-day basis. If a bond is in default, there is no accrued interest. Accrued interest also shows up as a current liability on a company's balance sheet.

accumulated dividend　A dividend that has been declared, but hasn't yet been paid to stockholders.

ACH　See *Automatic Clearing House.*

acid-test ratio　The ratio of current assets, minus inventories, to total current liabilities. This ratio shows how well a company is covering its short-term obligations. It also indicates how much of a company's short-term debt could be paid off if the company sold its liquid assets.

acquisition　An act by one company to acquire control of another company, either through an agreed-upon deal or a hostile takeover. Companies also may acquire units of a company, property, or other assets. Often used interchangeably with *merger.*

acreage report　A yearly report, produced by the U.S. Department of Agriculture, that surveys farmers to ask them what crops they have planted that will be harvested in the fall. The report also provides the total acreage planted for each crop.

across-the-board　An action or event that affects a market or a group of people in the same way. For instance, stocks may be rising across-the-board or a pay cut may be made across-the-board.

active income　Income that is actively earned such as a salary, hourly wages, fees, and commissions. For tax purposes, the Internal Revenue Service distinguishes between active income and *passive income,* such as income from real estate limited partnerships or other real estate activities that don't occupy more than 50 percent of a person's time.

active market　Heavy volume; can be used for an exchange or a specific security. An active market is more liquid and has a smaller *bid/ask spread,* which is the difference between the sell and purchase prices.

active month　In the futures market, the active month is the nearest base contract month that is not the current delivery month. For example, if the current delivery

month is August, the active month is September. The August contract will be significantly less active because traders will be closing out their positions in order to avoid having to buy or sell the actual product or financial instruments. See also *nearby month.*

acts of God　A phrase that is found in legal and financing agreements that refers to events that are beyond either party's control, such as earthquakes, floods, or riots.

actual/360　A method of calculating the accrued interest that is earned on a bond. The actual number of days in each month and a 360-day year are used to calculate the interest payments.

actual/actual　A method of calculating the accrued interest that is earned on a bond. The actual number of days in each month and the actual number of days in the year are used to calculate the interest payments.

actuary　A specialist in mathematics who is employed by an insurance company or other financial institution. For example, an insurance actuary reviews the data of claims filed by policyholders to determine how risk should be priced. The actuary recommends the amount of premiums that should be charged, the amount of reserves that should be kept, and the amount of dividends paid. Actuaries in other companies attempt to project results and potential outcomes by analyzing numerical data.

ACUs　See *Asian currency units.*

ad valorem　A Latin term that means "according to the value." It frequently is used to refer to a way of assessing taxes on property or duties on goods in which a percentage of the value of the item is paid as the tax or duty.

additional paid-in capital　Capital that is received from investors after the initial capital infusion from when the company was established. Also called *contributed capital.*

adequacy of coverage　The extent to which the value of an asset, such as real estate, an investment, or a security, is insulated from loss either through insurance coverage or by hedging using futures contracts.

adjustable-rate mortgage A mortgage with an interest rate that will rise or fall over time as interest rates fluctuate. The interest rate of an ARM, as they are frequently referred to, will change every year, every 3 years, or every 5 years. Lenders peg the interest rate on an ARM to an index. For example, a lender might use as a benchmark the interest rates that Treasury bills are paying for the equivalent time frame or a national or regional average cost of funds; alternatively, the lender may develop its own index. Thanks to low interest rates, adjustable-rate mortgages have grown in popularity in recent years, enabling people to buy homes that they normally couldn't afford. If interest rates rise, however, the monthly payment of an ARM will rise in kind.

adjustable-rate preferred stock Preferred stock in which the dividend changes according to a pre-set formula matched to movements in a benchmark such as the U.S. Treasury bill rate. Typically, these stock prices are less volatile than fixed-rate preferred stock. Adjustable-rate preferred stock is quite rare. May also be called *variable rate stock* or *floating rate preferred stock*.

adjusted basis The price of an asset or security that has been altered to reflect commissions paid, improvements made to the asset, or stock splits that have occurred. Adjusted basis is used for income tax purposes.

adjusted book value The value of an asset that has been adjusted to reflect market prices. Also referred to simply as *book value*.

adjusted funds from operations A calculation used for Real Estate Investment Trusts (REITs) that measures a real estate company's cash flow generated from operations. This calculation is often referred to as

AFFO, or may be called cash available for distribution (CAD) or funds available for distribution (FAD). To arrive at the adjusted funds from operations, two expenses are subtracted from funds from operations (FFO): 1) straight-line rents, which averages the tenant's fixed-rent payments over the life of the lease, and 2) routine expenses, such as carpeting, painting, or leasing expenses, which are capitalized by the REIT and then amortized.

adjusted gross income (AGI) The amount used in the calculation of an individual or couple's income tax liability after deductions, such as IRA contributions, half of self-employment taxes, and health insurance and alimony payments, have been subtracted. AGI is income before the standard or itemized deductions or personal exemptions are subtracted.

administrator

1. A person who is appointed by a probate court to manage the settlement of an estate of someone who died *intestate,* or without a will. If there is a will, the person who settles the estate is an *executor.*

2. A person who manages an organization, often a non-profit organization.

adoption credit A tax credit given by the Internal Revenue Service for expenses incurred in the adoption of a child. For 2002, the tax credit was $5,000 per child, unless the child has special needs, in which case the credit was $6,000.

adoption tax credit A tax credit of up to $10,000 for expenses associated with the adoption of a child, such as attorneys' fees, travel expenses, and other qualifying expenses.

ADP See *Alternative Delivery Procedure.*

ADR American Depository Receipts, sometimes called American Depository Shares. These represent shares of a foreign company that can be purchased in the U.S., with transactions settled and dividends paid in dollars. When an investor purchases ADR shares, the bank makes a deposit abroad to buy the actual shares of the foreign stock. Companies issuing ADRs have to follow U.S. regulatory and accounting rules.

advance refunding Issuing a bond or note with a longer maturity period than the original issue in order to pay off that original issue. Advance refunding is done to take advantage of decreased interest rates, which makes the new debt less expensive than the current debt. Also called *prefunding*.

advance/decline ratio A ratio that is commonly used to determine the strength of a stock market. The ratio is the number of stocks whose price rose compared with the number of stocks whose price fell. The more rising stocks, the more bullish the market; the more stocks declining, the less bullish the market.

advancing volume A breakdown of the trading volume produced during a trading session on an exchange by those stocks whose prices rose, in contrast to that produced by the stocks that declined, which is the *declining volume*. By looking at the volume of stocks advancing and comparing it to the volume of those stocks declining, it is possible to determine how strong the market move was. Advancing volume details are published daily in financial newspapers.

adverse opinion An opinion by an independent auditor that a company's financial statements are not accurate. An adverse opinion is worse than a *qualified opinion,* which says that only some areas of the financial reports are problematic. Adverse opinions occur infrequently and typically lead to investors selling their shares in the company.

AEX See *Amsterdam Exchange Index*.

affidavit A sworn, written statement made in the presence of a notary public or a person who is authorized to administer an oath. Affidavits are used in legal proceedings and may be submitted in lieu of having a person appear in court.

affiliated company The definition of "affiliated company" will vary, depending on the context in which the term is used. One way that companies are considered affiliated is when one company owns less than the majority interest in another company. Companies also may be affiliated when they are subsidiaries of a third company. Another test of affiliation is the amount of effective control that a company has over another company, even though a relatively small percentage of stock may be held, such as 10 percent or 25 percent.

affordability index An index that measures how affordable housing is, Compiled by the National Association of Realtors, it measures whether a family earning the median family income, as reported by the U.S. Bureau of the Census, could qualify for a mortgage loan on an existing single-family home priced at the national median. To make the calculation, the prevailing mortgage interest rate on loans closed on existing homes from the Federal Housing Finance Board and HSH Associates is used.

An index value of 100 means that the average family has exactly enough income to qualify for a mortgage. An index value over 100 means that the family has more than enough income, while a value below 100 means that a family doesn't have enough income to qualify for a mortgage loan. The calculation assumes a 20 percent down payment and that the loan doesn't exceed 25 percent of the median family income. The index is calculated for fixed mortgages, adjustable-rate mortgages, and composite mortgages.

afghani The currency unit of Afghanistan, comprised of 100 puls.

after-acquired clause A paragraph found in a mortgage that says that any additional mortgages acquired after the first mortgage is obtained will be additional collateral for the first mortgage.

after-hours trading The trading of securities after the official close of a market. The proliferation of Internet trading sites has allowed individuals to trade after the markets have closed, which once was something only institutional investors could do. Exchanges may have their own electronic trading services or traders may use ECNs (electronic communications networks). However, the liquidity may be limited, which means that the investor may not receive the best price after hours.

AG Stands for *aktiengesellschaft,* which is a German company designation, similar to *Inc.* Aktiengesellschaft translates to "stock corporation." In Germany, all publicly traded companies are AG's, but not all AG's are publicly traded.

AGA See *American Gas Association.*

against actuals A method of settling a futures contract that is used by two hedgers who want to exchange their futures positions for cash, instead of delivering the actual commodity or underlying financial instrument. Also called an *exchange for physicals.*

aged fail A contract or trade between two brokers or dealers that remains unsettled after 30 days of the settlement date. The account can no longer be treated as an asset for the firm on the receiving end of the transaction.

agency An arrangement in which a person, or agent, matches up buyers and sellers and charges a commission.

agency cross A trade in which one broker acts as the agent for both the buyer and the seller. This typically occurs when a broker receives orders from two different customers for the same number of shares for the same security. The order can be processed without sending it to the exchange because both parties already have been identified.

agency securities Fixed-income securities that are issued by U.S. government-sponsored entities (GSEs) that were started to reduce borrowing costs for students, farmers, and homeowners. Agency securities are issued by organizations such as Government National Mortgage Association

(Ginnie Mae), Federal Home Loan Mortgage Corporation (Freddie Mac), and Federal National Mortgage Association (Fannie Mae). Only the securities issued by the Farm Credit Financial Assistance Corp. are backed by the U.S. government. However, because of their special GSE status, the market doesn't demand as high of an interest rate as it would from an equivalent private sector issuer because of the perception that the government would step in to back the securities in the case of a default. However, the U.S. government does not actually back these debt issues.

agency trade A buy or sell order that is initiated by a brokerage firm on behalf of a customer. An agency trade is in contrast to a trade that is initiated directly by the customer. If a customer has given a brokerage firm discretion to manage his or her account, then any trades from that account are agency trades.

aggressive growth fund A mutual fund that invests primarily in common stock of small growth companies that have potential for capital appreciation. An aggressive growth fund does not attempt to generate income through dividends.

aging schedule A list of accounts receivables that is broken down into groups such as 0–30 days, 31–60 days, 61–90 days, and over 90 days from date of sale. A company uses an aging schedule to show how effectively it is collecting on its accounts receivables.

agreement among underwriters A contract signed by the members of an investment banking syndicate that has been established to sell stock or bonds for a corporation. It appoints the managing agents, defines how much each firm is allowed to sell, outlines each firm's liability, determines how costs will be allocated, and sets other rules as needed.

agricultural futures Futures whose underlying instruments are based on agricultural commodities, such as grains, cattle, coffee, or butter. Agricultural futures have had a long history, with the first contracts originating in 1865 on the Chicago Board of Trade. Wheat and corn futures and options have traded since 1877 on the Chicago Board of Trade. Agricultural futures are in contrast to financial futures, which are based on financial instruments such as the U.S. Treasury bond or stock market indices.

AICPA   See *American Institute of Certified Public Accountants.*

AIMR   See *Association for Investment Management and Research.*

air pocket   A sharp drop in the price of a stock or a futures or option contract in response to unexpected negative news gaps. Often air pockets are indicated on a price chart by a discrepancy between the previous day's closing price and the next day's price.

Allen, William M.   The president of Boeing Co. in 1945 when the U.S. government cancelled all of the company's World War II contracts, forcing Boeing to cut its workforce from 63,000 to 8,000 employees. To keep the company alive, Allen pushed Boeing into the commercial aircraft market. Although Boeing remained in the defense business, producing the B-52 bomber, it also produced the first commercial jet airplane, the Boeing 707.

alligator spread   A combination of call options and put options that produces excessively high commissions, making it nearly impossible for an investor to make a profit. The term is so named because such a combination, like an alligator, can eat an investor alive.

all-in cost   The total amount of costs that a bank incurs when it creates and sells a certificate of deposit to its customers. These costs include the interest rate it has to pay to the CD owner, the premium it pays for insurance from the Federal Deposit Insurance Corp., and the cost it incurs because it has to keep some of the money on deposit at the Federal Reserve in a non-interest bearing account in order to meet reserve requirements.

all-or-none   A type of buy or sell order placed with a broker to indicate it cannot be partially filled. The broker must fill the entire order or not fill it at all. Unlike a *fill-or-kill* order, an all-or-none order will not be automatically canceled if a broker can't fill it fully right away.

allotment   The number of securities that each company in an underwriting syndicate is given to sell.

allowance method   A method of writing off bad debts in which uncollectible accounts are expensed in the period when the related sales take place. The allowance method contrasts with the *direct charge-off method*, which directly debits an expense account when bad debts are discovered.

alpha   A measure of the risk-adjusted performance of an investment that factors in the individual risk of the security and not the overall market risk. A large alpha indicates that the stock or mutual fund has performed better than would be predicted given its beta, which is a measurement of an investment's volatility.

Alternative Delivery Procedure (ADP)   A provision in a futures contract that allows buyers and sellers to make and take delivery of the underlying product under terms or conditions that differ from those outlined by the contract. An ADP may be invoked at any time during the delivery period after long and short futures positions have been matched for the purpose of delivery.

alternative minimum tax (AMT)   A federal income tax provision that ensures that wealthy individuals, estates, trusts, and corporations pay a minimum level of tax. To arrive at AMT, certain items, such as passive losses from tax shelters, are added to adjusted gross income. The tax rate charged to individuals varies, though the tax rate a corporation pays is 20 percent.

amended tax return   A tax return, filed on a 1040X Form, that is filed because mistakes were made on the original tax return. Amended returns have to be filed within three years of the original filing date.

American Association of Individual Investors (AAII) A not-for-profit organization formed in 1978 whose purpose is to educate investors about investing in a variety of investment vehicles including stocks, bonds, and mutual funds. The AAII also provides information about tax planning, portfolio management, and retirement planning and offers guidelines about working with a broker.

American Corporate Accrual Receipts (ACARS) The coupon, or interest payments, of corporate bonds that have been separated from the principal payments. It is the corporate bond equivalent of STRIPS, which are U.S. Treasury bonds whose interest payments have been stripped from the principal payments.

American Eagle A popular bullion coin that is minted by the U.S. government. American Eagles are purchased by coin collectors and precious metals investors from traders in the secondary market. They are made of gold, silver, or platinum.

American Gas Association (AGA) The major natural gas industry trade association, based in Alexandria, Virginia. AGA conducts technical research and helps create standards for equipment and products involved in every facet of the natural gas industry. It also compiles the statistics that are considered to be industry standards. The AGA's weekly report on how much natural gas is in storage is closely watched by traders. If gas supplies increase, then prices are likely to decline and vice versa. AGA also creates outlooks for the industry and compiles heating degree and cooling degree data. See also *heating degree day and cooling degree day.*

American Institute of Certified Public Accountants (AICPA) The professional association of certified public accountants, formed in 1887. Membership is open to CPAs who pass an exam and agree to pursue continuing education, along with other requirements. The organization promotes continued learning, ethical behavior, and professionalism.

American Petroleum Institute (API) The primary U.S. oil industry trade association, based in Washington, D.C. API conducts research and sets technical standards for industry equipment and products, from wellheads to retail outlets. It also compiles statistics that are regarded as industry benchmarks. A widely watched statistics is its weekly stock report that shows what crude oil inventories are and how much product has been imported. The API also reports data for derivative products, such as gasoline.

American Stock Exchange (AMEX) The third largest exchange in the United States, behind the New York Stock Exchange and the NASDAQ. It offers trading on equities, options, and exchange traded funds (ETFs). Companies with shares traded on the AMEX are generally smaller than those listed on the New York Stock Exchange. In 1993, it created the first domestic product market for ETFs and listed 122 at the end of 2002. The AMEX is the listing exchange for most U.S.-registered ETFs and a variety of listed derivative securities including equity and index options.

The AMEX is the second largest options exchange in the United States. It also lists over 100 closed-end funds ranging from single-state tax-free bond funds to global equity funds. The benchmark index is the AMEX Composite whose symbol is XAX. The AMEX also allows trading on NASDAQ-listed stocks.

In 1998, AMEX was purchased by the National Association of Securities Dealers (NASD), which operates the NASDAQ stock market.

American-style option An option that can be exercised at any time before its expiration date. An American option contrasts with a European option, which can be executed on its expiration date only. (An option gives the holder the right to purchase or sell a security during a specific time and price.)

AMEX   See American Stock Exchange.

Amex Composite Index   A composite value of all of the stocks traded on the American Stock Exchange. The value of each stock in the American Stock Exchange is derived by multiplying the stock's market price by the number of shares outstanding. The trading symbol is XAX.

Amivest Liquidity Ratio   A liquidity measure that calculates the dollar value of trading that would occur if prices changed 1 percent. The Amivest Liquidity Ratio shows how well a stock or investment is able to absorb trading volumes without a significant move in its price. A high ratio means that large amounts of stock can be traded with little effect on prices.

amortization

1. An accounting technique that reduces the cost of an intangible asset, such as goodwill, by assessing the charge against income over a specific amount of time. For a tangible asset, such as machinery, the term *depreciation* is used.

2. The act of reducing debt by making regular principal and interest payments.

Amsterdam Exchange Index (AEX)   A weighted arithmetic average index of the top stocks that are traded on the Amsterdam Stock Exchange. The value of the exchange was adjusted to 538.36 on January 4, 1999, after the euro was adopted.

AMT   See *alternative minimum tax.*

analog   In telecommunications terms, an early technology that frequently has been superceded by digital technology. For example, to transmit sound in analog, as broadcast and telephone companies did, the frequency is altered by amplifying the strength of the signal or varying the frequency in order to transmit information. In contrast, *digital,* which is now the dominant technology, uses a series of electronic data represented by ones and zeros to store or transmit data.

analyst   An employee of a sell-side firm (a Wall Street broker), a buy-side firm (a mutual fund or investment management company), or an independent research firm that makes buy and sell recommendations on companies in a particular industry. Analysts also are employed by companies involved in commodities trading to recommend when customers should buy and sell futures contracts and suggest appropriate trading strategies.

anchor   A term used by Federal Reserve Governor Edward M. Gramlich in January 2003 to say that U.S. monetary policy needed an *anchor,* or a long-term strategy. He said that a clear strategy would help the Federal Reserve react to economic problems such as a surge in unemployment without riling financial markets.

angel   A wealthy individual who agrees to invest money with a start-up company in what is likely its first funding. Angels invest even before venture capital firms do so. Typically, the amount of money invested by an angel is smaller than the amount that would be received from a venture capitalist, and may be $10,000 up to about $200,000. *Angel* also is used in the context of a *fallen angel,* which is a bond that has been reduced to junk status.

Annan, Kofi   The secretary-general of the United Nations, as of this printing. He was awarded the Nobel Peace Prize for 2001.

annual meeting   Public companies hold an annual meeting once a year. During the meeting, members of the board of directors are elected, the selection of an auditor is voted on, and shareholders may bring forth other issues. Shareholders unable to attend may vote through a proxy, which may be mailed in or transmitted over the Internet or telephone. In an annual meeting, the chief executive officer or chief financial officer typically will discuss the company's performance during the last year as well as its outlook.

annual percentage rate (APR) The interest expense a consumer pays for debt that is expressed in simple, annual-percentage terms. The Federal Truth in Lending Act requires that each consumer loan agreement includes the APR.

annual percentage yield (APY) The effective interest rate from the standpoint of a person receiving interest. For instance, compare two interest-bearing accounts: one pays 1 percent interest monthly and the other pays 3 percent interest quarterly. The account paying monthly interest will have a higher annual percentage yield than the account paying quarterly interest, because interest is credited to the account more frequently, which increases the amounts of funds in the account that interest is paid upon.

annual report Once a year, public companies summarize their financial results, outline their competitive accomplishments, and outline the various areas of their business and product lines to shareholders. Typically, financial results will go back over a multi-year period. The annual report is mailed to all shareholders. Formats of the annual report vary depending on the financial health of the company. For instance, companies that are losing money may produce a plain report on white paper with black ink that is relatively inexpensive to print. Other companies that are established and profitable are likely to produce magazine-quality reports with lots of design elements, photography, and the use of color throughout.

annualized gain The amount of appreciation of an investment during a 12-month period. If an investment appreciates 1.5 percent during one month, the annualized gain is 18 percent, which is 12 multiplied by 1.5 percent.

annuitant A person who receives the benefits from an annuity. When the owner decides to receive regular payments, it is called annuitizing the policy or contract. See also *annuity*.

annuity A financial instrument that pays out the investor's earnings on a regular, periodic basis for a set amount of time. Annuities typically are used to provide funds for retirement. Annuities may be paid for the duration of a person's life or may be set for a certain period of time. Annuities are tax-deferred, so the earnings from investments in these accounts grow without tax liability until the benefits are paid out.

annuity certain A financial instrument which pays out the investor's earnings in a specific amount of money each month for a set amount of time, often ten years. If the annuitant dies before the time period is up, the payments are made to the beneficiary. See also *annuity*.

annuity in arrears An annuity whose first payment occurs at the end of the year rather than at the beginning. Annuity in arrears also may be used to refer to periodic payments that must be made by the annuitant that falls behind schedule.

annuity starting date The date on which annuity payments begin. The longer the annuitant waits to begin receiving payments, the higher the payments will be because the life expectancy period is shortened and the insurance company paying the annuity has a longer time to invest the money. Typically, people don't begin receiving an annuity until after 59½ years of age because withdrawals before then are subject to a 10 percent penalty from the Internal Revenue Service. See also *annuity*.

anticipated growth rate An approximation of the annual rate of return that an investor can expect for bond mutual funds based on the maturity of the fund's bond portfolio. The anticipated growth rate is calculated using the fund's weighted-average maturity and assumes that all dividends and capital gains are reinvested. The calculation also assumes that bonds are held until maturity and are not sold or recalled early by the issuers.

anticipated value at maturity Although this can be a generic term, for a mutual bond fund it indicates the expected redemption value of one share of a portfolio based on the portfolio's weighted-average maturities. There is no guarantee that the bond mutual fund's share price will reach its anticipated value at maturity.

antidilution right See *dilution protection*.

antitrust laws A collection of different laws and court rulings that have evolved over time to govern the anti-competitive behavior of large business. Some of the business practices that may be illegal are agreements among competing businesses, such as agreements on price or related matters; agreements to restrict output; group boycotts, which drive up prices; and agreements among competitors to divide sales territories or allocate customers.

The Sherman Antitrust Act of 1890 prohibits contracts, conspiracies, and combinations that would restrain trade or create a monopoly. The Act provides criminal penalties as an enforcement tool.

The Clayton Antitrust Act of 1914 outlaws exclusive dealing arrangements, tie-in sales, price discrimination, and mergers that would restrain trade and interlocking directorates. It carries only civil penalties and is enforced by both the Department of Justice and the Federal Trade Commission. The Clayton Act was significantly amended in 1936 by the Robinson-Patman Act and in 1950 by the Celler-Kefauver Antimerger Act.

The Federal Trade Commission Act was passed in 1914. It created a governmental agency whose responsibility is to protect consumers against illegal business practices and may catch loopholes in the other statutes.

The antitrust laws are enforced by the Federal Trade Commission and the Antitrust Division of the U.S. Department of Justice.

APAC The Asia Pacific Advisory Committee is a governmental committee that includes representatives from Asia-Pacific countries. It meets periodically to discuss economic and trade issues as well as topics important to the international capital markets.

API See *American Petroleum Institute*.

appraisal The evaluation of a property and assessment of its worth by an independent professional. Typically, appraisals are done on property before a bank approves a mortgage. Appraisals also may be done on other assets, such as jewelry or a business. The person conducting the appraisal is called an *appraiser*.

appreciation The increase in value, over time, of an asset, stock or investment. The opposite is *depreciation*.

apps Short for *software applications*; jargon that is often found in technology research reports written by Wall Street analysts.

APR See *annual percentage rate*.

APY See *annual percentage yield*.

ARA An abbreviation used in Europe, usually in conjunction with the futures market, which stands for *Antwerp, Rotterdam, and Amsterdam*.

arbitrage A situation in which a trader attempts to profit from minute differences in price for the same security on different stock or futures markets. Traders that employ this strategy are called arbitrageurs and use specially designed computer programs to identify price discrepancies.

arbitrage pricing theory A mathematical theory that attempts to determine the expected or required rates of return on risky assets based on the asset's systemic relationship to more than one risk factor. The theory was developed by Stephen Ross in the early 1970s and was initially published in 1976. It assumes that capital markets are perfectly competitive and investors always prefer more wealth to less wealth, even if less wealth comes with more certainty. In contrast, another popular theory, the *Capital Asset Pricing Model*, focuses on a single risk factor.

arbitrage trading program (ATP) A computer program that traders rely on to indicate when stocks or investments should be bought or sold. Because many people use the same program, program trading often produces excessive volatility in the market.

arbitration A binding dispute-resolution process in which an impartial person or group of people hear the facts and decides how the matter should be resolved. Arbitration has the effect of a court order. Many brokerage firms require their clients to sign agreements stating that they will use arbitration, rather than take legal action, in the event that there is a disagreement. Stock, futures, or options exchanges, and other professional or regulatory associations are often involved in administering arbitration proceedings. Arbitration contrasts with *mediation,* which isn't binding on the parties.

Archer Medical Savings Account (Archer MSA) A savings account that is set up to pay qualified medical expenses of the account holder or a family member. It is used by employees who work for a small business, which is usually 50 employees or less, and contrasts with a *Flexible Spending Plan,* which is offered by large corporations. In order to use the Archer MSA, a company must have a high-deductible health plan. For medical expenses to qualify for payment from an Archer MSA, they generally must be unreimbursed and could be deducted on Schedule A of the 1040 Income Tax Return form.

Arpanet The first generation of the Internet, which consisted of electronic mail and software that allowed users to transfer files. The second generation of the Internet is the World Wide Web, which allows people to connect to databases in addition to Arpanet services. Today, the third generation of the Internet allows people to connect directly to the Internet's computers via software.

ARPS See *Dutch auction.*

ARPU Average revenue per user is calculated by dividing revenues by the subscriber base. Non-service revenues, such as equipment or other sales, are included in the calculation. The definition often is used in the telecom industry. User refers to one customer, such as a cell phone user.

articles of incorporation This is a document that is filed by a company with the Secretary of State in the state where the company wants to incorporate. The articles include the names of the major shareholders, the officers, and the number of authorized shares, and describe the corporation's purpose. They also list the registered address for the business. Once the articles are approved by the state, the corporation is issued a *charter,* or right to do business.

artificial currency A substitute for an actual currency that is used in economic transactions. An example of an artificial currency is the special drawing rights (SDR) that were created by the International Monetary Fund (IMF). SDRs are used by the members of the IMF to pay their dues and transfer funds between countries. The value of the SDR is computed using a grouping of currencies and adjusts as the prices of the underlying currencies change.

ascending tops In technical analysis, a chart pattern in which the peaks in a security's price are increasingly higher than the previous peaks. A *descending top* is the opposite of an ascending top.

ascending triangle A price-chart pattern that indicates that a market is consolidating and is about to break out to either the upside or downside. Ascending triangles are identified by charting the closing prices of a stock, futures contract or other financial instrument in a technique called technical analysis.

ASEAN Association of Southeast Asian Nations. A cooperative group formed in 1967 that focuses on economic, social, and cultural issues. It has a political objective of regional peace and stability, but does not require member countries to adopt common political views. Member countries are Brunei Darussalam, Cambodia, Indonesia, Laos, Malaysia, Myanmar, Philippines, Singapore, Thailand, and Vietnam.

Asian currency units (ACUs) Dollar deposits that are held in Asian financial centers, such as Singapore. *Dollar deposits* are funds that have been deposited into a bank outside of the United States.

Asian Financial Crisis A chain of events that led to turmoil in the financial markets during the latter half of 1997 and continued into 1998. The crisis began when traders decided that Thailand's currency, the baht, was too highly valued given that country's financial situation. Thailand had a very large current account deficit, a growing foreign debt, and a governmental budget shortfall. To stop the baht from falling, the Thai government used its currency reserves to buy baht. The effort was short lived and the Thai government had to let the baht trade freely, instead of being linked to the U.S. dollar.

As the baht weakened, so, too, did other currencies in the region, particularly the Philippines' peso, Malaysia's ringgit, and Indonesia's rupiah. Stock markets, such as Hong Kong's market, posted sharp declines. South Korea was drawn into the turmoil when it spent much of its foreign currency reserves to protect the value of the won.

In January, attention turned to Indonesia, which agreed to implement economic reforms in order to continue receiving IMF assistance. In particular, the IMF wanted to reduce the country's use of crony capitalism, whereby many large businesses were controlled by members of the then-President Suharto's family.

In March, the Thai baht and South Korean won begin to firm as investors confidence began to return to the markets. However, by May riots in Indonesia left Jakarta in ruins, and President Suharto resigned after 32 years in office. Currencies

in emerging markets also begin to weaken. Although the situation has stabilized, the emerging Asian countries still haven't regained their former status as attractive places to invest.

Asian option A specialized form of option whose payoff is connected to the average value of the underlying security on specific dates. An Asian option's strike price is equal to either the lowest underlying security value (call option) or the highest underlying security value (put option) over a period of time that ends on the option expiration date. An Asian option is typically more expensive than a regular option. Also called *average rate option.*

ask The price at which someone is willing to sell a financial contract or security. Also synonymous with sell.

Aspirin An acronym for *Australian Stock Price Riskless Indexed Notes.* These are four-year, zero-coupon bonds that are guaranteed by the Treasury of New South Wales. The bonds are repayable at face value plus a percentage increase that the Australian All Ordinaries stock index rises above a predetermined level during the time period.

assay The process of testing a metal or an oil for its purity or quality. The term is often used in the context of metal and energy products that are delivered against futures contracts on futures exchanges and which have to meet certain minimum requirements.

assessed valuation The value that is assigned to a property by a state or municipality in order to assess taxes. The assessed valuation of properties is important to municipal bond investors when the bonds are backed by the property taxes collected by the governmental unit.

asset Cash, accounts receivables, property, or equipment that has value and is listed on a company's balance sheet. An asset may be bought or sold and its price can range from hundreds of dollars to millions of dollars.

asset allocation The allocation of investment dollars between major asset classes such as stocks, bonds, precious metals, real estate, and cash. Asset allocation is a highly recommended investment strategy because it lets investors diversify risk between different investments. For example, if the stock market is performing poorly, then it is likely that the fixed-income market is performing well as investors shift money from stocks to bonds in order to lock in a return. In this case, an investor with a well-allocated portfolio will lose money on stocks but gain money on bonds. Asset allocation is a way for investors to weather market downturns by spreading their risk.

asset allocation fund A mutual fund that invests in a set mixture of equities, fixed-income securities, and money market instruments. These funds are required to maintain a precise weighting in each asset class, unlike a flexible portfolio fund. See also *flexible portfolio fund*.

asset allocation mutual fund A type of a mutual fund that divides its investment dollars among stocks, bonds, and money market securities in order to maximize the return to investors and minimize risk.

asset class A class of investments that have similar characteristics, including risk factors and how returns are created. Stocks, bonds, real estate, precious metals, and cash are different types of asset classes.

Asset Depreciation Range (ADR) System A schedule that the Internal Revenue Service accepts for determining the depreciable lives of different assets. Business managers can select the ADR system or may elect a straight-line depreciation schedule.

asset financing A financing method available to businesses in which lenders look at the cash flow from a particular asset and base a loan on the asset's expected rate of return. The asset secures the loan. Most common forms of asset financing are loans made against account receivables and inventory. Second mortgages also are frequent sources of asset financing.

asset impairment Impairment occurs when the sum of the expected cash flows from the asset is less than the book value of the asset. Accounting practices require that long-term assets be evaluated for impairment. If a reduction is made in the carrying value because of impairment, it is recorded as a loss.

asset management The professional management of financial assets by managers who make investment decisions for individuals, institutions, or pension funds. Although asset management has existed since the early 1900s, it began to show strong growth in the 1970s. Concerns about the solvency of the Social Security Administration increased individual's attention to their retirement planning. The Employment Retirement Income Security Act (ERISA), which passed in 1974, created private retirement plans called 401(k) plans. Those changes paved the way for firms to specialize in managing money for individuals and institutions. Also called and often used interchangeably with *investment management*. A professional referring to the job he or she holds is likely to use the term *investment manager*. A person referring to the industry itself is likely to use the term *asset management industry*.

asset management account An account at a brokerage house or other financial services institution that combines checking account features and the ability to make investments including buying stocks, bonds, and other investments.

asset play A stock that is attractive because the current price doesn't reflect the true value of the company's assets. Companies that are an asset play are a tempting target for takeovers because they are an inexpensive way to buy assets, thereby guaranteeing a certain return.

asset stripper A type of corporate takeover in which the buyer is taking over a company in order to sell the company's assets. The income from the sale of the assets pays for the debt incurred in funding the takeover. The buyer will profit if the value of the assets sold exceeds the liabilities incurred in acquiring the target company.

asset turnover   Net sales divided by average total assets. Asset turnover measures how much each dollar of assets produced in sales.

asset/equity ratio   A ratio calculated by dividing total assets by stockholder equity. The ratio number is not important by itself and must be compared to other companies in the same industry to have relevance.

asset-backed commercial paper Commercial paper that is backed by assets of the issuer and is often abbreviated ABCP. *Commercial paper* is an unsecured promissory note that is sold by a corporation. It has a fixed maturity of 1 to 270 days and is usually sold at a discount from face value.

asset-backed security (ABS)   A fixed-income security that is collateralized, or backed by, mortgages, credit card or other receivables, installment contracts, or by some other type of asset. These securities have become increasingly popular during the last several decades. Government-sponsored entities, such as Fannie Mae and Freddie Mac, have issued an increasing amount of ABS securities that are backed by home mortgages. By removing those mortgages from their balance sheet, the agencies are able to loan additional money so that more people can receive home mortgages.

asset-for-asset swap   A situation in which creditors exchange the debt of one defaulting borrower for the debt of another defaulting borrower. Typically, debt is exchanged for new debt that reduces the amount owed but increases the interest that is paid. Debt also may be swapped for additional equity.

assign   To transfer ownership from one party to another by signing a contract. The *assignor* gives up ownership and the *assignee* becomes the owner.

assignment   The act of telling a futures or options writer that his or her contract has been exercised and that he or she must purchase or sell the underlying security at the specified strike price. At expiration, the exchange or clearinghouse *assigns* the futures or options contract to either a randomly or systematically chosen party.

assimilation   The absorption by the public of a new stock issue after it has been sold in its entirety by the underwriter.

associated gas   Natural gas that is present in a crude oil reservoir, either separate from the oil or mixed in with it. Associated gas may increase the value of the crude oil if the cost involved in extracting the gas doesn't exceed its value.

associated person   A person engaged in the investment-banking or securities business who is either directly or indirectly controlled by a member firm of the National Association of Securities Dealers. It doesn't matter whether this person is registered with the NASD or exempt from registration. An associated person also is every sole proprietor, partner, officer, director, or branch manager of any NASD member. An associated person is also someone who is involved in business dealings with a member firm of the National Futures Assocation that requires the person to be registered with the Commodity Futures Trading Commission.

Association for Investment Management and Research (AIMR)   An international, nonprofit organization of more than 50,000 investment practitioners and educators in over 100 countries. The organization was founded in January 1990 when the Financial Analysts Federation (FAF) and the Institute of Chartered Financial Analysts (ICFA) merged. Its purpose is to educate and examine investment managers and analysts and to ensure that high standards of professional conduct and financial analysis are followed. AIMR administers the Chartered Financial Analyst (CFA) program, which is a three-year testing and study program to certify that investment management professionals are qualified. Pass rates for the CFA exam in 1963, the first year it was introduced, was 94 percent. That rate declined steadily to 54 percent in 2001. AIMR's members are securities analysts, portfolio managers, strategists, consultants, educators, and other investment specialists who work in a variety of financial services companies.

assumed interest rate   An interest rate used by an insurance company to calculate the payout on an annuity contract. Typically, a monthly annuity payment correlates to the level of interest rates. See also *annuity.*

assumption   The act of taking responsibility for another person or corporation's liabilities. For example, a mortgage may be assumed by another buyer. In this case, the seller remains secondarily responsible for the mortgage payment unless the seller is relieved of those responsibilities by the lender.

ASX   See *Australian Stock Exchange.*

asymmetric information   Information that is known to some people but not to others. For example, in a merger situation, the parties involved in the deal have more knowledge than their competitors that the industry is about to undergo a significant change.

asynchronous transfer mode (ATM) A network that divides messages into small cells, or fixed-size units, that establish a switched connection between two computers. By separating the transmission into small pieces, different types of signals (such as data, voice, and audio) can be sent over a single line without any one type dominating the transmission. It provides fast transmission speeds.

at   In trading jargon, a stock is offered for sale "at" a certain price. In a trading transaction the syntax is "quantity-at-price."

at par   At a price that is equal to the *nominal,* or face value, of a security.

at risk   Exposed to the danger of loss. The concept of at risk is used in limited partnerships in which the investor deducting a loss must prove to the Internal Revenue Service that there was a chance of never realizing any profit and that the investment may be lost as well.

ATM

1. See asynchronous transfer mode.

2. Stands for *automatic teller machine,* which a consumer can use to withdraw funds from his or her bank account or to obtain a cash advance on a credit card.

ATP   See *arbitrage trading program.*

at-the-close order   A trade order for a stock, futures, or options contract that is to be executed at the closing price of the security. If the execution can't occur at the close, then the order is cancelled. In this respect, it is a particular type of all-or-none market order. On futures and options exchanges, there often is a closing period that lasts for approximately ten minutes when at-the-close orders can be executed.

auction markets   A securities market in which price is determined through the open and free interaction of buyers and sellers. In contrast, electronic trade processing systems are not auction markets.

auction rate preferred stock (ARPS) See *Dutch auction.*

audit   The process of verifying a company's financial information. Auditors are certified public accountants who are independent of the corporation. An auditor examines a company's accounting books and records in order to determine whether the company is following appropriate account procedures. An auditor issues an opinion in a report that says whether the financial statements "present fairly" the company's financial position and its operational results in accordance with Generally Accepted Accounting Principles (GAAP). Corporate financial statements are audited once a year.

audit committee A committee made up of some of the members of a company's board of directors that is responsible for the overall management of the auditing process and the auditors. The audit committee assists the board of directors in overseeing the integrity of the company's financial statements and also may be involved with legal and regulatory compliance, including the internal audit function. The board of directors appoints the audit committee. The audit committee also recommends whether shareholders should approve the choice of an independent auditor.

Under the 2002 Sarbanes-Oxley legislation, members of an audit committee must be independent directors. This means those members cannot be company executives and they must limit business involvement between their employer and the company on whose board they serve. The rules also require that the board of directors evaluate whether a board member serving simultaneously on more than two companies' boards would impair an audit member's performance; membership on different audit boards must be disclosed in the company's proxy statement. In addition, the rules require that at least one member have significant financial expertise, although exactly what constitutes significant financial expertise is left up to the companies.

The Sarbanes-Oxley law requires companies to have an internal audit function, which may be outsourced to independent auditors. The audit committee also is required to have a charter that specifies the purpose, duties, and evaluation procedures of the committee.

audit trail

1. The papers that validate accounting records. The audit trail shows how financial numbers and conclusions were developed.

2. The record of trading information that identifies the brokers participating in each transaction, the firms clearing the trade and its terms, the customers involved, and the time the transaction occurred.

Aunt Millie A rude term applied to an unsophisticated investor by a market professional. If an investment interests Aunt Millie, it is simple and not too complicated.

Australasia Australia and the Far East.

Australian All Ordinaries Index A market capitalization-weighted index comprised of the largest 500 companies listed on the Australian Stock Exchange. It was developed in 1979 with a base value of 500.

Australian Kangaroo A popular bullion coin that is minted by the Australian government. Kangaroos are purchased by coin collectors and precious metals investors from the Australian government or from traders in the secondary market. They are made of gold, silver, or platinum.

Australian Stock Exchange (ASX) An exchange formed in 1987 by the Australian Parliament by consolidating six independent stock exchanges that had operated in the capital cities of the Australian states. Those individual exchanges had been in existence since the 19th century. In 1994, the first stage of an electronic clearing and settlement system (CHESS) was introduced and was fully implemented in 1996. During that same year, the ASX voted to demutualize, and phase two of CHESS was implemented, which allowed the shares of foreign companies to be settled. During the latter half of the 1990s, the number of finance, insurance, communications, and media companies increased dramatically, thereby diversifying the stock market from its heavy concentration of mining and natural resources companies. Equities, fixed-income securities, and derivatives trade on the ASX. Its lead index is the *All Ordinaries Index,* which is comprised of the largest 500 companies.

Autex An automated trading system used by broker/dealers, exchanges, and others.

authentication The process of validating a bond certificate to determine that it is genuine and not a fraud.

authority bond A bond that is issued by a government entity to provide funds for revenue-producing agencies. The bond is paid for from revenues earned by the agency, or authority, which may operate toll roads, transportation hubs such as bridges and airports, or public utilities. The authority bond contract may include bondholder protections. Authority bonds are similar to *revenue bonds,* which are paid for from the taxing revenues of a public agency.

authorized shares The number of stock shares that a company may issue as authorized by its articles of incorporation or by its shareholders. Often, a company does not issue all of its authorized stock shares. If a company has issued all its authorized shares and wants to issue more shares, it usually has to obtain permission from the board of directors and/or the shareholders.

authorized stock The maximum number of shares of stock that a corporation is allowed to issue. If corporate management wants to exceed that limit, typically they have to obtain approval from shareholders in order to issue more shares.

automated bond system (ABS) An electronic bond information and trading system operated by the New York Stock Exchange that allows subscriber firms to automatically execute orders in corporate, agency, Treasury, and municipal securities. Most of the trading occurs in corporate debt, including convertible bonds. ABS allows trading for over 2,000 debt securities.

automated order system A computerized trading order-entry system that sends single-order entries directly to the appropriate specialist on the exchange floor. The New York Stock Exchange's system is called Super DOT. The Philadelphia Stock Exchange uses PACE (Philadelphia Automated Communication and Execution System) and Autom (Automated Options Market). The NASDAQ stock market uses the Small Order Execution System (SOES), which automatically executes agency orders in NASDAQ SmallCap securities for 1,000 shares or less. Another system is Auto-Ex.

Automatic Clearing House (ACH) A nationwide electronic funds transfer network that lets financial institutions distribute electronic credit and debit entries to bank accounts and settle them. The ACH enables banks to settle accounts with other banks.

automatic extension The extension that is granted by the Internal Revenue Service to taxpayers giving them 90 additional days beyond the April 15 deadline to file their tax returns.

automatic funds transfer The movement of funds from one account to another using electronic technology.

automatic investment program An investment plan where money is added automatically each month (or at another interval) to a checking account, savings account, mutual fund, or another investment vehicle.

automatic rebalancing A portfolio-management process in which investments that have appreciated are sold in order to take a profit and the profits are reinvested into sectors that are out of favor. Automatic rebalancing helps investors keep the asset allocation of their portfolios in line with their stated investment goals. Often, automatic rebalancing is used for managing mutual funds, retirement accounts and variable annuities.

automatic stay A provision allowed under U.S. Bankruptcy law that prevents the commencement or continuation of most judicial, administrative, or other proceedings against the debtor or the debtor's estate after bankruptcy is filed. The purpose behind an automatic stay is to give breathing room to a debtor filing a Chapter 11 or Chapter 13 bankruptcy, and to give a Chapter 7 trustee the time and protection to administer the assets of the estate. The automatic stay also stops Chapter 7 debtors from being pressured by collection agencies. However, anyone who doesn't want to abide by the automatic stay can file a motion with the bankruptcy court and ask for an exception.

automatic withdrawal   A type of mutual fund that lets shareholders receive a fixed payment from dividends on a monthly or quarterly basis.

average   A number arrived at by totaling a set of values and then dividing that sum by the number of values in the set. Averages, such as the Dow Jones Industrial Average (DJIA), are cited as a measure of the stock market's performance. To arrive at the DJIA, the prices of the 30 stocks in the DJIA are added and divided by an adjusted divisor whose value is printed daily in the *Wall Street Journal*.

average accounting return   The average return that is calculated on an investment. It is calculated by taking the average projected earnings after taxes and depreciation and dividing them by the average book value of the investment during its projected lifetime.

average annual return   While this term has many different uses, it generally means the annually compounded return that would have been produced for a mutual fund or other investment's cumulative total returns if the performance had been constant over the entire period. Average annual return is used to smooth out variations in a fund's return and is not the same as individual fiscal year results.

average cost

1. The average cost of shares of a stock or mutual fund that were bought at different prices over a period of time.

2. In a manufacturing context, the total amount of costs divided by the number of units produced.

average cost inventory method   A method of pricing inventory at the average cost of goods that are available for sale

during the period. The average cost is computed by dividing the total cost of goods available for sale by the total units available for sale. The average unit cost is applied to the units in ending inventory.

average daily balance

1. A method that credit card companies use to calculate how much interest is owed by a customer.

2. A method used by a bank or savings and loan to calculate how much interest is payable to the customer in the case of a savings account or interest-bearing checking account.

average days payable   A ratio calculated by dividing 365 days by the payables turnover ratio. *Payables turnover ratio* is calculated by adding cost of goods sold to any change in inventory and dividing that number by average accounts payable. Average days payable gives an idea of how much time passes before a company pays its accounts payables. If the time increases, then the company may be having difficulty paying its bills.

average days' inventory on hand   The number of days in the year divided by *inventory turnover*, which is cost of goods sold divided by average inventory. The ratio shows how many times inventory turns over during a year, which indicates how vibrant sales are.

average down   An investment strategy that reduces the average cost of shares purchased. When prices are falling, then the same amount of money buys more shares. See also *average up*.

average life   The average number of years before the principal of a debt or mortgage remains outstanding. Businesses calculate average life; individuals typically do not. Also called *weighted-average life*.

average maturity   The average time before bonds or other fixed-income investments mature. Often cited as a measure in mutual fund portfolios. The longer the average maturity, the greater the risk of rising interest rates.

average rate of return (ARR) The ratio of the average cash flow received to the amount of funds invested.

average receivable collection period The amount of receivables turnover (net sales divided by average receivables) divided by the average receivables to calculate how many times during the year that accounts receivable turns over. *Average receivables* are equal to the sum of beginning receivables and ending receivables, divided by two. The number alone doesn't provide much information. It must be compared to average receivable collection periods for other companies in the industry, as well as past collection periods, to find out if collection times are increasing or decreasing.

average tax rate The amount of taxes paid as a percentage of income. The average tax rate is calculated by combining the different rates weighted to the payment amounts in order to arrive at an average tax rate. Corporations usually have an average tax rate of 35 percent to 40 percent. The rate declines if a company's profits fall and it often rises as profits increase.

average up An investment strategy used in a rising market that is designed to reduce the overall cost of purchasing securities. For example, purchasing equal amounts of shares at $40, $43, $45, and $49 means that the average share cost is $44.25.

away from the market In a limit order, a situation in which an order to buy is lower than the current market price for the security or in which the offer price, or sell price, is higher than the current market price. The opposite is *in-line order*. Away-from-the-market orders typically are held for later execution, unless they are specified as fill-or-kill orders.

B

B share

    1. A type of mutual fund share that has a *back-end load,* a sales charge that is deferred until the money is withdrawn. Mutual fund shares also have other classes of shares with different fee structures.

    2. A Chinese stock share that can be purchased by foreign investors.

    3. A type of corporate stock. The characteristics of these class B shares will vary among each company.

B.T.U.   See *British thermal units.*

B2B   See *business-to-business.*

baby bond   A bond with a par value of $1,000 or less. Baby bonds allow small investors to invest in bonds and give smaller corporations a chance to sell bonds. The small issue size means that large institutional investors typically ignore this debt issue. Because baby bonds are sold to a smaller market, they lack the liquidity of large corporate bond issues and thus have higher costs associated with them.

back months   Futures contracts that have the longest time before expiration. In contrast to *front month,* which is the futures contract that will expire next. Typically the front month is the most actively traded futures contract.

back office   Departments that manage banks or financial companies' accounting, administrative, information technology, and trading settlement operations. Those departments support the firms' trading and underwriting activities but do not interact with clients. Typically, back offices are located in office space that is away from prime real estate, where the company's headquarters are.

back up   A term used in the fixed-income market when prices fall and yields rise. Another use for this term occurs when an investor moves funds from a five-year note and puts them into a two-year note. This term is also used to refer to a market that reverses an upward trend and *backs up.*

back-and-fill   Price action, for a stock or other financial instrument, that isn't indicative of a substantial trend; prices remain in a narrow range. Prices rise, but then fall back, filling in the space on a price chart inside a larger price movement.

back-end load   A sales commission paid by an investor who purchases shares in a mutual fund or an annuity. Back-end loads are charged when the investor sells the investment. Often the sales charge, which is called a *load,* decreases the longer the investment is held, until some point, often several years out, when the sales charge disappears. Also called *redemption fee* or *deferred sales charge.*

backstop   A type of insurance. Underwriters for a stock or bond issue have a backstop in place to make sure that the security issue will be purchased. To do so, the underwriters assemble a group of sub-underwriters, often institutional investors who are prepared to take a certain share of the offering that remains unsold. This type of underwriting deal may be called a *back-stopped deal* or a *firm-commitment underwriting deal.* Backstop also refers to a government agency or loan guarantee program that will insure a company's debt or its credit line.

backstopped deal   A type of underwriting deal in which the underwriter offers a firm commitment to purchase the company's securities, thereby assuming the risk if the deal is poorly received by the market. The underwriters' fee is the *spread,* the difference between the price at which the securities were purchased from the company and the price at which they were sold to the public. Also called *firm-commitment underwriting* or *bought deal.*

backwardation In the futures market, a situation in which the price of the nearest, or active contract, is higher than the price of contracts further in the future. Typically, prices increase as the delivery months extend into the future. Backwardation occurs because, as a commodity or financial instrument is held for a longer period of time, it carries charges (such as storage charges), interest expenses, and insurance that have to be paid. Backwardation occurs only in unusual circumstances. A current shortage of product is one situation in which backwardation occurs.

bad debt Accounts receivable that are unlikely to be paid. Companies typically write off bad debts, setting up a special reserve account that they then charge. In a recession or tough economic times, the amount of bad debt increases. Companies, as well as small business owners, can write off the bad debt as a business deduction on their income taxes.

baht The currency unit of Thailand, comprised of 100 satang.

balance of payments A country's international transactions over a specific time period, usually a quarter or a year. It tabulates the inflows and outflows of goods, services, and investment flows for a country. Balance of payment includes 1) a current account, which primarily measures the flow of goods and services and earnings on investments; 2) a capital account, which measures capital transfers, the transfer of fixed assets, and inheritance taxes; and 3) a financial account, which records transfer of financial capital and non-financial capital such as U.S.-owned assets abroad, foreign-owned assets in the United States, and the purchase and sale of non-produced assets such as patents, trademarks, copyrights, franchises, and leases.

balance sheet A financial statement that shows a company's level of assets, liabilities, and shareholders' equity. In the accounting system used in the U.S., the assets listed on a company's balance sheet equal both the liabilities and shareholders' equity of the company.

balanced fund A mutual fund that invests in a mix of equity securities and bonds with the objective of conserving the principal, providing income, and achieving long-term growth of both principal and income.

balboa The currency unit of Panama, comprised of 100 centesimos.

balloon mortgage A mortgage whose interest and principal payment won't result in the loan being paid in full at the end of the mortgage term. The final payment on the mortgage is significantly larger than the regular payment and is called a *balloon payment*. Balloon mortgages, as well as balloon loans, often are used when the debtor expects either to refinance the loan closer to maturity or expects a large cash infusion to pay off the debt.

bandwidth The amount of digital data that can be transmitted over a computer network, or another communications device, during a given time. Digital devices measure bandwidth in bits per second (bps) or kilobits per second (kbps). The term also may be used informally to refer to an ability to complete a project or task.

bank A financial business chartered by state or federal government that takes in deposits from individuals and businesses. Banks then lend the money to other individuals and businesses that need cash. Banks also offer a variety of financial and investment products, such as checking and savings accounts, certificates of deposit, loans, and mortgages. In recent years, banks have added online bill payment services and online banking. Accounts at banks are insured by the Federal Deposit Insurance Corp. (FDIC) for up to $100,000 per account.

bank examination A periodic review of: a bank's assets and liabilities, as listed on its balance sheet; the competence of bank management; the quality of bank assets, especially loans; and the bank's compliance with state or federal banking regulations.

Bank examinations are conducted by the bank's supervisory agency in order to detect problems at a bank before they become so serious as to result in the closure of the bank and investors' loss of funds.

bank holding company An entity that owns or controls one or more banks as well as insurance or brokerage firms. The Glass Steagall Act of 1933 prevented banks from owning brokerage firms or insurance companies, but that law was repealed in 1999 with the passage of the Financial Services Modernization Act. The 1999 law also did away with the prohibition against commercial banks engaging in underwriting activities such as raising debt and equity capital for their clients.

The Federal Reserve Board of Governors has responsibility for regulating and supervising bank holding companies. Typically, supervision includes approving acquisitions and inspecting the operations of such companies. The Federal Reserve still has authority even though a bank owned by a holding company may be under the primary supervision of the Federal Deposit Insurance Corp. (FDIC) or Comptroller of the Currency.

Bank of England The British central bank, which is responsible for printing money for England. In 1998, the Bank, which was founded in 1694 as the government's banker and debt manager, assumed the additional responsibility for setting interest rates, which makes it one of the world's oldest independent central banks. The Bank's Monetary Policy Committee sets interest rates. The Committee meets once a month and releases its minutes two weeks after its last meeting. The Bank's goal is to focus on price stability while simultaneously supporting the government's policy of growth and employment. In 1998 the Bank's regulatory functions were transferred to a newly created Financial Services Authority.

Bank of International Settlements (BIS) An international organization, based in Basel, Switzerland, that acts as a central bank for the banks of major industrial countries. The BIS was chartered in 1930 by a group of European central banks and has evolved since the 1960s into an influential institution that hosts periodic meetings of central bankers from the most developed countries. Through communication and research, the BIS attempts to create cooperation and set up the conditions for worldwide financial stability. In 1988, the BIS developed the risk-based capital standard, which classifies loans and other bank assets by risk. The risk-based capital standard was adopted by banks in the Group of 10 countries: Belgium, Canada, France, Germany, Italy, Japan, the Netherlands, Sweden, the United Kingdom, and the United States. A latecomer and an eleventh member Switzerland, however the name G-10 was retained.

Bank of Japan (BOJ) Japan's central bank, which is responsible for a variety of monetary policy functions. Its mission is to pursue price stability. It also is responsible for maintaining an electronic settlement system to transfer treasury funds, receiving tax payments, paying public works expenditures, and handling public pension accounts. The BOJ provides accounting services for government agencies, issues banknotes (called *Bank of Japan notes*), and issues securities for the government. The BOJ also carries out intervention policies in the foreign exchange market for the Ministry of Finance.

Bank Secrecy Act A federal law requiring banks to report cash transactions that are over $10,000. The law also increases the record keeping that banks have to undertake, and was passed with the purpose of cracking down on money laundering of funds received through illegal means. Banks must designate an employee as a Bank Secrecy Compliance Officer. Complying with the Bank Secrecy Act is this person's responsibility.

bank supervision The act of monitoring the financial performance and operations of banks in order to ensure that they are operating safely and soundly and following rules and regulations. Bank supervision is conducted by governmental regulators and occurs in order to prevent bank failures.

bank trust department A department in a bank that administers trusts and guardianships. Trust departments manage trust funds for their clients and decide what investments to make. Trust departments also may manage assets for businesses, such as administering pension funds and acting as a trustee for corporate bonds or as a transfer agent. Generally, investments made by trustees are fairly conservative because they are intended to maintain existing wealth and limit risk.

bank wire An electronic communications network owned by an association of banks. The bank wire transfers messages between subscribing banks and offers a check clearing service called *Cashwire*. The best-known bank wire is the Fed Wire, which is a high-speed computerized network that connects all of the Federal Reserve banks, their branches, and the U.S. Treasury. It lets the members transfer reserves between themselves and make transfers for business customers.

bankers' acceptance A short-term credit letter drawn on a bank that guarantees payment of a bill by the bank. Bankers' acceptance letters generally are used in export and import transactions. They are termed *accepted* when a bank writes on the draft its agreement to pay it at maturity, using the word *accepted*. A bank may accept the draft for either the drawer or the holder. Unlike a more traditional loan, a bankers' acceptance doesn't necessarily reduce a bank's lending capacity, because the bank can raise funds by selling the acceptance. The acceptance is nevertheless an outstanding liability of the bank and is subject to reserve requirements from the Federal Reserve.

bankruptcy A legal proceeding initiated by an individual or company that is unable to pay its debts. A bankruptcy can either liquidate the debts or attempt to develop a reorganization plan under which the debt, or some of it, will be paid. The most common type of bankruptcy filing is *Chapter 11,* in which a business is allowed to continue running while it reorganizes its debts. Creditors are prevented from attempting to collect debts from a company that is in a Chapter 11 bankruptcy proceeding. In a Chapter 11, the debtor and creditors meet to draw up an agreement for repaying some of the debt.

Some companies close down through a *Chapter 7* bankruptcy (also called a *liquidation*), instead of attempting to reorganize. In a Chapter 7 bankruptcy, a court-appointed interim trustee is given discretion to make management changes, arrange unsecured financing, and wind down the business. Individuals who want to get rid of their debt and not attempt to pay anything back file for Chapter 7 bankruptcy.

Individuals who want to reorganize their debts and pay back a portion file for a *Chapter 13* bankruptcy. Typically, people who make this type of filing pay something each month for several years to the bankruptcy court, which distributes the funds to the creditors. When the payments are completed, the debtor's debts are discharged. Chapter 13 bankruptcies allow individuals to hold onto more assets than Chapter 7 bankruptcies do.

Bankruptcies fall into two categories. A *voluntary bankruptcy* occurs when the debtor petitions the court to begin a bankruptcy proceeding. An *involuntary bankruptcy* occurs when the creditors petition the court to put the debtor into bankruptcy. The term *chapter* refers to the chapter of the bankruptcy law where the provisions are outlined.

bar chart A chart that describes price movement in an easy-to-understand format. Each day's price movement is represented by a vertical line that shows how high and how low the security traded. The closing price is indicated by a short horizontal line, called a *tick mark,* which runs through the vertical line. Sometimes the trading volume is depicted below the price information as a horizontal line that rises or falls in accordance with the volume. At the very bottom of the chart, *open interest,* which is the amount of futures or options contracts that are available for trading in the market, are drawn to scale using vertical lines. The higher the line, the higher the open interest.

barbell portfolio   A bond portfolio that has high concentrations of bonds in both short-term and long-term fixed-income instruments with only a few in intermediate-term bonds. A barbell portfolio implements a trading strategy that concentrates on investments in the short- and long-term end of bond maturities. A barbell strategy is useful when short-term and long-term interest rates are higher relative to interme-diate interest rates. This strategy allows investors to earn higher overall yields while still retaining the desired time frame for the bond portfolio.

barge   A ship that is used to carry heavy and space-intensive products in rivers, lakes, or other waterways. For example, inland river barges that carry oil products typically hold 25,000 barrels; ocean-going barges range in size up to 120,000 barrels.

Barings Bank collapse   The financial collapse, in 1995, of one of the world's old-est banks, Barings Bank, which had been the banker to the British royal family. Nick Leeson, a Singapore-based trader for the bank, made a series of bad trades over a sev-eral year period that incurred substantial losses that produced the Barings failure. Barings Bank was bought after the collapse by ING, a Dutch financial institution, for £1. The Barings Bank collapse is an exam-ple of what can go wrong when a bank fails to properly supervise its employees and their trading practices. Leeson took speculative positions (primarily in the futures market) that were linked to the Nikkei 225. He also took speculative positions in Japanese gov-ernment bonds and options on the Nikkei. By the end of 1994, Leeson had lost £208 million, which created a £827 million hole in the bank's balance sheet. By February 1995, half of the open interest in the Nikkei futures and 85 percent of the open interest in the Japanese Government Bond futures were attributed to Leeson.

barometer   In the financial markets, an important economic statistic or stock index that indicates market direction or senti-ment. Some of the more frequently cited barometers are the NASDAQ Composite Index, the Dow Jones Industrial Average, the U.S. unemployment rate, the rate of inflation, and the consumer price index.

barrel   A unit of measurement used for oil, gas, and other refined products. One barrel equals 42 U.S. gallons. Sometimes abbreviated *BBL* or *BL.*

barrier option   An option with a payoff that depends on whether the underlying investment trades through a barrier price. If the option doesn't reach a certain price level, it is worthless. There are many types of barrier options. Three types are: *down-and-out options, up-and-in options,* and *early-exercise trigger CAPS options.* Barrier options are one type of trading strategy that an options trader will use to create profits. Also called *knock-in* or *knockout options.*

barter   To trade goods or services for other goods or services of equivalent value. Currency is not used. While bartering is often associated with undeveloped econ-omies or thought of as a historical way of conducting commerce, it is still used in developed countries in certain circum-stances.

base metal   Any metal from the group of metals that includes copper, aluminum, lead, nickel, tin, and zinc. Traders on the London Metal Exchange, as well as other exchanges, such as the New York Mercantile Exchange, trade futures contracts on base metals. Base metals are in contrast to *precious metals,* such as gold and silver.

Basel Convergence Agreement   An international agreement to implement common standards for funds that banks are required to have on hand to maintain ade-quate capital. The agreement is named for Basel, the city in Switzerland where the Bank of International Settlements (BIS) is located. The BIS essentially is a central bank for central banks and is involved in developing many rules and regulations to ensure the safety of the international banking system.

Basel Standards for Market Risk A set of capital requirements for banks that is intended to protect against financial market risk. Banks are allowed to use their own internal risk model as long as minimum capital standards are met.

baseload The minimum amount of electric power that an electric company can deliver over time at a steady rate. Baseload capacity is determined by the kind of stress that electric generating equipment can handle if it is operated on an around-the-clock basis. On a hot day, demand for electricity increases as more people turn on their air conditioning. This demand can overwhelm the baseload, resulting in power surges, blackouts, or grayouts.

basic earnings per share Earnings per share that are calculated without taking into account stock options, warrants, and convertible debt. If a company has a large amount of those financial instruments outstanding, then diluted earnings per share provides a better measurement of the earnings that should be allocated to each share of stock. The diluted earnings per share calculation includes stock options, warrants and convertible debt. Typically, companies report both basic earnings per share and diluted earnings per share.

basis In the futures market, the difference between the cash and futures prices. For instance, if cash prices for cotton typically are 5 cents below the July futures price, the November basis is said to be "5 cents under." Separately, basis also is used to calculate the amount of capital gains tax that is due on the sale of an investment or asset. The basis is calculated by taking the purchase price and subtracting any commissions or expenses.

basis point (bp) One-hundredth of a percentage point (1/100 of 1%). One percentage point equals 100 basis points. This term is commonly used in a trading context for futures contracts or when talking about price movements of bonds and loans. Also used in the context of the Federal Reserve moving the federal funds rate or the discount rate by 25 or 50 basis points.

batch In the oil industry, a specific amount of crude oil or refined product shipments that are sent through a pipeline. A *batching sequence* is the order in which shipments of crude oil or refined products are sent through a pipeline.

BBX See *Bulletin Board Exchange.*

bcf *Billion cubic feet.* Typically refers to an amount of natural gas that is in storage or that has been sold. Sometimes *bcf/d* is used, which is billions of cubic feet produced in a day.

bear Someone who believes that the market will fall. Contrasts with a bull, who believes the opposite. See also *bear market.*

bear hug An uninvited takeover attempt that offers such a large premium for the target's shares that the board of directors of the target company has no alternative but to vote in favor of the acquisition or face the wrath, and lawsuits, of shareholders.

bear market A stock market, or some other financial market, that has traded sharply lower, usually falling 20 percent or more. In contrast, a *bull market* is a market that is rapidly rising.

The term may originate from an English proverb that warns against selling the bear's skin before one has caught the bear, which might describe a situation in which a speculator sells a stock with the assumption that it can be bought later at a lower price. An alternative origin may come from a 1709 issue of the United Kingdom's satirical paper, *The Tatler,* which told a story about a noble gentleman who bought a bear, sight unseen, from another officer. The deal went bad, and it was said that someone who confers real value upon an imaginary thing is selling a bear. The different descriptions for bull and bear markets may also be derived from the fact that a bear attacks by coming down on its prey while a bull attacks its prey by thrusting its horns upward.

bear spread   The simultaneous purchase of a call option with a higher exercise price and the sale of an option with a lower exercise price. A bear spread also can be created by the simultaneous purchase of a put option with a higher exercise price and the sale of a put option with a lower exercise price. A trader who sets up a bear spread expects prices to go lower but still wants a way to limit the amount of money spent purchasing options. A bear spread is the opposite of a bull spread.

bear trap   A situation in which a bear market (a downward-moving market) changes directions and prices rise. Bearish investors who expected the market to continue declining will continue selling short (selling what they don't own). Eventually they are forced to buy their investments back at a higher price in order to avoid further losses. Thus, the bears are caught in a trap.

bearer bond   A bond whose ownership is evidenced by whoever is holding it. The corporation that issued the bond pays the bearer the interest payments and ownership is not otherwise recorded. This contrasts with a registered bond, whereby the company issuing the bond knows who the owner is.

before-tax contribution   The part of an employee's salary that is contributed to a retirement plan before federal income taxes are deducted. Before-tax contributions reduce the taxpayer's gross income for federal tax purposes. A withdrawal from an account funded with before-tax contributions becomes taxable at the time of withdrawal.

beggar-thy-neighbor policies   Economic actions taken by one country to improve its economic situation that may have adverse effects on other economies. For example, a country may lower prices on certain goods or push down the value of its currency to increase exports in the hope

that more jobs will be created. In this case, surrounding countries may be harmed by cheap imports flowing into their borders. Retaliatory actions may ensue, and thus worsen economic situations for both countries.

behavioral finance   The study of behavior in market economies and businesses. Behavioral finance models focus on observed psychological factors that influence decision making during periods of economic uncertainty. For example, if a stock becomes highly sought after and its price rises sharply even though the company's fundamentals haven't changed, crowd psychology may be at work, according to behavioral finance psychologists. Another example of behavioral finance is when an investor is influenced to hold onto a stock that has decreased substantially because the investor wants to avoid admitting that he or she was wrong.

Beige Book   An assessment of the economic performance of each of the 12 regional Federal Reserve districts. The Beige Book is prepared by the Federal Reserve staff before the Federal Open Market Committee meeting, which happens eight times a year. The report examines economic activity, specifically employment trends, construction and housing activity, retail sales, consumer confidence, and any other relevant information. The Beige Book is used by financial analysts as a descriptive measure of economic performance within the regions of the U.S. Financial analysts scrutinize the book for clues about the Fed's future monetary policy decisions.

Belgian option   An option that pays off on a partial basis as the underlying security moves from its initial cash price to the strike price. If the instrument is in-the-money at expiration, then it also pays off just as a regular option does.

Bell, Alexander Graham   The inventor of the telephone. He patented the telephone on February 14, 1876, filing his application on the same day as Elisha Gray of Western

Union. He refined the telephone with the help of Thomas Edison. He also contributed to the education of the deaf, by researching a machine to make sound understandable, which fed into his ideas about the telephone.

bellwether A stock, index, bond, or other financial instrument that shows the direction of a market. Significant and widely owned stocks may become bellwethers of market direction. In the Treasury bond market, the 10-year note is a bellwether.

benchmark A tool for evaluating the performance of a company, department, or individual by comparing its performance to a set of standards. Benchmarks may be cited in terms of numbers, such as sales figures. They also may have to do with meeting specific goals.

beneficial owner A person or company who has direct or indirect voting or invest-ment power, according to the Securities and Exchange Commission. A beneficial owner also is someone who has the benefits of ownership even though the title might be held in someone else's name. For instance, stock certificates may be held in the name of the brokerage firm, but the beneficial owner is the person who actually owns the certificate, not the brokerage firm.

beneficiary The institution or person who receives cash or an investment; typi-cally used to refer to people who inherit money or property through a will, or people who receive the proceeds from a life insur-ance policy, annuity, or trust.

bequest The act of giving assets such as cash, property, cars, or stocks to a beneficiary through a will.

Bermuda option An option with aspects of American and European options. Bermuda options can be exercised on one of several specific dates before expiration, similar to American options, which can be exercised anytime up until expiration. However, the flexibility of Bermuda options is limited to only several specific dates, which resembles European-style

options, which can be exercised only at expiration.

Bernoulli trial A random event that has three important characteristics. Its result must be a success or failure; the probability of a success must be the same for all trials, and the outcome of each trial must be independent of the other trial's outcomes. A coin toss would meet the requirements of a Bernoulli trial.

best execution The best price of a trade that is reasonably available. A broker has a duty to obtain the best price, called an *exe-cution*. When making a trade, a broker must consider opportunities to get a better price than what is currently quoted, the speed of execution, and the likelihood that the trade will be executed. In doing so, the broker evaluates which markets, market makers, or electronic communications networks (ECNs) offer the most favorable terms of execution.

best practices The best method or approach to conducting business or trading. Best practices are customs that don't have the force of law.

best-efforts underwriting Underwriting in which the underwriter provides its best efforts to get the deal done, whether it is selling stock or debt. Contrasts with *firm-commitment underwriting,* in which the underwriter assumes the risk of the issue being poorly received. In best-efforts underwriting, the underwriter assumes the role of an agent. If the issue can't be sold at the desired price, the price will either be lowered or the issue withdrawn and sold at a later date.

beta A measure of a stock's relative volatility. The Standard & Poor's 500 Stock Index has a beta coefficient of 1. The beta of individual stocks, mutual funds, or portfolios is measured in comparison to this index. For example, a stock that has a high beta of 1.5 and thus high volatility has 50 percent more movement than the rest of the market. Although high betas can result in strong gains, they also can produce substantial losses. Similarly, stocks with a beta below 1.0 move less than the market as a whole.

bid

1. The purchase price of a stock, futures contract, or other investment. The term is used by market makers and other traders who are prepared to purchase an investment. In contrast, *ask* is the price of a stock or other investment that a market maker or trader is willing to sell an investment for. See also *bid-ask spread.*

2. In the context of a merger agreement or attempted merger, *bid* indicates a proposed price.

bid-ask spread   The difference between a bid and an ask price. The *bid* is what a trader or market maker is willing to pay to buy a stock or other investment and the *ask* price is what the trader is willing to sell it for.

bid-to-cover ratio   In U.S. Treasury auctions, the ratio between the number of bids received and the number of bids accepted. The measurement indicates how strong investor demand is for U.S. Treasuries. The higher the ratio, the stronger the demand. Typically a ratio over 2.0 is an indicator of a strong auction. A low ratio indicates weak demand and is said to have a *long tail* (a wide spread between the average and the high yield).

Big Bang   A significant change, often as a result of legal or regulatory changes. The term has acquired many different uses in the financial markets. For example, in the U.S., a Big Bang occurred in 1975 when stockbrokers stopped receiving fixed commissions, which opened the way for the first discount brokerage firms to set up business. As investment banks earned smaller trading commissions, they began to look for other ways to generate income to support trading-related services, such as research. Investment banking revenues replaced trading commissions as a way to pay for research analysts,

so analysts began working more closely with each other. The Big Bang reached a crescendo during the 1990s as the stock market reached historic highs. After the stock market began to fall sharply in the first half of 2000, investigations by regulators and legal authorities put a damper on the close working relationship as they alleged conflicts of interest.

In the U.K., Big Bang refers to the deregulation of the financial markets that occurred in 1987 and 1988, when a series of reforms of the London Stock Exchange were implemented; these reforms allowed investors to trade without going through *market makers,* or companies that were given exclusive rights to trade stocks on the exchange. The reforms also allowed financial institutions to expand into many different areas of financial services so that customers could deal with one bank for various investment purposes instead of dealing with several. Japan experienced a Big Bang when the foreign exchange market was deregulated in 1998.

Big Blue   A nickname for IBM Corp. It comes from the color used in the company's logo.

Big Board   A nickname for the New York Stock Exchange (NYSE).

Big Four   The four largest U.S. accounting firms. They are Deloitte & Touche, Ernst & Young, KPMG International, and PricewaterhouseCoopers. The Big Four once were the Big Six, and before that the Big Eight, but mergers have reduced the number of competitors.

Big Three   Ford Motor Co., General Motors Corp. and Chrysler Corp. These were the three large U.S. automotive companies. However, Chrysler was bought in 1998 by Germany's Daimler-Benz in a $37 billion deal, which at that time was the largest ever takeover of a U.S. firm by a foreign company. The deal created DaimlerChrysler. Even though Chrysler is no longer independent, the term *Big Three* is still used.

bill pass The purchase by the Federal Reserve (Fed) of Treasury bills in the open market from dealers. A bill pass injects money into the monetary system because the Fed pay cash to the sellers of the bills.

bill-over-bond spread The difference in yield between a Treasury bill and a bond, which is the inverse of a bill-over-bond spread.

binder

1. Money that is paid as part of a contract to show good faith until the transaction is completed.

2. In the insurance industry, a binder provides proof to the insured that coverage has been approved until the actual insurance policy is delivered and the payment is submitted to the insurance company. A binder is a letter guaranteeing insurance coverage.

Birdseye, Clarence The originator of the frozen food industry in the United States. He invented quick-freeze machinery. Postum Company, a major food manufacturer, paid $22 million for the equipment and rights to the freezing process. The purchase created the basis for General Foods Corporation and made frozen food a staple for Americans and others throughout the world.

birr The currency unit of Ethiopia, comprised of 100 cents.

BIS See *Bank of International Settlements.*

bi-weekly mortgage A mortgage on which payments are made every two weeks. Mortgages are typically paid monthly. The bi-weekly payment amount is calculated by dividing a monthly amount in two. However, 26 payments are made over the course of a year, because some months are longer than just the two bi-weekly payment periods. The effect is an accelerated payment schedule, in which principal is paid down faster and the amount of interest paid over the life of the mortgage is decreased.

black box A complex software program that is used to determine a price that a security should be sold at, indicate what trades should be done, or give the result of a financial calculation. The inner workings of a black box pricing formula are not explained to the users or are very complex and hard to understand, so users refer to the end result as black box number.

black knight A slang term for a company that makes a hostile takeover bid for another company.

black market An illegal market, typically one that sells goods or services that are in short supply or that are prohibited by government policy. Determined consumers seek out the goods on the black market, and purchase them at drastically inflated prices.

Black Monday

1. October 29, 1929. Stock market volume was huge this day, with nearly 16.4 million shares of stock traded. Prices fell drastically: For example, General Electric was off 48 points, Westinghouse was off 34 points. The big bankers of the time, such as J.P. Morgan, refused to do anything to support prices. Instead, their concern was that the market remain orderly.

2. October 19, 1987. On this date, the U.S. stock market lost nearly one-fourth of its value in a matter of hours. The Dow Jones Industrial Average fell 22 percent, or 508 points, its biggest one-day point fall to date.

Black Thursday October 25, 1929, when the U.S. stock market crashed and a record volume of 12.9 million shares traded, beating the previous peak of 4 million. Stocks sustained substantial losses. This crash was exceeded by the crash that occurred on the following Monday, October 29, when prices fell again on record volume of 16.4 million shares.

Black Wednesday Wednesday, September 16, 1992, the day the British government withdrew the British pound from the Exchange Rate Mechanism (ERM), a European monetary agreement. The value of the pound was quickly declining and the ERM required it to remain within a price range. The British government tried to stop the price slide by purchasing sterling in the market. However, the government spent a significant amount of money and was not going to be able to continue its buying campaign. Instead, it decided to stop buying the pound, and thus had to withdraw from the ERM because the pound would no longer be in the prescribed trading range.

blackout period   A period when a public company's directors, officers, and specified employees can't trade the company's stock. Blackout periods occur prior to the release of annual or quarterly financial earnings information, and may extend for a time period after the release of the earnings information. The company, not the Securities and Exchange Commission, sets the blackout period. Rule 10b5-1 of the SEC Act of 1934, however, creates a "safe harbor" in which officers, directors, and employees of a company, through the adoption of a *trading plan,* may trade a company's securities even during a blackout period or other times when they have knowledge of material nonpublic information. A trading plan might be an established employee stock ownership program that calls for a set number of shares of the company to be purchased each month. In general, a trading plan removes discretion for the sale or purchase of stock from the individual and creates an automatic program.

Black-Scholes Option Pricing Model
A formula to calculate the value of European style options. The formula was introduced in 1973 by Fischer Black and Myron Scholes. The Black-Scholes formula assumes that the primary factors affecting the price of an option are the value of the underlying asset, the exercise price of the option, the volatility of the underlying asset, the risk-free rate of interest, and the remaining time to expiration.

blind pool   A type of limited partnership that doesn't specifically state what kind of investments the general partner will make. Those in this limited partnership are blind to the intended investments.

blind trust   A trust whose owner cannot be informed about which investments have been bought or sold. This kind of trust is created when someone puts his or her assets into a trust and gives a fiduciary party, such as a bank or asset manager, complete authority to make investments on his or her behalf. Blind trusts are often set up by politicians or high-ranking government officials as a way of avoiding potential conflicts of interest by investing on issues or creating government policies that could benefit individual investments.

block trade   The purchase or sale by a wealthy individual, corporation, or institution of a large quantity of stocks, bonds, futures, options, or other investments. Although definitions about what constitutes a block trade vary, typically over 10,000 shares or contracts or a trade with a value of $200,000 or more is considered a block trade. Often the term is associated with the equity market; however, block trades can occur in any market.

blowoff top   A chart pattern identified in technical analysis, in which a trading system attempts to determine future price movements by looking at patterns on price charts. A blowoff occurs at major market tops when prices suddenly stage a sharp rally after a long advance. Trading volume and open interest rise sharply.

Blue Dog Coalition   A budget watchdog group of Democrats in Congress who emphasize the necessity of reducing budget deficits.

blue sky law   A state law that is designed to protect the public against securities fraud. Kansas was the first state to enact a securities registration law, in 1911. When announcing the legislation's passage, lawmakers said, "The State was the hunting ground of promoters of fraudulent enterprises...so barefaced...that it was stated they would sell building lots in the blue sky." Since then, state securities laws have been referred to as blue sky laws.

blue-chip company A company that is very strong financially, with a solid track record of producing earnings and only a moderate amount of debt. A blue-chip company also has a strong name in its industry with dominant products or services. Typically, blue-chip companies are large corporations that have been in business for many years and are considered to be very stable. However, there is no formal requirement for being a blue chip. Often, blue-chip companies are found in the Dow Jones Industrial Average.

board independence A relatively new concept in corporate governance that calls for a majority of board members to be independent from the company. Independence occurs when a board member has not been and is not currently employed by the company or its auditor and the board member's employer doesn't do a significant amount of business with the company. Each company creates its own definition of *significant*. Board independence was given legal definition and direction in 2002 in the Sarbanes-Oxley legislation. Stock exchanges, such as the New York Stock Exchange and the NASDAQ also passed their own rules governing the behavior of their listed companies.

board of directors The body that manages a U.S. corporation. The board appoints top managers, approves their compensation, votes to issue dividends, decides whether to approve a merger, and handles many other big-picture issues. The size of boards vary.

Board of Trade Clearing Corporation
An independent corporation that is responsible for settling all of the trades at the Chicago Board of Trade. It is a guarantor for all the trades it clears. It reconciles the accounts of the clearing member firms daily and sets and adjusts clearing member firm margins when market conditions change.

Boesky, Ivan F. An American stock speculator who used inside information to strategically buy and sell stocks and profit from the mergers and takeovers of businesses. He is remembered for declaring that "greed is healthy" in 1985 at a college commencement address. Just over a year later, in November 1986, Boesky pleaded guilty to insider trading charges and agreed to pay a $100 million fine and to cooperate with the Securities and Exchange Commission's ongoing inside trading investigation. He also received a three-year sentence. The fine was by far the largest settlement obtained by the SEC for insider-trading activity at that point. His cooperation with federal authorities also led to the convictions of others, including junk-bond king Michael Milken and Boesky's employer, Drexel Burnham Lambert.

Boesky testified that he had gained his $200 million fortune using illegal inside information about impending mergers to trade stock in the companies involved. As a result of Boesky's confession, subpoenas were issued to some of the world's most famous financiers, including "Junk Bond King" Michael Milken. Boesky's testimony directed investigators to Milken and Drexel for their participation in the illegal schemes. As a result of this insider trading scandal, the U.S. Congress increased the penalties for securities violations.

boiler room A stock brokerage firm that targets unsophisticated or otherwise vulnerable people in an attempt to pressure them to purchase stock. The brokers that work for a boiler room use sales tactics designed to exert significant pressure on people to make them buy stock without any regard to whether it is a wise investment for their age, risk tolerance, and investment goals. Brokers who work for boiler rooms may also lie or provide misleading information in order get the sale. Generally, the stocks that boiler room brokers sell are very risky and likely will result in investors losing money. Boiler rooms operate out of inexpensive, obscure locations that can be easily moved or abandoned. They generally operate outside of the law.

BOJ   See *Bank of Japan.*

bolivar   The currency unit of Venezuela, comprised of 100 centimos.

boliviano   The currency unit of Bolivia, comprised of 100 centavos.

Bollinger bands   A technical analysis system that plots two standard deviations above and below a moving average and on the moving average itself. *Standard deviation* measures volatility, so these bands will be wider during increased volatility and narrower during decreased volatility. Technical analysts believe that a market that approaches the upper band is overbought, while a market that approaches the lower band is oversold. *Overbought* means that too many buyers have entered the market and prices are likely to fall. *Oversold* means that too many sellers have sold, and the next price direction will likely be upward.

bolsa   The Spanish word for "stock exchange." One well-known bolsa is the Bolsa de Madrid, Spain's largest regional stock exchange.

Bolsa de Madrid   Spain's stock exchange, which is comprised of regional markets in Madrid, Bilbao, Barcelona, and Valencia. Stocks, bonds, and derivatives are trading on the exchange. The primary stock index is the IBEX-35.

Bolsa Mexicana de Valores (BMV) Mexico's stock exchange, which dates back to 1850, the year Mexican mining stocks were first traded. In 1975 it incorporated stock trading with the Guadalajara and Monterrey exchanges. In 1995 the BMV introduced the electronic trading system for debt instruments, BMV-SENTRA Titulos de Deuda, which was developed by the Bolsa. Debt market trades occur entirely on an electronic platform. The introduction of the electronic trading system for equities, BMV-SENTRA Capitales, came in 1996. In 1998 a new Bolsa subsidiary, Financial Integration Services (SIF), was created to administer the operation of debt market and trading through the electronic trading system for debt instruments. On January 11, 1999, the entire stock market migrated to the electronic trading system. Since then, the stock market has operated via the BMV-SENTRA Equities System. The main price index on the exchange is the IPC Index.

Bombay Sensex   India's benchmark stock index. The Sensex is a value-weighted index comprised of 30 companies whose beginning index value was set at 100 in April 1979. These companies account for about 20 percent of the market capitalization of the Bombay Stock Exchange.

Bombay Stock Exchange (BSE) India's largest stock exchange, which began operations in 1875. There are more than 6,000 companies listed. Its benchmark index is the Bombay Sensex.

bond anticipation notes   Short-term debt that is issued by cities or states in order to provide interim financing for projects that will be funded by future bond issues.

bond spreads   The difference in interest rates between the yield on a corporate bond and the yield on a U.S. Treasury bond with similar maturities. Spreads also are calculated against Treasuries for federal agency debt, such as Fannie Mae notes, or other government debt. For example, the spread on a 10-year corporate bond will trade 75 basis points over a 10-year Treasury note.

bond swap   The act of liquidating a current bond position while simultaneously buying a replacement issue that has similar attributes but increases the chance for a higher return. Swaps are done to increase the return, or yield. Other reasons to do a swap may be to take advantage of shifts in interest rates or to realign yield spreads to improve the quality of the portfolio.

bond valuation analysis   A strategy in which a bond portfolio manager attempts to buy bonds based on their intrinsic value. Using this strategy, the bond portfolio manager compares the different characteristics of bonds, such as whether they have a deferred call feature, a sinking fund, or other factors that would affect their yield and price. When those characteristics are compared, some bonds will be better values than other bonds.

bonding The process of carefully checking an employee's background and then taking out insurance to protect the company against theft or fraud losses caused by that employee. Financial firms or other companies whose employees handle cash are some of the firms that bond their employees.

bond-over-bill spread The difference in yield between a specific bond and a Treasury bill. It is the inverse of a bill-over-bond spread.

bond-over-stock warrant A *warrant* (a right to purchase a stock) in which the payout is based on the performance of a bond index. However, the payout will be reduced by the amount of return on the stock index that is used. Typically, bond-over-stock warrants are issued on many different fixed-income and equity indices.

book

1. A trader's *positions,* or list of investments.

2. A broker's or investment manager's list of clients, which is called a *book of business.*

book transfer The act of transferring ownership of a product or asset without actually delivering the physical goods.

book value A company's total assets, minus its liabilities. To calculate the book value per share, divide the company's book value by the number of shares outstanding.

book-entry

1. A method used by the U.S. Treasury and some agency issuers, such as Fannie Mae, to confer ownership of the bonds and notes. Book-entry consists of an entry on the computerized records of the U.S. Department of the Treasury, a Federal Reserve Bank, or a financial institution. No actual certificate is given to the owner.

2. Refers to stock certificates and corporate bonds that are held on behalf of customers using only the brokerage firm's name. The brokerage firm keeps track of who the owners are.

book-entry callable corpus (BECC) Principal zero-coupon bonds that have been converted from paper to an electronic form. The term is often used in conjunction with written materials on bond mutual funds. The significance of the conversion is that the bonds can be wire transferred instead of physically delivered.

The U.S. Department of the Treasury's Bureau of the Public Debt (BPD) also lets holders of the principal portions, or *corpora,* of U.S. Treasury bearer securities that have been stripped of some or all of their non-callable coupons to have an opportunity to convert their stripped corpora to book-entry form by using the Bearer Corpora Conversion System. Keeping the Treasuries in book-entry form makes them easier to transfer.

bookkeeping The process of recording financial transactions and maintaining the financial records to support a company's financial statements. Bookkeeping is only one small part of accounting, which is the overall examination of a company's financial results.

book-to-bill A ratio that shows the relationship between semiconductor orders and billings. A book-to-bill of 1.28 means that $128 worth of new orders were received for every $100 of product billed for the month. A San Jose, California-based trade association, the Semiconductor Equipment and Materials International (SEMI), reports book-to-bill data monthly for North America using three-month moving averages. Companies in the semiconductor industry often release their own book-to-bill ratios. The statistic is widely watched in the technology market to judge how well semiconductor companies are performing.

bootstrapping

   1. The act of an individual starting a company with very little money and very little credit and doing everything on the cheap. A start-up company that has little money is said to be bootstrapping its way to profitability. Originated from the expression "pulling yourself up by your bootstraps," from a Horatio Alger story of moving from rags to riches.

   2. The process of creating a theoretical spot-rate curve by using one yield projection as the basis for creating the yield of the next maturity. Traders use this method to determine what various interest rates will be along the yield curve when they have only one interest rate.

borrowed reserves   Funds that eligible depository institutions, such as banks, obtain by borrowing from the Federal Reserve in order to meet minimum reserve requirements. Typically, reserves are borrowed only for a short period of time.

borrower   A legal term for a person or entity that obtains funds from a business or individual for a specified period of time upon condition of promising to repay the loan. The terms of the loan are spelled out in a written document that is signed by both the lender and the borrower.

borsa   The Italian word for "stock exchange." Italy's largest stock exchange is the Borsa Italiana, which was created when the stock exchange was privatized. See *Borsa Italiana.*

Borsa Italiana   Italy's stock exchange. Privatized in 1997, the Borsa Italiana is Europe's fourth largest stock exchange. Its benchmark index is the Milan MIB 30, a market capitalization-weighted index of the 30 top Italian companies.

bottom feeding   Bargain hunting in a market, whether it is the stock, real estate, or another market. Bottom feeding occurs

when investors begin to return to a market after a sustained downturn that has lowered prices significantly. See also *bottom fisher.*

bottom fisher   A trader or investor who looks for bargains among stocks or other investments whose prices have fallen sharply. When a market rises after a period of a strong decline, traders say that the bottom fishers have come into the market. The term is borrowed from the sport of fishing and comes from fish such as catfish that sit on the bottom of a lake or river and feed on food particles and waste products that come floating down to the bottom.

bottom line   Another way of saying net income. It draws its name from the fact that net income is the bottom line on an income statement.

bought deal   An underwriting deal in which the underwriter offers a firm commitment to purchase the company's securities, thereby assuming the risk if the deal is poorly received by the market. The underwriter's fee is the difference, or *spread,* between the purchase price and the price the instrument sells for on the open market. Also called *firm-commitment underwriting.*

bounce

   1. A quick, but moderate, upward rise in a market that had previously traded lower. Also called a *dead cat bounce* when price gains aren't expected to last.

   2. To write a check without having sufficient funds to cover it. A *bounced check* is one that has been rejected by a bank because there are insufficient funds in the checking account.

bourse   The French word for "stock exchange." The Paris Bourse is France's national stock exchange, created in 1991.

boutique   A small, specialized brokerage or financial firm that offers a limited number of services and products. Typically, boutiques are started by people who leave large Wall Street firms, either because of a desire to create their own company or as a result of losing their job through a down-sizing or firing. A boutique typically employs anywhere from a few people to several hundred people, compared with a global financial company that employs several hundred thousand people.

Bowie bond Asset-backed bonds whose interest and principle payments are collater-alized by the music publishing royalties of rock musician David Bowie. Originally $55 million of the bonds were sold in 1997. Since then, other asset-backed issues based on intellectual property have been issued, including bond issues based on revenue from James Brown and the Isely Brothers.

box spread An arbitrage play in the options market in which both a bull spread and a bear spread are established in order to create a risk-free profit. One spread includes put options and the other includes call options. An arbitrage attempts to profit from the difference in prices on two different markets. See also *arbitrage, bull spread,* and *bear spread*.

boycott An agreement among competitors to not have any dealings with a person, company, or organization. A boycott can violate the law if it is used to force another party to pay higher prices or in any way restrict competition. If boycotts are launched to prevent a company from entering a market, they are illegal. Often boycotts are used by consumer or social action groups to prompt a company to change its behavior or policies that are deemed harmful to the group.

bp See *basis point.*

bracket creep The effect that inflation has on pushing incomes higher and, thus, into higher income tax brackets.

Brady bond A bond issued as part of a bailout plan launched in the early 1990s to exchange commercial banks' loans to emerging market countries that were in default for new bonds. Developed in conjunction with the International Monetary Fund (IMF) and the World Bank, Brady bonds give the commercial banks guarantees that principal and interest will be paid along with cash payments. The debtor governments benefit from having their principal, interest payments, and interest arrears reduced. The principal and some interest are collateralized by U.S. Treasury zero-coupon bonds and other high-grade instruments. Brady bonds are associated with Latin American countries, however, they are also available to other countries. Brady bonds still trade today and can be issued in new instances of default. The bonds are named for Nicholas Brady, President George Bush's treasury secretary.

breadth of the market The number of stocks that are participating in either the market's upward or downward movement. If the stock market rises during a trading session and a large number of stocks also rise, then the market has good breadth. Inversely, if the market rises, but only a relatively small number of stocks rise, the upward price movement is said to lack breadth. The same is true of a declining market. Breadth often is measured by the *advance-decline ratio,* which compares the numbers of stocks rising against the number of those that are falling.

break A quick and sharp price decline; a term frequently used in trading.

breakaway gap A chart pattern that is identified through technical analysis of price patterns. It shows a pattern that is interrupted by a gap on the chart, which indicates a market spiking either up or down.

break-even point The point at which income equals costs. Typically, before investing in a business or new plant or equipment, a company does a break-even analysis to determine what sales revenues are needed in order to cover costs. Sales above the break-even point create profit. The break-even point also may be used to refer to the price at which an investment can be sold so that the investor neither profits nor loses money.

breakpoint In mutual funds sales, the minimum amount of money that an investor must invest to earn a reduction in sales charges. As the amount invested rises, fees are discounted even further. Typically breakpoints occur with Class A mutual funds shares, which have a front-end sales load.

Brent crude oil A particular type of crude oil that is a light, sweet oil produced in the North Sea with most of it being refined in Northwest Europe. Brent can be thought of as a benchmark oil for Europe. Futures and options are traded primarily on Brent on the International Petroleum Exchange in London. Futures contracts also are traded on the New York Mercantile Exchange.

Bretton Woods An agreement struck in the summer of 1944, in which the U.S., the U.K., and their wartime allies set up the rules for the post-World War II monetary system. The meeting set the structure for the International Monetary Fund (IMF) and the International Bank for Reconstruction and Development (IBRD), which in the U.S. is more commonly known as the World Bank. The comprehensive agreement called for the participants to limit the movement of their currencies, which were set against the dollar. The gold standard was maintained and the dollar retained its value of $35 to an ounce of gold. That standard allowed the U.S. to finance its balance of payments deficit by using dollars instead of gold. However, the U.S. also retained the responsibility of converting dollars into gold on demand from foreign central banks. The name Bretton Woods comes from the city in New Hampshire where the wartime allies met.

bricks and mortar A term that came into vogue during the Internet boom of the late 1990s. It describes actual retail stores that a person can visit, in contrast with retail Web sites.

bridge financing Short-term financing used as a stop-gap measure until medium- or long-term funding can be arranged. Often, bridge financing is provided in conjunction with a deal that will provide the necessary long-term funding but needs more time to close. Also called a *bridge loan*.

bring-down comfort letter A letter that updates the *comfort letter* issued prior to closing an initial public offering. The bring-down comfort letter reconfirms the assurances given in the comfort letter that the accountants are comfortable that the unaudited financial data in the company's prospectus follows generally accepted accounting principles. The bring-down comfort letter also says that no material changes have occurred since the financial reports were prepared.

British thermal unit (B.T.U.) A unit of measure used when referring to natural gas. Technically, it is the quantity of heat required to raise the temperature of one pound of water from 60 to 61 degrees Fahrenheit at a constant pressure of one atmosphere. In the same way that ounces is the typical unit of measure used when pricing gold, B.T.U. is used when pricing natural gas.

broadband A digital technology that gives users high-speed Internet access where data, e-mail, videos and music can be downloaded at speeds significantly faster than those available through dial-up modems. Often, broadband service is provided through cable lines from a cable telephone company. Another type of broadband connection, digital subscriber lines (DSL) provides high-speed broadband service using a special telephone line.

broker An individual or firm who acts as an intermediary between a buyer and seller. A broker usually charges a commission for services. A broker also may be a person who sells insurance products offered by different companies or someone who sells real estate.

broker loan rate An interest rate charged to brokers who need funds to cover the margin loans that they have extended to their customers. These loans can be called with short notice, even within 24 hours.

Interest rates on broker loan rates usually are only about a percentage point above short-term interest rates like the federal funds rate. Also called *call loan rate.*

brokered CD A certificate of deposit (CD) that is bought from a brokerage firm rather than from a bank or savings and loan. Brokerage firms choose CDs from many banks around the country and as a result the CDs they offer often pay higher interest rates than CDs issued by banks. Brokered CDs tend to be easier to sell than CDs bought from a bank directly because they can be sold on the open market. Unlike a bank CD, there is no penalty for selling a brokered CD before it matures. Because brokered CDs are originally issued by banks, they are insured by the Federal Deposit Insurance Corp. (FDIC) for up to $100,000.

brokers' loan Money borrowed by brokers from banks in order to pay for inventories of stock, finance the underwriting of corporate or municipal debt, or provide financing for their customers' margin accounts.

Brown, Gordon The Chancellor of the Exchequer for the U.K., which is an equivalent position to the U.S. Treasury Secretary, as of this printing.

bubble Markets that rise significantly above what rational expectations would dictate. Recently, the stock market run-up in the late 1990s that ended in 2000 is cited as an example of a stock market bubble. Historically there have been many bubbles, such as the South Sea Bubble and the Dutch Tulip Bubble. See also *Tulipmania* and *South Sea Company Bubble.*

buck A slang term used to refer to one U.S. dollar; in traders' jargon, $1 million.

budget deficit The difference between expenditures and income, when expenditures exceed income. The term is usually used in reference to the deficit of the U.S. government, or another government's deficit. Federal deficits are funded by issuing government debt, which may take the form of bills, notes, or bonds. Corporations also can have budget deficits; however, steps are quickly taken to reduce the deficit by cutting costs or increasing sales.

Buffett, Warren A famed investor who took over the management of Berkshire Hathaway in 1964. Buffett shunned investments in technology during the bull market of the late 1990s. Although some pundits questioned whether Buffett had lost his touch, when the technology bubble burst, his strategy proved sound.

Some of Buffett's investments include insurance companies Geico Corporation, General Re Corporation, and investments in the Washington Post Company. When Buffett buys companies, he looks for those that are undervalued, and he believes in keeping management in place. He is sometimes called "the sage of Omaha," after the city where his company is headquartered.

bulge Typically, a quick run-up in the price of a futures contract, although the term can be used to refer to stocks, the entire stock market, or another investment.

bulge bracket A loosely defined group of investment banks that dominate the industry. Those in the bulge bracket are Morgan Stanley, Goldman Sachs, Merrill Lynch, Credit Suisse First Boston, Citigroup, and Lehman Brothers. Because there are no formal membership requirements, other banks may argue that they, too, are included.

The concept of bulge bracket came from the early part of the 1900s when a small group of investment banks cooperated, or colluded, in the market for investment-grade debt offerings. In the 1960s and 1970s, Frederick B. Whittemore, a syndicate chief for Morgan Stanley in the 1960s and 1970s who was known on Wall Street as Father Fred, was incredibly influential in deciding who was included in the bulge bracket. Since he retired, no one person, or Morgan Stanley, has had the clout to determine who could declare themselves bulge bracket members and who should be excluded.

Bulge bracket described how the top firms' names on tombstones bulged out from the smaller underwriters listed on them. *Tombstones* are the ads that appear in newspapers and magazines that announce deals. In addition to prestige, the underwriters at the top of a bond or stock offering made the most money from the deal. Before the 1970s, Morgan Stanley reinforced who was able to participate in deals because it was the dominant banker to the largest U.S. companies and didn't let other banks participate as co-managers. As the 1970s drew to a close, the status quo began to change as companies demanded that other bankers participate on their deals and the banks own syndicate networks grew and the iron-clad relationships that determined who corporations hired diminished.

bull   Someone who believes that the market will rise. Contrasts with a bear, who believes the opposite. See also *bull market*.

bull market   A stock market, or some other financial market, that has traded sharply higher. A market up by approximately 20 percent is considered a bull market, though that percentage can vary.

One of the strongest bull markets ever was the bull market in the latter half of the 1990s, when record gains were recorded until the market peaked in 2000. A bull market is in contrast to a bear market, which is a market that is trading sharply lower by at least 20 percent.

The term bull market came into use in 1714 soon after the term "bear market" was introduced. One of its first uses was in Charles Johnson's comic play, *The Country Lasses*. The citation was, "Instead of changing honest staple for Gold and Silver, you deal in Bears and Bulls." Another reference was made in Colley Cibber's play *The Refusal* in 1721.

bull spread   The simultaneous purchase of a call option with a lower exercise price and the sale of a call option with a higher exercise price. A bull spread also can be accomplished with the simultaneous sale of a put option with a higher exercise price and the purchase of a put option with a lower exercise price. The trader using this strategy expects the price of the underlying security to rise and wants to limit the cost of purchasing options.

bulldog bond   A British pound-denominated bond that is issued by a corporation that maintains its accounting records in another currency.

Bulletin Board Exchange (BBX)   The system that will replace the OTCBB (Over-the-Counter Bulletin Board) system. It was scheduled to launch in the fourth quarter of 2003, pending approval by the Securities and Exchange Commission (SEC). BBX will have higher listing standards than OTCBB. BBX companies will have to meet many of the corporate governance requirements that NASDAQ-listed companies are required to meet. However, there will be no financial requirements for listing, which means that BBX companies will not have to meet minimum share price, market capitalization, or shareholder equity requirements. Higher listing standards include requiring that a company be engaged in a legitimate, lawful business, and that it not be a shell company.

BBX companies will have to comply with the Securities Exchange Act of 1934 and be current with required filings. They also will have to produce annual and quarterly reports and are required to adhere to good practices for corporate governance and shareholder rights. See also *OTC Bulletin Board*.

bullion   A precious metal such as gold or silver that is in a tradable form, typically a bar or wafer.

bund   A German Treasury security.

Bundesbank The German central bank. The Bundesbank is responsible for maintaining price stability, ensuring the orderly execution of domestic and foreign payments, and contributing to the stability of payment and clearing systems. The Bundesbank has nine regional offices throughout Germany.

bundled Two companies jointly selling similar, complimentary products or services. One example of bundled services is when a telecom company offers its fixed phone service combined with another company's mobile phone service.

burn rate A measure of how quickly a company will exhaust its cash or available liquidity, used frequently in the venture capital industry. Burn rate is calculated by taking the total amount of cash on hand and dividing it by the monthly expenditures to see how many months the company could stay in business. The term was often used during the Internet boom

business An organized entity whose purpose is to sell services or goods to customers in order to earn a profit for the owners.

business cycle A long-term pattern of improvements and downturns in the economy. A business cycle typically has four stages: expansion, prosperity, contraction, and recession. Eventually a recession will be followed by expansion. A business cycle typically is tracked by looking at gross domestic product data. Employment levels, retail sales, and industrial productivity are some of the other economic indicators that show whether a business cycle is shifting from one stage to another. Business cycles may also be used in reference to an industry or company.

business day A day that banks or securities firms are open for business. Typically, business days are Monday through Friday, excluding various national holidays.

business incubator A business, either for-profit or non-profit, that assists start-up companies with establishing their business. An incubator provides below-market rent on office space and shared services such as teleconferencing equipment, a conference room, and secretarial services. Marketing, legal, and accounting services also may be provided. Private businesses and developers, public agencies, or universities may operate business incubators.

business plan A comprehensive plan written by a potential or current small-business owner who is attempting to obtain venture capital financing, a bank loan, or other financing. The business plan is a blueprint for how the company intends to perform. It must spell out the company's product or service, give a synopsis of its history, explain how the company is superior to its competition, and outline how it intends to be successful in its target market. Sales projections must be included in the business plan, along with financial performance statistics and future projections. The background, qualifications, and job functions for key players and managers also are included.

business process management A management technique that scrutinizes the processes that a company goes through to perform certain tasks. The intention is to create a more efficient way of working, thereby saving time and money.

business sales and inventories A lesser-watched economic statistic that is released monthly by the U.S. Department of Commerce. The statistic is usually released about six weeks after the end of the fiscal quarter that the data covers. The business sales and inventories statistic studies trends in inventory accumulation. If inventories are accumulating quickly, that may indicate a slowdown in business growth. If the inventories are declining, it may indicate that business is improving and there will be future growth.

business-to-business (B2B) An e-commerce business relationship in which a company's customers are other businesses. B2B businesses sell goods and services online to other companies, and are similar to wholesalers and distributors in the bricks-and-mortar marketplace. This term was frequently heard during the technology boom of the late 1990s. See also *bricks and mortar.*

busted convertible security A convertible security whose current stock price is substantially below its strike price. For instance, if the strike price is $20 and the stock is trading at $5, there is no reason to convert the security into stock at $20. Generally, a busted convertible security's value as a debt instrument or preferred stock obligation is much higher than its conversion value. Thus, busted convertible securities trade like debt instruments because there is little likelihood that it will be converted into equity.

butterfly spread An option strategy to sell several call options and at the same time buy several call options on the same security or futures contract. The options have different maturity dates and the exercise price of the options will differ. If the underlying security makes no dramatic moves, the options trader hopes to make a profit by collecting income from the premiums. The strategy limits both risk and profit potential. For instance, one call is bought at the lowest strike price, $35 for Company A's stock. Then two calls are sold at $40, which is the middle strike price. Then a call is bought at $50, the highest stock price.

Buttonwood Agreement A 1792 trade agreement that created an investment community out of the original 24 brokers in New York. The name comes from a Buttonwood tree that was their informal meeting site on Wall Street.

buy on the dips To take advantage of a *pullback,* or temporarily lower prices, in order to purchase stocks or other investments in a market that is rising. A *dip* is a small move downward in prices that have been steadily rising.

buy the rumor, sell the fact A phrase often quoted by stock or futures traders that explains price declines that occur after an anticipated positive event has happened.

For example, stocks prices may rally ahead of the monthly unemployment report on the anticipation that employment will be weaker than expected. The weaker numbers are interpreted to mean that the Federal Reserve is likely to cut interest rates, which is a positive event for stocks because it lowers a company's borrowing costs. However, when the actual unemployment numbers are released and match the lower expectations, stocks may trade lower.

buy-and-hold strategy A passive investment strategy, often associated with purchasing bonds, whereby a manager selects a portfolio of bonds aligned to his client's objectives and intends to hold the bonds to maturity. A *modified buy-and-hold strategy* follows this process; however, portfolio managers still actively look for attractively-priced opportunities. A buy-and-hold strategy also may be applied to stock selection or other investments.

buyback

    1. The purchase of a company's stock by that company.

    2. The purchase of a position to offset a previously established short position.

buydown A large, unscheduled payment made by a borrower to a creditor in order to reduce some or all of the borrower's outstanding debt. If allowed by the terms of the loan, a buydown reduces the amount of the regular payment.

buyer's market A market situation in which there are plenty of goods or services available to choose from and buyers can afford to be selective. The availability of goods or services drives selling prices down and can pressure the profits of the seller. The opposite is a *seller's market,* in which there are few items available for sale and prices are driven upwards.

buying climax The end to a rapid price rise in a security, commodity, or overall market for a type of asset, such as real estate or bonds, characterized by all of the likely buyers jumping on the bandwagon. After a buying climax, the market will fall sharply. A dramatic run-up on strong volume is a sign of a buying climax.

buying hedge A position that is established by purchasing futures contracts in order to protect against a possible increase in the future cost of commodities. Also called a *long hedge.*

buying power The amount of money that is available to fund a purchase. Often people will say that the dollar doesn't have the buying power it did many years ago. The term also is used in the context of taking all the cash held in a brokerage account and purchasing securities on margin.

buying the basis Buying an investment in the cash markets, such as wheat or S&P 500 futures, and then selling a futures position in an attempt to profit from a narrowing of the basis. Also called *cash-and carry trade.*

buy-side analyst A securities analyst who works in the research department of an institutional firm that is on the *buy-side* (so-called because these companies buy stocks and other securities on behalf of their clients). A typical buy-side firm is a mutual fund. A buy-side analyst's research product is distributed only internally or to the firm's best clients. In contrast, the research of a *sell-side analyst* (whose firm is selling its trading and investment banking services to clients) is widely distributed to the public at large as well as the firm's clients.

buy-side trader A person who trades on behalf of an institutional investor such as a pension or mutual fund portfolio manager.

buy-stop order A buy order that won't be executed until the market price rises to the price level listed by the stop order. At that point it will become a market order to buy the security at the best price possible. For instance, a buy-stop order may be entered for a S&P 500 futures contract calling for it to be bought at 850. If the current price is 835, the order won't be executed until 850 is reached. A technical trader might use this type of order because he or she isn't willing to purchase the contract unless it reaches a certain point. Also called *suspended market order.*

bylaws Rules written by a corporation or non-profit organization that establish the policies the corporation or organization will follow. Bylaws must be adopted by the board of directors. Such policies cover the election of officers, the appointment of auditors, how many shares of stock will be issued, and other topics.

bypass trust A trust that is created to minimize estate taxes by taking full advantage of a tax credit available when the first spouse dies. However, other estate planning tools must be used to minimize taxes when the second person dies.

A bypass trust takes advantage of a person's *lifetime unified gift and estate tax credit,* which is the amount of money that can be left to beneficiaries without paying federal estate taxes. The credit is $1 million and is scheduled to increase to $3 million by 2009. If a married couple has $2.4 million of assets, the assets of the first spouse to die can be included in an estate that can give $1 million tax free to the couple's children or other beneficiaries. The living spouse can also use the $1 million credit, and only the remaining $400,000 is taxed. Also called *A/B trust,* a *unified credit trust,* and *credit shelter trust.*

C

C shares In a mutual fund with more than one class of shares, C shares are typically those shares that have a permanent sales charge component in the fee structure.

cabinet security A stock or bond that is listed on a major exchange but is no longer actively traded.

cabinet trade A trade made in an inactive stock or bond. A cabinet trade also may be an off-market transaction that is completed in order to close out a nearly worthless option contract because it is out of the money.

cable The exchange rate between the U.S. dollar and the British pound sterling. The rate was transmitted over the transatlantic cable from 1866, and the initial novelty of the communication method gave the exchange rate this name. Cable also refers to sending a message electronically or transferring funds.

CAC-40 Index A stock market index that measures the performance of 40 top companies listed on the Paris Bourse, which is the Paris stock exchange. It is a narrow-based capitalization-weighted index that was developed with a base level of 1,000 on December 31, 1987.

California Public Employees Retirement System (CALPERS) The United States' largest public pension fund; it manages assets of $128 billion. It provides retirement and health benefits to nearly 1.4 million state and local public employees and their families. It also has become a major voice in corporate governance issues.

call The right, but not the obligation, to sell a security at a predetermined price.

call date A specific date on which a bond can be redeemed before it reaches maturity. A bond typically can be redeemed at the discretion of the issuer at *par* (face value). In some circumstances there may

be special requirements surrounding the specific call-date features. Those will be spelled out in the bond's prospectus. If a bond can be called, it is a *callable bond*.

call loan rate The interest rate on short-term secured loans that can be called, or cancelled, by giving a 24-hour notice.

call money Money obtained from banks or brokers to finance margin loans. Generally, call money can be obtained by giving a two-day notice. The interest rate charged is flexible.

call option An option that gives the purchaser the right, but not the obligation, to purchase the underlying stock, commodity, or other financial instrument at a set time and price from the writer of the call option. Typically, one option contract for a stock confers the right to buy 100 shares of the stock. A purchaser of a call option believes that the price of the underlying security will rise and is willing to pay a premium for the right to be able to purchase it at a lower price in the future, thereby avoiding the inflated market price.

call premium A premium that bond issuers must pay to purchasers of their callable bonds to compensate them for the fact that the bonds may be called before maturity and the bondholders may not receive as much interest over the life of the bond as anticipated. The call premium is the amount above the value at maturity that the issuer must pay to the bondholder for possibly calling the bond.

call protection A situation in which a bond or note cannot be redeemed by the issuer prior to a certain date.

call provision A provision in a bond indenture that gives the bond issuer the option to call the bond for redemption or refund at a specific time (before the bond's stated maturity) or at a certain price. Also called *redemption provision*.

call ratio The key interest rate that Korea uses to set monetary policy. The call ratio is the rate at which the Bank of Korea buys and sells short-term government securities. In the past Korea has had an explicit inflation target between 2 and 4 percent.

call risk A lender's potential opportunity loss associated with premature repayment of principal on a debt instrument. Call risk is a reinvestment risk, because it is usually impossible to reinvest the funds in a similar instrument with an equal yield.

call swaption A swaption is an option to enter into an interest rate swap at a specified future date with the call giving the purchaser the right, but not the obligation, to receive a fixed interest rate. A swaption is short for *swap option,* which is an over-the-counter option on an interest rate swap.

callable A bond that the issuer can call before maturity. The issuer can decide to redeem the bond and pay the investor the *par,* or face value, of the bond, or, in some cases, a slight premium. If interest rates fall, companies often call bonds because they can issue new bonds at a lower interest rate and save money. If a bond is called it is referred to as *called away.*

callable bond A bond that the issuer can demand the investor return before its stated maturity date. The issuer repays the investor the principal amount. Because the purchaser may lose future interest payments that he or she would have received, if the bond can be called that risk is reflected in the bond's price. Corporations call bonds when interest rates have fallen below what they are currently paying on the outstanding bonds. The bonds can be called and then reissued at a lower interest rate, which saves the company money. This is a similar process to refinancing mortgages in order to take advantage of lower interest rates.

callable preferred stock Preferred stock that can be retired or redeemed at the option of the issuing corporation at the price stated in the preferred stock contract. The investor can either receive cash for the preferred stock based on the call price (redemption price), or can convert it into common stock. If a preferred stock is called, the stockholder is entitled to receive the par value of the stock, a call premium, any dividends in arrears, and part of the current period's dividend.

called away Eliminating an underlying security position by exercising a call option. A common stock position may be called away if a short call option is exercised. A bond position also may be called away by the issuer under call provisions that are embedded in the bond indenture.

CALPERS See *California Public Employees Retirement System.*

cap A limit on a price outlined by a contract or other agreement. Adjustable rate mortgages or adjustable rate credit cards often have a cap.

capacity utilization An economic statistic that shows what percentage of the capacity at U.S. manufacturing plants is being used. It is cited as a percentage, such as 75.6 percent. The data is included in the monthly industrial production statistics that are released by the Federal Reserve Board each month around the 15th.

capex See *capital expenditures.*

capital

  1. The amount of funds that represent an ownership stake in a business or new venture that can be used to create wealth.

  2. The net worth of a business, or the amount by which assets exceed liabilities.

  3. Accumulated wealth such as cash, stocks, and other investments.

capital adequacy A ratio that can indicate a bank's ability to maintain equity capital sufficient to pay depositors whenever they demand their money and still have enough funds to increase the bank's assets through additional lending. Banks list their capital adequacy ratios in their financial reports. It is stated in terms of equity capital as a percent of assets. Capital requirements imposed by regulators tend to be simple mechanical rules rather than applications of sophisticated risk models.

capital asset pricing model (CAPM) A model that shows the relationship between expected return and expected risk. CAPM shows that the return on an asset depends on 1) the time value of money (the total interest rate or return that can be earned on money over a period of time) 2) the reward for bearing systemic risk (the risks inherent in a market, such as the possibility of the stock market selling off) and 3) the amount of systemic risk. The risk is systemic because even if a stock is purchased and the company performs well, poor performance by a competitor in the same industry may mean that the entire market trades sharply lower. Because investors are risk-averse, they require higher rewards for higher risks.

capital budget A budget used to plan major, long-term, cash-intensive projects, such as building a new plant or office building or funding long-term research. Several financial tools can be used to evaluate potential capital budget plans, such as internal rate of return (IRR), a payback period, and a net present value analysis. See also *internal rate of return*.

capital consumption allowance The percentage of the gross domestic product (GDP) that is due to depreciation. GDP minus capital consumption allowance equals net national product. The capital consumption allowance measures the amount of expenditure that a country needs to undertake to simply maintain, as opposed to grow, its productivity.

capital expenditures (capex) Expenditures for big-ticket items that are expected to last several years. In the telecom and technology markets, the amount of money companies spend on capital expenditures has a direct influence on the sales growth that their suppliers can expect.

capital flight The exodus of large sums of money from a country that is experiencing political or economic turmoil. Funds typically flee to a safe haven, such as the U.S. Treasury bond market. Capital flight is very disruptive because it tends to multiply on itself. That is, if one country is experiencing turmoil, then there is the danger that investors will pull their funds from other countries in the region to avoid potential future losses. The term is associated with smaller, emerging market economies, such as Asia Pacific in 1997 and 1998, Russia in 1998, and countries in Latin America at many different times. In contrast, an *investment outflow* indicates that money is leaving a country in a more orderly fashion.

capital gain The income derived from selling an investment for an amount of money greater than its purchase price. To be considered a capital gain, and not an ordinary gain, the investment must have been held for one year or longer. Capital gains are taxed at a lower rate than ordinary income is taxed at. Capital gains can be offset by capital losses in order to reduce the amount of the taxpayer's overall bill.

capital gains tax An income tax assessed on investments or assets that are held for at least 12 months. The U.S. capital gains tax rate was lowered in 2003 to 15 percent by 20 percent, which is lower than the rate for ordinary income, which can be as much as 35 percent. For individuals in the 10-percent or 15-percent income tax bracket, the capital gains tax rate is 5 percent, down from 10 percent. Unless Congress takes further action, the pre-2003 capital-gains rates will reappear after 2008.

capital lease A lease that in an economically substantial way transfers nearly all of the risk and rewards inherent in the leased property to the lessee. Payments for a capital lease should not be treated as a current expense, but rather should be capitalized by recording them on the balance sheet as both an asset and a liability. Under the "Statement of Financial Accounting Standards 13" criteria, a lease must be treated as a capital lease if it meets one of the following four criteria: (1) the lease transfers ownership of the property to the lessee when the lease ends; (2) the lease has a purchase option at a price discounted from the regular market price; (3) the length of the lease is equal to 75 percent of the estimated economic life of the leased property, although this isn't applicable if the lease term begins during the final 25 percent of the estimated economic life; and (4) the present value of the minimum lease payments equals or exceeds 90 percent of the fair value of the leased property. A capital lease contrasts with an operating lease, which does not meet any of those four criteria. An *operating lease* is an expense item and no asset or liability is recorded on the company's financial statements.

capital loss   The cost of selling an investment for a price that is less than its purchase price. To be considered a capital loss, and not an ordinary loss, the investment must have been held for one year or longer. Capital losses can offset capital gains in order to reduce the amount of the taxpayer's overall bill.

capital markets   The markets in which debt and equity are raised and then traded in the secondary market.

capital rationing   The action that a corporation takes when capital is either difficult or expensive to obtain and many projects must compete for the limited capital available. Companies ration capital when companies increase the minimum return required to fund a new project or investment.

capital structure   The long-term financing arrangements that a corporation has established. A company's capital structure may include long-term debt, retained earnings, and common and preferred stocks. Capital structure contrasts with financial structure, which includes short-term debt and accounts payable.

capitalism   An economic and business system that rewards individual effort by giving successful individuals and companies the right to keep the profits from their activities.

Most of the land, factories, manufacturing, transportation, and communication systems are privately owned and operated in relatively competitive environments, where businesses and individuals seek to increase their profits. Capital is raised in order to fund activities and produce profits. Property and businesses are privately owned and typically the government plays a minor role in directing business.

capitalization–weighted index   A stock index in which each stock affects the index in proportion to its market value. The NASDAQ Composite Index, the S&P 500 Index, the Wilshire 5000 Equity Index, the Philadelphia Stock Exchange's Gold & Silver Sector Index, and the Utility Sector Index are examples of capitalization-weighted indices. Also called *market-value weighted indices.*

capitalized interest   Interest that is paid for a capital asset that is treated as a regular asset and amortized on the income statement over a multiyear period. Capitalized interest contrasts with *regular interest,* which is treated as an expense in the current period and charged against income.

CAPM   See *capital asset pricing model.*

captive insurance company   An insurance company that is owned or controlled by another insurer or a small number of client firms. The owner or company controlling the insurance company helps to fulfill its business objectives by having a captive company. The arrangement also may provide some tax advantages to the owner.

Capture Theory of Regulation   A theory developed by George Stigler that says an industry can benefit from regulation if it can *capture* the regulatory agency involved. This can happen if the industry's political influence and technical knowledge makes the regulatory agency dependent on it. Political appointees from the industry, along with the agency's need for informal cooperation from the industry, help create a situation in which the agency is captured.

car   A unit quantity of an item, such as a contract, that is traded in the commodities market. For example, a *car of bellies* may refer to a contract on pork bellies. The term comes from the fact that quantities of the product specified in the futures contract correspond to the capacity of goods that can be packed into a railroad car.

Carnegie, Andrew   A day laborer who began his career earning $1.20 a week in a Pittsburgh Steel mill and became wealthy as the head of a steel empire. Carnegie's Union Iron Mills produced beams and plates for his bridge-building company. He created his steel empire through acquisitions and good management processes. He also bought steamships and railroads. He sold his steel company to J.P. Morgan's U.S. Steel Corporation for $492 million, which made him the world's richest man. He gave away much of his fortune to charitable organizations and endowed libraries throughout the United States.

carry   The interest cost of financing securities. A *positive carry* occurs when the return from a security exceeds the financing cost. A *negative carry* occurs when the financing cost exceeds the return on the security that has been financed.

carrying charge   The cost of storing a physical commodity over a period of time, including storage, insurance, interest, and opportunity cost.

carrying value   The portion of an asset's value that is not depreciated. Also called *book value*. Carrying value is not market value, which is determined by market forces, such as stock prices. A company assigns carrying value to its assets.

cartel   A group of countries or companies that work in concert to limit production of a product in order to influence the price of the product. OPEC, the Organization of Petroleum Exporting Countries, is one of the better-known cartels. Many western countries, including the United States, have laws prohibiting cartels, but many other countries don't.

carve out   To separate part of a company's business, such as a product or division, from the company and turn it into a totally independent firm by selling shares in the new firm.

cash & carry   An arbitrage transaction that includes the purchase of a commodity in the cash market using borrowed money while selling the corresponding futures contract. See also *arbitrage*.

cash available for distribution   A measure of a Real Estate Investment Trust's (REIT) ability to generate cash and distribute dividends to shareholders. Put another way, it is the amount of money left over after the bills are paid. Normal monthly expenses, non-cash items, and one-time expenditures are subtracted from the funds received from operations in order to determine how much cash is available for distribution.

cash basis accounting   An accounting system that records income when it is received and records expenses when they are paid. In contrast, the most common account method records income when it is earned and expenses when they are incurred.

cash collateral   Items such as cash, negotiable instruments, titles, securities, deposit accounts, or other cash equivalents in which the debtor's estate and an entity other than the estate have an interest. Cash collateral may not be used, sold, or leased in the ordinary course of business unless the creditor with an interest in the collateral consents or the court, after notice and a hearing, authorizes the transaction.

cash commodity   The actual physical commodity underlying the futures contract. Also called *actuals* or *spot commodity*.

cash equivalent   A readily marketable financial instrument that has a highly stable value.

cash flow   The cash available to a business generated from its operations. A positive cash flow means that the net operating income is sufficient to cover expenses.

A negative cash flow shows that expenses exceed revenues. A corporation issues a statement of cash flow with its quarterly and yearly earnings report. The statement shows where the company received its funds from and where they were spent. A popular measurement of cash flow, especially among Wall Street analysts, is *free cash flow*, which is cash flow left after expenses, capital expenditures, dividends, and debt service has been paid, although some companies may slightly vary what comprises free cash flow. The concept of free cash flow gained followers after the bear market that started in 2000 brought into question the quality of companies' financial statements.

cash flow coverage ratios Cash flow analysis tools that add back certain expenses that are normally deducted to arrive at net income, such as adding back interest expense because it was already subtracted to obtain net income. Because earnings and cash flow may vary significantly, cash flow coverage ratios may be more important indicators of a company's financial condition than earnings. See also *cash flow to long-term debt ratio*.

cash flow from operations Cash flow (net income plus depreciation expense, which is a non-cash charge, and deferred taxes) adjusted by increases in accounts receivable and accounts payable. Increases in accounts receivable are a use of cash if the company didn't collect all of its sales or used cash to produce the increase. However, an increase in accounts payable or another current liability account means that the firm acquired some assets but hasn't paid for them, which has the effect of boosting cash.

cash flow management The process of planning a company's schedule for paying bills and estimating when income is likely to be received. Cash flow management helps a company avoid damaging its relationship with creditors by not paying bills on time and being forced into bankruptcy.

cash flow to assets A financial ratio that measures how well a company is able to generate cash from its current operations. Calculate cash flow to assets by subtracting net cash flows from operating activities and dividing the resulting number by average total assets. This ratio measures a company's cash-generating efficiency using cash flow to assets. Other ratios accomplish a similar objective by using cash flows and cash flows to sales.

cash flow to long-term debt ratio A cash flow coverage ratio that measures how much cash is available to pay for long-term debt. This ratio is a good indicator of potential bankruptcy. To arrive at the ratio, compute cash flow by adding net income, depreciation expense, and changes in deferred tax, then dividing that amount by the book value of long-term debt.

cash flow to sales A financial ratio that measures how well a company is able to generate cash from its current operations. Calculate cash flow to sales by subtracting net cash flows from operating activities and dividing the resulting number by net sales. This ratio measures a company's cash-generating efficiency using cash flow to sales. Other ratios accomplish a similar objective by using cash flows and cash flows to assets.

cash flow yield A financial ratio that measures how well a company generates cash from its current operations. Calculate cash flow yield by subtracting net cash flow from operating activities and dividing the resulting number by net income. This ratio measures a company's cash-generating efficiency using cash flow. Other ratios accomplish a similar objective by using cash flows to sales and cash flows to assets.

cash flows from financing activities Funds that a company receives through its financing activities. It is computed by taking the amount of funds received from financing (*inflows*) and subtracting *outflows*, or the uses of financing, which come from paying down liability accounts or the payment of dividends. *Inflows* of cash from financing are created by increases in notes payables, long-term liabilities, and equity accounts from stock and bond issues.

cash management account (CMA)
An account that is offered to consumers by a brokerage firm. A cash management account combines the ability to trade securities while earning money market interest with the ability to write checks and make deposits. A CMA often requires a minimum initial deposit amount.

cash management bill A short-term, fixed-income security issued by the U.S. Treasury to cover cash needs for a very short period of time. Cash management bills may be issued before income tax payments are received, or before the government has to make a large payment of some sort. Cash management bills range in duration from as little as four days to several months. They are issued on an as-needed basis, in contrast to a regular schedule that the Treasury follows for issuing its other bills and notes.

cash market A market for an actual commodity or financial instrument, in contrast to the futures market. Commodity markets often have locations where buyers and sellers meet, and where commodities are bought or sold for immediate delivery For example, there are actual sales locations where cattle and oil are delivered for sale. In contrast, a cash market for a financial instrument doesn't have a centralized meeting place. Instead, transactions occur over a computer system or the telephone. Also called *spot market*.

cash rate The key interest rate that Australia uses to set monetary policy. The cash rate is the interest rate charged on overnight loans between banks. Australia uses an explicit inflation target, which in the past has been around 2 to 3 percent a year.

cash ratio The most conservative liquidity ratio for judging the financial stability of a company on a short-term basis. To calculate cash ratio, add the value of the company's cash and short-term marketable securities and divide the total by current liabilities. This ratio shows the ability of the company's cash on hand to fund short-term liabilities.

cash settlement An obligation or financial instrument, such as a futures or options contract, that is paid for in cash. In a banking transaction, cash settlement is the process of recording the debit and credit positions of the parties in the transaction and making the respective cash transfers. In the money market, a transaction is a cash settlement if the securities that have been purchased are paid for by Federal Reserve funds on the same day the trade is made.

cash surrender value The amount of money the holder of a cash-value life insurance policy would receive from the life insurance company if the insurance policy were cancelled. A cash-value life insurance policy, in addition to being a life insurance policy, is also an investment and savings account whose value increases each year that it is held. Policyholders also can borrow against the value of the policy.

cash-and-carry trade A trade in which an investment or index-equivalent position is purchased in the cash market and an equivalent futures contract is sold. The purpose is to profit from a narrowing of the basis. Also called *buying the basis*.

cash-balance pension plan A benefit plan that gives an employee a specific amount of money based on salary and years of service. The employer bears the investment risk. Cash-balance pension plans have come under criticism because often they pay more to a younger person leaving the company than to an older person nearing retirement age. In early 2003, regulations were proposed to require pension plans converting to a cash-balance plan to make it age-neutral. A cash-balance plan establishes a hypothetical account for each employee and credits the account with hypothetical pay and interest credits.

cash-generating efficiency The ability of a company to generate cash from continuing operations. Three ratios measure a company's cash-generating efficiency: cash-flow yield, cash flows to sales, and cash flows to assets.

cash-realization ratio A financial ratio that is used in the telecom industry, among others. It is calculated by dividing cash flow from operating activities by net income. It measures how close a company's net income is to being realized in cash. Cash flow from operating activities is taken from the statement of cash flows. The net income figure is taken from the income statement. Companies that are less risky have cash realization ratios that exceed 1.0, indicating that income may not be dependent on non-cash sources such as mark-to-market accounting valuations, which can be affected by aggressive valuation decisions by management. This ratio is considered a good measure of earnings quality. Cash-realization ratio is calculated by dividing cash flow from operating activities by net income.

cash-value life insurance A life insurance policy that combines life insurance with the features of a savings and investment account. The gains from the investments accumulate tax-deferred and the cash value of the policy can be borrowed against. A cash-value life insurance policy pays a death benefit to the named beneficiaries when the policyholder dies. The three primary types of cash-value life insurance are

> A *whole life insurance policy,* which lets the cash value of the policy accumulate depending on the return of the life insurance company's investments in stocks, bonds, and other financial instruments.

> A *variable life policy,* which lets the policyholder choose the investments for the life insurance policy, selecting from a variety of mutual fund or other investment options.

> A *universal life policy,* which lets investors choose their investments among money market and Treasury securities; universal life policies were widely popular during the 1980s, when interest rates were high, but are less popular today.

CAT bond Short for *catastrophe-linked bond.* CAT bond is a debt obligation that is often issued by an insurance company. The interest payments are tied to the insurance losses of a portfolio of property and casualty insurance contracts. Large losses from a hurricane or flood result in investors receiving smaller-than anticipated interest payments; if losses are small, then investors receive above-market interest payments. Also called *Act of God bond.*

catch-up contribution The additional money that can be contributed to a 401(k) retirement plan that is offered to employees. The catch-up contribution was allowed as part of the Economic Growth and Tax Relief Reconciliation Act passed in 2001. The law allows employees age 50 and older to contribute an extra $2,000 in 2003 on a pre-tax basis. The catch-up contribution will increase $1,000 per year until it reaches $5,000 in 2005. Many employers will not match the catch-up contribution, however.

CATS See *certificates of accrual on treasury securities.*

cats and dogs A stock market term that refers to speculative companies with little history of earnings or revenues. In a strong market, traders will sometimes say that everything is going up, even the cats and dogs.

cattle placements A monthly statistic reported by the U.S. Department of Agriculture as part of its monthly cattle-on-feed report. It shows how many cattle are being put in feedlots in preparation to go to slaughter. The report is presented in terms of a percentage. For instance, the report will say that placements are down 1 percent from last year.

cattle-on-feed report A monthly report, produced by the U.S. Agriculture Department, that details the number of cattle being placed in feedlots as a precursor to going to market. Three stages of getting cattle to market are detailed by the report: The first is *placements,* which are cattle that are taken out of pastures, where they eat grass, and put on corn to start gaining weight. The second stage is *cattle on feed,* which is the number of cattle that are eating corn to gain weight in preparation for slaughter; the corn may be mixed with some extra protein, such as soymeal. The third stage is the *number of marketed cattle*, which are cattle that have been sent to slaughter.

The cattle-on-feed report is stated in percentage terms compared to the previous year. For example, if cattle on feed are placed at 99 percent compared with a year ago, that means that placements are down one percentage point from a year ago.

caveat emptor   A Latin term that means "let the buyer beware." It is typically used in reference to consumer transactions.

caveat venditor   A Latin term meaning "let the seller beware," in contrast to the more widely known saying *caveat emptor* (let the buyer beware). The principle of *caveat venditor* cautions that the seller is responsible for any problem that the buyer might encounter with a service or product.

CBO   See *Congressional Budget Office.*

CBOE   See *Chicago Board Options Exchange.*

CBOT   See *Chicago Board of Trade.*

CCPU   Short for *cash cost per user;* the average cost that a telecom carrier spends to retain current customers.

CD   See *certificate of deposit.*

CDC   See *Community Development Corporation.*

CDCU   See *Community Development Credit Union.*

CDMA   Short for *code-division multiple access;* a technology used in wireless communications for second-generation and third-generation wireless networks. It allows many signals to occupy a single transmission channel in order to optimize the available bandwidth, a process called *multiplexing.* CDMA is used in UHF (ultra-high-frequency) cellular telephone systems in the 800-MHz and 1.9-GHz bands. Wireless companies that use the CDMA technology

include Sprint, PCS and its affiliates, Verizon Wireless, and Qwest Communications International Inc.

CDO   Stands for *collateralized debt obligations;* a collection of debt instruments that have been grouped together to provide greater flexibility for the issuer and a good return for the investor. Repayment is collateralized by the assets underlying the CDO.

cease-and-desist order   A court or regulatory order that directs a company or official to stop unlawful behavior. Regulatory agencies such as the Securities and Exchange Commission can issue cease-and-desist orders.

cedi   The currency unit of Ghana comprised of 100 pesewas.

Central African Economic and Monetary Community   A monetary union consisting of six West African countries: Cameroon, Central African Republic, Chad, Republic of Congo, Equatorial Guinea, and Gabon. These countries use the CFA franc, or the franc de la Coopération Financiére Africaine, which is issued by the Banque des Etats de l'Afrique Centrale. The CFA franc was pegged, or linked, to the French franc starting 1947, but became pegged to the euro when France adopted that currency in 1999. Only one devaluation has occurred during the history of the currency peg. In January 1994, the CFA was devalued to CFA 100 from CFA 50. The countries using the CFA franc have an arrangement with the French treasury to maintain their currency peg and to take the sole responsibility for guaranteeing convertibility of CFA francs into euros. See also *West African Economic and Monetary Union.*

CEO   See *chief executive officer.*

certificate of deposit (CD)   A deposit with a specific maturity date and a specific interest rate. Many individual investors buy CDs from a bank, although corporations also purchase commercial CDs that are extremely large. CDs also are sold by savings and loans and credit unions. CDs sold by banks or S&Ls that are Insured by the Federal Deposit Insurance Corp. are insured up to $100,000. Interest earned on CDs are taxable by federal and state governments. If the CDs mature in 1 year or less, they can be used as a cash reserve.

certificates of accrual on treasury securities (CATS) Zero-coupon instruments created by stripping U.S. Treasury securities. Also may be called *STRIPS* or *Stripped Treasury Securities*, although zero-coupon bonds were created and issued by broker/dealers before the U.S. Treasury Department started its STRIPS program in 1985. CATS were issued by Salomon Brothers, which is now part of Citigroup Inc.

certified check A check guaranteed by the bank it is written on. When the check is certified, it becomes a legal obligation of the bank. The bank immediately deducts the funds to cover it from the depositor's account. A certified check cannot bounce.

Certified Development Company (CDC) A non-profit corporation that provides small businesses with 10- or 20-year private Small Business Administration (SBA) guaranteed financing. CDCs must meet SBA guidelines. Also called *504 corporation*.

certified financial planner (CFP) A professional designation given by the Certified Financial Planner Board of Standards to applicants who complete course work on six subjects: investment planning, financial planning, income tax planning, insurance planning, retirement planning, and employee benefits and estate planning; pass a two-day examination; and meet ethics and experience standards. Continuing education is also required. Those who want to help people plan their finances and invest their money can obtain this qualification.

certified investment management consultant (CIMC) A designation for a person who has completed certain course work and has passed exams that are administered by the Institute for Investment

Management Consultants. They must have experience in the industry, adhere to a code of ethics, and satisfy continuing education requirements.

certified public accountant (CPA) A type of qualified accountant. Although rules vary by state as to the requirements for becoming a CPA, generally speaking a CPA must have 150 semester hours of college coursework, which may be a combination of undergraduate and graduate classes. A CPA must also pass a two-day exam that is administered by the Board of Examiners of the American Institute of Certified Public Accountants (AICPA). Some states also require a certain amount of work experience as a public accountant before CPA status is achieved.

certified stocks Stocks of a commodity that have been inspected and found to meet the quality requirements for commodities in order to fulfill the delivery requirements specified by a futures exchange. When certified stocks are delivered, they must be transported to one of half a dozen or so locations that the futures exchange has specified as delivery warehouses.

CFA See *chartered financial analyst*.

CFA franc A currency used by many West African countries. See also *West African Economic and Monetary Union* and *Central African Economic and Monetary Community*.

CFO See *chief financial officer*.

CFP See *certified financial planner*.

CFTC See *Commodity Futures Trading Commission*.

chaebol A South Korean conglomerate. South Korean banks sometimes work on a buddy system, making unsound loans to companies just because they are associated with the same chaebol. A chaebol often is controlled by one family or a small group of families.

chain store sales report A weekly report of retail sales activity in the largest U.S. retail stores. The Bank of Tokyo-Mitsubishi Ltd. and UBS Warburg compile sales figures from stores that have been open for one year or longer, called *same-store sales.* The seven stores that are surveyed for their sales activity are Target, Federated, JC Penney, Eckerd, May Department Stores, Sears, and Wal-Mart. The chain store sales index shows a percentage change from the previous week and previous year. It is timely and it closely tracks changes in consumer spending; however, its volatility can limit its impact, so the monthly chain sales number is more closely watched. The importance of chain store sales increases during the holiday selling season. The data is released every Tuesday morning unless there is a holiday during the week, in which case it is likely to be released on Wednesday.

chairman   Short for *chairman of the board,* this is the highest-ranking corporate officer. The chairman presides over board meetings. Often one person may hold the positions of chairman and chief executive officer. Depending on the personality and clout of the chairman, the chairman may have a lot of power and authority or may take a distant back-seat to the chief executive officer of the company. A chairman may be more of an honorary position for a long-term employee or another prominent person, large shareholder, or a member of the founding family.

Challenger Report   A monthly job cut report, produced by the recruiting firm Challenger, Gray and Christmas, that tallies the number of layoffs throughout the United States. The report has some effect on the stock market because job cuts can be expected to positively impact corporate profits when employee costs decrease. The data gives some sense of future layoff activity and tracks layoffs by industry and region, as well as providing reasons for the layoffs. However, the data has some limits: Layoffs are listed by the company headquarters, but the job cuts may be spread across the United States. The layoff data is gleaned from press reports and isn't a comprehensive compilation. The workforce reduction may occur over a long period of time; if conditions change, more or fewer jobs could be cut or saved. The data also doesn't count workforce reductions that occur through retirement or voluntary resignations. The report is published one week after the previous month end.

Chancellor of the Exchequer   The United Kingdom equivalent of the U.S. Treasury Secretary.

change agent   A person or company that initiates wide-reaching changes within a company or industry.

channel   A pattern in a technical analysis that shows a straight line occurring in an upward or downward "channel." It is a very strong chart pattern that is occurring in a definite direction.

channel inventory   The amount of inventory that is in the process of being made available for delivery to the end customer.

chaos theory   An area of mathematics that deals with non-linear dynamic systems. Although the results may seem to be random, they actually arise from a deterministic process. Chaotic systems have a fractal dimension and are highly dependent on initial conditions. *Fractals* are geometric structures that appear to be similar when viewed at a wide range of magnifications.

Chapter 11 bankruptcy   A type of bankruptcy that allows a business to retain control of its operations while it plans how to reorganize its debts. Chapter 11 is the most common type of bankruptcy. Creditors are prevented from pursuing a company that is in a Chapter 11 proceeding. The debtor and creditors meet to draw up an agreement for repaying some of the debt. In a Chapter 7 bankruptcy, in contrast, the company closes its doors and liquidates its business. See also *Chapter 7 bankruptcy, Chapter 13 bankruptcy.*

Chapter 7 bankruptcy   A type of bankruptcy in which a business sells its remaining assets, shuts its doors, and goes out of business. There is no attempt to reorganize in order to pay some of the debts and remain in business. A court-appointed interim trustee is given discretion to make management changes, arrange unsecured financing, and wind down the business. Individuals can also file for Chapter 7 bankruptcy. See also *Chapter 11 bankruptcy, Chapter 13 bankruptcy.*

Chapter 13 bankruptcy A type of bankruptcy used by individuals who want to reorganize their debts and pay back a portion of the money they owe to creditors. The debtor pays something each month for several years to the bankruptcy court, which distributes the funds to the creditors. When the payments are completed, the debts are discharged. Chapter 13 bankruptcies allow individuals to hold onto more assets than Chapter 7 bankruptcies, which involve total liquidation. See also *Chapter 7 bankruptcy, Chapter 11 bankruptcy.*

charitable lead trust A trust that allows a charity to receive income during the grantor's, or donor's, lifetime. Upon the death of the grantor, the balance of the trust goes to the grantor's beneficiaries. This trust reduces estate taxes while enabling the family to retain the assets. See also *charitable remainder trust.*

charitable remainder trust An irrevocable trust in which property, investments, or money is donated to a charity, but the grantor, or donor, continues to use the property or receive income from the investments or money while still alive. Upon the death of the donor, the charity receives the balance of the trust. The trust is tax-efficient because the grantor avoids paying capital gains tax on the assets in the trust and can deduct the earnings of the trust. The trust also removes the assets from the grantor's estate, which reduces the amount of estate taxes that will be due after death. Often a charitable remainder trust is created by someone who doesn't have any family members or children that he or she needs to support. See also *charitable lead trust.*

chart of accounts A listing of all of a company's account names and numbers used in its *general ledger,* its accounting books. Typically these accounts include codes that indicate the type of transaction and the department or project the expense is associated with.

chartered financial analyst (CFA) A professional designation that may be obtained by analysts or portfolio managers working for asset managers or pension funds. The designation takes at least three years to obtain and involves passing three tests that are considered very difficult. The CFA designation has grown in popularity since 1999 as many people have been laid off and are looking for ways to increase their qualifications. Also, the criticism leveled at brokerage firms' research analysts for their conflict of interests has encouraged some people to obtain this qualification.

chartered financial consultant (ChFC) A qualification that life insurance agents typically obtain, along with the chartered life underwriter (CLU) designation. The ChFC designation typically takes several years to obtain and involves passing an exam.

chartered life underwriter (CLU) A common qualification for life insurance agents. Typically those holding a CLU also hold a chartered financial consultant (ChFC). The CLU designation typically takes several years to obtain and involves passing an exam and meeting ethical standards and continuing education requirements.

check A piece of paper that is a negotiable instrument drawn on a bank and payable on demand to the person identified as the payee.

check kiting Writing a check on an account without sufficient funds to cover the amount of the check, then depositing a check from a second account to cover the first check, and leaving the second account short of funds to cover its obligations. The process repeats itself, resulting in little more than a share game. Check kiting is illegal.

checking account An account targeted at investors that allows them to write drafts and make deposits. The sizes of the transactions are completely flexible. Typically, checking accounts pay very low interest rates, if they pay anything at all; therefore, they aren't useful as a way to save money. Banks, credit unions, and savings and loan institutions offer checking accounts. Checking accounts are insured by the U.S. government up to $100,000 per account through the Federal Deposit Insurance Corporation (FDIC). Interest earned on checking accounts is taxable. They are useful for keeping ready cash reserves.

cherry picking

1. In a bankruptcy action, the process in which competitors purchase only the best assets and leave behind the rest.

2. The action of a new portfolio manager in selecting only the best investments from a predecessor's portfolio.

3. Assigning winning trades to the trader's own account or the account of a favored client.

ChFC See *chartered financial consultant.*

Chicago Board of Trade (CBOT) The oldest futures exchange in the United States, which began trading futures contracts in 1865. The oldest continually traded contracts on the CBOT are corn and wheat futures, both traded since 1877. The CBOT trades a variety of futures and options contracts. Agricultural futures and options include wheat, corn, oats, soybeans, soybean meal, soybean oil, and rough rice. Financial futures and options are traded on the U.S. Treasury bond, 10-year Treasury notes, 5-year Treasury notes, 2-year Treasury notes, and 30-day Fed Funds rate. Stock index futures and options are traded on the Dow Jones Industrial Average. Trading occurs using open-outcry pit trading during regular trading hours. After hours, contracts can be traded on the CBOT's Electronic Trading System.

The CBOT is governed by a board of directors that includes a chairman, a vice chairman, 11 member directors, 3 public directors, and the president. The exchange is managed by an executive staff headed by the president and chief executive officer.

Chicago Board Options Exchange (CBOE) A subsidiary of the Chicago Board of Trade that operates as an independent entity, the CBOE trades options on over 1,500 equities and equity index futures. It was founded in 1973 to provide standardized, listed stock options as an alternative to options that were unregulated and created on an individual basis. Now the CBOE accounts for over half of all U.S. options trading and 91 percent of index options trading. Trading began April 26, 1973, with 16 call options that were traded on 16 underlying stocks. Put options were added in 1977. The first option on stock indices was introduced on March 11, 1983, when options on the Standard & Poor's 100 Index (ticker symbol OEX) were introduced. The CBOE also trades options on the Standard & Poor's 500 Index (SPX).

Options on interest rates were introduced in June 1989: options based on the 13-week U.S. Treasury bill yield and options on the 5-year, 10-year, and 30-year yields to maturity of U.S. Treasury notes and bonds. The underlying value of these options moves up or down as a result of shifts in the U.S. Treasury yield curve.

In 1993, the CBOE created FLEX (flexible exchange) options on the S&P 100, S&P 500, and Russell 2000 indices. FLEX options allow institutional investors to customize the terms of an option contract, the expiration date (up to 5 years), the strike price, and the exercise style and settlement basis, with a minimum opening underlying contract value of $10 million. In 1997, options on the Dow became eligible for FLEX trading.

Trading on sector indices began on the CBOE in October 1992. Options on sector indices in the automotive (AUX), banking

(BIX), chemical (CEX), software (CWX), environmental (EVX), gaming (GAX), gold (GOX), healthcare (HCX), internet (INX), insurance (IUX), oil (OIX), retail (RLX), and transportation (TRX) industries are now listed. In 1994, the CBOE Mexico Index (MEX), the Nikkei 300 Stock Index (NIK), and the CBOE Israel Index (ISX) were launched to give U.S. investors the ability to hedge the risks associated with holding stocks in foreign markets. In 1995, new CBOE sector indices in REITs (RIX) and technology (TXX) were added.

Chicago Fed National Activity Index
A monthly economic report prepared by the Chicago Federal Reserve Bank that tracks economic activity in the 7th district, which is comprised of Indiana, Iowa, Illinois, Michigan, and Wisconsin. The Chicago Fed National Activity Index is a coincident indicator of broad economic activity that is a weighted average of 85 indicators based on economic data covering production and income, employment, personal consumption, housing, manufacturing, trade sales, inventories, and orders. It is useful in tracking economic growth and identifying potential inflation. An index value of 0 indicates that the economy is growing at its long-run potential; a value over 0 indicates that the economy is growing above its potential. A negative value indicates that the economy is growing below potential. The data has a lag of about one month. It is a relatively new report that has not yet gained a following in the financial markets.

Chicago Mercantile Exchange (CME)
A futures and options exchange that trades contracts in four main areas: interest rates, stock indexes, foreign exchange, and commodities. In 2002, a record 558.4 million contracts with a value of $328.6 trillion traded at the CME, which the CME says is the largest notional value traded that year on any futures exchange. Among the well-known contracts that trade on the CME are futures and options on the S&P 500 index, the Eurodollar, and currency futures. Agricultural products traded include lean

hogs, frozen pork bellies, milk, feeder cattle, and live cattle.

The CME was founded as a not-for-profit corporation in 1889 as the Chicago Butter and Egg Board and became the Chicago Mercantile Exchange in 1919. At the time it was founded, the only futures traded were contracts based on butter and eggs. In December 2002, the CME became the first publicly traded U.S. financial exchange when it launched an initial public offering of the Class A shares of its parent company, the Chicago Mercantile Exchange Holdings Inc. The shares trade under the ticker symbol CME. Trading is based on open-outcry pit trading during regular trading hours. The CME also operates GLOBEX, an after-hours electronic trading system.

Chicago Purchasing Managers Index (PMI)   An index released monthly on the last business day of the month to which it refers that indicates how vibrant regional manufacturing activity is. An index value of 50 or higher indicates increasing business activity; below that indicates decreasing activity. The index breaks out readings for production, new orders, order backlog, inventories, prices paid, employment, and supplier deliveries. The PMI is a timely look at the strength of manufacturing industry in the Chicago Federal Reserve regions, which comprise Illinois, Iowa, Indiana, Michigan, and Wisconsin. The new orders and orders backlog indices are useful in predicting future production activity.

The Chicago PMI draws much of its influence from the fact that it is released one day before the ISM Index, which used to be called the NAPM index, and is produced by the Institute for Supply Management. The Chicago PMI index, is perceived by market traders to be a good leading indicator for the ISM, which typically affects the financial markets. Shortcomings of the PMI include the fact that it is only an opinion survey and relies on people's perceptions, not data. It also doesn't capture any technology improvements or increasing production efficiencies that might alter expectations and actual results.

Chicago School   Monetary theories that are closely linked with Milton Friedman, a noted monetarist and long-time professor at the University of Chicago. The monetarist theories that the Chicago School espouses say that the quantity of money in circulation and its rate of growth determines the level of economic activity and whether inflation occurs.

chief executive officer (CEO)   The person responsible for running a corporation. The chairman of the board or the president may also hold the title CEO.

chief financial officer (CFO)   The person responsible for the company's finances, whose duties include producing financial reports; signing checks; and devising long-term financial plans, including capital raising activities. The CFO may also hold multiple positions including treasurer or controller.

chief operating officer (COO)   A corporate executive who is responsible for day-to-day operations of the company. Typically the COO reports to the chief executive officer.

child tax credit   A tax credit of $600 for each child who is younger than 17 years of age, as of this printing. The credit is phased out when adjusted gross income exceeds $110,000 for married couples filing jointly, $55,000 for married separate filers, and $75,000 for all other taxpayers.

China Mint Panda Bear   A coin that is minted by the Chinese government from gold, silver, or platinum. Panda Bears are popular with coin collectors and investors. They can be purchased from the Chinese government or from traders in the secondary market.

Chinese Hedge   A hedge in which stock in a company is owned and a convertible bond in the same company is *sold short,*

meaning that the seller does not own the sold bond. The hedge is undertaken on the belief that the premium on the convertible will fall. A typical hedge would be to short the stock and purchase the convertible. Also called *reverse hedge.*

Chinese Wall   The separation that should exist between a bank's investment banking department and its research department. The separation is intended to protect research analysts who issue reports about companies' financial situations from being influenced by investment bankers who are trying to sell merger advisory services or capital raising services to those same companies. As the stock market fell after record gains in 2000, and regulators began looking at conflicts between investment banking and research, it became apparent that the Chinese Wall had developed some gaping holes.

chi-square test   A statistical measure of the fit, independence, or homogeneity of data. The chi-square test can be used to determine whether a sample of data comes from a normally distributed population by comparing its frequency distribution with that of the normal distribution. It can also be used to determine whether two variables are independent by comparing their observed joint occurrence with their expected joint occurrence. Finally, it can be used to determine whether categories of a single variable are represented in the same proportions in two or more populations.

churn   The rate of subscriber or customer turnover. If a company has a high rate of churn, it means the company may attract a large number of customers but will typically lose them at a rapid rate. The churn rate measures the number of customers that discontinue service in a typical month, and often is expressed as a percentage of a company's average subscriber base for the time period. The term often is used in conjunction with subscribers to wireless telephone companies.

churning The illegal practice of making a large number of trades in a client's account in order to increase the broker's commission.

CIF See *cost, insurance, and freight.*

CIMC See *certified investment management consultant.*

circuit breaker A circuit breaker in a stock or futures exchange works in the same way as the circuit breakers in a home; both cut off electricity before the system becomes dangerously overloaded. Circuit breakers are designed to stop the market from going into a free-fall and are intended to restore stability by helping rebalance the number of sell and buy orders. Separate circuit breakers are triggered when the Dow Jones Industrial Average (DJIA) drops 10 percent, 20 percent, and 30 percent; the point value of each of these thresholds is calculated at the beginning of each quarter by the New York Stock Exchange. The amount of time that trading is halted depends upon the severity of the drop. Circuit breakers were instituted after Black Monday in October 1987, when the U.S. stock market crashed, and have been revised after various market sell-offs, including October 1989.

Each stock and futures market also sets its own individual circuit breakers. In the future market, circuit breakers are referred to as *price limits,* which also limit upward movements. Trading *collars* limit index arbitrage trades by allowing those trades to be placed only if they are the opposite of the market's direction. For example, a buy order could be processed in a declining market. See also *collar* and *price limits.*

Class A shares Mutual funds shares that typically charge investors a front-end load, or sales charge assessed when the account is opened, that amounts to 1 percent to 5 percent of the total amount invested. Definitions for each class vary with each fund. See also *Class B shares, Class C shares,* and *Class I shares.*

class action lawsuit A court action in which many people file similar lawsuits and a judge agrees to group them together because of their similar claims. In such a case, a lead attorney for the class is appointed; however, the attorneys who filed the individual lawsuits also are allowed to share in any eventual fees. Class action lawsuits proliferated after the stock market began its descent following its peak in 2000. Hundreds of class action lawsuits were filed against different companies, especially telecom and technology companies that had experienced a disproportionate share of the gains from the bull market.

Class B shares Mutual funds shares that typically have a deferred sales charge, or back-end sales charge, that is assessed when shares are redeemed. Typically the fee declines the longer the investment is held. Definitions for each class vary with each fund. See also *Class A shares, Class C shares,* and *Class I shares.*

Class C shares Mutual funds shares that typically have no up-front or back-end sales load, or sales charge. If the shares are held for a minimum amount of time there is usually no redemption fee. However, they likely will have the highest 12b-1 fee (sales and marketing fee). This fee is paid each year by being deducted from the fund's assets. Each mutual fund defines its own definition Class C shares. See also *Class A shares, Class B shares,* and *Class I shares.*

Class I shares Mutual funds shares that are sold only to institutional investors. Fees and expenses for Class I shares vary widely. Depending on the fund, this type of share may be known by a different letter. See also *Class A shares, Class B shares,* and *Class C shares.*

clawback A word used in the venture capital industry to describe a common term found in partnership agreements. A clawback requires venture capitalists to refund fees to their investors if it turns out that the venture capitalists received more than their 20 percent share of a fund's overall profits. Clawbacks became common in 2002, occurring when a venture capitalist took its

20 percent share of a fund's early investment success, but the fund later lost money. Clawbacks also are used in other financing contexts, such as private equity.

Clayton Act An antitrust law passed in 1914 that prohibits a variety of pricing violations, such as *discriminatory rebates,* pricing or discounts that favor one group of customers over another. Section 7 of the Clayton Act prohibits mergers if the effect would be to substantially lessen competition or to create a monopoly. Within that section, the Hart-Scott-Rodino Act requires prior notification of mergers over $50 million to both the Federal Trade Commission (FTC) and the Justice Department, who are jointly charged with monitoring compliance. The $50 million will adjust beginning October 1, 2004 to take into account changes in the U.S. economy, based on gross national product from the previous year. Although the Clayton Act was passed in 1914, it has been updated and amended, including the Hart-Scott-Rodino Act, which was passed in 1976.

clean-vehicle tax deduction A deduction of $2,000 (as of this printing) that is available for people who buy eligible gasoline-electric hybrid vehicles.

clear Describes a situation in which a trade has been matched with its appropriate buyer or seller, the payment has been made, and the product has been delivered.

clear title A title that doesn't have any liens or other legal problems that call into question the ownership of the property. The term may apply to real estate or to personal property such as cars. In real estate transactions, title searches are conducted by companies specializing in this service. After a title company has completed a search and found no problems, the title company offers insurance certifying that the title is clear. The term *free and clear* also may be used to mean that there is a clear title.

clearing Moving checks from the bank where they were deposited to the bank on which they were drawn. This gives a credit to the bank where funds are deposited and a corresponding debit to the account of the paying institution. The Federal Reserve operates a nationwide check-clearing system. *Clearing* also is used to signify matching buyers and sellers in stock, futures, and options transactions.

clearing member The member of a futures exchange who accepts responsibility for all trades cleared, or settled, through him or her. The clearing member is responsible for matching the buy orders with the sell orders to make sure that the transactions are settled. Clearing members share secondary responsibility for the liquidity of the clearing operation. Clearing members earn commissions for matching their clients' trades with the counterparty, and they pay lower margins than non-clearing members and their customers. They must meet minimum capital requirements.

clearinghouse A business where mutual claims are settled between the accounts of member depository institutions. Banking clearinghouses manage check-clearing activities along with electronic fund transfers. A clearinghouse in the futures industry assists the transfer of funds and contracts between members who execute trades. A clearinghouse is a central point for depositing and paying out funds that need to be credited or debited into the accounts of its member firms. A futures clearinghouse also guarantees the performance of the futures contract, despite what the individual member may do. If a member defaults, the collective resources of the members are used to satisfy the claim as necessary. Another role that a futures clearinghouse undertakes is assigning and overseeing the deliveries of future contracts at maturity. In order to be a member of a clearinghouse, a firm generally must be a member of the futures exchange.

CLEC See *competitive local exchange carrier.*

CLN See *credit-linked note.*

closed-end fund   A type of investment company that offers a set number of shares that are traded on a stock exchange in the same manner as equities. The fund is managed according to its investment objectives and may invest in stocks, bonds, or a combination of both. Closed-end funds issue a fixed amount of shares through an initial public offering. In contrast, open-ended funds are commonly called *mutual funds.* Open-ended funds constantly offer new shares for sale and redeem shares at the end of any business day at a price of net asset value that is calculated at the end of each trading day. Closed-end funds can be bought or sold throughout the business day at a market price that may be above or below their net asset value, which fluctuates according to demand.

closely held corporation   A corporation that is owned by only a few shareholders. Shares of such a company are not available for trading in any meaningful way. If an investor wants to sell or purchase shares, the investor needs to locate existing shareholders and obtain their cooperation.

closing range   The range of prices as the market closes. Each exchange determines what precise time period the closing range covers. Closing ranges are used in futures trading because, as the trading session ends, it takes time to determine what the actual closing price, called the *settlement price,* is.

CLU   See *chartered life underwriter.*

cluster analysis   A statistical technique that identifies clusters of stocks whose returns are highly correlated within the cluster. However, the returns are relatively uncorrelated between clusters. Cluster analysis has the ability to identify groups such as growth, cyclical, and stable stocks.

CMA   See *cash management account.*

CMBS   See *commercial mortgage-backed securities.*

CME   See *Chicago Mercantile Exchange.*

CMO   See *collateralized mortgage obligation.*

CMO Swap   A swap based on a specific collateralized mortgage obligation (CMO). The swap transaction depends on the a specific criteria, such as cash flow or principle repayments.

coal   A dark brown to black combustible sedimentary rock that is used as a fuel source. It accounts for the generation of about 55 percent of the total electricity output in the United States. The United States has 30 percent of the world's bituminous and anthracite coal reserves, more than any other country except China, which consumes nearly all of its own production. Coal futures are traded on the New York Mercantile Exchange (NYMEX). Coal futures are a relatively new addition to the NYMEX, with trading beginning only in the late 1990s. Its trading symbol is QL.

COBRA   See *Consolidated Omnibus Budget Reconciliation Act.*

CoCo   See *contingent convertible.*

cocoa   A raw-foods good whose futures are traded on the Coffee, Sugar & Cocoa Exchange (CSCE), which is a subsidiary of the New York Board of Trade (NYBOT). Futures and options contracts are traded on the CSCE, as well as other exchanges. One of the important reports followed by the industry is the quarterly cocoa grind report that is published by the Chocolate Manufacturers Assoc. of the U.S.A. and the New York Board of Trade. Cocoa contracts are traded by cocoa growers and chocolate processors in order to protect themselves against sharp price movements that could create a loss.

cocoa grind report   A quarterly report that is closely followed by cocoa traders and others in the industry. It is produced by the Chocolate Manufacturers Association of the U.S.A. and the New York Board of Trade. It typically comes out about a month after the end of the previous quarter. It measures the amount of cocoa beans that have been ground, melted into chocolate liquor, and melted into cocoa butter. About a dozen chocolate processors contribute their data to the report.

code of ethics A set of standards for professional behavior. Since the 2002 Sarbanes-Oxley legislation, a publicly held company is required to create its own code of ethics to deter wrongdoing and to promote ethical behavior. A code of ethics also should outline potential conflicts of interest for company employees and board of directors. A code of ethics also would call for the company to disclose potential conflicts of interest or waivers from the code of ethics.

coffee An agricultural product and one of the most popular drinks in the world. Coffee futures and options are traded on the Coffee, Sugar & Cocoa Exchange (CSCE), which became a subsidiary of the New York Board of Trade in 1998. The coffee futures contract traded on the CSCE calls for delivery of washed Arabica coffee beans which are grown in several Central and South American, Asian, and African countries.

cogenerator A power-generation facility that produces electricity as well as a byproduct, such as heat or steam, that is used for heating and cooling.

COGS See *cost of goods sold*.

coin A metal piece that is used as legal tender and is inscribed to show that it is backed by the government that issued it.

coincident indicators Four indicators that are part of the composite index produced monthly by the Conference Board to signal peaks and troughs in the business cycle. Coincident indicators are those economic statistics that are expected to move in conjunction with the business cycle, in contrast with leading indicators, which are expected to improve before the overall economy does, and lagging indicators, which are expected to increase only after the economy improves. The same holds true in times of declining economic activity. Coincident indicators are: employees on non-agricultural payrolls, personal income less transfer payments, industrial production

and manufacturing, and trade sales. These four categories also may be referred to as *coincident indicators of economic activity* in situations separate from the Conference Board.

COLA See *cost-of-living adjustment*.

cold calling To make unsolicited telephone calls to potential customers without the benefit of any prior introduction or familiarity. Many stockbrokers typically find clients through cold calling. People selling financial services, such as financial planners and life insurance salespeople, also make cold calls. Cold calling occurs frequently in the United States and to a lesser extent in other countries.

COLI See *corporate-owned life insurance*.

collar

1. A restriction on index-arbitrage trading, which is also called *program trading*. Collars are imposed to keep markets stable by restricting extreme price movements. An example of a collar is the one instituted by the New York Stock Exchange. Under New York Stock Exchange rules, if the Dow Jones Industrial Average moves up or down 2 percent from the average closing value of the DJIA for the last month during the previous quarter, collars are instituted. If the market erases half of that move, the trading collars are removed. The NYSE sets the equivalent point level quarterly. Other exchanges may have their own collars. Also called *trading collars*.

2. In the context of mergers, collars may be used to set minimum and maximum prices the acquiring company will pay. Setting collars is often necessary in the acquisition of publicly traded companies because the price of the companies' stock may vary greatly between the time the deal was announced and when it actually closes many months later.

3. A supply contract between a buyer and seller of a commodity, in which the buyer is assured that he or she will not

have to pay more than some maximum price, and the seller is assured of receiving some minimum price. Also called *option fence* and *range forward*.

collateral An asset pledged as payment for a loan if the debtor fails to make regular payments. Collateral on a consumer loan may be an automobile, real estate, or other significant personal property. Collateral on a business loan may be property, equipment, or other assets of the company. On asset-backed debt, the collateral is the underlying mortgages or credit-card receivables.

collateralized mortgage obligation (CMO) A security that is backed by real estate. Payments on CMO obligations are paid using interest and principal payments from a pool of mortgages that have many different coupon rates, final maturities, and prepayment schedules. The term CMO usually indicates that the issuer is not a governmental issuer, such as Fannie Mae. Payments to the bondholders are pass-through payments from the homeowners, consisting of both principal and interest payments. CMOs are subject to early retirement if the mortgage is prepaid or if the mortgage is refinanced. CMOs were first introduced in 1983; since then, issuance has exceeded $1 trillion. They have since been replaced by *Real Estate Mortgage Investment Conduits* (*REMICs*), with nearly all types of CMOs issued in the form of a REMIC, though the terms are used interchangeably.

collectibles Objects collected either for their investment value or because the collector has a personal interest in the objects. Any object can become a collectible, but typically the most popular collectibles are coins, stamps, antiques, and baseball cards. Often these items have historical value; however, occasionally a new collectible item emerges. Collectibles should be insured to protect against loss.

Collectibles may not be easy to sell because there are few organized places where trades can be made. However, some organizations hold periodic trade fairs where hundreds of people come to trade their collectibles.

colon The currency unit of Costa Rica, comprised of 100 centimos, and El Salvador, comprised of 100 centavos.

co-manager An underwriter in a stock or debt offering who is a member of the syndicate, or group that is selling the offering, but is not one of the lead managers.

combination utility A utility company that provides both gas and electric service.

comfort letter A letter from an accounting firm given to a company before the company goes public. The letter states that the accountants are comfortable with the unaudited financial data in the company's prospectus and that the company follows generally accepted accounting principles. The letter also states that no material changes have occurred since the financial reports were prepared. Investors use the comfort letter to assure themselves that the company's financial statements are accurate.

comment letter A letter written by a corporation or stock or futures exchange outlining its thoughts on a particular topic under review by the Securities and Exchange Commission (SEC) or other regulatory agency. When the SEC is considering changing rules or procedures, the commission receives input on the proposed changes during a *comment period*.

commercial and industrial loan A bank loan that is given to businesses such as retail, wholesale, industrial, or manufacturing companies. Typically, commercial and industrial loans have been syndicated, securitized, and repackaged to take them off the bank's balance sheet, so that the bank can make additional loans.

Commercial Book-Entry System A system operated by the U.S. Treasury Department to sell Treasury bills, notes, and bonds to banks, brokers, and large institutional or individual investors. The Treasury, as well as all of its primary dealers, use this system, therefore making it easier to conduct trades. This system is different from *Treasury Direct,* which is the system used to sell securities to individuals.

commercial mortgage-backed securities (CMBS) Securities that are based on mortgages written on commercial or industrial properties, in contrast to residential mortgages, which are written on houses.

commercial paper An unsecured promissory note that is typically sold by a corporation. Commercial paper has a fixed maturity of 1 to 270 days and is usually sold at a discount from face value.

commingling

1. In the securities industry (investment management companies or trust companies), combining customers' money and securities with the broker's funds.

2. For law firms, combining client funds that are received in settlement of a lawsuit with the firm's money; this is strictly prohibited by lawyers' ethics rules.

commission broker Often used in conjunction with the commodities market, an agent who executes the public's buy and sell orders.

commission house An individual or business that accepts orders to buy or sell futures contracts or options on futures on behalf of customers. A commission house generally refers to the largest stock brokerage firms that have diversified into numerous financial services products and businesses. Also may be called a *wire house,* which refers to the fact that in the early days of the stock market only the biggest companies could have their customers wire, or telegraph, their trades.

commitment of traders report A biweekly report put out by the Commodity Futures Trading Commission that shows the number of long and short positions held by traders in the U.S. commodities markets. *Long positions* are futures contracts

that have been purchased; *short positions* are contracts that have been sold without the seller owning the underlying contract. The reports also show the *open interest,* or number of contracts that exist, in the market. Traders look at the report for signals about whether the market is likely to move higher or lower.

Committee on Uniform Securities Identification Procedures (CUSIP) A security's CUSIP number identifies the security and makes it easier to settle trades. CUSIPs are assigned to securities such as stocks of North American companies and government debt issued by federal and local governments and corporations. Non-North American securities use a system called CINS, which stands for CUSIP International Numbering System. The American Bankers Association owns the copyright and propriety rights to CUSIP and CINS.

commodities index An index compiled to track the price movements of any of a group of around 20 commodities. These indices are created by a variety of brokerage firms and news agencies. The best-known index is the CRB Index, which began in 1934. Other indices include the Reuters/CRB index, Dow Jones-AIG Commodity Index, Goldman Sachs Commodity Index, JP Morgan Commodity Index, and the S&P Commodities Index (SPCI).

commoditization The process of prices moving substantially lower because of strong competition. Commoditization happens because too many competitors enter a market when they see the large returns that can be earned on certain products. However, those returns soon disappear as competition drives prices lower.

commodity Products that can be traded on a commodities exchange, for example, agricultural products, metals, petroleum, gasoline, heating oil, and natural gas. The term *commodity* may refer to physical products, such as oil, gasoline, or building supplies that are purchased in the cash market that have nothing to do with a futures exchange. The term can also refer to the fact that over time, as more companies enter a market, competition drives prices down, resulting in a product moving from being profitable to being little more than a commodity.

Commodity Exchange Act A law that governs commodity and futures trading in the United States. It established the Commodities Futures Trading Commission (CFTC) and outlines what types of investments the CFTC can regulate. It also includes the Shad-Johnson Agreement, which describes the division of authority and responsibility for regulation of financial contracts between the CFTC and the Securities and Exchange Commission (SEC).

Commodity Futures Trading Commission (CFTC) A commission created by Congress in 1974 as an independent agency with the mandate to regulate commodity futures and option markets in the United States. The CFTC protects market participants against manipulation, abusive trade practices, and fraud. The CFTC has five commissioners who are appointed by the U.S. president to five-year terms and confirmed by the Senate. One of the commissioners is appointed by the president to be the chairperson.

commodity pool A cooperative effort in which funds contributed by a number of people are combined in order to trade commodity futures or options contracts. Professional traders and investment managers make the decisions about which investments to make, thereby relieving the individual investors of the investment research and decision-making process. By combining funds with other investors, individuals can obtain access to a larger range of investments and size of trade than by doing their own trading. Commodity pools work on a similar concept as mutual funds for individual stock and bond investors.

commodity trading adviser (CTA) A person who directly or indirectly advises investors about buying or selling commodity futures and options. Indirect advising includes providing information through the media or through written communications.

Commodity Trading Advisor (CTA) Index A benchmark that is based on the performance of a group of CTAs, who advise investors on purchasing and selling futures contracts.

common stock An ownership interest in a company. Unlike preferred stock, common stock has no priority for dividend payments or any repayment in bankruptcy. Investors holding common stock can lose only as much as the amount invested. An owner of common stock is referred to as a *stockholder* or *shareholder*. Common stockholders may earn dividends and may see the share price rise, which produces profits. Common stock is more risky than preferred stock in that if funds are limited to pay dividends, preferred stockholders are paid first. In the case of liquidation or bankruptcy, preferred shareholders may receive preferential treatment over common shareholders. Common stockholders, however, typically have more voting rights than do preferred shareholders.

common stock equivalent A convertible security that trades like its underlying common stock because the stock is trading substantially above its conversion price. Common stock equivalents also may be calculated for convertible bonds in order to calculate a company's fully diluted earnings.

Community Development Block Grant Flexible federal aid given to cities to promote neighborhood revitalization through economic development and improved community facilities and services in depressed neighborhoods. Local government can decide how to use the funds, which are administered by either state or city economic development offices.

Community Development Corporation (CDC) A community organization, owned by the residents in the neighborhood, that promotes affordable housing and commercial development. Most CDCs are non-profit, tax-exempt corporations.

Community Development Credit Union (CDCU) A non-profit credit union chartered to serve a low-income community. The structure is similar to that of a regular credit union, however, because CDCUs are non-profit, they are tax-exempt. CDCUs offer services not provided by mainstream banks, such as small loans at below-market rates to people who might not qualify for bank loans in a competitive situation. CDCUs rely heavily on banks, foundations, and other investors for deposits to support their work. Federally chartered CDCUs are regulated by the state they operate in.

Community Reinvestment Act (CRA) A federal law passed in 1977 that encourages banks and other financial institutions to help meet the credit needs of the low- or moderate-income communities where they operate. The CRA requires that a bank's lending record in the community be evaluated periodically. Federal officials examine that record when considering an institution's application for deposit facilities or other administrative services, and look to see that the bank is meeting the needs of all its customers. A poor evaluation of a bank's CRA effort also can impede a merger if one of the companies has a poor lending record.

company-specific risk Risk that comes from a company's operations and business environment. A company-specific risk differs from systemic risk or any other risk coming from the economy.

comparables In the world of retail sales, the term comparables, or *comps,* refers to sales in stores that have been open for longer than one year. Investors can use comps to figure out how much of the company's overall sales growth was the result of the opening of new stores.

comparative advantage The ability of one country or region to produce a product at a reduced cost compared with another country or region. The nation with the lower cost structure is said to have a comparative

advantage over the other country. Often countries attempt to use trade law or trade monitoring bodies to allege price dumping or violations of expected labor practices that unfairly allow companies in that country to be low-cost producers and thus grab a comparative advantage. One company may also have a comparative advantage over others if its cost structure is lower.

compensation committee A committee of a board of directors that sets the compensation level of senior management. In addition to salary, the compensation committee determines the level of stock option compensation and stock warrants. Under the 2002 Sarbanes-Oxley legislation, members of the compensation committee all have to be independent directors by the middle of 2004. If a company is controlled by another company, it is not subject to the full independence requirement. The compensation committee also must have a charter specifying its purpose and the evaluation procedures of the committee.

competitive bid A bid made by a bank that is a primary dealer in the U.S. Treasury auction. These banks purchase large amounts of securities at the most competitive rate they can get. In contrast, *non-competitive bids* are submitted by individual investors who are willing to take whatever price is offered because their purchase is too small to be competitive.

competitive local exchange carrier (CLEC) A telecom company that was created to compete with the established local telephone service providers, such as the former regional Bell operating companies. In contrast to an *unbundled network element provider,* a CLEC competes with telecom companies by using its own switching equipment and network. The opportunity to establish CLECs was created in the Telecommunications Act of 1996, which was intended to promote competition among long-distance and local phone service providers. See also *UNE-P.*

compliance The state of being in accordance with relevant federal or regional authorities and their regulatory requirements. In financial services, the most important compliance is adhering to the rules of the Securities and Exchange Commission (SEC). Most large financial services companies have compliance departments that are charged with making sure that the company is following all the necessary rules and regulations.

compound annual growth rate (CAGR) A year-over-year growth rate that is calculated on an investment that has been made or a stock that has been purchased.

compound interest Interest that is calculated not only on the *principal* of the investment or loan (the original amount invested or borrowed), but also on the interest accrued when periodic repayment is received. Compound interest causes the interest that is earned or paid to be higher than interest calculated under the simple interest method. *Simple interest* pays interest only on the initial principal amount of the investment or loan.

comps See *comparables*.

comptroller The chief accountant of a company, who is responsible for preparing financial reports and supervising internal audits. The comptroller also may act as the treasurer in small companies. The terms *comptroller* and *controller* are used interchangeably.

comptroller of the currency An officer of the U.S. Treasury Department who is responsible for chartering national banks and regulating and supervising them in order to ensure safe, sound, and competitive banking systems. The Comptroller has six district offices in the United States and one office in London that supervises the international activities of national banks.

The office of the comptroller of the currency was created in 1863. The comptroller is appointed by the president and is confirmed by the Senate for a five-year term.

The comptroller also is a director of the Federal Deposit Insurance Corporation and a director of the Neighborhood Reinvestment Corporation. The comptroller office examiners conduct onsite reviews of national banks and supervise their activities; issue rules and legal interpretations about banking investments and operations; and analyze banks' loan and investment portfolios, levels of capital and liquidity, earnings, and market risk. The comptroller's examiners ensure that banks comply with consumer banking laws such as the Community Reinvestment Act. The comptroller also reviews the banks' internal controls and audit operations and evaluates management's ability to identify and control risk.

concept release A report by the Securities and Exchange Commission (SEC) outlining a proposed rule change. The concept release is made in order to solicit the public's viewpoints before an actual proposed rule is announced. The SEC specifies how long the public has to submit opinions, known also as the *comment period*. Concept releases also may be used by other regulatory agencies, such as the Commodity Futures Trading Commission.

condor A complex option spread that has two short options with different strike prices. The spread can be expensive to initiate because of the large number of contracts and resulting commissions.

Conference Board A private, economic research organization that produces the monthly index of leading economic indicators, which predicts the direction of the U.S. economy over the next six months. The Leading Economic Indicators are widely watched in the financial markets to glean clues about the direction of the economy. Also included in the data are the coincident indicators and lagging indicators. The Conference Board is a business membership and research network that was founded in 1916. Since 1919 it has measured cost of living data in the United States. In 1995, the U.S. Department of Commerce handed over to it responsibility for the composite indexes. It also produces business cycle indexes for Australia, France, Germany, Korea, Japan, Mexico, Spain, and the United Kingdom.

The Conference Board also produces the monthly consumer confidence index, a survey based on a representative sample of 5,000 U.S. households. Included with the consumer confidence index data are the expectations index and the present situation index.

confidence letter   A letter written by an investment bank that says it is highly confident that specific financing will be obtained. Such a letter is sent ahead of some capital market activity, such as a debt or equity offering.

confirmation

1. A trading document sent by a broker to a customer confirming that a trade has taken place and stating its terms.

2. A letter sent by an auditor to the company's customers asking them to verify the terms of their accounts receivable or payable transactions. A confirmation also may be sent to account holders asking them to verify their account balances. A positive confirmation asks that all of the appropriate information be confirmed. A negative confirmation requests a reply only if a difference is noted.

3. In technical analysis, a situation in which one technical indicator confirms another technical indicator. The term can also mean that the requirements of a technical pattern have been met, which confirms the pattern and resulting trend.

congestion   An area on a pricing chart that indicates where previous heavy trading volume occurred or an area in which closing prices on successive trading days tended to cluster. Congestion often looks like a rectangle on a price chart, as prices have remained in a narrow range. Usually, when prices break out of the range they resume the price direction that prices had before entering the area of congestion.

Congressional Budget Office (CBO) The U.S. government agency that reports to Congress on matters dealing with the federal budget. The office makes projections about the budget surplus or deficit along with what effect various spending or tax proposals will have on the budget. The CBO is set up to be nonpartisan. It reports its calculations twice a year to the House and Senate Budget committees.

consensus estimate   An opinion about a company's financial performance. Analysts' earning expectations are averaged by an information provider such as Thomson/ First Call. Sometimes there may be a consensus estimate on revenues or other financial measures, but the earnings per share (EPS) consensus is the most commonly used.

conservative   An investment or investment style that is likely to result in modest returns. However, the investor is unlikely to lose the amount of money that has been invested. Typically, people approaching retirement or in retirement opt for a conservative investment approach.

consignment   An agreement by a retailer to sell merchandise owned by another person or corporation (the consignor). No payment is made to the consignor until the merchandise is actually sold. Unsold items are returned to the consignor.

consolidated financial statements Financial statements produced when one company, a parent, owns 50 percent or more of another company, which is its subsidiary. Once the 50 percent threshold is crossed, the subsidiary's balance sheet, income statement, cash flow statement, and any other financial statements are combined with those of the parent company into a single set of statements. For a consolidated balance sheet, loans to the subsidiary from the parent are removed, along with any sales and purchases between the two entities. By eliminating these accounts, duplications are avoided and the statements more closely reflect the financial position of a single entity. For consolidated income statements, inter-company sales and related expenses, as well as income and expenses related to loans, receivables, or other debt, also are eliminated. These entries to consolidate the financial statements are called *eliminations.*

Consolidated Omnibus Budget Reconciliation Act (COBRA) Federal legislation that allows an employee to continue group health insurance coverage after leaving his or her job or after losing coverage because of divorce or legal separation. The coverage of dependents can be continued until they marry or reach the age of 23. However, anyone obtaining COBRA coverage has to pay the entire cost. The coverage expires after a certain period of time.

consolidator

1. A provider of electronic bill payment services over the Internet. Companies that operate Internet banks and financial Web sites contract with consolidators to allow their customers to receive and pay their bills online.

2. A company that helps indebted consumers pay off their bills by consolidating all of their obligations into one monthly payment, which is then remitted to the appropriate company.

consortium A group of companies that join together to attain a specific goal. When the goal is achieved the consortium typically disbands. It is a way for companies to work together that is less formal than a joint venture or a strategic partnership.

consortium bank A banking subsidiary set up by several banks that may be headquartered in different countries. Consortium banks are commonly formed in Europe. A consortium is created to fulfill a specific project or goal or to complete deals, such as selling loans for a client in the loan

syndication market. When the deal is completed, the consortium bank disbands.

constant dollars In economics, dollars that are part of the base year. Constant dollars are used to adjust for the effects of inflation by converting economic information into a standard era dollar term, such as 1990 dollars. The gross domestic product reports (GDP) produced by the United States and other governments often list GDP in constant dollar terms. For example, GDP in the most recent quarter may show a growth of 2.5 percent, however in constant dollar terms the growth rate might only be 2.0 percent using a base year of 1990. In contrast, *current dollars* refers to the value of a dollar today. Current dollars have not been adjusted for the effects of inflation, and thus may not be useful for comparing economic activity in different time periods.

Constant Maturity Treasury A rate used by the U.S. Treasury Department that represents a daily determination of what the yield on a U.S. Treasury bill, note, or bond would be if it were issued on that day. The Treasury Department publishes these rates on a daily and weekly basis in reports called *Special Interest Rates.*

construction loan A loan given to a company in order to pay for building construction. Construction loans are relatively short term and the lender takes an ownership interest in the building. At the end of construction, the loan is repaid from the proceeds of a mortgage obtained on the finished building. Because of the risk inherent in construction, such as cost overruns and the potential for not completing the building, the interest rate charged is typically higher than the prime rate.

construction spending report A monthly economic statistic report that measures the amount of construction spending for home building, which is the major component of the report. Home building is a widely watched indicator of activity, because as new homes are built, a significant amount of follow-on consumer spending is created for durable goods such as carpets, washers, dryers, dishwashers, and so on, as well as non-durable items such as dishes, sheets, and other furnishings. Construction spending data is produced by the Department of Commerce. In addition to residential spending, the data also tracks spending on government projects and office buildings.

consumer confidence index The University of Michigan's consumer sentiment index that is closely watched by those who follow the economy and the financial markets. Typically traders react not so much to what the index says, but rather to how closely the results matched analysts' expectations. The present situation index measures consumers' current attitudes about the economy and their finances.

consumer credit Credit extended to consumers for any of a variety of purposes. Funds to purchase a car or boat, funds disbursed through credit cards, and personal loans for many other uses are types of consumer credit. A variety of federal regulations have been written over the years to protect consumers from unfair or misleading consumer practices.

Statistics on outstanding consumer debt are released each month by the Federal Reserve (Fed). The report is closely watched because it gives economists and traders an idea of consumer buying patterns. About two-thirds of expenditures in the U.S. economy are driven by consumer spending, and a slowdown could potentially spell trouble for the U.S. economy. The Fed's report measures revolving credit, which includes credit card debt, and non-revolving debt, which includes loans for cars, mobile homes, tuition, and other items.

Consumer Credit Protection Act of 1988 Important federal legislation that requires lenders to disclose important financial terms to consumers who are borrowing funds. The law requires that consumers be told what the annual percentage rate on their loan is, the total cost of the interest

they will pay, and any other relevant loan terms. The act, enforced by the Federal Reserve Bank, is also known as the *Truth in Lending Act*.

consumer goods Items purchased by consumers that are characterized by their short-term use and are differentiated from capital goods. Food, personal-care items, entertainment, and clothing are examples of consumer goods. Consumer goods loosely defined also can include consumer services such as dry cleaning and haircuts.

Consumer Leasing Act Legislation that requires lessors to disclose specific financial information about the terms of a lease, such as the monthly payment, the total amount of payments, and the allowance for a trade-in. The act also requires lessors to give an estimated value of the property, typically a car, at the end of the lease period. The legislation was passed in 1976 and is intended to protect consumers.

consumer price index (CPI) An important inflation measure computed by the U.S. Department of Commerce, Bureau of Labor Statistics (BLS), which is released monthly around the 15th of the month at 8:30 A.M. Eastern Time. The CPI reports price changes in over 200 categories, which are grouped into eight major areas; it also includes income taxes and Social Security taxes. The CPI compares the cost of a "market basket" of some 385 goods and services with the cost of the same items during the previous month or year. In order to reduce volatility, the *core CPI* data exclude food and energy prices. Data for the previous three months are revised monthly. Typically they are not substantial revisions. Major benchmark revisions occur about every ten years.

The CPI measures prices of goods and services for two population groups. The All Urban Consumers index (CPI-U) represents around 80 percent of the total U.S. population. It also measures prices that urban wage earners and clerical workers (CPI-W) pay. To produce the CPI, the Bureau of Labor Statistics surveys retail stores throughout the United States and gathers price information on thousands of items. Each price is put into one of the 200 expenditure categories and weighted by importance, which allows price changes in the categories to be estimated.

consumption tax A taxation system in which taxes are assessed on how much the taxpayer spends instead of on the taxpayer's income. The idea of a consumption tax in the United States picked up steam in early 2003 when President George W. Bush and his Council of Economic Advisors backed it. However, a consumption tax draws criticism from some people who argue that it is a regressive tax that would hurt poor people more than the rich. One type of consumption tax is a value-added tax (VAT), which is common in Europe. Businesses pay a VAT tax, which is passed on to the end consumer.

contagion Unanticipated negative events in one market or region that may spread to another market or region. Contagion often is a concern in emerging markets, where one country's poor economic performance, high inflation, or lack of investor confidence may cause investors to flee nearby markets as well.

contango A pricing situation in which the prices of futures contracts are higher the further out the maturities are. This is the normal pricing pattern because carrying charges such as storage, interest expense, and insurance have to be paid in order to hold onto a commodity. It is the opposite of *backwardation.*

contingency plan A plan a business has for continuing to operate in the event of a disaster such as a fire, severe weather, terrorist attack, or any other dire situation. A contingency plan includes an emergency plan with offsite offices and a management structure if senior management can't be located. Back-up procedures should be in place for telephone and computer systems. Important company data should be kept in a separate place that is accessible no matter what happens. A contingency plan also may

be referred to as a *continuity plan,* although that term also has the additional connotation of planning for corporate succession in the event that one or more senior executives is no longer able to fulfill his or her duties.

contingent conversion clause A provision in a convertible bond or other convertible investment that limits the issuer's ability to force conversion until a specific event has occurred. One example of a possible contingent conversion clause is that a stock price must exceed the strike price for a period of two months.

contingent convertible (CoCo) A mandatory convertible security that allows investors to sell their shares back to the issuer within a certain time period, which may be as short as one year. CoCos are a specific type of mandatory convertible that is created by Merrill Lynch & Company and that has a structural variation that defers the dilution of earnings per share caused by debt being converted into stock shares. CoCo limit when investors can convert their debt to equity, tying that right to price appreciation of the stock. In general, a *mandatory convertible* is a bond that must be converted into equity by a specific time in the future, often three years. Ratings agencies typically count 80 cents out of each $1 in the mandatory convertible as equity, since the debt will be turned into equity within three years. A mandatory convertible is an attractive alternative for companies that have too much debt, because it helps protect their debt rating. Most companies assume that their stock will remain at its present level or higher and there is little likelihood that investors will want to cash out. Moreover, the conversion price is often set so high that investors are unlikely to ever be able to convert it to cash.

contingent deferred sales charge A fee that is imposed if mutual fund shares are sold back to the fund within a certain time frame during the initial years of ownership. Typically, the sales charge decreases over time and is eliminated after a certain period, such as four years.

contingent liability   A potential liability that may develop into an actual liability if some specified event occurs, such as not paying a bill. The Financial Accounting Standards Board (FASB) says that a company should record a contingent liability in its accounting records if the liability is probable; it also must be reasonably estimated. A contingent liability may be a potential judgment from a lawsuit, lines of credit that may not be repaid, loan commitments that the company may have, or the impact from foreign exchange transactions or other financial contracts. A contingent liability also occurs when a company sells its accounts receivables to a purchaser; however, if the customer defaults on payment, then the seller of the accounts receivable is contingently liable.

contingent order   An order to sell or buy a security that depends on the execution of another order or the achievement of a certain price level in the trading of another instrument. Contingent orders are frequently used in futures, options, and swap transactions.

contra account   An account that is paired with a separate, related account. The balance of the contra account is shown on the balance sheet. An accumulated depreciation account is an example of a contra-asset account, which shows how much depreciation has been deducted against an asset. The remaining value of the asset shows up on the balance sheet.

contract   A legal agreement that sets up the terms for a purchase or sale of property or rights, or outlines an agreement about a common business venture or other business deal. Part of a contract is the receipt of money, known as *lawful consideration*. In general, for a contract to be considered valid, it must be entered into by competent parties, must pertain to a legal transaction, and must possess mutuality and a meeting of minds.

contract grade   A physical commodity or cash market instrument that qualifies as an acceptable delivery to settle a futures contract. The contract grade must meet specific qualifications outlined by the respective terms of the futures contract.

contract month   The month that an exchange-traded option or futures contract expires or settles.

contrarian investment theory   A trading theory that recommends making investments contrary to the apparent direction of the market or commonly accepted wisdom. The theory holds that if everyone is certain something is going to happen, then it won't. Contrarians also draw their conviction from the viewpoint that if everyone believes the market will rise, they have already bought. Thus, there are few investors remaining to create additional buying, which means it is likely that the market will decline. Some mutual funds have adopted a contrarian trading strategy as their main focus.

contributed capital   A line item on a company's balance sheet that reflects payments of cash or assets that the owners have made to the company in order to increase the company's equity. It also includes additional *paid-in capital*, which occurs when stock is issued and the value received is greater than par value. Also called *paid-in capital*.

controlled equity offering   A strategy that allows small companies to issue additional equity in small, periodic increments in order to manage their capital needs. Typically the stock can be issued in increments as small as 50,000 shares, compared with other follow-on offerings that consist of millions of shares. Controlled equity offerings can be done over a period of months. The controlled equity offering allows companies to have increased flexibility in raising capital, specifically in reacting quickly to changing market needs and being able to place equity quickly. Cantor Fitzgerald has been a leader in developing this equity product. Its fee ranges from 2 percent to 3 percent of the funds raised, compared with a typical fee charged by investment bankers for a follow-on offering of about 5 percent to 6 percent of the funds raised.

controlling interest Typically, an ownership interest of 50 percent or more of a company's voting shares. In large corporations, however, a significantly smaller ownership interest may be enough to give the owner enough of an interest to exert significant control over how the company is managed.

convenience yield A premium that is earned by people who hold a physical commodity. A convenience yield reflects the near-term scarcity of the commodity or underlying asset and it also reflects the preference that consumers have for holding the equivalent cash position. Convenience yields show up as an adjustment to the theoretical forward, or future, price of a commodity or the future contract delivery price. Sometimes convenience yields are earned by holders of a government bond that is in short supply in the repo market.

convergence The degree to which the price in a futures or forward market moves toward, or converges, with prices in the cash market as the expiration date approaches. Generally, if convergence is reached at expiration, then that market is likely to be more liquid and easily traded. A trader can be fairly certain that a stock index contract closely matches the cash settlement value of the actual stocks, so it serves as a good hedge. If convergence is less definite, then the pricing relationships between the futures contract and the cash product are less defined and may pose problems for traders or arbitrageurs who want to use the financial instruments to hedge their risk.

conversion price The share price at which a convertible bond or convertible preferred share is eligible to be converted into common stock.

conversion ratio The number of common shares that an investor can receive in exchange for a single convertible bond or convertible preferred share.

convertible adjustable-rate mortgage (ARM) A mortgage in which the interest charge can be converted into a fixed-rate mortgage in order to avoid rising interest rates, which would make the cost of the adjustable-rate mortgage rise sharply. Typically, a bank or other financial institution charge a service fee to transfer an ARM into a fixed-rate mortgage.

convertible bond A bond that the bondholder may exchange for a predetermined amount of common stock. For example, a company could issue $10,000 face-value convertible bonds that could be converted into 30 shares of the company's common stock after three years. Convertible bonds are attractive because they provide regular cash flow, along with the possibility of future price appreciation.

convertible currency A currency that can be exchanged for another currency. Some governments may place limits on the convertibility of their currencies. In order to be actively traded, a currency must be convertible. The U.S. dollar is an example of a currency that is fully convertible.

convertible exchangeable preferred stock Preferred stock that can be exchanged at the issuer's option for convertible debt that has the same yield and conversion terms. A convertible exchangeable preferred stock is designed to permit an issuer to switch to a tax-deductible obligation when its earnings become taxable.

Convertible Mark The currency of Bosnia and Herzegovina, comprised of 100 fening.

convertible preferred stock Preferred stock that can be exchanged for shares of common stock according to the ratio stated in the preferred stock contract. The conversion feature is attractive because if the market value of a company's common stock rises, the preferred stockholders share in the appreciation, either through the rising price of the preferred stock price or by converting to common stock at the fixed ratio, which may provide a greater return.

convertible security A bond, preferred stock, or warrant that is convertible to the issuer's common stock or some other security under certain circumstances. The conversion may come with a payment of cash or usable securities.

convexity

1. For a bond or note, a measure of the way duration and prices change when interest rates change, as represented in the curvature of the price-yield relationship. A bond or note has a positive convexity if the instrument's value increases at least as much as duration indicates when rates drop, and decreases less than duration indicates when rates rise. Investors want positive convexity because it makes a bond more valuable after a price change than its duration value suggests.

2. For options, a measure of the way the value of the position changes in response to the change in the volatility or price of the underlying instrument. An option with positive convexity holds or increases its value more than *delta* (the change in the price of the option with respect to a one-dollar change in the price of the underlying asset) would predict when volatility increases or when prices change by a large percentage.

conveyance A document that transfers ownership of real property from one person or entity to another.

COO See *chief operating officer.*

cookie jar accounting An accounting technique that involves setting aside reserves during good years and using the reserves during unprofitable years. This makes earnings appear more even and helps create the impression of consistency, which investors are keen to see.

cooking the books A slang term that means illegally falsifying financial statements. A company may try to cook the books in order to hide a loss, a drop-off in sales, or a liability that it doesn't want to

disclose; in order to protect the share price from falling; or to keep creditors from demanding additional collateral or the immediate repayment of loans. It also may be done in order to decrease the amount of income tax that the company has to pay.

cooling degree day A measurement used in the energy market to gauge demand. A cooling degree day is accumulated for each degree the average temperature for a day moves above 75 degrees Fahrenheit. For example, if the average temperature for the day was 80, that would count as 5 cooling degree days.

coop See *cooperative.*

cooperative (coop) A form of housing in which residents form a corporation for the purpose of owning and managing a multi-unit property collectively. Instead of owning an individual apartment, residents legally own a set number of shares in the coop that gives them the right to use the apartment. If a resident wants to move, those shares are sold to another buyer who then moves into the apartment. Owners pay a maintenance fee each month that covers the expense of utilities, an underlying mortgage on the building, salaries for staff members, and other costs of upkeep. The maintenance fee may also cover a reserve fund, which is a savings account that can be drawn on in the event that an expensive repair needs to be made. As a result of part of the maintenance payment going to pay for a mortgage, some of the monthly maintenance payment, often half, may be deducted from income taxes on Schedule A of the Form 1040.

Typically, coop owners hold an annual meeting at which owners elect members to the board of directors and vote on any other coop issues. Although coops are a typical form of housing in New York City, with over 80 percent of the housing stock comprised of coops, they are a relatively rare phenomenon in other parts of the United States.

co-opetition A principle of game theory that says businesses succeed by combining their cooperative strategies with competitive strategies. The premise is that they cooperate in order to increase the pie of available business opportunities and then compete against each other in order to divide the pie up and obtain a greater share. Implicit in the theory is that one competitor doesn't have to fail in order for another company to succeed.

copper One of the world's oldest known commodities and the world's third most widely used metal, after iron and aluminum. It is used in highly cyclical industries such as construction and industrial machinery manufacturing, which ties its price direction to the state of the world economy. Chile is the world's largest copper producer.

The largest futures and options market for copper is the London Metal Exchange (LME), where a variety of copper contracts trade. Three-months copper is the benchmark issue. The name "three-month" comes from the delay that it took to ship copper mined in Chile to London when trading began on the LME. The forerunner to the LME was the Royal Exchange that began in 1571 when metals traders first began to meet on a regular basis. In 1877, the London Metal Market and Exchange Company was formed as a direct result of Britain's industrial revolution of the 19th century.

Copper futures also are traded on the Comex Division of the New York Mercantile Exchange, where the trading symbol is HG, as well as on other exchanges around the world.

copyright The exclusive right, as recognized separately in each country, to publish and sell literary, artistic, or musical materials or computer programs during the author's lifetime plus 50 years. Accounting regulations require that the value of a copyright be recorded at its acquisition cost and amortized over its useful life, which is often much shorter than the legal life. Amortization can't exceed 40 years.

cordoba oro The currency unit of Nicaragua, comprised of 100 centavos.

core competency A company's primary area of business and greatest expertise. If a company grows by acquiring diversified businesses, then goes through a period of sluggish growth and disappointing earnings, it may shift back to its core competencies and sell off businesses that are non-core.

core earnings An accounting system developed by Standard & Poor's (S&P) that attempts to clarify corporate accounting for a company's income from day-to-day operations. To arrive at core earnings, S&P calculates the cost of stock options and gains or losses from pension plans and deducts them from corporate earnings. Also subtracted are one-time gains or losses. Under current accounting rules of the Financial Accounting Standards Board, companies aren't required to deduct the cost of options, but can include gains from pension funds.

core-satellite investment strategy An asset allocation program utilized by an exchange-traded fund (ETF) that uses a broad index fund (the core) and sector funds (the satellites) in order to enhance overall portfolio performance or provide diversification while controlling risks. A core-satellite investment strategy also may be a simplified ETF-oriented risk budgeting program that uses active equity funds to add *alpha,* the estimate of the amount of return expected from an investment.

corn An agricultural product that is grown throughout the Midwestern United States, as well as other areas. Futures and options on corn have been traded on the Chicago Board of Trade since 1877. Corn also is traded on other futures exchanges throughout the world. Monthly crop reports produced by the U.S. Department of Agriculture are closely watched by corn traders because they give information about expected supply, which directly affects prices.

cornering the market Purchasing a stock or commodity in such a significant amount that trading in that item is no longer competitive. Cornering the market is illegal. One of the most notorious instances of cornering the market was the attempt by Nelson Bunker Hunt and William Herbert Hunt to corner the silver market in the 1970s. They bought silver throughout the 1970s as a hedge against inflation, and by 1980 they, along with some Arab investors, were estimated to hold anywhere from one-third to one-half of the world's supply of silver. In 1973, the price of silver was $1.95 an ounce; by the early 1980s, it had shot up to $54. The Hunt brothers ended up suffering substantial losses due to rules changes enacted by Comex, which is the New York futures market where silver was traded, and the intervention of the Federal Reserve.

corporate bond fund A mutual fund that seeks a high level of income by investing two-thirds or more of its portfolio in corporate bonds.

corporate bond intermediate-term fund A mutual fund that seeks a high level of income by keeping two-thirds or more of its portfolio invested constantly in corporate bonds with an average maturity of 5 to 10 years.

corporate bond short-term fund A mutual fund that seeks a high level of current income by keeping two-thirds or more of its portfolio invested at all times in corporate bonds with an average maturity of 1 to 5 years.

corporate charter The articles of incorporation and bylaws that establish how a company should be governed. Corporations that are the subject of an unwanted takeover attempt may try to change their charter to make the takeover more difficult. One common tactic is to increase the number of shareholders that must vote to approve a takeover.

corporate credit A term that is used in written investment materials and commentaries to refer to a corporation's debt or to the corporate debt market as a whole.

corporate finance The industry of raising debt and equity capital for corporations.

corporate governance The policies, procedures, and rules that determine how a corporation is managed, as defined by the company's bylaws, corporate charter, policies, and applicable laws. Following the flurry of record-setting corporate bankruptcies in 2001 and 2002, corporate governance became a high-profile topic.

corporate governance committee A committee comprised of some of the members of a board of directors. Under the 2002 Sarbanes-Oxley legislation, companies are required to have all of the members of the corporate governance committee be independent from the company. At a basic level, that means they can't be board members who are employed by the company. Companies have a grace period until 2004 to make certain that all of their members are independent. A company that is controlled by another company is not subject to the full independence requirement. The corporate governance committee must have a charter that specifies the purpose, responsibilities, and evaluation procedures of the committee. This committee also may be incorporated with or under the nominating committee.

corporate governance guidelines Publicly traded corporations are required to adopt guidelines for their ethical behavior that include a code of business conduct and charters for ethics and key committees that have oversight of corporate governance. The documents have be to published on companies' web sites and included in their annual reports. These guidelines were required with the passage of the Sarbanes-Oxley legislation in 2002.

Corporate governance guidelines must cover directors' qualifications, responsibilities, compensation, management succession, an annual performance evaluation of the board, and must list the access to management and independent advisors. The codes of business conduct and ethics should address: conflicts of interest and corporate confidentiality, protection and use of company assets, and the steps to report illegal or unethical behavior. Companies also have to disclose any waivers of the code that have been granted by the board of directors or by one of its committees for directors or executive officers.

corporate-owned life insurance (COLI) A life insurance policy that is taken out on employees for the benefit of the corporation. The company pays the premiums. Tax breaks can be earned for five years on the cost of the premium. COLI differs from *group life insurance,* which is provided to employees as a benefit and is payable to a beneficiary that the insured employee chooses. COLI has come under fire for the large tax breaks it generates and for the fact that it pays the company when an insured person dies even after the person has left the company or has retired.

corporation A legal entity that exists under authority granted by state law. A corporation has its own identity, separate from its shareholders or owners, and as such can be sued, enter into contracts, buy or sell real estate or property, and even break the law. A corporation is responsible for its debts; typically, responsibility can't be directly assessed to shareholders or corporate directors or officers. A corporation continues indefinitely and is not affected by the death of shareholders, directors, or officers.

correction The movement of a stock or market to lower levels (often 10 percent or more) after the market or stock has been at unrealistically high levels. Gains from the too-high period are erased. Although a market may correct, it doesn't necessarily mean that the long-term upward trend is broken. While the term is usually applied to falling markets, it is possible to have an upward correction that breaks a downward trend. In technical analysis, a correction is a short-term movement, either up or down, that is contrary to the dominant price trend.

However, correction often is used in a more generic sense to refer to a market that has fallen, regardless of the principles of technical analysis.

correlation A statistical concept that shows the tendency of two or more variables to change their values at the same time, either in the same direction (*positive correlation*) or opposite directions (*negative correlation*).

correlation coefficient A statistical measurement that shows to what extent two variables move together.

correlation risk The probability that the actual correlation between two assets or variables will be different from the correlation that was assumed. As a result, the portfolio could be riskier than anticipated.

correspondent bank A bank that takes deposits for and performs banking services for other depository institutions in exchange for a fee. Correspondent banks typically provide banking services when the others banks, often foreign banks, aren't able to offer the services or find that it is more cost effective to outsource this need. Commercial banks typically provide correspondent banking services.

Corrigan, Gerald The named managing director of Goldman, Sachs & Co. in 1996 after serving as president of the Federal Reserve Bank of New York from 1985 to 1993.

cosigner A person who signs a credit card or loan application agreeing to guarantee payment if the signer is unable to repay the loan. The cosigner of a loan assumes legal responsibility for the loan.

cost basis The purchase price of a security or physical asset that has been adjusted to subtract depreciation expense and capital gains tax payments. The cost basis is used to calculate how much capital gains tax is owed when the investment or asset is sold.

cost of capital The minimum return that is required on a new investment. The *required return* is what a company must earn on its capital investment in order to break even. Another way of looking at cost of capital is as the opportunity cost associated with a company's capital investment. An opportunity cost is not being able to make an investment because the limited funds available have already been committed.

cost of carry The net cost of holding a cash market position. For physical commodities, cost of carry includes storage costs, insurance costs, transportation costs, and any interest paid to purchase the goods. For financial transactions, cost of carry is limited to any interest charges incurred to hold onto the position, as well as any opportunity cost that might be incurred.

cost of goods sold (COGS) A financial ratio that shows how much a company paid to be able to sell its product or services. It doesn't include interest expense or taxes. To arrive at cost of goods sold, subtract sales from gross profits.

cost, insurance, and freight (CIF) A sale in which the buyer agrees to pay a unit price that includes the free-on-board (FOB) value at the port of origin plus all insurance and transportation costs.

cost-benefit analysis A calculation that totals the benefits of making a capital purchase expenditure or an investment decision, then separately totals the costs of that decision. If the benefits outweigh the costs, then the action makes sense. A government may also do a cost-benefit analysis to determine if a government program or regulation is justified.

cost-of-living adjustment (COLA) A provision in wage contracts or government payments such as Social Security that provides for automatic increases in wages or benefits. Often COLA agreements are linked to the consumer price index (CPI); when the CPI, or inflation, rises, so do the payments.

cost-push inflation Inflation that is caused by rising wages and benefits. As a result of rising compensation, employees may feel relatively wealthy and increase their purchases, which can produce inflation. Federal Reserve policymakers closely watched for cost-push inflation during the market boom of the late 1990s, but none emerged.

cotton An agricultural product that is used to produce cloth and cloth-based products. Futures and options are traded on the New York Cotton Exchange (NYCE), which became a subsidiary of the New York Board of Trade in 1998.

cotton-on-call report A weekly report produced by the Commodity Futures Trading Commission (CFTC) that tracks the amount of futures positions in the cotton market. The report is closely watched by cotton traders who trade futures and options on the New York Board of Trade (NYBOT).

Council of Economic Advisors A group of economists appointed by the U.S. president that advises him on economic policy. The chairman of the council can be a strong spokesman for the president's economic policies.

counter-party risk The probability that the other party in an investment or trading transaction may not fulfill his or her part of the deal and may default on the contractual obligations.

country risk A risk that an investor must bear when investing in a foreign country. Strikes or political or financial turmoil are just a few of the country risks that may cause an investment to be wiped out or seriously impaired.

coupon The interest payment that must be made on a note or bond until it matures. For example, a note with a 7 percent interest rate pays $70 annually on a $1,000 bond, which typically would be split into semiannual payments. The $70 is the coupon. The term *coupon* reflects the portion of a bond that the bond holder separates and presents to the bond issuer in order to obtain the interest payment the bearer is entitled to. This type of bond is called a *bearer bond*. In contrast, the name and address of the holder of a *registered bond* are known to the bond issuer.

coupon pass The purchase by the Federal Reserve (Fed) of Treasury notes or bonds from dealers. The term *coupon* refers to the coupons that are attached to the notes and bills. If the Fed purchases bills it is called a *bill pass*. The coupon pass and the bill pass are tools that the Fed can use to conduct open market operations and keep a stable supply of reserves in the monetary system.

coupon reinvestment risk The probability that when a bond or note matures, its coupon, or interest rate, will be lower than what the investor is currently receiving. As a result, when the investor tries to reinvest the proceeds from the bond or note, he or she will have to be satisfied with a lower interest rate. However, if interest rates rise, then the investor benefits.

covariance A statistical tool that measures the likelihood of two random variables moving together.

covenant The rules on a loan agreement that require certain financial conditions be met or prohibit other financial actions by the borrower. A covenant may limit how much additional debt can be issued, require financial targets such as sales and earnings to be met, limit the payment of dividends, and require that certain cash levels be maintained. If a covenant is violated, then the bank or loan issuer can require that the loan or note be immediately repaid.

cover

1. In the futures market, to offset a short futures or options position by buying back contracts.

2. In corporate finance, to be able to meet fixed annual interest charges on bonds or other obligations out of funds generated from earnings.

3. In insurance, the requirement that the expenses of an insured person be reimbursed.

Coverdell Education Savings Account See *Education IRA*.

covered call A short call option that gives the buyer the right to purchase the underlying security at a pre-determined price that is collateralized by the call writer who actually owns the underlying security. Also called *covered call writing*.

covered option An option contract where the person writing the option protects him- or herself by owning the underlying shares. In contrast, when the writer doesn't own the shares, it is called a *naked option,* and the shares may have to be purchased at an unfavorable price in the market in order to deliver them.

covered put A short put option that gives the buyer the right to sell the underlying security to the put writer at a pre-determined price. The put writer holds cash or a cash-equivalent investment that is sufficient to pay for the purchase of the underlying security if the put purchaser decides to exercise the contract at expiration and sell it to the put writer. Also called *covered put writing*.

covered writing The selling of a futures or option contract to someone when the seller owns the underlying instrument.

covering shorts In the futures market, when prices rise for little apparent reason, traders are often said to be "covering their shorts." *Shorts* occur when traders have sold contracts that they didn't own, expecting prices to continue falling. When prices begin to rise, they must buy those contracts to cover their position so that they maintain a neutral position and stop their losses.

CPA See *certified public accountant*.

CPF See *certified financial planner*.

CPGA Short for *cost per gross add*; the average cost that a telecom carrier spends to prompt a new user to sign up for its service.

CPI See *consumer price index*.

crack spread The difference in price between the purchase of crude oil futures and the sale of heating oil and gasoline futures, or vice versa. It is an *inter-commodity spread,* which is the difference between the prices of a commodity, such as crude oil, and its products, such as heating oil and gasoline. The crack spread reflects the profit margins of oil refiners. Typically, heating oil prices are higher during the winter months, reflecting strong demand, and they usually rise more than the price of crude oil, which often increases the crack spread's value ahead of winter. Spreads are typically traded by commercial users such as oil companies or gasoline refiners. By trading spreads, hedges can be moved from one contract month to another. Trading spreads also provides a method to recover costs incurred by storing or financing inventories.

cram-down deal A merger or leveraged buyout that shareholders, typically of a financially troubled company, are forced to accept because a better option doesn't exist.

crawling peg A system for automatically revising the exchange rate between two currencies. Initially, central banks establish a *par value,* around which the rate can vary up to a given percent. The par value is revised regularly, usually by using a formula.

CRB Index A pricing index that measures changes in the price of 22 commodities that are believed to be among the first to react to changes in economic conditions. The CRB Index may serve as an early indicator of changes in the business climate and thus it is one of the economic statistics watched by analysts and economists. The index includes raw materials or products close to the beginning stages of production. Highly fabricated commodities are not included because they have large fixed costs, which causes them to react less quickly to changing market conditions.

Milton Jiler, a journalist, started *Commodity Research Bureau* in 1934 to provide commodity pricing information, which was virtually non-existent at the time. The company was sold in 1984 to Knight-Ridder Financial Publishing. In 1997, Knight Ridder Financial Publishing was purchased by Bridge Information Systems Inc. and the index adopted the name CRB/Bridge Index. Bridge Information was liquidated in bankruptcy proceedings, and in September 2001, Logical Systems Inc. of Chicago, purchased the CRB division from Bridge and restored the CRB name. Products include the CRB Commodities Yearbook, price charts, and daily market commentary.

creation unit The number of shares in an exchange traded fund (ETF). An ETF is similar to a mutual fund, but it has the objective of achieving the same return as a particular market index. The size of the creation unit varies by fund and ranges from 25,000 to 600,000 shares. Participants engaging in the creation and redemption process are charged a fee, which varies. One well-known ETF is Spiders, or SPDRs, which invests in all the stocks included in the S&P 500 Composite Stock Price Index.

creative accounting Using one or more accounting options to present financial results in the most favorable light. Although creative accounting is not illegal per se, if the rules are pushed too far, a corporation may run into trouble with regulatory authorities. If particular creative accounting techniques become too popular, the Financial Accounting Standards Board or another agency with regulatory authority may change the rules.

credit Any money lent through bonds or loans, for any of a variety of purposes. Credit must be paid back or the borrower risks defaulting.

credit analysis A bond portfolio investment strategy that involves undertaking a detailed analysis of the bond issuer in order to determine the likelihood of changes in its credit status or the likelihood of default.

credit balance

1. The amount of money in a financial account that is in favor of the account holder.

2. The amount of cash or securities in a brokerage account that exceeds the payment amount needed to pay for securities purchases.

credit bureau An agency that collects information on the credit histories of consumers and businesses. A credit history includes a record of bill payments and whether payments have been late or missed. A credit history also includes information on bankruptcy or legal filings. Credit bureaus use different methods of credit scoring to rank borrowers and advise companies on whether credit should be granted. See also *credit scoring*.

credit card A plastic card with a magnetic strip on one side. It is used to buy goods and services, and is the means by which consumers take out small loans. The bank or financial institution issuing the credit card pays the merchant and then sends a monthly bill to the holder of the credit card. The issuer charges interest for the amount of time that the money is outstanding, although many credit cards offer a 25-day grace period during which no interest is charged.

Credit card companies often require only a very small monthly payment, which may get the consumer into debt trouble if he or she pays only the minimum monthly payment. In recent years, banks have been aggressive about pushing cash advances to their credit card customers in the form of checks that the customer can use at stores or to pay off other high-interest credit card balances. Consumers who don't pay their credit card bill on time can incur a variety of different fees. In contrast, the cost of items purchased with a *debit card* is debited, or deducted, from the account of the debit cardholder at the time of purchase.

credit crunch A reduction in the supply of credit that occurs when lenders become reluctant to lend funds and tighten their borrowing requirements. A credit crunch typically drives up interest rates and is often associated with a tightening monetary policy.

credit default swap A financial transaction in which the holder of a debt instrument pays a premium for protection from a loss in the case of default. This may be accomplished by purchasing an option or credit insurance, rather than a true swap. All of the credit risk can be transferred by using a total return swap.

credit history A compilation of how a person or corporation has paid its bills. A credit history shows whether the subject is typically late with payments, has defaulted on an obligation, or has filed for bankruptcy. Consumer credit agencies compile this data and then sell it to financial institutions interested in checking a person's credit history before extending a mortgage, loan, or credit card. A credit history is judged by a credit scoring system that adds or subtracts points depending on certain behaviors such as a large income or late bill payments. In recent years, some companies have required potential employees to agree to having a credit history run on them before being hired.

credit insurance An insurance policy that protects the insured against unusually high losses from unpaid accounts receivable. Often a bank requires credit insurance before it issues a loan backed by a company's receivables.

credit limit A limit on the total amount of credit that will be extended. A credit limit might apply to a consumer credit card or to an individual or corporation's line of credit. If credit limits are exceeded, the account can be suspended and the borrower may be required to immediately pay the debt down.

credit quality rating An evaluation of a company's creditworthiness, and thus the creditworthiness of its debt, that is made by an independent rating service. Typically, ratings services issue a rating that ranges from AAA, the best, to D, which indicates that the company is in bankruptcy, or soon will be.

credit rating A formal evaluation of an individual's or company's credit history and ability to repay obligations. Many firms investigate, analyze, and maintain records on the credit responsibility of individuals and businesses. A credit rating is based on the number of outstanding debts and whether debts have been repaid in a timely manner in the past. The best-known business credit rating agencies are Standard & Poor's, Moody's Investors Service, and Fitch Ratings. Other agencies specialize in credit ratings of individuals.

credit risk The risk that a party to a loan, trade, or financial transaction will not be able to pay for the transaction or repay the loan at maturity.

credit scoring A numerical method of ranking the creditworthiness of individuals, companies, and governments. Each credit bureau has its own ranking system and scoring method. Some credit bureaus target only individuals, others target businesses. Corporations that issue debt and other obligations are scored by credit rating agencies such as Standard & Poor's, Moody's Investors Service, Fitch Ratings, and D&B Corporation (formally known as Dun & Bradstreet Corporation).

credit shelter trust See *bypass trust*.

credit union A not-for-profit financial institution formed by employees of a company, a labor union, a professional association, or some other group and operated as a cooperative. Account holders are members, rather than customers. Credit unions may offer a full range of financial services including loans and checking and savings accounts. They typically pay higher interest rates on deposits and charge lower rates on loans than commercial banks. Federally chartered credit unions are regulated and insured by the National Credit Union Administration, which charters and supervises federal credit unions. Depositor's accounts are protected up to $100,000 through the National Credit Union Share Insurance Fund (NCUSIF). There are more than 80 million credit-union account holders in the United States.

credit watch A list that is used by ratings agencies to signal that they may downgrade a company's credit rating because of a declining business environment characterized by declining sales, pressure on profits, or extreme competition. Just because a company is placed on a credit watch list by Standard & Poor's, Moody's Investors' Service, or Fitch Ratings doesn't necessarily mean that the company will be eventually downgraded.

credit-linked note (CLN) A debt instrument that pays investors a return that is dependent on the issuer's credit rating.

creditor An entity that has a monetary claim against a debtor.

creditors' committee A group that represents all the firms that have lent money to a company that is in bankruptcy or nearing bankruptcy. A creditors' committee negotiates on behalf of all the lenders owed money, and thus has considerable clout. Typically only the largest creditors are represented on the creditors' committee.

creditors' life insurance A life insurance policy that is held for the benefit of the company granting credit to the insured. If the insured borrower dies before paying off the loan or debt, then the policy will be paid to the creditor so the loan balance can be paid off.

creditworthiness The ability of an individual, business, or government to repay money that has been loaned. Generally, creditworthy customers have an easy time borrowing funds; those who are not judged to be creditworthy have a difficult time.

critical mass The point at which a company can achieve self-sustaining viability because its revenues have risen enough to make the business activity profitable because the related costs are spread across a wide range of customers.

CRM See *Customer Relationship Management*.

Crockett, Andrew General manager of the Bank for International Settlements, as of this printing.

crop report A monthly report released by the U.S. Department of Agriculture for a large number of agricultural commodities. The reports are closely watched because their contents explain what the supply is likely to be, which causes prices to rise or fall. The reports focus on the amount of acreage that has been planted and the expected and actual *crop yield* (how much product is produced from one acre of land). Crop reports are watched closely for commodities markets such as the wheat, corn, cotton, and soybean markets.

crop reports Reports on the state of agricultural crops that are compiled by the U.S. Department of Agriculture. The crop reports include estimates on planted acreage, yield, and expected production, and include details from the previous year. Crops reports are just as important to the agricultural markets as the unemployment or gross domestic product reports are to the financial markets. When crop reports are released, trading can be very volatile if the information outlined in the report was unexpected.

crop year The time period between harvests, which varies according to the commodity. In general, the wheat crop year runs from July 1 to June 30 and the soybean crop year runs from September 1 to August 31.

cross hedge Offsetting a risk in a cash market security or commodity by buying or selling a futures contract for a similar investment. A cross hedge is done when there is a high degree of correlation between the two investments but an exact futures contract doesn't exist.

cross margining The procedure for margining related futures or option contracts and stocks together when different clearinghouses are clearing each side of the position. Cross margining allows traders to apply the same margin funds to different trading positions.

cross trading The non-competitive matching of one customer's buy order with the sell order of another customer. This practice is regulated and is permitted only when it follows specific rules established by the Commodity Exchange Act or the Commodity Futures Trading Commission.

cross-border carry trade A trade in which the investor borrows money in a country that has low interest rates and lends or invests the funds in a country that has high interest rates. The trade relies on currency and interest-rate stability in order to succeed. If the spot currency rate changes too much to keep the interest rate advantage, even though the trade is profitable, money can be lost on the change in the currency's value. The yen carry trade in the latter part of the 1990s was a popular use of the trade. Traders bought yen and then invested the proceeds in the U.S. Treasury market to earn the differential between the relatively high U.S. interest rates and the very low Japanese interest rates.

cross-rate The exchange rate for a non-U.S. currency expressed in terms of another non-US currency.

crowding out The effect that occurs when governments borrow heavily to fund budget deficits. Governments that are heavy debt issuers may supply all of the debt that the market needs, which makes it that much more difficult for other less highly-rated borrowers, such as corporations, to issue debt. If the supply of debt increases, the prices of bonds and notes fall. Because interest rates move inversely to the price of bonds or notes, the cost of borrowing rises.

crown jewel A part of a company that is the most attractive or lucrative. Often a company's crown jewels are the primary reason that another company attempts to take it over. The crown jewels may be a product line, a group of assets, a service, or a trademark.

crude oil The raw material refined into gasoline, heating oil, propane, petrochemicals, jet fuel, and other products. A mixture of hydrocarbons, crude oil exists as a liquid underground and remains a liquid in the atmosphere after going through separating processes. Crude oil futures trade on the New York Mercantile Exchange as well as other futures exchanges throughout the world.

crude oil futures   The world's most actively traded commodity based on crude oil, which is unrefined oil that is a popular source of energy and energy-related products. Contracts on many different types of oil are traded on exchanges throughout the world. In the United States, the New York Mercantile Exchange (NYMEX) is the major trading exchange for crude oil futures contracts. In the United Kingdom, the major trading venue is the International Petroleum Exchange.

Light sweet crude oil is preferred by refiners because of its ability to yield high levels of gasoline, diesel fuel, heating oil, and jet fuel. Other trading exchanges throughout the world also trade futures and options on many different varieties of crude oil. The benchmark light, sweet crude oil contract that NYMEX bases its contract on is the West Texas Intermediate (WTI) crude oil that is delivered in Midland, Texas. Cash prices for WTI are quoted at Cushing, Oklahoma, which is a major crude oil shipment point that has extensive pipeline connections to oil producing areas and Southwest and Gulf Coast-based refining centers.

crude oil inventories   The actual inventories of crude oil, gasoline, and distillate, such as jet fuel, as reported on a weekly basis. The numbers are watched closely by the energy markets, and if the results differ greatly from the expected inventory levels, the market can react strongly. The inventory data can be skewed by holidays and seasonal factors. Weekly data can be unreliable and should be viewed as a part of longer-term trends, so a four-week moving average may be more useful.

There are two sets of inventory data that comprise the crude oil inventory reports. The American Petroleum Institute, a private trade group, compiles a voluntary survey of its members and releases the data weekly. The Energy Information Agency, a U.S. government agency, compiles mandatory reports from firms in the energy industry and releases the data on Wednesday mornings.

crush spread   The purchase of soybean futures and the simultaneous selling of soybean oil and soymeal futures, or vice versa. It is an *inter-commodity spread,* which is the difference between the prices of a commodity, soybeans, and its two products, soybean oil and soybean meal. Crush strategies can be a profitable way to take advantage of price differences between the underlying product and those that are derived from it. Spreads typically are traded by commercial users such as food manufacturers. By trading spreads, hedges can be moved from one contract month to another. Trading spreads also provides a method to recover costs such as storing or financing inventories.

CUBES   An acronym that stands for the *Coupons Under Book-Entry Safekeeping* program that is operated by the U.S. Treasury Department's Bureau of Public Debt. The CUBES program gives investors holding coupons that were previously stripped from bearer Treasury securities the opportunity to convert those coupons to book-entry form so they can easily be transferred. A *bearer Treasury security* is one for which ownership rights are established by whoever holds it, in contrast to a registered security, for which the owner is identified.

cubic foot   A unit of measure used with natural gas volume. One cubic foot of gas is the amount needed to fill a volume of one cubic foot at 14.73 pounds per square inch absolute pressure and 60 degrees Fahrenheit. One cubic foot of natural gas contains an average of 1,027 BTUs.

cuffing trades   Delaying the filling of customer orders to benefit another trader. Cuffing is an illegal trading practice and falls in the category of an *accommodation trade,* a transaction in which a floor broker lets another trader profit from a customer order that is held by the floor broker through any arrangement other than open-outcry trading.

cumulative dividends Dividends on preferred stock still owed to the shareholders, even if they are not paid out during the year. These dividends are carried forward to the next year. Cumulative dividends aren't liabilities of the corporation because the directors can defer the preferred dividends indefinitely. In contrast, *noncumulative dividends* are lost and do not carry over to the next year if they are not paid.

cumulative effect of an accounting change The effect that the implementation of a new accounting principle would have had on net income in previous periods had it been used then. Accounting rules require that changes in accounting systems or principal must be included in financial statements in order to compare results with and without the change.

cumulative preferred stock Preferred stock with a fixed dividend that is owed each year. If a company's board declines to declare a dividend, then the per share dividend accumulates each year and the whole amount must be paid before any dividends on common stock can be paid. Dividends not paid in the year they are due are called *dividends in arrears.*

cumulative voting A voting system that lets shareholders give all their votes to one candidate for the board of directors, which gives minority shareholders more power. In contrast, in *regular* or *statutory voting,* shareholders may not cast more than one vote per share to any single nominee. For example, in an election for four directors, a shareholder with 500 shares has one vote per share. Under the regular method, the shareholder could vote a maximum of 500 shares for each of four candidates. Under cumulative voting, however, the shareholder could choose to vote all 2,000 votes for one candidate, 1,000 each to two candidates, or otherwise divide his or her votes.

curbs in A term used in a volatile market to signal that predefined trading limits have been reached and further trades can't take place until the market stabilizes. For example, if the stock market sells off substantially, curbs would be instituted to prevent more sell orders from being executed. Often financial television stations will put "curbs in" at the bottom of the television screen when this situation exists. See also *circuit breaker.*

currency Money, such as coins or paper, that is used as a medium of exchange.

currency board A method of controlling the value of a currency by rigidly fixing the currency's value to a more widely used and dominant currency, often the British pound or the U.S. dollar. The local currency can be exchanged only for the dominant currency at the fixed exchange rates. Two countries that use currency boards are Hong Kong and Panama.

currency futures Exchange-listed currency futures contracts that can be bought and sold. Currency futures are traded on the Chicago Mercantile Exchange's International Monetary Market (IMM) division. They also trade on other smaller U.S. exchanges and on the Singapore International Monetary Exchange (SIMEX).

currency peg The policy of controlling the value of a currency by linking it to another currency. The U.S. dollar is used as a peg for many currencies.

currency speculator A person who trades currencies with the sole purpose of making a profit.

currency swap A trade that shifts a loan from one currency to another or shifts the currency of an asset. Companies use a currency swap to borrow in a currency different from their own currency and to be protected from changes in exchange rates that would affect the value of the loan. A currency swap also is a way to diversify a company's borrowing requirements to different capital markets or to shift cash flow from foreign currencies.

current assets   Cash or other assets that are expected to be converted into cash, consumed, or sold within one year or during the normal operating cycle of the business, whichever is longer. Current assets are listed on the company's balance sheet and include cash, accounts receivable, prepaid insurance, and office supplies. *Non-current assets* are items such as land, buildings, and office equipment.

current dollars   Value of a dollar without adjusting for the effect of inflation. This term frequently is used in economic discussions and in monthly economic reports that refer to the dollar at today's price. For example, gross domestic product (GDP) data for the most recent quarter may show a 2.5 percent growth rate, which is the actual rate quoted in current dollar terms. In contrast, *constant dollars* have been adjusted for inflation. A constant dollar GDP growth rate with a base year of 1995 may show a 2.0 percent growth instead of the 2.5 percent current-dollar rate.

current enterprise value   A value derived from subtracting out the debt of minority-owned companies from a corporation's financial statements. This is typically done if the revenues or earnings of the minority-owned company are not included, or *consolidated,* with the parent's financial statements. The term is frequently used in the research reports of Wall Street analysts.

current issue   In the Treasury market, the Treasury bond or note that has been issued most recently. Trading also is most active in the current-issue market.

current liabilities   Obligations that are expected to be paid or performed within one year or within the normal operating cycle of a business, whichever is longer. Current liabilities are listed on the company's balance sheet and include accounts payable, notes payable, taxes payable, and salaries payable.

current ratio   A frequently used indicator of short-run liquidity that measures a company's ability to pay its bills over the next 12 months. To calculate current ratio, divide current assets by current liabilities. *Current assets* are cash, accounts receivables, or other depositary accounts. *Current liabilities* are accounts payable and other obligations coming due in less than a year.

current yield   The coupon payment on a fixed-income security, such as a bond or note, that is a percentage of the security's market price. This value should include accrued interest. Current yield is to bonds what a dividend yield is to a stock. To calculate current yield, divide the annual coupon payment of the bond by the bond's current market price. The result is the amount of interest that the investor actually earns.

Curtis, Cyrus H.K.   A pioneer in the magazine publishing industry who founded the *Ladies' Home Journal* and the *Saturday Evening Post.* Curtis discovered that advertisers would pay more money to advertise in magazines with large circulations, which allowed publishers to sell the magazines to readers at lower prices. His tactics paved the way for the success of other mass-circulation magazines.

CUSIP   See *Committee on Uniform Securities Identification Procedures.*

custodian   A bank or financial institution that holds stock certificates or other investment documents for individuals, corporations, or mutual funds.

Customer Relationship Management (CRM)   An information technology system. Software programs provide customer-relationship-management tools that allow companies to manage aspects of their relationships with their customers, including ordering history, billing information, and accounts receivables.

cyberbanking   Using the Internet to perform banking functions. Also called *electronic banking, remote banking,* and *online banking.*

cybercash A commercial payment system whereby a user digitally purchases cash credits and then spends them when making electronic purchases over the Internet. Most merchants accepting digital cash use it as an alternative to other forms of payment, such as credit cards. Cybercash had its heyday during the Internet boom of the late 1990s.

cyclical stock A stock whose value moves upward when the economy rises and declines when the economy slows. Companies in the fields of automobile manufacturing, travel, lodging, entertainment, and large equipment manufacturing, for example, are cyclical stocks. Non-cyclical stocks, in contrast, are those in companies whose business remains fairly static regardless of the economy. Food, consumer products, and drug companies, for example, are non-cyclical stocks.

cyclical unemployment Unemployment that rises or falls in conjunction with the business cycle. As economic growth slows and corporations' profits decline, cyclical unemployment rises because corporations lay off workers in order to reduce costs. The opposite is *structural unemployment,* which remains constant irrespective of what the economy is doing.

D

D&O insurance *Directors' and officers' liability insurance,* which protects the personal assets of a company's executives and company assets in the event of a management-related legal judgment.

DAC See *deferred acquisition cost.*

daily settlement The amount of money that has to be paid at the end of each trading day by a futures trader in order to make an additional margin payment required by the price change of the futures contracts. The accounts of futures traders are marked-to-the market at the end of each trading day, meaning that current prices are applied to calculate the brokerage account balances that traders have.

daily trading limit A maximum rise or fall in prices that futures or options contracts are allowed to have in one day. When the daily trading limit is met, the trading is stopped on the instrument for the day. Exchanges create their own rules governing daily trading limits.

daisy chain A series of linked trades that are done in order to manipulate the market and increase trading volume to make it appear that there is an active market for a security. The activity makes prices rise and allows the market manipulators to sell their holdings at a higher price. However, when unsuspecting investors attempt to place sell orders, they receive sharply lower prices than they expect because there is no one on the other side willing to purchase the shares.

dalasi The currency unit of Gambia, comprised of 100 bututs.

dark fiber An optical fiber network that is not actively used but is available as extra capacity.

DARPA *Defense Advanced Research Projects Agency,* a research agency of the Pentagon. DARPA looks for existing or developing products that have military applications for the United States. DARPA was a major force behind the formation of the Internet.

DAX Stock Index An index of 30 selected German blue-chip stocks that are traded on the Frankfurt Stock Exchange. The index was created with a base value of 1,000 on December 31, 1987. Typically, a company must be listed for at least three years prior to the inclusion of its stock in the DAX. Also, the free-floating capital must be at least 15 percent.

day order An order from a customer to buy or sell a stock that is good only on the day it is given. A day order expires if it hasn't been executed by the end of the trading day.

day trading Trading by investors who rapidly buy and sell stocks throughout the day in the hope that their stocks will either rise or fall in value for the seconds or minutes that they own the stock, allowing them to lock in quick profits. Day trading is extremely risky and can result in substantial financial losses in a very short period of time. Day traders became part of popular culture during the stock market boom in the late 1990s, but many found other work when the bear market began in 2000. In the futures market, however, day traders have been a continual presence. A futures market day trader is a speculator who takes positions in futures or options contracts and liquidates them before the close of the same trading day.

daylight overdraft An intra-day debit in a trading firm or bank's account at its clearing bank, clearinghouse, or central bank. While the overdrafts will be covered by the end of the business day, they still expose the clearing bank or the members of a clearinghouse to default risk. The Federal Reserve Board has a rule that assesses a charge against the average intra-day overdraft, which is designed to encourage banks to actively manage the potential default risks that can be introduced into the banking system with overdrafts.

DBA See *doing business as.*

DCF See *discounted cash flow.*

dead-cat bounce

1. A quick, but modest, upward movement in a market that previously traded lower.

2. A term that is used by traders to indicate that they don't expect a stock's upward price movement to last.

dead-hand poison pill A technique used to fight unwanted takeover attempts that dilutes the stock holdings of an unwanted acquirer. The dead-hand poison pill allows only members of the board of directors who were on the board of directors when the poison pill provision was enacted, or their successors, to redeem the poison pill rights, which gives them the rights to additional shares of stock and makes it that much harder for the unwanted acquirer to gain control of the company. It is a controversial provision that has been challenged in some states.

dealer Any person or company that sells or buys securities for his or her own account. The dealer realizes profit or loss from the difference between the price paid and the price sold. A dealer is in contrast to an *agent,* who trades on behalf of someone else.

dealer commercial paper A high-quality unsecured note that is sold by corporations through dealers. It is generally high-quality debt, because if the company isn't financially healthy, no one will be willing to purchase the commercial paper.

dealer market A market where market makers can buy and sell for their own account or for customer accounts. Usually, at least one side of the transaction is conducted on behalf of the dealer's account.

death spiral convert A convertible bond that gives the holder the ability to convert it into enough shares to protect the bondholder's principal in the event of a sharp decline in the price of the stock. In other words, if a death spiral convert holder has $1 million of equity in a company, and stock shares decline, the holder can convert the bond into enough new shares to push his or her equity back up to $1 million. This can lead to the original shareholders losing control of a company, if the company's share price posts a sharp decline.

debenture In general, an unsecured debt, often an unsecured bond backed only by the integrity or creditworthiness of the issuer (and not by any form of collateral, such as property or inventory or some other asset). Debentures are governed by agreements known as *indentures,* which are subject to the Trust Indenture Act of 1939.

debit card A plastic card that has a magnetic strip on one side that can be swiped. A debit card is used to pay for goods and services. The bank or financial institution issuing the debit card pays the merchant and then deducts the amount of the transaction from the debit card holder's bank account immediately. In contrast, a credit card balance doesn't have to be paid for many months after a purchase.

debt An obligation that a person or organization has to another person or organization. Debt may be in the form of a bond, note, mortgage, line of credit, or other financial instrument. Debt may be secured by assets, which means that the assets will be seized in the event of default, or be unsecured.

debt covenants Restrictions that are put on a borrower by the bank or other entity that granted the loan. The restrictions might specify that a certain level of sales or profits be generated or might limit the company's ability to take on other debt. If debt covenants are broken, often the loan becomes due immediately.

debt instrument A catchall term that refers to a bond, note, commercial paper, or a line of credit.

debt limit   A limit put on the amount of funds that a government is allowed to borrow. Debt limits are created in order to restrain the government's ability to overspend, which would eventually drive up taxes.

debt retirement   The act of repaying debt. This may be accomplished by recalling notes and bonds that have been issued and returning the principal to those who have purchased the debt. Often debt is retired by creating a sinking fund when the debt is issued. The issuer deposits a certain amount of money received from the debt issue into the sinking fund. When the debt has to be repaid, the funds are available. Another debt retirement method is issuing serial bonds, which requires the debt to be retired at different times according to a schedule.

debt service cost   The annual cost of paying interest on a company's outstanding debt.

debt-equity swap   A refinancing technique where debt holders forgive some of the debt they hold in exchange for equity in the company. Often this is done in bankruptcy or near-bankruptcy situations if the company is unable to pay back the debt. While the lender gambles by taking equity, the lender bets that the stock price will rise and dividends will eventually be paid, thus making up the debt.

debt-financed stock   Stock that is purchased by using a margin account. A margin account lets an investor purchase stock by borrowing money from a brokerage firm.

debtor   A person or entity who seeks voluntary relief under the Bankruptcy Code or who has been forced involuntarily into a Chapter 7 or 11 bankruptcy case by petitioning creditors.

debtor in possession financing (DIP)   A financing situation in which a bank extends credit to a company in or approaching bankruptcy but takes possession of agreed upon assets before making the loan.

debt-reducing exchange offer   An offer made by the equity owners of a company to their bondholders asking them to cancel the bonds they hold in return for obtaining equity in the company.

debt-to-equity ratio   A company's total liabilities divided by stockholders' equity. The ratio shows how indebted a company is. A higher proportion of debt compared to equity as a contributor to a firm's capital makes earnings more volatile and increases the likelihood that the company will not be able to meet its interest payments and may default. A company with a high debt-to-equity ratio can become a potential credit risk if the economy slows down or if competition increases.

decimal trading   See *decimalization.*

decimalization   Quoting stock prices in decimals (dollars and cents), as opposed to the old-style one-eighth of a dollar increments, in order to make prices easier for investors to understand. This also cuts down on the amount of commission that traders receive on the large spread between prices when they are quoted in one-eighth of a dollar increments.

declaration date   The date on which a company's board of directors votes to issue a dividend. There are several days between a declaration date and the date when new shareholders lose the right to receive the dividend, called the *ex-dividend date.*

declining volume   The number of companies whose price fell during the trading session. Volume is separated into declining volume, advancing volume, and unchanged. By comparing the volume of stocks that are advancing and the volume of stocks that are declining, it is possible to determine how strong the market move was. Volume details are published daily in financial newspapers.

declining-balance method of depreciation   The most commonly used accelerated method of depreciation, which results in large depreciation expenses being taken in the early years of an asset's life with smaller amounts of depreciation allocated to later years. Depreciation is computed by applying a fixed rate to the *carrying value,* or resale value, of the assets. Any fixed rate can be used; however, if twice the straight-line percentage is used, then it is referred to as the *double-declining-balance method*. The declining-balance method may be appropriate in industries where equipment and technology changes quickly. It also makes sense from the perspective that an asset has more value and provides better results in its early years.

decoupling The tendency of U.S. Treasury bonds to rise significantly when the stock market trades lower. Decoupling is caused by investors liquidating stock holdings and putting their funds in the safety of U.S. Treasury bonds. Decoupling makes the purchase of Treasury securities a good way to diversify a portfolio because losses in stocks will typically produce gains in bond prices.

decoupling trade A transaction that is designed to profit from a change in the spread relationship between two or more indices, rates, or other financial relationships.

deduction An expense that is subtracted from taxable income in order to reduce the amount of income tax that has to be paid. Charitable donations and business expenses, such as entertainment expenses and office supplies, are examples of items that can be deducted.

de-escalation clause A section of a contract that requires prices to be lowered in the event that certain conditions are met. For example, if the price of raw materials that are used to fulfill the contract decreases, then the cost to the customer also decreases. This is in contrast to an *escalation clause,* in which prices can be raised in the event certain conditions are met.

default Failure to meet the terms of a loan or other debt; such terms may include making periodic payments or repaying the principal by a certain date. When a corporation defaults on a loan, the lender can take legal action toward the company, including pushing it into bankruptcy.

default risk The risk that a partner in a business transaction will not live up to its obligations; for example, that a financial institution such as a bank or savings and loan may collapse and not be able to return the investors' principal, or may not continue paying interest. Default risk also is found in a variety of other financial scenarios. The U.S. government helps protect against default risk by banks through the *Federal Deposit Insurance Corporation* (FDIC) program, which insures deposits for up to $100,000 in the event that a bank defaults. Although various insurance programs exist to protect against default risk, including the Securities Investor Protection Corporation (SIPC) program for brokerage account holders, U.S. Treasury bonds are the only investment that does not have default risk. That is because the U.S. government pledges that Treasury bond investments are protected by the "full faith and credit obligation" of the U.S. government.

defeasance

1. The ability of a debtor to offset a liability by purchasing government securities or a specialized risk management contract.

2. Voiding a contract or deed because a certain prohibited action has occurred.

defensive securities

1. Stocks with a beta of less than 1, which means that the stock will move less than the overall market. See also *beta*.

2. Bonds that have an investment-grade rating.

deferred acquisition cost (DAC) An asset that is accumulated by life insurance companies because they are allowed to spread out the expenses from selling policies, such as commissions, over a multi-year period.

deferred annuity An investment whose earnings accumulate tax-deferred and that, at a specific point in the future, begins making a series of regular payments. These are sold by insurance companies and often used to plan for retirement.

deferred compensation   A technique that employees can use to defer taxes and save money. An employee defers part of his or her salary into a deferred compensation plan. The money grows tax-free until it is withdrawn, at which time taxes are owed. Deferred compensation plans are part of pension, stock option, and profit-sharing plans.

deferred contingency sales load   Another name for a commission charged on a mutual fund that has a back-end sales load. That means that no commission is paid when the investment is purchased, but the commission is charged when investors liquidate their holding. However, if the mutual fund is held for a minimum time period, such as five years, then the investor doesn't have to pay the sales commission at all.

deferred equity   Securities, such as convertible securities, that will be convertible into common stock at some point in the future. A convertible security is debt that is issued that at a particular point can be converted into equity at a predetermined ratio.

deferred interest bond   A bond that pays interest at maturity, or at a later date. A typical bond pays interest regularly, often twice a year. A *zero-coupon bond* is a type of deferred interest bond that pays no interest until maturity, at which point all the interest due and the face value of the bond is paid. Zero-coupon bonds are sold at a deep discount.

deficit

1. A budget in which expenses are greater than income. Money must be borrowed to make up the shortfall or assets must be sold.

2. A situation in which liabilities exceed assets.

deficit financing   Financing undertaken by a corporation or government to make up for a shortfall in revenue. Typically, the term is associated with government spending. Governments may undertake deficit financing in order to provide an economic stimulus.

deficit net worth   See *negative net worth*.

deficit spending   Spending that exceeds revenues. The term typically is associated with government spending. Governments issue debt to fund their deficit spending.

defined benefit plan   A type of retirement plan that is committed to paying a specified amount to a recipient based on years of employment and annual salary. The plan may be funded by employees' contributions, employer's contributions, or a combination of the two. The employer has the responsibility to see that the plan is solvent. An employer can contribute the amount of money needed to provide an annual benefit that is no larger than the smaller of $140,000 or 100 percent of the employee's average taxable compensation (as of this printing) for his or her most highly paid three consecutive years.

defined contribution pension plan   A retirement plan in which the level of contributions are fixed and most of the contributions come from employees. The contributions that employees make and the return on the investment determine the amount of pension funds paid. This type of plan provides an individual account for each plan participant. Employers can put away the smaller of $35,000 or 25 percent of the participant's compensation (as of this printing) regardless of whether the employee makes the contributions or funds are provided through a separate profit-sharing plan. Gains or losses in the underlying investments and plan expenses affect the benefits paid.

deflation   Declining prices for goods, services, and/or assets that are caused by decreases in personal, government, or investment spending. Deflation can also be caused by a reduction in the supply of money or credit, according to monetarists. *Inflation,* which is an increase in prices, is the opposite of deflation. Both can be damaging to the economy if they are at excessive levels.

deflator A statistical factor that converts current dollars into inflation-adjusted dollars. Deflators are used with gross domestic product statistics to remove the influence of inflation.

degearing The process of replacing debt in the capital structure with equity in a debt-for-equity swap.

delayed opening A situation in which a stock is unable to begin trading on a given day because of an extraordinary situation. For example, a delayed opening may occur if there is a flood of buyers or sellers due to news announced before the opening of the stock exchange, resulting in an imbalance between buyers and sellers. Alternatively, the opening may be delayed if there is pending news that a company needs to announce. Sometimes entire stock or futures markets experience a delayed opening, caused by weather conditions, for example.

deleveraging

1. Reducing the amount of debt that is held by a company.

2. A situation in which traders attempt to sell the same holdings, or position, at the same time. That context was used more frequently during the Asian financial crisis.

delist To remove a company from a U.S. stock exchange. Exchanges delist companies if the company's stock falls lower than a minimum closing price, often $1, for a certain period of time. Exchanges also have minimum market capitalization levels.

deliverable A commodity or financial instrument that meets the settlement requirements outlined by a futures or options exchange.

deliverable grades A standard for a commodity or financial instrument that must be met in order to deliver the commodity to a futures exchange to meet the requirements of the futures contract. Also called *contract grades*.

delivery The process of fulfilling the terms of a futures contract, called a *settlement*, by delivering the underlying physical product.

delivery date The first day during the month when delivery is expected to occur under the terms of a futures contract. It is up to the seller to determine exactly when the delivery will be made during that month.

delivery month The month, specified by a futures contract, in which the actual physical commodity or cash for a financial instrument must be delivered to the purchaser.

delivery notice

1. A notice that informs the holder of a futures contract when the actual commodity will be delivered. Many futures contracts are cash-settled, rather than involving the delivery of the actual commodity. Because futures transactions are used as a financial hedge, most traders don't want several tons of wheat arriving on their doorstep. Instead, a check is sent.

2. In a business setting, a notification that informs a customer when purchased goods will be delivered.

delivery specifications The list of characteristics a commodity or financial instrument must meet in order to settle futures or options contracts traded on organized exchanges. Such characteristics might include the grade, or quality, of the commodity, its size, and where the physical product must be delivered.

delivery versus payment (DVP) The delivery of the underlying instrument for a futures or options contract made in exchange for the receipt of payment. That system is in contrast to *delivery versus receipt,* where delivery is made in exchange for a signed receipt for the securities.

delivery versus receipt (DVR) In a futures or options contract, DVR means the seller delivers the securities in exchange for a signed receipt. DVR contrasts with *delivery versus payment* (DVP), in which payment is received when the item is delivered.

delta The measurement of how much an option's premium changes when there is a unit change in the underlying price of the financial instrument, which may be a futures contract, a stock, or some other financial instrument. Another way to interpret delta is as an indication of whether an option will still be *in the money,* or have value, at its expiration.

delta neutral spread A spread where the total delta position on the long side and on the short side add up to approximately zero, thereby making the commodity risk neutral. Sometimes, a rise or fall in prices is attributed to traders attempting to get a delta neutral spread.

demand deposit A type of checking account from which funds can be withdrawn at any time by check or cash withdrawal without giving the bank or financial institution any prior notice.

demand shock The sudden rise or fall of prices based on the expectation that demand for a product will soar or fall. For example, the energy market often is impacted by demand shocks. Typically, the anticipation of extreme cold snaps in areas of the United States, such as the Northeast, that use heating oil drive demand and prices substantially higher. Prices have even doubled within a month in extreme situations. It is the market's perception of demand, rather than the actual demand, that creates demand shocks.

demand-pull inflation An inflationary condition that occurs when demand outpaces supply. People are competing for a too-small amount of goods, which drives prices up. In order to monitor demand-pull

inflation, traders and investors watch the producer and consumer price index statistics produced by the U.S. government. Demand-pull inflation is the opposite of *cost-push inflation,* where increasing costs drive inflation up.

demutualization The process of converting a mutual insurance company, or a mutually owned bank or savings and loan, into a company that has publicly-traded stock. A mutual company is one that is owned by its account holders or policyholders. Demutualization requires approval from mutual shareholders and policyholders. Typically, management advocates demutualization if it believes that reorganization is needed to enable the company to grow by having greater access to capital or being able to offer stock options to employees to attract the most qualified people.

denar The currency unit of Macedonia, comprised of 100 deni.

denomination The face value of currency or securities.

Department of Justice A government agency that, along with the Federal Trade Commission, administers antitrust laws. Both agencies work together on antitrust matters, including holding joint hearings. Under the Hart-Scott Rodino Act, passed in 1976, both the Federal Trade Commission and the Department of Justice review merger agreements for deals above $50 million in order to prevent potential anti-competitive harm to individuals and businesses. If the agencies decide to sue a company for unfair trade practices, the Department of Justice's lawyers in the Antitrust Division try the case. The Department of Justice also handles issues such as fraud, civil rights, personal safety, and prison issues.

depletion An accounting method used by mining, oil, or other natural resource companies to write off natural resource assets such as oil, gas, precious metals, or minerals as they are withdrawn from the ground. Depletion functions much like depreciating a building or equipment to reflect the fact that its value decreases over time. Depletion is a non-cash expense that is deducted from revenues; it increases expenses and thus lowers net income.

depletion account An account set up by a company to take charges against earnings as the amount of natural resources in reserves is depleted. Reserves may be oil, gas, metals, and timber, which are depleted over time. This is a non-cash charge but is charged against earnings to account for the decrease in the amount of the asset that the company owns.

depo rate An interest rate that is paid on deposits in the interbank market. It is a bid rate, or an interest rate that a bank will pay on eurocurrency deposits. It is similar to the *London Interbank Offered rate (LIBOR)*, which is the rate that international banks typically charge each other for loaning Eurodollars overnight in the London market. It is a frequently quoted rate that is used to price a variety of financial issues and short-term debt. Often, interest rates are quoted at an amount above LIBOR. It also may be called a *London Interbank Bid rate (LIBID)*.

deposit insurance Insurance that is charged to banks, savings and loans, and credit unions to fund federal insurance programs that reimburse depositors in the event that a financial institution collapses. The charge for the insurance is based on the amount of assets on deposit. See also *Federal Deposit Insurance Corporation*.

depositary bank A bank that manages the administration of American Depositary Receipts (ADRs), which are U.S.-based shares of foreign companies that have met specific underwriting and listing requirements to be able to sell their shares in the United States. Typically, a depositary bank is part of a large U.S. banking institution or trust company.

depository trust company A company that is collectively owned by banks and broker-dealers for the purpose of holding the securities of its shareholders and clients. The company also arranges for the receipt, delivery, and settlement of securities transactions.

depreciated cost The original value of an asset minus depreciation.

depreciation The loss, over time, in the value of an asset such as plant, equipment, and vehicles. Depreciation accounts for the decline in the value of the asset as it ages. Several methods are used for calculating depreciation, including straight-line depreciation, accelerated depreciation, and the accelerated cost recovery system. See also *straight-line depreciation method*.

depression An economic situation that is characterized by decreased business activity, high unemployment, and falling prices. Depressions are relatively infrequent occurrences in the United States. The most famous depression is the Great Depression that began with the collapse of the U.S. stock market in 1929 and continued until 1942, when production activity picked up to meet the demand for goods during World War II.

depth of market The number of shares of a security that can be bought or sold near current prices without causing a sharp change in prices. A widely traded security is said to have a *deep market*.

deregulation The process of reducing the number of laws and rules that apply to an industry in order to allow more innovation and less constraints on companies. Two well-known examples in the United States are the deregulation of the stock brokerage industry in 1975, when brokers were allowed to set their own commission rates, and the deregulation of the telecom industry in 1996.

derivative pricing model A financial model that analyzes various factors in an attempt to find the fair price of a futures or options contract. The best-known model is the Black-Scholes Option Pricing Model. See also *Black-Scholes Option Pricing Model*.

derivatives Financial instruments whose performance is derived, at least in part, from the performance of an underlying asset, security, or index. For example, a stock option is a derivative because its value changes in relation to the price movement of the underlying stock. Futures contracts also obtain their value from the underlying product.

Designated Order Turnaround System An electronic order system that has been developed by the New York Stock Exchange to execute small market and limit orders by directly routing them to the specialist on the NYSE floor. Also called *SuperDOT.*

desk A short way of saying *trading desk.* The term is used across all financial and commodities markets. A trading desk is the department that is responsible for executing securities transactions.

Deutsche Börse The German stock exchange, which trades a variety of other financial products such as bonds, options, and exchange traded funds. The Deutsche Börse has one of the largest electronic cash markets in the world, the Xetra trading platform. It also runs one of the world's largest derivatives markets, Eurex, which has joined with the Chicago Board of Trade in a strategic alliance.

development drilling program A program for drilling for oil or natural gas only in areas where known reserves exist. Investors or companies undertaking a development drilling program are more likely to find oil or gas, and thus make a profit, than those conducting an exploratory drilling program, which is risky and may result in a loss.

diagonal bear spread An option-trading strategy that involves purchasing a relatively long-term option contract and simultaneously selling a shorter-term contract that has a lower strike price. The investor profits if the price declines, within limits. This spread can be constructed using either puts or calls.

diagonal bull spread An option-trading strategy that involves purchasing an options contract that expires later and has a lower strike price than an option that the investor sells simultaneously. The investor profits if the price increases. This spread can be constructed using either puts or calls.

diagonal spread The price spread between two call options or two put options with different strike prices and different expiration dates. See also *spread, diagonal bear spread,* and *diagonal bull spread.*

Diamonds Jargon for DIAMONDS Trust Series 1, which is a unit investment trust that holds all 30 stocks in the Dow Jones Industrial Average. Diamonds attempt to produce investment results that correspond to the price and yield performance of the Dow Jones Industrial Average. Diamonds are traded on the American Stock Exchange (AMEX).

differentials Price differences between classes, grades, and locations of different stocks of the same commodity. Differentials describe discrepancies in price because of different characteristics of the product. For example, grocery products may be more expensive in a gourmet food store than they are in a regular or warehouse-type grocery store even though they are the same product.

diffusion index An index that indicates how pervasive a particular sentiment is on economic conditions or a forecast of price levels.

digital A format in which bits of data (information represented by 1s and 0s) are stored, transmitted, or manipulated. Each individual digit is a *bit.* Contrasts with *analog* format, in which data is transferred by amplifying the strength of the signal or varying its frequency in order to transmit information.

digital money Electronic payments systems that are used to pay bills. Also called *electric money* or *e-money.*

Digital Pearl Harbor A concern, which is so far unfounded, that computer hackers or terrorists could illegally gain access to a computer system and wreak national or even global havoc by destroying or manipulating data. Computer viruses are one relatively low-risk example of the problems that could be caused by a hacker.

digital piracy The illegal trade in software, videos, digital video devices (DVDs), and music. Piracy occurs when someone other than the copyright holder copies the product and resells it for a fraction of the cost that the legitimate producer charges. It is a serious problem in many countries outside the United States, particularly China.

digital subscriber lines Technology used to obtain a high-speed connection to the Internet by residential or small business users. Telephone companies typically provide the service.

diluted earnings per share An earnings per share measure that is calculated by dividing earnings by the number of outstanding shares of common and preferred stock, certain unexercised stock options, warrants, and some convertible debt. In contrast, a *basic earnings per share* calculation doesn't take into consideration the shares that would be outstanding if all of the options, warrants, or convertible debt were exercised. For companies with a large number of options, warrants, and convertible debt outstanding, the diluted earnings per share measure provides a more accurate picture of earnings. Companies are required to report basic and diluted earnings per share on their income statements. Also called *fully diluted earnings per share.*

dilution A ubiquitous term that refers to a decrease in an investor's ownership level or a company's market value, book value, or earnings per share. Ownership levels are diluted when additional shares are sold and existing shareholders don't buy the shares. An increase in the shares outstanding also dilutes a company's book value and earnings per share. Often, merger transactions are said to be dilutive to current shareholders.

dilution protection A provision in an investment that is designed to protect existing shareholders from reduced earnings. *Dilution* occurs when earnings have to be spread among an increased number of shares. One dilution protection measure adjusts the conversion ratio used to calculate the value of convertible securities if a stock dividend is paid. Another dilution protection technique is a *full-ratchet provision,* which automatically increases the equity percentage held by the original investors if subsequent investment rounds decrease a company's value. A dilution protection provision is typically found in venture capital funding agreements.

dinar The currency unit of Algeria, comprised of 100 centimes; of Iraq, Kuwait, and Bahrain, comprised of 1000 fils; of Jordan, comprised of 100 piasters; of Libya, comprised of 100 dirhams; of Sudan, comprised of 10 pounds; of Tunisia, comprised of 1,000 millimes; and of Yugoslavia, comprised of 100 paras.

dip A slight drop in prices of stocks, bonds, or other investments that presents a good buying opportunity. Traders often attribute rising prices to investors "buying on the dips."

DIP See *debtor in possession financing.*

direct charge-off method An accounting method for uncollectible accounts that directly debits, or charges, an expense account when a bad debt is discovered. Contrasts with the allowance method, which accounts for uncollectible accounts by expensing estimates of uncollectible accounts in the period when the related sales take place.

direct investment The purchase of a controlling interest in a business or subsidiary. If the investment is in a foreign company or subsidiary, it is called *foreign direct investment.*

direct issuer A company that does not use an investment bank to sell its commercial paper or other securities to investors. Instead, the company sells the securities directly to investors.

direct overhead Costs, such as warehouse rent, electricity costs, and insurance, that are directly related to the cost of a manufacturing activity. These costs are tabulated and become part of cost of goods sold.

direct participation program An investment program that lets investors receive the cash flow and tax benefits directly from an investment. Direct participation programs typically are structured as limited partnerships and most often are used as a tax shelter. However, their use as a tax shelter has been curtailed by legislation affecting passive investments.

direct placement Selling securities to professional investors and thereby avoiding registering the issue with the Securities and Exchange Commission. These securities are sold only to institutions such as mutual funds, banks, and pension funds or to wealthy investors. The securities may be for debt, equity, limited partnerships, or venture capital. Also called *private placements.*

direct rollover The transfer of funds out of a 401(k) plan or qualified plan directly into another account, such as an Individual Retirement Account (IRA) or a specially established account. By doing a direct rollover, the plan owner avoids paying withholding taxes and a penalty (typically between 10 and 20 percent). If, instead of doing a direct rollover, the owner opts to have plan money paid directly to him- or herself, taxes and penalties withheld reduce the amount of the payout.

dirham The currency unit of Morocco, comprised of 100 centimes, and the United Arab Emirates, comprised of 100 fils.

dirty float A term used in the currency market to refer to currency exchange rates in which a government intervenes relatively frequently in order to alter the direction of a country's currency. This is in contrast to a currency that freely trades, which has minimal government intervention.

disability income insurance An insurance policy that pays part of a person's salary, typically 60 or 70 percent, in the event that the person is unable to work for an extended period of time. Often, disability insurance policies are broken down into short- and long-term policies. Disability payments begin after a predetermined time period. If the individual pays for the disability insurance, then the insurance payments are tax free. However, if an employer paid the premiums, then the disability payments are taxed. Disability benefits are also available through the Social Security Administration.

disability insurance Insurance that can be purchased by an individual or provided by an employer. It pays a fixed amount, often 60 percent or 70 percent of the employee's salary, if the employee becomes disabled and unable to work. If an individual pays the premium for disability insurance, then future disability payments are tax free. However, if an employer pays for disability insurance, then the disability payments are taxed.

disbursement A payment that fulfills a contractual or business arrangement. For example, an investor closing out a 401(k) plan and rolling that money into another account receives a disbursement from the 401(k) plan.

discharge of bankruptcy A court order that terminates a bankruptcy proceeding after the terms of the bankruptcy are met. The discharge frees the debtor of all legal responsibilities for the listed debts.

discharge of lien A court order that removes a lien on a property after the court-ordered payment has been completed. A discharge of lien frees up the property to be sold.

disclosure Information released to the public by companies in order to comply with stock exchange and Securities and Exchange Commission rules requiring that the public and professional investors have simultaneous access to information about the company, its products, and specific transactions.

disclosure statement A pleading filed by a debtor with the Bankruptcy Court Clerk and sent to creditors. It contains information about the debtor and his or her plan for reorganization.

discontinued operations A company's operations that have been sold or shut down because they are no longer profitable or strategically beneficial. Often a company takes a charge against its quarterly earnings to account for the expense involved in discontinuing the operation. Both income and expenses from discontinued operations must be reported separately on a company's income statement in order to give investors a clear picture about the company's ongoing operations.

discount A term with many uses. Often discount refers to the difference between a bond's face value and its current market value. A discount occurs when the bond is selling at a price less than its face value. Treasury bills are sold at a discount to their face value. On maturity, the investor gets the full face value returned. Discount also may refer to a price that is lower than it ordinarily would have been if circumstances were different.

discount bond

1. A debt instrument, such as a Treasury bond, that has its coupon stripped away from the debt. Thus, no periodic interest is paid. It trades at a discount from its settlement value at maturity.

2. A bond that sells below its value at maturity because market interest rates are higher than its coupon rate.

discount rate The interest rate charged to commercial banks and other depository institutions on loans they receive from the *discount window,* the Federal Reserve Bank's lending facility. Typically, these loans are given only to meet a bank's short-term need, such as overnight or for the weekend. Banks must use all other sources of funds before applying for a Federal Reserve loan, which is given at below-market rates.

discount window A Federal Reserve Bank's lending facility through which a bank may borrow funds. The Federal Reserve gives loans to banks for short-term needs such as keeping sufficient reserves on deposit for overnight or over the weekend. Banks can borrow funds at the Federal Reserve's discount rate, which is a below-market rate. The term derives its name from when Federal Reserve banks all had teller's windows and at least one of them was the discount window. Bankers needing funds would bring their loans to their regional Federal Reserve Bank for discounting, which is selling loans for less than face value. Later, they would buy the loans back from the Federal Reserve at face value. The law has been changed to let the Fed lend money through advances that are collateralized by loans or securities.

discount yield The return on a security that is sold at a discount, such as money market instruments, commercial paper, and Treasury bills. These instruments are priced at a discount from par value (face value). Discount yield is calculated by dividing the annual discount rate earned on the investment by par value.

discounted A frequently heard market term that refers to an event, economic statistic, or other development whose effect has been minimized or discounted. If the stock market has been expecting the Federal Reserve to cut interest rates, once the actual news is received the effect will likely be muted because the news already has been discounted.

discounted cash flow (DCF) A valuation for an investment created by estimating future cash flows using a measure of risk, which can be thought of as the required rate of return, and considering the time of the investment period. To calculate valuations of stocks using discounted cash flows, the value is estimated using some measure of the present value of a cash flow. These cash flows can be either dividends, earnings, or free cash flow.

discounted cash-flow valuation A valuation technique that calculates the present value of expected cash flows to arrive at the current value of an asset or investment. One shortcoming of the discounted cash-flow valuation model is that the value it indicates may be drastically different than current prices that can be received in the market. The type of cash flow inputs can vary among dividends (dividend discount model), operating cash flow (present value of operating cash flows), or free cash flow (present value of free cash flows to equity).

discounting A method that is used to finance receivables by discounting or selling them. The financier, usually a bank, deducts the interest from the maturity value of the note and then gives the proceeds to the receivables holder, who then endorses the receivables note and delivers it to the bank. If the maker of the note or receivable doesn't pay the obligation, then the original receivables holder is liable to the bank for payment.

discretionary account An investment account that gives the broker discretion to purchase and sell stocks and other investments without obtaining the prior approval of the account owner. The broker should have broad guidelines to follow that spell out what types of investments are allowed and explain what types of risks are permissible.

discretionary order An order to purchase a stock, futures contract, or other investment that lets the broker determine at what price the order will be executed at and when it will be executed. The investor trusts the broker to find the best deal.

disintermediation The removal of a middleman from a transaction. This term was used in the 1970s when relatively wealthy investors realized they could invest their funds directly in money market funds to earn higher interest rates and cut their bank out from the transaction. Disintermediation is also used in other industries where middlemen can be eliminated. With the advent of the Internet, disintermediation can also occur when a company selling its product online bypasses traditional distribution channels and directly links with buyers and suppliers.

dismal science A nickname for economics that took hold in the nineteenth century due to the dismal outlook that economists had of strong population growth and the weak industrial structures that were unable to support strong population gains. Thomas Carlyle coined the phrase.

Disney, Walt The founder of a self-named company that made animated feature films and later opened theme parks. He began his career as a cartoonist who created feature-length films such as *Snow White and the Seven Dwarfs, Pinocchio,* and *Fantasia.* The Walt Disney Company is now a large multimedia conglomerate.

disposable income An individual's available cash after living expenses are paid. The amount of disposable income that individuals have directly affects the economy because consumer spending accounts for about two-thirds of the economic activity in the United States.

dissolution The process of legally dissolving a corporation. Dissolution is achieved when a company's lenders are paid off, property and assets are sold, and any remaining cash is distributed to the company's shareholders.

distribution

1. The payment of dividends to shareholders.

2. The payment of capital gains to mutual fund shareholders.

3. A company spinning off the shares of another company that it owns or a partial interest in one of its business units.

4. The ability of an institution to sell new equity or debt issues of a corporation to its clients.

distribution capability An investment bank's ability to sell shares in a stock or bond offering that it has underwritten. Banks that are global, or have a particularly large presence in the retail or institutional market, have large distribution capabilities.

divergence In technical analysis, price movements that fail to confirm a trend or that bring a pattern on a price chart into question.

diversification A principle of investment management that calls for spreading investments across a number of different assets, securities, and industries. Diversification is important because it reduces the investor's risk because each asset class is likely to have different risks. Diversification also can occur within asset classes, such as buying equities of both small companies and large companies, which typically move in different cyclical patterns. Companies may also diversify by selling different products or by entering different industries.

divestiture The sale of part of a company or an important company asset, either by spinning off a company's unit, selling a unit to another company or group of employees, or liquidating it. The term also refers to a company's sale of the stock of another company that was purchased for investment purposes.

dividend A distribution, typically quarterly, of a corporation's earnings to its shareholders. Dividends can be paid in cash or stock. Sometimes, if a company has had a particularly good year, a special year-end dividend may be paid. If a company failed to make a profit, likely no dividend is paid. Some companies, such as growth companies, don't issue dividends even when the company makes a profit. Their belief is that they can create a higher return for shareholders, through stock appreciation, by keeping the money and using it to expand the business. Often technology companies have this strategy.

dividend cover The number of times that a dividend can be divided into after-tax profit for the period. Dividend cover indicates the level of profits that will be available to pay dividends. Typically dividend cover is a British term. To calculate the dividend cover, divide the per share dividend into after-tax profit. In the United States, it is more common to refer to a *payout ratio*.

dividend discount model A technique that estimates the price that a stock should be trading at by calculating the present value of all future dividends. The model assumes that dividends will grow at a constant rate and that growth will continue for an infinite period. It also assumes that the required rate of return is greater than the infinite growth rate.

dividend payable A line item on a company's income statement. Dividends become payable after the board of directors declares them so. Typically, there is a lag of several weeks between when dividends are declared payable and when they are actually paid. Dividends that are payable become a legal obligation of the corporation.

dividend reinvestment plan (DRIP) A plan that allows investors to purchase a company's stock directly from the company, without using a broker. DRIP investors don't have to pay a broker's commission, which reduces costs. Companies typically let individuals use their dividends to purchase additional shares. Many DRIP programs let investors invest only a small amount of money each month, called *dollar-cost averaging,* making the program affordable to moderate income investors.

dividend yield Dividend per share divided by price per share. Dividend yield measures how much income a stock generates. The higher the yield, the more income.

dividends in arrears Dividends on preferred stock that were not paid in the year that they accumulated. Dividends in arrears must be satisfied before common shareholders receive their dividends. However, dividends in arrears are not recognized as a liability on the company's books because no liability exists until a dividend has been declared by the board.

divisor　A number that Dow Jones & Company uses to compute the value of the Dow Jones Industrial Average (DJIA). The value of the 30 DJIA stocks are divided by the divisor to arrive at the DJIA. The divisor changes as stock splits occur. The divisor is reported daily in the Wall Street Journal.

DJIA　See *Dow Jones Industrial Average.*

dobra　The currency unit of São Tomé and Principe, comprised of 100 centimos.

Dodd, David　See *Graham and Dodd.*

Dogs of the Dow　A trading strategy that recommends buying equal amounts of the ten highest yielding stocks in the Dow Jones Industrial Average. Many people adopt this strategy and buy the stocks at bargain prices to get the high yield. The buying activity pushes the price of the stocks up. The Dogs of the Dow typically receive renewed attention from shareholders at the end of the year who are looking to make trades to produce higher returns for the next year. The strategy also has been adapted to other world stock indices.

Doha Round　A series of trade liberalization negotiations initiated under the World Trade Organization (WTO) in late 2001. The Doha Round focuses on trade liberalization for a wide-range of agricultural products. In particular, this round of trade talks is aimed at helping developing countries whose exportable goods are heavily concentrated among agricultural products develop their international trade. Poor countries complain that rich countries spend $1 billion a day on trade subsidies. By enacting trade liberalization on agricultural products, developing countries can be helped the most and poverty reduced. Other subjects covered by the trade talks include trade in services and intellectual property issues.

The round draws its name from the WTO Ministerial Conference that was held in Doha, Qatar, from November 9 to November 14, 2001. Actual talks commenced in January 2002 with their completion scheduled for Jan. 1, 2005.

doing business as (DBA)　Used to mean that a name is not the legal name of the individual or business. For example, sole proprietorships often do business under a name other than the legal name of the owner: Jane Smith DBA Jane's Flowers. DBA certificates are filed with governmental authorities. The filing allows governmental units or anyone having a legal claim against the company to discover who the legal owner is.

dollar　The currency unit of the United States, comprised of 100 cents. Traders shorten it to USD. The U.S. dollar is the world's most frequently used currency in business transactions. Even transactions not involving a U.S. party often are cited in dollars. The dollar is also the name for the currency unit of Antigua, Australia, Bahamas, Barbados, Belize, Brunei, Canada, Dominica, Fiji, Grenada, Guyana, Hong Kong, Jamaica, Liberia, Marshall Islands, Micronesia, Namibia, Nauru, New Zealand, Palau, Saint Kitts and Nevis, Saint Lucia, Saint Vincent and the Grenadines, Singapore, Solomon Islands, Taiwan, Turk and Caicos, Trinidad and Tobago, Tuvalu, and Zimbabwe.

dollar bear

1. A U.S. Treasury Secretary who doesn't believe in a strong dollar.

2. A trader who thinks the U.S. dollar is overvalued and due to fall.

dollar bond　A bond that is quoted and traded in dollars instead of yield. It also is a bond whose principal and interest is denominated in dollars, versus a bond whose principal and interest is denominated in another currency.

dollar-cost averaging　An investment concept that calls for investing the same amount of money each month in a security. When prices are high, a smaller amount is bought, and when prices are lower, more securities are purchased. Over time, the price averages out and the investor gains by investing regularly, rather than waiting for the right time.

domestic corporation

1. A corporation that is doing business in its home country. A domestic corporation in the United States is considered a foreign corporation in the United Kingdom.

2. A corporation doing business in the state in which it is incorporated.

domicile A legal place of residence, used when filing corporate reports with the state's secretary of state and when filing income taxes. Domiciles are established when the corporation files papers of incorporation with the secretary of state. For individuals, domicile is established by having a permanent home, registering to vote, or obtaining a driver's license.

domino theory The concept that a default or financial instability at one financial institution will cause other defaults or instability at other firms, in a ripple effect that spreads throughout the financial system.

don't know Also called DK, slang for "don't know the trade," a Wall Street phrase that is used when one party doesn't have any knowledge of a trade or has received conflicting information from another trader. Sometimes brokers in an open-outcry trading pit may not recognize each other's trades, especially in a volatile futures market.

Donaldson, William H. The chairman of the Securities and Exchange Commission, as of this printing, appointed by President George W. Bush in February, 2003. He was a co-founder in 1959 of Donaldson, Lufkin & Jenrette, an investment bank that was purchased by Credit Suisse First Boston in 2001. He was a founder of Yale University's Graduate School of Management, served as its first dean, and held a tenured chair there from 1975 to 1980.

donated capital See *donated surplus.*

donated surplus An account found in the shareholders' equity section of a corporation's balance sheet that consists of donations of cash, stock, or property made by shareholders. The account also may be called *donated capital.* Donated surplus contrasts with *contributed surplus* (or *contributed capital*), which is capital that exists in excess of par value.

dong The currency unit of Vietnam, comprised of 100 hao.

dot–com One of the terms to come into common usage the quickest, it refers to any number of Internet companies that began in the later half of the 1990s during the technology and Internet boom. It takes its name from the companies that included a ".com" at the end of their name. As the technology bubble burst and dot-com companies were discredited, many firms that were still in business changed their names to get rid of the ".com."

double bottoms A chart pattern of price movements that shows a resistance to falling prices. This pattern reflects a period of falling prices followed by a period of rising prices. That pattern is repeated a second time to create what looks like twin bottoms on a price chart. Despite the decline, prices can't break lower as there is strong support for prices to remain above a minimum level. Technical analysts say that double bottoms indicate a reversal of pricing trends because they indicate that although prices tried to move lower, they were unable to do so, and the next price move will be upward. A double bottom is the inverse of a *double top.*

double dipping The ability to deduct interest expense in two different tax jurisdictions at the same time. This is a creative, cross-border financing arrangement. Double dipping can also refer to any other similar situation in which a system is used to a person or company's benefit.

double exempt Refers to municipal bonds that are exempt from both federal and state income taxes.

double hedging A hedging strategy that uses both a futures contract and an options contract to protect against losses caused by changes in the cash prices of the underlying instrument. See also *hedge.*

double taxation　A situation that occurs when corporations issue dividends, which they cannot deduct from their income. Shareholders receiving the dividends have to pay tax, resulting in so-called double-taxation of dividends.

double top　A chart pattern identified by technical analysis that represents a period during which prices have risen and have remained elevated, followed by a dip, succeeded by another rising top, and then another dip, which creates the appearance of twin peaks. In this pattern, prices are unable to break through resistance, or a ceiling, to move higher. When technical analysts see a double top they say it indicates a reversal of a price trend because prices tried to move higher and failed and will be moving lower. A double top is the inverse of a *double bottom*.

double witching hour　The simultaneous expiration of stock option and index option contracts, which may create market volatility. Occurs on the third Friday of the month, excluding March, June, September and December. In these four months, futures contracts also expire, in an event called *triple witching hour.*

double-barreled bond　A revenue bond issued by a municipal or state authority that ultimately is guaranteed by the overlying municipal or state authority. For example, if a turnpike authority for a state issues a bond, in the event of a default (if revenues from the turnpike are not enough to pay back the bond), the state government would use its tax revenues to make the interest and principal payments.

double-declining-balance method of depreciation　An accelerated depreciation method that assumes that the most useful life of an asset is its early years. Thus, it takes a larger than normal amount of depreciation expense in the first years of an asset's life. The double-declining-balance method is calculated by doubling the annual depreciation expense that would be calculated by the *straight-line depreciation method,* which spreads the depreciable cost of the asset evenly over the estimated useful life of the asset.

double-entry bookkeeping　An accounting system that requires two entries, a debit and a credit, for each transaction, so that they equal each other. It is the standard bookkeeping method today. Debit entries increase assets while they reduce liabilities and stockholders' equity. Credit entries decrease assets while increasing liabilities and stockholders' equity. Double-entry bookkeeping began during the Renaissance: One of its first written descriptions appeared in 1494 in a math book written by Fra Luca Pacioli.

double-taxation agreement　An agreement between two countries that reduces the tax bill for an individual who is a resident of one country but has citizenship in another country. The agreement strives to prevent the taxpayer from paying tax to both countries. Often the tax owed is based upon the number of days that the taxpayer actually worked in both countries.

Douglas, Donald　An aviation entrepreneur. The company he founded, Douglas Aircraft Co., created the Cloudster, which was the first aircraft to lift its own weight in payload and the first to circle the globe, and the DC-3, a two-engine plane that was introduced in 1935.

Dow Jones Euro STOXX 50　A market capitalization-weighted index of 50 blue-chip stocks from the countries that participate in the European Monetary Union. The index was created with a base value of 1,000 on December 31, 1991.

Dow Jones Industrial Average (DJIA)
The world's most well known stock index, comprised of 30 stocks that represent leading companies in major industries. Charles H. Dow, the founder of Dow Jones & Co, introduced the DJIA in 1896. It is the oldest stock price measure in continuous use. All the companies in the index are large and stable (blue-chip) companies and are widely held by both individual and institutional investors. Although many companies

have remained in the DJIA for a length of time, some are occasionally removed due to poor financial performance or a merger. The ticker symbol is DJIA.

Dow Jones Transportation Index An index that tracks the share price movement of 20 of the largest transportation companies. These companies include railroads, trucking companies, and airlines. While many companies have remained in the Dow Jones Transportation Index for a length of time, some are occasionally removed due to poor financial performance or a merger. The ticker symbol is TRAN.

Dow Jones Utilities Index An index that tracks the share performance of 15 companies that are spread across the United States and represent the utilities sector as well as the industry's sub-sectors. Companies listed in the utilities index will be added and removed due to poor financial performance or a merger. The ticker symbol is DJU.

Dow Theory The theory that any major stock market trend must occur both in the Dow Jones Industrial Average and the Dow Jones Transportation Average; both indices must reach either new highs or lows, otherwise the market will fall back to its previous trading range. Dow Theory is based on a technical analysis theory pioneered by Charles Dow, one of the founders of *The Wall Street Journal* and Dow Jones & Co.

down payment An upfront payment that is made on an item that will be paid for over time, such as a house or a car. The down payment reduces the amount of money that needs to be borrowed, and thus decreases the monthly payment. For homes, typically down payments are equal to at least ten percent of the purchase price of a house; however, in some circumstances the down payment may be less.

down round A second or subsequent round of venture capital or private equity financing for a start-up company, in which it is not able to raise as much as it did in previous financings because its valuation is lower

than the previous round. The valuation may have fallen because the price per share decreased or because investors demanded a larger equity stake in the company while decreasing the amount of financing.

downgrade An action that communicates concern or an increasingly negative outlook for a stock or bond. Typically, Wall Street analysts downgrade a company's stock if they think the outlook for the company is worsening. Other times, analysts lower a stock's rating if the stock has performed strongly and has little room left for its price to appreciate. Ratings agencies also downgrade the credit ratings of companies, countries, and specialized financial instruments.

downside risk The risk that an investment will decline in value.

downsizing A reduction in a company's workforce, typically accompanied through layoffs. A company downsizes in order to reduce costs. Downsizing is done in a period of declining sales and is one of the few things a company can do to improve its profitability when it isn't able to sell more goods. Companies usually take restructuring charges that are applied to their income statement in order to account for the costs associated with laying people off, such as severance pay.

downstream A term used in the energy industry to refer to commercial oil and gas operations beyond the production phase. Downstream operations include oil refining, marketing, and natural gas transmission and distribution.

downtick A trade that occurs at a lower price than the previous trade. To indicate that it is a downtick trade, a minus sign is displayed next to the last price where the stock traded. Short sales can't be executed on downticks.

downturn A downward shift in a business cycle or a market cycle. A downturn reverses a previous period of rising prices or increased business activity.

dragon bonds   Debt instruments that are priced in U.S. dollars but are largely sold in Hong Kong. They are similar to Eurobonds, which are dollar-denominated bonds that are sold outside of the United States.

dram   The currency unit of Armenia, comprised of 100 lumma.

DRAM   Shorthand for *dynamic random access memory*. A type of computer memory chip that is typically used in personal computers or large computers. DRAM needs to have its storage cells refreshed by giving it a new electronic charge every few milliseconds.

drawback   A rebate given by a government on duties or taxes that were paid on imported goods that were used to create other goods, or repackaged and exported again.

DRIP   See *dividend reinvestment plan.*

drive-by investing   A relatively new term that came into common usage during the technology and venture capital boom in the late 1990s. It refers to the practice of venture capitalists (VCs) agreeing to fund start-up companies without doing any substantial due diligence to verify whether the company's product and management is worthy of receiving an investment. During the technology boom, VCs were anxious to fund the next big company before their competitors. Drive-by investing occurred because they believed that they didn't have enough time to do their due diligence.

DSL   See *digital subscriber lines.*

dual banking   A banking system in the United States in which banks can be chartered either by the federal government or by a state government.

dual listing   Listing the stock of a company on more than one exchange. Stocks may be listed on one of the major stock exchanges, such as the New York Stock Exchange, American Stock Exchange, or the NASDAQ stock market, along with one of the regional stock exchanges, such as the Pacific Stock Exchange. Companies may also list their stock on foreign exchanges as well as domestic exchanges.

dual trading   In the futures industry, the act of a trader simultaneously trading for his or her own account while executing trades for his or her customers. This practice poses a potential conflict of interest if the trader engages in *front-running,* a practice in which traders take a position for their own accounts with the advance knowledge that a large order will be coming to the market, potentially making the personal trade profitable.

dual-option bond   A bond that has an embedded option that gives the investor a choice of currency to receive payments of interest and principal. Also called *cross-currency option.*

due diligence   The amount of reasonable investigation that must be made by a prudent person to determine whether an investment or business arrangement makes sense and to determine whether it is likely that the information he or she has contains omissions or misstatements. Due diligence involves looking through public documents related to a company and talking with people in the industry who have knowledge of the company's performance.

Duisenberg, Willem F.   The first president of the European Central Bank (ECB), selected in 1997. As of this printing, he planned to resign in July 2003. Duisenberg, who is Dutch, ran the Dutch central bank for 11 years before becoming head of the ECB. He was a Dutch finance minister from 1973 to 1977. He began his career as an economist and was on the staff at the International Monetary Fund in Washington, D.C. He also taught at Amsterdam University.

Duke, James Buchanan   A pioneer in the tobacco and utilities industry who built American Tobacco Co. and Duke Power & Light Company in North Carolina, now called Duke Energy Corporation. In 1890 he become president of American Tobacco Co., which was made up of the five largest domestic cigarette makers. The Supreme Court disbanded American Tobacco in 1911 on antitrust grounds. The breakup created R.J. Reynolds Tobacco Company, Liggett & Meyers, and P. Lorillard Tobacco Company. He then turned his attention to the utility industry and founded Duke Power Corp. His $100 million bequest created Duke University.

dumping

1. Selling goods or commodities in another country at prices that are substantially below the going market price. International trade regulations attempt to prevent dumping. Violations may be reported to the World Trade Organization.

2. Selling a large amount of securities in a market with no concern for what effect that is likely to have on the price or the product.

DuPont System A system for analyzing a firm's return on equity in which return on equity is broken down into three component pieces. The first is net income divided by net sales, which gives a net profit margin. The second is net sales divided by total assets, which indicates total asset turnover. The third is total assets divided by common equity, which indicates the financial leverage. Those calculations are multiplied against each other in order to come up with a firm's return on equity according to the DuPont System.

durable goods A monthly economic report produced by the U.S. Commerce Department that tracks new orders received by manufacturers of durable goods, such as machinery and aircraft. Durable goods are those products that are expected to last more than one year, in contrast to non-durable goods such as food items, clothing, and consumer-disposable products. The durable goods report differentiates between spending that is connected to military and non-military orders. It also tracks sector spending, such as technology. Economists and investors look at the report to get a sense of how the economy is performing: If durable goods orders are strong, then often the economy is doing well.

durable power of attorney A legal document written by a person giving another person, the executor, the right to make legal and financial decisions. If the writer of the durable power of attorney becomes incapacitated, the executor of the durable power of attorney begins to make decisions for the writer of the durable power of attorney. The durable power of attorney may narrowly define areas in which the executor has the ability to make decisions or it may broadly give away those rights. A durable power of attorney might cover buying or selling investments or assets. Another type of a durable power is a durable power of attorney for health care that authorizes someone to make decisions about health care, such as whether a person should remain on life-support equipment.

duration A measurement of a bond's price sensitivity to changes in interest rates. A high-duration bond, or one whose maturity date is a long way out in the future, is more sensitive to interest rate changes than a bond with a shorter maturity date. The duration is defined as the weighted average of the maturities of the bond's cash flows, which include periodic interest rate payments and principal repayment cash flows. The weights are the proportionate share of the bond's price that the cash flows in each time period represent.

Modified duration is a measure of Macaulay duration, which was named for Frederick Macaulay. It is calculated by dividing the yield maturity by the number of interest payments per year that have been adjusted to help estimate a bond's price volatility. Modified duration allows an estimate of bond price changes for a small change in interest rates. For larger changes in interest rates, convexity is used. Convexity measures the way duration and price change when interest rates change. It does this through a mathematical formula that measures the curvature of the price-yield relationship.

Dutch auction An auction with one seller and many buyers in which the price is reduced from a high starting point until the bidders find a point that is attractive to enough buyers. This is the auction system that is used by the U.S. Department of the Treasury to sell its debt obligations.

duty A tax or payment imposed by a government on the goods that a company imports or exports. Goods that do not require the payment of a duty are called *duty free.*

DVP See *delivery versus payment.*

DVR See *delivery versus receipt.*

dynamic asset allocation See *dynamic hedging.*

dynamic hedging A portfolio insurance technique that creates an option-like return by increasing or reducing the position in the underlying security or futures, options, or forward contract. The intent is to simulate the delta change in the value of an option position. One example of dynamic hedging is increasing or decreasing a short stock index futures position (selling stock index futures that you don't own) to create a synthetic put on a portfolio, This will create a return that is similar to portfolio insurance.

E

E Can be attached as a fifth letter of a NASDAQ stock symbol to specify that the company has not met the reporting date for the company's Securities and Exchange Commission (SEC) regulatory filing requirements. This happens infrequently because companies can be delisted or face penalties from the SEC if they do not meet regulatory requirements.

early stage Financing provided by a venture capital firm to a company after it has received its initial, or seed, financing. At this early stage, the company has a product or service that it is testing or still developing, but it isn't completely ready to go to market. In some cases, the product may be commercially available in a limited manner but not yet generating revenue. Typically, a company that receives early stage financing has been in business for less than three years.

earned income credit A tax credit that is given to qualified, lower-income taxpayers who have at least one child living at home for half of the year.

earnest money A good-faith deposit paid before a transaction closes that ensures that the sale will be completed or a deal closed. Typically, earnest money is put down by a home buyer at the time the contract is signed.

earnings A common term that refers to a company's net income.

earnings per share A financial measurement that takes a company's total amount of net income and divides it by the number of shares outstanding. Two calculation methods used are basic and diluted earnings per share. See also *basic earnings per share* and *diluted earnings per share*.

earnings report A quarterly or annual release that shows a corporation's income statement, balance sheet, and statement of cash flows. Earnings reports often have a substantial effect on the market, especially if the actual results vary greatly from expectations.

earnings season The time period in which corporations typically announce corporate financial results for a quarter. Earning season begins about two weeks after the close of the previous quarter and lasts for about four weeks. Earnings seasons begin around January 15, April 15, July 15 and October 15. Companies don't have to report during this time frame, but many companies do.

earnings surprise A situation in which a company's earnings differ from Wall Street analysts' expectations. Negative earnings surprises often cause stock prices to fall, while upward surprises may cause prices to bounce up.

earnings yield A measure that is derived by dividing the expected earnings by the stock's price. The resulting figure estimates how much in earnings stockholders can expect to receive for each dollar paid for the stock. Earnings yield is the inverse of the *P/E ratio,* which is the price of the stock divided by earnings per share.

earnout In a merger transaction, an additional payment or series of payments that is based on the performance of the company after the acquisition. In essence, the final amount that the acquirer pays is dependent on the company's financial performance after the sale. On a present-value basis, the seller likely is not receiving the full amount that he or she wanted by waiting several years for future payments, but the seller is getting more funds than he would have without the earnout. Earnouts can be based on revenue or earnings or any other financial measure.

ease To increase the amount of credit in the banking system, which the Federal Reserve does by lowering interest rates. This is accomplished by lowering the federal funds rate, the discount rate, or both. Increasing the available credit has the effect of stimulating the economy.

Eastman, George An innovator in the world of photography, Eastman produced the first dry photographic plate. He created paper-backed film and, in 1886, produced a fixed-focus camera that sold for $25. Because Eastman liked the letter "K," he called the camera a Kodak. He started Eastman Kodak, which produced smaller and less expensive cameras that made photography available to the masses.

easy money policy See *accommodative monetary policy.*

Eaton, Cyrus The founder of Republic Steel Corporation, which was formed from six small steel firms that he owned. Eaton also took over Goodyear Tire & Rubber Co. and battled for control of the Chesapeake & Ohio railroad with the House of Morgan banking concern and won. He also built the St. Lawrence Seaway. Eaton wrote books that criticized capitalism.

Ebbers, Bernard J. The former chief executive officer of WorldCom, Inc. who was investigated for his role in WorldCom's collapse and bankruptcy.

EBIAT *Earnings before interest after taxes* is a financial measurement that subtracts the cost of goods sold as well as selling, general, and administration expenses (SG&A) from revenues. It is equal to earnings before interest and taxes (EBIT) minus cash.

EBIT *Earnings before interest and taxes* is a financial calculation that subtracts cost of goods sold along with selling, general, and administrative expenses (SG&A) from revenues. EBIT is a measure of operating and nonoperating profit before interest and income taxes are deducted.

EBITDA *Earnings before interest, taxes, depreciation, and amortization,* pronounced ee-bit-dah. To arrive at EBITDA, interest, taxes, depreciation, and amortization are added to net income. EBITDA is measure of debt-paying capabilities of a company.

EBITDA margin Total EBITDA divided by total revenue. It measures the extent to which operating expenses use revenue. See also *EBITDA.*

EBRD See *European Bank for Reconstruction and Development.*

ECI See *employment cost index.*

ECM See *equity capital markets department.*

ECN See *Electronic Communications Network.*

e-commerce See *electronic commerce.*

econometric model An empirical method of economic forecasting that uses an equation based on the statistical relationship among economic variables, such as housing starts and equipment purchases.

econometrics Use of computer analysis and modeling techniques to describe in mathematical terms the relationship between key economic forces such as labor, capital, interest rates, and government policies. The model allows variables to be changed so that different situations can be examined. An econometric model could show the relationship of unemployment to housing starts, for example.

Economic Growth and Tax Relief Reconciliation Act of 2001 The Republican tax cut program that was approved in 2001 during the first year of George W. Bush's presidency. The act reduced personal income tax rates by three percentage points for each income tax rate over 10 years except for the top rate, 39.6 percent, which was reduced to 35 percent. These tax reductions are scheduled to disappear in 2011 unless the changes are made permanent. In addition, this act created a new 10 percent rate for the first $12,000 of taxable income for married couples filing jointly.

economic growth rate The rate of change in the Gross National Product, as expressed in annual percentage terms. If adjusted for inflation, it is called the *real economic growth rate.* Two consecutive quarterly drops in the growth rate mean recession, and two consecutive advances in the growth rate reflect an expanding economy.

economic indicator Any of a number of important economic statistics that are typically announced monthly. Investors and economists look at economic indicators to gauge the overall health of the economy and use them as a guide to develop their expectations for the stock market. Examples of economic indicators are the non-farm payroll report, or the unemployment report as it is referred to in news reports, and inflation reports, such as the producer price inflation and consumer price inflation reports.

economies of scale An economic principle that says as production or sales increase, the cost of each unit decreases. For example, a company that increases the production capacity of a factory by adding a second shift can create economies of scale because many costs (such as the lease for the property) do not increase, or increase only slightly, while output doubles. Executives announcing merger agreements often tout economies of scale as one of the advantages of merging.

ECRI Weekly Leading Index An index, released each Friday by the Economic Cycle Research Institute, that identifies turning points in the economic cycle that are indicated by pronounced changes in the index. The index contains money supply data, stock prices, an industrial markets price index developed by the organization, mortgage applications, bond quality spread, bond yields, and initial jobless claims. An advantage of the index is that it is very timely. However, it is relatively new and its predictive ability is relatively untested.

ECU See *European currency unit.*

EDGAR The Securities and Exchange Commission's electronic system for receiving, organizing, and electronically disseminating corporate information, such as quarterly and annual financial statements, securities filings, and other disclosure documents. EDGAR stands for *Electronic Data Gathering, Analysis, and Retrieval.* EDGAR filings can be found on the SEC's web page, www.sec.gov.

Edison, Thomas A. An inventor who had received more than 1,000 patents by the time he died at age 85 in 1931. Among his inventions were the incandescent light bulb, the phonograph, the movie projector, and the carbon transmitter that helped make the telephone a reality.

education IRA A type of Individual Retirement Account (IRA) that allows parents to save money to pay for their children's' education. This type of IRA has very little to do with retirement. Education IRAs were first created in the Taxpayer Relief Act of 1997. As of this printing, a maximum of $2,000 a year can be contributed, if certain conditions are met. Investments accumulate tax free and the account creator decides how to invest the funds and how the funds will be spent. Eligible expenses include college, elementary, and secondary tuition and the purchase of books and supplies. If the money is drawn for non-education expenses, federal taxes will be owed at the taxpayer's tax rate, along with a 10 percent penalty. Also called *Coverdell education savings account.*

effective debt The total amount of debt that a firm owes, including the capitalized value of lease payments or other periodic contractual payments.

effective tax rate The income tax rate that is actually paid by a taxpayer. To calculate it, divide the amount of tax paid by taxable income for the year. The percentage is the effective tax rate. Although a person may be in a 31 percent tax bracket, by the time deductions and credits are taken, the person's effective tax rate may be less than 31 percent.

efficient market A theory that says market prices reflect everything that investors currently know and includes their expectations about future behavior. Attempting to find undervalued investments is futile because the market already has priced in any new information, making it impossible to best the market. Instead, results just as good would be produced by randomly picking stocks. See also *Random Walk theory.*

efficient portfolio A portfolio whose return is maximized according to expected returns or risk levels. An efficient portfolio is mathematically calculated and takes into account the expected return for each security and its standard deviation.

EFP See *exchange for physicals.*

EFT See *electronic funds transfer.*

E-Government Act Legislation that was signed into law in December 2002 that aims to give the public easier online access to the data and services that the federal government collects and disseminates. The law is intended to remove information barriers between the various federal agencies. The legislation encourages different government agencies to use the same software system, which would allow the agencies' computer systems to communicate with each other. The law also increases public input on what government forms and information should be published on the Internet by establishing public comment periods. Agencies also are required to conduct a privacy impact assessment each time they buy new technology systems.

Eichel, Hans Germany's Finance Minister, as of this printing. He is a member of the Social Democratic Party.

either-or order A trade order given to a broker where the execution of one of the orders automatically cancels another order. One example is a buy-limit order that is executed only if the market price is below a certain price. It is combined with a buy-stop order that is executed only if the market price is above a certain price.

El Niño A disruption of the oceanic-atmospheric system in the tropical Pacific that strongly affects weather conditions across the globe for a few months to up to one year with a seemingly random frequency. El Niño is watched in the agricultural commodities markets because the phenomenon can have substantial effects on crops in affected areas. El Niño increases rainfall across the southern part of the United States and in Peru. Drought conditions can be produced in the West Pacific, which leads to brush fires in Australia and Indonesia. Its most severe effects occur close to the equator. Warmer water near Central America spawns more frequent and stronger hurricanes, which can occur as far west as Hawaii. El Niño occurs in contrast to La Niña, which produces cold events.

El Niño was first recognized by fishermen off the coast of South America when unusually warm water in the Pacific Ocean arrived near the beginning of the year. The term El Niño means "the little boy" or "Christ child" in Spanish. The name was given because the warm water arrived around Christmas.

elasticity of demand A measure of buyers' responsiveness to price changes. Items that have a high elasticity of demand, such as luxury cars and expensive jewelry, are very likely to experience decreasing demand if prices rise. In contrast, goods with *inelastic demand* are resistant to changing prices. Items with inelastic demand include electricity, heating oil, and groceries.

electronic banking A form of banking in which funds are transferred electronically between financial institutions instead of cash, checks, or other negotiable instruments being physically exchanged. The ownership of funds and transfers of funds between financial institutions are recorded on computer systems connected by telephone lines. Customers of the financial institutions can access their records using a password or personal identification number (PIN).

electronic commerce (e-commerce) Buying and selling on the Internet. E-commerce is subdivided into two areas: B2B, short for *business to business,* or businesses selling to other businesses on the Internet; and B2C, which is *business-to-consumer* sales.

Electronic Communications Network (ECN) A trading system that brings customer orders to the market but doesn't commit any capital. This system widely disseminates quotes to third parties. Price quotes are entered into the system by an exchange or over-the-counter market maker. Third parties buy or sell stocks.

Electronic Data Gathering, Analysis, and Retrieval See *EDGAR*.

electronic data interchange A technique that lets one bank communicate electronically with another bank.

electronic funds transfer (EFT) The transfer of funds using computer systems, electronic terminals, the telephone, or any other non-paper-based method. A well known EFT method is automatic teller machines (ATMs).

elephants A slang term that refers to large investors, typically institutions. Some institutions that fall into that group include mutual funds, pension funds, insurance companies, and banks that trade securities worth millions of dollars at one time.

elevator pitch An entrepreneur's very brief explanation of his or her business, given to a potential investor. It is named from the idea that the entrepreneur could corner a potential investor in an elevator.

Elliott Wave Theory Named after Ralph Elliott, who said that the stock market moves in predictable patterns that reflect the basic harmony of nature. The Elliott Wave Theory describes the stock market's behavior as a series of waves up and another series of waves down to complete a market cycle. Those cycles are grouped into eight waves, with five of those following the main trend, and three being corrective trends. After the eight moves are made, the cycle is complete. Stock market behavior can be predicted by identifying those patterns, the Elliott Wave Theory says.

Elliot's theory was described in 1938 when *The Wave Principle* was published. A 1978 book called the *Elliott Wave Principle*, written by Robert Prechter and A.J. Frost, is now considered the definitive text on the subject.

embargo

1. The prohibition by a government or organization that prevents goods from being shipped into or out of a country. One of the most memorable embargoes was the oil embargo imposed by the Organization of Petroleum Exporting Countries (OPEC) in the early 1970s to protest U.S. policies toward Israel. It had the effect of drastically raising oil prices and led to long lines for motorists at gas pumps.

2. The act of passing along economic reports or news releases to the press but requiring that the information not be disseminated until some future time or date. Embargos give reporters a chance to prepare their stories without rushing and potentially making a mistake. U.S. economic statistics, such as the unemployment report, are released 30 minutes ahead of the time that they become public information. During that time reporters prepare their stories so they are completely available at the release time.

embedded loss An economic loss that has not yet been recognized for income tax or reporting purposes. Also called *unrealized loss.*

embedded option An option that is an inseparable part of another instrument. Embedded options often are conversion features granted to the buyer or early termination options reserved by the issuer of a security. For example, this feature could be a call provision in corporate bonds that lets the issuer repay the borrower before the scheduled maturity date. Another example of an embedded option is the homeowner's ability to repay the mortgage principal early; in this case, the option of early repayment is embedded within the mortgage agreement.

emergency fund A cash reserve that individuals should have on hand that is easily accessible and doesn't involve selling securities. Financial experts generally recommend having three to six months of living expenses on hand in case income or a job is lost.

emerging market A foreign country that is beginning to adopt capitalism and is showing promise as a good place to invest. The country is beginning to reduce restrictions on foreign exchange transactions, start stock markets, and allow companies to compete with one another.

emerging market equity fund A mutual fund that invests primarily in equity securities of companies located in less-developed regions of the world.

eminent domain The right of a government to seize private property for what it deems the public good. The government must fairly compensate the property owner for the property. Eminent domain often is invoked when government officials want to construct roads, although it can be invoked for other uses as well.

e-miNY futures A type of futures contracts offered by the New York Mercantile Exchange for its liquid crude oil and natural gas futures contract. The contracts are 50 percent of the size of the standard futures contracts and are financially settled, versus being settled by delivering the physical commodities. E-miNY futures trade around the clock through electronic, after-hours exchanges such as the Chicago Mercantile Exchange's GLOBEX electronic trading platform. They clear through the New York Mercantile Exchange clearinghouse.

empirical Based upon analysis of data or experience rather than on deduction or speculation.

Employee Retirement Income Security Act (ERISA) A federal law, passed in 1974, that regulates private pension plans. The law set up the Pension Benefit Guaranty Corp., which created guidelines for managing pensions, and made qualifying for a pension easier for individuals. The Pension Benefit Guaranty Corp. is a quasi-federal agency that protects the retirement income of over 44 million U.S. workers in more than 35,000 defined benefit pension plans if the companies operating the plan go bankrupt.

Employee Stock Ownership Plan (ESOP) A qualified retirement plan that has tax advantages. An ESOP is are set up by the company and nearly all of its assets are invested in the employer's stock. The plan must include all full-time employees meeting minimum age and longevity requirements. Employees gradually become vested and receive their money when they leave the company.

Employee Stock Purchase Plan A plan that allows employees to buy stock in the company through payroll deductions. Often the stock price is discounted, typically 15 percent from the market price. After purchasing the stock, the employee can sell it for a quick profit or hold onto it. Often ESPPs are set up as tax-qualified Section 423 plans, which means that all employees at the company two years or longer must be able to participate.

employer matching contribution The amount of money that an employer matches to the amount that employees pay. Matching contributions may occur for 401(k) plans, for charitable contributions, or for other benefits or payments.

employment cost index (ECI) A survey of employers' payrolls during the third month of each quarter. It is a probability sample of about 3,600 private companies and 700 public employers, such as government agencies and school systems. Subcategories include information broken down into white-collar and blue-collar professions, goods and services industries, and benefit information for each of those subgroups. The index also has data categorized by region. The index is released quarterly by the federal Labor Department's Bureau of Labor Statistics and is widely watched by the financial markets to catch any signs of wage-driven inflation.

encryption A data protection strategy for electronic information that is transmitted over the Internet. Encryption prevents the unauthorized access of the transmitted information.

encumbrance A lien, charge, or claim that is attached to real property. Properties with mortgages are encumbered.

endorse To sign one's name on a document, the back of a check, or another negotiable instrument. The signature serves as an authorization to follow the directions on the document.

endowment A donation of money, stock, or property that is given to a non-profit organization, or the total assets that a nonprofit organization has invested. Usually funds given to endowments are significant. An endowment may be used to fund capital improvements or build new buildings, or it may be used to fund special programs or ongoing expenses. Often people leave money for an endowment in their will.

Enronitis Nervousness over a company because of suspected accounting problems. The term was coined in the fourth quarter of 2001 after Enron Corp. collapsed and filed for Chapter 11 bankruptcy amid substantial financial irregularities that its auditor, Arthur Andersen, failed to detect.

enterprise value A calculation used to compute financial ratios, frequently cited by Wall Street analysts in research reports. To arrive at the enterprise value, minority interests are valued at a level that the analyst considers to be fair value. If corporate management doesn't control the minority interest, the current market value is used.

enterprise zone An area identified by a city, county, or state government that makes a business moving into the zone eligible for special tax considerations, financing, special access to bids on government contracts, or other benefits from the government. Governments create enterprise zones because they want to revitalize depressed areas.

entrepreneur A person who starts his or her own business. The entrepreneur assumes the risk but stands to gain the profits. The entrepreneur may continue to operate the business, or may decide to sell out to a larger competitor or sell the company to the public in an initial public offering.

entrepreneur A person who starts a business from scratch. The risk, as well as the possible reward, for an entrepreneur is very high. Funding for the business may come from personal funds, cash advances on credit cards, or loans from friends or family. If the entrepreneur has a technology-related business, he or she may look for funding from *angels,* who are wealthy investors who fund start-up businesses, or venture capitalists.

EPS See *earnings per share.*

equilibrium price The price that is reached when the supply of goods in a market matches the demand for those goods. If a chart is made with supply on one axis and demand on the other axis, the point where the two lines intersect is the equilibrium price.

equipment trust certificates A type of corporate bond that is issued by railroads (the largest issuer), airlines, or other transportation firms. The proceeds are used to purchase equipment such as railroad cars or airplanes, which then serve as collateral for the certificates. The maturity of equipment trust certificates is usually from 1 to 15 years, reflecting the fact that the equipment's useful life is limited.

equity

1. Stock, either common or preferred.

2. The difference between the value of a house, or other real estate, and the amount owed on the mortgage.

3. An ownership stake in a partnership or joint venture.

equity capital markets department (ECM) A department in an investment bank that is the intermediary between the firm's investment banking activities, which include debt and capital raising and merger advice, and the firm's traders. Because the firm's investment bankers may be working on confidential deals that could cause turmoil in the markets, the equity capital market department serves as a buffer between the bankers and the market traders.

equity financing Issuing stock in order to raise funds. Equity financing may be an *initial public offering,* which is the first equity that a company raises. All subsequent offerings of equity are called *secondary,* or *follow-on, offerings.*

equity kicker Giving an ownership stake to someone who lends money to a company as part of the loan arrangement. An equity kicker may be given to a mortgage REIT (real estate investment trust) or a limited partnership that lends money to a developer. In exchange for the equity kicker, the interest rate on the loan may be slightly lower.

equity REIT A real estate investment trust that owns rental real estate, rather than making loans secured by real estate collateral. See also *REIT.*

equity risk premium The earnings yield on an equity benchmark, such as the S&P 500 Index, minus the risk-free rate of money. Typically, the risk-free rate is the rate paid on Treasury bills.

equity-linked annuity A series of equal payments that are made at equal intervals to the owner of an annuity in exchange for investing a fixed amount of cash. The return on an equity-linked annuity is determined by the equity index that it is linked to, such as the S&P 500. Annuities typically are used as an investment tool to plan for retirement. In contrast, the return on variable annuities changes depending on the direction of the equity index that it is linked to.

ergonomics The study of how computers, machines, office furniture, and other furnishings can be designed to prevent injuries and to make the equipment easy to use. Ergonomic chairs and keyboards are frequently seen in offices today.

ERISA See *Employee Retirement Income Security Act.*

ERM See *Exchange Rate Mechanism.*

escalator clause A paragraph in a contract that sets the terms for regular price increases. Escalator clauses may be found in labor contracts. Such a clause also may be part of a long-term supply contract, in which case the clause provides for regular price increases to the seller or allows the seller to pass along increased prices of raw materials or goods.

escheatment A requirement that financial institutions report to the appropriate state when a brokerage account or other investment has been abandoned or unclaimed after a certain period of time. Each state specifies the length of the inactive period. A firm must make a diligent effort to find the account owner. If the owner is not found after a certain period of time, the state claims the account through the escheatment process. The state can hold the account, or its sales proceeds, indefinitely. Some Web sites, such as the National Association of Unclaimed Property Administrators' site, www.naupa.org, allow people to search for unclaimed property.

escrow An account that holds money or securities until some agreed upon event or condition is met. Escrows typically are used when purchasing a home. The down payment, or good faith deposit, goes into an escrow account and is held until the funds are disbursed to the seller at closing.

escudo The currency unit of Cape Verde, comprised of 100 centavos.

ESOP See *Employee Stock Ownership Plan.*

estate All the assets that a person has at the time of his or her death. This includes cash, stocks, bonds, real estate, personal property, and other investments. The estate is distributed to the deceased's heirs as prescribed in the will.

estate planning Creating an orderly plan to disperse a person's assets upon the person's death. Estate planning involves writing a will, creating trusts, and consulting with a tax planner to minimize estate taxes.

estate tax   A state or federal tax assessed on property left to heirs. In 2002, the amount of an estate that could be excluded from federal taxes was raised to $1 million, and this figure will continue to rise until it tops out at $3.5 million in 2009. Once the $1 million threshold has been passed, estates are taxed at 50 percent, which decreases to 45 percent in 2007.

ETF   See *exchange traded funds.*

EU   See *European Union.*

Eurex   A European-based, computerized trading system for futures and options across a variety of financial products. Eurex is the successor to Germany's first fully computerized exchange, the Deutsche Terminborse. Eurex has plans to offer trading in the United States on a full range of derivatives on U.S. interest rates, indexes, and equities through a registered U.S. exchange beginning in 2004.

euro   The currency used by 12 Western European countries that agreed to give up their own currency and monetary policy. The countries using the euro are: Austria, Belgium, Finland, France, Germany, Greece, Ireland, Italy, Luxembourg, the Netherlands, Portugal, and Spain. The euro was introduced to bring the countries of Europe and their economies closer together and to reduce the cost of doing business among these countries. The European Central Bank was created to set monetary policy for the 12 member countries. The euro came into existence for financial transactions on January 1, 1999. Euro notes began circulating on January 1, 2002. The symbol is €.

eurobond   A U.S.-dollar denominated bond, or a bond of another currency, that is issued and traded outside of the country whose currency is used. Typically it is a bond that is issued by a non-European company for sale and trade in Europe. An example of a eurobond is a bond issued by a Russian corporation in the European market that pays interest and principal in U.S. dollars.

eurodollar   A U.S. dollar that is held in banks outside the United States, often received as payment for goods or services in international transactions. Some fixed-income securities are issued in eurodollars and pay interest in dollars deposited into foreign bank accounts. Most, but not all, eurodollars are located in Europe.

Euronext   A cross-border European market where equities, options on equities, bonds, derivatives, and commodities are traded. Euronext was created on September 22, 2000, when three stock exchanges merged: Société des Bourses Françaises SA (SBF), Amsterdam Exchanges NV (AEX), and Société de la Bourse de Valeurs Mobilières de Bruxelles SA/ Effectenbeursvennootschap van Brussel NV (BXS). After the merger, the three stock exchanges became wholly owned subsidiaries of Euronext NV, a newly created Dutch holding company, and changed their names to Euronext Paris, Euronext Amsterdam, and Euronext Brussels, respectively. This created Europe's first integrated stock exchange and the first time three stock exchanges in different countries merged to form a single entity. Cash, derivatives, and over-the-counter transactions occur on Euronext.

Commodity products are traded on Euronext.liffe, previously the London International Financial Futures Exchange, which was purchased by Euronext in January 2002. It allows trading for futures and options contracts across five different currencies and product lines: bonds, short-term interest rates, swaps, equities and equity indices, and commodities. Stock options on corporations located in five European countries, Belgium, France, Holland, Portugal and the U.K., can be traded on Euronext.liffe.

European Bank for Reconstruction and Development (EBRD)   A bank, owned by 60 countries and two intergovernmental institutions, established in 1991 to jumpstart private-sector activity in the former Eastern Bloc and Soviet Union. Its mandate says that it works only in countries that are committed to democratic principles and that have respect for the environment. The EBRD is now the single largest investor in the region. The EBRD provides project financing for banks, industries, and businesses. This includes both new ventures and investments in existing companies. It also works with publicly-owned companies to support privatization, the restructuring of state-owned firms, and the improvement of municipal services. The EBRD also promotes strong financial institutions and legal systems and strong corporate governance, structure, and reforms. It also promotes co-financing and direct investment and provides technical assistance.

European currency unit (ECU) A currency, created from the first attempt at European economic and monetary union, that was replaced when the euro was introduced in 1999 as a financial unit. The ECU was a basket of currencies from countries across Europe. ECUs could not be spent and thus were an artificial currency.

European Union (EU) A treaty-based organization that was set up to manage economic and political cooperation among 15 European member countries. The European Union began in the 1950s with six countries: Belgium, France, Germany, Italy, Luxembourg, and the Netherlands. Their theory was that by creating communities that shared sovereignty in matters of coal and steel production, trade, and nuclear energy, another war in Europe would be unthinkable. Since then, common EU policies have evolved in a number of other sectors. The members of the EU are Austria, Belgium, Denmark, Finland, France, Germany, Greece, Ireland, Italy, Luxembourg, The Netherlands, Portugal, Spain, Sweden, and the United Kingdom. During 2003, ten new countries were undergoing the process of becoming a member of the EU. Those countries are the Czech Republic, Cyprus, Estonia, Hungary, Latvia, Lithuania, Malta, Poland, Slovakia, and Slovenia.

The European Council makes the decisions to define and implement common foreign and security policy and coordinates the activities of member states, including police and judicial cooperation in criminal matters. The council is made up of the heads of the member-country governments and meets at least twice a year. The president of the council organizes meetings and works out compromises to resolve difficulties. The presidency rotates every six months.

European-style option An option that can be exercised only on its expiration date, in contrast to an *American option,* which can be exercised at any time up to its expiration date.

euro-zone The group of countries that have adopted the euro. Typically this term is used in conjunction with economic data that is now compiled for the 12 countries that have adopted the euro. Those countries are Austria, Belgium, Finland, France, Germany, Greece, Ireland, Italy, Luxembourg, the Netherlands, Portugal, and Spain.

event risk A risk that comes from an unexpected and unpredictable event, such as a negative industry report, a competitor reporting unexpected, poor financial results, or a ratings downgrade by a Wall Street analyst or by a ratings agency.

evergreen stock option plan A plan that automatically gives boards of directors an annually renewable pool of stock shares to distribute to the company's executives as compensation. Typically, the distribution is calculated as a fixed percentage of shares outstanding. The term *evergreen* comes from the fact that a board needs to obtain authorization from shareholders to institute such a plan only once instead of each year.

exact interest Interest paid by a financial institution that is calculated on a 365-days-per-year basis. This contrasts with *ordinary interest,* which is calculated on a 360-day basis. When a very large amount of money is drawing interest, the difference between exact interest and ordinary interest can be significant.

examiner An individual who may be appointed by a bankruptcy court with duties limited to conducting an investigation of specified acts and business affairs of the debtor. The appointment of an examiner does not change the status of a debtor who remains in control of the property of the estate during the Chapter 11 bankruptcy case.

excess margin   The amount of money in a customer's brokerage account that is above the minimum required amount. If a customer's holdings decline in value, the excess margin helps prevent the customer from receiving a *margin call,* which directs him or her to deposit more money into the account. If an account is required to have a margin of $20,000 and actually has $30,000, then the excess margin is $10,000.

excess reserves   The amount of money that a bank has on deposit with the Federal Reserve that is above what is required by the Federal Reserve. If a bank is required to have $300 million in reserves and has $350 million on deposit, then its excess reserves are $50 million.

exchange   An organized market where stocks, commodities, futures, and options contracts are sold. Exchanges bring together brokers and dealers who buy and sell securities. Well-known stock exchanges are the New York Stock Exchange and the NASDAQ. However, there are hundreds of less well-known exchanges throughout the world, such as the Minneapolis Grain Exchange.

exchange controls   Government regulations that limit or prevent currency or bank deposits from being moved out of the country. Governments apply exchange controls with the intention of maintaining orderly capital flows and preventing a run on their currency, in which businesses and individuals quickly sell the currency in exchange for another currency that is perceived to be more stable and valuable, such as the U.S. dollar. Free-market advocates disapprove of exchange controls because they restrict trade and business transactions.

exchange for physicals (EFP)   The exchange of a long or short position in a futures contract for the equivalent position in the cash market. The exchange for physicals transaction allows a futures trader to get out of position when the futures market is closed. An EFP allows the trader to respond to a new development in the market.

exchange offer   A situation in which a company, typically one that is bankrupt or nearly bankrupt, asks bondholders to exchange their bonds for new ones that typically pay higher interest rates but have lower face values. Often the maturity of the bonds is lengthened in the exchange offer in order to give the troubled company more time to fix its problems.

exchange rate   The expression of one nation's currency in terms of another nation's currency. It is the price at which one currency can be traded for another.

Exchange Rate Mechanism (ERM)   An agreement among most of the members of the European Economic Community to maintain relatively fixed currency rates by limiting movements of the currency to a narrow band of between plus/minus 2.25 percent from an agreed upon relationship between the values of the currencies. The ERM was effective in the early 1990s and since has been replaced by the euro.

exchange ratio   In an acquisition or merger, the number of shares of the acquiring company that a shareholder of the purchased company receives for each share of stock that he or she holds.

exchange-traded funds (ETF)   An investment that is popular with large investors that resembles a mutual fund. Its objective is to achieve the same return as a particular market index. ETFs trade on stock exchanges. One well-known ETF is Spiders, or SPDRs, which invests in all the stocks included in the S&P 500 Composite Stock Price Index.

Although an ETF is legally called an *open-end company* or a kind of mutual fund called a *unit investment trust,* these terms are not interchangeable. ETFs don't sell individual shares directly to investors and only issue their shares in large blocks of approximately 50,000 shares. These blocks are called *creation units,* which are frequently purchased by institutions. The creation units may be split up into individual shares and sold on a secondary market. An advantage to exchange-traded funds is that they can be sold short and bought on margins. They also allow traders to quickly buy or sell equities.

Although both closed-end funds and ETFs are investment companies whose shares trade in the open market, the shares are issued and redeemed differently. *Closed-end funds* issue a fixed number of shares in an initial public offering (IPO), and sometimes trade at a premium or discount to their net asset value (NAV) in the secondary market. ETFs allow their outstanding shares to increase or decrease but prevent a significant premium or discount from occurring to NAV. Closed-end funds are based on an actively managed portfolio of stocks; ETFs are based on index portfolios.

The American Stock Exchange (AMEX) was a pioneer in introducing ETFs, which have grown to $100 billion in assets in less than a decade. There are over 100 ETFs that trade on AMEX. In contrast, only three ETFs were listed on the New York Stock Exchange in early 2003. The iShares S&P Global 100 Index Fund (IOO) tracks the performance of the S&P Global 100 Index. It was the first ETF to be listed on the NYSE, in December 2000. Nearly two years later, two more ETFs were listed on the NYSE: the Fresco Dow Jones Euro STOXX 50 Fund (FEZ) and the Fresco Dow Jones STOXX 50 Fund (FEU).

exchequer Another name for the U.K. Treasury. The person in the United Kingdom who is responsible for the treasury is the chancellor of the exchequer.

The word *exchequer* comes from an oblong, cloth-covered table with squares like those on a chequer (checker) board. In times past, the table was used as an abacus using the place value of the squares to tally tax revenues.

ex-dividend A stock on which the current owner has no right to a declared dividend. When a company declares a dividend, it sets a *record date* on which a person must hold the stock in order to receive the dividend. When the company sets the record date, the stock exchange set the ex-dividend date, which typically is two business days before the record date. If the stock is purchased on or after its ex-dividend date, the shareholder is not eligible to receive the next dividend payment. Instead, the dividend payment goes to the seller.

execution risk The risk that a transaction won't be executed within the range of recent market prices or within the stop order limits that have been set by an investor. Execution risk exists on virtually all financial instruments.

executor (executrix) The administrator of the estate of a deceased person. The executor (masculine) or executrix (feminine) manages the settlement of the estate by gathering and disbursing the assets of the estate after paying the debts and filing the estate's tax returns and any personal income tax returns for the deceased. The executor/executrix may be a family member, a friend of the deceased, a lawyer, or a bank trust officer.

executrix See *executor.*

exercise To invoke the right to buy or sell the financial instrument specified by an option.

exercise price The price at which the underlying security for an options contract can be purchased. If the exercise price of an option is $35, then the stock can be purchased at $35 a share, irrespective of the current market price. Also called *strike price.*

exhaustion gap A pattern on a technical chart that shows a strong upward or downward movement that is soon followed by a movement in the opposite direction.

Ex-Im Bank See *Export Import Bank of the United States.*

existing home sales   A monthly statistical report compiled by the National Association of Realtors of sales of existing homes. These statistics are closely watched by the financial markets as a sign of the strength of the economy; The purchase of a house typically prompts additional sales of furniture, appliances, and new decorations, which help to fuel consumer demand and thus economic growth. The report also includes sales on a seasonally adjusted annual rate, which reflects the number of homes that would be sold if the same number of sales in one month occurred for twelve months. In 2002, a record 5.56 million homes were sold, which beat the previous record of 5.3 million in 2001.

exit strategy   A strategy developed by a venture capitalist or a private equity investor for selling his or her ownership stake in a company to realize a profit and the return of his or her principle.

exotic options   A name given to options products developed beginning in the mid-1980s that were created to manage financial risk in increasingly creative ways. Several examples of exotic options are barrier options, Asian options, and Bermuda options. See also *barrier option* and *Bermuda option*.

expansion stage   Financing provided by a venture capital firm to a company whose service or product is commercially available. Though the company's revenues may look strong and show significant growth, the company may not be profitable. Typically, a company that receives an expansion stage investment has been in business three years or longer.

expense ratio   A measure of the operating expenses of a mutual fund as a percentage of the average net assets. These expenses cover the costs of providing services to shareholders, professional money managers, and administrative staff. The expenses are deducted from the fund's income. Expense ratios vary, but typically they range from 0.3 percent up to about 1.80 percent of the average net assets,

although the latter number can easily be exceeded.

expenses   The costs incurred by a business. Expenses include everything from lease payments to payments for office equipment to salaries. Expenses are subtracted from revenues to arrive at net income.

expiry month   Options terminology that refers to the month a futures or options contract expires and in which the terms of the contract are fulfilled, if the buyer decides to take delivery.

export   To sell goods or services to a company in another country. The level of exports helps to determine a country's trade balance. If exports exceed the amount of imports, then the country has a *trade surplus*. If imports exceed exports, then the country has a *trade deficit*.

Export-Import Bank of the United States (Ex-Im Bank)   An independent federal government agency that helps finance the sale of U.S. exports, primarily to emerging markets. Financing is accomplished by providing loans, guarantees, and export credit insurance. In many cases, without financing guarantees, companies would decline to sell goods to companies in foreign countries because they would have little redress through the country's legal system if the foreign company defaulted. In fiscal year 2002, the Ex-Im Bank authorized financing to support about $13 billion in U.S. exports.

ex-rights   Losing the right to buy a stock at a particular price because those rights expired. Once the rights expire, the stock becomes ex-rights.

extra dividend   A dividend that is paid to shareholders in addition to regularly scheduled dividends. Extra dividends are paid to reward shareholders for a company's strong performance. Typically they are awarded after the end of the company's fiscal year.

extraordinary item   A revenue or expense that is unusual and infrequent, as defined by the Accounting Principles

Board in its Opinion No. 30. Examples of extraordinary items include expenses to deal with a fire, earthquake, or uninsured losses from a flood, the gain or loss from early retirement of debt, or the expropriation of a property by a foreign government. Companies' financial statements separate extraordinary items from regular expenses in order to give investors what the companies consider a more accurate picture of their ongoing business and expenses.

ex-warrant Stock that is sold without a warrant attached to it. Warrants let the owner buy stock at a future date at a specific price, which typically is below the market price.

F

fabless A semiconductor company that designs chips but outsources the actual production of the chip because it doesn't have any production facilities. Fabless companies are a fairly new development. Typically semiconductor companies construct and operate extremely expensive factories (called *silicon foundries*), which are capable of the high standards of precision and cleanliness required to make these complex circuits. Many of these plants are located in foreign countries where wages and other costs are low or grants are available. Operations usually are restricted to the manufacture of components, and these silicon foundries have no research or design facilities. These factories are known in the business as *fabs,* short for "fabrication plants," which is where the term *fabless* comes from.

face value

1. The value of a bond or another type of debt instrument at maturity. Also called *par value.*

2. The amount of the principal on a futures, option, swap, or forward contract.

face-amount certificate A debt instrument issued by a type of mutual fund that is called a *face-amount certificate company.* An investor who owns a face-amount certificate makes periodic payments to the company issuing the certificate. At the end of the payment period, the issuer pays the investor the face value of the certificate. If the certificate is presented before maturity, the investor is paid the surrender value.

factoring The selling or transferring of accounts receivable in order to gain funds that are immediately available. A company sells its receivables to another company, which is called a *factor.* Factoring can be done *without recourse,* which means that the company that buys the accounts receivable bears the risk of repayment. One example of factoring without recourse is taking a charge such as American Express, Visa, or MasterCard to pay for a purchase. Factoring can be done *with recourse,* which means that the company that originally sold the goods will be liable to the purchaser if the receivable is not collected. Discounting is another form of financing accounts receivables.

factory orders report A monthly report produced by the Census Bureau on factory orders in the United States. It measures new orders, shipments, and unfilled orders for major industries such as the electronics, textile, and automobile industries. Its shortcomings are that it can be excessively volatile and that it excludes data on imports. Because the report follows the durable goods release, its information is anticipated and has little broad impact.

fair value

1. The price that an asset or investment can be bought or sold at. Quoted market prices of instruments traded on exchanges give an accurate reading of fair value.

2. The theoretical value of a futures or options contract that is derived from a mathematical valuation model. Also called *non-arbitrage value.*

fairness opinion A valuation of a merger, a joint venture, or some other financial arrangement or investment by an independent organization. Typically, fairness opinions are written by investment banks or other financial advisors who are hired by companies to provide an independent opinion about a merger and the price being paid.

fallen angel A bond that was investment-grade quality when it was issued but which has been reduced to junk, or non-investment grade, status. These bonds become fallen angels because the company has added too much debt or because sales have fallen drastically and no longer enable the company to sufficiently cover its interest payments.

family of funds A group of mutual funds that are managed by the same company. An investment company manages financial instruments that have different investment objectives, such as large-cap growth, small-cap, or fixed income. It is very easy to transfer money between funds within the same family.

Fannie Mae A private agency that is congressionally chartered to promote home ownership among low to moderate income people. It buys home mortgage loans in the private market that aren't insured by the Federal Housing Administration (FHA) or guaranteed by the Department of Veterans Affairs (VA). Fannie Mae may retain the mortgages for a short period of time, but most of the mortgages are packaged and resold to investors in the market as mortgage-backed securities. By reselling the mortgages it purchases from the primary issuers, Fannie Mae gives banks and savings and loans the ability to issue more mortgages. Fannie Mae offers additional programs to encourage home ownership among low-income people.

Originally created in 1938 by Congress to bolster the housing industry after the Great Depression, Fannie Mae was part of the Federal Housing Administration (FHA) and authorized to purchase only FHA-insured loans. In 1968, it became a private company operating with private capital whose role is to buy mortgages beyond government-linked mortgages and to establish a national secondary market for government-insured mortgages. Fannie Mae's debt is perceived to be nearly as safe as U.S. Treasury debt, which allows it to pay lower interest rates to its debt holders. Even though Fannie Mae is now a private company that continues to be active in the secondary market for conventional and FHA and VA loans, it still operates under a congressional charter and the Department of Housing and Urban Development and the U.S. Treasury Department continue to have oversight of the agency.

FASB See *Financial Accounting Standards Board.*

fast market A situation in open-outcry futures or options trading in which transactions occur so quickly that volume data and precise prices can't be determined. Instead, the exchange lists volume as "fast" and shows a range of prices instead of citing a precise volume figure. See also *open outcry.*

Fastow, Andrew S. The former chief financial officer of Enron Corp. who was indicted on 78 felony charges in conjunction with the collapse of Enron. As of this printing, he had pled not guilty.

fast-track trade authority A congressionally approved trade process that gives the president the authority to negotiate trade agreements and requires Congress to vote on such agreements within 90 days (an expedited schedule) without amending them. Enacted in December 2001, fast-track trade authority was intended to speed up the approval of trade agreements in order to show foreign countries that the United States would act quickly on the provisional agreements. The U.S. president had not had fast-track authority since April 1994, when concerns over the impact of trade agreements on the environment and on labor practices temporarily ended the authority.

FCF See *free cash flow.*

FCM See *futures commission merchant.*

FCOJ Stands for *frozen concentrate orange juice futures.* See *orange juice futures.*

FDIC See *Federal Deposit Insurance Corporation.*

fear premium A rise in prices based on the fear that an event will happen. For example, a fear premium was present in the crude oil market in the months leading up to the United States' military action against Iraq in March 2003. Prices rose because of fears that a war would severely interrupt the supply of oil to the market, which would drive up prices. Once fears abated, prices fell substantially and quickly, often by as much as 10 to 20 percent. Fear premiums can occur in any market.

Fed A nickname for the Federal Reserve. See *Federal Reserve System*.

fed funds rate The interest rate that the U.S. central bank, the Federal Reserve (Fed), charges on overnight loans between banks. The federal funds rate is used by the Federal Reserve to set monetary policy with the intention of maintaining price stability, or the absence of inflation. At the end of 2002, the fed funds rate stood at a four-decade low of 1.25%. The fed funds rate influences many interest rates throughout the economy and may vary daily and between the different Federal Reserve banks.

Fed Model A model that compares the returns from the 10-year Treasury note and the Standard & Poor 500 to determine whether stocks are overvalued. The expected return from both instruments should be roughly the same. The Treasury's return, or its yield, is compared to the stocks' earnings yield, which is the expected earnings divided by price. Rising stock prices that surpass expected earnings cause the earnings yield to fall. If earnings fall below the 10-year Treasury yield, stocks are overvalued. There is little incentive to buy potentially risky stocks if they don't even earn as much as risk-free Treasuries.

The Fed Model was constructed by Ed Yardeni, the chief investment strategist at Prudential Securities as of this printing. He constructed the model from comments made in a Federal Reserve report to Congress in July 1997. The report included a paragraph that said the yield on the 10-year Treasury note at that point far exceeded stocks' earnings yield.

Federal Deposit Insurance Corporation (FDIC) An independent agency of the U.S. government that insures bank deposits. It was established by Congress in 1933 following the numerous bank failures that occurred during the Great Depression. The FDIC's mission is to maintain the stability of and public confidence in the U.S. financial system. FDIC-insured deposits are backed by the full faith and credit of the U.S. government. Most, but not all, accounts in banks and savings and loans are insured. Institutions that are insured by the FDIC must display a sign at each teller window. Each bank account held is insured up to $100,000. Examples of insured accounts include checking and savings accounts, NOW accounts, Christmas Club accounts, and certificates of deposit. The FDIC charges financial institutions a fee on their assets that helps pay for the insurance.

Stocks, mutual funds, and other investments are not covered by deposit insurance. Neither are Treasury securities (bills, notes, and bonds) purchased by an insured depository institution on a customer's behalf. However, in the event of a bank's default, the Treasury securities held by that bank on behalf of the customer remain the customer's property.

Federal Farm Credit Banks Funding Corp. A federal agency that issues note and bond debt securities on behalf of the 105 member banks that make up the federal farm credit banks. Unlike commercial banks, farm credit banks don't accept deposits. Instead, the funds for loans come from the issuance of notes and debt by the Federal Farm Credit Banks Funding Corp. The money raised is used to benefit domestic agricultural producers and cooperatives by creating a source of funds for loans. The Farm Credit System meets approximately one-third of the credit needs of U.S. agricultural producers.

The Farm Credit System is a nationwide network of borrower-owned lending institutions and affiliated service entities that make loans to agricultural companies. It is the oldest government-sponsored enterprise (GSE), and was created by Congress in 1916. The system institutions are federally chartered under the Farm Credit Act and are subject to supervision, examination, and regulation by a Federal agency, the Farm Credit Administration. The Farm Credit Debt Securities are the joint and several obligations of the System Banks. In the late 1980s the Farm Credit System Insurance Corp. was created. It is an independent U.S. government-controlled corporation that insures the debt securities to the extent that funds are available.

Federal Home Loan Bank Board (FHLBB)

A federal agency that supervises all federal savings and loan associations and federally insured state-chartered savings and loan associations. The FHLBB also directs the Federal Home Loan Bank System, which provides a flexible credit facility for members to promote home financing; the Federal Savings and Loan Insurance Corp., which insures accounts at federal savings and loan associations and some state-chartered associations; and the Federal Home Loan Mortgage Corp., which was established in 1970 to promote secondary markets for mortgages.

Federal Home Loan Bank System

A system of banks that were created in 1932 to improve the supply of funds to local lenders, thus making more funds available to finance home mortgages. Today, there are just under 8,000 member banks of the FHLB system, compared with the 12 that existed in 1932. These banks make up a cooperative partnership system that continues to help finance the United States' urban and rural housing and community development needs. The partnership supports community-based financial institutions and facilitates their access to credit. They are privately capitalized, government-sponsored enterprises.

The Federal Home Loan Finance Board ensures that the federal home loan banks operate safely, carry out their housing and community development finance mission, and remain adequately capitalized so they are able to raise funds in the capital markets. The five-member finance board is an independent, regulatory agency of the U.S. executive branch. The president appoints four board members for seven-year terms. The fifth member is the Secretary of the Department of Housing and Urban Development, or the secretary's designee. The Finance Board is supported solely by assessments from the banks and no government funds are used to fund its operations.

Federal Home Loan Mortgage Corp.

See *Freddie Mac.*

Federal Housing Administration (FHA)

An agency of the U.S. Department of Housing and Urban Development that insures home mortgage loans to people with low income or poor credit. The insurance allows private-sector banks and savings and loans to underwrite a mortgage in circumstances that would otherwise disqualify potential home buyers. The FHA also provides low-income housing through public-housing developments and manages the Section 8 rental program, which allows renters to locate and rent apartments using vouchers issued by the FHA. Section 8 refers to the section of the law that created the rental program.

Federal Open Market Committee (FOMC)

A Federal Reserve committee charged with setting the federal funds rate as well as managing open market operations such as the buying and selling of government securities. If the U.S. Treasury secretary decides to intervene in the foreign currency market by buying or selling foreign currency, the FOMC carries out the transaction. The Federal Reserve and U.S. Treasury coordinate on policy. The FOMC holds day-long meetings eight times a year. However two of those meetings, usually in January or February and June or July, are two-day meetings. During the two day meetings, the FOMC develops the Federal Reserve Board's semiannual monetary policy report delivered to Congress.

Federal Open Market Committee minutes

The minutes of the meeting held by the Federal Reserve committee, which decides whether to raise or lower interest rates. The minutes of the previous meeting are released several days after the most recent meeting has been held. Typically this creates about a six-week lag for the minutes to be released. The minutes show what was discussed during the meeting and list those who voted with the majority and the dissenters.

Federal Railroad Administration (FRA)

The Federal agency set up in

1966 to promote railroad safety, consolidate government activities for railroads, and rehabilitate rail passenger service in the Northeast United States. The agency manages federal law pertaining to rail safety and educates the public about safety at highway railroad crossings. The agency's safety force inspects 230,000 miles of railroad track, 1.4 million freight cars, 20,000 locomotives, and signal and train control systems on 89,000 miles of tracks. The FRA oversees and provides financial assistance to Amtrak, the passenger railroad service.

Federal Register The official daily publication for rules, proposed rules, and notices of federal agencies and organizations as well as Executive Orders and other presidential documents. Proposed laws and regulations, including those involving securities matters, must be published in the Federal Register, often for a 30-day period, before they become law. Governmental agencies and Congress pass the regulations or laws that are published in the Federal Register, which is maintained by the U.S. government's Office of the Federal Register.

Federal Reserve Board of Governors The manager for the Federal Reserve System. The seven members on the Board of Governors of the Federal Reserve System are nominated by the U.S. president and confirmed by the U.S. Senate. Terms are for 14 years, and terms begin every two years on February 1 of even-numbered years. A member who serves a full term can't be reappointed, however a member who completes an unexpired portion of another person's term can be reappointed to a full term. All terms end on their statutory date regardless of when the member is sworn into office.

The chairman and vice chairman of the board are selected by the president for a four-year term and confirmed by the Senate. They may be renominated until their terms as governors expire.

Federal Reserve System Also called the Fed, the Federal Reserve System is the central bank of the United States, created in 1913. The purpose of the system is to provide a safe, flexible, and stable monetary policy and financial system. It conducts monetary policy by influencing the amount of money and credit available in the financial system. It is charged with pursuing policies that promote full employment and avoid inflation. It also has other duties, which include promoting the stability of the financial system and providing banking services to depository institutions and the U.S. government. It also is charged with protecting consumers from bad banking policies. Twelve regional Federal Reserve Banks, located in Atlanta, Boston, Chicago, Cleveland, Dallas, Kansas City, Minneapolis, New York, Philadelphia, Richmond, St. Louis, and San Francisco, are the system's operating arms. (Eleven of the regional banks are located in the eastern U.S. because that is where the majority of the nation's population was located when the Federal Reserve System was chartered.)

Federal Rules of Bankruptcy Procedure Rules that outline the procedural laws that are used in bankruptcy proceedings. Each court district or each bankruptcy judge also may have individual rules.

Federal Trade Commission (FTC) A government agency that, along with the Justice Department, administers antitrust laws. The law setting up the FTC was passed in 1914 and outlaws "unfair methods of competition," however, it doesn't define *unfair*. In addition to antitrust laws, the FTC enforces consumer protection laws in order to ensure that the U.S. markets function competitively and are vigorous, efficient, and free of undue restrictions. Under the Hart-Scott Rodino Act that was passed in 1976, both the Federal Trade Commission and the Department of Justice review mergers agreements for deals over $50 million in order to prevent potential anti-competitive harm to individuals and businesses.

federal unemployment insurance tax (FUTA) A tax that is designed to help unemployed workers. It is paid only by employers, whose tax rate rises as more workers are laid off. The federal program allows a credit to be taken for taxes paid to state unemployment insurance programs.

Fedwire A payment system that is used by the 12 Federal Reserve Banks, their 24 branches, the Federal Reserve Board, and the U.S. Treasury Department. Banks can instantaneously transfer money between themselves as well as transfer money for business customers. The transaction is made in real time so the recipient immediately has the funds.

feed ratio The relationship of the cost of feed to the sale price of animals, which is expressed as a ratio. For example, the corn/hog ratio is one popular feed ratio that is used. Feed ratios are indicators of the level of profit margin that a farmer can expect.

feeder cattle A futures contract based on young cattle that are sent to feedlots in preparation for slaughter. The feeder cattle are the basis of the Chicago Mercantile Exchange's (CME) Live Cattle contracts. Feeder cattle futures began trading in 1971 and in 1987 options began trading.

Feldstein, Martin S. An influential economist from Harvard University who was an advisor to George W. Bush in the 2000 presidential campaign. He also worked in the Reagan administration. He was a proponent of the 2001 tax cut and also favors the partial privatization of Social Security by introducing private investment accounts.

FHA See *Federal Housing Administration.*

FHLBB See *Federal Home Loan Bank Board.*

FHLMC See *Freddie Mac.*

FIA See *Futures Industry Association.*

FICA See *Social Security tax.*

fiduciary A person who is entrusted to manage financial assets, matters, and property for a beneficiary's benefit. People who are fiduciaries have a fiduciary trust that requires actions taken on behalf of the beneficiary benefit that person and not result in

misappropriating funds or making decisions for the fiduciary's benefit. Many people have fiduciary responsibilities, including money managers and administrators of wills and estates.

FIFO See *first in, first out.*

fill A trading term that indicates that the customer's order to buy or sell stocks, bonds, futures, or options has been successfully completed. Orders that are only partly filled are called *partial fills.*

fill or kill A customer order that must be filled immediately or cancelled. It also is a *price limit* order, which means the trade must take place at a specific price or not at all. It is used in different securities markets, including stock and futures markets.

finance charge The cost of obtaining and using credit; typically applied to credit cards or other consumer loans, such as car loans. Finance charges typically include interest due on outstanding balances as well as fees for special services, such as cash advances. The federal Truth in Lending Act requires that the finance charges must be disclosed to customers before issuing credit.

Financial Accounting Standards Board (FASB) A private sector organization, established in 1973, that has established standards and rules for financial accounting and the production of financial reports. The standards help create an efficient economic system because investors, auditors, and creditors can rely on credible financial information that is transparent and comparable among different companies.

The mission of the FASB is to establish and improve standards of financial accounting and reporting to guide and educate securities issuers, auditors, and investors. To fulfill its mission, the FASB focuses on improving the usefulness of financial reporting by focusing on how relevant, reliable, comparable, and consistent financial information is; keeps standards current to reflect changes in methods of doing business and changes in the economic environment; watches for any deficiency in financial reporting that might be improved by additional standards; promotes the international convergence of accounting standards; and improves the understanding of information in financial reports.

While the Securities and Exchange Commission (SEC) was given legal authority for establishing financial accounting and reporting standards for publicly held companies through the Securities Exchange Act of 1934, the SEC frequently relies on the FASB to set rules governing financial standards and reporting requirements. The American Institute of Certified Public Accountants also recognizes FASB standards as authoritative. The Financial Accounting Standards Advisory Council advises FASB on issues related to new issues or ongoing evaluation of financial standards. Chief executives, chief financial officers, academics, and senior executives in accounting firms are on the council.

financial engineering The creative application of financial technology to solve financial problems or create financial opportunities. Financial engineering involves creating desirable cash flows from new or existing investments. Financial engineering may tackle a problem such as determining how to allocate investment capital in order to maximize investment returns. Techniques that might be used include optimization technologies such as linear and quadratic programming.

financial expert A term defined by the Sarbanes-Oxley legislation that was passed in 2003, which requires that least one member of the audit committees of boards of directors is a financial expert. Although the law issues guidelines for what a financial expert is, it is up to each board of directors to make a determination using five key qualities outlined in the law. A financial expert must: 1) understand Generally Accepted Accounting Principles (GAAP) and financial statements; 2) be experienced in preparing or auditing financial statements of comparable companies; 3) have experience accounting for estimates, accruals, and reserves; 4) understand internal accounting controls; and 5) understand the functions of an audit committee.

financial future A futures contract whose underlying instruments are securities such as U.S. Treasury bonds, eurodollars, currencies, or stock market indices. Financial futures contrast with agricultural futures contracts, which are based on agricultural products such as wheat, cattle, hogs, coffee, and butter.

financial institution A company that takes in money from individuals or companies and uses those funds to purchase financial assets such as deposits, loans, and securities as opposed to tangible property. Financial institutions are split into two types: depository and non-depository. Depository firms are banks, credit unions, and savings and loans that pay interest on deposits and then lend money in the form of interest-earning loans. Non-deposit firms offer pension funds, life and property/casualty insurance policies, and retirement income in exchange for receiving premiums payments or contributions to retirement accounts from their clients.

financial leverage The ability of a company to earn more on its assets by taking on debt that allows it to buy or invest more in order to grow its business. If a company can borrow funds at 8 percent and receive a 10 percent return, then it has financial leverage. If the market turns down, a heavily leveraged company can be in danger.

Financial Market Working Group A financial group that examines governmental finance policy. Its job is to research and give opinions about the regulation of the financial markets. The group is comprised of the Treasury Secretary, the chairman of the Board of Governors of the Federal Reserve System, the chairman of the Securities and Exchange Commission, and the Chairman of the Commodity Futures Trading Commission.

financial plan An outline of a person or family's financial goals and the steps that are necessary to reach them. The goals can include establishing a cash reserve for emergencies, purchasing a home, funding children's education, or setting up a retirement account.

In order to establish a financial plan, it is important to gather current financial data. Then the data must be analyzed in conjunction with the goals that have been selected. Alternatives should be evaluated and decisions made. The plan must be monitored to make sure that it is being implemented correctly.

A financial planner can be hired to set up a financial plan. A planner can be effective in helping examine current savings, investment, and insurance strategies along with budgeting practices. A planner also helps evaluate retirement planning efforts and tax planning. Financial professionals who may work as financial planners including accountants, life insurance advisors, stockbrokers, investment advisors, and attorneys specializing in tax or financial planning. Some people have a more general professional background and are simply financial planners.

Several organizations for financial planners give out professional designations that are designed to set their members apart from others who call themselves financial planners but may not have as strong qualifications. The Certified Financial Planner Board of Standards Inc. of Denver, Colorado issues a certified financial planner (CFP) designation. Those who hold the CFP designation must past a test, have minimum education and experience levels, and promise to adhere to ethical standards.

Financial planners use a variety of methods to charge for their services. Some fee-based financial planners charge an hourly rate or a flat rate for their advice. They don't earn a commission for investments that their clients purchase. Some financial planners charge a percentage of the assets under management. Other financial planners make their money through commissions they earn when an investment they recommend is purchased by their client. Some financial planners may be compensated through a combination of fees and commissions.

Financial Services Authority (FSA)
An independent, non-governmental organization, created in 1997, that regulates the financial services industry in the United Kingdom. The FSA has four main objectives:

1) Maintain confidence in the United Kingdom financial system by supervising exchanges, settlement houses, and other market infrastructure providers. The FSA also conducts market surveillance and monitors transactions.

2) Promote public understanding of the financial system so consumers can be informed and manage their financial affairs.

3) Protect consumers.

4) Reduce financial crime, such as money laundering, fraud, and reduce criminal market misconduct, such as insider dealing.

The FSA is financed by the financial services industry. The board of directors is appointed by the U.K. Treasury. The board consists of an executive chairman, three managing directors, and eleven non-executive directors (including a lead non-executive member, the deputy chairman). The board sets overall policy, but daily decisions and manage-ment of the staff is the responsibility of the executive chairman.

The Chancellor of the Exchequer announced financial services reform and the creation of a new regulator in May 1997. The Chancellor merged banking supervision and investment services regulation into the Securities and Investments Board (SIB), which changed its name to the Financial Services Authority in October 1997. In June 1998, the responsibility for banking supervision was transferred to the FSA from the Bank of England. The Financial Services and Markets Act, which received Royal Assent in June 2000 and was implemented on December 1, 2001, transferred to the FSA the responsibilities of several other organizations such as the Building Societies Commission, Friendly

Societies Commission, Investment Management Regulatory Organization, Personal Investment Authority, Register of Friendly Societies and Securities, and Futures Authority.

The FSA also took on new responsibilities under the regulation reform process, including Mutual Societies Registration. The FSA is responsible for the registration and public records of about 9,500 industrial and provident societies, 3,000 societies registered under the Friendly Societies legislation, 700 credit unions, and around 70 building societies. It also has power under the Unfair Terms in Consumer Contract Regulations to take action to deal with unfair terms in financial services consumer contracts.

The FSA is responsible for regulating Lloyd's Insurance Market and Recognized Overseas Investment Exchanges (ROIEs). The FSA is responsible for tackling market abuses.

Financial Services Modernization Act of 1999   See *Gramm-Leach-Bliley Act*.

Financial Times Stock Exchange Index (FTSE) 100 Index   A capitalization-weighted index of the 100 largest-capitalization companies that are traded on the London Stock Exchange. The index was developed by using a base level of 1000 as of January 3, 1984.

firm commitment underwriting   An underwriting assignment in which the underwriter gives the issuing company a commitment to purchase the company's securities, thereby assuming the risk if the deal is poorly received by the market and the price needs to be lowered. This is the most common type of underwriting assignment undertaken in the United States.

first generation   See *1G*.

first in, first out (FIFO)   An inventory accounting method in which the first goods that are purchased are counted as being sold. FIFO is calculated by taking the inventory at the beginning of the period, adding purchases during the accounting period, and then subtracting the ending inventory to arrive at the cost of goods sold. In times of inflation, FIFO produces a higher ending inventory, a lower cost of goods sold, and a higher gross profit, which means that income taxes may be higher.

first mortgage   A real estate mortgage that gives the lender the first claim on the property in case of a default. It is in contrast to a second mortgage, which is paid only after the first mortgage holder is paid in the event of a default.

first notice day   In the futures or options market, the first day that the clearinghouse notifies its members of delivery allocations, which are dictated by the futures contracts that it holds. If positions on the futures or options exchange aren't closed out before expiration, then the contract holder risks having to fulfill the terms of the contract by either delivering or buying the underlying commodity.

fiscal policy   A government's taxation and spending policies.

fiscal year (FY)   The 12-month period that a corporation uses to report its financial results; a company's fiscal year does not necessarily correspond to the calendar year. Companies choose their own fiscal year over using a calendar year when it is to their advantage.

five 9s   99.999. In computer terms, a system should be operating 99.999% of the time, which works out to be 5.4 minutes of downtime in a year. Companies talk about their technological systems as being able to achieve five 9s.

fixed annuity   An annuity investment that guarantees a fixed payment for a specific period or for the life of the insured. Insurance companies sell annuities and assume the risk that the insured will live for a long time. In contrast, a *variable annuity* is an annuity for which payments depend on the return earned on investments and are uncertain.

fixed asset   An asset that will not be consumed in the short term, such as a building, equipment, and furniture. These assets are quantified on a company's balance sheet and depreciation expenses are taken on them.

fixed cost   A cost that is constant regardless of the level of sales or production. For instance, in a manufacturing plant, expenses such as rent, depreciation, and insurance must be paid even if the factory closes down for a two-week period. Fixed costs contrast with variable costs, such as temporary labor or materials that are used to produce goods, which vary depending on the level of sales or production.

fixed exchange rate   An exchange rate that is set by the central bank or governmental monetary authorities. This is in contrast to *floating exchange rates* that are determined by the market. One country that uses a fixed exchange rate is China, which pegs its yuan to the U.S. dollar.

fixed-charge coverage ratio   A ratio calculated by dividing profits before payment of interest and income taxes by interest paid on bonds and other long-term debt. The larger the ratio, the safer the company is because it has more of a cushion to pay its debts and avoid default. The ratio illustrates how many times interest charges have been earned by the corporation on a pretax basis. If the ratio is five, the company has earned five times its interest charges, for example.

fixed-income investment   An investment, typically a government, municipal, or corporate bond or note, that pays a fixed rate of return. *Preferred stock,* which pays a fixed dividend, also is an example of a fixed-income investment. If interest rates decrease, or if inflation remains low, then fixed-income investments provide a steady return. However, if interest rates increase or if inflation rises, returns will fall.

fixed-rate mortgage   A home loan in which the interest rate remains unchanged throughout the life of the loan. This results in a constant payment that won't rise during the life of the mortgage even if interest rates rise. During the early years of a fixed-rate mortgage, most of the monthly payment goes to pay interest on the loan and only a small portion goes to pay down the principal. This situation reverses itself toward the end of the mortgage term. In contrast, an *adjustable-rate mortgage* has an interest rate that can increase or decrease depending on market interest rates.

flag   A technical analysis chart pattern that looks like a flag. A flag pattern shows upward price movement followed by declining price movement that is in a channel formation (meaning that is it constant and definite). The flag formation typically lasts just several weeks and shows a period of price congestion, or little movement, in prices. When the flag pattern ends, prices typically resume the direction of the trend that occurred before the flag.

flash memory   A type of memory that is used in digital cell phones, digital cameras, personal digital assistants, and PC cards for notebook computers. Flash memory is constantly on. It can be erased and reprogrammed in units of memory called blocks. The term takes its name from the memory's design, which allows a section of memory cells to be erased in one action, or in a flash. Flash memory is a popular product that is sold by semiconductor companies.

flat

1. In trading, a term used to indicate a market or a price that is neither rising or falling. Low trading volumes often produce flat trading conditions.

2. The trading position of a trader who has sold all of his or her holdings and is neither long or short.

flat tax   A system of income tax in which each taxpayer pays the same percentage of tax on their income, irrespective of income level. It contrasts with the progressive income tax system presently used in the United States, in which those making more money have a higher tax rate than those who have less income. Critics of a flat tax say that it is regressive and unfairly hurts poor people. Proponents of a flat tax approve of its simplicity and say that everyone should pay the same rate.

flatline A market that returns to where it opened, having neither a gain nor a loss. A chart of the market shows a line that looks flat. The term is used more frequently on financial television programs than in news articles or magazines.

Flexible Exchange (FLEX) options Investment vehicles that combine the benefits of customizable options with the advantages of a listed security. FLEX options are available on all option products listed on the American Stock Exchange. FLEX options let investors customize the key contract terms such as expiration date, exercise method, exercise price, and the ability to take advantage of expanded limits on the number of open positions that can be held by one trader at a time.

flexible portfolio fund A mutual fund that seeks high total return by investing in common stock, bonds, and other debt and money-market securities. The portfolio may hold 100 percent of its funds in any one of these asset classes in order to maximize returns. Most funds invest only in large-cap equities or only in bonds. This type of fund can invest in everything.

flipping Purchasing shares in an initial public offering (IPO) from the underwriter and then immediately selling them to retail investors in the secondary market at much higher prices. Institutional investors typically flip IPO shares, but many brokerage firms have policies that prevent retail customers from flipping. If investors violate the policy, they will be prevented from participating in future IPOs.

float

1. The difference between the funds that a bank has on deposit with the Federal Reserve and the funds that have been paid out of its account. Float adds to the money supply and is one of the money supply statistics collected and reported weekly by the Federal Reserve Bank of New York.

2. The number of shares of stock available to be traded multiplied by the price of the shares. The bigger the float, the greater the stock's liquidity.

floater Debt securities that have a variable interest rate that is tied to another interest rate instrument, such as the 10-year U.S. Treasury note rate. A floating debt issue spreads the risk that interest rates will change unfavorably between the debt issuer and the debt purchaser.

floating an issue A slang expression used to refer to raising capital by issuing new debt or equity.

floating exchange rate An exchange rate that is determined by the market, not by a central bank or governmental authorities.

floor

1. The main trading area of a stock, futures, or options exchange.

2. A minimum price level received by the seller in a financial transaction.

floor broker A person who buys and sells stocks or other securities on an exchange. Floor brokers are the largest single membership group of the New York Stock Exchange (NYSE). There are two types of floor brokers: commission brokers and independent floor brokers. *Commission brokers* are employed by brokerage houses and trade for the public on the NYSE floor. They make money on commissions charged to execute trades. *Independent floor brokers* are self-employed and execute orders for brokerages that don't have full-time commission brokers.

floor committee A committee made up of experienced traders on futures, options, or stock exchanges. These committees have a variety of responsibilities, such as recommending changes to trading rules and monitoring compliance with them. The responsibilities of the floor committee varies from exchange to exchange. The floor committee also rules on trading disputes.

floor official An employee of a securities exchange who is responsible for overseeing the trading process. Floor officials can settle disputes and also monitor any trading violations by members.

floor trader A member of a future or options exchange who buys or sells futures and options for his or her own account. Also called a *local trader.*

flow of funds report Shorthand for the *Flow of Funds Accounts of the United States,* a quarterly survey published by the Federal Reserve that shows the movement of funds between households, businesses, the government, and financial institutions. It also shows whether debt levels increased or decreased and what the savings rate is. The report is released during the second week of March, June, September, and December.

FOB See *free on board.*

follow-on offering The sale of additional shares of stock to the public after a company's initial public offering has been completed. Also called a *secondary offering.*

FOMC See *Federal Open Market Committee.*

FOMC Minutes See *Federal Open Market Committee minutes.*

footprint The process, that a company goes through to expand its market or locations. Expanding the company's footprint is a favorite justification for a merger. By purchasing another company the acquirer increases its footprint.

Footsie A nickname for the Financial Times' FT-SE 100 index, which is a capitalization-weighted index of 100 blue chip stocks that are traded on the London Stock Exchange.

for A market term that connects the price paid to the quantity bought. The syntax is price-for-quantity.

Forbes 400 A listing of the richest 400 Americans that is published annually by *Forbes Magazine.*

force majeure A standard clause in a contract that *indemnifies,* or protects from loss, either or both parties to a transaction if events that prevent the realization of the contract are judged to be unanticipated or uncontrollable and reasonably beyond the terms of the contract or agreement. For example, when workers at the state-owned Venezuelan oil company went on strike in late 2002, a force majeure on oil exports was declared that suspended contractual obligations due to circumstances beyond the company's control.

Ford, Henry The founder of Ford Motor Company, which created the first inexpensive, mass-produced cars. In 1908, Ford introduced the low-cost Model T, which sold for $850 to $1,000. Later the price was lowered to $300. Ford also is known for creating a production line that removed excess movement and processes from the production process. He also reduced the work day to eight hours from nine.

forecasting Making an informed guess about the direction of an individual investment, a market, or the economy as a whole. Research analysts forecast their view on the price direction of individual stocks. A market strategist forecasts what direction he or she thinks the market will head. Chief economic strategists forecast a variety of their views on what direction they think economic growth, inflation, and interest rates will take.

foreign corporation A corporation that is chartered under the laws of one country but is operating in another county.

foreign direct investment Private-sector investments that are made by a company into a foreign country. Foreign direct investments create a strong demand for a local currency and help boost the economy. With money coming into a country, strong foreign direct investment is one way governments can finance current account deficits. However, just as funds flow in, they also can flow out, creating economic turmoil.

Levels of foreign direct investment are closely watched to determine how attractive a country is to investors. If foreign direct investment levels drop, then other investors may become cautious about investing in that country. As a result, others may limit their foreign direct investment activities and also limit their purchases of stock or bonds issued by the country's corporations.

foreign exchange The value of one currency stated in terms of another currency. A person who exchanges one country's money for currency issued by another country has acquired foreign exchange.

foreign exchange market The world's largest and most liquid financial market, which operates 24 hours a day, 365 days a year. Turnover in the foreign exchange market, where one country's currency is traded for another, is estimated to be about $1.5 trillion a day. Trades may be conducted over computer or Internet-based trading systems, over the phone directly with a bank, or with a broker. A limited amount of trading is conducted on futures markets such as the Chicago Mercantile Exchange. Four main currencies, representing the world's largest economies, are traded against the U.S. dollar: the British pound, or sterling, (GBP); the Swiss franc (CHF); the euro (EUR); and the Japanese yen (JPY). These currencies, along with many minor ones, are traded by governments, corporations, fund managers, and speculators.

foreign tax credit A credit received for taxes paid to a foreign government or for taxes that a foreign government withheld from earnings or investments.

forfeiture The act of giving up the right to the ownership of an asset.

forint The currency unit of Hungary, comprised of 100 fillers.

Form 10-SB A report filed with the Securities and Exchange Commission by small businesses for the registration of securities.

Form 11-K An annual report filed with the Securities and Exchange Commission that outlines employees' stock purchases and contains information on employee savings plan.

Form 20-F A Securities and Exchange Commission form that is used by foreign companies to file annual reports. These reports must be filed within six months of the end of the company's fiscal year. The Form 20-F also may be used as a registration statement to comply with other requirements. The form also is used by domestic companies to report a change in their fiscal year.

Form 4 A form that must be submitted to the Securities and Exchange Commission when stock is sold by a company director, a company officer, or an individual or institution that owns 10 percent or more of a company's stock. The form must be filed within 10 days of the end of the month in which the ownership change occurred. Also called *Statement of Changes in Beneficial Ownership.*

Form 6251 The federal income tax form that is used to calculate the Alternative Minimum Tax, which ensures that individuals with substantial economic income pay at least a minimum amount of tax.

Form 6-K A Securities and Exchange Commission form that is used by non-U.S. companies that have issued debt or equity securities in the United States to make periodic reports to the Securities and Exchange Commission. These reports may communicate financial information or important changes in the company.

Form 8-K See *8-K*.

Form F-1 A Securities and Exchange Commission form that is used to register the securities of a non-U.S. company that will be issued through a public stock or debt offering. Although there are other forms that can be used for non-U.S. offerings, the Form F-1 is the most common.

Form S-8 A form used to register securities that will be offered to employees through employee benefit plans. The securities are registered with the Securities and Exchange Commission.

Fortune 500 Index A stock-market index based on *Fortune* magazine's annual list of the largest 500 U.S.-based public and private companies that produce and file annual reports with the Securities and Exchange Commission. The companies are ranked by revenue. The list is a market-capitalization-weighted index whose value is calculated during 15-second intervals during the trading session. It was set at a base level of 1,000.00 using the closing price on December 31, 1999.

forward contract A non-standardized transaction to buy or sell a specific financial instrument or asset at some period in the future at a specified price. Forward contracts may be written on Treasury debt, currencies, commodities, or any number of other investments. Unlike a *futures contract,* which has standardized terms and can easily be traded in a secondary market, a forward contract has unique terms. Forward contracts also are subject to the credit risk factors of the *counterparty,* or the person with whom the transaction is done, which is eliminated in the futures market because the clearinghouse guarantees payment.

forward exchange contract An agreement to exchange sums of currencies at a time in the future.

forward rate agreement (FRA) The over-the-counter equivalent of the Eurodollar futures contract. The FRA represents an interest rate similar to that indicated by a futures contract. FRAs are quoted on a money market yield basis, which uses the actual number of days in a month and a 360-day year.

forward swap agreement A transaction that has two parts: The first is a spot transaction, where something is bought or sold today, and the second is a transaction in the future that reverses the previous trade. Forward swap agreements occur in many different markets. Often forward swap transactions are created to make a bet on the direction of interest rates in the two different countries. Forward swap transactions are also conducted in the foreign exchange market: A company operating in a foreign market may undertake a forward swap in order to bring its profits back to its home country. Or, a central bank may provide some of its own currency to another central bank in exchange for an equal amount of its currency. Typically this is used when central banks intervene in the foreign exchange market. The swap is reversed at a time specified from the swap when the market pressure on the weaker currency ends.

forward trade An agreement to trade financial instruments at some time in the future. For foreign exchange, a forward trade creates a forward exchange rate, which is the price that someone is willing to pay in the future to purchase a currency. Forward trades frequently are used in the foreign exchange market, although they apply across investment groups.

FRA

1. See *Federal Railroad Administration.*

2. See *forward rate agreement.*

fractionation A term used in the energy industry to describe the separation of saturated hydrocarbons from natural gas into distinct parts or fractions (such as propane, butane, ethane, or other elements).

franc The former currency of France before it joined the European Monetary Union and adopted the euro. Many West African countries also use their own version of the franc, including Benin, Burkina

Faso, Burundi, Cameroon, Central African Republic, Republic of Congo, Chad, Djibouti, Equatorial Guinea (its franc is comprised of centimos), Gabon, Guinea, Guinea-Bissau, Ivory Coast, Madagascar, Mali, Niger, Rwanda, Senegal, and Togo. Martinique and St. Pierre also use the franc. The franc is comprised of 100 centimes. See also *Swiss franc*.

franchise A business that can be purchased for a fee and continued payment of royalties to the parent company. Examples of franchises are McDonalds and Dunkin' Donuts Inc. The franchise comes with a brand name, established policies, and procedures for operations, and may have regional or national name recognition. A franchise allows an entrepreneur the opportunity to run his or her own business without the time and expense of having to start a business from the ground up. The franchiser also will likely serve as a consultant and offer advice, promotional assistance, and financing for the franchisee.

franchise license A license that confers the right to market the franchiser's product or service in an exclusive territory or location using the franchiser's business process, name, and products. The cost of the franchise license is amortized over its reasonable life, which can't exceed 40 years.

franchise tax A state tax that is imposed on corporations that are chartered within the state. Franchise taxes are usually based on a percentage of profits, capital stock, or the amount of property held within the state.

fraud A legal term that refers to the intentional misrepresentation or concealment of the truth in order to manipulate or deceive a company or individual. When companies undergo severe financial problems and end up in bankruptcy, fraud by senior management may be involved.

fraudulent financial reporting The intentional preparation of misleading financial statements. Those involved in fraudulent reporting may be stripped of their professional designation and subjected to civil and criminal penalties. Fraudulent reporting can result from distorted records, falsified transactions, or misused accounting principles.

Freddie Mac A shareholder-owned company that was set up by Congress in 1979 with the objective of stabilizing the U.S. mortgage markets and expanding opportunities for home ownership and affordable rental housing. Freddie Mac does not issue mortgages itself, but purchases them from lenders throughout the U.S. Those loans are packaged together and sold to investors in a process called *securitization*. When Freddie Mac buys mortgages, it allows mortgage lenders to make additional loans to homeowners, which ultimately provides low- to middle-income homeowners and renters with lower housing costs and better access to home financing. Freddie Mac also invests directly in mortgages. It funds the purchases by selling bonds to investors. Through the purchases Freddie Mac is able to give investors another way to indirectly invest in mortgages in the U.S. and thus provide people with more affordable mortgage financing. The full name of Freddie Mac is the Federal Home Loan Mortgage Corp. (FHLMC), which is infrequently used.

free cash flow (FCF) The amount of cash that remains after deducting the funds that a company has to spend to fund its current operations. Often dividends are included; while they don't have to be paid, not paying them will be a significantly negative event for shareholders. This is a favorite financial measurement of companies that have high overhead as a routine part of their business. The free cash flow calculation assumes that the company must pay for financing and business activities before it can use its cash for other purposes.

To arrive at free cash flow, take net cash flow from operating activities and subtract dividends and purchases of plant assets and add in sales of plant and equipment assets.

free on board (FOB) A term used in the transportation industry to describe a transaction in which the seller provides a commodity at an agreed unit price at a specified loading point during a certain time period. The buyer has to arrange for transportation and insurance from that specified loading point.

Free Trade Area of the Americas A trading coalition comprised of the United States and five other countries: Costa Rica, El Salvador, Guatemala, Honduras, and Nicaragua. These Central American countries import approximately $9 billion in products from the United States each year; the United States imports about $11 billion in goods from these five countries. Because of special-preference programs established within the coalition, nearly 75 percent of the products exported to the United States by the countries in the coalition arrive *duty free* (meaning taxes are not paid on them).

free-riding Selling a stock before it has been paid for, which violates the credit extension provisions of the Federal Reserve Board. If an investor free-rides, the broker is required to freeze the account for 90 days. This means that while trades can still be made, they must be paid for in full on the day the purchase is made, not three days later, as is typically allowed.

Friedman, Milton A prominent economist who believes that managing the money supply, not government spending or taxation policies, is the key to economic growth. Thus, Friedman belongs to the monetarist school of thought. He won the 1976 Nobel Prize for economics.

front office In the brokerage industry, the company employees who work literally in the front part of the office and deal with clients. Front-office employees produce revenue, in contrast with back-office employees who provide support for client operations, such as managing the firm's trading and accounting systems.

front running Illegally making a trade for a personal account or a preferred customer's account with the advance knowledge that a large order is in the market or will be coming to the market that likely will create a profit. Front running is possible in situations in which traders in the futures or stock markets trade both for their own accounts and their customers' accounts, a practice known as *duel trading.* However, just because a trader engages in dual trading doesn't mean that the trader is involved with front running.

front-end load A sales charge on a mutual fund that is assessed when shares of the fund are purchased. This charge often goes to pay the selling broker in the form of a commission. A front-end load charge is different from a *12b-1 fee,* which is deducted from the fund's assets and used to pay for marketing and distribution expenses. A mutual fund without a sales charge is called a *no-load fund.*

frozen account

1. A bank or brokerage account that has been *frozen,* meaning no funds can be withdrawn. Accounts are frozen by a court or regulatory authorities for an alleged violation of a rule or law. Bank accounts remain frozen until the owner satisfies a lien against the account. Although the owner of a frozen account cannot access the funds, he or she remains the owner of the funds or investments in the account.

2. A brokerage account that the Federal Reserve Board has frozen because the Board's margin rules, outlined in Regulation T, have been violated.

FSA See *Financial Services Authority.*

FTC See *Federal Trade Commission.*

Fukui, Toshihiko As of this printing, the governor of the Bank of Japan (BOJ). He took over for Masaru Hayami, who retired after his term ended in April 2003. Before becoming governor, Fukui, like Hayami, had rejected establishing an inflation target or taking other radical steps to stop the effects of deflation and move the economy forward.

Fukui is a career bureaucrat and previously had been a deputy governor of the bank. He headed the research and credit management bureaus and became executive director before becoming deputy governor.

In 1998, while serving as deputy governor, he and then-BOJ-governor, Yasuo Matsushita were forced to resign over a bribery scandal that involved leaks of financially sensitive information. Fukui then became chairman of the Fujitsu Research Institute, a private policy group. In April 2001, he became vice chairman of the Japan Association of Corporate Executives, a business lobbying organization better known as Keizai Doyukai. That appointment won Fukui strong support among the business community and helped win his appointment as governor of the BOJ.

full faith and credit Refers to debt obligations that are guaranteed by the U.S. government. Government debt or other obligations are "backed by the full faith and credit of the U.S. government." Because the U.S. government is very strong and stable, its taxing authority can be used to ensure that the debt obligations are honored in the event of a default by the issuer.

full-ratchet A provision found in financing agreements in the venture capital industry that automatically increases the equity percentage of the original investors in the event that a new round of financing occurs. The original venture capital investors are protected if a company has a "down round" of financing, which is financing that values the company at a lower price. This provision protects the venture capital investors; however, it hurts the founders because their share of the company is decreased.

full-service bank A bank that offers services to both retail customers, such as individuals or small businesses, and large corporations and institutions.

full-service brokerage A firm that offers a full range of financial services beyond purchasing and selling stock. Other products that a full-service brokerage might offer include mutual funds, financial and tax planning, tax shelters, limited partnerships, and commodity trades. A full-service brokerage contrasts with a discount brokerage.

fully depreciated A fixed asset that has had all of its legally allowable depreciation charged against it. On a company's balance sheet, a fully depreciated asset may be listed at a minimal resale value even though it may have a value greater than what is listed.

fully diluted earnings per share An earnings-per-share calculation that assumes that all stock warrants and options have been exercised and that all convertible bonds have been converted into equity. Those investments are said to be dilutive to earnings. Accounting rules require that companies report earnings per share on a basic and fully diluted basis.

fully distributed A new debt or equity securities issue that has been completely sold to investors. The underwriters have no unsold shares.

fully invested A condition in a portfolio in which only a minimum amount of cash is being held and virtually all funds are invested in stocks, bonds, or other investments. When a portfolio manager is uneasy about the market, the manager will not be fully invested and is said to be *sitting on the sidelines*.

fully valued A stock or other investment that has reached the target set for it by an analyst or trader. A fully valued stock is one whose value has been recognized by the market. If the stock or investment continues to rise, then it may become overvalued.

fully-loaded dividend payout ratio A financial measurement used in the Real Estate Investment Trust (REIT) industry that calculates how much it costs to get a tenant into a domicile in order to produce a dividend for investors. The ratio is EBITA (earnings before interest, taxes, depreciation, and amortization) minus the gains on the sale of property, leasing commissions, tenant improvements, maintenance capital expenditures, and straight-line rent, divided by the cost of capital, which includes interest expense, preferred dividends, optional distributions, and common dividends.

fund family See *family of funds.*

fund manager A person who manages the investments of mutual funds, insurance funds, or pension funds. The manager decides what investments to buy and sell and is compensated in relation to how well the funds he or she manages do. It is a good idea before investing money with a fund to understand the manager's strategy, which may be an aggressive, growth-oriented strategy or a conservative, value-oriented approach.

fund of funds A mutual fund that invests in other mutual funds. The logic behind a fund of funds is that the fund of funds will maximize investors' returns by knowing which fund is performing the best. A fund of funds also can offer additional diversification. However, a fund of funds assesses a fee on the funds under its management, which the fund investor pays in addition to the fees assessed by the underlying funds. Some have criticized a fund of funds as doing nothing more than just adding an extra layer of management fees.

fund of hedge funds Intermediary funds that advise pension funds or asset management companies on hiring hedge fund managers. They help the pension funds and asset management companies find the right hedge fund, advise them on investment strategies, and help them track the performance of the hedge fund.

Fund of funds is a relatively new development in the hedge fund industry and is one of the fastest growing segments of the hedge fund industry. Its growth has come in part from the increasing use of hedge funds by conservative money managers, such as pension plans, who are looking for ways to boost returns since the market sell-off beginning in the spring of 2000. By hiring a fund of funds, pension funds and asset managers, who often are required to invest funds conservatively, can become more comfortable investing some of their money with hedge funds, which often are known for their risky investment style.

fundamental analysis The practice of valuing companies by looking at revenues and earnings and then analyzing the company's management and the prospect for its products or services to be successful. Fundamental analysis also can be used to look at entire industries or commodities markets. Fundamental analysis of a company or commodity is in contrast to technical analysis, which looks only at price charts to form an opinion about the company's or market's direction. As applied to the economy, fundamental research involves analyzing economic statistics, such as unemployment.

funded debt A debt issue whose repayment has already been provided for in some manner. One example of funded debt is a bond issue that has a *sinking fund,* which is a fund to which regular payments are made. When the bond matures, the issuer will have the money on hand to redeem the bonds.

funded pension plan A pension plan in which there are sufficient funds to pay for all liabilities. Both contributions from participants and earnings on investments provide cash to cover the plan's liabilities. Funded pension plans are relatively easy to achieve during periods of rising markets. However, during a bear market, the situation is much different, and companies may have to provide additional capital to fund their pension plans. The Pension Guaranty Corp. guarantees pension plans and can make a company contribute additional funds to an under-funded pension plan.

funded status The amount by which a pension plan's assets exceed the plan's projected benefit obligations (the amount the plan will have to pay in the future). The funded status is important because it forecasts whether or not the plan is fully funded.

A fully funded pension plan is one in which the market value of the plan's assets is enough to cover at least 100 percent of current benefits earned by employees. The pension plan's funded status also is important because it impacts the magnitude of off-balance sheet liabilities that the company will eventually have to pay.

funding

1. A term that is used by a company that is *funding* its operations by issuing debt.

2. Refinancing debt before maturity, typically referred to as *refunding*.

3. Initial investments in a start-up, provided by a venture capitalist or private equity investor.

fungibility The interchangeability of financial instruments, such as futures and options, because the instruments have identical terms. Fungibility allows a trader with an open position to close it out with an identical contract. For example, an S&P 500 futures contract is fungible with another contract that has the same expiration date.

fungible Interchangeable. Fungible products can be substituted for each other for shipment or storage purposes. Options that have the same strike price and expiration date also are fungible.

fungibles Goods or investments that are equal and can be interchangeable, or substituted. Stock shares of the same company and future contracts for commodities such as pork bellies or wheat are fungible.

furthest month The contract month that is the furthest away from the expiration of the futures or options contract. For some commodity contracts, the furthest month may be several years into the future.

future value The amount that an investment will be worth at a future date if it is invested at a compounded interest rate. Future value is calculated using a future value table that gives a factor based on interest rate and the time period for which

the investment will be held. The principal is then multiplied by the factor to arrive at the future value.

futures commission merchant (FCM) A company or individual who solicits orders to buy or sell futures contracts or options that are traded on organized exchanges. Also called *commission house* or *wire house.*

futures contract A contract between a buyer and seller in which the buyer is obligated to accept delivery and the seller is obligated to provide delivery of a fixed amount of a commodity at a fixed price and at a specified location. In contrast, option contracts don't obligate the holder to execute the contract. Futures contracts are traded exclusively on regulated commodities exchanges and are settled daily based on their current value in the marketplace. Their terms are the same; the only thing that changes is the price, which is determined usually through an auction system, called *open-outcry trading,* conducted on the floor of the exchange.

futures exchange A central marketplace with established rules and regulations where buyers and sellers trade futures contracts and options on futures contracts. There are dozens of futures exchanges throughout the world that have been formed to trade specific futures contracts. Typically, a futures exchange trades about 10 to 20 different types of contracts. The futures exchanges are physical locations, many of which have open-outcry trading that takes place in a pit, and others that use computer systems.

Futures Industry Association (FIA) A national not-for-profit industry trade group that represents the interests of the futures industry. It lobbies Congress and regulatory bodies, conducts research, and provides educational opportunities for its members.

futures market An organized exchange where futures contracts and options are traded.

fuzzy numbers A quantity whose value is imprecise, in contrast to an ordinary number. A fuzzy number is a number whose value is influenced by a set of numbers, which can produce many different outcomes. One analogy is driving a car on the highway. Even though the driver attempts to keep driving steadily at 65 miles per hour, the actual results will vary. If the speed were plotted each minute, there would be many different speeds, such as 63 mph, 67 mph, and 65 mphs. Fuzzy numbers are used in computer programming, engineering for communications products, and experimental science. Computer software and consulting companies increasingly are making use of fuzzy numbers.

FY See *fiscal year.*

G-10 See *Group of Ten.*

G-24 See *Group of 24.*

G-30 See *Group of 30.*

G-4 See *Group of Four.*

G-5 See *Group of Five.*

G-7 See *Group of Seven.*

G-77 See *Group of 77.*

G-8 See *Group of Eight.*

GAAP See *Generally Accepted Accounting Principles.*

gaijin A term that refers to a non-Japanese investor or business person in Japan. The term also refers to a large U.S. or European brokerage firm operating in Japan.

game theory A branch of mathematics that has indirect applications to computer science, information technology, and engineering. It involves studying the interactions among groups of people who make use of an increasing number of technologies and increasing types of technologies to achieve their goals. Game theory was first devised by John von Neumann.

gamma A measure of how quickly an option's delta will change. *Delta* measures the change in the price of a call option when the underlying futures asset price changes. Gamma is a mathematical formula that is used in pricing options.

GAO See *General Accounting Office.*

gap

1. In trading terms, the price movement when the opening price of a trading day is higher or lower than the previous day's level, which leaves a gap on the price chart. In that situation, a stock or futures contract is said to gap open lower or higher.

2. A company's lack of financing, such as a gap of $1 million that hasn't been filled by investors.

garnishment A notice to an employer or to a financial institution that funds from a person's paycheck or bank account need to be deducted and turned over to a court to pay for a judgment against the person.

gasoil The term used in Europe to refer to No. 2 heating oil and diesel fuel. No. 2 heating oil is a specific type of heating oil that is used for specific purposes, such as heating homes. Gasoil futures are traded on the International Petroleum Exchange in London.

gasoline A commodity product derived from crude oil; it is the largest refined product sold in the U.S. and accounts for about half of national oil consumption. Futures and options contracts on gasoline are traded on the New York Mercantile Exchange based on New York harbor unleaded gasoline, a particular type of gasoline. The futures contracts are based on delivery at petroleum products terminals in the New York harbor, which is the major East Coast trading center that handles much of the imported and domestic shipments. Trading also occurs on other futures exchanges throughout the world.

gather in the stops A trading technique, particularly used in the futures market or stock market, that involves selling a sufficient amount of futures or stocks in order to drive prices down to a level where sell or buy stops (traders' orders to purchase or sell stocks at a specific level) are thought to be. Once the stops are activated, then the market will trade higher or lower.

GATT See *General Agreement on Tariffs and Trade.*

GDP See *gross domestic product.*

GDP implicit price deflator Current-dollar gross domestic product (GDP) divided by constant-dollar GDP. This ratio is used to account for the effects of inflation.

GDR   See *global depositary receipt.*

geisha bond   See *shogun bond.*

General Accounting Office (GAO)
The arm of Congress that investigates the
performances of governmental agencies or
programs. The GAO evaluates how public
funds are spent and whether federal programs are meeting their stated goals.
Congress usually requests the reports and
investigations that it wants the GAO to
conduct, though some reports are required
by law, such as periodic reviews of programs
that Congress created. The GAO also serves
as Congress's investigative arm and provides
analytical, investigative, and legal services in
order to provide Congress with information to use in creating policy and making
decisions.

**General Agreement on Tariffs and
Trade (GATT)**   The first attempt to promote free trade after World War II. The
agreement came into effect on January 1,
1948. GATT created most-favored nation
status among all the member countries,
which said that any advantage, favor, privilege, or immunity granted to exports or
imports going to one country in the group
must be given to all of the countries in the
group. GATT was the forerunner of the
World Trade Organization (WTO), which
continues to lobby for trade liberalization
across many different product and services
categories.

The original members of GATT were
Australia, Belgium, Brazil, Burma, Canada,
Ceylon, Chile, China, Cuba, the
Czechoslovak Republic, France, India,
Lebanon, Luxembourg, Netherlands, New
Zealand, Norway, Pakistan, Southern
Rhodesia, Syria, South Africa, the United
Kingdom of Great Britain and Northern
Ireland, and the United States. The WTO
has over 140 members.

general ledger   The accounting records
of a company that contain all of the financial accounts of a business. The financial
accounts categorize and keep track of
income and expenses.

general lien   A lien against an individual
that includes all personal property but
excludes real property. Liens are authorized
by a court in order to satisfy a judgment
against the person.

general obligation bonds   Municipal
securities that are secured by the tax
receipts of the issuing government body.
Often, in the event of default, general
obligation bonds have a superior claim on a
municipal's assets or tax receipts over other
debt securities.

general partner   The person or persons
responsible for managing a partnership or
venture capital fund. They make investment
decisions, handle day-to-day issues, and are
responsible for the debts of the partnership.
General partners are full-time employees,
while limited partners invest money without participating in investment decisions or
daily operations.

**Generally   Accepted   Accounting
Principles (GAAP)**   A set of accounting
rules for recording financial transactions
and creating financial statements. The
Financial Accounting Standards Board
(FASB) creates and updates the principles.

generation-skipping trust   A trust that
is created upon the person's death. The
income for the trust goes to the person's
children while they are alive. When the
children die, the trust transfers to the
grandchildren. Tax regulations have been
tightened to limit the tax-free transfer to
grandchildren to $1 million.

George, Edward   The governor of the
Bank of England, as of this printing.

ghosting   Collusion between at least two
market makers (specialists who have been
authorized to conduct trades in certain
companies' stock) to manipulate the price
of a stock. Ghosting is accomplished by one
firm pushing a stock price higher or lower,
with the other firms following the first
firm's lead. The stock is sold at the new levels, resulting in a guaranteed profit. It is
illegal because market makers are required

to compete against each other and create a fair marketplace.

Giannini, A.P. An important figure in American banking in the first part of the 20th century. When the 1906 San Francisco earthquake struck, he salvaged $1 million in gold and currency from the Bank of Italy and buried it in his backyard. He set up a tent on a waterfront pier and made loans while many of his competitors were still attempting to dig out their funds. In 1909, he went on to create the first statewide banking network in the United States, in California. He focused his efforts on the banking needs of small investors and businesses. He purchased banks, including New York's Bank of America, which he used to create his financial empire. When he died in 1949, Bank of America had 493 branches and more assets than any other commercial bank in the world.

GIC See *guaranteed investment contract.*

gift splitting Dividing a gift into two pieces in order to avoid paying a gift tax. The current amount that is allowed to be given as a gift without incurring taxes is $11,000. A married couple that wants to give $22,000 to a child or family member would each write a check for $11,000 in order to avoid the gift tax.

gift tax A tax that is assessed on a person who gives assets or money to another person without receiving fair compensation. Gifts up to $11,000 a year are exempt from the gift tax. A married couple may give a total of $22,000 to one person as a gift if each person writes a separate check. A spouse may receive unlimited gifts free of tax, unless the spouse is a foreigner. Top gift tax rates are at 50%.

gilt-edged bond A high-grade bond that is issued by a strong and stable company. Investors in these bonds have confidence that they will regularly receive their interest payments and that their principle will be paid back.

gilts Bonds issued by the U.K. and Irish governments. The term comes from the

original British government certificates, which had gilded edges. Gilts are considered risk-free investments because they are backed by the government. The term may include issues of local British authorities and some overseas public sector offerings.

Ginnie Mae The common nickname for the Government National Mortgage Association (GNMA). Ginnie Mae guarantees pass-through securities that are backed by pools of home mortgages. Ginnie Mae occasionally comes under fire for its unfair competitive advantage over private businesses. Because Ginnie Mae was started by the federal government but functions as a private business, there is a perception that in the event of a default the U.S. government would bail out Ginnie Mae. That perception allows Ginnie Mae to borrow funds in the market more cheaply than its competitors. There have been no defaults to determine what the actual procedure would be.

ginzy trading A trade practice in which a floor broker in the process of executing an order fills part of the order at one price and the remainder of the order at another price. This tactic is done in order to avoid exchanges' rules against trading at fractional increments, or *split-tick trading.* Essentially, ginzy trading is the unethical practice of quoting different prices to customers on the same buy and sell order. Regulators have rules that this is a noncompetitive trading practice and violates the Commodity Exchange Act.

give up A term used to describe a transaction between three brokers in which one does not use his/her name. For example, a broker receives a buy order that he or she can't transact. The broker asks a second broker to handle the order. So the second broker buys the stock from a third broker on behalf of the first broker's client. The transaction is recorded in the records of the firms and exchange as if the first broker was never involved.

Glass-Steagall Act A law passed in 1933 in response to the banking collapse that occurred in the wake of the Great Depression. The law created deposit insurance, prohibited commercial banks from owning insurance companies or brokerage firms, and prevented banks from conducting underwriting activities such as raising debt and equity for companies. The terms of the Glass-Steagall Act that prevented banks from owning insurance companies and brokerage firms and underwriting activities were repealed in 1999 by the Financial Modernization Act.

global depositary receipt (GDR) A negotiable certificate that shows ownership of a company's shares. GDRs let companies offer shares in markets throughout the world, and they let investors purchase an equity stake in foreign companies without having to use the company's home exchange. That saves the investor the time, difficulty, and cost of trading shares on a foreign exchange. GDRs convert dividends and share price into the investor's home currency. Often companies in emerging markets such as China and South Korea issue GDRs. A GDR is similar to an ADR, which represents ownership of foreign companies that trade on U.S. exchanges.

Global System for Mobile Communication (GSM) A digital mobile telephone system that is the most widely used wireless standard in the world. It is the dominant standard in Europe. It uses a type of TDMA (time-division multiple access). GSM digitizes and then compresses data before transmitting it down either a 900 MHz or 1800 MHz channel with two other streams of data, each with its own time slot. In the United States, AT&T Wireless Services Inc., Cingular Wireless, and Voice Stream Wireless Corp. use GSM technology.

globalization The spreading influence of companies beyond their national borders and increased interconnectivity between the economies and cultures of countries. Since 2000, there have been increasingly vocal protests against the ill affects of globalization. Critics have increasingly demonstrated against globalization at international monetary and trade meetings of organizations such as the International Monetary Fund and the World Trade Organization.

GLOBEX An after-hours, global, electronic trading system for futures contracts that is operated by the Chicago Mercantile Exchange.

GmbH A German corporate designation that stands for *Gesellschaft mit beschränkter Haftung* and is translated as a "company with limited liability." A GmbH is incorporated, but it is not publicly traded. GmbHs are essentially partnerships without a legal name, and there must be at least two partners. They also must meet minimum capital requirements. Public companies must be AGs and AG subsidiaries can be GmbHs. Switzerland also uses this designation. See also *AG*.

GMT See *Greenwich Mean Time*.

GNP See *gross national product*.

going concern A company that is in solid financial shape and can continue operating for the foreseeable future. The concept of going concern comes to investors' attention when a company's auditor questions whether the company can continue as a going concern.

going long Purchasing an investment, usually a futures contract or stock. Long refers to buying, in contrast to *short,* which means to sell.

going short A term that refers to selling a stock or futures contract that is not owned by the seller. An investor going short typically borrows the stock or futures contract from his broker and then sells them. The goal is to later buy the actual stock or futures contract at a lower price, close out the position, and return the securities to the broker. The profit is the difference between the price that the stock was sold at and the price that was paid to buy it back. Also subtracted from the profit are commissions and the interest charged to borrow the securities. If the price rises, however, the short seller will have to buy the securities at a higher price than what they were sold at and will incur a loss.

gold A precious metal that has functioned as a currency or served as a long-standing investment since the early days of civilization. Gold is a *safe haven investment,* which means that investors will put their money in gold during times of extreme uncertainty such as war, terrorist attacks, or financial uncertainty such as a sell-off in the stock market, or during times of high inflation.

Investors can invest in gold by purchasing gold *bullion,* which is a precious metal that is in a tradable form, typically a bar or wafer. Gold coins also are minted by governments or by a private company as an investment piece. Popular gold coins issued by governments include the American Eagle, the Canadian Maple Leaf, the South African Krugerrand, the Isle of Man Gold Cat, the Australian Kangaroo, and the China Mint Panda Bear.

Gold future and options also provide a way to invest in gold. They trade on Comex, a division of the New York Mercantile Exchange. They trade in a unit that is based on 100 troy ounces. Price quotations are in dollars, such as $360.70. Trade occurs from 8:20 a.m. ET until 1:30 p.m. ET. Trade after hours occurs on NYMEX's Internet-based electronic trading platform, ACCESS. Gold futures and options also are traded on other exchanges throughout the world.

Gold & Silver Sector Index A benchmark index in the precious metals industry that is used by investors to track the performance of companies in the industry. It was created and is traded on the Philadelphia Stock Exchange. It also is referred to as XAU, which is its trading symbol. The Gold & Silver Sector index is a capitalization-weighted index composed of the common stocks of nine companies involved in the gold and silver mining industry. The XAU was set to an initial value of 100 in January 1979. Options began trading on December 19, 1983. A capitalization-weighted index is a stock index in which each stock affects the index in proportion to its market value.

gold bullion Gold that is in its purest form, usually in the form of ingots or bars, and is regarded as a raw material. It is investment-grade, pure gold, which may be smelted into gold coins or gold bars.

gold coin A coin that is minted in gold that may be issued by a government or created by a private enterprise. Those minted by governments are called *bullion coins.* Popular bullion coins include the American Eagle, the Canadian Maple Leaf, the South African Krugerrand, the Isle of Man Gold Cat, the Australian Kangaroo, and the China Mint Panda Bear.

Another type of gold coin is a numismatic coin, which is minted in smaller quantities by governments or private businesses and often traded at a markup, based on aesthetics, to its gold content.

gold standard A monetary system that allows the conversion of currency to gold at a fixed price. The U.S. quit using the gold standard in 1971.

gold/silver ratio The price of gold divided by the price of silver. The result is the number of silver ounces that are required to buy one ounce of gold using current prices. The gold/silver ratio is a frequently traded precious-metals spread. If the ratio is expected to decline, traders sell gold futures while buying silver futures, and vice versa.

goldbug An enthusiastic gold investor who expects the price of gold to move higher due to economic, political, or market turbulence. Historically, gold has been a secure investment that hasn't lost its value because of inflation or because a country has cancelled one currency and started another.

golden handcuff A substantial financial incentive that is given to top corporate managers or bank and brokerage managers that encourages them to remain with their firm. Golden handcuffs are used to cut down on employees jumping from one firm to another in order to make more money.

golden handshake An early retirement incentive program that provides the member with additional age and/or service credits. This enables the member to receive a higher pension allowance earlier than would otherwise be possible.

golden parachute A large payment that is made to top corporate executives in the event that the executive's job is somehow eliminated, perhaps because the company is taken over. The payment may include cash, stock options, or a bonus.

gold-fixing An international benchmark for pricing that is published every business day in London at 10:30 a.m. and 3 p.m. There are four members of the gold fixing committee, all of whom also are market makers on the London Bullion Market Association. The committee meets at NM Rothschild & Sons Ltd., the offices of the fixing chairman. The other three members are Bank of Nova ScotiaScotiaMocatta, Deutsche Bank AG, and HSBC Bank. The purpose behind the gold fixing is to give market participants a single price that can be used to transact business. Many other financial instruments are priced from the fixing, including options and cash-settled swaps. During the price-fixing process, the price of gold fluctuates and orders can be changed until both the buyers' and sellers' orders are satisfied and the price is set or "fixed." The gold fixing began in 1919.

Goldilocks economy A term coined during the mid-1990s, when the economy was neither growing too quickly nor too slowly. Many give credit to the U.S. Federal Reserve for producing a monetary policy that encouraged growth but kept inflation in check.

good delivery Approved brands or types of commodities that are acceptable for delivery to fulfill a futures contract. Often used to refer to metals contracts.

good faith deposit Money that a buyer deposits with a seller, or deposits with a third party, as a guarantee that a contract or sales agreement will be completed. If the buyer backs out of the contract, the deposit may be kept by the seller.

good until cancelled (GTC) An order to buy or sell a stock, future, or other financial instrument that remains valid until it is cancelled. Also called *open order.*

good until executed (GTX) An order to buy or sell a stock, future, or other financial instrument that remains in effect until it is executed.

goodwill An intangible asset above and beyond the concrete value of a business or asset. For example, the value of a business's good name and customer relationships. Goodwill is listed as an asset on a company's balance sheet and must be amortized over its reasonable life, which can't exceed 40 years. If a large corporation purchased a small business for $25 million, but its actual value is determined to be $35 million, goodwill is valued at $10 million.

Gordy Jr., Berry The creator of the Motown Record Corporation. This innovative music label produced hits from black artists such as Diana Ross and the Supremes, The Temptations, Smokey Robinson and the Miracles, and the Four Tops. Gordy started the studio with $700 he borrowed from his family.

Gould, Jay A 19th-century stock speculator and entrepreneur who attempted to corner the gold market, owned half of the railroad tracks in the southwestern United States, and was involved in the Western Union Telegraph Company, the New York City elevated railways, and publications such as the *New York World.*

gourde The currency unit of Haiti, comprised of 100 centimes.

Government National Mortgage Association (GNMA) Pass-Through Certificates These are debt securities that are collateralized by residential mortgage debt whose payment of interest and principal is guaranteed by GNMA, which is commonly called *Ginnie Mae.*

government paper Debt that is issued by the U.S. Treasury Department or guaranteed by it.

Government Securities Clearing Corp. (GSCC) A nonprofit organization that provides trading and settlement services for government securities, such as U.S. Treasury bonds and bills and municipal bonds. It brings operational and risk management benefits to the government securities market by providing automated trade comparison and settlement services for U.S. government securities. The GSCC is registered with and regulated by the Securities and Exchange Commission. It was established in September 1986 by the National Securities Clearing Corp. as a wholly-owned subsidiary, capitalized with $1 million. It was incorporated in November 1986 under New York law.

grace period

1. A time period between when a cost is incurred and when a payment is due. Grace periods often are associated with credit cards that don't start charging interest on new purchases until 25 days after the item has been charged.

2. A time period in which insurance won't be cancelled if a payment isn't received.

graduated call writing An options strategy that involves writing, or selling, call options at progressively higher exercise prices. As the price of the underlying stock rises and the options are exercised, the writer earns a higher average *premium,* or income, from writing the option. This occurs because premiums typically rise as the underlying stock rises.

Graham and Dodd Benjamin Graham and David Dodd are the authors of a very prominent book published in 1940, *Security Analysis.* The book explains their fundamental approach to investment and laid the groundwork for modern security analysis. They recommend a growth-oriented investment strategy, which is characterized by purchasing the stocks of undervalued assets because the market eventually will recognize their value. The book advocates finding stocks with low price-earnings ratios.

grain stocks report A quarterly report that details grain exports and how much grain has been used in production. It details production for food processing, feeding livestock, creating ethanol, or deriving products such as oils.

Gramm-Leach-Bliley Act Legislation that broke down the long-time prohibition against one bank offering commercial loans and providing investment banking services. The act allows one bank within a holding company structure to own an insurance company, sell securities to the public, and provide loans to companies. It repeals the 66-year old Glass-Steagall Act, which prevented banks, securities firms, and insurance companies from being affiliated. However, non-financial companies are prevented from owning banks.

grandfather clause A provision that allows a practice or procedure to continue, even though it is now prohibited. For example, if new energy legislation is passed that mandates power plants meet certain emissions standards, existing plants may be excused from these standards by means of a grandfather clause.

graveyard market A bear market where investors don't want to sell because they would incur substantial losses. Potential buyers are also on the sidelines, because they want to keep their funds in cash or cash-equivalent securities.

gray knight A potential acquirer who outbids a white knight in an unfriendly takeover attempt. A *white knight* is a person who is asked to acquire a company as an alternative to an unwanted *black knight,* who is the investor initiating a hostile takeover bid. The new bidder, the gray knight, is not as preferable as the white knight, however the gray knight is still a better option than the black knight.

gray market

1. The sale of stocks or bonds by a bank that isn't a member of the underwriting syndicate. If sales in the gray market are strong, it is a good indicator of strong demand for the new stock or bond issue.

2. The sale of products by distributors that haven't been authorized by the manufacturer. Often these goods are sold at discounted prices. However, if there is any problem with the product, the manufacturer may refuse to honor its warranty.

Great Depression A period that began with the stock market crash in October 1929 that turned into a worldwide economic collapse. Real gross national product in the U.S. declined from October 1929 until March 1933 by 24 percent. A large number of banks and businesses failed, which added to the malaise. International trade also declined sharply as countries passed trade protectionist legislation. When recovery began, it failed to make up the earlier losses and the effects of the depression continued until World War II began in 1939. During the 1929 to 1933 period, unemployment was above 20 percent.

greater fool theory The theory that a questionable stock purchase or investment can be sold at a later date. The person was a fool to make the purchase, but the purchase can be sold to a greater fool.

green coffee warehouse stocks A monthly report published by the Green Coffee Association Inc. that lists all the coffee held in 11 warehouses in the United States, with New York, New Orleans, and Miami among the largest warehouses. The data is collected from warehouses in the ports. The report is closely watched by coffee traders.

green shoe An offering in which the company issuing securities agrees to issue an additional 10 percent or 15 percent of an offering to their underwriters in order to accommodate strong demand. The lead underwriter will distribute the shares to the members of the underwriting group in proportion with their orders at the issuing price. Also called *overallotment option*.

In order for an underwriter to actually sell the intended number of shares of common stock in an offering, it may have to make commitments to sell a larger number of shares. For example, if there are 100,000 shares to be sold, commitments will be made for 110,000 shares. Brokers often overcommit because a certain number of potential purchasers will likely change their mind when the shares are actually offered. To cover themselves in those cases where purchasers commit for more than the 100,000 shares, the underwriter arranges with the company to purchase additional shares. A 15 percent maximum overallotment option is the standard set by the National Association of Securities Dealers.

The name is derived from the first offering containing an overallotment option, underwritten by Paine, Webber, Jackson & Curtis for the Green Shoe Manufacturing Company in October 1960. Very few offerings are done without an overallotment option.

greenback A nickname for the U.S. dollar that often is used in foreign exchange commentary.

greenmail A payment made to the potential acquirer of a company in a hostile takeover attempt. The company agrees to buy the potential acquirer's shares at a premium if the acquirer agrees to stop the takeover attempt and not undertake any more for a certain period of time. This process is also called a targeted stock repurchase payment; critics of it say it is little more than a bribe, hence the term *greenmail*.

Greenspan, Alan The chairman of the Federal Reserve Board of Governors since 1987, when he was appointed by President Ronald Reagan to succeed Paul Volcker. Greenspan was a private economic consultant from 1954 until 1987, excluding a 3-year period when he was Gerald Ford's chairman of the President's Council of

Economic Advisors. He chaired a bipartisan National Commission on Social Security Reform from 1981 until 1983.

Greenwich Mean Time (GMT) A time consistent with London's time zone. Typically, GMT is referenced in stories about stock, bond, or foreign exchange trading activity in order to avoid confusion about when events occurred.

gross The total amount of something before various factors deduct from the total. For example, *gross revenue, gross sales,* and *gross income.*

gross adds The total number of new subscribers added by a company. Gross adds aren't adjusted to include the number of customers that cancelled service. Typically gross add numbers are used in the telecom industry, however, they may be used in other industries and contexts as well.

gross domestic product (GDP) The total production and consumption of goods and services in a country. GDP measures production by totaling the labor, capital, and tax costs of producing the output. To calculate consumption, GDP adds up expenditures by households, businesses, government, and net foreign purchases. GDP is a closely watched economic indicator that provides a wide and encompassing picture of economic activity. In the United States, the Department of Commerce assembles GDP data in its Bureau of Economic Analysis. The report is produced one month after the quarter's end and then is updated a month later followed by another update a month later.

GDP is closely watched because it is a very comprehensive measure of economic activity. It also measures inventories, which is an important indicator of economic activity. If inventories are growing strongly, then that suggests a slowing economy because products are sitting on the shelf and not being sold. However, GDP is problematic because the date is not as timely as monthly or weekly indicators. There also is not regional breakout for GDP.

The data also includes the GDP price deflator, which is used to convert output measured at current prices into constant-dollar GDP. This data is used to define business cycle peaks and troughs. Total GDP growth of between 2.0 percent and 2.5 percent is generally considered to be optimal when the economy is at full employment (unemployment between 5.5 percent and 6.0 percent). Higher growth than this leads to accelerating inflation, while lower growth indicates a weak economy.

gross estate The total value of a deceased person's cash, assets, and properties before liabilities, such as debts, taxes, and funeral expenses, are subtracted. The beneficiaries receive the remainder of the estate, which is split according to the deceased person's instructions.

gross lease A property lease in which the landlord pays all of the expenses associated with owning property, or all of the expenses up to a certain amount. These expenses typically include insurance, taxes, repairs, and utility expenses. A gross lease is commonly used with short-term leases.

gross margin Gross income divided by net sales, expressed as a percentage. Gross margins reveal how much a company earns, taking into consideration the costs that it incurs for producing its products and services. Gross margin is a good indication of how profitable a company is at the most fundamental level. A company with a gross margin of 35 percent is more profitable than a company with a gross margin of 20 percent, at least when analyzing that particular measure of profitability. Companies with higher gross margins have more money to spend on other business operations or to pay dividends.

gross national product (GNP) Gross domestic product (the total market value of all final goods and services produced within a country), plus the income earned by domestic residents from investments made in other companies, minus the income earned by foreigners in the domestic economy. GNP is not a closely followed statistic in the financial markets.

gross profit margin A frequently used financial ratio that is one indicator of a company's financial health. Companies often refer to the fact that their gross margins are improving, which means that the expenses involved in selling their goods are decreasing, thereby leading to increased profits. *Gross profit* is sales, or revenues, minus the cost of goods sold. That number is divided by sales to get the gross profit margin, which is expressed in percentage terms.

ground floor The beginning or first stage of a new company. This phrase is used to describe an investment opportunity that is potentially lucrative because the investor can get in at the beginning, therefore sharing in maximum price appreciation.

group depreciation A depreciation method in which a company calculates one depreciation amount for each group of assets, such as a fleet of company cars, instead of calculating individual schedules for each asset. Large companies can save a significant amount of effort and record keeping by doing group depreciation of their assets such as office equipment, cars, and trucks. Accounting regulations require that companies depreciate the value of their large assets each year. Group depreciation commonly is used by large businesses, with more than half using this depreciation method.

Group of 24 (G-24) A chapter of the Group of 77 that was established in 1971 to coordinate the positions of developing countries on international monetary and development finance issues. The official name for the group is the *Intergovernmental Group of 24 on International Monetary and Development Affairs.* The G-24 also has been involved in negotiations on international monetary matters and has worked to make certain that the interests of the developing nations are represented. The G-24 meets twice a year and its membership is limited to just 24 countries; however any country that belongs to the G-77 can join the discussions. See also *Group of 77.*

The members of the G-24 are: Algeria, Argentina, Brazil, Columbia, Côte D'Ivoire, Democratic Republic of Congo, Egypt, Ethiopia, Gabon, Ghana, Guatemala, India, Islamic Republic of Iran, Lebanon, Mexico, Nigeria, Pakistan, Peru, Philippines, South Africa, Sri Lanka, Syrian Arab Republic, Trinidad and Tobago, and Venezuela.

Group of 30 (G-30) A private, non-profit, international body that includes senior people from the public and private sectors and academia. The G-30's purpose is to deepen the understanding of international economic and financial issues and to consider the effect of governmental and private sector policy decisions. The members of the group meet twice a year to discuss economic, financial, and policy developments. For instance, in January 2003, the group proposed a plan to reduce risk with cross-border processing of stock and bond trades. As part of that plan, the group recommended harmonizing technical standards and market practices. Banks, corporations, central banks, foundations, and private individuals fund the activities of the G-30.

Group of 77 (G-77) The G-77 was established on June 15, 1964, by the Joint Declaration of the Seventy-Seven Developing Countries that was issued at the end of the first session of the United Nations Conference on Trade and Development (UNCTAD). G-77 was started to promote the economic interests of its members, who are primarily developing countries, and to strengthen their joint negotiating capacity on all major international economic issues addressed by the United Nations. The membership of the G-77 has expanded to 133 member countries, but the original name has been retained because of its historical significance. See also *Group of 24.*

Group of Eight (G-8) A group of major industrial countries that was started in 1994 when Russia joined the Group of Seven (G-7) at the group's 1994 Naples Summit. At that time, and in 1997 at the Denver Summit, Russia participated only in political conversations, not economic ones. However, Russia joined as a full member in 1998 at the Birmingham Summit. The other member countries are the U.S., the U.K., Canada, Japan, France, Germany, and Italy.

Group of Five (G-5) The finance ministers of the U.S., Japan, Germany, France, and the UK. This was the main group that led international economic cooperation during the 1970s and into the late 1980s. Later, Canada and Italy would join the group, which became the G-7.

Group of Four (G-4) The four countries perceived as the world's largest and strongest economies. G-4 is comprised of Canada, Japan, the United Kingdom, and United States. The term G-4 isn't frequently used; when it is used it is often in the context of foreign exchange trading or in relationship to the International Monetary Fund.

Group of Seven (G-7) Major industrial countries that share common economic and political interests. The members are the U.S., the U.K., Canada, Japan, France, Germany, and Italy. Typically, the head of the G-7 countries meet once a year in a ministerial meeting that is hosted by each country once every seven years. Finance and foreign ministers also attend their own annual meeting. Russia joined the group in 1998, and the group is now called the Group of Eight (G-8).

Group of Ten (G-10) Major industrial countries that have banded together because they share joint interests in economic and political issues. Specifically, the countries in the G-10 have agreed to participate in the International Monetary Fund's General Arrangements to Borrow, which was established in 1962 when the governments of 10 IMF members agreed to make money available to the IMF to loan out to member countries, or, in some cases, non-member countries, at market-interest rates during times of crisis. The IMF Executive Board renewed GAB in November, 2002 for a period of five years,

beginning December, 2003. Members of G-10 include Belgium, Canada, France, Italy, Japan, the Netherlands, the U.K. and the U.S. The central banks of Germany and Sweden are also members. Switzerland joined in 1964 when it wasn't a member of the International Monetary Fund, which administers the group, but the G-10 name remained.

group rotation A shift of funds by investors into sectors that have become favored, such as automobiles, consumer products, or leisure companies. Share prices in those groups rise as investors buy stocks in those sectors on expectations that the current economic conditions favor companies in those sectors. For instance, if the economy is slowing, consumer product stocks likely will benefit because consumers still will have to purchase basic products. However, shares of steel or transportation companies may falter, since consumers don't have to buy their products.

growth company A company that is known for its rapid earnings growth. Typically stocks of these companies don't pay dividends, because management reinvests earnings to fuel growth. *Growth* also refers to a style of investing that seeks out higher risk companies that have strong growth prospects.

growth investing A type of investing style that focuses on purchasing stocks with strong earnings and revenue growth expectations. Because the stocks that are purchased are issued by companies that are attempting to grow their business, dividends are rarely paid. Instead, the companies retain the money to boost their growth. Sometimes growth companies also may have a lot of risk associated with them, especially in declining markets. Mutual funds call themselves a growth fund if they purchase the stock of growth companies.

growth stock See *growth company*.

Grubman, Jack A former telecommunications analyst for Citigroup/Salomon Smith Barney who was one of the superstar analysts during the stock market boom in the late 1990s, which was in part led by telecom. After the market crashed, however, federal investigators began focusing on how investment-banking revenues influenced his investment recommendations.

GSM See *Global System for Mobile Communication.*

guarani The currency unit of Paraguay, comprised of 100 centimos.

guarantee A legal responsibility to pay a bill or fulfill a contract in the event that the company or person who has promised to make the payment defaults. If the guarantor is a corporation, the guarantee is a contingent liability that isn't recognized on the company's balance sheet until it appears that it will become an actual liability.

guarantee of signature A document that is issued by a bank or brokerage firm that attests to the authenticity of a person's signature. A guarantee of signature is needed in order to process certain transactions, such as transferring stocks or bonds from one person to another.

guaranteed bond A bond that is issued by a subsidiary but guaranteed by the parent company. Guaranteed bonds, which are most common in the U.K., are usually issued by financial institutions and mature in one to ten years. The investment is based on an individual purchasing a policy whose value is linked to the performance of one or more of the world's stock markets. Guaranteed bonds provide a fixed income or a predetermined amount of growth for the set period of the bond.

guaranteed insurability A type of life insurance policy where the insurance company is required to renew the policy for a specified amount of time regardless of changes in the person's health. Also called *guaranteed renewable* or *convertible term insurance.*

guaranteed introducing broker A broker who matches up traders with brokerage firms that will execute the orders. A guaranteed introducing broker doesn't take any payment, but his or her operations are guaranteed by the futures commission merchant (FCM), which does accept money from clients and executes trades. A guaranteed introducing broker has no minimum capital or financial reporting requirements. All of the accounts of a guaranteed introducing broker must be carried by the guaranteeing FCM.

guaranteed investment contract A debt instrument such as a note that is issued by an insurance company, usually in a large denomination, which is often bought for retirement plans. The investor pays money upfront and then the principal and interest rate payments are guaranteed.

guaranteed investment contract (GIC) An investment product issued by an insurance company. The investor pays the issuer and in turn receives regular interest payments. The terms of a GIC vary significantly. Some offer a high initial return guarantee, which imposes some restrictions on the investor's ability to withdraw funds. Similar contracts offered by banks are called *bank investment contracts* or *bank deposit agreements.*

guaranteed renewable insurance policy An insurance policy that is guaranteed to be available for renewal for the time period that is specified in the policy. Changes in the health of the insured can't prevent the policy from being renewed, as long as premiums are paid on time. The only change the insurance company is allowed to make is the premium, as long as it is changed for all policyholders. Also called *guaranteed insurability.*

guaranteed replacement cost insurance A homeowner's or renter's insurance policy that promises to pay for the full replacement cost of damaged or stolen property. It contrasts with a cash-value policy that accounts for depreciation before paying for stolen or damaged items.

guaranty A contract whereby one person or corporation becomes liable to perform a specific act or duty for another person or corporation if that person or corporation doesn't fulfill a responsibility. The responsibility usually is financial. For example, a corporation may guarantee that its subsidiary will fulfill the terms of a contract that the subsidiary signs with one of its customers.

guardian   A person legally entrusted with the care of another person, usually a minor, and who manages that person's financial affairs.

guidance   Information provided by company officials about the company's outlook for future sales, earnings, and product expectations. Guidance can be positive or negative, and is watched very closely by analysts and investors because it is often a strong indicator of that company's future performance.

guilder   The currency unit of the Netherlands, comprised of 100 cents, and Suriname.

gunslinger   A portfolio manager with an extremely aggressive investing style who chooses risk stocks and investments in the hopes of obtaining a high return.

Gyohten, Toyoo   A former Japanese finance ministry official who is well-known for working on foreign exchange and other financial issues during Paul Volcker's tenure as chairman of the Board of Governors of the Federal Reserve System, from 1979 to 1987. Gyohten and Volcker co-authored "Changing Fortunes: The World's Money and the Threat to American Leadership," which was published in 1992. Gyohten spent his career at the Japanese Finance Ministry where he was vice minister for international affairs. He retired in 1989. He was educated in the U.S.

H

hacker Someone who illegally gains access to a computer system or Internet site. Hackers can damage computer systems or Internet sites and cause users to experience delays.

haircut Formulas that reduce the value of any given security based on its class, market risk, or maturity date. Haircuts come into play when the borrowers become unable to make payments or repay the loan or when companies value the securities they hold.

half-life The point at which half of the principal has been repaid in a mortgage-backed security. A typical time assumed for half-life is 12 years. If interest rates fall, that time decreases because more homeowners will refinance their mortgages, which will have the effect of paying off the principal more quickly than normal. If interest rates rise and refinancing slows, then the inverse is true.

hallmark A stamped impression on a bar of precious metal that lists the serial number, producer, weight, and purity of metal content.

handle The largest number in a price or index value. For instance, if the S&P 500 is at 860, traders talk about the "8" handle. If a foreign exchange dealer quotes a price for dollar/yen as 85/95, the dealer means he or she would sell it at 120.85 and buy it at 120.95. The handle of 120 would be left out. Handle is a form of short-hand that traders use to save time; in the examples above, suppose that it is general knowledge that the S&P 500 is 800-something or that dollar-yen is 120-something. Communicating those two pieces of information would waste time in a quick trading conversation.

hands-off investor An investor who contributes capital to a business but stays out of the daily management. Typically, hands-off management occurs in a business that is going well. If the venture begins to lose money, then a hands-off investor may become a hands-on investor. Also called *silent partner.*

hands-on investor An investor who has contributed capital to a business and who is involved in the daily management.

Hang Seng Index A capitalization-weighted index of 33 companies representing about 70 percent of the market capitalization of the Hong Kong Stock Exchange. The index has 4 subindices: Commerce and Industry, Finance, Utilities, and Properties. The index began on July 31, 1964 with a base of 100.

hard currency A currency that people have a great deal of confidence in, such as the U.S. dollar and the Swiss franc. In contrast, currencies of countries with unstable governments or weak economies are *weak.* Gold coins or other forms of gold are another form of hard currency.

HARM Jargon used to refer to a group of boutique investment banks that were dominant in technology underwriting during the 1980s and 1990s, before many larger banks, such as Goldman Sachs and Morgan Stanley, began to actively seek business in the market. The HARM group was Hambrecht & Quist Inc., Alex.Brown & Sons Inc., Robertson Stephens, and Montgomery Securities Inc. All of the four have since been sold to commercial banks, with Robertson Stephens being shut down in July 2002.

Hart-Scott-Rodino Act Federal antitrust legislation that requires an automatic review of planned merger agreements if the size of the deal is over $50 million. That size will adjust beginning in fiscal 2005 (October 2004) to reflect changes in the gross national product from the previous year. The act was passed in 1976 and gives power to both the Federal Trade Commission (FTC) and the Department of Justice (DOJ) to review merger agreements in order to prevent potential anti-competitive harm to individuals and businesses.

Hayami, Masaru   A former Governor of the Bank of Japan who retired in the spring of 2003. Hayami held a variety of senior management positions with the Nisssho Iwai Corp. He also has been chairman of Keizai Dayukai, the Japan Association of Corporate Executives, from 1991.

head of household   A tax filing status allowed by the Internal Revenue Service to people who provide over 50 percent of the financial support for their household. Heads of households must have dependent children, grandchildren, parents, or other relatives living at home who they support. They can be single or married. The designation modestly reduces the amount that the taxpayer has to pay by extending the income range so that more income fits into the lower tax bracket.

head-and-shoulder bottom   A pattern in technical analysis that shows an even level of prices followed by either an upward or downward level of prices that soon returns to the original level. The pattern takes its name from the fact that the charted prices look like the head and shoulders of a person either upright or inverted.

Health Maintenance Organization (HMO)   An insurance company that provides a range of services and coverage for a flat monthly fee with no deductible. The HMO network requires that patients use only doctors in the HMO network. If patients use out-of-network doctors, the patient has to shoulder a greater proportion of the expense. Visits to specialists or hospitals have to be approved in advance by either the HMO staff or the insured's primary care physician.

heating degree day   A measurement commonly used in the energy market to determine how warm the weather is for a specific region. One heating degree day is accumulated for each degree that the average temperature for a day falls below 65 degrees Fahrenheit. For example, if the average temperature for the day was 60, that would count as 5 heating degree days (5 degrees multiplied by 1 day).

heating oil   A product of crude oil that is used to heat homes and businesses, particularly in the northeast United States. Heating oil, also known as No. 2 fuel oil, accounts for about 25 percent of the yield of a barrel of crude oil, second only to gasoline. Heating oil futures and options are traded on the New York Mercantile Exchange and are based on delivery to New York harbor. Trading also occurs on other exchanges throughout the world.

heavy crude   A grade of crude oil. Heavy crude oil is challenging to produce because its low gravity level and high viscosity restrict its ability to flow. Technically speaking, heavy crude oil contains a large number of heavy hydrocarbon fractions because it has a high specific gravity, a low API gravity, which is lower than 20 degrees, and its viscosity is higher than 1,000 centipoise.

hedge   A position created when a financial contract is purchased in the futures or options market. The purpose of the hedge is designed to protect against price changes in the actual commodity or financial instrument. By selling a futures contract, a producer or trader can protect against potential price declines. Buying a futures contract protects against rising costs. In essence, a hedge works somewhat like insurance.

hedge fund   Private investments, open to large customers and wealthy individuals, that use borrowed funds to invest in the stock, bond, and foreign exchange markets. Hedge funds are exempt from regulation by the Securities and Exchange Commission (SEC) under federal securities laws. Thus, hedge funds are not required to limit the types of financial instruments included in their fund and don't have to disclose information about their holdings beyond what they voluntarily want to disclose. Hedge funds often take 20 percent of the annual return for their profit, with an annual fee of about 2 percent.

hedge ratio   The ratio of the value of futures contracts to the value of the cash commodity whose value the trader is attempting to protect by using a hedge. The ratio is calculated to make certain that there are enough futures contracts to provide financial protection in the event that the price of the cash commodity either rises or falls. Hedge ratios are calculated for options using the option's *delta* (rate of change between the option price and the underlying price of the stock or futures contract). For example, a hedge ratio of 4 (4 options for each futures contract) would be needed if a $1/barrel change in the underlying futures price led to a 25 cent per barrel change in the options premium.

hedger   A trader or commodity producer who places a trade in order to protect against price fluctuations in commodities or financial instruments. A hedger may be someone who owns Treasury bonds and is concerned that prices might decline, for example. He doesn't want to sell the actual bonds, but instead sells Treasury bond futures contracts to hedge his position. If the price of bonds does fall, his profit on the futures contract transaction will cover, or *hedge,* the loss.

heir   A person who receives money or assets from the estate of a person who has died. An heir may receive the property and funds through the direction of a will or, if the deceased hasn't left other instructions, by legal statute as the family member who is lawfully eligible to receive the estate's proceeds.

Herfindahl-Hirschman Index (HHI) A mathematical calculation that uses market-share figures to determine whether a proposed merger will be challenged by the government. The HHI is calculated by squaring the market share of each merging firm competing in the market and then adding the results. For example, if four merging firms have market shares of 30 percent, 30 percent, 20 percent, and 20 percent, the HHI is 2,600 ($30^2 + 30^2 + 20^2 + 20^2 = 2,600$). The HHI takes into account the relative size and distribution of the firms in a market and approaches zero when a market consists of a large number of

firms, all of which are relatively small. The HHI increases when the number of firms in the market decreases and as the disparity in size between firms increases in a specific market.

If the HHI is between 1,000 and 1,800 points, the market is moderately concentrated. If the HHI is over 1,800 points, the market is called concentrated. Transactions that increase the HHI by more than 100 points in concentrated markets presumptively raise antitrust concerns under the Horizontal Merger Guidelines issued by the U.S. Department of Justice and the Federal Trade Commission.

Herstatt risk   The risk that the other party in a transaction may not fulfill the terms of the contract or trade. The term originated and is used in the foreign exchange market. For example, Herstatt risk is the danger that one party in a foreign exchange transaction faces after delivering the currency it sold to the buyer until it receives the currency it bought from the other party. The term comes from an actual situation that occurred in the 1970s when Germany's Herstatt Bank failed to pay what it owed in a forex transaction after the other side had met its obligations. Quicker settlement periods enabled by the improvement of computer systems have helped diminish Herstatt risk. The danger of Herstatt risk is that the failure of one party to fulfill the transaction will cause a ripple effect of other parties defaulting.

Hewlett, William   The founder of computer company Hewlett-Packard, Inc., along with David Packard. See *Packard, David.*

HHI   See *Herfindahl-Hirschman Index.*

HIBOR   See *Hong Kong Interbank Offer Rate.*

hidden load   A sales charge assessed by life insurance companies on life insurance policies. The specific load is not disclosed; instead, the purchaser of the policy is told what amount of the first year's premium will go to build the cash value of the insurance policy. This indirectly shows what sales loads are taken out of the premium payment. Another hidden load that may come as a surprise to investors who don't read the fine print of their prospectus is charges assessed on their mutual funds. One example of a "hidden" load is the 12b-1 fee that is assessed annually as a percentage of the fund's assets. The fee covers marketing and distribution expenses and typically it is under 1%.

high net worth individual A person who has investable assets of $1 million or more. Typically, investment or brokerage firms that cater to this group of people have a private client services division. High-net worth individuals with $5 million or more in assets will be served by a Private Bank.

high-beta A high level of volatility and therefore risk; used to refer to investments. While high-beta investments tend to outperform the market when the market is going up, they also will accelerate their losses when the market moves down. Stocks with a beta above 1 are considered to have a high-beta. See also *beta*.

high-valuation stock A stock that is expensively priced in comparison to stock in other companies in the same industry. Typically, when a stock is referred to as high-valuation, its price-earnings ratio (P/E ratio) is higher than other companies in its industry.

high-yield bond See *junk bond*.

high-yield fund A mutual fund that seeks a high level of income by investing at least two-thirds of its portfolio in lower-rated corporate bonds. Bonds rated Baa or lower by Moody's Investors Service or BBB or lower by Standard & Poor's are considered to have a lower rating.

HIPC Initiative The *Heavily-Indebted Poor Countries Initiative* was adopted in 1996 by major industrialized countries to provide a comprehensive approach to helping poor countries with their debt burdens with a goal of getting the debt to sustainable levels. By granting debt relief, the HIPC Initiative hoped to reduce the constraints on economic growth, reduce poverty, and allow countries to pay future interest payments without needing further debt relief. The HIPC Initiative works with other creditors clubs such as the Paris Club. The HIPC Initiative is led by the World Bank and the International Monetary Fund.

historic rehabilitation tax credit A credit that can be used to offset up to $25,000 of income for owners of residential rental property that provides low-income housing. The credit isn't available for upper income taxpayers.

historical cost An accounting principle that requires that all assets included on a company's balance sheet be based on the original, or acquisition, cost. Items are depreciated as needed.

historical volatility The standard deviation, or variation, of the change in the price of a stock or other investment over a specific time period. It indicates past volatility in the market and doesn't guarantee that there will be future volatility.

HKEx See *Hong Kong Exchange*.

HMO See *Health Maintenance Organization*.

hog-corn ratio A ratio that is used to express the relationship of feeding costs and the dollar value of livestock. The ratio is measured by dividing the price of hogs (as calculated by the dollar per hundredweight) by the price of corn, which is calculated by the dollar per bushel. When corn prices are high in relation to pork prices, fewer units of corn equal the dollar value of 100 pounds of pork. Conversely, when corn prices are low in relation to pork prices, more units of corn are required to equal the value of 100 pounds of pork. Because corn is a major cost for hog producers, higher pork prices and lower corn prices signify more profits in feeding hogs.

hogs and pigs report A monthly and quarterly report produced by the U.S. Department of Agriculture that outlines hog production and gives insight into the supply-and-demand factors affecting the hog market. The quarter-end reports are published in March, June, September, and December and are more closely watched than the monthly reports.

The three most important measures of the hogs and pigs report are: *hogs and pigs,* which shows how many pigs are in the market compared to last year, in percentage terms; *hogs and pigs kept for breeding,* which is how many animals producers are going to hold on to; and *hogs and pigs kept for marketing,* which outlines how many animals are going to slaughter.

holding company   A corporation that owns a sufficient amount of another company's stock to influence its board of directors and control its management and policies. A holding company may own companies in its industry or in non–related industries. The holding company must own 80 percent or more of the subsidiary's voting stock in order to gain tax benefits such as tax-free dividends from the company that it holds.

holding company depositary receipts (HOLDRs)   A security developed by Merrill Lynch that represents an exchanged-traded fund (ETF). By purchasing HOLDRs, investors become owners in the common stock or American Depositary Receipts of companies in a particular industry or sector. For instance, investors can purchase Telecom HOLDRs, Semiconductor HOLDRs, or Oil Services HOLDRs. These trade on the New York Stock Exchange and the American Stock Exchange. HOLDRs were developed to let an investor own a moderately diversified group of stocks by purchasing a single investment that is transparent and liquid. The purchase is economical because one sales commission is paid, in contrast with multiple commissions that would be owed on the purchase of individual shares.

holding period   The length of time that an asset or investment is likely to be held. For instance, in order to lessen capital gains taxes, the asset or investment must be held for 12 months or longer.

HOLDRs   See *holding company depositary receipts.*

home equity credit line   Credit that is offered to homeowners by banks based on the amount of equity that they have in their house, condo, or coop apartment. A fee may be charged for setting up the credit line. If the credit line is used, interest is charged for the period that the money is outstanding. The homeowner may access a small portion of the credit line or the entire amount. Because funds accessed through a home equity credit line are essentially a home loan, the homeowner can deduct interest paid from income taxes on Schedule A.

home sale gain exclusion   The ability to exclude up to $250,000 of gain from the sale of an owner-occupied house for a single tax filer and up to $500,000 of gain for married joint filers. Those claiming the exclusion must have lived in the house for two of the last five years. A person or married couple can only use the exclusion once.

homeowner's insurance   Insurance that protects the homeowner from financial loss due to damage to the insured property in the event of bad weather, such as a hail storm or tornado, or damage or loss of the contents of the house in case of fire or theft.

Hong Kong Exchange (HKEx)   The holding company of The Stock Exchange of Hong Kong Limited, Hong Kong Futures Exchange Limited, and the Hong Kong Securities Clearing Company Limited. The stock exchange trades securities including equities, debts, unit trusts, exchange-traded funds, and warrants. HKEx went public in June 2000, when the securities and futures market were integrated. Its lead index is the Hang Seng Index.

Hong Kong Interbank Offer Rate (HIBOR)   The rate of interest offered on Hong Kong dollar loans by banks in the interbank market for a specified period ranging from overnight to one year. HIBOR is a benchmark for interest rates and debt issues in the Far East.

Hope Scholarship A tax credit that covers 100 percent of the first $1,000 and 50 percent of the next $1,000 of tuition and fees paid for the first two years of post-secondary education. Another credit, the Lifetime credit, allows a credit for 20 percent on the first $5,000 of tuition and fees, with a limit of $10,000 in 2003. The credits begin to be phased out for single filers with an adjusted gross income of $41,000 and married joint filers at $82,000.

horizontal agreement An agreement among competitors to cooperate among themselves to provide goods or services to their customers. Horizontal agreements can trigger antitrust violations because competitors may be making agreements that restrict competition.

horizontal spread A trading strategy in the options market that involves the purchase of a call or put option and the simultaneous sale of the same type of option with the same strike price and a different expiration month. Option spreads allow investors to speculate on relative price changes, and thus create another way to make profits, instead of just betting on a direct price change in one investment. Also called *calendar spread*.

hostile takeover A takeover of a corporation that is launched without the approval or agreement of the target corporation. A takeover doesn't technically become hostile until the potential acquirer formally bypasses the board of directors and takes its offer directly to shareholders in a proxy contest. Even though a takeover is hostile, if the price being paid is high enough, the board may feel compelled to recommend the deal. However, management can mount various tactics to repel an unwanted takeover such as greenmail, finding a white knight, or a poison pill. See also *greenmail, white knight, poison pill*.

hot money Money that runs from one sector or investment to another very quickly. Hot money may be hedge funds attempting to take advantage of a trend.

Hot money also may be funds that flow into another country and will just as quickly flow out if the fundamentals seem to be changing even slightly.

hot stock A stock that is in high demand, either because of its performance or because it is in a sector whose popularity has soared. During the stock market boom of the late 1990s, technology and telecom stocks were frequently called hot stocks. The term often was applied to shares of an initial public offering that were in high demand and quickly ran up in price after they were issued.

house poor An informal term that indicates that an individual or family has little spare cash because a large percentage of income is going to pay a mortgage.

housing starts Widely-watched economic statistics that measures the number of new houses and apartments that are being built. The statistics are released monthly by the Commerce Department. The data splits out construction on both homes and apartments. It also is broken out into regions such as the Northeast, West, Midwest, and South. The data is seasonally adjusted. In 2002, construction began on 1.7 million new homes and apartments, compared with 1.6 million in 2001. The 2002 numbers were the best showing since 1.81 million homes and apartments were built in 1986.

hryvnia The currency unit of Ukraine, comprised of 100 kopiykas.

HUBZone Program The *HUBZone Empowerment Contracting Program* is a governmental program designed to stimulate economic development and create jobs in depressed urban and rural communities by giving small businesses incentives to hire employees who live in a HUBZone. The Small Business Administration regulates and manages the program. In return for hiring people in that area, small businesses are given priority treatment when federal agencies contract with vendors.

human capital A term often used by banks and corporations to describe the knowledge and skills their employees possess.

humped yield curve A yield curve in which the yields on intermediate-term issues are above the yields on short-term issues, and the rates on long-term issues decline to levels below those for the short-term issues before leveling out.

Humphrey-Hawkins Act Also known as the Full Employment and Balanced Growth Act of 1978. Legislation that required the Federal Reserve to set one-year target ranges for money supply growth and to report those targets twice a year to Congress. The legislation also required the chairman of the Federal Reserve to speak to Congress on the state of the economy twice a year in what was called the Humphrey-Hawkins report. That legislation expired in 2000 and the Fed said it would no longer set money supply growth targets. Indeed, the use of money supply growth targets had ceased through much of the 1990s. Even though the Federal Reserve chairman is no longer required to address Congress, that practice has continued; he typically goes before Congress in January or February and July.

hurdle rate

1. The minimum rate of return that would justify a capital investment.

2. The minimum return that an investment manager must earn before he or she can earn a performance-based fee.

hybrid annuity An annuity that lets the purchaser mix the characteristics of fixed and variable annuities. Part of the assets may be invested in a fixed annuity and the remainder invested in a variable annuity.

hybrid debt A combination of a debt instrument and either an equity instrument,

option, or swap agreement or a currency or commodity forward agreement. Hybrid debt is a variation of a hybrid security. See also *hybrid security.*

Hybrid REIT A Real Estate Investment Trust that combines the strategies of both equity REITs and mortgage REITs by purchasing properties and making loans to real estate owners and operators. See also *Real Estate Investment Trusts.*

hybrid security A financial security that has two or more characteristics of other financial instruments such as equities, bonds, swaps, forward agreements, futures, or options. The return often is based on the return of two or more underlying instruments such as exchange rates, interest rates, or equities. Also called a *structured financial transaction.*

hyperinflation A significantly high rate of inflation that damages an economy because it restricts people's ability to purchase goods and services. The level at which inflation becomes hyperinflation is arbitrary. Some economists say that the monthly inflation rate must be 50 percent in order to be considered hyperinflation; others say that monthly inflation must be 100 percent or more. Hyperinflation has mostly been a problem in the 20th century, with Germany as a prime example. From August 1922 to November 1923, Germany's monthly inflation rate was 322 percent, which means that prices effectively quadrupled each month during that period.

hypothecation The act of pledging property to another person for collateral without transferring the possession of the title or ownership of the asset. For example, hypothecation occurs when a trader pledges securities as collateral for his or her margin account.

Iacocca, Lee A. A force in the auto industry who is credited with rescuing Chrysler Corp. from the brink of bankruptcy in the late 1970s. Iacocca obtained loan guarantees from the U.S. government and was able to return the company to profitability in the 1980s, after he negotiated concessions from the company's union. Prior to joining Chrysler, he helped launch the Mustang, one of Ford's most popular cars.

Iara In Islamic finance, the capital advance (loan) that is repaid through the profit on rental income. Islam has a set of strict rules that forbid making or receiving interest payments, and this is one way to get the benefits of leasing without charging interest.

IB See *introducing broker.*

IBEX 35 The official index of the Spanish Continuous Market, which is comprised of the 35 most liquid stocks traded on the market. The Sociedad de Bolsas publishes the index. It began with a base level of 3,000 on Dec. 29, 1989.

I-bond An inflation-index bond, issued by the U.S. government, with a value ranging from a minimum of $50 to a maximum of $10,000 and a 30-year maturity. Inflation-indexed bonds were issued beginning in 1998 as a hedge against inflation. I-bond holders have a tax-deferred investment. Bondholders receive a fixed rate of interest and then they receive an extra interest rate payment that is based on the rate of inflation, which is indexed to the inflation rate as calculated by the consumer price index. Also called *TIPS,* which is short for Treasury inflation-protected securities.

IBRD See *International Bank for Reconstruction and Development.*

ICC See *Interstate Commerce Commission.*

ICSID See *International Centre for Settlement of Investment Disputes.*

IEA petroleum reserves Reserves of crude oil that are held by the Paris-based International Energy Agency (IEA), which is an independent agency that is aligned with the Organization for Economic Cooperation and Development, a think-tank and economic development agency for Europe. The stocks of oil remain the property of the European countries that contributed them, along with the United States. The reserves are released during times of supply disruption, such as the Gulf War in 1991. They also can be released at other times.

IFC See *International Finance Corporation.*

IFO Business Climate Index A monthly economic report that is issued in Germany toward the end of the month. The IFO surveys over 7,000 companies in Germany to obtain their opinion of the current business situation and asks them to quantify their response by selecting *good, satisfactory,* or *poor* and provide their expectations for the future business climate using the same criteria. The index measures the changes in business confidence and is an early indicator for economic development in Germany. It shows whether business spending and capital investment is likely to increase or decrease. The indicator is a leading indicator of future business activity, however it asks respondents about *expected* business activities, which may not actually occur.

The index is weighted according to the influence of the company's industry or the sector. The index values start from a base of 100. East Germany and West Germany have separate indexes, though the West German index is used to represent the business outlook for Germany as a whole.

Ijara Wa Iktina An Islamic finance strategy that governs financial and operating leases where the lessee makes rental payments and then purchases the assets on previously agreed to terms when the payments are completed. Islam has a set of strict rules that forbid making or receiving interest payments, and this is one way to get the benefits of leasing without charging interest.

ILEC An *incumbent local exchange carrier* is U.S. telephone company that was providing service when the Telecommunications Act of 1996 was passed. ILECs include the former Bell operating companies, such as Verizon Communications Inc. and SBC Communications Inc. The "local" refers to the central office of a local exchange carrier. Telephone lines from businesses and homes end at a local exchange.

illiquid

1. An investment that can't be quickly converted into cash. Such investments include limited partnerships, real estate, or investment into securities or debt of a company that is thinly traded or which doesn't trade on major exchanges.

2. A company that doesn't have sufficient cash flow to pay its interest charges and expenses.

imbalance of orders In a financial market, either too many sell orders or too many buy orders. An imbalance of orders occurs after a major event, such as a company announcing that earnings will be lower than expected. An imbalance also may occur after an announcement of a takeover or any other major event. The stock market will delay the opening of a stock that has made a major announcement until the imbalance can be worked out. Trading of the particular stock also may be suspended during the trading day.

IMF See *International Monetary Fund.*

impaired capital Capital that is worth less than its stated value in the company's capital stock account. Impaired capital occurs when an investment has declined in value and is now worth less than what it was recorded as being worth on the company's capital stock account on its balance sheet. Also called *deficit net worth.*

impaired credit Credit that has deteriorated. In a corporate setting, this may result in a decrease in the amount of funds that banks are willing to lend the creditor.

Impaired credit also occurs with individuals who are late paying their bills or who have filed for bankruptcy.

implied price volatility An estimate of the expected volatility of the security that an option is based upon, determined by the price, or premium, of the option. Factors affecting implied volatility are the exercise price of the options, the risk-free rate of return, the option's maturity date, and the price of the option. Pricing models, such as the Black-Scholes option pricing model, can be used to solve for implied price volatility.

import To purchase goods or services from a company in another country. If imports exceed exports, then the purchasing country has a trade deficit.

import and export prices report A monthly economic report prepared by the Bureau of Labor Statistics that tracks import and export prices. These price statistics provide important information about the U.S. economy, since imports make up about 15 percent of the goods purchased in the United States. The report also gives an indication about pricing pressures affecting U.S. firms. If import prices are low, U.S. companies have to compete with lower prices, which reduces their profits. The data is useful for economists, but has less effect on the financial markets.

imputed value The value of an asset that hasn't been actually recorded in any accounts, but can be deduced from the end product or result. If historical comparisons are being made, and certain data isn't available, then an imputed value can be estimated. An imputed value might be calculated for cash that is waiting to be invested. There is an imputed value of the opportunity cost that is being incurred because the company is holding onto the money rather than investing it in a project that would return a certain percentage.

in play Refers to a firm that has become an acquisition target by virtue of the fact that another company has mentioned it as potential merger target.

in the tank A favorite term among traders that means that prices have fallen sharply. It may also be shortened to say that the market *tanked*.

Inc. See *incorporated*.

income equity fund A mutual fund that intends to create income by investing primarily in equity securities of companies with good dividends. Capital appreciation is not a goal.

income mixed funds A mutual fund that seeks a high level of current income by investing in a variety of income-producing securities, either fixed-income or equities. Capital appreciation is not a primary objective.

income statement One of the major financial statements produced by a company, it shows the amount of money that is earned, the expenses incurred, and the resulting net income. Corporations produce income statements quarterly as well as annually. Publicly-traded companies meeting minimum size requirements must file their income statement with the Securities and Exchange Commission.

income stock A stock that produces income through the payment of dividends. It contrasts with a *growth stock,* which typically doesn't pay dividends. Instead the would-be dividends of a growth stock are reinvested in the company to help it to grow faster.

income tax An annual federal tax that U.S. citizens, residents, and corporations have to pay on income. Some state and local governments have income taxes as well. Income tax was created in 1913 by the Sixteenth Amendment to the Constitution. The federal tax is *progressive,* meaning that it taxes an increasingly large percentage of personal income as individuals become wealthier.

incorporated A company that has filed incorporation papers with the Secretary of State in one of the 50 states. Incorporation limits the liability of owners' losses up to the amount of their investment. It also relieves individuals of personal liability in the event that the company has been sued, except in certain rare situations when top corporate executives may be judged to have been at fault. Many large U.S. corporations are registered in Delaware, because its state laws are perceived to be most favorable to the companies.

incubator A dynamic process of business development that helps start-up businesses grow and create a stable base for their operations. Incubators provide a variety of services, such as management assistance, financial assistance, and access to other professional and technical services. They also may provide marketing support. Incubators provide entrepreneurial firms with shared office space and equipment, support services, conference rooms, access to equipment, and flexible leases. Incubators also may focus on companies in one industry or in a niche industry. Often they are non-profit.

U.S. business incubators began in the 1970s, although the oldest one began in Batavia, New York in 1959. They were created from three concurrent events, according to the National Business Incubation Association, which was formed in 1985. Incubators came from an attempt to use old, abandoned factory buildings in distressed areas of the Midwest and Northeast by subdividing them for small firms. Incubators also received a boost from an experiment funded by the National Science Foundation to foster entrepreneurship and innovation at universities. Finally, successful entrepreneurs wanted to encourage others and provide support to emerging companies.

The U.S. Small Business Administration also was a strong promoter of incubators, especially from 1984 until 1987. During that time, the number of incubators grew from just over 20 annually to more than 70 by 1987. The agency held a series of regional conferences and published a newsletter and incubator handbooks.

indemnify To agree to compensate for any damage or loss. Insurance contracts may state that the policyholder will be *indemnified,* or restored to his or her original financial position, should a loss occur.

Indemnification agreements also may be signed by one party to protect the other party against claims from the other.

indenture A written agreement between a company and its lender that spells out the terms of the debt issue. The terms include the amount of bonds issued and their type, the interest rate that is paid, a description of the property that is being used as collateral, repayment provisions, and call provisions in the event that a company wants to redeem the bond before it matures. The indenture also lists any financial covenants that the company has to follow, such as maximum debt level ratios or minimum cash flow.

independent bank A locally owned and operated commercial bank. It derives its funds from, and it lends money to, the community where it operates, and it is not affiliated with a multibank holding company. Also called *community bank.*

independent director A member of a company's board of directors who does not otherwise have substantial connections with the company whose board he or she sits on. According to the rules passed by the New York Stock Exchange, an independent director is someone who does not have a "material" relationship with the company, although "material" is not defined. NASDAQ rules specify that in order to be independent, a director can't make any charitable contributions of more than $200,000 or contribute more than 5 percent of a company's gross revenues in situations in which a director also is an officer of the company or charity.

Companies also have created their own guidelines that go beyond those specified by the stock exchanges. For example, General Electric Corp. (GE) defines a material relationship as one in which the transactions between GE and the director's company equal more than 1 percent of the revenues of the director's company. A director also won't be deemed independent if he or she is associated with a charity to which GE contributes more than 1 percent of the charity's annual receipts.

Other common terms for independent director are *outside director* and *non-executive director,* which is commonly used in the United Kingdom.

independent introducing broker An introducing broker who works with many different futures commission merchants to match potential clients up with companies that can process their trades. An independent introducing broker works for himself or herself, as opposed to working exclusively with one company. The independent introducing broker is subject to minimum capital and financial reporting requirements in order to meet the requirements of the futures exchanges and regulatory authorities.

independent research Research on stock and bond investments that is free of investment banking conflicts, because it is offered by firms that are not involved in investment banking. In December 2002, to settle conflict-of-interest accusations, securities regulators reached an agreement with ten of the largest investment banks that called for them to spend $450 million to provide independent research to their customers, in addition to their own research.

index A statistical indicator that measures changes in financial markets or the economy. In the case of economic indicators, the Producer Price Index (PPI) is one example of an index. An index also can be a group of stocks representing a particular segment of the market. Well-known indices are the Dow Jones Industrial Average, the S&P 500 Index, the NASDAQ Composite Index, and the Russell 2000 Index.

index arbitrage The simultaneous purchase of stock index futures and the sale of some or all of the component stocks that make up the particular stock index, or the sale of the index futures and purchase of the stocks. The trading intention is to profit from sufficiently large intermarket spreads between the futures contract and the index itself.

index funds Funds that mimic the performance of a specific index, such as the S&P 500. The holdings of the fund mirror the stocks that make up the particular index. Because the funds don't require managers who pick stocks, the fees are lower than for other types of funds.

Investors in index funds are considered passive investors. Those who manage index funds are often called indexers.

index of manufacturing activity A monthly report produced by the Institute for Supply Management that reports on manufacturing conditions. The index is updated each month and often includes revisions of the previous month's data. For example, in December 2002 the index was at 55.2. A level above 50 indicates that manufacturing activity is expanding, while a level below 50 means that the sector is contracting.

index-linked bond A bond or note whose principal and interest payments are linked to the performance of a stock market or inflation index. Also called *equity index-linked note*.

indication An approximate value that a stock market, stock, or investment is likely to open at when trading resumes after a trading delay caused by extreme volatility or news that is imminent. Indications also are given for expectations about where a market is likely to open for its regular trading session based on what trading has done overnight in Asia and in Europe.

indirect labor costs Costs that are not charged to a specific product or project, such as administrative overhead (the human resources and accounts payable departments), cleaning and maintenance crews, or other expenses not directly related to the actual production of a good or service. Often indirect labor costs are found at

headquarters, while an employee on a manufacturing line will have his or her salary charged to the product that is being produced. The salary of the person in the accounting department who processes the paychecks and the human resources person who answers questions for that line worker won't be charged to the product that is being manufactured.

Individual Retirement Account (IRA) A trust or custodial account that is set up in the United States to accumulate funds on a tax-deferred basis to fund retirement. Individuals can contribute up to $3,000 during one year. The Economic Growth and Tax Relief Reconciliation Act of 2001 increases the limits to $5,000 per person by 2008. For people over age 50, additional catch-up contributions are allowed. These rise to $1,000 in 2006.

An IRA account can be set up with a bank, savings and loan, brokerage firm, mutual fund, or other financial institution. IRA funds can't be used to buy life insurance. The assets in the IRA account cannot be combined with other property, unless it is in a common trust fund or common investment fund.

To be able to deduct the contributions to an IRA from income taxes, a married couple can't earn more than $53,000, or $63,000 for a qualified widower. A single person is limited to $33,000 in income or $43,000 for a single individual or head of household. That limit does not apply if the individual and spouse are not covered by a retirement plan at work.

Withdrawals from IRA accounts are prohibited before age 59½, however in emergencies withdrawals can be made but are subject to a 10 percent penalty tax on top of the regularly owed tax, as determined by income. After age 59½, withdrawals can be made and are taxed at the retiree's income tax rate.

industrial production A monthly statistical report, released around the 15th of each month at 9:15 a.m. Eastern Time by the Federal Reserve Board, that measures the production of goods and power for domestic sales in the United States and for export. It excludes production in the agricultural, construction, transportation, communication, trade, finance, and service industries, as well as government output and imports. The industrial production index is developed by weighting each component according to its relative importance in the base period.

This data gives insight into the performance of the economy. *Capacity utilization,* which measures the extent to which U.S. factories are busy producing goods, also is an important indicator. The industrial production data that is released is preliminary and may be revised during the successive three months as new sources of data become available. At the fourth month, the indexes are not revised until the data is revised annually.

industrial revenue bonds   Bonds that are designed to promote economic development. The proceeds from the bond sale are loaned to businesses to pay for buildings or other capital investment projects. The bonds must be paid back by the company; the government gives its name to the bond issue, but not its credit rating. Typically, these bonds are tax exempt. Also called *industrial development bonds.*

inefficient market   A market, such as a stock market, in which investors fail to realize that a stock or other investment is undervalued or overvalued. The *efficient market theory* says that prices reflect all information that is in the market, and that prices are therefore realistic calibrations of the value of a financial instrument. However, there are gaps in the efficient market theory and that creates an opportunity for an inefficient market.

inelasticity of demand   See *elasticity of demand.*

inflation   The rise in prices of goods and services. Inflation is measured by the percentage of price increase. For example, a moderate rate of inflation, approximately 1 to 3 percent, is seen as healthy for an economy. When prices rise more than 3 percent, inflation can produce economic turmoil. People who don't have the ability to increase their income at the same rate as inflation, such as retirees or students, are particularly hurt. If inflation rises to excessively high levels, that is called *hyperinflation.* Inflation is caused by too many dollars chasing too few goods.

inflection point   A dramatic change to a company's business, often caused by the development of a new product. Typically, the term is used in conjunction with a technology company.

infrastructure

1. The physical underpinning of a country that support activities and transportation, such as roads, railways, electrical systems, and so on.

2. In contemporary jargon, the basic abilities and structure of a company.

ingot   A bar of metal, such as gold. Gold is often stored in ingots.

inheritance   The money or property that is received from a deceased person's estate through his or her will.

initial margin   The amount of money up to 50 percent of the purchase price of securities that can be bought on margin, which is a loan from a broker. The Federal Reserve's Regulation T sets rules governing margin. Even though 50 percent can be borrowed, some firms require that more than 50 percent of the purchase price be paid with by the trader before he or she can begin to trade. The investments purchased on margin are used as collateral for the loan. A margin call occurs when the amount of money in a trader's account has decreased below required levels because the prices of his securities have fallen.

initial performance bond   The funds that are required to be deposited as collateral when a futures position or a short option on futures position is opened with a brokerage firm.

initial public offering (IPO) A company's first sale of stock to the general public. Typically, a company hires an underwriter, which is an investment bank that specializes in selling stock to the public, to handle the IPO. The sales process is highly regulated by the Securities and Exchange Commission (SEC), which approves all public stock sales.

Initiative Terrorist Information Awareness A project of the Pentagon to allow it to detect terrorism by electronically monitoring foreigners in the United States. The original plan allowed the Pentagon to investigate U.S. citizens as well, but in February 2003, Congress disallowed that. The data is gathered by looking at a variety of electronic records of tools people use every day, such as e-mail, ATM systems, online shopping purchases, online travel reservations, cell phone networks, credit card usage, and electronic toll-collection systems. To monitor the activity of suspected terrorists, the Pentagon uses software technology to weave data into a form useful for anti-terrorism activities. This includes comparing electronic travel reservations with surveillance camera information at airports, along with credit card and phone calling records. Such information is fed into software that attempts to link activities together. The project is overseen by John M. Poindexter, President Ronald Reagan's former national security advisor. Formerly called *Total Information Awareness.*

injunction A court order that requires a person or company to stop an action that would hurt a plaintiff in a court proceeding. If an injunction is ignored, the violator can be fined or jailed.

inside director A member of a company's board of directors that also is an employee of the company. Also called *executive director.*

inside market The range between the highest price a buyer is willing to pay (bid) and the lowest price a seller is willing to sell (ask), as dictated by NASDAQ market makers for their own inventories. If an order doesn't fall within the inside market range, it is considered outside of the inside market. This is different from a retail market, where price quotes reflect the prices that customers pay dealers.

insider Someone who knows about important information before it becomes public. An insider may be an employee, a company director, someone who works closely with the company, or someone who owns at least 10 percent of the company. Insiders, including their friends and family members, are prohibited from trading on inside information that has not yet been announced to the public.

insider trading Trading by people who have access to material, non-public information that allows them to make a substantial profit by either buying or selling the company's securities (usually stock). Insider trading is strictly prohibited by securities law and violators are subject to large fines and jail time.

insolvency The condition of being unable to pay debts that are due. An insolvent person or company is likely to end up in bankruptcy.

installment refund annuity A refund option offered to the beneficiaries of a person who buys an annuity that allows the beneficiaries to receive a minimum amount of money after the annuitant dies. An installment refund annuity makes installment payments that consist of the difference between the purchase price of the annuity and the total annual benefits received by the annuitant. An installment refund annuity provides some compensation for the annuitant's beneficiaries to account for the fact that had the annuitant lived, he or she would have been entitled to more annuity payments.

Instinet An electronic network that facilitates trading in stocks for its clients, which are large institutions. Because the trading is done electronically, clients can trade stocks at any time. After regular market trading hours end, news reports will often say that a specific stock was "higher on Instinet." Instinet has access to over 40 securities markets throughout the world. It also provides its clients with research conducted by its staff and third party organizations. Instinet is owned by Reuters Plc., which also owns Island ECN, a rival that it acquired on September 20, 2002. Island also owns ProTrader and Lynch, Jones & Ryan, which provide trading-related services.

Institute of Supply Management (ISM) A trade association based in Tempe, Arizona that is best known for its monthly forecast of index of manufacturing activity, the ISM Index, which is widely watched by the financial markets to gauge how the nation's economy is performing. The Institute also produces a less widely known report that tracks non-manufacturing activity. ISM used to be known as the National Association of Purchasing Management (NAPM).

institution A company holding assets for others. Institutions include banks, insurance companies, pension funds, and mutual funds. The term also is used in the trading context to talk about the companies that trade securities in very large volumes.

insurability The circumstances under which an insurance company is willing to insure a person or a company. Each company rates the risks that it is willing to insure and determines the cost of the insurance. The higher the judged risk, the higher the premium, and vice versa for lower risks.

insurance A product that a person or business buys, typically through monthly payments, that provides financial protection against risks. The monthly payments, called *premiums,* are made by a large group, which spreads out the risk for the company issuing the insurance. Losses are paid for from premium revenue that has been invested to earn a return that will cover the insurance company's expenses and produce a profit.

Consumers can buy insurance to protect against financial loss due to health issues, car accidents, damage to a home, and to protect against the negative financial effect of a relative's death, among other things. Businesses can buy insurance to protect their property against damage and theft and to protect themselves against liability.

insurance agent A person who sells insurance policies. There are two main types of insurance agents: A *captive agent* can sell only the insurance policies of the company that employs him or her. An *independent agent* sells the policies of many different companies and attempts to find the best policy for the insurance buyer. An independent agent may also be called an *insurance broker.*

insurance broker See *insurance agent.*

intangible asset An asset (something beneficial to an organization) that is not actual physical property. Examples of intangible assets are patents, trademarks, copyrights, goodwill, and various kinds of permits. Real estate and cash are *tangible assets.*

intellectual property The knowledge of how to develop products or processes. Typically intellectual property is protected by patents, trademarks, or copyrights.

inter vivos trust A revocable trust whose terms become effective while the donor is still alive. The trust becomes the legal owner of a person's property, investments, and assets, in a process called *funding.* Those assets are used for the benefit of another person, called a *beneficiary.* A trustee manages the trust. However, the trust creator, called the *grantor,* does not give up any control over the assets and can still buy or sell them. An inter vivos trust in many ways resembles a will. It includes instructions and details for handling the grantor's estate at death. However, unlike a will, it does not go through probate and prevents the court from controlling the assets of the deceased. Also called *living trust.*

interbank rate An interest rate that is charged by banks to each other. Often interbank rates are cited in financial agreements and contracts between corporations or investors. See also *LIBOR* and *HIBOR*.

intercommodity spread A situation in which a futures contract in one commodities market is purchased and futures contracts are sold in a different, but usually related, market. For example, an intercommodity spread would cause crude oil futures to be purchased and heating oil futures to be sold. Also called *intermarket spread*.

interdelivery spread See *intramarket spread*.

interest

1. A fee that is charged by a lender to a borrower for the right to use the borrowed funds. The funds can be used to purchase a house, a car, or goods that were charged on a credit card, for example. The interest charge typically is expressed as an annual percentage rate.

2. An amount of money that an investor receives for leaving funds on deposit in an interest-bearing account, usually expressed in annual percentage terms.

3. Partial or total ownership in an asset.

interest coverage ratio Income before interest expenses and taxes (EBIT) divided by the amount of interest that a company pays on its debt. The ratio indicates how well the company's earnings are able to cover the company's debt.

interest deduction Interest that is deducted from income taxes. Corporations can deduct their interest expense as a cost of doing business. Individuals can deduct the interest that they pay on their home mortgage, if they live in the house.

interest rate differential The average U.S. interest rate subtracted from the average foreign interest rate. This concept is discussed in the foreign exchange market as one factor that accounts for the difference in relative values between currencies.

interest rate futures Futures contracts based on fixed-income securities such as U.S. Treasury bonds or notes.

interest rate parity A theory that says the differences in values of currencies are directly related to the differences in short-term interest rates of each of the countries.

interest rate risk The risk of losing money because interest rates move up or down. For example, the value of bonds in a portfolio can be reduced if interest rates move higher and the value of the interest rate paid on the bond remains set.

interest rate swap The exchange of cash flows according to a predetermined agreement, usually between two parties. Upon the payment date of the swap, typically only the difference between the two payment amounts is given to the party that is entitled to it, which results in very little cash being spent.

interest-sensitive stock A stock that is particularly sensitive to changes in interest rates. Often interest-sensitive stocks are bank stocks. When interest rates rise, shares of banks may move lower. That occurs because banks are locked into long-term loan contracts with borrowers and can't raise their interest rates up to the market rate, which can pressure earnings. The interest rate they have to pay to deposit holders increases also.

interexchange carrier (IXC) A telecom term that refers to U.S. long distance companies, such as AT&T Corporation, Sprint Corporation, and MCI Corporation. An interexchange carrier is a telephone company that provides connections between local exchanges in different geographic areas. Interexchange carriers provide interLATA service, which is a term used in the U.S. for a geographic area that is covered by one or more local telephone companies, or *local exchange carriers* (LECs).

interim loan A short-term loan that is paid back after a permanent loan is received.

interlocking directorate   Having members of corporations' boards of directors or management serve on each other's boards. This is illegal if the companies are competitors, but if the companies are in separate industries and don't compete with each other, it is legal.

Intermarket Surveillance Information System   A data sharing tool that collects information on equity and options transactions. It allows exchange officials and regulators to monitor the market and protect the investing public. The information is provided online to give surveillance personnel complete and timely data about transactions and to help them spot potential violations.

intermediary   A person who has been given the legal right to work for another person. An intermediary such as an investment banker may help in arranging a deal between two companies that want to merge. An intermediary also may be an investment advisor who determines how to invest funds for his clients.

intermediate term   A time period that falls somewhere between short- and long-term. *Intermediate term* has many different definitions depending on who uses the term. Stock analysts typically are referring to a period ranging from 6 months to 18 months when they use *intermediate term*.

internal audit   The steps a company takes to make certain its financial reports and information are accurate.

internal auditor   The person or department that independently evaluates a company's financial records to make certain that there are no mistakes or deliberate misstatements. The role of the internal auditor was strengthened through the passage of the Sarbanes-Oxley legislation in 2002. The legislation requires the internal auditor to report directly to the board's internal audit committee, which is responsible for the corporation's audit.

internal controls   The means by which a company monitors its accounting systems for conformance with an expected behavior. Before the Sarbanes-Oxley Act of 2002, the term was used mainly in an accounting sense to refer to financial controls that a company established. Now, an extra layer of internal controls has been added with the emphasis on making sure that management is carrying out its internal auditing duties. The Securities and Exchange Commission, which was charged with writing rules to implement the Sarbanes-Oxley Act, requires that companies include an internal control report in their annual reports. The report should outline management's responsibilities for establishing and maintaining internal controls and procedures for financial reporting. A company also has to evaluate how effective the controls are, and the chief executive officer has to certify that the company's internal controls have been followed. The company's outside auditors have to verify management's evaluation in writing.

internal expansion   Expanding a company by creating growth internally as opposed to buying a company or product. Also called *organic growth*.

internal financing   Receiving funds from a company's operating activities, as opposed to borrowing money from a bank or through means such as issuing equity or debt. A company with a strong business and solid sales is able to raise funds internally to fund new projects or initiatives.

internal rate of return (IRR)   The discount rate at which the present value of future cash flows equals the current market price of the investment or opportunity. Also called *dollar-weighted rate of return*.

Internal Revenue Code   The body of laws and regulations that govern the U.S. federal income tax paying process for individuals and corporations.

Internal Revenue Service (IRS) The U.S. government agency that is in charge of collecting federal income tax from individuals, corporations, and estates, as well as excise taxes and other taxes. The IRS is part of the U.S. Treasury Department.

International Accounting Standards Board A professional organization that encourages cooperation in developing accounting principals and has passed more than 30 international standards of accounting. The forerunner of the Board was the International Accounting Standards Committee, which was the focal point for international accounting standards until 2001. The Board works in conjunction with the Financial Accounting Standards Board.

International Bank for Reconstruction and Development (IBRD) An affiliated agency of the World Bank whose mission is to reduce poverty in middle-income and credit-worthy poorer countries by promoting sustainable development. The IBRD does this by making loans, issuing guarantees, and offering analytical and advisory services. IBRD doesn't intend to maximize profit; however, it has earned net income every year since 1948. It was started in 1945. In fiscal 2002, it lent $11.5 billion for 96 new operations in 40 countries.

The IBRD is owned by its 184 member countries, with those contributing the most money having the greatest influence. The United States is the greatest contributor.

International Centre for Settlement of Investment Disputes (ICSID) An organization that works in conjunction with the World Bank to resolve investment disputes between foreign investors and their host countries through arbitration or conciliation.

International Development Association An organization that works in conjunction with the World Bank to help the world's poorest countries reduce poverty by giving them *credits,* which are loans at zero interest that have a 10-year grace period and maturities of 35 to 40 years.

international equity funds Mutual funds that invest at least two-thirds of their portfolios in equity securities of companies that are located outside of the United States.

International Finance Corporation (IFC) An organization affiliated with the World Bank that promotes private sector investment, which may be either foreign or domestic, in developing member countries. The IFC's investment and advisory activities are intended to reduce poverty and improve people's lives in an environmentally and socially responsible manner.

International Fisher Effect A theory that says that differences in interest rates between two countries should be an unbiased estimator of the future change in the cash exchange rate between currencies in the foreign exchange market.

International Monetary Fund (IMF) An international organization whose purpose is to ensure the stability of the international financial system. Specifically, the IMF promotes international monetary cooperation, international trade, and exchange rate stability; the organization also assists member countries that are having trouble paying their debt obligations. The IMF was first proposed in July 1944 at a United Nations conference held at Bretton Woods, N.H. Those at the conference were looking for a way to cooperate economically in order to avoid another Great Depression. The organization came into existence on December 27, 1945, when its articles of agreement were signed. It began financial operations on March 1, 1947.

The IMF is composed of 184 countries. It is managed by an Executive Board consisting of 24 Executive Directors, headquartered in Washington, D.C. Its Executive Board meets as least three times a week in formal sessions. Today, the IMF has three main functions. One is to appraise its members' exchange rate policies, in what is called an Article IV consultation. The IMF surveys its members' economic and exchange rate policies because it believes this will lead to stable exchange rates and a growing world economy. The IMF also provides financial and technical assistance to member countries.

International Petroleum Exchange of London Ltd. (IPE) Europe's leading energy futures and options exchange. It provides a regulated marketplace where over $2 billion in underlying value is traded daily. It is organized as a Recognised Investment Exchange (RIE) under British law. The Financial Services Authority supervises the members of the IPE.

Futures and options for four commodities trade on the IPE: Brent Crude (Oil), Gas Oil, Natural Gas, and Electricity. Trade occurs at the exchange through *open outcry*. Orders from clients are taken over the telephone by brokers and transmitted to the appropriate traders in the pit, who shout out their orders. Hand signals may be used to supplement spoken words but can't replace them.

A group of energy and futures companies founded the IPE in 1980, and it began trading its first contract, Gas Oil futures, in 1981. In June 1988, the IPE successfully launched Brent Crude futures. In 1997, the IPE began trading its first non-oil contract, Natural Gas futures, which are traded electronically. In March 2001, the IPE began trading an Electricity futures contract.

International Swap Dealers Association The trade association for the swaps industry. Swaps are a method of creating financial investments by agreeing to trade different investments at a set time in the future. The trade group attempts to promote standardized practices, terminology, and agreements. Swaps are used across the financial services industry and by corporations to lock in returns or minimize risk.

international trade data A monthly statistic, reported by the U.S. Commerce Department's Bureau of the Census and Bureau of Economic Analysis, that shows the trade balance of the United States. The report is watched closely to detect trends in the balance of payments, including the strength of exports. Exports are closely

watched because they show how competitive U.S. goods are overseas. If the demand for U.S. goods is strong, then that provides a reason for the U.S. dollar to strengthen. The export data in the trade statistics also provide insight into what the export component to gross domestic product will look like. However, trade data is sensitive to short-term shocks because of the cyclical nature of many of the components. For instance, aircraft exports comprise a large part of exports and any delay in shipment, which commonly can happen, will affect the monthly export data.

Internet Bubble The period in the late 1990s that was one of the biggest periods of market euphoria ever seen. Venture capitalists raced to fund Internet companies before their competitors,. When start-up companies had been funded for several years, often no more than three years, venture-capital backers rushed to take them public, with investment bankers fighting for the business. (During normal situations, it would take a start-up company about seven to ten years to develop its business to the point where it was ready to become a public company.)

The Internet boom had its beginning when Netscape Inc. did its initial public offering (IPO) in 1995. The price of Netscape stock soared once trading began. That captured the attention of Wall Street, which previously had not thought of technology companies as a lucrative source of business. As more companies did IPOs, the demand for Internet-company shares shot up and prices spiked. Many people who got in on the ground floor of IPOs became millionaires. The hype soon died down as reality began to seep back into the market and investors began to question whether many of the companies could ever generate earnings that justified their stock prices. The NASDAQ stock market peaked in March 2000, and began its descent into a technology bear market, as well as an overall bear market, which burst the bubble.

Internet Protocol (IP) The method used to break data into small pieces, called *packets,* to send them from one computer to another across the Internet. IP is used to send a single chunk of data (in several packets) across various routes on the Internet to a gateway destination. At this point, a second protocol, called Transmission Control Protocol (TCP), reassembles the packets and completes the data transmission. IP and TCP work so closely together that they are often referred to as a single protocol (TCP/IP), even though they are distinct. Each computer connected to the Internet has a unique IP address.

Interstate Commerce Commission (ICC) A federal agency whose purpose is to protect the public and make sure that the public receives fair and reasonable rates and services from transportation companies. The agency was created in 1887. Many of its regulatory activities were curtailed in the 1970s and 1980s during a period of deregulation.

intervention When a government or central bank buys or sells a currency in the foreign exchange market in order to increase or decrease its relative value to other currencies. Intervention policies vary widely, with some countries, such as Japan, being more active in the foreign exchange market, and others, such as the U.S., being in the foreign exchange market less frequently. Historically, the U.S. actively intervened in the foreign exchange market in order to affect foreign exchange policy, but since approximately 1990, the general approach has been to let market forces determine the direction of currencies. However, if the U.S. believes that one currency is too strong or weak relative to others, it may intervene. Also, sometimes a foreign government will ask the U.S. to help it either strengthen or weaken its currency through intervention.

When the U.S. does decide to intervene, the Department of the Treasury and the Federal Reserve work together. Typically, the Department of the Treasury decides when to intervene, while the intervention is carried out by the foreign exchange desk of the Federal Reserve Bank of New York. Intervention usually is paid for evenly between the Treasury's Exchange Stabilization Fund and the Federal Reserve's System Open Market Account. Such interventions are typically *sterilized,* which means that the expansion or contraction in the monetary supply that resulted from the intervention is offset by the Federal Reserve's domestic monetary actions.

in-the-money An option that has value. Call options, which give the holder the right to buy a security, are in-the-money when the price of the underlying security is above the option's strike price, or price at which the security can be bought. The option allows the holder to buy the security at a cheaper price than is available in the market. Put options, which give the holder the right to sell a security, are in-the-money when the security currently is priced lower in the market. The put option allows the holder to get more money from the sale.

intraday Occurring within the trading day. Typically stock and futures exchanges give the intraday high and low of stock, futures, and options contracts.

intramarket spread A situation in which futures contracts for the same commodity are bought for one month and sold for another month. For example, August heating oil contracts are purchased, and September heating oil contracts are sold. Intramarket spreads are very common. Spread trades on most exchanges qualify for lower commission rates and lower margin requirements. Traders use intramarket spreads to make a profit in the future direction of prices. They also use this to roll over their position from one month to another. Also called *interdelivery spread.*

intrinsic value The value of an option that is in-the-money, or that still has value. If a call option can be used to buy a stock at a *strike price* (the price at which the option allows the stock to be bought) of $50, and the market price is $55, then the intrinsic value is $5.

introducing broker (IB) A person or firm that solicits orders to buy or sell futures contracts or options, but who does not accept money or other assets to pay for those orders. An IB turns the client over to the futures commission merchant who accepts the money and does the transaction. An IB must be registered with the Commodity Futures Trading Commission.

inventory

1. A corporation's stock of goods, such as raw materials, that are used to produce final products.

2. A company's goods that have been produced and are waiting to be sold. Inventory is valued by a company using methods such as first in, first out (FIFO) or last in, last out (LIFO).

inventory financing

1. Financing provided by a bank or finance company that is secured by the inventory of the company receiving the financing. Also called *wholesale financing.* Inventory financing may be extended to companies to purchase raw materials and finished goods. Other names for inventory financing are *floorplanning, wholesale financing, floorplan financing,* and *distribution financing.*

2. Financing provided by a company to a business customer who needs to pay for a purchase from the company providing the financing. Technology companies and telecom companies, whose orders often total millions of dollars, often provide financing to their customers.

inventory turnover A financial calculation that shows how quickly a company's inventory is being turned over. A high inventory turnover is an indicator of business's health. Inventory turnover is calculated by dividing annual sales, or the cost of goods sold, by the average inventory for the year. The resulting number is the number of times that the inventory turned over.

inverted market A futures market where the nearer months' contracts are more expensive than the distant months' contracts. An inverted market occurs during periods of shortages. Typically, the further

months are more expensive because the goods have the additional costs of insurance, storage, and interest costs incurred in borrowing funds to hold the commodities.

inverted yield curve A rare situation in which short-term interest rates are higher than long-term rates. An inverted yield curve occurs when there is strong demand for short-term credit, which drives up the demand for Treasury bills and other short-dated credit. During periods of strong inflation, the Federal Reserve raises interest rates, which tends to invert the yield curve; long-term rates remain low because investors are reluctant to make long-term commitments. An inverted yield curve suggests an unhealthy economy that is racked by high inflation. A normal yield curve is called a *positive yield curve.*

investment A commitment of dollars for a period of time with the expectation or hope of receiving future payments that will cover any inflation and compensate the investor for the time that the funds are committed and the uncertainty of any future return. An investment may be made by any person or entity, including corporations, pension funds, or a government, and be made in land, equipment, stocks, bonds, commodities, or any other financial instrument.

Investment Advisers Act of 1940 A law that regulates investment advisers and requires that firms or sole practitioners who are paid to advise others about investments register with the Securities and Exchange Commission (SEC) and conform to regulations designed to protect investors. Since its amendment in 1996, typically only advisers who manage more than $25 million of assets or who advise a registered investment company must register with the SEC.

investment advisory service A business service that provides investment advice to its clients for a fee. The advice may come through personal or telephone meetings, through the Internet, or through a paper-based newsletter or other publication. Investment advisors must register with the Securities and Exchange Commission.

investment climate The general mind-set of investors. An investment climate might be extremely bullish where everything is being bought and funded, as was the case during the technology boom of the late 1990s. Or, the investment climate might be very bearish, like the markets in the several years after the market peaked in the spring of 2000 and the tech bubble burst and venture capitalists virtually quit funding new companies and the initial public offering market slowed to a trickle.

investment club A group of friends or associates who pool their money together and make joint investment decisions about what stocks to invest in. Each member contributes money, usually on a monthly basis, and shares in the profits or loss of the club. Investment clubs have grown in popularity during the last two decades. The National Association of Investors Corporation is a well-known association of investment clubs.

Investment Company Act of 1940 A landmark law passed in 1940 that established the laws and regulations for the mutual fund industry. Its purpose is to ensure that investors receive adequate and accurate information about mutual funds. The law regulates what type of investments that mutual funds may make and attempts to ensure that investors' money will be protected and not subjected to too much risk. The law outlines what information mutual funds must disclose to investors about the fund's fees and expenses, share holdings, management, and financial performance. The law applies stringent financial requirements on funds; for example, it severely restricts a fund's ability to borrow against the securities in its portfolio. Funds also are required to own the underlying securities if they purchase futures, options, forward contracts, or do short selling (selling stocks or futures that they don't own).

Investment Company Institute A national association for the U.S. investment company industry, founded in 1940. Its members include nearly 9,000 mutual funds, over 500 closed-end funds, and a handful of sponsors of unit investment trusts. It represents its members in matters of legislation,

regulation, taxation, public information, economic and policy research, and business operations. It prepares weekly, monthly, and annual statistics on the industry.

investment consultant An individual who helps wealthy institutions or individuals find an appropriate investment manager. The investment consultant sends out a request for proposal (RFP) to investment managers and then helps the client narrow down the list of managers. The investment consultant helps the client interview the managers that most closely fit the client's needs. Investment consultants also evaluate the performance of the investment management firm after it has been chosen. During the last decade, the role of investment consultants has grown as the number and complexity of financial instruments has grown.

investment credit A tax credit that is given to a company for making a certain type of investment. The investment may be in building a new plant, purchasing certain equipment, or undertaking other investments that the government wants to encourage.

investment horizon The length of time that an investor expects to hold onto a specific investment.

investment income Income that is earned from investments, such as dividends from stock, interest from bonds or savings accounts, payment from an annuity, or options premiums earned by writing an option.

investment letter A letter that is written by the issuer of a new security when the security is sold through a *private placement*. The letter is written because the security is not registered with the Securities and Exchange Commission. Because the securities are not registered, they cannot be sold until two years after they are purchased, which is stated in the investment letter.

investment management The professional management of financial assets. Investment managers make investments on behalf of people, institutions, or pension funds. Although investment management has existed since the early 1900s, it really began to grow in the 1970s as concerns about the solvency of Social Security increased individuals' attention to their retirement planning. In 1974, the *Employment Retirement Income Security Act* (*ERISA*) was passed, creating 401(k) private retirement plans. Those changes paved the way for firms to specialize in managing money for individuals and institutions.

The term *asset management* can be used interchangeably with *investment management*, but asset management is more likely to be used in reference to the industry as a whole, while individual investment managers are more likely to use the term investment management to describe what they do.

investment objective The guiding principle that an investor uses to decide where to invest his or her money. If the objective is to make cash grow, then he or she will invest in higher-risk companies that have the greatest possibility of growth potential. If current income is the objective, investments generating income, such as bonds or stocks with a high dividend, are purchased.

investment portfolio The collection of all the assets, such as stocks, bonds, and cash, that an individual or company has invested in.

investment strategy A strategy for allocating investments among different categories, such as stocks, bonds, and cash. The decisions are made based on the investor's expectation about each categories' potential performance and the investor's tolerance for risk. Before an investment strategy is formed, investors have to know what their goals are, such as buying a home or saving for college or retirement.

investment-grade debt High-quality notes or bonds that are the least likely to default. Standard & Poor's investment grade ratings are AAA, AA, A, and BBB. Moody's Investors' Service breaks investment grade debts into an A rating and three 'B' categories, Baa1, Baa2, and Baa3. Fitch Ratings considers debt with a rating of A or B to be investment-grade.

investor relations (IR) department A department set up by large public corporations to answer inquiries from shareholders and potential shareholders about a variety of topics.

invisible earnings A phrase that is commonly used in the United Kingdom to mean earnings from services, which are "invisible," in contrast to physical goods or manufactured products that are "visible."

invisible supply Inventory of a commodity that is uncounted because its is held by wholesalers, manufacturers, and producers and is not available to be accurately counted. However, it is still available to the market.

invoice A bill that is produced by a company or individual that shows how much money is owed to that company or individual. The invoice details the nature of the charge, including a listing of any items that might have been purchased or the type of services rendered.

involuntary bankruptcy A bankruptcy in which the creditors petitioned a court to put the debtor into a bankruptcy proceeding. This contrasts with a *voluntary bankruptcy,* which occurs when the debtor petitions the court to begin a bankruptcy proceeding.

IP See *Internet Protocol.*

IPE See *International Petroleum Exchange of London Ltd.*

IPE Brent Crude futures A futures contract based on Brent crude oil, a particular type of oil and one of the most important oil price benchmarks in the world. Brent Crude futures have been traded on the London-based International Petroleum Exchange (IPE) since June 1988, using open-outcry trading. Three related markets comprise the Brent oil complex, as follows: Brent that is available immediately, which is called dated or physical Brent; forward Brent, which is for purchase or sale at a future date; and Brent futures, which have standardized delivery times and amounts. Companies trading Brent futures, such as users of oil products, can take actual delivery of the oil by using an *exchange-for-physicals technique,* which allows traders to close out their futures contracts by trading them with the physical products. Traders of the futures contracts use cash to settle contracts after expiration. IPE options contracts also are based on the underlying IPE futures contract.

IPE Electricity futures A futures contract launched by the London-based International Petroleum Exchange (IPE) in March 2001, coinciding with the deregulation in the electricity market that was occurring in England that occurred when the New Electricity Trading Arrangements was passed. The contracts are traded electronically on the IPE's automated Energy Trading System. The electricity contract was designed to allow natural gas traders and electricity traders to arbitrage, or exploit the differences in prices between natural gas and electricity because they are closely related, since their end uses are similar. Margins on deposit with member firms of the exchange also can be applied to both products, which is called *cross-margining.* Cross-margining substantially reduces the amount of cash that traders have to keep on hand.

IPE Gas Oil futures The first futures contract launched by the London-based International Petroleum Exchange (IPE) in 1981. It has evolved into a benchmark for spot middle distillate oil across northwest Europe. In the United States, gas oil is often referred to as *heating oil.* The contract is traded on the IPE floor using open outcry trading. Physical delivery for the contract occurs near Amsterdam, Rotterdam, and Antwerp; however, most contract users employ the contract as a financial mechanism to protect against losses and close out their positions before they have to deliver or receive the gas oil. The options contract is based on the underlying IPE futures contract.

IPE Natural Gas futures A futures contract based on natural gas, the first non-oil contract on the London-based International Petroleum Exchange (IPE) that began trading in January 1997. Natural

Gas futures contracts are traded electronically on the IPE's automated Energy Trading System. Physical delivery takes place within the U.K. natural gas grid at the National Balancing Point (NBP).

IPO See *initial public offering.*

IRA See *Individual Retirement Account.*

IRR See *internal rate of return.*

irrational exuberance A phrase uttered by Federal Reserve Chairman Alan Greenspan in December 1996 to refer to the stock market's phenomenal gains. At that point, the Dow Jones Industrial Average was below 6,500. The comment caused the stock market to drop sharply the next day as traders were afraid that Greenspan's concerns would lead the Federal Reserve to take actions to stop the market's climb, such as raising interest rates or limiting the amount of *margin,* or borrowed funds, that investors could obtain from their broker when buying stocks or other investments. The phrase was often repeated as the market continued to climb to record highs through early 2000.

irrevocable life insurance trust A trust that pays estate taxes out of the proceeds of a life insurance policy. An irrevocable life insurance trust is created when a married couple, or a single person, gives money to an irrevocable life insurance trust. The individuals' children, or other beneficiaries, are named as trustees and beneficiaries. The children also can use the money in the trust to buy a survivorship life policy, which also is called a *second-to-die* policy. The life policy insures both spouses and is owned by the trust and names the trust as the beneficiary. The life insurance policy pays only when the second spouse dies. The children or trustees use the proceeds to pay the estate taxes. There are no estate taxes after the first spouse dies. This insurance may be obtainable even if one spouse is in bad health, because it doesn't pay until the second, healthy person dies.

IRS See *Internal Revenue Service.*

Islamic finance A set of strict rules that forbid making or receiving interest payments. To get around this prohibition, trade financing is obtained by buying inventory that will be resold at a pre-determined price on a future date, which is called *Murabaha*. Financing for capital projects is called *Musharaka*, which is funding by two or more parties who may be active managers in a partnership. Losses are shared on the basis of the capital contribution. Profits may be shared in any way the partners decide. See also *Istisna, Qardhul Hasan,* and *Riba*.

ISM See *Institute of Supply Management.*

ISM Index A monthly composite index, released by the Institute for Supply Management, that is based on surveys of 300 purchasing managers throughout the United States in 20 industries in the manufacturing area. The index is released on the first business day of the month and covers the previous month's data, which makes it particularly timely. If the index is above 50, it indicates that the economy is expanding. Values below 50 indicate a contraction.

Within the overall index, there are nine subindices: new orders, production, supplier delivery times, backlogs, inventories, prices, employment, export orders, and import orders. The index is believed to reflect future movements in gross domestic product, thereby making it a closely watched economic data release. The subindices for new orders and backlogs predict well future production. Formerly, it was called the *National Association of Purchasing Management's survey.* A limitation of the survey is that it doesn't include any questions on wages, which is an important component of overall costs.

ISM non-manufacturing index An index produced by the Institute for Supply Management Non-Manufacturing that is based on surveys of 370 purchasing and supply executives. Its shorter name is *ISM Services Survey,* and it was started in 1997. If the index is over 50, it typically indicates expansion among non-manufacturing components of the economy. A value under 50 indicates contraction. There are ten subindices. Of those, the business activity

subindex is most influential. The other nine indices are new orders, supplier deliveries, employment, inventories, prices, backlog of orders, new export orders, imports, and inventory sentiment. A limitation of the survey is that it doesn't include any questions on wages, which is an important component of overall costs.

ISO 9000 A quality management standard created by the International Organization for Standardization (ISO). ISO establishes and defines effective quality systems for many manufacturing and service industries, but the ISO 9000 is the most well-known. Companies can be certified as meeting ISO 9000 standards by going through an evaluation process. There are 350,000 ISO-9000 certified organizations in over 150 countries. ISO is a standard that frequently is used in Europe, while in the U.S. companies are more likely to follow Total Quality Management procedures.

issue A security that will be sold to public or private investors. Those securities may be stocks or bonds. The term may also be used as a verb to indicate that a company plans to issue a bond offering.

Istisna In Islamic finance, a contract to manufacture goods, assemble or process them, or to build a house or other structure according to exact specifications and a fixed timeline. Payments are made as work on the property is finished. Istisna avoids making or receiving interest payments, which is forbidden by the Islamic religion.

itemized deduction A deduction that is taken off of federal income taxes by totaling individual expenses such as charitable expenses, mortgage interest expense, and health care expenses, which are deducted on Schedule A. These expenses have to be greater than 2% of the taxpayers adjusted gross income in order to be deducted. An itemized deduction contrasts with a *standard deduction,* which is an amount that can be deducted by every taxpayer filing in that particular category.

IXC See *interexchange carrier.*

J

Japanese Auction An auction with one seller and many buyers, in which the auctioneer raises the price from a low starting point. The buyers must bid at each price in order to remain in the auction.

JASDAQ Average A capitalization-weighted index of all Japanese over-the-counter stocks. It began with a base value of 100 on October 28, 1991. Its name was changed in October 2002 to the Nikkei JASDAQ Stock Average. Typically, it is referred to as the Nikkei JASDAQ Average.

J-curve phenomenon The tendency of a country to run a larger trade deficit immediately after its currency depreciates. Eventually, the trade deficit will decrease after consumers begin to change their behavior and exporters, who initially didn't want to lose business when their products became more expensive, begin to increase their prices. The J-curve gets its name from the shape of the curve, which looks like a capital J.

JGBs *Japanese Government Bonds.* Just as U.S. government bonds are frequently called Treasuries, JGBs typically is used instead of the full name. JGBs are traded in the over-the-counter market, as well as on organized exchanges throughout the world.

JIBOR *Jakarta Inter Bank Offered Rate,* an interest rate that is charged between Asian banks. JIBOR is the equivalent of LIBOR, applied to the Asian market. See *LIBOR.*

jobless claims report A weekly report published by the U.S. Department of Labor that shows how many people have filed initial claims for unemployment insurance. The report is published on Thursdays at 8:30 a.m. eastern time. A four-week moving average of initial claims for unemployment insurance is created in order to smooth out the volatile weekly figures. The report also includes the number of continuing claims for unemployment insurance and the insured unemployment rate. If initial filings move above the benchmark 400,000 level, the labor market is said to be contracting. The jobless claims report is useful because it gives a timely picture of the economy. It also breaks out information by state, however that information may have a lag period. The report's usefulness is limited because weekly claims are very volatile and the data can be affected by holidays. The report has very little industry-specific information. Although the jobless claims report is watched by the financial markets, it has a lower profile than the monthly non-farm payroll report, or the unemployment report, as it is referred to in the non-business press.

Jobs, Steven The creator of the Apple computer, along with Steve Wozniak. They used a color television monitor that was designed to appeal to non-technical people to create the Apple in 1976, which formed the basis of Apple Computer, Inc. and was targeted at educators and schools. In 1984, the Macintosh, the next-generation Apple, was produced. In 1985, Jobs was forced out of the company he had started, so he and a few Apple employees started a company called Next Inc., which was acquired by Apple. He later rejoined Apple Computer Inc. and is its chief executive officer, as of this printing. In 1986 he co-founded Pixar, the Academy-Award-winning animation studio.

Johnston, Donald J. The secretary-general of the Organization for Economic Cooperation and Development (OECD), which is a Paris-based think tank whose purpose is to forward democracy and free-market policies. Johnston was a member of the Canadian Parliament and a practicing lawyer before taking this position at the OECD. See also *OECD.*

joint and survivor annuity An annuity for which payments are made for as long as the insured or a designated survivor lives. An annuity is an investment sold by an insurance company that guarantees payments based on a fixed or variable return for a certain time period. The investor in the annuitant purchases it by paying the life insurance company a lump sum.

joint tenancy with right of survivorship   A method of property ownership by more than one person. Under joint tenancy with right of survivorship, when one of the owners dies, the property passes to the surviving owners. In contrast, under *tenants in common* ownership, when one of the owners dies, the ownership interest in the property passes through inheritance as directed in the will or trust and is not divided among the other owners. Also called *joint tenancy ownership.*

joint venture   An agreement between two or more companies to cooperate on a specific initiative. The joint venture may involve marketing a product, offering a service, or expanding into a new geographical territory. Often, companies undertake joint ventures with companies in other countries as a way to expand into new markets. While the local company will have the business relationships and current business operations, the foreign company may bring a brand name and managerial skills.

jointly and severally   In legal terms, an agreement that if a member of a group is unable to fulfill his or her contractual obligations the other members of the group are responsible. For example, if an underwriter agrees to buy a specific amount of a new securities issue and a member of the underwriting group is unable to meet its obligation, the other members of the group are responsible.

jumbo certificate of deposit (jumbo CD)   A certificate of deposit with a minimum denomination of $100,000. Jumbo CDs are usually bought and sold by large institutions such as banks, pension funds, money market funds, and insurance companies.

junk bond   Bonds that have a credit rating of BB or below. Bonds that have a junk rating are often issued by companies or municipalities that have a bad or uncertain credit rating. Also called *high-yield, high-risk,* or *below-investment grade* bonds.

just-in-time   A production and inventory system that has supplies arriving just as they are needed. Just-in-time systems save companies money and time because they don't have to pay for storage space or manage as much inventory. Just-in-time inventory strategies were embraced by the Japanese when they rebuilt their industry after World War II. In the U.S., just-in-time was slower to catch on, but it now is frequently used.

K

Kaiser, Henry J. The founder of a string of health care clinics and hospitals in the Western United States during the 1930s. Kaiser also led contracting consortiums that built hydroelectric power projects and owned a company that produced automobiles, Kaiser-Frazer Corp., which at one time was the fourth largest car maker in the United States. However, the car company failed because of Korean War restrictions on using industrial materials and an insufficient dealer network.

kangaroo Slang for an Australian stock.

Kansas City Fed Manufacturing Survey A survey of 300 manufacturing firms located in the 10th Federal Reserve District, which includes Colorado, Kansas, Nebraska, Oklahoma, Wyoming, western Missouri, and northern New Mexico, that gives data about manufacturing trends. The survey is a good indicator of current manufacturing conditions and near-term expectations. It is particularly helpful in providing an early indication of price changes and ordering patterns. Index values greater than zero generally suggest expansion, while values less than zero indicate contraction.

This survey typically has little impact in the financial markets, but it can be useful to either confirm or discredit trends seen in the monthly ISM Index. The Kansas City Fed Manufacturing Survey particularly has a stronger role when the Federal Reserve Board is focusing on manufacturing as an important variable to gauge economic strength.

kappa A measurement of the effect of volatility on an option's price. Kappa is a value that is the change in the price of option that likely will result if the underlying investment has a 1 percent change.

karat A measure of the amount of gold that is in a piece of jewelry. Pure gold is 24-karat. A 14-karat ring, for example, is $\frac{14}{24}$th gold and $\frac{10}{24}$th alloy.

KBW Bank Sector Index A benchmark index used in the banking industry and by investors to track the performance of banks. The index was created and is traded by the Philadelphia Stock Exchange. It also is referred to as the bank index, or BK, which is its trading symbol. The BKX is a capitalization-weighted index composed of 24 geographically diverse stocks representing national money center banks and leading regional institutions. BKX is based on one-tenth of the value of the Keefe, Bruyette & Woods Index (KBWI). Founded in 1962, Keefe, Bruyette & Woods is recognized as a banking industry authority. The index was initiated at the time of the firm's founding and was calculated retroactively to 1947. The index is evaluated at least annually by Keefe, Bruyette & Woods to assure that the composition is highly representative of the banking industry. Options trading began on September 21, 1992.

keiretsu A Japanese term used to describe a loose collection of firms that share one or more common links of ownership or business dealings.

Kennedy, Joseph P. Best known as the father of U.S. president John F. Kennedy and two U.S. senators, he also was the first chairman of the Securities and Exchange Commission in 1934. Kennedy made the SEC a credible agency by obtaining a large budget from Congress, hiring a strong staff, and vigorously pursuing swindlers. He was appointed by Franklin D. Roosevelt on the principle that through his experiences as a bank president and a stock manipulator, he would know the tricks of the trade and would be able to help create laws that would favor small investors.

Keogh Plan A retirement plan for self-employed people or owners of unincorporated businesses. Employers contribute to a Keogh on behalf of their employees. Contributions are limited to up to 25 percent of compensation or $30,000. Employees can take loans or withdrawals according to plan provisions. Withdrawals made prior to age 59½ may incur automatic tax withholding of 20 percent, plus a

10 percent early withdrawal penalty, unless a permitted exception applies. Tax-free rollovers are permitted to an IRA or qualified retirement plan.

kerb trading   An informal trading period on the London Metal Exchange that takes place in the ring beginning at 1:15 p.m. GMT, and ending at 3:10 p.m. At this time, eight non-ferrous metals contracts and the silver index contract trade simultaneously.

At 1:15 p.m. every day, following ring, or exchange, trading, the official pricing is issued for non-ferrous metals futures contracts and a period of trading begins. The name *kerb* came from the practice of members in the early 1900s gathering on the roadside by the kerb to continue trading after the official session ended.

key performance indicator   Measurements such as market share growth, number of new products launched, number of stores opened, or any other benchmarks that show how well a company is performing. The concept of key performance indicators was forwarded with the passage of corporate governance reform proposals that became law in 2002 through the passage of the Sarbanes-Oxley legislation. When companies report key performance indicators, investors know what criteria company management is looking at to judge its success and progress.

key person insurance   Life or disability insurance that is purchased by a company for its key executives. The insurance benefits are payable to the company and help to provide a financial cushion while finding solutions for business problems caused by the executive's death. Some policies also may have a smaller amount of money that is payable to the employee's designated beneficiary.

Keynes, John Maynard   A prominent economist who believed that governments should spend money or cut taxes in order to stimulate a slowing economy. In 1936, he wrote *The General Theory of Employment, Interest, and Money,* a revolutionary pronouncement. It came at the right time because the economic theory of the time fell drastically short of being able to explain why unemployment reached such high levels in the U.S. and Europe during the Great Depression and remained high until World War II broke out and stimulated demand.

Keynesian economics   An economic theory, created by John Maynard Keynes, that advocates governments becoming involved in the markets and economy in order to produce price stability and economic growth. Keynes said that insufficient demand results in unemployment, and too much demand results in inflation. To influence demand levels, the government should adjust its spending and taxation policies. He outlined his theory in *The General Theory of Employment, Interest, and Money,* which was published in 1935. His ideas clash with those of classical economists, such as Adam Smith, who believe the government should not get involved in the markets or economy. The severe level of unemployment in the U.S. and Europe following the Great Depression of 1929 gave Keynesian economists more prominence.

kickback   An illegal, secret payment made by a company to a person or company in exchange for awarding the first company a contract.

kicker   An extra feature added to a note or bond that provides additional incentive for an investor to purchase it. Often, the kicker will be a provision that lets the investor take a portion of the note or bond and exchange it for equity.

kina   The currency unit of Papua New Guinea, comprised of 100 toea.

King, Mervyn   The governor of the Bank of England, who took over in July 2003, replacing Sir Edward George who retired. Previously he was the deputy governor at the Bank, a position that began June 1998. Before that he was the Bank of England's chief economist and executive director since March 1991. From October 1984 he was a professor of economics at the London School of Economics.

kip The currency unit of Laos, comprised of 100 at.

kitchen sink bond A bond that is formed from a wide collection of collateralized mortgage obligations (CMOs). The name comes from the saying that everything is included except the kitchen sink. The underlying bonds in a kitchen sink bond have a wide variety of different characteristics, such as credit quality, maturity dates, and prepayment dates. Kitchen sink bonds are the obligation that is created from a Secured Investor Trust.

KK The abbreviation for a joint stock company in Japan. It stands for kabushiki (stock) kaishi (company). This designation is the equivalent of Plc. in the United Kingdom or Corp. in the United States.

knock-in option See *barrier option*.

knock-out option An option that will become worthless, or be *knocked out,* if the underlying investment, such as a commodity, currency, or stock, reaches a particular price level. An option gives the buyer the right, but not the obligation, to purchase a security at a specific time and price, or the right to sell a security at a specific time and price. A knock-out option contrasts with a regular option, which only becomes worthless on the day of expiration, if it hasn't been exercised.

knowledge management The process of creating, institutionalizing, and distributing knowledge among people for the purpose of improving and organizing business processes and practices. In recent years, companies have created knowledge management departments and selected certain people to manage those activities.

Köhler, Horst The managing director of the International Monetary Fund (IMF), as of this printing; appointed in May 2000. From September 1998 to May 2000, Kohler was president of the European Bank for Reconstruction and Development. He served as president of the German Savings Bank Association from 1993 to 1998. From 1990 to 1993 he was Germany's Deputy Minister of Finance, and was responsible for overseeing Germany's international financial relations. In that role, he led negotiations of the Maastricht treaty, which laid the groundwork for the European Economic and Monetary Union, the precursor for the formation of the euro.

koruna The currency unit of the Czech Republic, comprised of 100 haliers, and the Slovak Republic, comprised of 100 haliers.

Kospi Composite Index A market capitalization-weighted index of the top 691 stocks that trade on the Kospi stock market, South Korea's Stock Exchange.

Kozlowski, Dennis L. The former chief executive of Tyco International Ltd. Indicted on corruption and grand larceny charges in 2002 for allegedly stealing $600 million from Tyco, Kozlowski resigned before he was indicted by the state of New York on charges of evading $1 million in sales taxes for allegedly having paintings that were purchased in New York shipped to Tyco offices in Exeter, New Hampshire, before being returned to New York. He pled not guilty. In December 2002, Tyco sued Kozlowski and former chief financial officer Mark Swartz for allegedly making dozens of short-swing stock trades (totaling $40 million), beginning in August 2000. See also *short-swing stock trade*.

Kravis, Henry One of the principals of Kohlberg Kravis Roberts & Co., which pioneered the leveraged buy-out, which uses debt to take control of companies from shareholders. Kravis and his company are known for the $25 billion leveraged buyout of RJR Nabisco in the late 1980s, which was the largest U.S. takeover up to that time.

Kroc, Raymond A. The creator of fast-food restaurant chain McDonald's Corporation, which started the standardized, fast-food industry. Kroc was a 52-year-old milkshake-machine salesman who, in 1954, bought the franchise rights to a small chain of Southern California hamburger stands run by the McDonald brothers; seven years later, in 1961, he bought the company for $14 million.

krona The currency unit of Iceland, comprised of 100 aurar, and Sweden, comprised of 100 øre.

krone The currency unit of Denmark, comprised of 100 øre, and Norway, comprised of 100 øre. Greenland uses the Danish krone.

kroon The currency unit of Estonia, comprised of 100 senti.

kruggerand A gold bullion coin minted by South Africa that is popular with investors and traders.

kwacha The currency unit of Malawi, comprised of 100 tambala, and Zambia, comprised of 100 ngwee.

kwanza The currency unit of Angola, comprised of 100 lwei.

kyat The currency unit of Myanmar, comprised of 100 pya.

La Niña A cold-weather event, or cold episode, in contrast to *El Niño*, which is often referred to as a "warm event." In the United States, La Niña causes winter temperatures that are warmer than normal in the Southeast and cooler than normal in the Northwest. The effects of both El Niño and La Niña are seen more in the winter than in the summer. La Niña impacts agricultural products and thus is watched by traders and others involved in agricultural commodities. Typically the effects last for several months to a year. La Niña is Spanish for "the little girl." See also *El Niño*.

labor productivity The amount of output per average worker in one hour. This measure is used in cost accounting to calculate the cost of goods sold for end products.

ladder option An exotic option that lets the option owner capture and lock-in gains on the underlying security during the life of the option. If the price of the underlying security reaches certain thresholds, such as 25 percent or 50 percent above the exercise price, then the holder of the warrant receives a minimum payment. Also called *lock-step option* and *step-lock option*.

laddering

1. A practice of initial public offering (IPO) underwriters that requires investors to buy shares at higher prices in the after-market as a condition for receiving lower-priced shares of the IPO. Following the stock market bubble that burst after reaching historic highs in early 2000, laddering has been mentioned as one possible explanation for the unique run up in first-day trading prices of IPOs during the bubble. Some IPOs even made triple-digit one-day gains.

2. In portfolio management, the practice of purchasing equal amounts of bonds with staggered maturity risk. Staggered maturity risk spreads out the risk of interest rate changes over time.

Laffer, Arthur An economist who argued that reducing marginal personal income tax rates would lead to a rise in government revenues because individuals would be more likely to work harder and longer to generate higher income. His theory is embodied in the Laffer Curve, which contributed significantly to *supply-side economics*, also known as *Reaganomics*. See also *Laffer Curve*.

Laffer Curve A key underpinning of supply-side economics that says that tax cuts produce non-inflationary economic growth and increase productivity. The theory derives its name from economist Arthur Laffer.

lagging indicators One of three composite indices published monthly by the Conference Board (an international, independent organization that creates and distributes information about management and the marketplace) around the 20th day of every month in the *Index of Leading Economic Indicators*. These indices comprise an analytical system that is designed to signal peaks and troughs in the business cycle. The other two composite indices are the leading indicators and the coincident index.

The lagging indicators index is comprised of economic statistics that reflect economic activity after it has occurred. The seven lagging indicators are unemployment, unit labor costs for manufacturing, the average prime rate charged by banks, the ratio of manufacturing and trade inventories to sales, commercial and industrial loans, the ratio of consumer installment credit to personal income rate, and the consumer price index for services. Traders and analysts pay attention to the indices to determine whether the U.S. economy is doing well or is slowing down. See also *leading indicators*.

laissez-faire A doctrine that says government involvement in business and financial affairs should occur only at a very minimal level. It is French for "let them do as they please." Adam Smith originated this theory in

1776, in his book *The Wealth of Nations.* Advocates of a laissez-faire policy believe that businesses should be able to pursue all opportunities as they see fit, and that the marketplace should act as an *invisible hand* in order to create the maximum good for everyone. Although this theory was popular during the 19th century, and businesses in the United States and Great Britain generally were able to do as they wished, the laissez-faire philosophy was severely restrained in the United States in the 20th century when the federal government broke up several large monopolies. Later, the Great Depression further changed the thinking of government officials, who felt compelled to take action to cope with severe unemployment.

lambda The ratio of the percentage change in an option's price to the percentage change in an underlying price. Lambda measures the change in option premiums for a percentage point change in the option's implied volatility. If lambda is high, the value of an option is very sensitive to even small changes in volatility. A low lambda means that volatility changes have little impact on the value of an option.

land bank A public agency that provides inexpensive financing for the purchase or refinancing of undeveloped land so that affordable housing and economic revitalization projects can be developed.

large cap Short for *large capitalization,* this designates the largest company type. A large-cap company typically has a market capitalization of over $5 billion, although exact guidelines for what constitutes a large-cap company vary greatly among different classification systems. Market cap is derived by multiplying the price of a company's stock by the number of outstanding shares. For example, a company with a stock price of $30 and 10 million shares outstanding has a market capitalization of $300 million. Often mutual funds are classified by the type of companies that they invest in, such as large-cap companies.

lari The currency unit of Georgia, comprised of 100 tetri.

last in, first out (LIFO) An inventory accounting method that uses the price of the most recently purchased goods as the cost basis for cost of goods sold. During periods of inflation, LIFO produces higher costs, reduced profits, and reduced taxes paid on profits. LIFO contrasts with *FIFO* (*first in, first out*), another inventory accounting method that uses the prices of goods that were purchased first to calculate cost of goods sold.

last notice day The last day on which notices of intent to deliver on futures contracts may be issued.

LATA A U.S. telecom term, which stands for *local access and transport area.* A LATA is a particular area that is covered by one or more local telephone companies, called *local exchange carriers* (LECs). *IntraLATA* is a connection between two local exchanges within the same LATA. *InterLATA,* which essentially is long distance service, is a connection between a carrier in one LATA to a carrier in another LATA. Rules governing what companies can provide both types of service were established in the Telecommunications Act of 1996.

later-stage financing The type of financing that is awarded to a start-up company by a venture capital firm when the company's product or service becomes widely available. Financially, the company is generating strong revenues and likely has positive cash flow. It may or may not be profitable. Companies receiving later-stage financing may include spinouts of operating divisions of existing private companies.

lats The currency unit of Latvia, comprised of 100 santimi.

laundered money Money that has been transmitted through many different accounts, usually foreign, in an attempt to disguise its illegal origins. Money laundering is illegal and in recent years there has been a push by regulatory and legal officials in developed countries to attempt to stop money laundering.

Lay, Kenneth L. The former chairman of Enron Corp., who resigned under pressure after the company collapsed and filed for bankruptcy protection.

LBO See *leveraged buyout*.

LDC See *Local Development Corporation*.

lead investor The bank or investor that is a company's principal provider of debt. The lead investor organizes other investors in a syndication process.

leading indicators One of three composite indices published monthly by the Conference Board (an international, independent organization that creates and distributes information about management and the marketplace) around the 20th day of every month in the *Index of Leading Economic Indicators*. The other indicators are the lagging indicators and the coincident index. These indices comprise an analytic system that is designed to signal peaks and troughs in the business cycle.

The 11 components of the leading indicators index are average weekly hours worked in manufacturing, average weekly initial unemployment insurance claims, manufacturers' new orders for consumer goods and materials, vender performance, the slower deliveries diffusion index, manufacturers' new orders for non-defense capital goods, building permits for new houses, stock prices, M2 measures of money supply, the interest rate spread measured by the ten-year Treasury bonds less federal funds, and the index of consumer expectations.

league table A list that shows how various investment banks stack up against their competitors in a variety of categories, such as mergers, debt, equity, and initial public offerings. Thomson Corp. has software that tracks the deal data and that produces league tables. In recent years, other competitors have launched competing products. Information providers such as Thomson charge a yearly fee to corporations to access their database, using Internet-based software, in order to create the league tables.

lean hogs A futures contract traded on the Chicago Mercantile Exchange (CME). The lean hog contract began trading in November 1995 with the February 1997 contract and improved upon the live hog futures and options contracts that previously had been traded. Both futures and options are traded on lean hogs at the CME.

LEAPS (long-term equity anticipation securities) Long-term equity options. Instead of expiring in several months, LEAPS can remain in effect for up to three years after their initial listing. LEAPS are not available on every stock. They have their own unique ticker symbol and trade on the major stock exchanges.

learning curve In economic terms, the anticipated improvements that are likely following early mistakes. Companies refer to mastering learning curves following troubled product introductions, difficult entries into new markets, or even to refer to improvements that a company has made in consolidating the acquisition of subsequent companies.

lease A temporary transfer of ownership of an asset, such as real estate or a car, for a set period of time. Regular monthly payments are due on the lease and the lessee is responsible for any maintenance or upkeep expenses. At the end of the lease period, the property reverts back to the owner. However, the lessee may have an option to buy the property at the end of the contract period. Leases often enable a company or individual to have the use of the equipment or property for a significantly lower cost than an outright acquisition. A lease also has the benefit of allowing the lessee to use the most up-to-date equipment or property that is available while avoiding any of the market risk that comes with ownership.

leaseback A transaction in which one person or business sells property to another person or business. The seller agrees to lease the property back from the buyer for a fixed period of time at a set cost. The advantage for the seller is that a leaseback provides cash from the sale while retaining the beneficial use of the property. The purchaser acquires an asset, as well as a guaranteed income stream. Leasebacks may be used on the sale of airplanes, motor vehicles, and other valuable long-term assets.

leasehold   An asset that gives the holder the right to use the property under a lease. A leasehold is a fixed asset and thus depreciates over time. Improvements to the property are called *leasehold improvements*. The cost of the improvement is added into the fixed asset. A leasehold may be used by businesses that rent an office or factory. In some situations, houses may be sold through a leasehold, which gives the purchaser the legal right to occupy property for a specific period of time, such as 99 years. This practice is more common in the United Kingdom than in the United States.

leasehold estate   A system of property ownership in which the property is purchased for a defined period of time, often a maximum of 99 years. When the period is up, ownership returns to the original freehold owner. This is a rare form of property ownership in the United States, but is more common in the United Kingdom and other countries.

lease–purchase agreement   An agreement to lease property or equipment for a certain period of time that allows some or all of the lease payments to be applied to the purchase price of the property or equipment.

legacy system   An information technology or other automated system that is technologically obsolete. It may be too expensive to update or replace, but it is still needed for the company's operations and thus is kept operational even though a newer system is in use.

legal risk   The risk that a legal contract or financial transaction won't be fulfilled because it breaks the law or there is a regulatory conflict. Other legal risks include documentation or contractual problems.

Lehman Brothers Commercial Mortgage-Backed Securities (CMBS) Index   A performance benchmark for commercial mortgage-backed securities. All of the bonds in the index must be private transactions and cannot be agency deals. The collateral for each transaction must be new issues. The minimum transaction size must be at least $500 million to be included and $300 million to remain in the index.

The CMBS Index has four subsectors:

The *CMBS Investment Grade Index* measures return for investment-grade classes.

The *CMBS High-Yield Index* measures return for non-investment grade and nonrated classes.

The *CMBS Interest-Only Index* measures return for interest-only classes.

The *Commercial Conduit Whole Loan Index* measures return for all bond classes and interest-only classes.

Lehman Brothers Emerging Markets Index   A market index that measure the performance of emerging markets throughout the world. The index was introduced in January 1997, and the existing Emerging Americas Bond Index was folded into the new index. The index measures the performance of bonds in emerging markets that meet certain criteria, such as being denominated in U.S. dollars, meeting minimum liquidity requirements, and having at least one year to maturity.

lek   The currency unit of Albania, comprised of 100 qintar.

lemon

1. A used car that develops numerous mechanical problems shortly after being purchased. Some states have *lemon laws* to protect consumers from these and other similar purchases.

2. An investment that performs poorly.

lempira   The currency unit of Honduras, comprised of 100 centavos.

lender of last resort   A central bank, such as the Federal Reserve in the United States, to whom member banks turn if they are not able to obtain needed funds anywhere else. When the Federal Reserve functions as a lender of last resort, member banks borrow funds from what is called the discount window. The *discount window* refers to loans that the Federal Reserve makes to its member banks that are used either to pay for large withdrawals or to meet reserve requirements. Banks are discouraged from using the privilege unless they are short of reserves.

leone The currency unit of Sierra Leone, comprised of 100 cents.

less-developed countries Countries that have lower per capita incomes and that have a greater dependency on commodity prices. Their capital markets and business system aren't well developed, compared with those of Western countries such as the United States and the United Kingdom.

letter of credit A document written by a bank that guarantees the payment of a customer's bills up to a certain amount. The letter eliminates the seller's credit risk because it pledges that the bank intends to use its assets to pay for the purchase. It typically is used in international trade. There are various types of letters of credit:

A *sight letter of credit* is payable when the required documents have been presented.

A *revolving letter of credit* is issued for a certain amount of money and can be renewed as long as the limit is not exceeded.

A *traveler's letter of credit* typically lists banks that will accept payment requests.

A *performance letter of credit* guarantees performance of a contract's terms.

letter of intent

1. A document that formalizes the agreement between a company and an underwriter. The letter of intent outlines the process for an initial public offering or for a secondary debt or stock issue and outlines the underwriter's fees,

ranges for stock or debt prices, and other pertinent terms.

2. A document that is signed by two companies that plan to merge. The document contains pertinent terms of the merger such as the price the company will be purchased for, the preliminary merger schedule, and who will have leadership positions in the new, combined company.

3. A document created by a bank that outlines the terms on a loan that it is willing to make to a corporation.

leu The currency unit of Moldova and Romania, comprised of 100 ban.

lev The currency unit of Bulgaria, comprised of 100 stotinka.

level playing field A situation in which all competitors have the same advantages and disadvantages and have to adhere to the same rules. Companies may attempt to argue before Congress or regulators that their competitors have an unfair advantage because the playing field is not level.

level-premium insurance A type of insurance policy whose premiums do not change during the entire term of the policy. Although the amount of a level premium is higher than necessary for the protection given in the early years of the contract, it is less than necessary for coverage in the later years of the policy. A life insurance policy can be a level-premium policy.

leverage

1. The amount of debt a company has. A highly-leveraged company has a relatively large amount of debt when compared to the level of assets it owns. Although becoming highly leveraged can create significant profits if things go according to plan, it can severely hamper a company that is caught in a slowing market or experiences unanticipated competition.

2. To purchase stocks or other investments by using borrowed funds (on

margin). An investor who borrows money from his or her broker to purchase stocks uses leverage in order to increase his or her potential gain. However, if the investment declines in value, then the amount of money the investor loses likely increases well.

leveraged buyout (LBO) A transaction by a small group of individuals that turns a public company into a private company. An LBO involves using a significant amount of debt to pay for the purchase. The interest payments on the debt are paid out of the cash flows of the acquired company. Management also may use this technique, which then is called a *management buyout*. One of the largest LBOs was the LBO of RJR Nabisco in 1989 for $30 billion, which was financed by junk bond sales. See also *junk bond* and *management buyout*.

leveraged loans Speculative-grade or unrated loans that are priced above LIBOR by approximately 2 percentage points or higher. Leveraged loans have a greater chance of defaulting, so investors demand higher interest rate payments in exchange for investing. See also *LIBOR*.

Levitt, Arthur The longest-serving chairman of the Securities and Exchange Commission (SEC). Appointed by President Bill Clinton in July 1993, Levitt was reappointed to a second five-year term in May 1998. He resigned in February 2001. Levitt's term was characterized by a strong emphasis on investor protection. He was considered an advocate for small, individual investors, and in 2002 published a book that lists the seven deadly sins that the financial industry commits against investors. Before becoming SEC chairman, Levitt owned *Roll Call*, a newspaper that covers Capitol Hill. From 1989 to 1993, Levitt was the chairman of the New York City Economic Development Corporation. He was the chairman of the American Stock Exchange from 1978 to 1989.

Levitt, William A real estate developer who created a major innovation in the U.S. housing industry by building a mammoth residential subdivision after World War II. It consisted of over 17,000 homes that were nearly identical. The subdivision, which soon took the name Levittown, was built on Long Island in New York state.

Lewis, John L. A labor union leader who was the president of the United Mine Workers in the mid-1930s. He set up the rival Congress of Industrial Organizations when the American Federation of Labor ignored his attempt to organize unskilled workers. He obtained a landmark wage and benefit package for United Mine Workers' members when workers went on strike in the 1940s.

liability An obligation to make a payment to a person or company in exchange for a benefit that has been received or money that has been lent. The liability section on a company's balance sheet is one of the three major parts of the balance sheet.

LIBID See *depo rate*.

LIBOR See *London Interbank Offered Rate*.

life annuity with period certain An investment whose payouts are made to the insured during his or her lifetime or to his or her beneficiary according to the terms of a guarantee provision. If the insured dies within a certain time period after starting to receive income, usually 10 or 20 years, the insured's beneficiary will receive regular payments for the balance of the period.

life cycle A versatile term that applies to the lifetime of a product or business. Business life cycles are characterized by a start up phase, a period of growth, maturity, and closure.

life expectancy The age to which an average person is expected to live, based on the person's sex, health factors, and other demographic data. Life expectancy rates are calculated by actuaries and are used extensively by life insurance companies to determine how much to charge for life insurance policies. Life expectancy varies according to a person's current age: A baby born today may be expected to live until 85 years of age; a 50-year-old may be expected to live only until age 75.

life insurance A contract that pays the insured's beneficiaries a specified amount of money, called a *death benefit,* upon the insured's death. In return, the insured pays the life insurance company monthly or yearly premiums.

There are many types of life insurance. Permanent insurance policies remain in effect throughout the life of the insured as long as premiums continue to be paid. These policies increase in value over time, allow the insured to borrow against the policy, and offer financial flexibility to use the cash value to pay the policy's premium, if the policy holder is short on cash. Types of permanent policies are whole life, variable life, and universal life.

Term life insurance policies are cost-effective alternatives to permanent insurance policies. Term policies cover the insured for only a specified amount of time, which is usually one year. When that term is up, a new policy has to be obtained, but the insurer isn't obligated to issue the policy if the person's health condition worsens.

life insurance cash value The value in a permanent life insurance policy that can be withdrawn if the policy is surrendered. The cash value also indicates how much can be borrowed against the policy by the policy holder.

LIFFE *London International Financial Futures Exchange.* See *Euronext.*

LIFO See *last in, first out.*

light-weight vehicle sales An economic indicator, little-watched outside of the automobile industry, that tracks total sales and leases of domestic and imported new cars and lightweight trucks, which are trucks that weigh up to 10,000 pounds. The data measures both consumer and business sales, and is collected by Ward's Automotive Reports and the American Automobile Manufacturers Association (AAMA). It is seasonally adjusted by the U.S. Commerce Department, and released every 10 days, or 3 times a month.

lilangeni The currency unit of Swaziland, comprised of 100 cents.

limit

1. In the futures market, the maximum daily allowable amount that a futures contract may advance or decline during one trading session.

2. The number of positions that one trader may hold in the market.

limit down In the futures market, the maximum downward price movement allowed during one trading session for a specific future contract. Once a limit down is reached, trading halts unless a sell order comes into the market to change the market's direction. *Limit up* is the opposite of limit down.

limit order Used when placing a trade for a stock or futures contract to make certain that the order isn't bought above a certain price or sold below a particular level. For example, an investor may want to buy 1,000 shares of AAA, which is currently priced at $10.25. The investor could submit a limit order that stipulates that he or she will buy shares of AAA until either 1,000 shares are bought or the price hits $12.00.

limit up The maximum price movement allowed for a futures market during one trading session. When the limit is reached, trading halts unless a sell order comes into the market to change the market's direction. See also *limit down.*

limited A term that is used in the United Kingdom to designate a private company whose owners have limited liability. The abbreviation *Ltd.* is placed after a company's name to identify it as limited.

limited liability partnership (LLP) A business structure that limits a partner's liability to the amount of his or her investment. It is a designation often used by law or accounting firms. Also called *limited liability company*.

limited partner　See *limited partnership*.

limited partnership　A business organization or investment structure in which the general partners manage the business and assume the legal risk and obligation. The limited partners share in the partnership's returns, but they aren't liable for the partnership's debts, so they can lose only the amount of their investment A limited partnership often exists to make specific investments or is created to make venture capital investments.

Lipper Ratings　A firm that ranks the performance of mutual funds by the investment objective of the fund, such as a small-cap growth or a fixed-income fund. Lipper Ratings produces rankings for different time periods, such as the most recent quarter, 1 year, 5 years, and 10 years. The rankings are based on total return with capital gains and dividends reinvested. Lipper is owned by Reuters Plc.

liquid　An investment or asset that can be quickly converted into cash at a price that closely resembles a fair market value. Treasury bills and widely-traded stocks are examples of liquid investments. Real estate and private equity investments are not liquid. A *liquid market* can accept large sell or buy orders without causing an inordinate influence on price. *Liquidity risk* is an uncertainty that is created from the inability to buy or sell an investment in a secondary market.

liquid asset　Either cash or an asset that is easily convertible into cash, such as bank deposits or money market fund shares. Typically, a company's liquid assets are cash, marketable securities, and accounts receivable. Examples of illiquid assets are real estate, venture capital investments, and limited partnerships.

liquid crystal display (LCD)　A technology used in monitors for notebook and desktop computers. LCD's popularity likely will diminish as flat-panel displays, which have thin display screens, decrease in price and thus become more popular.

liquidate

1. To sell all of a business's assets and close down the business. An involuntary liquidation is called a *Chapter 7 bankruptcy.*

2. To close a brokerage account and sell its stocks and investments.

3. To close open futures and options positions. If futures are owned, an equivalent amount is sold to liquidate a position. If futures have been sold short, then the equivalent position is bought to liquidate a position.

liquidity event　Describes how an investor is going to realize a profit on an investment in a non-public company. The term is typically used in the venture capital industry. Liquidity events typically occur by issuing stock through an initial public offering (IPO) or through an acquisition by a larger company. Also called *exit strategy.*

liquidity ratio　A measure of how quickly a company can liquidate its securities and cover its short-term liabilities. It is a measure of a company's financial strength. To calculate the liquidity ratio, divide the total value of all cash and marketable securities by current liabilities. Also called *cash ratio.*

liquidity risk　A risk that comes from not being able to sell an asset quickly. Some assets that come with a potential liquidity risk include real estate, cars, limited partnerships, or an ownership interest in a small business. These items may be hard to sell if: 1) there is an inefficient secondary market, 2) the asset is not highly sought after, or 3) the economy is sluggish and therefore potential buyers are cautious. In contrast, investments that don't have liquidity risks include stocks of publicly traded companies, mutual fund shares, or futures or options contracts that are traded on an exchange.

liquid-yield option notes　See *LYONS.*

lira　The currency unit of Malta, comprised of 100 cents; the currency unit of Vatican City, comprised of 100 centesimos;

the currency unit of San Marino, comprised of 100 centesimos; the currency unit of Turkey, comprised of 100 kurus.

listed company A company whose stock trades on a major stock exchange such as the New York Stock Exchange, American Stock Exchange, or the NASDAQ stock market. In order to be listed, a company has to meet stringent financial and performance requirements.

listing and maintenance agreement A written agreement between a company and an exchange, such as NASDAQ or the New York Stock Exchange, in which the company agrees to maintain the market's qualitative and quantitative listing standards.

listing broker A licensed real estate professional who obtains the contractual right to sell a house or commercial property. Often, a listing broker shares the commission earned with the selling broker. Listings may be exclusive to the real estate office, or may be advertised among all brokers through a multiple listing service. Also called *listing agent*.

litas The currency unit of Lithuania, comprised of 100 centas.

live cattle futures A futures contract that is traded on the Chicago Mercantile Exchange (CME). When live cattle futures were introduced in 1964, the concept of trading futures on a live and non-storable commodity was revolutionary.

live hogs See *lean hogs*.

living benefit A type of life insurance policy where the insured can receive a payout from the policy while still alive. Typically, this benefit is allowed in cases of terminal illness or other long-term, severe health problems.

living trust A revocable trust whose terms become effective while the donor is still alive. Although the trust is the legal owner of property, investments, or assets in the trust, the creator of the trust (called a *grantor*) does not give up any control over the assets and can still buy or sell them.

Those assets are used for the benefit of another person, called a *beneficiary*. A trustee and a successor trustee manage the trust. A living trust in many ways resembles a will. It includes instructions and details for handling the writer's estate at death. However, unlike a will, it does not go through probate and prevents the court from controlling the deceased person's assets. Also called *inter vivos trust*.

living will A document that lets the creator state his or her preferences about what type of medical treatment should be given in the event that he or she becomes terminally ill or severely injured and is unable to declare his or her intentions. A living will dictates whether the person is to be fed intravenously or to be put on a respirator, among other health-care directives.

LLC A *Limited Liability Company* is a legal company that has a limited existence. It is neither a corporation nor a partnership. The LLC can be dissolved when a member dies, resigns, or files for bankruptcy protection, unless the remaining members unanimously vote to continue the business. The LLC has a termination date in the Articles of Organization, but the operating agreement can be written to avoid that end result. An LLC allows taxes that are owed on income to pass through directly to the owners, who have to report the income on their income tax forms.

Lloyd's of London A group of insurance underwriters located in London, England. When a risk is underwritten, it is shared by many different member underwriting syndicates. Each syndicate decides what risks it wants to underwrite. Individual investors in the syndicate are called *names* and are wealthy people with a significant amount of money to invest who are attracted by the large returns. Freak events, such as strong hurricanes in the United States or an unnaturally large number of disasters, can wipe out profits and require the names to invest more money and incur a substantial loss. Lloyd's doesn't issue policies itself but it does set standards for its members. Separately,

Lloyd's is also a major reinsurer, which is an insurance company that insures other insurance companies against large payouts, thus allowing other insurance companies to limit their risks.

LLP   See *limited liability partnership.*

load   A charge added to the sale of shares in a mutual fund. The load covers sales commissions and other market costs. A mutual fund without a sales charge is called a *no-load mutual fund.* Typically loads range from 0.5% to 2.0% of the mutual fund's assets under management.

loan commitment   A written commitment that obligates the lender to provide a certain amount of funds at a specific interest rate for a limited time period. Typically, loan commitments have an expiration date. A commitment fee may be charged.

loan value

1. The maximum amount that a lender is willing to lend against collateral. For example, if a lender is willing to loan 80 percent of the appraised value of a $1 million house, then the loan value is $800,000.

2. The maximum value of securities that a broker can lend to a customer through a margin account, mandated by the Federal Reserve through Regulation T.

3. The amount of a whole life insurance policy that the policyholder may borrow against.

loan-loss reserves   Money that a bank sets aside to offset potential losses from loans or other receivables that aren't paid. By setting aside money for loan-loss reserves, a company lowers the amount of its quarterly profit. However, when the actual losses occur, the company has set aside funds to be able to cover the anticipated losses. As the economy weakens, companies typically increase their loan-loss reserves.

loan-to-value ratio   The relationship between the dollar amount that has been borrowed and the value of the asset that was purchased with the borrowed funds.

local   A floor trader on an options or futures exchange who trades contracts for his or her own account. Locals help to provide liquidity to the markets by being present to either buy or sell securities.

Local Development Corporation (LDC)   An investment company that has been certified by the Small Business Administration (SBA) to help finance small businesses. An LDC can obtain special financing from the SBA that enables it to extend long-term, fixed-asset financing to local small businesses.

lockbox   An accounts-receivable management system in which customers mail payments to a post office box affiliated with the company's bank. Bank employees check the box frequently, deposit checks into the company's checking account, and then either electronically transmit or telephone the check details to the company's accounts receivable department. The process gives the company access to its money more quickly and saves the company from hiring more staff to process the checks. The bank charges a fee for the lockbox service.

locked in

1. A situation in which an investor has made a profit on an investment but is reluctant to sell it because the gain will be subject to ordinary income taxes rather than capital gains taxes, which are assessed after a minimum holding period and are lower than regular tax rates.

2. A situation in which a hedged position can't be lifted without offsetting both sides of the hedge.

locked market   A temporary condition in which the selling price, or *offer,* of one security is the same as the *bid,* or buy price, of another security. Locked-market conditions are rare, and occur most frequently in fast-moving markets. Also called *locked quotations* or *crossed quotations.*

lock-limit   A term used in the futures market to describe upward or downward limits to price moves during a trading session. Once the lock-limit is reached, prices can't move any further in that direction during the trading session; trading comes to a halt. If prices begin to move in the opposite direction, then trade will resume and the market will no longer be locked.

lock-step option See *ladder option.*

lockup A restriction made when giving shares in an initial public offering that limits when the buyer can sell the shares after the IPO begins trading.

London Club An informal group of commercial banks that jointly negotiate their claims against debtor countries. The banks band together to ensure that their interests are being protected. The composition of the group depends on which banks have given loans.

London Interbank Bid rate See *depo rate.*

London Interbank Offered Rate (LIBOR) The rate that international banks typically charge each other for loaning euro dollars overnight in the London market. Frequently quoted, the rate is used to price a variety of financial issues and short-term debt. Often, interest rates are quoted at an amount above LIBOR.

London Metal Exchange (LME) A U.K. commodities exchange that trades futures and options contracts on non-ferrous industrial metals. These are high-grade aluminium alloy, copper grade A, standard lead, primary nickel, tin, and zinc. The LME also trades contracts on silver. An index contract, the LMEX tracks the six primary base metals that are traded. Trading on the LME is a combination of floor trading and trading that is conducted over the phone or by electronic means.

London Stock Exchange (LSE) The primary stock exchange of the United Kingdom, where more than 470 companies' stocks from more than 60 countries trade. A variety of financial instruments are traded on the LSE, including stocks, bonds, warrants, and exchange-traded funds. Its

leading index is the London Financial Times Stock Index 100 (FTSI, pronounced FOOT-sie).

long A synonym for buy. If an investor owns 50 futures contracts and 100 shares of common stock, the investor is said to be long 50 futures contracts and long 100 shares of common stock. A trader who is long expects prices to rise. Long is the opposite of *short,* which corresponds to a sale of shares of futures contracts or common stock.

long bond Another name for the 30-year Treasury bond. It derives its name from the fact that it has the longest maturity on the Treasury yield curve, which ranges from the 3-month Treasury bill up to the 30-year bond. See also *Treasury bonds.*

long hedge A strategy in which futures contracts are purchased in order to protect against price changes in a cash commodity. A hedge is a trading strategy that creates a position in the futures or options market that is designed to protect against price changes in the underlying commodity or futures or options instrument. See also *hedge.*

long the basis Purchasing futures contracts to protect against possible rising prices of commodities. Traders will "go long the basis." It is the opposite of *shorting the basis,* which is the selling of futures contracts to protect against falling prices.

Long-Term Capital Management LP A U.S. hedge fund that became a household name when it collapsed in the fall of 1998. The hedge fund wrongly bet that interest rates would rise. Instead, in August 1998 Russia devalued its ruble and defaulted on some of its debt, which produced a worldwide flight to the safety of the U.S. Treasury bond. As buyers flooded into the market, bond prices increased and interest rates decreased. At the same time, large investors sold risky debt instruments, further depressing prices. Both of those actions were directly counter to Long-Term Capital's expectations. The hedge fund was founded by two men. John Meriwether was a pioneer of fixed-income arbitrage trading at Salomon Brothers, and was prominently featured in the book, *Liar's Poker*. Meriwether was caught in Salomon's government bond trading scandal in 1991. The other founder was David W. Mullins, Jr., who previously had been named an assistant Treasury secretary in 1988 and afterwards was named vice chairman of the Federal Reserve Board. The fund also had two partners who were Nobel Prize-winning economists: Myron Scholes and Robert Merton. They won a Nobel Prize for Economics in 1997 for their work on the Black-Scholes options pricing formula.

After the events that devalued the Long-Term Capital Management LP, government officials and the Federal Reserve Bank of New York arranged for a large group of financial institutions to invest $3.5 billion in the fund in order to prevent its losses crippling the financial system. Treasury officials from around the world, however, were afraid that the turmoil would lead to a credit crunch, and as a result many major industrial countries lowered interest rates in a concerted action. In the U.S., the Federal Reserve lowered interest rates three times during the fall of 1998, something that the Fed rarely does with such frequency. One of those reductions even occurred between meetings, which is very uncommon.

long-term care insurance Insurance that is purchased to pay for the costs of long-term health care, such as the cost of a nursing home. Long-term care insurance must be purchased separately from health insurance.

long-term debt Debt held by a company that will mature in a year or longer. Debt on a company's balance sheet is separated into short- and long-term debt.

long-term debt-total capital ratio A financial ratio that shows what proportion of long-term capital comes from long-term debt. It is calculated by dividing total long-term debt by total long-term capital. *Long-term capital* is defined as long-term debt plus shareholders' equity.

Long-Term Equity Anticipation Securities See *LEAPS*.

long-term gain A gain that occurs on an investment that was held for a year or longer. A long-term gain allows investors to pay a lower tax rate on the profit by paying a capital gains tax instead of the ordinary tax.

long-term liability An obligation that won't be due for one year or longer or that is beyond the normal operation cycle of the business. Examples of long-term liabilities are mortgages payable, long-term notes, employee pension obligations, and long-term lease liabilities. Balance sheets contain a long-term liability section.

lookback option An option in which the strike price is equal to either the lowest underlying security value (call option) or the highest underlying security value (put option) over a period of time that ends on the option expiration date. Lookback options are typically more expensive than regular options because they have more of a chance to be exercised than regular options do.

loophole A technicality that allows a law or tax rule to be bypassed without violating the law. The term is commonly used to refer to ways of avoiding paying taxes. When a tax loophole is discovered, the U.S. Treasury attempts to close the loophole and prosecute any current and future offenders.

loose credit policy A monetary policy that is characterized by low, or declining, interest rates. A loose credit policy is implemented by the Federal Reserve Board in order to increase growth and stimulate a slowing economy. If interest rates decrease too quickly, the economy may become over-heated and cause inflation. As a result, interest rates will rise.

Approximately every six weeks the Federal Reserve's Open Market Committee (FOMC) meets to determine interest rate policy. The FOMC implements its interest rate policy by setting a target for the federal funds rate, which is the rate that it charges its member banks for short-term loans. The inverse of loose credit policy is a tight monetary policy, which is characterized by high interest rates. Also called *easy money policy* or *accommodative money policy*.

loss-leader A product that is priced and advertised at very low levels to attract customers into a retail store. The price may be so low that the store loses money on the sale of the item. The hope is that customers will be enticed into the store by the loss leader, and while they are there will purchase other regularly priced items. The business recoups any money lost on the loss leader and marketing costs by selling more goods than otherwise would have been sold.

loti The currency unit of Lesotho, comprised of 100 sente.

Louvre Accord A declaration made at the Louvre in Paris February 1987 by finance ministers and central bank governors of major industrial countries. The Louvre Accord resolved that the value of the dollar had fallen far enough and should be stabilized. In a public statement, these ministers and central bank governors declared that their currencies were roughly at the right levels and were within ranges broadly consistent with underlying economic fundamentals. They promised to cooperate closely to foster the continued stability of foreign exchange rates at the current levels. The signers of the Louvre Accord also agreed to a variety of economic initiatives, such as reducing budget deficits, stimulating demand, and enacting tax reform. The impact of the statement was short-lived, however, as market forces reasserted themselves.

low-income housing tax credit A deduction-equivalent credit that offsets up to $25,000 of income, available to owners of residential, low-income rental property. Depending upon when the property was purchased, income limitations may apply.

LSE See *London Stock Exchange.*

Ltd. Short for *limited,* which is a term inserted after a company's name. It indicates that a company is incorporated and that the owners have limited liability. It is used in the United Kingdom and many former British colonies. It appears in other countries as well, including Japan and the United States.

Luce, Henry A pioneer of magazine publishing, Luce started *Time* magazine in 1923, which was aimed at his contemporaries, people who were college-educated and enjoying the Jazz Age. He also started *Fortune,* a business magazine, during the Great Depression. *Life,* which chronicled American life, was started in 1936. His final magazine was *Sports Illustrated,* which appeared in 1954.

Luddite An opponent of technology. The term comes from Ned Ludd, a leader of workmen in England who conducted campaigns early in the 19th century against replacing workers with machines.

lumber A product created from trees that is used in constructing homes, offices, and furniture. Futures contracts are traded on the Chicago Mercantile Exchange (CME), among other exchanges throughout the world. The CME's contract is random-length lumber futures, which began trading in 1969. Options also are traded on lumber.

luxury tax A tax assessed on expensive, non-essential goods that primarily affects wealthy people. A luxury tax in the United States on automobiles expired in January 2003. It was repealed in the Taxpayer Relief Act of 1997 and had been decreasing by one percentage point each year since then.

Lynch, Peter A strong performer in the mutual fund industry who was instrumental in bringing mutual funds as an investment option to the attention of the general public. Lynch helped push Fidelity Magellan Fund to become one of the largest mutual fund companies in the United States.

LYONS (liquid-yield option notes) A type of zero-coupon bond instrument that is convertible into equity. The product allows corporations to raise cash by issuing debt, pay lower interest rates than they would with ordinary debt, and earn a tax break. LYONS were invented by Merrill Lynch executive Thomas H. Patrick in the mid-1980s. Other Wall Street firms have their own brand of liquid-yield option notes.

M

M1 A measure of monetary supply tracked by the New York Federal Reserve Bank and reported every Thursday. See also *money supply*.

M2 A measure of monetary supply tracked by the New York Federal Reserve Bank and reported every Thursday. See also *money supply*.

M3 A measure of monetary supply tracked by the New York Federal Reserve Bank and reported every Thursday. See also *money supply*.

Ma Bell A slang term referring to AT&T Corp., which provided the original telephone service in the United States, and thus was considered the "mother" of the telecom industry. It is no longer commonly used.

Maastricht Treaty A 1991 treaty, signed in Maastricht, the Netherlands, that was designed to establish a single European currency and create economic cooperation in Western Europe. From the treaty a currency union was created that set up narrow ranges restricting the value of each countries' currency. The Maastricht Treaty was replaced by the agreement to create the euro, which began to circulate Jan. 1, 2002.

MAC Clause See *Material Adverse Change clause*.

Macaulay Duration A method developed by Frederick Macaulay to measure the interest rate risk of a bond. Macaulay demonstrated that the duration of a bond is a more appropriate measure of the bond's worth than its time to maturity because duration considers both the repayment of capital at maturity and the size and timing of coupon payments before maturity. The Macaulay Duration is the weighted average of the maturities of the bond's coupon and its principal repayment cash flows. The weights are the fractions of the bond's price that occur in each time period.

macroeconomics The study of economic activity by looking at the economy as a whole. Macroeconomics analyzes overall economic issues such as employment, inflation, productivity, interest rates, the foreign trade deficit, and the federal budget deficit.

MACRS See *Modified Accelerated Cost Recovery System*.

maintenance call A call to the owner of a brokerage account to inform the owner that more funds have to be deposited into the account because the account has fallen below the minimum equity requirements of the exchange or regulatory authorities. If additional cash isn't deposited within a specified time, some of the securities will be sold in order to bring the account up to required levels.

maintenance margin A minimum margin, or cash balance, that a customer must maintain on deposit with his or her brokerage firm in order to continue purchasing securities on margin, or with borrowed funds.

major medical insurance Medical insurance that pays for more than just basic hospital coverage. In addition to hospital room charges, it will pay for drugs used, bandages, X-rays, physician fees, and other charges that are incurred while in the hospital.

majority shareholder A shareholder who owns 51 percent or more of a company's stock. A large publicly traded company may have no majority shareholder. In that case, the majority shareholder may be someone with a significantly smaller percentage but who exerts effective control or influence over the company.

Malcolm Baldrige Award The Malcolm Baldrige National Quality Award recognizes companies that have successfully implemented total quality management principles to prevent errors and create high-quality products or services. The award is named for Malcolm Baldrige, who was President Ronald Reagan's Secretary of Commerce until he died in 1987. The Foundation for the Malcolm Baldrige National Quality Award was established in 1988.

malfeasance The performance of an illegal act, particularly by an elected official.

Maloney Act A law that provides for the regulation of the over-the-counter securities markets through national associations that are registered with the Securities and Exchange Commission (SEC). The National Association of Securities Dealers Inc. (NASD) is the only association that has ever registered under the act. It was passed in 1938 and added onto the Securities Exchange Act of 1934.

managed account An investment account that is managed by an investment advisor who makes the choice about what investments will be made. The account holder pays a management fee, which is usually based on a percentage of assets managed.

managed float The policy of allowing a currency to trade within a defined set of parameters. Those parameters are set by the government.

managed futures An industry made up of professional money managers who manage their clients' funds on a discretionary basis using futures contracts.

management accounting A system that provides company managers with financial information they use to monitor the company's operations and make financing and investment decisions. The system enables managers to evaluate the company's overall profitability as well as individual departments' income and expenses.

management buyout A heavily leveraged transaction that involves management and outside investors taking a public company private. The acquirers borrow a significant amount of money to purchase the company. They plan to pay the debt payments from the acquired company's earnings.

management fee A fee that is paid to the managers of a mutual fund, pension fund, or other investment fund.

management information system (MIS) The computer system a company uses to maintain the information that it needs to manage its business.

managing underwriter The investment banker or bankers for a specific debt or equity offering charged with coordinating the offering. The underwriting agreement lists who the managing underwriters are and outlines their responsibilities. Managing underwriters receive more of the issue to sell to their clients, thus making the issue more lucrative for the underwriter. Managing underwriters determine how much of the issue other underwriters will receive to sell to their clients. They also engage in open market transactions during the underwriting period to stabilize the securities' market price. See also *underwriter.*

manat The currency unit of Azerbaijan, comprised of 100 qepiq, and Turkmenistan, comprised of 100 tenge.

mandate A declaration that indicates that an investment banker has won the opportunity to do debt or equity underwriting for a corporation or to advise it on merger discussions

mandatory convertible A debt issue that is converted into equity within a certain time period, often three years. A mandatory convertible is an attractive alternative for companies that have too much debt. Ratings agencies typically count 80 cents out of each $1 in the mandatory convertible as *equity,* which helps protect the company's debt rating. The debt can be ranked as equity because within three years the debt will be turned into equity.

manipulation The intentional deception of investors by controlling or artificially affecting the market for a security. Manipulation can involve a number of techniques to affect either the supply or demand of a stock. Traders might spread false or misleading information about a company; improperly limit the number of publicly-available shares; or rig quotes, prices, or trades to create a false or deceptive picture of the demand for a security.

Manley, John Canada's Minister of Finance who was appointed in June 2002. Previously, Manley was the Deputy Prime Minister of Canada (January 2002 to June 2002), Minister of Foreign Affairs (in 2000) and the Minister of Industry (in 1993). He was first elected to the House of Commons in 1988 and he is a member of the Liberal Party of Canada. He is a business and tax lawyer by training and was the chairman of the Ottawa-Carleton Board of Trade in 1985.

Maple Leaf A bullion coin minted by the Canadian government in gold, silver, and platinum. These coins are collected by investors and coin collectors and are actively traded. They can be purchased from the Canadian government or from traders in the secondary market.

margin The amount of money (or the value of assets) deposited by a customer to a broker in order to qualify for a loan to trade securities, or for a margin loan. Similar to collateral, margin may also be deposited by a broker with a clearing member of a futures exchange. If conditions become volatile in the futures market, margin requirements are raised. A clearing member of a futures exchange is also required to pay margin to the clearinghouse.

A margin is not a partial payment on a purchase. At the end of each trading day, profits and losses on open positions are calculated (using the mark-to-market process). If an investor has lost money and his or her margin account is therefore below minimum balance requirements, the broker makes a margin call to inform the investor that he or she needs to deposit additional funds in the account. The Securities and Exchange Commission regulates margins charged on investment accounts used to purchase stocks, bonds, and other financial instruments.

margin call A demand made of a customer of a stock brokerage or futures commission merchant firm to add more money into his or her account. Margin calls are made in order to bring investors' accounts up to a minimum level. This happens when the price of a stock, futures contract, or other security declines after it has been purchased on margin. In the futures market, a clearinghouse also may make a call asking the member to increase the amount of money on deposit.

margin requirement The minimum amount of money that a client must have on deposit, either in cash or approved securities, in a margin account at a brokerage office. Margin requirements for stock trading are governed by the Federal Reserve through Regulation T. Generally, investors are required to have a minimum margin of 50 percent of the purchase price of securities or 50 percent of the proceeds of short sales. Also called *initial margin*.

marginal revenue The change in revenue that can be attributed to the sale of an additional unit of output. When marginal revenue exceeds marginal costs, it is profitable to produce and sell an additional unit.

marginal tax rate The tax rate that is paid on an additional dollar of taxable income. In progressive tax systems, the tax rate paid increases as income rises. The U.S. and many European companies have a progressive tax system. For example, suppose the tax rate is 25% for the first $25,000 of a person's income and 35% for the next $10,000. A person earning $30,000 a year would have a marginal tax rate of 35%, as any additional income earned by the person would be taxed at 35%. The actual percentage rate of tax that ends up being paid will vary according to the amount of deductions that are taken.

marginal utility The additional satisfaction received from goods or services that is derived from consuming one more unit. For example, if a person is hungry, one hamburger may provide a great deal of satisfaction, or utility. The second hamburger provides less utility, and the third one provides little or no utility. The value of a good depends on its utility.

mark-to-market An accounting standard by which companies value their assets and liabilities on their balance sheet using the assets' current market values. Traders in the futures industry also have to mark-to-market their books at the end of each day.

market cap   Short for market capitalization. See *market capitalization*.

market capitalization (market cap)
The value of a corporation derived by multiplying its stock price by the number of outstanding shares. For example, a company with a stock price of $20 and 10 million shares outstanding has a market capitalization of $200 million.

The value of a company's market capitalization determines whether it is *small cap, mid cap,* or *large cap.* However, cap size definitions vary greatly among financial firms. A general guideline is that a small-cap company has a market capitalization of $300 million to $1 billion; a mid-cap company ranges from $1 billion up to $5 billion; and a large-cap company is over $5 billion. Sometimes, companies under $300 million are called *micro-cap* companies. To calculate the market capitalization of foreign companies that have issued American Depositary Receipts (ADR) in the United States, only the outstanding ADR shares are used, and shares that are issued and traded in other countries are excluded.

market correction   In technical analysis, a reversal in the direction of prices following a period of sustained price movement. The term often is used informally to indicate that the market or the price of a stock or commodity has changed directions.

market interest rate   The rate of interest paid in the bond market on bonds that are in a similar risk category. Also may be called an *effective interest rate.*

market maker   A firm or individual that is ready to buy or sell a particular stock on a continuous basis by giving a publicly quoted price. They attempt to make a small profit from differences between the buy and sell prices. Market makers typically are found on the NASDAQ or other over-the-counter exchanges. Market makers on

an exchange, such as the New York Stock Exchange, are called *third-market makers.* Many stocks have more than one market maker. Market makers provide a two-sided market and add liquidity to the market.

market order   An order to buy or sell a futures contract or a stock at a market price. In the futures market, the order is for a futures contract that must be filled at the best price right away.

market perform   A rating issued by Wall Street analysts that indicates lukewarm approval of a company's prospects. If an analyst rates a company a market perform, the common expectation is that the analyst is really saying "sell" but doesn't want to be that blunt for fear of offending the company and preventing his or her employer from winning future lucrative banking business from the client. The term *neutral* may be used instead.

market portfolio   A collection of all of an investor's assets such as stocks, bonds, real estate, cash, and so on.

market reporter   Someone who is employed by a futures exchange to record prices as they are shouted out during trading. Market reporters are located near the trading pit so that they can see and hear all the trades as they happen.

market research   A study of a market or potential market for a company's product. Market research is done before developing or changing a product to ensure that there is demand for the product and that the product will be distinct from similar products. Market research involves surveying current and potential customers about what types of products or services they might want. It also may involve looking at other research conducted on the demographics of a region or a group of potential customers.

market share   The percentage of a market, or sales, that a particular company has in a certain industry or region.

market timing   A strategy used by some investors when deciding whether to buy or sell securities. Investors look at current trends such as interest rates, market volatility, and expectations for an industry and then predict how stock prices will respond.

market value of portfolio equity The net present value of a company's existing assets, liabilities, and off-balance sheet investments.

marketable security A security that is easily bought or sold. Stocks and futures contracts are examples of marketable securities. In contrast, a venture capital investment or a limited partnership may not be able to be easily sold.

market-if-touched order A trade order that becomes a market order when a certain price is reached. A *sell market-if-touched order* is placed above current prices. A *buy market-if-touched order* is placed below current prices. These trade orders are placed to protect investors from rapidly falling prices or to trigger action when a certain price is believed to signal a rapid, significant move above or below that price. See also *market order.*

market-on-close A trading order to purchase or sell a futures or options contract at the end of the trading session at a price within the closing range of prices.

market-on-open A trading order to purchase or sell a futures or options contract at the opening of the trading session at a price that is within the opening range of prices.

market-value-weighted index See *capitalization-weighted index.*

marriage penalty A term that refers to the situation in which a married couple pays more in taxes to the Internal Revenue Service than two single people with identical tax liabilities would. The marriage penalty was eliminated in 2003 after a tax cut was enacted by Congress.

Marshall Jr., George C. The developer of the Marshall Plan that rebuilt Europe after World War II. Marshall was the U.S.

secretary of state after World War II and had been the U.S Army chief of staff throughout World War II. See also *Marshall Plan.*

Marshall Plan A plan put forth by George C. Marshall Jr. to rebuild postwar Europe. The plan called for giving about $12 billion of U.S. aid to Western Europe in the late 1940s. Marshall won the Nobel Peace Prize in 1953, the only professional soldier ever given that award.

Martin Act A state law enacted in New York in 1921 that gave the attorney general jurisdiction over securities trade. The law was used by New York Attorney General Eliot Spitzer in the wake of the stock market slump of the late 1990s as a justification to investigate and bring civil and criminal penalties for conflicts of interest between investment banks and their research departments, as well as a number of other allegedly illegal abuses.

master limited partnership (MLP) Publicly traded partnerships that trade similar to common stock by issuing limited liability units to their shareholders. MLPs are an investment that combines the tax benefits of a limited partnership with the liquidity of publicly traded securities. MLPs are required to pay out quarterly dividends, which may be around ten percent.

matched sale-purchase agreement The outright sale by the Federal Reserve of securities for immediate delivery to a dealer or foreign central bank. The sale includes an agreement to buy the securities back on a specific date, typically within seven days, at the same price. Matched sale-purchase agreements have the effect of withdrawing reserves on a temporary basis. They are the opposite of *repurchase agreements,* which put reserves, or more money, into the economy.

matching rule An accounting rule that says revenues must be assigned to the accounting period in which the goods were sold or the services performed. Likewise, expenses must be assigned to the accounting period in which they are used to produce revenue.

Material Adverse Change (MAC) clause A clause in a merger agreement that gives both parties remedies, or the right to cancel the merger, in the event that prescribed negative events occur. The negative events may be a sharp decline in sales or a regulatory change or problem that would seriously impair the ability of the merged company to function.

material event News or details that may reasonably be expected to affect a company's stock price and thus decisions that investors make about buying or selling the company's stock. Material events may be the addition or loss of a large customer, falling or rising sales, a merger agreement, financial results above or below expectations, or a change in the company's dividend policy. Material events must be disclosed to the public and to the Securities and Exchange Commission in an 8-K.

May Day

1. In the United States, May 1, 1975, the day when fixed minimum brokerage commissions ended and brokers were free to set their own commission rates. Discount brokerage firms developed as a result. The end of fixed brokerage commissions planted the seeds for conflicts of interest between research analysts and investment bankers. Without inflated brokerage commissions to pay the salaries and bonuses of research analysts, they soon began to work more closely with investment bankers. By the time of the stock market boom in the late 1990s, research analysts in many instances were actively involved in helping the bankers at a firm take companies public in what was a crumbling of the so-called "Chinese Wall" that was supposed to separate the two departments.

2. In Europe, May 1 is International Workers' Day, which commemorates the struggle of working people to obtain decent working conditions and fair pay. It is celebrated throughout the world with the notable exception of the United States and Canada.

MBA Mortgage Applications Survey A weekly index that is a leading indicator of home sales activity. The four-week moving average of the indices, which includes indices for composites, purchases, refinancing, fixed mortgage rates, and adjustable mortgage rates, smoothes out the volatile weekly figures. Because many homebuyers apply for a mortgage before purchasing a home, the mortgage application purchase index is a leading indicator of future home sale activities and is an early gauge of economic strength. Refinancing activity is important because it often leads to increased levels of consumer spending. The data is timely, with a lag factor of only five days. However, the data is limited because it covers less than half of the U.S. residential mortgage market and the historical data goes back only to 1990. The Mortgage Bankers Association of America (MBAA) produces the data.

MBS See *mortgage-backed securities.*

McCarran-Ferguson Act of 1945 A law passed by Congress that gave states the right to regulate the insurance business. Often states have a Department of Insurance that is responsible for regulating insurers.

McDonough, William The chairman of the Public Company Accounting Oversight Board, as of this printing, who was appointed in May 2003. McDonough had been the president and chief executive of the New York Federal Reserve Bank since July 1993.

MD&A *Management's discussion and analysis,* an interpretive section in a regulatory filing, quarterly report, annual report, or prospectus that explains management's view of the events or challenges facing a company. Also called a *financial review.*

mean The average, or arithmetic mean. To calculate the mean of a series of numbers, the numbers are added together and then are divided by the number of terms. For example, the average of 5, 10, and 15 is 10. The answer is calculated by adding the three numbers, which equal 30, and then dividing 30 by the number of terms, 3, to get 10.

mean income　The total income of area residents, divided by the number of residents. The mean income measurement allows relative incomes in one area to be compared with mean incomes in another area.

median　The middle number in a series of numbers. To find the median, first arrange the numbers from the smallest to the largest. If the number of items is odd, the median is the number that is in the middle of the series. If the number of items is even, the median is the average of the two middle numbers. For example, the median of the odd-numbered series of 2, 5, 7, 9 and 12 is 7. The median of the even-numbered series of 1, 6, 8 and 15 is 7.

median income　The middle point of area incomes. Median income divides the income distribution range in half, one with residents having incomes above the median, and the other with residents having incomes below the median. Median family income and median household income are based on the distribution of the total number of families, including those with no income. However, median income calculated for individuals excludes information from those who have no income.

Medicare tax　A tax deducted from employees' paychecks that goes to pay for medical benefits for people over 65 years of age. Medicare tax is paid by both employee and employer.

medium-term notes (MTN)　Notes that are sold continuously, often weekly, that have all the features of corporate bonds. (A typical bond offering is made only every three to four years.) The maturities of medium-term notes range from 9 months up to 30 years, although 30 years isn't a common issuance. Companies that sell MTNs are the highest-quality companies.

megabits per second (Mbps)　A measure of the amount of information that can be transmitted over a computer network each second.

MEMS　*Microelectro-mechanical systems* are tiny sensors and other devices that have small moving parts. Such devices are commonly found in consumer electronics products such as DVD players, cell phones, and hand-held computers, expanding from their early markets in industrial and military applications.

Mer, Francis　As of this printing, the Finance Minister of France, whose official title is the Minister of the Economy, Finance, and Industry. Mer has been Chairman of the National Association for Technical Research since 1991. From October 1997 to October 1998, he was Chairman of the International Iron and Steel Institute. He also was chairman of Eurofer, the European steel manufacturers' association, from 1990 to 1997.

Merc　See *Chicago Mercantile Exchange*.

merchant bank　A term commonly used in the U.K.; the equivalent to an investment bank in the U.S. Merchant banks advise companies on mergers and on raising capital, managing portfolios, dealing in bullion, and other financial services. Typically merchant banks don't make loans.

Mercosur　The world's third largest trading group, comprised of Argentina, Brazil, Paraguay, and Uruguay. Bolivia and Chile are associate members. The four main countries created Mercosur in March 1991 when the Treaty of Asunción was signed. The group took effect on December 31, 1994. Mercosur was established with the purpose of creating a common market and customs union among the countries using the economic cooperation between Argentina and Brazil since 1986 as a model. Mercosur also established common external tariffs and adopted a common trade policy in relationship to other countries.

merger　The process of two or more companies combining. In one model, one company retains its name and often most of its top management. This company acquires all the assets and liabilities of the firm being acquired, which ceases to exist after the merger is completed. Another type of a merger is a *consolidation,* in which a completely new firm is created and both the other two firms cease to exist. Often, mergers are classified into three types: vertical, horizontal, or conglomerate.

A *vertical merger* involves combining a company with its supplier or customer.

A *horizontal merger* combines two companies that are direct competitors making the same products.

A *conglomerate merger* involves two companies that are not in related industries or businesses.

merger of equals   A merger in which two equal companies come together. The term is frequently used when two companies are announcing a friendly merger. It implies that the merger will bring two happy "families" together. In reality, a merger of equals rarely occurs since one company will usually have more power and retain more management and employees in the new venture.

Merrill, Charles E.   One of the founders of the largest U.S. stock and bond firm, Merrill Lynch. Before the crash of 1929, he advised his clients to sell some of the stocks in their portfolios. During the 1930s he concentrated on building the Safeway supermarket chain. In the 1940s he returned to Wall Street and focused on bringing stock investments to small investors.

metical   The currency unit of Mozambique, comprised of 100 centavos.

metrics   A general term that refers to financial performance measures, such as earnings per share or revenues. An analyst may say that one company beat its competitors in certain metrics.

Metropolitan Statistical Area (MSA)   A federally designated area with an urban population of at least 50,000 residents and a regional population of 100,000. A metropolitan statistical area includes major cities plus the suburban areas surrounding them. Federal banking regulations allow financial institutions that do business within an MSA to use a single master account with

the Federal Reserve for computing reserve requirements, check processing, and sending electronic fund transfers.

Mexico Bolsa Index   A market capitalization-weighted index of the leading stocks that are traded on the Mexican Stock Exchange. It began with a base level of 0.78 on October 30, 1978. This index also is called the IPC (Indice de Precios y Cotizaciones) All-Share Index.

mezzanine   Debt given to middle-market companies that is subordinated to other higher-ranking debt. Typically mezzanine financing is used for buyouts, recapitalizations, or acquisitions, and the amount of the debt often ranges from about $5 million to $25 million. Mezzanine debt also may incorporate stock warrants. Mezzanine financing may be used in the venture capital industry to describe a funding for a company that is beyond the startup stage but is not yet ready for an initial public offering.

Michael R. Milken   Dubbed the "junk bond king" for his role in creating the junk bond market and using the proceeds to help companies mount hostile takeovers, or leveraged buyouts, during the 1980s. He worked at Drexel Burnham Lambert, which folded after legal investigation of Milken and the firm's activities. Drexel filed for bankruptcy protection in 1990 and was dismantled. Milken pled guilty to six counts of securities fraud in 1990, served nearly two years in prison, and paid more than $1 billion in fines, penalties, and restitution. He was barred from the securities business for life.

micro cap   A very small corporation with a market capitalization of $300 million or less. The exact cutoff for the market capitalization of a micro-cap company varies depending upon who is citing the criteria.

microeconomics   The branch of economics that examines how economic decisions are made by individual businesses, households, and industries. In contrast, *macroeconomics* analyzes big-picture economic decision-making throughout the economy and examines the effect that employment or inflation is likely to have on the economy. See also *macroeconomics.*

midcap Short for *mid-capitalization,* a measure of the size of a company by market capitalization. Market capitalization is calculated by multiplying the price of a company's stock by the number of shares outstanding. The definition of what is midcap will vary, but generally a midcap company has a market capitalization that ranges from $1 billion to $5 billion.

MIGA See *Multilateral Investment Guarantee Agency.*

mil A tenth of a cent ($0.001). Typically a mil is a unit of measurement used by cities to assess taxes on property, such as real estate or cars. The mil is multiplied by an asset's assessed valuation to arrive at the amount of tax that must be paid.

Milan MIB 30 A market capitalization-weighted index of the 30 top Italian companies traded on the Milan Stock Exchange. It had a base value of 10,000 on December 31, 1992. This index is revised twice a year, typically in March and September, based on companies' liquidity and market capitalization.

minimum bid repo rate The interest rate used by the European Central Bank (ECB) to set interest rate policy. The minimum bid repo rate is the rate at which the ECB buys and sells short-term government securities.

minimum-variance hedge ratio The minimum number of options or futures contracts needed to hedge a position in the cash market to prevent the least change in the total hedged position.

minority interest Less than 50 percent ownership in a company or joint venture.

minutes of use See *MOU.*

MIPS See *Monthly Income Preferred Shares.*

MIS See *management information system.*

mixed Market activity that is marked by some indices being up while others are down. For instance, if the Dow Jones Industrial Average and the S&P 500 are up, but the NASDAQ market is down, the market is mixed.

MLP See *master limited partnership.*

MM An abbreviation for million that typically is used in the financial markets. 5MM means 5 million.

MMbpd *Million barrels per day.* A term used in the oil industry to indicate how many barrels of oil a company can produce in one day. May also be shortened to *mpd.*

mnemonic The abbreviation that appears on the trading badges that individuals wear on the floors of exchanges. The badge has a few letters that serve as a quick shorthand when a trader needs to record the counter party to a trade. Mnemonic badges are worn by stock, futures, and options traders. In a broader context, mnemonics is the system of improving memory by using formulas.

MOB spread Short for *municipal over bond* spread, which measures the difference between the yield on the municipal bond futures contract and the yield on the Treasury bond futures contract on the Chicago Board of Trade. The MOB spread is often traded by those who want to exploit changes in the direction of interest rates.

mode The number in a series of numbers that occurs most frequently. If each observation occurs an equal number of times, there is no mode. If two or more observations occur the same number of times, then there is more than one mode, in which case the sample is called multimodal. For example, the mode of 2, 1, 5, and 1 is 1.

modeling A mathematical representation of a potential financial outcome if certain conditions fall within the specified parameters. Models are very complex financial instruments.

Modified Accelerated Cost Recovery System (MACRS) A method for writing off costs associated with purchasing assets. MACRS was introduced as part of the Tax Reform Bill of 1986. It does away with the concepts of estimated useful life and residual value in calculating the value of recorded assets. The intent was to encourage businesses to invest in new plants and equipment by allowing them to write off assets rapidly. MACRS accelerates the write-off of investments by allowing a recovery period shorter than the estimated useful life of the asset, in contrast to standard depreciation rules. MACRS allows businesses to recover the majority of the cost of the investments early in the depreciation schedule. Despite its acceptance by Congress, this type of a depreciation schedule isn't accepted for financial reporting under generally accepted accounting principles because the recovery periods are shorter than the depreciable assets' estimated useful life.

modified duration A measure of the Macaulay Duration adjusted to help estimate a bond's price volatility. Calculating modified duration gives an estimate of how bond prices would change if interest rates changed a small amount. Measuring the effect that large changes in interest rates would have on bond prices requires examining a bond's *convexity,* or the measure of the curvature of the price-yield relationship.

mom and pop store A small business managed by the owners, who make up a large percentage of the company's workforce.

momentum

1. A measure of the rate of change in prices, instead of the actual price levels. Momentum is a tool used in technical analysis.

2. The impetus of rising or falling prices.

monetarist An economist who watches the money supply to predict how the economy will perform. Monetarists dislike government initiatives that influence the economy. Instead, slow but steady growth in the money supply is seen as the key to growth. One of the most prominent monetarists was Milton Friedman. In contrast, Keynesian economists believe in active governmental initiatives to encourage economic activity.

monetary aggregates The measure that the U.S. Federal Reserve uses to monitor the United States's monetary assets using M1, M2, and M3. M1 is travelers' checks and the currency in circulation, in checking accounts, or in other accounts upon which checks can be written. M2 includes M1, plus savings accounts, time deposits under $100,000, and funds in retail money market mutual funds. M3 includes M2 plus time deposits over $100,000, balances in institutional money funds, repurchase liabilities issued by depository institutions, and eurodollars held by U.S. residents at foreign branches of U.S. banks and at all banks in the United Kingdom and Canada.

monetary policy The plan undertaken by a central bank, such as the Federal Reserve Bank in the U.S., to influence the cost and availability of money and credit. Monetary policies are put into effect in order to help promote national economic goals. For example, a monetary policy may be followed to raise or lower short-term interest rates. Printing more money and putting it into circulation is a monetary policy that is followed when a country faces *deflation,* or falling inflation, because this strategy tends to increase inflation.

monetary policy lag The time between a change in interest rates and when an effect is felt in the economy. A typical lag time is 6 to 12 months.

money An instrument that serves as a medium of exchange, has a standard of value, and is a means to save or store purchasing power. In the United States, money takes the form of paper currency and coins issued by the U.S. Treasury. Paper notes and coins issued by other governments also are considered money. Gold, silver and other metals have been used as money in the past with limited usage now.

money laundering   Making money that is generated through criminal activities appear as if it was earned through legitimate business activities. Detecting money-laundering activities is often very difficult because the money often is transferred between several accounts in order to conceal its true origins. As terrorism activities have increased, so too has the motivation for money laundering.

money market   See *money market securities.*

money market account   An account that usually pays higher interest rates than checking or savings accounts, but that may require a higher initial deposit. Money market accounts are offered by brokerage firms and they are not federally insured, unlike most checking and savings accounts.

money market certificate   A certificate of deposit in a minimum denomination of $10,000 that typically has a maturity of six months. The interest rate on a money market certificate is related to the yield on six-month Treasury Bills, in accordance with regulations issued by the Depository Institutions Deregulation Committee. See also *certificate of deposit.*

money market instruments   Financial instruments that usually mature in less than one year. They typically have only small fluctuations in price and involve minimal risk. Money market funds or 13- or 26-week Treasury bills are some examples of money market instruments.

money market securities   Interest-bearing securities that mature within one year. Included in this group are short-term certificates of deposit, repurchase agreements, and commercial paper. Generally, money market securities are low risk and have yields that are similar to Treasury securities with short maturities.

money order   A financial instrument that is equivalent to cash. A money order is purchased at a bank, a post office, or a busi-ness that cashes checks by paying cash. There is no chance that the money order will bounce because of insufficient funds, since cash is paid upfront for it. The money order lists both the payee and the person who purchased it.

money supply   The amount of money in the economy. There are three measures of money supply: M1, M2, and M3.

M1 is currency in circulation, travelers' checks, and checking accounts or other accounts upon which checks can be written.

M2 includes M1, plus savings accounts, time deposits under $100,000, such as certificates of deposit, and funds in retail money market mutual funds.

M3 includes M2 plus time deposits over $100,000, balances in institutional money funds, repurchase liabilities issued by depository institutions, and eurodollars held by U.S. residents at foreign branches of U.S. banks and at all banks in the U.K. and Canada.

The New York Federal Reserve Bank releases money supply data every Thursday. The Full Employment and Balanced Growth Act of 1978 (also called the Humphrey-Hawkins Act), required the Federal Reserve to set one-year target ranges for money supply growth twice a year and report the targets to Congress.

Money supply was a widely watched economic indicator in the 1980s. If money supply jumped, the financial markets anticipated that the Federal Reserve might attempt to limit money supply growth by raising short-term interest rates. However, by 1993 Federal Reserve Chairman Alan Greenspan said that money supply, or M2, had been downgraded as a reliable indicator of financial conditions because its forecasting ability declined. As a result, money supply has decreased substantially in its importance to the financial markets. When the Humphrey-Hawkins legislation requiring the Fed to set target ranges for money supply growth expired, the Fed announced that it was no longer setting such targets because doing so wasn't useful.

Monte Carlo Simulation   A process for valuing options by using numerical probability to generate a series of prices for the underlying instrument. The Monte Carlo Simulation randomly generates values for uncertain variables over and over. The results are analyzed to decide which variables are most likely to occur. It derives its name from Monte Carlo, the Monaco city near the South of France, which is known for its casinos.

Monthly Income Preferred Shares (MIPS) A creative financing arrangement that lets companies list a transaction on its balance sheet as preferred equity instead of debt. MIPS was one of the aggressive accounting techniques that Enron Corp. used to hide the true amount of debt it held.

monthly unemployment report See *nonfarm payrolls report.*

Moore's Law A law that states that the number of chips on a transistor, and thus the transistor's computing power, will double about every two or three years. The law also states that this increase in computing ability will not require an equivalent increase in cost. The law is named after Gordon Moore, a pioneer in the semiconductor industry, who articulated his theory in 1965. He was one of the founders of Fairchild Semiconductor in 1957, but left that firm with other colleagues to co-found Intel Corp. in 1968. To date, Moore's law has held true.

moral hazard A dilemma that arises when government officials take steps to bail out countries or businesses that are in serious financial trouble. Although the action may help prevent widespread financial turmoil, thereby protecting innocent parties, it creates an expectation that governments will always come to the aid of failing countries and companies, potentially increasing risky behavior because there is no penalty.

Morgan Stanley Capital International World Index A market capitalization weighted index that is comprised of equities from 23 developed economies in North America, Europe, and Asia/Pacific.

Morita, Akio As of this printing, the chairman of Sony Corporation, who has been instrumental in exporting Japanese goods to the United States and other countries around the world. He created the Sony Walkman, which combined tiny earphones with a small radio and was a major commercial success.

Morningstar Ratings A rating system for mutual funds that ranks performance on a scale ranging from one star (lowest rating) to five stars (highest rating). Morningstar is a Chicago-based global investment research firm that sells advisory products and services for individuals and institutional investors. It provides information on stocks, mutual funds, exchange-traded funds, closed-end funds, and variable annuity/life products.

mortgage A debt instrument that enables the borrower *(mortgagor)* to receive funds to purchase real estate. In return, the lender receives a lien on the property as security that the loan will be repaid. The borrower receives access to needed funds and the lender earns interest. The borrower has full use of the property and ownership rights. The lien is removed when the mortgage is paid off in full.

mortgage bond A bond secured by a mortgage on property. Mortgage bonds are backed by real estate or physical equipment that can be liquidated. Mortgage bonds are usually considered high-grade, safe investments and safer than unsecured bonds. If an issuer in default has both secured and unsecured bonds outstanding, secured bondholders are paid off first, then unsecured bondholders. Because unsecured bonds carry greater risk than secured bonds, they usually pay higher yields.

mortgage broker Someone who locates banks that are willing to issue a mortgage that will meet the borrower's criteria. The mortgage broker does not issue the mortgage but instead receives a fee for matching the home buyer with the financial institution issuing the mortgage.

mortgage insurance See *private mortgage insurance.*

Mortgage REIT A Real Estate Investment Trust that issues or owns loans that are secured by real estate collateral. See also *REIT.*

mortgage-backed funds A mutual fund that invests at least two-thirds of its portfolio in pooled mortgage-backed securities. *Mortgage-backed securities* are debt instruments whose principal and interest are backed up by underlying mortgage assets.

mortgage-backed securities (MBS) Securities that are created when a financial institution, such as Fannie Mae or Freddie Mac, purchases mortgages from the banks that issued the mortgages. The financial institutions package the mortgages and resell them into the secondary market where investors purchase them to earn current income in a relatively safe investment. The banks sell their mortgages so that they can make additional mortgage commitments and earn more fees. The payments on the underlying mortgages are used to make payments to the security holders. Mortgage-backed securities, such as those issued by Fannie Mae are secured by conventional mortgages with interest payments and the principle guaranteed.

most active list A list of the most active stocks on a stock exchange, as measured by volume for a specific trading day. This list typically is printed daily in financial newspapers.

MOU An acronym that stands for *minutes of use;* often used in the telecom industry. MOU is the total time, measured in minutes, that a customer uses his or her mobile phone during a day, month, or year.

moving average The average of closing prices for a set period of time. Typical moving averages are calculated on a 3-, 10-, or 20-day basis, though averages can be calculated using any number of days. To calculate a 3-day moving average, three suc-

cessive days of price moves are used. The average for the fourth day is figured and added, and the closing price for day one is dropped. The 3-day moving price average gives an indication of short-term price movements. A 20-day moving average smoothes out short-term price fluctuations; 3- or 10-day moving averages smoothes out short-term price changes to a lesser extent.

moving-average price chart A statistical-based trading tool that provides one method of analyzing a variety of price trends. A moving average is calculated by adding the prices, over a certain number of days, of the stock or investment being analyzed. The total is divided by the number of days. The advantage of a moving average price chart is that it smoothes price spikes and gives a truer indication of the market's trend.

MSA See *Metropolitan Statistical Area.*

MSCI ACWI The *Morgan Stanley Capital International All Country World Index,* a free float-adjusted market capitalization index that is designed to measure equity-market performance in the developed and emerging markets throughout the world. There were 49 developed- and emerging-market country indices included in the MSCI ACWI as of April 2002: Argentina, Australia, Austria, Belgium, Brazil, Canada, Chile, China, Colombia, the Czech Republic, Denmark, Egypt, Finland, France, Germany, Greece, Hong Kong, Hungary, India, Indonesia, Ireland, Israel, Italy, Japan, Jordan, Korea, Malaysia, Mexico, Morocco, the Netherlands, New Zealand, Norway, Pakistan, Peru, Philippines, Poland, Portugal, Russia, Singapore, South Africa, Spain, Sweden, Switzerland, Taiwan, Thailand, Turkey, the United Kingdom, the United States, and Venezuela.

MSCI EAFE Index The *Morgan Stanley Capital International Europe, Australasia and Far East Index,* a free float-adjusted market capitalization index that is designed to measure developed-market equity performance, excluding the United States and

Canada. As of April 2002, the MSCI EAFE Index consisted of the following 21 developed-market country indices: Australia, Austria, Belgium, Denmark, Finland, France, Germany, Greece, Hong Kong, Ireland, Italy, Japan, the Netherlands, New Zealand, Norway, Portugal, Singapore, Spain, Sweden, Switzerland, and the United Kingdom.

MSCI EM EMEA Index The *Morgan Stanley Capital International Eastern Europe, Middle East, and Africa* Index, a free float-adjusted market capitalization index that is designed to measure equity-market performance in the emerging market countries of Eastern Europe, the Middle East, and Africa. As of August 2002, the MSCI EM EMEA Index consisted of the following ten emerging market country indices: the Czech Republic, Hungary, Poland, Russia, Turkey, Israel, Jordan, Egypt, Morocco, and South Africa.

MSCI EMF Index The *Morgan Stanley Capital International Emerging Markets Free* Index, a free float-adjusted market capitalization index that is designed to measure equity-market performance in the global emerging markets. As of April 2002, the MSCI EMF Index consisted of the following seven emerging market country indices: Argentina, Brazil, Chile, Colombia, Mexico, Peru, and Venezuela.

MSCI Europe Index The *Morgan Stanley Capital International* Europe Index, a free float-adjusted market capitalization index that is designed to measure developed market equity performance in Europe. As of September 2002, the MSCI Europe Index consisted of the following 16 developed market country indices: Austria, Belgium, Denmark, Finland, France, Germany, Greece, Ireland, Italy, the Netherlands, Norway, Portugal, Spain, Sweden, Switzerland, and the United Kingdom.

MSCI World Index The *Morgan Stanley Capital International* World Index, a free float-adjusted market capitalization index that is designed to measure developed-market equity performance throughout the world. As of April 2, 2002, the 23 developed-market country indices included: Australia, Austria, Belgium, Canada, Denmark, Finland, France, Germany, Greece, Hong Kong, Ireland, Italy, Japan, the Netherlands, New Zealand, Norway, Portugal, Singapore, Spain, Sweden, Switzerland, the United Kingdom, and the United States.

MTN See *medium-term notes.*

Multilateral Investment Guarantee Agency (MIGA) An organization affiliated with the World Bank that promotes growth in emerging economies by encouraging foreign direct investment. To do this, it offers guarantees to investors and lenders in order to protect them against political risk.

multinational corporation A corporation that has offices or production facilities in many countries around the world, giving it a global presence. The term is typically used only for those corporations that have a presence in more than just a few countries.

multiple listing service A system that shows all the houses available for sale in a certain area. Multiple listing services help buyers because they quickly show what property is available in a specific area and at what price ranges. If a real estate agent other than the one who listed the property for sale ends up selling it, then both agents split the commission. Although the amount of the listing agent's commission decreases in such a sale, the system effectively increases the agent's chances of selling a property and thereby earning at least a partial commission.

municipal bond A bond that is issued by a city, state, or local government agency or entity, such as a school district, to finance public works projects or raise money. Municipal bondholders don't have to pay federal income tax on interest received from municipal bonds and also may be exempt from state and local taxes. Also called *munis.*

munis Pronounced MU-nees, a shortened name for *municipal bonds,* which are bonds issued by cities and states to finance the government's expenses. Investors in munis don't have to pay federal income taxes on the bonds and are sometimes exempt from state and local taxes as well.

murabaha A concept found in Islamic finance that governs a contract between a bank and its client, by which the bank purchases goods and then sells them to the client at a cost that includes a profit margin. The contract requires specific installment payments to the bank. This arrangement allows the bank to avoid charging interest, which is forbidden under some interpretations of Islamic law.

Muriel Siebert The first woman to buy a seat, or membership, on the New York Stock Exchange, in 1967 at the age of 35. After 1975, when brokers stopped earning fixed commissions, Siebert started her own firm, Muriel Siebert & Co., the first discount brokerage. She also was New York State's superintendent of banking in 1977.

musharaka An Islamic technique to provide funds to a partnership. Both parties provide capital and both may be active in managing the venture. Losses are shared on the basis of how much capital has been contributed. Profits are shared in any way the partners decide.

mutual fund An investment company that pools money from shareholders and invests it in a portfolio of securities. More than 82 million Americans own shares in mutual funds. There are four primary types of mutual funds: *stock, bond, money market,* and *hybrid* (a mixture of stocks and bonds). In August 2002, 43 percent of mutual fund assets were stock funds; 35 percent were money market funds; 17 percent were bond funds, and 5 percent were hybrid funds.

There are four laws that govern the mutual fund industry:

The Investment Company Act of 1940 requires all funds to register with the Securities and Exchange Commission and to meet certain operating standards.

The Securities Act of 1933 mandates certain disclosures.

The Securities Exchange Act of 1934 sets out antifraud rules regarding the purchase and sale of shares.

The Investment Advisors Act of 1940 regulates fund advisors.

Additionally, the National Association of Securities Dealers Inc. oversees most mutual fund advertising and sales materials.

Investors typically need to make a minimum initial investment, which may be $1,000 or $2,500. For Individual Retirement Account investments, often the initial investment is a minimum of $500.

Fees fall into two categories: shareholder fees and annual operating expenses. Typically, shareholder fees are front-end loads that essentially are a sales charge assessed when a mutual fund is bought. Back-end loads assess the sales charge when fund shares are sold. A no-load mutual fund does not have any sales charges.

Annual operating expenses pay for the ongoing cost of running a fund, such as the fund manager's salary and record keeping, printing, and mailing expenses. Also included in this category are 12b-1 fees, which are fees that are deducted from fund assets to pay for marketing and distribution expenses, such as a broker's commission.

Some mutual funds have more than one class of shares available for purchase by the public: Class A, Class B, and Class C shares. (Another class, Class I shares, can be sold only to institutional investors.)

Definitions vary among mutual funds. Often Class A shares have a front-end sales load, while Class B shares charge a fee only when investors redeem fund shares. The fee may decrease to zero if the investor holds the shares for a certain period of time, or may just convert to a regular 12b-1 fee. Class C shares may have a 12b-1 fee and a contingent deferred sales load that would be lower than the other fees assessed on the Class A or Class B shares. See also *12b-1 fees.*

N

Nader, Ralph A consumer protection advocate and former candidate for the U.S. presidency. Nader wrote *Unsafe at Any Speed*, a 1965 book about poorly designed cars that brought him to national attention. He also has fought on behalf of consumers against many other businesses and government agencies.

NAFTA See *North American Free Trade Agreement*.

naira The currency unit of Nigeria, comprised of 100 kobo.

NAIRU See *Non-Accelerating Inflation Rate of Unemployment*.

naked

1. Undertaking either a long or short market position without having an off-setting short or long position.

2. Executing one side of a spread without executing the other side.

3. Writing an options contract without owning the underlying investment.

naked option An option contract whose underlying shares are not owned by the person writing the option. The writer of a naked option exposes him- or herself to risk if the option contract is exercised by the buyer and the writer doesn't own the shares. The writer will have to purchase the underlying shares in the market at what could be an unfavorable price in order to deliver them according to the terms of the option contract. Also called *uncovered option*.

nakfa The currency unit of Eritrea, comprised of 100 cents.

nanometer A nanometer is one billionth of a meter, or about three to five atoms wide. See also *nanotechnology*.

nanotechnology The building of very small machines. Nanotechnology involves manipulating matter at the atomic scale, resulting in faster, more powerful technology that uses smaller parts. A nanometer, which is a billionth of a meter, is only about three to five atoms wide. In early 2003, some companies were working on creating a manufacturing technology for computer chips that were 90 nanometers across, which is 30 percent smaller than the 130-nanometer computer chip technology that was common in 2002.

NAPM Index Short for the *National Association of Purchasing Management Index,* which has been renamed the ISM Index. See *ISM Index*.

NAREIT See *National Association of Real Estate Investment Trusts*.

NASAA See *North American Securities Administrators Association Inc.*

NASD Regulation Inc. (NASDR) An independent subsidiary of the National Association of Securities Dealers, which operates the NASDAQ stock market. NASDR:

Is responsible for regulating brokers and dealers on the NASDAQ stock market and the over-the-counter securities markets

Conducts market surveillance

Registers securities personnel

Undertakes disciplinary actions for rule violations

Investigates customer complaints

Provides forums to resolve disputes through arbitration proceedings

Educates the investing public

Reviews advertising and underwriting to ensure that firms are not making inappropriate claims

Regulates the sale of mutual funds, direct participation programs, and variable annuities

NASDAQ The *National Association of Securities Dealers Automated Quotation Service* is a computerized trading system established by the National Association of Securities Dealers (NASD) for trading over-the-counter stocks, which don't qualify for trading on the older, established exchanges. NASDAQ gained tremendous popularity for trading technology stocks in the late 1990s. NASDAQ's listing requirements are more lenient than those of the New York Stock Exchange and the American Stock Exchange.

NASDAQ 100 Stock Index A modified capitalization-weighted index that includes the largest non-financial U.S. and non-U.S. companies listed on the NASDAQ stock market across a variety of industry groups, such as retail, healthcare, telecommunications, wholesale trade, biotechnology, and technology. The index is designed to limit the influence of a few large stocks. To be included in the index, companies must meet some general guidelines: Companies listed in the NASDAQ 100 have been publicly traded for two years, are listed on the NASDAQ National Market (made up of the largest stocks), and have an average daily trading volume of at least 200,000 shares. Companies must not be in bankruptcy or involved in a potential merger transaction. NASDAQ reviews the companies in the index quarterly in order to adjust the weightings. The NASDAQ 100 began in January 1985.

An exchange-traded fund (ETF), QQQ, tracks the NASDAQ-100 Index. It allows large investors to buy or sell shares in the collective performance of the NASDAQ 100 Index in a single transaction as if purchasing or trading just one stock. QQQ trades on the American Stock Exchange and is one of the most actively traded ETFs.

NASDAQ Bank Index A measure of the performance of financial companies listed on the NASDAQ stock market, such as banks, savings institutions, and related holding companies that perform banking-related functions. It began in February 1971 with a base of 100.00.

NASDAQ Biotechnology Index A measure of the performance of NASDAQ-listed companies involved in biotechnology research that is targeted to discover and develop treatments for human diseases. The index began on November 1993 with a base of 200.00. It is calculated using a modified capitalization-weighted methodology.

NASDAQ Composite Index An index that includes all NASDAQ domestic and foreign common stocks. It is the most commonly cited index when referring to the performance of the NASDAQ stock market. The composite index is market-value weighted so that each company's stock price affects the index in proportion to its market value. During the technology boom of the late 1990s, the NASDAQ composite often was cited as technology heavy. However, since the technology boom ended and many of the start-up dot-com companies have failed, that description is rarely used. Securities on the NASDAQ composite index typically are assigned to subindices.

NASDAQ Computer Index A measure of the performance of NASDAQ-listed computer hardware and software companies that provide products or services. It began in November 1993 with a base of 200.00.

NASDAQ Industrial Index A measure of the performance of NASDAQ-listed companies that are not in one of the other NASDAQ indices, such as the computer, biotechnology, or banking indices. This leaves agricultural, mining, construction, manufacturing, retail and wholesale trade, services, and public administration enterprises, as well as health maintenance organizations and companies not included in NASDAQ's Biotechnology Index. It began in February 1971 with a base of 100.00.

NASDAQ National Market A market that consists of stocks of the largest companies on the NASDAQ stock market that are the most actively traded. The National Market includes more than 3,900 companies.

NASDAQ Quotation Dissemination Service (NQDS) A provider of real-time quotation pricing information for market makers and electronic communications networks (ECNs) in the NASDAQ National Market and the NASDAQ SmallCap Market. The ECNs and the market makers are the stock-trading professionals who are responsible for fulfilling the investing public's buy and sell orders.

NASDAQ Telecommunications Index
An index of 308 telecommunications companies, radio and television broadcast companies, and communications equipment and accessories manufacturers that are traded on the NASDAQ stock market. Before November 1993, the Telecommunications Index was called the NASDAQ Utility Index. It was reset to a base of 200.00 in 1993, using a factor of 5.74805.

National Association of Real Estate Investment Trusts (NAREIT) A nonprofit trade association, headquartered in Washington, D.C., that represents the interests of businesses involved in the real estate investment trust (REIT) industry. (REITs consist of businesses that invest in commercial real estate or housing or provide related services.) The association lobbies Congress on behalf of the industry, conducts research on the industry, and monitors trends.

National Association of Securities Dealers (NASD) A private, not-for-profit provider of financial regulatory services that owns the NASDAQ stock market as well as NASD Regulation Inc., which is an independent subsidiary that regulates brokers and dealers on the NASDAQ stock market and the over-the-counter securities market. NASD registers member firms and creates rules to govern their behavior, monitors their actions for compliance, and disciplines firms or brokers that break the rules. It also operates arbitration and mediation programs to resolve securities disputes. Federal law requires that nearly every securities firm conducting business with a U.S. public company must be a member of NASD. Members of NASD include about 5,300 brokerage firms with 91,000 branch offices and

662,000 registered securities representatives. NASD is headquartered in Washington, D.C., with offices and a market site in New York City. NASD also has district offices throughout the U.S.

National Association of Securities Dealers Automated Quotation system See *NASDAQ.*

national bank A commercial bank that receives its *charter,* or permission to operate, from the Comptroller of the Currency instead of a state banking department. National banks must be members of the Federal Reserve System and the Federal Deposit Insurance Corp. (FDIC). They also must own stock in their regional federal reserve bank.

National Credit Union Administration (NCUA) The agency of the U.S. government that charters, supervises, and insures federal credit unions. The NCUA also insures state-chartered credit unions that apply and qualify for insurance. Credit union members may also tap a credit facility that is offered by the NCUA.

national debt The amount of money owed by a federal government. Typically, a government's debt is comprised of obligations such as Treasury bonds, notes, and bills. The U.S. Congress has put limits (or a *ceiling*) on how much debt the United States can undertake. If those limits are exceeded, then Congress either has to raise them, or, as has happened occasionally in the past, threaten to shut down the government as a way to keep spending under control. As the economy performs well and individuals and businesses make more money and pay more taxes, the debt can disappear and turn into a surplus. When the economy slows and profits fall and unemployment rises, the amount of money the government receives decreases, which can lead to a budget deficit. When the deficit is significant, interest expense on the debt is one of the larger budget outlays. The national debt is distinct from a *budget deficit,* which is the difference of the amount of money raised and spent for one year.

National Futures Association (NFA)
A self-regulated industry organization for the futures and options markets. The NFA's purpose is to enforce ethical standards, protect customers, screen professionals for membership, and monitor members for compliance rules. The association also provides a venue to arbitrate disputes over futures deals. It also is responsible for the registration and supervision of commodity pool operators and commodity trading advisors. The NFA began operations in October 1982.

national municipal bond fund A type of mutual fund that primarily invests in municipal bonds that have either an average maturity of more than five years or no stated maturity. This type of bond fund usually is exempt from federal income tax but may be taxed under state or local laws.

national municipal short-term bond fund A bond mutual fund that invests predominately in municipal bonds that have an average maturity of one to five years. This type of bond fund is usually exempt from federal income tax but may be taxed under state or local laws.

National Securities Clearing Corp. A clearinghouse that matches and settles traders' buy and sell orders. It began in 1977 when the National Clearing Corp. (which was owned by the National Association of Securities Dealers Inc.) and the clearing units of both the New York Stock Exchange and the American Stock Exchange merged. See also *clearinghouse*.

national tax-exempt money market fund A mutual fund that looks for investments whose income is not taxed by the federal government. This type of mutual fund invests in municipal securities that have relatively short maturities.

nationalization The takeover by a government of a private company's assets and business. Nationalization is a risk to companies doing business in foreign countries that don't have a strong court system and don't value democratic principles. A government nationalizes companies in order to obtain their profits and to avoid what it considers to be exploitation of the country's resources by the foreign company.

Nationally Recognized Statistical Ratings Organization (NRSRO) A designation awarded by the Securities and Exchange Commission (SEC) to select credit ratings agencies. It confers a high status among those firms that receive it and helps them gain traction in the marketplace. The SEC has been criticized for the lengthy process that companies are involved in to acquire the designation and for the lack of clear criteria to achieve the designation, especially amid the corporate scandals and defaults that occurred in 2001 and 2002. Those companies with the NRSRO designation are Moody's Investors Service, Standard & Poor's, Fitch Ratings, and Dominion Bond Rating Service. Another firm, Egan-Jones Ratings of Wynnewood, Pennsylvania, applied for NRSRO status in 1998, but as of this printing had yet to receive it.

natural gas A commodity that is used to heat homes and businesses. Other uses include heating water, running air conditioning in the summer, and generating power. Industrial uses include serving as the base ingredient for products such as plastics, fertilizers, antifreeze, and fabrics. Futures and options contracts are traded on natural gas on the New York Mercantile Exchange (NYMEX). The Natural Gas Policy Act of 1978 deregulated the natural gas industry, which opened up the possibility for trading. In April 1990, NYMEX launched the world's first natural gas futures contract, and in October 1992, it launched options on natural gas futures. NYMEX contracts are based on natural gas that is deliverable to the Henry Hub trading complex in Louisiana.

natural gas storage report A report issued by the American Gas Association (AGA) that comes out each week at 2:00 P.M. ET on Wednesday and shows how much natural gas is in storage in the United

States in billions of cubic feet. It is widely watched by traders in the natural gas market. If storage levels are low, or if the data is lower than had been anticipated, then prices will likely shoot higher. Conversely, if the amount of natural gas in storage exceeds expectations or is at historically high levels, then prices are likely to fall, because there is too much supply relative to demand.

NAV See *net asset value*.

nearby contracts Futures contracts that are closest to expiration. See *nearby month*.

nearby month The futures contract month that is closest to expiration. If the current month is March, the nearby month is likely April for a futures contract that has 12 contracts per year. Also called *spot month* or *delivery month*.

negative amortization A repayment schedule in which the monthly payments are insufficient to fully *amortize*, or pay off, the loan. Interest expense that has been incurred but not paid is added to the principal, which increases the amount of the debt. Typically this occurs with a balloon mortgage where the payments don't cover the debt and at the end of the term a large payment must be made.

negative carry The result that occurs when the cost of borrowing money to pay for a securities purchase is greater than the expected return. If funds are borrowed at 8 percent, for example, and the stock or bond investment has a return of only 6 percent, the securities purchase has a negative carry. See also *positive carry*.

negative goodwill A situation that occurs when the market value of goodwill falls below the goodwill value that is stated on a company's balance sheet. Corporations take a write-off on their income statement to reflect the amount that goodwill has declined.

negative net worth A condition in which a company's liabilities exceed its assets plus shareholders equity. Negative net worth can occur because a company borrowed too much money and subsequently had its income fall as its debt payments rose. It also may occur if the value of assets declines.

negative yield curve A yield curve characterized by interest rates that are higher on short-term debt than on long-term debt. This is an abnormal circumstance, because typically investors want to be compensated for taking on the greater risk of tying their funds up for a longer period of time. A negative yield curve has a downward slope. This contrasts with a *positive yield curve*, which is characterized by higher long-term interest rates and lower short-term interest rates. Also called *inverted yield curve*.

negotiable instrument A written order to transfer money from one person to another. A negotiable instrument may be a check, a bill of exchange, or a promissory note but most often it is a check written on a checking account. The instrument must be signed by the writer, have the payee's name on it, and must list a specific amount of money that is payable upon demand.

negotiable order of withdrawal (NOW) account An interest-earning account on which checks may be written. NOW accounts are offered by commercial banks, mutual savings banks, and savings and loan associations. They may be owned only by individuals, some nonprofit organizations, and government agencies or bodies.

NERC See *North America Electric Reliability Council*.

nest egg Money that an individual has saved, often for retirement.

net adds The number of new subscribers, or gross adds, minus the number of customers that drop service, which is called *churn*. Though this term can be used in many different contexts, it is frequently used in the telecom industry.

net asset value (NAV)

1. Effectively, the price of one share in a mutual fund. NAV is calculated by

taking the market value of the fund's securities, subtracting liabilities, and dividing by the number of shares outstanding. As prices of the securities rise or fall, so does the net asset value.

2. The book value of a company's different types of assets.

net capital rule A Securities and Exchange Commission rule that requires all broker/dealers to maintain no more than a 15-to-1 ratio between indebtedness and liquid assets. Examples of indebtedness includes money owed by the firm, margin loans, and commitments to purchase securities. *Liquid assets* consist of cash and other assets that are easily converted into cash.

net fixed asset turnover A financial measurement that shows how well a company is utilizing its fixed assets. It is net sales divided by average net fixed assets. The resulting number must be compared to the net fixed asset turnover of other firms in the industry, as well as the company's historical data, in order to be relevant. An unusually high asset turnover can mean that the company doesn't have enough productive capacity to meet sales demand or is using old equipment that may be obsolete. A low turnover implies that capital is tied up in fixed assets.

net inflow In the mutual fund industry, a situation in which more money is flowing into a mutual fund than is flowing out of it. See also *net outflow.*

net interest cost The total expense that a bond issuer will end up paying in order to issue debt securities. The net interest costs includes the interest payments, sales charges to underwriters, and any premiums paid. Underwriters who can offer the lowest net interest costs to the issuer often win the business.

net interest rate spread The difference between the average yield on loans, mortgage-related securities, and investments earned by the bank or savings and loan and the average rate that the institution has to

pay on deposits and borrowings. It is a key determinant of a bank's profitability.

net new cash flow The amount of new funds flowing into a mutual fund. Net new cash flow subtracts out reinvested dividends, redemptions, and investors' movement of money between different funds.

net outflow In the mutual fund industry, a situation in which more money is flowing out of a mutual fund than is flowing into it. See also *net inflow.*

net portfolio capital flows Foreign acquisitions plus U.S. divestitures of foreign securities. Strong net portfolio capital flows help to support a country's currency. This is a statistic that tracks how much money is being invested in a country by foreigners and the extent to which domestic companies are selling their foreign holdings.

net present value The present value of an investment's future net cash flow minus the cost of the initial investment. If the net present value is positive, then the investment will be profitable.

net profit margin A calculation that shows how profitable a company is after paying income taxes. Divide net income by net sales to arrive at the net profit margin, which is expressed in percentage terms. Typical net profit margins vary substantially between industries. The ratio is based upon sales and earnings from continuing operations, not discontinued operations, because the point of the calculation is to provide insight about future activity.

net redemptions In the mutual fund industry, a measurement that describes the difference between money that is flowing into mutual funds (net inflow) and money that is flowing out (net outflows). If the outflows are more than the inflows then net redemptions occur.

net worth

1. For individuals, the value of all assets minus any liabilities, such as a mortgage, a car loan, or credit card balances.

2. For corporations, assets plus shareholders equity, minus liabilities.

Neuer Markt The growth segment of the German stock market (the Deutsche Börse) that collapsed in 2001 as the technology and telecom markets crashed in the United States.

neutral A rating used by Wall Street analysts. Even though *neutral* implies the lack of an opinion, a neutral rating is a code phrase for a sell rating. The word *sell* is rarely used in order to avoid offending clients and preventing the investment bank that the analyst works for from winning future lucrative banking business from the client. The term *market perform* also may be used to indicate a neutral opinion.

new high/new low A tabulation of how many stocks have hit a new 52-week high or low during the previous day's trading session. The number of New York Stock Exchange and NASDAQ stocks that have hit new highs and new lows, as well as a list of the stocks, is published in *The Wall Street Journal*.

new residential construction A monthly report, produced by the U.S. Bureau of the Census, on privately owned residential construction activity. The data shows how many new building permits have been issued and the number of housing units started. Also, it focuses on the number of housing units under construction and the number of housing units completed. The data gives an indication of the potential impact on the number of construction-related jobs, as well as giving some insight into what gross domestic product (GDP) data is likely to look like. One shortcoming of the data is that it is difficult to determine what type of housing is being constructed, since the only differentiation is between single-family housing and multi-family housing. The report has only a minimal impact on the financial markets.

New York Board of Trade (NYBOT) A futures exchange located in New York City that was formed in 1998 when it became the parent company of the Coffee, Cocoa and Sugar Exchange (CCSE) and the New York Cotton Exchange (NYCE). Coffee, cocoa, and sugar contracts are traded on the CCSE, along with the Standard & Poor's Commodity Index futures. Cotton and orange juice futures are traded on the NYCE. Futures on 25 currency pairs also trade on the NYBOT. Also on the exchange is the New York Futures Exchange (NYFE), where futures contracts trade on the CRB/Bridge Index, the Reuters CRB Index, the Russell 1000 Index, the NYSE Composite Index, and the U.S. Dollar Index.

New York Empire State Manufacturing Survey A survey, sent out to companies in the manufacturing industry in New York state, that provides an early indication of business conditions, such as price levels and employment trends. The survey gives an indication of changes in sentiment and may give an indication of what the ISM Manufacturing Index will show. The survey's most watched statistic is the general business conditions index: If the index is above zero it indicates that business sentiment is improving. The index also has sub-indices, such as shipments, new orders, employment, and prices paid. The survey is produced by the Federal Reserve Bank of New York and is released around the middle of the month.

New York Futures Exchange (NYFE) A wholly-owned subsidiary of the New York Cotton Exchange (NYCE), which was combined into the New York Board of Trade in 1998 along with the Coffee, Cocoa and Sugar Exchange (CCSE). The NYFE trades futures and options on the NYSE Composite Index, which is based on approximately 2,000 common stocks, and the CRB/Bridge Index, based on the Commodity Research Bureau/Bridge Index of 21 commodity components. Futures also are traded on the Pacific Stock Exchange's Technology Index, representing 100 listed and over-the-counter stocks from 15 different technology industries. The NYCE was acquired from the New York Stock Exchange (NYSE) in December 1993.

New York Mercantile Exchange (NYMEX) A futures exchange that trades a variety of metals and energy futures and options contracts. Futures and options contracts that are traded on the exchange, using open-outcry trading in pits devoted to each product, include the following: energy products such as crude oil (Brent and West Texas Intermediate crude oil and light, sweet crude), gasoline, heating oil, natural gas, propane, electricity, and coal. Metals contracts include gold, silver, platinum, palladium, copper, and aluminum. Gold, silver, copper, and aluminum contracts are traded on COMEX, a wholly-owned subsidiary of NYMEX.

NYMEX ACCESS is the Exchange's electronic trading system, which is available when open-outcry pit trading is not available.

New York Stock Exchange A stock exchange that was founded in 1792 by 24 men who created an investment community in New York. The NYSE is the largest stock market in the U.S., and trades an average of 1.3 billion shares a day, representing $42 billion in market capitalization. The exchange lists 2,800 companies with a global market capitalization of $15 trillion. It is owned by its 1,366 seat-holding members.

NGO See *non-governmental organization.*

ngultrum The currency unit of Bhutan, comprised of 100 chetrum.

Nielsen, A.C. A pioneer in television ratings, which he began tabulating in 1950. Prior to his work in television ratings, he measured sales in drug stores and grocery stores and measured the size of radio audiences.

Nikkei 225 A price-weighted index of the 225 top Japanese companies (called the First Section) that are listed in the Tokyo Stock Exchange. The Nikkei Stock Average began on May 1949, with an average price of 176.21 with 225 companies in the index.

Nikkei 300 Index A capitalization-weighted index of important equity securities traded on the First Section (the top companies) of the Tokyo Stock Exchange. It began on October 1982 with a value of 100.

no-action letter A letter written by the Securities and Exchange Commission (SEC) that says it will not take any action against a corporation that might potentially be violating the letter of the law. No-action letters are requested by corporations from the SEC before it undertakes any action that might potentially violate the letter of the law.

NOB Spread See *note over bond spread.*

no-fault A legal distinction that doesn't require opposing parties in a lawsuit or claim to prove who is at fault. No-fault commonly is used in divorce law and for automobile insurance. For auto insurance, each party seeks reimbursement from their own insurance company regardless of who was at fault. No-fault laws vary among states.

noise Factors that can be cited as the reason that prices for a stock or other investments rose or fell, but that the person making the comment doesn't think had much of a substantial effect.

no-load A term used to refer to a mutual fund that has no sales charge. It is in contrast to a load mutual fund, which does have a sales charge that pays the person selling it a commission and covers other marketing charges. However, the fund still charges an asset-management fee based on a percentage of the assets under management, which provides its profit.

nominal A number that hasn't been adjusted. For example, a sales number that hasn't been adjusted for price changes is a nominal sales number. A nominal interest rate is the interest rate that is actually paid, as opposed to the amount that is owed. If a consumer pays 8 percent on a car loan, the nominal interest rate is 8 percent. Nominal income means income that hasn't been adjusted for any changes in the dollar's purchasing power. Nominal dollar means money that hasn't been adjusted for inflation.

nominal yield The coupon rate of a bond. A bond with a 7 percent coupon has a 7 percent nominal yield. However, the nominal yield does not equal how much the bond will pay, which is determined by the current yield on the bond, which takes into consideration the current yield of a bond and its current price.

nominating committee A committee comprised of some of the members of a board of directors with responsibility for finding members of the board of directors and hiring top corporate executives. Under the Sarbanes-Oxley legislation passed in 2002, all members of a company's nominating committee must be independent from the company, which means that they can't be board members employed by the company. A grace period until 2004 exists for companies to make certain that all of their members are independent. Companies controlled by another company are not subject to the full-independence requirement. The nominating committee must have a charter that specifies the purpose, responsibilities, and evaluation procedures of the committee.

Non-Accelerating Inflation Rate of Unemployment (NAIRU) The rate of unemployment that can't be avoided without causing the inflation rate to rise. NAIRU is said to be the "natural" rate of unemployment, meaning that some people always are going to be unemployed because they have gone back to school, are raising a family, or taking a break from work. They also may have secured another job but haven't started it yet. There are various theories about what NAIRU is. At one time it was thought to be about 5 percent. However, that theory was disposed of after the unemployment rate went below 4 percent during the stock market and technology boom of the late 1990s and no increase in inflation was seen. Determining what NAIRU is has been a topic of discussion among Federal Reserve policy makers over a long period of time.

non-callable bond A bond that can't be called, or repaid, by the issuer before its maturity. The U.S. Treasury is the most common issuer of non-callable bonds. Corporate bonds usually have some type of call option, except during periods of low interest rates when there is little incentive for a company to issue new bonds with call protection. See also *callable bond*.

noncash charge Charges that don't involve the payment of cash, such as depreciation, amortization, or depletion. Rather, these are "paper" charges that account for the decreasing value of an asset.

non-clearing member A member of an organized exchange that does not have a trade clearing operation to match up buyers and sellers of futures and options contracts. In order to settle its trades, it has to pay a fee to another firm that is a clearing member.

noncompetitive bid Treasury auction bids that come from small investors over the Internet, from a Federal Reserve Bank, or from some commercial banks. When entering their bids, purchasers of noncompetitive bids agree to accept the interest rate offered, which is determined through the bids of the competitive bidders. The competitive bidders are large banks that buy millions of dollars of the Treasury issues at a time.

non-contributory pension plan A pension plan that is entirely funded by the employer; the employee makes no contributions. Also called *defined benefit pension plan*.

non-cumulative preferred stock A stock for which, if the board of directors of the company does not declare a dividend for preferred stockholders in a particular year, the company has no obligation to make up a missed dividend in future years.

non-current asset An asset that isn't going to be consumed or converted into cash within one year. Non-current assets are listed separately from current assets on a company's balance sheet. Examples of non-current assets are buildings, plants, and equipment.

non-cyclical stock A stock whose performance is minimally affected by upward or downward movements in the economy. Companies whose stocks fall into the non-cyclical category produce, for example, food and pharmaceuticals. These are goods that people must continue purchasing, even if the economy is not doing well. See also *cyclical stock.*

non-durable good A product that has a short life and usually will be consumed in three years or less. A non-durable good contrasts with a durable good, which is expected to last three years or longer.

non-farm payrolls report The report called the *monthly unemployment report* by the mass media. It is released by the U.S. Department of Labor's Bureau of Labor Statistics on the first Friday of the month, unless a holiday disrupts the schedule. The report is one of the most widely watched economic indicators because of the strong influence it has on future interest rate actions by the Federal Reserve. It also is a major indicator of the economic health of the economy and an indication of likely future consumer spending levels. The statistics that are reported include average hourly earnings, which shows whether wages are rising, which could signal a potential source of inflation.

non-governmental organization (NGO) A term commonly used by developmental organizations such as the World Bank and the International Monetary Fund (IMF) to refer to organizations that lobby and otherwise attempt to influence policies enacted by the World Bank and IMF, along with governments. NGOs typically have a particular purpose, focused on a social agenda that may include ethical, cultural, political, scientific, environmental, religious, or philanthropic considerations.

non-investment-grade debt Low-quality notes or bonds that may be in danger of default because of the relatively high levels of debt that the issuing company has relative to the amount of equity.

Standard & Poor's non-investment grade ratings are BB and lower; Moody's Investors' Service are Ba1 and lower. Anything below B is considered non-investment grade by Fitch Ratings.

non-manufacturing business activity index An index of activity in the services sector that is put out monthly by the Institute for Supply Management. Any rating above 50 denotes expansion in the services sector. Ratings below 50 indicate contraction in the services sector.

nonoperating expenses Expenses that aren't incurred as a part of a company's operating, or main business, activities. Examples of non-operating expenses are the cost of the human resources department or upkeep expenses associated with the corporation's headquarters.

non-operating revenues Revenues that are not derived from a company's operating activities. These may include revenues from investments, such as dividends earned on stock held in other companies, or income from notes or credit extended to customers. In contrast, *operating revenues* are derived from the company's main businesses.

non-performing asset A judgment that is made by banks when they haven't received a payment on one of their bank loans within the last 90 days. However, each financial institution has its own criteria for judging when an asset is non-performing.

non-profit organization An organization, such as a charity, that is not established to make a profit. The term doesn't necessarily refer to an organization that is charitable; it could refer to activities to save the environment or preserve historical sites.

nonrated A company's or government's debt issue that hasn't been rated by one of the rating agencies, such as Standard & Poor's. The issue may not be rated because the company or government hasn't contracted with one of the ratings agencies or the issue is so small that it doesn't warrant rating.

non-refundable A provision in a bond indenture that stops or limits the issuer from retiring the bonds by using proceeds from another issue, which is called a *refunding*. Non-refundable bonds protect bondholders from having their bonds called and thus losing out on interest payments. Also called *call protection*.

nonresident alien A non-U.S. citizen who lives outside of the U.S. but who has taxable business activities in the U.S. A nonresident alien is subjected to a withholding tax of 30 percent on dividend payments unless the alien's country has a tax treaty with his or her native country. A nonresident alien is subjected to higher income tax withholding in other financial areas as well.

non-statutory stock option A type of employee stock option. A non-statutory stock option program is easier to set up and administer than an incentive stock option, however, taxes must be paid on the non-qualified stock options, while taxes do not have to be paid on incentive stock options. Also called *non-qualified stock options*.

non-systemic risk A risk that is particular to a company and doesn't affect other companies. Investors can protect against non-systemic risk by diversifying their investments. Non-systemic risk contrasts with *systemic risk,* which is risk that applies to all companies in a market or industry.

non-voting stock Stock issued by a company that doesn't come with any voting rights. Preferred stock often is non-voting stock. In the case of unwanted hostile takeovers, non-voting stock may be issued.

no-par stock *Capital stock,* which is stock that is held by a corporation that hasn't been issued yet, that doesn't have a *par value,* which is nominal dollar value applied to a stock or a bond. Typically, a stock's par value is $1. Stock is issued without a par value because most states prohibit an original stock issue below par value and thereby limit a corporation's flexibility in accessing capital.

normalized earnings Earnings that have been adjusted by a company to omit irregular expenses against earnings. Generally, when a company adjusts earnings statements for this reason, it's because the expenses aren't representative of its true business. For example, expenses that are deducted often include the cost of stock options for employees. Other omitted items include extraordinary items, charges for discontinued operations, and one-time charges. Normalized earnings are in contrast to GAAP earnings (Generally Accepted Accounting Principles), which follow set rules developed by accountants. Also called *pro-forma earnings*. See also *GAAP.*

North America Electric Reliability Council (NERC) A group that was formed in 1968 by electric companies to promote the reliability and adequacy of power supplies. NERC produces reliability reports to draw attention to situations that might restrict the available power supply. Every spring, NERC conducts a widely watched study of reliability to identify any areas of potential supply problems during the summer, when strong demand for air conditioning may potentially cause power shortages. NERC is made up of ten regional reliability councils and encompasses essentially all the power regions of the contiguous United States, Canada, and Mexico. The NERC regions are Alaskan System Coordination Council (ASCC); East Central Reliability Coordination Agreement (ECAR); Electric Reliability Council of Texas (ERCO); Mid-America Interpool Network (MAIN); Mid-Atlantic Area Council (MAAC); Mid-Continent Area Power Pool (MAPP); Northeast Power Coordinating Council (NPCC); Southeastern Electric Reliability Council (SERC); Southwest Power Pool (SPP); and Western System Coordinating Council (WSCC).

North American Free Trade Agreement (NAFTA) A free-trade zone created by the governments of the United States, Canada, and Mexico to encourage trade among themselves. By eliminating barriers to trade in goods and services in the North

American region, NAFTA also provides a dispute-resolution process for its members to solve trade issues before they get out of hand. The protection and enforcement of intellectual property rights also is a goal of the treaty.

North American Securities Administrators Association Inc. (NASAA) A professional association of securities commissioners that represents a variety of investor security and protection agencies. Founded in 1919, the NASAA membership consists of securities commissions from all 50 states, the District of Columbia, Puerto Rico, Canada, Mexico, and other entities. It is headquartered in Washington, D.C. Though federal regulators, such as the Securities and Exchange Commission (SEC), come to mind when thinking about securities regulation, individual states have their own set of securities laws that actively protect investors and must be followed by issuers.

note

1. A debt instrument with a maturity between one year and ten years. For longer-term debt instruments, the term *bond* typically is used. However, both *note* and *bond* often are used interchangeably, especially when speaking in general terms about a debt issue.

2. A written promise to pay a specified amount to the lender at a specified time in the future. It may be in the form of a promissory note.

note over bond (NOB) spread A yield curve spread that is created when the 10-year U.S. Treasury note futures contract is sold and the 30-year bond futures contract is purchased, often on the Chicago Board of Trade. This spread also can be created in the cash or repo (repurchase) market. Investors who expect interest rates to rise and thereby steepen the yield curve for the longer-dated maturities would purchase the note contract and sell the bond contract in a certain proportion. If interest rates are expected to move lower for shorter-dated maturities and thereby cause the yield curve to invert, then the bond contract would be purchased and the note contract sold.

not-for-profit An organization that exists to fulfill a charitable, educational, or humanitarian purpose instead of making a profit. These organizations are exempt from paying sales and income tax, unless they undertake profit-making activities that are extensive enough to risk their tax-free status. Donations to not-for-profit corporations are tax deductible for the donor. Also called *nonprofit*.

notice day The day that begins the process of notifying futures traders that they will have to fulfill the terms of their futures contracts. In the futures market, if a contract is not closed out by the notice day, the holder will receive a notice. At this point, the clearing corporation that settles trades must match the buyer with the *oldest long* (the person who has held the contract the longest) or another trader who is randomly chosen by another method. Both parties to the transaction are notified.

notional settlement A reference price based on trading activity during a specific time period that is close to the end of the day. The notional settlement is used to calculate the maximum daily price fluctuations for electronic trading that occurs in after-hours trading on the New York Mercantile Exchanges' ACCESS trading system. The notional settlement is used when the regular settlement price hasn't been established before NMEX ACCESS trading begins. It is discarded later in the session, when final settlement prices are available.

NOW account See *negotiable order of withdrawal account*.

NQDS See *NASDAQ Quotation Dissemination Service*.

NV Similar to *Inc.* or *Co.*, but signifying a Dutch company. NV is short for

Naamloze Vennootschap and is commonly used in The Netherlands and Belgium.

NYMEX See *New York Mercantile Exchange.*

NYMEX ACCESS Stands for the *New York Mercantile Exchange's ACCESS trading,* which is an internationally accessible after-hours trading system. ACCESS stands for *American Computerized Commodity Exchange System and Services.* The system is accessible over the Internet and is available after regular trading hours have ended for the day. NYMEX ACCESS trading opens at 3:15 p.m. Eastern time, Monday through Thursday, and runs as late as 9 a.m. the next morning, depending on the specific contract. Sunday evening sessions open at 7 p.m. Trades are executed on the basis of price and time submitted, with the first order at the best price taking priority in execution. The system provides anonymity.

NYSE Composite Index A stock index established by the New York Stock Exchange (NYSE) in 1966 that was intended to be a comprehensive measure of market trends. This index includes all the common stocks listed on the NYSE and four subgroup indices: Finance, Industrial, Transportation, and Utility. The index measures changes in the market value of NYSE common stocks. It is adjusted to eliminate the effects of capitalization changes, new listings, and delistings. The trading symbol is NYA.X.

NYSE International 100 Index A New York Stock Exchange index that tracks the 100 largest non-U.S. stocks that trade on the NYSE. The index covers 27 percent of the international stock market, has a total market capitalization of $3.8 billion, and represents 18 countries. Its ticker symbol is NYI.ID.

obsolescence The process of becoming out of date. It is one of the underlying concepts of depreciation, because obsolescence limits the useful life of an asset.

OCC See *Options Clearing Corporation*.

odd lot In the stock market, a trade that isn't divisible by 100. In the money market, an odd lot is a trade that doesn't meet the minimum amount required for dealers' quotes. The minimum ranges from $100,000 to $50 million, depending on the size and liquidity of the issue traded. Odd lots in the futures markets vary depending on the contract. The opposite is a round lot, which is exactly 100 shares.

OECD The *Organization of Economic Cooperation and Development* is a Europe-based think tank that focuses on promoting democracy and free-market policy theories. It publishes a variety of statistics and research on subjects such as good government, trade, education, employment, and technology, among others. The OECD is headquartered in Paris and is made up of 30 countries. Those countries are Australia, Austria, Belgium, Canada, Czech Republic, Denmark, Finland, France, Germany, Greece, Hungary, Iceland, Ireland, Italy, Japan, Korea, Luxembourg, Mexico, the Netherlands, New Zealand, Norway, Poland, Portugal, Slovak Republic, Spain, Sweden, Switzerland, Turkey, U.K., and the U.S.

The OECD began after World War II in order to administer U.S. and Canadian aid under the Marshall Plan. It originally was called the Organisation for European Economic Co-operation (OEEC). The OECD took over from the OEEC in 1961. The OECD increasingly is turning its attention to emerging market economies.

OEX The symbol for the Standard & Poor's 100 stock index, which comprises stocks that have options traded on the Chicago Board of Options Exchange. To pronounce it, say each of the letters: O-E-X. Options on the OEX are traded on major exchanges, such as the Chicago Board of Trade. Futures contracts are traded on the Chicago Mercantile Exchange.

off-balance sheet transactions Financial deals and arrangements that can have a material affect on a company but are structured in such a way that they do not show up on a company's balance sheet and do not affect a company's borrowing capacity. Off-balance sheet activities took on huge importance in 2001 when the off-balance sheet deals that Enron Corp. had engaged in came to light. Because the details about off-balance sheet activities are unknown to investors, the off-balance sheet transactions can hide a significant amount of liability.

off-balance-sheet debt Debt that is owed by a company, but because of alternative accounting or financing techniques, is not included on a company's balance sheet. Investors need to read through the fine print in the footnotes of a company's financial statements to find this debt. One type of off-balance-sheet debt that a company typically has is a lease for property or equipment that commits the company to a fixed-payment schedule for a multiyear period. Because the payment schedule is fixed, it isn't much different than having a bank loan. While a *capital lease* (a long-term lease) is likely to be reported on a company's balance sheet, an operating lease is generally only disclosed in a footnote.

Another example is when companies sell accounts receivables or credit card receivables through *securitization* (packaging debt into a group and then issuing new securities that are backed by the income from the pool). These transactions may be reported in the footnotes of a company, however they aren't on the balance sheet as debt. They are more like debt because in many instances the companies remain liable if a borrower or customer defaults on payment.

However, if the company has actually transferred the risk associated with owning them, and there is no danger that they will have to make the payment if the borrower defaults, then they really aren't a debt of the company. Details of these types of obligations are found in a company's financial statements, usually its form 10-K, which is filed annually with the SEC.

offering circular   See *prospectus.*

offering memorandum   See *private placement memorandum.*

off-floor order   An order to buy or sell a security that comes from off of the exchange floor, meaning that it is from a broker who is processing an order for a customer, in contrast to an on-floor order, which often comes from a floor member trading for a personal account. Off-floor orders are required to be executed before on-floor orders.

Office of Management and Budget (OMB)   An agency within the office of the President of the United States that is responsible for preparing the president's budget for Congress and working with the Council of Economic Advisors and the Treasury Department to develop a fiscal program.

Office of Thrift Supervision (OTS)   The primary regulator of all federally chartered and many state-chartered *thrift institutions,* which include savings banks and savings and loan associations. The goal of the OTS is to ensure that thrift institutions don't default and to support their role as home mortgage lenders and providers of community credit and financial services. It was established as a bureau of the U.S. Department of the Treasury on August 9, 1989, and has four regional offices located in Jersey City, New Jersey; Atlanta, Georgia; Dallas, Texas; and San Francisco, California. The office is funded by assessments and fees levied on the institutions it regulates.

offshore   A term used to refer to a domestic company that is registered to do business in a country other than where most of its business is transacted. For instance, in the United States, an offshore company would be one that is incorporated in Bermuda even though the vast majority of its business operations are in the United States. Offshore investment companies, such as mutual funds, still must comply with all U.S. regulations if they are doing business in the United States.

offshore bank   Any financial institution that has its headquarters outside of its home country. Banks, hedge funds, or mutual funds based in the U.S. may be located in Bermuda, the Cayman Islands, or the Isle of Man, near the U.K., just to name a few popular locations. While financial institutions can be headquartered offshore, they still have to comply with all U.S. securities regulations for products sold in the U.S. Offshore banks are used by individuals and companies to avoid paying higher tax rates that would be due if funds were left in their home country. Income on deposits in the offshore bank account will be taxed at a lesser rate than if the account was located in the U.S.

off-the-run   Old bond issues that have been replaced by a newer issue. When a new Treasury or federal agency debt issue comes to market, the older issues become off-the-run. As those issues move further away from their issue date, they become more difficult to trade because they have less liquidity. Most investors actively trade only on-the-run issues, which decreases liquidity by lessening interest in the old, or off-the-run, issues.

oil and gas limited partnership   A limited partnership whose purpose is to find, extract, and market oil and natural gas. The limited partners risk no more than the amount of money they contributed. Oil and gas limited partnerships were popular investments to avoid taxes during the 1980s; however, tax law changes have tightened the rules for deducting the losses and their popularity has declined.

oil patch An informal term that applies to a region in the United States that produces a significant amount of U.S. oil. The oil patch states include Texas, Oklahoma, Kansas, and Louisiana. Although Alaska is a large oil producer, it is geographically outside of the oil patch.

Oil Service Sector Index (OSX) A benchmark index used in the oil industry that was created by the Philadelphia Stock Exchange (PHLX), where it trades. The Oil Service Sector Index is a price-weighted index composed of the common stocks of 15 companies that provide oil drilling and production services, oil field equipment, support services, and geophysical/reservoir services. The OSX was set to an initial value of 75 on December 31, 1996. Options began trading on February 24, 1997.

oligopoly A situation in which a few companies share control of the market for selling a good or service. Therefore, they are jointly able to exert a good deal of influence over consumer prices. Firms in an oligopoly situation have a great deal of interdependence, because if one firm changes its prices or competitive structure, it affects all members in the industry. The airline and tobacco industries are examples of oligopolies.

oligopsony A situation in which a small group of companies share control of the market for buying a good or service. Because there are few buyers, they can jointly exert strong influence over wholesale prices. It is the buy-side counterpart to an oligopoly. Food processers, such as beef and pork processors, may hold oligopsony power.

OMB See *Office of Management and Budget*.

omega A model used to price derivatives that measures the effect of volatility. Also called *vega, zeta,* or *kappa*.

omitted dividend A dividend that was expected to be paid but was not declared by the board of directors and therefore went unpaid.

OneChicago LLC A joint venture between three Chicago-based futures exchanges that created an electronic exchange for trading futures, stocks, and exchange-traded funds. The venture began in November 2002. The joint venture members are Chicago Board Options Exchange (CBOE), Chicago Mercantile Exchange (CME), and Chicago Board of Trade (CBOT). Current members of these exchanges are automatically allowed to trade on OneChicago. In December 2002, the exchange began trading some single-stock futures.

one-time home sales income tax exemption A one-time federal income tax exemption that lets homeowners avoid paying some capital gains taxes on the sale of their home. In order to qualify, the home must have been the principal residence for at least two of the past five years. Married couples filing jointly can exempt up to $500,000 of capital gains taxes while single people can exempt $250,000 from the gain on the sale of their house. Proceeds don't have to be reinvested in another home to earn the tax exemption. Originally this exemption was only available to people 55 years and older, but it was expanded to include all homeowners in 1997.

online bank A bank that does not do business at a physical location and is accessed only through the Internet and the telephone. Accounts at online banks may earn higher rates of interest, since the banks are attempting to attract capital. Online banks allow checking accounts to be viewed online. Electronic funds transfers between different banks also are allowed. Bills may be paid online as well.

online bill paying Paying bills and transferring funds between accounts, and making other account transactions through a personal computer via the Internet. Typically, banks and other financial institutions charge a nominal amount each month to provide online banking services.

OPEC The *Organization of Petroleum Exporting Countries* is an association of 11 countries that attempts to maximize the member countries' profit from oil sales by coordinating the amount of oil that they sell. Another goal of OPEC is bringing stability and harmony to the oil market by adjusting oil output to help ensure a balance between supply and demand. The group typically meets twice a year, but can schedule more dates in response to market events. OPEC nations produce about 40 percent of the world's oil output and have over 75 percent of the world's total proven crude oil reserves. OPEC members are Algeria, Indonesia, Iran, Iraq, Kuwait, Libya, Nigeria, Qatar, Saudi Arabia, the United Arab Emirates, and Venezuela.

open interest   The number of futures or options contracts of a given commodity that are currently being traded. These contracts have not yet been offset by an opposite transaction or filled by delivery of the commodity. Open interest increases when a new buyer purchases a contract from a new seller. It decreases when an existing owner of a futures contract sells to an existing *short* (a trader who has sold something that he or she doesn't own). However, open interest is unaffected if a new buyer purchases from an existing long or a new seller sells to an existing short. Rising open interest indicates increased interest in the market because there are more contracts beings traded.

When contracts are new, their open interest is limited, making them illiquid, which lessens their attractiveness to trade. It will take months, if not several years, to build up their open interest, and thus their liquidity. Liquidity is impaired when open interest levels are approximately below 5,000 contracts or the average daily trading volume is below approximately 1,000 contracts.

open-market operations   The purchase and sale of government securities in the open market by the New York Federal Reserve Bank. Open market operations are undertaken at the direction of the Federal Reserve Open Market Committee (FOMC) with the intention of influencing interest rates and the supply of money in the economy. If the FOMC purchases securities, reserves are injected into the depository system. If the FOMC sells securities, then reserves are removed. The securities buyer gives up cash to buy the securities, which removes money from the system. In return, the buyer receives the securities.

open order   Essentially, a good-until-cancelled order for the purchase or sale of a security. See also *good-until-cancelled*.

open outcry   A method for conducting trades that involves traders shouting out offers and bids in a pit where futures and options are being sold. Open outcry also is used on some foreign stock and futures exchanges. The London Metal Exchange mixes two short periods of open outcry with trading that occurs over the telephone or through an electronic trading system.

opening range   The range of prices at which sell and buy transactions occurred during the daily opening of a market. Opening ranges are found in many futures and financial markets.

open-market operations   The Federal Reserve's purchase and sale of financial securities in order to affect the level of money supply. This tactic influences short-term interest rates. When the Fed wants to increase the money supply, it buys debt instruments, such as repos (repurchase agreements). When it wants to decrease the money supply, it sells debt instruments.

operating budget   A company's planned budget, which takes into account income and expenses that the company is likely to produce through its current operations. An operating budget lists expenses such as advertising, salaries, and general and administrative expenses. The budget should be periodically compared with actual expenses. The operating budget focuses solely on operating income and expenses, in contrast with a company's overall budget, which includes items such as income from investments and other non-operating items.

operating free cash flow EBITDA (earnings before interest, taxes, depreciation, and amortization) minus total capital spending. The term is frequently used by Wall Street analysts who often will customize the number to make it useful for their own comparisons. Operating free cash flow is popular because it shows how much cash from operations is available to cover a company's interest payments.

operating income The income from a company's main businesses. It is the difference between a company's gross profit and its operating expenses.

operating lease A lease that does not transfer the risk or rewards of the leased property to the lessee in any economically substantial way. Operating leases are treated as an expense, and no asset or liability is recorded on the company's financial statements. In contrast, a *capital lease* transfers nearly all of the risk and rewards of leased property to the lessee and the company records lease payments on the balance sheet as both an asset and a liability.

operating leverage Occurs when fixed costs comprise the company's total costs. As sales increase, the operating costs are spread across a wider number of units of sale, which increases the operating margin and, thus, profits. A higher ratio of fixed costs implies greater operating leverage, as incremental profits are higher than for a company with lower operating leverage.

operating profit A financial measurement that is calculated by subtracting sales, general, and administrative expenses (SG&A) from gross profit. Operating profit shows how much money a company has to spend in order to sell its goods. It is an indicator of profitability.

operating profit margin A financial measurement that is derived by dividing operating profit by net sales, in dollars. Operating profit is calculated by subtracting sales, general, and administrative expenses (SG&A) from gross profit. Operating profit

margin indicates how profitable the company's operations are. If the margin decreases, then the company's profitability is declining.

opportunity cost The cost of pursuing one opportunity or action, measured by what had to be given up in the course of choosing that opportunity. For example, opportunity cost may be not having the money to make an alternative investment because it has been spent on something else. Another type of opportunity cost occurs when a company can't expand in a certain area because expansion is already occurring in one region and the company's resources would be stressed.

option A contract that gives the buyer the right to purchase (call) a security from the option writer or to sell (put) a security to the writer. A writer is the investor who creates the option, hoping to profit from the premium that the purchaser pays. An option specifies a price at which the option can be executed (called the strike, or exercise, price), and a time period during which the option is valid. Exchange-traded options have standardized terms, while those traded between individuals are customized. Options provide a type of insurance for investors who want to lock in a maximum price that they can buy a stock or other investment for or a minimum price at which the stock can be sold.

option clearing corporation A company that has been set up by an options exchange to monitor margin accounts of options traders, guarantee their performance, and settle exchange-traded option trades.

option price The price at which an option contract is quoted. An option contract gives the holder the right to buy or sell a certain security at a specific future time at a set price. If the option is purchased, it is based on 100 shares of stock, so purchasing one option priced at $15 means that the purchaser bought an option for $1,500.

option writer A person who *writes,* or sells, an option contract in order to earn the *premium,* which is the fee that the purchaser pays the writer. A writer of a call option promises to sell the underlying investment to the call purchaser, who has bought the right to purchase it at a specific price. A writer of a put option has promised to buy the underlying investment from the put buyer, who has bought the right to sell the investment at a specific price.

Options Clearing Corporation (OCC) An equity derivatives clearing organization, founded in 1973. The OCC acts as guarantor to options contracts by acting as a counter-party to options transactions. The OCC is under the jurisdiction of both the Securities and Exchange Commission (SEC) and the Commodities Futures Trading Commission (CFTC). Under the SEC jurisdiction, the OCC clears, or matches, transactions for put and call options on common stocks and other equity issues, such as stock indexes, foreign currencies, interest rate composites, and single-stock futures. As a registered Derivatives Clearing Organization (DCO) under the CFTC's jurisdiction, the OCC offers clearing and settlement services for transactions in futures and options on futures.

The OCC is equally owned by the American Stock Exchange, the Chicago Board Options Exchange, the International Securities Exchange, the Pacific Exchange, and the Philadelphia Stock Exchange. The clearing members of the OCC serve both professional traders and public customers and they comprise approximately 140 of the largest U.S. broker-dealers, futures commission merchants, and non-U.S. securities firms.

optiputer A new style of a supercomputer that derives its name from combining optical networking, Internet protocols, computer storage, and processing. The optiputer consists of about 500 processors linked through fiber optical switching systems. Parts of the computer can share information at the speed of light.

This new design allows the communications lines to become the fastest part of the computer. In the past, the processors have been the fastest part of the computer. The optiputer is part of a new trend for supercomputers called *grid computing,* which allows complex problems to be solved by linking processors that may be thousands of miles apart.

oral contract An agreement to do business or a sales transaction that has been spoken but not put on paper. Oral contracts are legally enforceable; however, it is a better business practice to put contracts in writing.

orange juice futures These are traded on the New York Cotton Exchange (NYCE), a subsidiary of the New York Board of Trade. Orange juice futures are based on frozen concentrate orange juice (FCOJ) products from either Florida or Brazil. Officially the exchange lists the product as FCOJ-2, which replaced FCOJ-1 in 1999.

order imbalance An unusually large number of buy or sell orders for a futures contract, stock, or other investment. Order imbalances often cause the exchange to halt trading until other buyers or sellers appear. Sell imbalances may occur when a company experiences bad news, such as a negative earnings pre-announcement. A buy imbalance may occur if there is unexpected good news.

ordinary annuity A series of equal payments that are made at equal intervals to the owner of the annuity in exchange for the owner's investment of a fixed amount of cash. Annuities typically are used as an investment tool to plan for retirement. In contrast, the returns of *variable annuities* change depending on the direction of the market. Returns from *equity-indexed annuities* are linked to the performance of a specific equity index, such as the S&P 500.

ordinary interest Interest that is based on a 360-day year instead of a 365-day year.

In contrast, *exact interest* is based on a 365-day year. If large sums of money are involved, the difference can be significant. The ratio of ordinary interest to exact interest is 1 : 1.0139. Also called *simple interest*.

ordinary shares A term used in the United Kingdom and other English-speaking countries, such as Australia, to refer to common stock. Ordinary shares may be voting or non-voting shares.

organic growth Growth of a company that comes by increasing sales. Organic growth contrasts with growth that comes from buying another company or a product line.

Organization of Petroleum Exporting Countries See *OPEC*.

orphan stock A stock that is not covered by Wall Street research analysts. As investment banks laid off employees during 2001 and 2002 after the bear market settled in, an increasing number of small- to medium-sized stocks lacked coverage by Wall Street analysts.

Ortiz, Guillermo The governor of the Central Bank of Mexico, as of this printing, who is responsible for its operations. He also is a member of the Group of 30 (G-30), which is a private, non-profit international body that includes senior people from the public and private sectors and academia. The G-30's purpose is to deepen understanding of international economic and financial issues and to consider the effect of policy decisions.

oscillator A tool used in *technical analysis,* which attempts to identify price direction by using pricing charts. Oscillators are useful in *nontrending markets,* in which prices move sideways. They also can be helpful to alert traders to short-term market conditions when markets are moving up or down and become overbought or oversold. Oscillators can signal that a trend is ending its run, even before that is evident in the price movement. Oscillators are calculated by using *momentum,* which measures the rate of change in prices, instead of actual price levels.

The formula for momentum is $M = V \times V_x$.

V is the last closing price and V_x is the closing price ten days ago, or the price from some other interval. A ten-day momentum is commonly used.

oscillators Technical analysis tools that are used to examine price movements and make trading decisions. Some types of oscillators are relative strength index (RSI), stochastics, moving averages, and momentum. Momentum is one of the simplest oscillators and is the difference between the price of a security today and the price at a specific point, such as ten days ago. This example would be called ten-day momentum.

OTC Bulletin Board (OTCBB) An over-the-counter market used to trade stocks of small or financially risky companies. Another OTC market is Pink Sheets. In 2003, a new system, the Bulletin Board Exchange (BBX), is to begin replacing the OTCBB. See also *over-the-counter.*

OTS See *Office of Thrift Supervision.*

ouguiya The currency unit of Mauritania, comprised of 5 khoums.

out-of-the-money An option that has no value. A call option, which gives the holder the right to buy a security, is out-of-the-money when the price of the underlying security is below the option's strike price. If the security can be bought for less money in the open market, no option is needed. A put option, which gives the holder the right to sell a security, is out-of-the-money when the security can be sold in the market for a higher price.

outright-forward transaction A transaction in which one currency is purchased for another. The transaction is settled on a predetermined date three or more business days after the deal date. Outright-forward transactions are very flexible and can be customized. They may be used to hedge, to speculate, or as investments. Similar to a *spot transaction,* which doesn't have a predetermined settlement date.

outside director A director on a company's board who isn't employed by the corporation. With the passage of the Sarbanes–Oxley legislation in 2002, a greater emphasis has been placed on having outside directors on a company's board of directors. It is illegal for outside directors to sit on the boards of competing companies.

outside the market An order whose price didn't fall between the highest bid (the price a buyer is willing to pay) and the lowest ask (the price a seller is willing to sell) among all market makers competing in the security.

outsourcing An increasingly popular process in which a company contracts with another company to manage services that it needs but that it doesn't want to provide itself. Typically, outsourced services are non-core activities such as janitorial services, information technology, and food catering for the employee cafeteria. Sometimes companies outsource manufacturing and focus on sales and marketing. Outsourcing is popular because it allows companies to reduce short-term costs.

outstanding stock Stock of a corporation that has been issued and is tradable. If a company buys back stock, the repurchased shares are no longer outstanding and are either held in the company's treasury or retired.

over-allotment See *green shoe.*

overbought A trading condition in which a stock or other financial instrument has had a quick run up in its price, making the price higher than it should be. A market with prices that are too high is said to be overbought, and the prices may decline in a correction. The opposite is *oversold.*

overdraft Credit issued by a bank if a check is written on an account that does not have sufficient money to cover it and the bank chooses to approve the check. Often banks link a customer's savings account or credit card to the checking account to cover overdrafts, and an overdraft fee will be charged.

overdraft checking account A checking account that allows the account holder to write checks for more than the actual balance in the account. A finance charge, which may be quite expensive, is assessed on the amount of the overdraft. Sometimes overdraft checking accounts draw money from a linked credit card, in which case a debit to the credit card puts cash in the checking account and increases the amount of money owed on the credit card.

overfunded pension plan A pension plan in which the projected benefit obligations are smaller than the fair value of the plan assets. Overfunded pension plans don't require a contribution from the corporation, and the amount by which they are over-funded can be added to the company's bottom line as profit. In periods of increasing stock or fixed-income markets, a company's pension plan and the corporate bottom line will be boosted, thanks to stock market gains.

overhang A condition in the stock market in which a large number of shares of stocks of a particular company are expected to be sold in the near future, which likely will depress the share price. A large number of stock sales may occur when the lock-up period of an initial public offering expires or when a corporation that owns the stock of another company wants to liquidate that holding. The overhang may occur because the company is planning on issuing new shares in a follow-on stock offering. It also may occur because a company is planning to sell shares of another company that it acquired as an investment.

overhead Expenses that aren't directly related to the production of goods or services, but are more general and company-wide in nature. Examples of overhead are salaries for staff positions at headquarters and in human resources, accounting, payroll, and security departments.

overhead financing A lending program that is designed to help companies meet their monthly payroll expense when they have signed long-term contracts with customers who are billed on a monthly basis. Overhead financing may be provided by banks, but is often a product offered by specialty financing companies. To access overhead financing, a company submits an invoice for work that has been completed through a given time cycle. Advances are made to provide funds to coincide with the payroll periods. At the end of the month, when an invoice to the client is created, the overhead financing that has been provided is rolled into accounts receivable financing. That financing is usually converted into accounts receivable loans within 30 days.

overheating A term that refers to an economy that is growing too quickly and is in danger of producing inflation. In this circumstance, the central bank often will raise interest rates to slow borrowing, and thus spending.

overnight position A financial investment that is held after the close of daily trading. This term is used mainly in the futures market, since some futures traders typically close out their positions at the end of the trading day in order to avoid any overnight developments that might produce a loss. It applies much less to stock positions, which typically are held for long periods of time.

overnight rate The interest rate used by Canada to set monetary policy. The overnight rate is the rate charged on overnight loans between banks, similar to the Federal Reserve rate in the U.S. Canada in the recent past has had an explicit core inflation target between 1 percent and 3 percent per year.

overshoot Surpassing a financial target or earnings projection. A company may overshoot its revenue projection.

oversold A market state that is determined by using technical analysis; an oversold condition exists when prices have declined too

steeply and quickly compared to fundamental conditions. The next direction will be upward because everyone who wanted to sell already has done so.

oversubscribed A term used in underwriting to describe a new stock or bond issue that has more buyers than available shares. If an offering is oversubscribed, its price will often shoot up once it begins trading in the market. By using a *green shoe provision,* which allows the underwriter to sell more shares, the underwriter can modestly increase the number of shares offered.

over-the-counter (OTC) A trading market that isn't part of an exchange or a formal, regulated market. The OTC market is unregulated, and parties interact directly with each other, creating transactions with terms that are mutually agreeable (as long as they are allowed by law). In the foreign exchange market, the OTC market also is called the *inter-bank market.*

over-the-counter (OTC) stocks Stocks that aren't listed on an organized stock exchange. OTC stocks are traded by broker-dealers who communicate using computer networks or the telephone.

over-trading

1. The excessive buying or selling of securities in a discretionary trading account.

2. The expansion of a company's operations so quickly that it doesn't have enough working capital to pay for its expenses and may face default.

overvalued Describes a stock or other investment whose price is higher than what is justified by current fundamentals, such as its earnings or level of sales. Often the price of overvalued stocks will fall, sometimes rapidly.

overweight Having a large percentage of a portfolio invested in a particular sector. For example, an analyst may tell investors to overweight their holdings of healthcare stocks, meaning that healthcare stocks should take up a larger percentage of the investors' portfolios than they do on a broad market index, such as the S&P 500. The term also may be applied to individual stocks. Overweight contrasts with *underweight,* which indicates that a portfolio has a disproportionately small amount of funds in a particular stock or sector.

over-withholding Occurs when an employer withholds too much money from an employee's paycheck. Over-withholding means that the employee will receive a tax refund at the end of the year. There is no penalty assessed by the Internal Revenue Service for over-withholding; however, the taxpayer has essentially lent his money free of charge to the government. To reduce withholding, the taxpayer can file a new W-4 form and increase the number of exemptions that are claimed. That will trigger a reduction in the amount of money that is withheld from each paycheck.

overwriting Writing more call or put options than what are expected to be exercised. Call options are overwritten because the writer considers the underlying investment either overvalued or undervalued. Often, this strategy is used when the options writer has a concentrated stock position that he or she plans to hold indefinitely.

P

P&L See *profit and loss statement.*

P/GF See *price-to-growth flow.*

pa' anga The currency unit of the Tonga Islands, comprising seniti.

Pacific Exchange (PCX) A marketplace in which individual and institutional investors buy and sell options on more than 1,200 stocks. It was founded in 1882 as the San Francisco Stock and Bond Exchange and is headquartered in San Francisco. It was the first U.S. stock exchange to demutualize, establishing PCX Equities, Inc. as a for-profit corporate subsidiary of the Pacific Exchange in 1999.

Pacific Rim A region comprised of countries that border the Pacific Ocean. Pacific Rim countries include Australia, Cambodia, China, Hong Kong, Indonesia, Laos, Malaysia, New Zealand, Papua New Guinea, the Philippines, Singapore, South Korea, Taiwan, Thailand, and Vietnam. Although Japan is in the same region, its size as the world's second largest economy usually prevents it from being included in the group when talking about economic fundamentals or characteristics of the region. Instead, Japan is cited on a standalone basis and compared with the United States or Europe.

Packard, David The founder of computer company Hewlett-Packard Inc., along with William Hewlett. The company began in 1939 by filling niche demand for technology-based equipment, which the two constructed in Packard's garage. Their first product was a resistance-capacitance audio oscillator based on a design developed by Hewlett when he was in graduate school. After that, the company moved into computer equipment, such as printers, as well as other accessories and products.

packet services Telecommunications services that enable customers to transmit large volumes of data in a secure and economical manner. Packet services are used for local area network interconnection, remote site, point of sale, and branch office communications. Technically speaking, packet services include frame relay, ATM (asynchronous transfer mode), and IP (Internet Protocol) connectivity services. *Frame relay services* are provided by telecommunications companies that connect local area networks to national or regional networks. *Internet Protocol* sends data from one computer to another on the Internet; each computer has at least one unique address.

paid-in capital Equity listed on a company's balance sheet that is above the amount of equity that is listed at par value, which is usually $1. Paid-in capital is calculated by subtracting the par value of equity from the amount of money that actually was raised by a stock issue. Also called *additional paid-in capital, capital surplus,* or *capital in excess of par value.*

painting the tape Manipulating the market for a security by reporting fictitious trades on the consolidated trading tape of an exchange. These trades are not submitted for trade matching and clearing purposes. Those intending to commit fraud engage in this activity to increase the apparent trading volume of a security or to affect the reported closing price. The term is left over from the day when a paper-based ticker carried stock trade information. However, the tactic can still be used with electronic trading systems. In that case, traders can buy or sell a security to create the illusion of high trading activity and to attract other traders in order to push up the price.

PAIR See *productive asset investment ratio.*

Paley, William S. The builder of the CBS radio and television networks, which at the time he gained control was a 16-station chain of radio stations formally called the Columbia Broadcasting System. He lured radio talent away from the other networks during the 1940s, which helped make CBS the top-rated network in radio and television until 1976.

palladium An important industrial metal that has a variety of uses. Automotive catalysts use 63 percent of the demand for palladium; electronic equipment accounts for about 21 percent; dental alloys make up about 12 percent; and the remainder is used for jewelry. Most of the production, around two-thirds, comes from Russia; South Africa makes up just under one-fourth of production; the remainder comes from North America. Palladium futures are traded on the New York Mercantile Exchange; however, the volume is very modest. Other exchanges also trade palladium futures.

panic A widespread and significant fear that the market or economy is going to collapse. A panic leads to massive bank deposit withdrawals and possible banking collapses, as well as falling stock prices. Panics occurred at the height of the Great Depression in the U.S. when bank depositors by the hundreds descended on their banks to withdraw their deposits for fear that the bank would fail and they would lose all of their money. A panic is usually a relatively short-lived phenomenon, in contrast to a recession or depression, which last six months to several years.

Panitchpakdi, Supachai The Director-General of the World Trade Organization (WTO), as of this printing, appointed to a three-year term in 2002.

paper Short for *commercial paper*, which is a debt instrument issued by corporations for a short period, usually less than 270 days. The definition of paper may be expanded to refer to all of the short-term debt that the company has outstanding.

paper loss The extent to which a current market value of a holding is less than the value at which it was purchased. A paper loss is an unrealized loss that exists only on paper.

paper profit The extent to which a current market value of a holding exceeds the value at which it was purchased. A paper profit is an unrealized profit that exists only on paper.

par The face value of a security. For common stock, the company sets the par value before it is issued. Typically, par value is $1 a share. The par value of a bond is the amount that will be paid upon maturity, such as $1,000. Par value has nothing to do with a stock or bond's market value, which varies as trading occurs.

par value A value that is printed on the face of a stock or bond certificate when it is issued. Par value is of little significance once the stock or bond begins trading because the price will be influenced by market activity. For a bond, the typical par value is $1,000; the typical par value for one share of stock is $1.

parallel shift in the yield curve A shift that occurs in the yield curve when the yield on all maturities move by the same amount, or number of basis points. This is in contrast to *non-parallel shift in the yield curve*.

parent company A company that owns another company. The company that is owned is called a *subsidiary*.

Pareto's Law A theory developed by Vilfredo Pareto (1848–1923) that is applicable in numerous situations. It holds that 20 percent of the work or effort produces 80 percent of the return or benefit. The theory is quite ubiquitous and is used in a number of situations, such as commenting that 20 percent of the people on a team do 80 percent of the work.

Paris Club An informal group of developed countries that seek solutions for heavily indebted countries that are having trouble making their payments. The creditors, who typically are industrial countries, agree to reschedule the debts they are owed. The Paris Club began in 1956 when Argentina met its public creditors in Paris. The Paris Club and related groups have made more than 300 agreements with 76 debtor countries. The Paris Club works closely with the International Monetary Fund (IMF) and often requires countries to be IMF members in order to receive debt assistance.

parity Equality. The term is used in the foreign exchange market to talk about two currencies' parity with each other. For instance, as the exchange rate for the dollar and euro both approach 1, they are said to be at parity.

partnership A business that has two or more owners who agree to share profits and are liable for any debts or losses. The partnership agreement outlines how profits and losses are to be allocated. A partnership agreement may terminate upon the death or withdrawal of one member, or may include other arrangements in such situations, including allowing the remaining partner or partners to purchase the withdrawing partner's share of the business.

passed dividend A regularly scheduled dividend that has been omitted. A dividend is passed if the board of directors doesn't vote to declare it.

passive income Income from activities, in which an investor is not actively involved. It is a distinction, established by the Internal Revenue Service that governs how the income is taxed. Real estate investments used to be considered passive, but now if the taxpayer spends half his or her time involved in real estate property or services, then income from the real estate is not considered passive. In 1993, the IRS rules were changed to require that losses and credits from passive activities are deductible only from passive income.

passive portfolio strategy A strategy that relies on diversification to match the performance of some market index. The investor is minimally involved in directing the portfolio. A passive strategy assumes that the marketplace will reflect all available information in the price paid for securities.

pass-through security A security through which income passes from the debtors to investors. An example of a pass-through security is collateralized mortgage obligations.

pataca The currency unit of Macau, comprised of 100 avos.

patent An exclusive right, given to a person or company by the U.S. government, that lets the person or company "exclude others from making, using, offering for sale, or selling" a particular product or a specific process in the United States or importing the product or process into the United States. The U.S. Patent and Trademark Office grants a patent for a period of 17 years. Patent holders may apply for a renewal of their patent in certain cases. There are three types of patents: A *utility patent* may be granted to anyone who invents or discovers any new and useful process, machine, or article of manufacture, or creates any new useful improvement. A *design patent* is given for a new, original, and ornamental design for an article of manufacture. A *plant patent* may be granted to anyone who invents or discovers and reproduces any distinct and new variety of plants.

Accounting regulations call for the value of a patent to be amortized over its useful life, which may be less than the legal life of 17 years. If a patent has to be defended in court in a patent infringement suit, it is added to the acquisition cost of the patent.

pattern A trend that can be detected by connecting the prices on a price chart. Technical analysts interpret patterns in order to predict likely future price movements.

pawn shop A business that lends money at high interest rates in exchange for collateral such as jewelry, electronic items, or anything else that is judged to have a resale value. The pawn shop keeps the collateral, and if the loan is repaid, the item is returned. If the money isn't repaid, the item is sold and the pawn shop keeps the proceeds. Typically pawn shops lend money to people at a lower economic level who don't have access to other forms of credit, such as credit cards or a credit line from a bank.

payables turnover The sum of the cost of goods sold and the change in inventory, divided by average accounts payable. The resulting ratio shows the number of times on average that a company's accounts payable turns over, and it shows the relative size of accounts payable.

pay-as-you-go

1. A budgeting technique that requires expenses to be paid for when they are incurred. It doesn't allow for debt to be incurred. Typically state and local governments adopt this type of budgeting process.

2. The federal income tax collection system, in which employees have taxes taken out of each paycheck and submitted to the federal government.

payday loan A short-term cash advance that is made to an employee in exchange for the employee's post-dated check in the amount of the cash advanced plus a transaction fee. Authorization also may be given to do a debit transaction in the future. Usually, the interest rate charge is quite high, especially when calculated in terms of an annual percentage rate. In the spring of 2003, the Federal Deposit Insurance Corp. issued new guidelines, designed to protect borrowers, for banks to follow when making payday loans. The FDIC recommended that banks establish cooling-off periods between loans and verify that customers have only one payday loan outstanding at a time.

payment In trading terms, an instruction to transfer funds or a financial asset to pay for a transaction. In the case of transferring money to pay for stock or another investment, until the transaction settles, it is not yet final.

payment for order flow A payment made by a brokerage firm to its Wall Street counterparts for directing trades to the firm. The practice has been criticized because customers may not get the best available price if their trade is directed at someone who specifically is paying to receive those orders. And the payment usually won't be passed along to retail customers. The practice has

occurred in the past with options exchanges, which have paid brokerage firms to steer orders to their traders.

payment-in-kind (PIK) A program run by the U.S. Department of Agriculture that pays farmers for stopping or limiting the planting and production of specific products. For instance, the USDA offered sugar cane and sugar beet growers the choice of not producing some of their 2001 crop in exchange for receiving sugar that was already in storage that the farms could sell. The PIK program was started by USDA Secretary John Block in 1983, during Ronald Reagan's administration.

payout ratio The percentage of earnings that are paid in dividends. To calculate the ratio, dividend per share is divided by earnings per share.

pay-to-play

1. Refers to a company pressuring investment banks to provide it with ordinary loans and credit facilities in exchange for the company giving the bank the desired investment banking work. Investment banks typically want to provide lucrative advisory services, such as merger advice and helping companies raise equity and debt. Less lucrative is providing loans or credit facilities, so companies attempt to entice investment banks into providing those services through pay-to-play. The term increasingly came into use after the market boom of the late 1990s ended and credit became harder to get.

2. Refers to underwriters contributing to the election campaigns of elected officials in order for the underwriter to have an advantage in securing contracts to underwrite municipal bonds. This usage is now rare, as legal changes have made the practice difficult, if not illegal.

PCX See *Pacific Exchange.*

PDA See *personal digital assistant.*

peace dividend The increase to gross domestic product that comes from reallocating defense spending at the conclusion of a conflict to peacetime activities. The peace dividend was prominently seen after World War II.

pennant A term used in technical analysis to refer to a pattern created by price movements. When the price points are connected, the pattern looks like a pennant. Pennants are created by a sharp initial move upwards or downwards, followed by a limited trading range, which creates a shape like a pennant after the upward and downward trendlines merge. Usually these are short-lived patterns lasting only a few weeks.

penny jumping A term that was created in the early 1990s when the stock exchanges changed the minimum size of their trading transactions to pennies from one-eighth of a cent. Penny jumping occurs, for example, when a specialist on the stock exchange sees that there is a buyer for shares of stock at $20. The specialist could then step in front of the order, or *penny jump,* and sell the shares to the buyer at $19.99 using shares in his or her own account. The specialist takes the trade away from the other seller.

penny stock Very low-priced stocks that are viewed as speculative and typically sell for less than $1 per share. However, the definition of a penny stock can be expanded to include stocks that are priced less than $5 a share. Penny stocks are almost exclusively traded on over-the-counter markets because they don't qualify for exchange membership.

penny stock fraud Fraud that is committed by speculators in *penny stocks,* which are the stocks of very small companies with a limited number of shareholders. The insiders purchase the shares and put out false rumors about the company's prospects; then when buyers emerge, they sell their shares and make a huge profit. The new investors are left with virtually worthless shares.

Pension Benefit Guaranty Corp. (PBGC) A quasi-federal agency that protects the retirement income of over 44 million U.S. workers in more than 35,000 defined benefit pension in the event that the companies operating the plan go bankrupt. Defined benefit plans guarantee a minimum monthly payment upon retirement. The PBGC was created as a federal corporation through the Employee Retirement Income Security Act of 1974 (ERISA). The purpose of the PBGC is to encourage the continuation and maintenance of defined benefit pension plans and provide timely and uninterrupted payments of pension benefits to participants and beneficiaries in plans covered by PBGC. Analysts typically say that when plan assets fall below 85 percent of the projected benefit obligations, then the Pension Benefit Guarantee Corp. will ask companies to begin funding the pension plan with cash.

pension fund A fund that is set up by a corporation, government, or labor union to pay benefits to retired workers. While workers are employed, contributions may be made through payroll contributions and through employers' contributions. Pension funds manage billions of dollars and are major investors in the financial markets. The Pension Benefit Guaranty Corporation insures pensioners' benefits. See also *defined benefit plan* and *defined contribution pension plan.*

pension reversion The termination of a pension plan by a corporation because the plan is overfunded and the company wants to take ownership of the surplus assets. The money that is withdrawn is invested with an insurance company in a fixed-annuity plan, from which employees will receive future retirement benefits. A pension reversion usually is viewed negatively by employees. The action also eliminates insurance protection for the pension fund from the Pension Benefit Guaranty Corporation, an additional level of protection for pensioners in the event that something unexpected occurs to the fund.

per-capita income An income measure that is calculated by taking the total personal income of the residents of a given area and dividing this number by the population. Per capita income is the mean income for each person in the group. It is used to determine how wealthy the area is and provides guidance to companies considering expanding their business into the area.

percentage of net sales method A method of estimating uncollectible accounts that assumes a predictable percentage of each sales dollar will not be collected. All businesses that bill customers for goods or services, instead of requiring payment upfront, likely make some allowance for uncollectible accounts.

perfect competition A market condition in which individual buyers and sellers have no power to affect the market price of a good or service. This would theoretically happen if there were large numbers of both buyers and sellers, a similar good or service was being traded by all of them, and complete information about market prices was available to all participants.

perfect hedge A hedging strategy in which the profit and loss are equal. In a perfect hedge, for example, loss in a cash Treasury bond exactly equals the gain on the futures contract.

performance bond A surety bond that one party to a transaction provides to a second party to protect the second party in the event the terms of the contract are not met. In the event that the terms are not met, the company providing the insurance (the first party) is required to reimburse the second party. A similar concept occurs in the futures or options market. In that case, both the buyer and seller of contracts deposit money to ensure that each will meet the terms of the contract. This deposit is called a *performance bond margin,* which is a security deposit, not a down payment.

permanent life insurance A type of life insurance policy that requires premiums to be paid for as long as the insured lives. A permanent life insurance policy accumulates cash value over time, and, upon the

death of the insured, a death benefit is paid. The policy holder may borrow against the cash value of the policy, but if the insured dies before the loan is repaid, the balance is deducted from the life insurance proceeds.

personal digital assistant (PDA) A hand-held computer that holds names and phone numbers, a calendar, to-do lists, and may be able to connect to the Internet using a wireless Internet service. Additional features may include a foldable, small keyboard. Some units also serve as wireless telephones.

personal exemption A fixed amount of money ($3,000 per person in 2003) that can be deducted from income when calculating the amount of personal income tax owed. A personal exemption is allowed for each person, dependent, and spouse claimed on the 1040 form.

personal finance The industry that is concerned with advising individuals on financial and investment opportunities. Personal finance consultants give advice on life insurance, retirement savings, and investing in stocks and bonds, among other things. It is distinguished from *corporate finance,* which advises companies on raising money, and *public finance,* which helps governments raise funds.

personal identification number (PIN) A series of numbers that consumers use to access their checking or debit accounts from automated teller machines (ATMs), financial institution Web sites, and telephone banking services. PINs typically have four digits. PIN accounts also allow consumers to obtain credit card cash advances from ATM machines.

personal income A monthly economic statistic report produced by the U.S. government's Bureau of Economic Analysis. It is released about three or four weeks after the end of the month that it refers to. The impact of the personal income data on the financial markets is limited because it is released after other important indicators that indirectly give clues about personal income, such as retail sales and employment data. Personal income measures income from employment, self-employment, investment income, dividends, and transfer payments (such as Social Security). Income from wages is the largest component. The data's value comes from showing trends in personal income growth that can indicate future consumer spending patterns. Because consumer spending contributes about two-thirds to gross domestic product (GDP), any downward changes in consumer spending have a significant impact on consumer activity. The release also is the only source for data on consumption of services.

personal property Property that is owned by an individual that is not real estate. Personal property often is covered by homeowners' insurance. Clothing, televisions, and dishes are examples of personal property.

peseta The currency unit of Andorra, comprised of 100 centimos.

peso The currency unit of Argentina, comprised of 100 centavos. The currency unit of Chile, Columbia, Cuba, Dominican Republic, Mexico, the Philippines, and Uruguay, comprised of 100 centesimos.

petrodollars An informal term that refers to U.S. dollars that are received by oil-producing countries in payment for oil exports and are deposited in U.S. or European banks.

PGM See *platinum group metals.*

phantom stock plan An incentive plan that awards executives a bonus based on the market appreciation of the company's stock over a certain period of time, usually a year. The plan awards key employees for increasing the value of a company's stock without giving out actual stock; instead, a cash payment is used. A phantom stock plan works, for example, by giving an executive 1,000 shares of phantom stock at $20 a share. The phantom stock is not actual shares but is tied to the value of the company's stock. A formula is developed to determine the

phantom stock's value. If the valuation formula shows that the company's stock has risen by $20 a share, the executive would receive a $40,000 check. The company would deduct the $40,000 and the employee would pay taxes on the $40,000, which would be considered wages. The payout isn't made immediately, however. Participants usually must remain employed by the company for a certain number of years or until retirement to receive the payout. They also may have to agree not to compete with the employer.

In the case of private companies, a measure other than stock appreciation would be used. Phantom stock plans are popular with family-owned companies or closely-held companies that don't want to give up equity in the company. The amount of payment is related to the person's salary. A phantom stock plan also may be called a *shadow stock plan* or *unit stock plan.*

Philadelphia Fed Survey A survey of businesses in the manufacturing industry that gives an early indication of price direction, employment levels, and general business conditions. The survey covers manufacturers in the Third Federal Reserve District, which is headquartered in Philadelphia and includes the eastern two-thirds of Pennsylvania, southern New Jersey, and Delaware. The data is released at the end of the month that has been surveyed. Traders in the financial markets pay attention to the survey because it may give early insight into what other, broader manufacturing surveys, such as the ISM Index, will show. However the Philadelphia Fed Survey usually isn't a market-moving release. The data is presented as a diffusion index for current conditions and a six-month outlook.

Philadelphia Semiconductor Index A price-weighted index composed of 17 U.S. companies that design, manufacture, and sell semiconductors. This index was created by the Philadelphia Stock exchange on December 1, 1993, with an initial value of 200 and was split two-for-one on July 24,

1995. The ticker symbol for the index is SOX.

Philadelphia Stock Exchange (PHLX)
The first organized stock exchange in the United States, founded in 1790. The exchange trades more than 2,200 stocks, over 1,180 equity options, 13 index options, and multiple currency pairs. The PHLX's Philadelphia Automated Communication and Execution system (PACE) was one of the first automated equity trading systems on any exchange.

The PHLX offers popular index options such as the Oil Service Sector (OSX) Index Option, which is a widely quoted benchmark of the oil industry. Other popular industry benchmark indices include the PHLX's Gold/Silver Sector (XAU); the Semiconductor Sector (SOX); the KBW Bank Sector (BKX); and the Utility Sector (UTY).

The PHLX also trades both standardized and customized currency options. Customized currency options offer choice of expiration date, strike (exercise) price, and premium payment.

Phillips Curve An economic theory that describes the relationship between the rate of inflation and unemployment. It says that there was a consistent, inverse relationship between wage inflation and unemployment in the United Kingdom from 1861 to 1957. When unemployment was high, wages were slow to increase. The opposite happened when unemployment was low. The only exception was the period between the two world wars when inflation was extremely high. The theory is named after A.W.H. Phillips (1914–1975) who published a study in 1958 that was viewed as a milestone macroeconomic theory. However, recent economic performance has questioned this theory, as low inflation in the U.S. has coincided with low unemployment.

PHLX See *Philadelphia Stock Exchange.*

PHLX Gold & Silver Index A capitalization-weighted index composed of the common stocks of nine companies in the gold and silver mining index. The index is a product of the Philadelphia Stock Exchange and began trading in January 1979 with an initial value of 100. Its ticker symbol is XAU.

physical commodity The actual commodity that is delivered to a futures contract buyer when the expiration of the commodity contract occurs. Metals such as copper, gold, and silver and agricultural products such as cattle, wheat, and soybeans are examples of physical commodities.

physical verification An auditing process in which the auditor inspects the actual assets of the company to make certain that they match up with written records. Often the auditor verifies only a sampling of physical products.

pickup Extra value that is gained when bonds are swapped by traders. For instance, when bonds with the same coupon payment and maturities are *swapped,* or exchanged, one bond may be more valuable because of a difference in credit quality; this results in a pickup on the transaction for the trader ending up with the higher-quality bond.

piggybacking An illegal practice in which a broker mimics a client's trade. The assumption on the part of the broker is that the client may be making the trade because he or she has access to non-public information that will make the trade profitable.

PIK See *payment-in-kind.*

PIN See *personal identification number.*

Pink Sheets A private company that publishes the bid and ask price of stocks of very small companies that trade on the over-the-counter (OTC) market (as opposed to one of the major stock exchanges). Pink sheet companies derive their name from the color of paper they historically were listed on. Market makers who commit to buying and selling the securities of OTC issuers can publish their prices in the pink sheets. Pink Sheets began in 1904 as the National Quotation Bureau, which began as a paper-based inter-dealer quotation service.

Companies whose stock is listed on the pink sheets tend to have little trading volume. They don't meet the minimum listing requirements for a national exchange and many are small enough that they aren't required to file reports or audited financial statements with the Securities and Exchange Commission. Because of this lack of disclosure, purchasing shares of these companies can be very risky.

pip The smallest amount by which a price can move in a market. For example, in the foreign exchange market, a pip is one-hundredth of one percent for most currencies. Also called *tick*.

pipeline

1. A ubiquitous term that often is used to refer to the amount of business that a company expects to receive in the coming months or year. Typically it is used when companies have a long time between the placement of orders and when the goods or services actually are delivered. Companies talk about the pipeline being full to indicate that they have a solid backlog of orders.

2. In the energy market, the way crude oil, gasoline, or natural gas is delivered to refiners.

PIPES *Private investments in public entities* are an investment vehicle that enables small, private companies to turn themselves into a publicly-traded companies without going through the initial public offering process and the scrutiny that it involves. Typically, a private company that is viable will buy the stock of a public company that has ceased to operate but which still exists as a shell. The two companies in effect merge, with the operations and the management of the private company running the new company.

piracy The illegal copying of music or software programs, which deprives record and software companies and their artists of profits. In the music industry the piracy of compact disks (CDs) has become a significant problem that may significantly cut into the industry's profits. Software companies also have faced the same problem, especially in areas outside the United States where copyright laws aren't as strict.

pit The location of trading activity on futures or options exchanges that use *open-outcry trading,* a system in which traders shout out the prices they are willing to buy or sell contracts at. Around the pits are ascending steps, called *rings,* where support staff for traders stand.

placement ratio A ratio that indicates the percentage of municipal bond offerings that have been purchased from the underwriters during the previous week. The statistic is published by the *Bond Buyer,* an industry publication.

plan of reorganization A document that a debtor submits to a bankruptcy court in order to list what debt should be restructured or forgiven. In bankruptcies under Chapter 11, Chapter 12, and Chapter 13, the debtor proposes a reorganization plan.

plan sponsor A business or organization that establishes and manages a pension or insurance plan. Plan sponsors are required to follow legal guidelines to manage the plan and to inform the participants about the financial health of their investment.

plant An asset category that describes certain fixed assets listed on a company's balance sheet, such as buildings, manufacturing facilities, and offices. See also *fixed asset.*

platinum A metal that has a variety of uses in jewelry and industrial applications. Just over half of its demand comes from jewelry production, while automotive catalyst uses take up about one-third and chemical and petroleum refining takes up about 13 percent. The remainder of its demand comes from the computer industry and high-technology applications. Platinum is one of the world's scarcest materials.

Eighty percent of platinum supply comes from South Africa, about 10 percent from Russia, and the rest from North America. Futures and options contracts for platinum trade on the New York Mercantile Exchange, as well as other exchanges around the world. Platinum is the principal member of a six-metal group called platinum group metals (PGM). The other members of the group are palladium, rhodium, ruthenium, osmium, and iridium. All have chemical and physical qualities that make them vital industrial materials.

platinum group metals (PGM) Platinum and palladium, when the term is used in the U.S. financial markets. However, there are four other members of PGM: rhodium, ruthenium, osmium, and iridium. All six metals have unique chemical and physical qualities that make them vital industrial materials. Platinum is used in jewelry, along with industrial uses; palladium is used primarily for industrial purposes, such as manufacturing cars.

Plaza Agreement An agreement made in 1985 by the United States and four other industrial countries (the G5) that the dollar was too strong and that they wanted other currencies to appreciate against the dollar. The Plaza Agreement states that some further orderly appreciation of the main non-dollar currencies against the dollar was desirable, which told the foreign exchange market that the G5 intended to intervene in the market. Six weeks later, the Plaza agreement had the desired effect of pushing the dollar down more than 10 percent. The G-5 countries are the United States, Japan, Germany, France, and the United Kingdom.

Plc Stands for *Public Limited Company Means,* which is a commonly used term in the U.K., Ireland, and other English-speaking countries other than the U.S. It is equivalent to *Inc.* in the U.S.

plus-tick rule See *short-sale rule.*

PMI

1. See *Chicago Purchasing Managers Index.*

2. See *private mortgage insurance.*

point A finance charge that is paid up front on mortgages by the borrower. A point is 1 percent of the loan value. For instance, on a $200,000 mortgage, $2,000 is the point the borrower would pay as a finance charge. Points are tax deductible because the money paid is mortgage interest. However, points likely may have to be deducted across the life of the loan.

point-and-figure chart A technical analysis tool that has no time line at the bottom of the chart but instead indicates shifts in the direction of price movements. Entries are made when a price change occurs. Xs represent price increases and Os represent price declines. To simplify matters, point-and-figure charts indicate when a security should be bought when the current column of Xs rises one box higher than the top box in the immediately prior column of Xs. A sell signal occurs when the current column of Os falls one box lower than the lowest O in the immediately prior column of Os.

point-of-sale network A computer system that uses an electronic card reader at the cash register that records purchases. Point-of-sale systems give businesses up-to-the-minute information about sales, inventory, and customer purchases. They also are used to accept credit card payments.

poison pill A financial tactic that is designed to make an unfriendly takeover very difficult to accomplish. Often poison pills come in the form of share-rights plans that allow existing stockholders to purchase stock at some fixed price if a takeover bid occurs. At that time, all shareholders, except for the new, outside shareholders, are given the option to buy stock at a sharp discount, which dilutes the ownership of the new shareholder, and thus effectively makes it more difficult for it to exert influence.

poison put A provision in a bond or note that gives bondholders the option of redeeming the bond or note at its par value if certain events occur. Those events may include a restructuring that reduces the credit quality of the issue, a hostile takeover, or the payment of a large dividend.

Policy Board of the Bank of Japan The governmental agency in Japan that is responsible for setting monetary policy, including setting interest rates. One of the tools the Bank of Japan uses to implement monetary policy is targeting its current account balances held at the Bank of Japan to stay within a range, such as 15 to 20 trillion yen.

Ponzi, Charles See *pyramid scheme.*

pool factor The percentage of mortgage-based securities that is left over after the initial issuance of mortgage-backed securities has been made. A pool factor is often applied to a mortgage pool, such as Ginnie Mae or Fannie Mae securities, to help investors estimate what future prepayment rates will be.

pork bellies A futures contract, traded on the Chicago Mercantile Exchange (CME), for frozen, stored pork, which comes from hogs and provides products such as ham and bacon. The futures contract was designed to help meat packers and warehouse operators cope with price risks, as the price can be volatile. Futures and options are traded on the CME.

PORTAL An automated trading system operated by the National Association of Securities Dealers (NASD) to trade unregistered foreign and domestic securities.

portfolio All of the assets and investments, such as stocks, bonds, real estate, and cash, that a person or business owns. A professional who manages a portfolio is called a *portfolio manager.* Often, investors group their portfolios into different asset classes with a targeted percentage of each asset. For instance, one potential asset allocation formula for a portfolio is 60 percent stocks,

30 percent bonds, and 10 percent cash. Asset allocation protects the value of a portfolio. If equities decline, for example, then bonds likely will rise, which helps protect the portfolio's value.

portfolio beta score A beta score calculated for an entire investment portfolio, not just individual stocks. *Beta* measures the volatility of an investment relative to the market as a whole. A beta of 1 indicates that the stock moves in tandem with the market. A score over 1 indicates that the stock will rise or fall to a greater degree than the market.

portfolio insurance The use of stock index futures, or other hedging devices, to protect the value of an investment portfolio if the market declines. Portfolio insurance can be created by selling stock index futures short (selling futures that you don't own) or buying *stock index put options,* which give the right to sell the stock index futures contract at a specified price.

portfolio manager A professional who earns a fee for managing investments for individuals or institutions. Portfolio managers are employed by insurance companies, mutual funds, pension funds, banks, and other financial institutions; they owe a fiduciary responsibility to investors. Also called *money manager.*

portfolio theory The quantitative analysis of how investors can diversify their portfolio in order to minimize risk and maximize returns. The theory was introduced in 1952 by University of Chicago economics student Harry Markowitz, who published his doctoral thesis, "Portfolio Selection," in the *Journal of Finance.* Markowitz assumed that investors wanted to avoid risk, so he advocated analyzing individual security vehicles to determine how they contribute to the portfolio's overall risk. The analysis requires close examination of how investments move in relation to one another. Portfolio theory also is called *modern portfolio theory* or *portfolio management theory.* In 1990,

Markowitz received the Nobel Prize in Economics for his research.

There are four aspects of portfolio theory: individual security valuation, which describes a universe of assets by their expected returns and risks; asset allocation, which determines how much an individual should invest into stocks, bonds, or other asset classes; portfolio optimization, which determines which investments offer the best return given the level of the risk; and performance measurement, which divides each investment's performance into risk categories based upon its own performance, market-related risk, and industry-related risk.

portfolio turnover The frequency with which stocks and other investments are bought and sold within a portfolio. A high turnover ratio isn't usually positive, as it means that the portfolio manager spends a large amount of money on trading commissions. High turnover also likely means that the gains are taxed as ordinary income rather than at the long-term capital gains rate, which is lower. A mutual fund's portfolio turnover ratio is disclosed in its prospectus.

position A trader's or investor's financial commitment to a particular security. A *long position* means that the person owns shares or futures contracts. A *short position* means that shares or contracts have been sold even though the trader does not own them.

position building The process of buying or selling shares of stock, futures contracts, options, or other investments in order to accumulate a long or short position. By gradually adding to a position over time, the trader avoids pushing the price of the stock or contract up. If a trader builds a position in a particular stock, he or she is betting that the price of that stock will rise and make the investment profitable.

position trader A futures trader who holds onto his or her investment for a long period of time, perhaps even for several months or longer. Position traders are looking to make money from strong fundamental changes in the market, rather than short-term price moves. Position traders may attempt to take advantage of the spread between prices for different delivery months for the same commodity.

positive carry When the cost of borrowing money to pay for a securities purchase is less than the yield on the securities. For instance, if funds are borrowed at a cost of 6 percent, and the stock or bond investment yields 8 percent, there is a positive carry. The inverse is a *negative carry.*

positive spread investing Refers to the ability to raise either equity or debt capital at a cost that is significantly less than the initial returns that can be made on an investment. The phrase is typically used in conjunction with real estate investments.

positive yield curve An upward sloping yield curve that is characterized by interest rates that are higher on long-term debt than on short-term debt. This is the normal situation, because investors have to be compensated more for taking on the greater risk of tying their funds up for a longer period of time. If short-term interest rates are higher than longer-term interest rates, the graph is called a *negative yield curve.* A *yield curve* is a visual representation of interest rates on a graph shown for various points in time. For instance, the Treasury yield curve begins with 3-month bills and has points representing 6-month bills, 52-week bills, 2-, 3-, 5- 10-year notes, and the 30-year bond.

potentially dilutive securities Stock options, convertible preferred stocks, or bonds that potentially can be converted to common stock and therefore may dilute current shareholders' earnings at some point in the future. The dilution would occur because earnings have to be spread among a greater number of stock shares.

pound The currency unit of Great Britain, comprised of 100 pence. The pound is also known as the *sterling.* Traders write it as *GBP.* The Falkland Islands, Gibraler, St. Helena, and the Sudan Republic also use the pound. It is also the currency unit of Cyprus, comprised of 100 cents, and the currency unit of Egypt and Syria, comprised of 100 piasters.

power marketer A wholesale power company that has registered with the Federal Energy Regulatory Commission in order to buy power at wholesale prices and sell the power to other marketers or public entities at market prices. Power marketing companies may be financial intermediaries, companies affiliated with utilities, natural gas marketers, or entrepreneurs. Power marketers usually do not generate the power; they just sell it.

power of attorney A written, legal document that authorizes another person to act for the writer of the power of attorney. The power of attorney may be narrowly defined, in which case it would be called a *limited power of attorney*. A power of attorney also may be limited to deciding health care issues, in which case it is called a *health care power of attorney*.

PPI See *producer price index*.

PPO See *preferred provider organization*.

prearranged trading An arrangement that is made before trading commences in the futures or options pit to trade with another broker at a set price. Prearranged trading is illegal, whether the arrangement is implied or expressly stated.

precious metals A group of metals that are expensively priced relative to other metals, such as base metals. Precious metals include gold, silver, platinum, and palladium. Gold is especially valued, because its value is resistant to political turmoil and falling currency values.

predatory lending An unscrupulous lending practice that targets low-income or otherwise vulnerable people. Predatory lending involves making high-cost loans to borrowers based on their level of assets and not on their ability to repay the debt. This practice also may require a borrower to refinance the loan repeatedly, which lets the lender charge high points and fees. Another predatory practice is using fraud or deceit to conceal the true cost of the loan from an unsophisticated borrower.

preemptive right A right given to shareholders to retain the same percentage of ownership they currently have if new shares are issued. Preemptive rights prevent the current owners' stake and control from being diluted. Preemptive rights usually are transmitted by giving existing shareholders a subscription warrant that spells out how many new shares they are entitled to buy. Preemptive rights often exist only if they are listed in the corporation's charter.

preexisting condition A medical condition that a person has before becoming covered by a new health insurance plan. Insurers can refuse to cover people for preexisting conditions. Often there is a waiting period before insurance becomes effective, which may allow preexisting conditions to be discovered. Typically this situation is bypassed in the case of a job change; preexisting conditions are not an issue because the employer's plan is obligated to cover employees whether they have a preexisting condition or not.

preferred dividend coverage The amount of money that is available to pay preferred dividends after interest expense and taxes have been paid. Preferred dividend coverage is calculated by taking net income after interest and taxes (before common stock dividends are paid) and dividing that amount by the amount of preferred dividends to be paid. The resulting number tells how many times the preferred dividend requirement is covered by current earnings.

preferred provider organization (PPO) A network of doctors and health care providers who agree to offer discounted care to the members of an employer- or union-sponsored health insurance plan. The medical professionals receive a significant number of clients, which makes offering the discount worthwhile. Employees can see doctors and other professionals outside of the network, but they have to pay a higher percentage of the cost than if they stay with an in-network doctor.

preferred stock A class of stock that pays dividends at a set rate. Holders of preferred stock receive their dividends before common-stock holders if the company reduces or eliminates its common dividend payment. In the case of a bankruptcy or liquidation, preferred-stock holders receive the proceeds before common-stock holders. Preferred stocks do have some drawbacks. If the company's earnings rise, the preferred stockholders' dividend payment remains fixed at the initial dividend level. Typically preferred stockholders don't have voting rights.

Dividends can be cumulative, which means that if they are not paid in a particular year then they will be carried forward. However, these are not debts of the company because the directors can defer preferred dividends indefinitely. Noncumulative dividends are lost if they are not paid in a particular year. Preferred stock dividends can have tax advantages for corporate investors, which is one reason they are the primary purchasers of preferred stock.

preliminary prospectus The first document that is given by the underwriter of stock or bond offerings to prospective purchasers. It outlines the terms of the offering. The preliminary prospectus lists all the details about the company's structure and its strategy, but it is incomplete; in particular, it does not contain the amount of money that the company hopes to raise through the offering or the offering price. Also called *red herring*.

premium

1. A price that is above market prices.

2. The amount that a policy holder pays an insurance company for coverage.

3. In the options market, the cost of the option.

4. In the futures market, an upward adjustment in price that is allowed for delivery of a commodity of a higher grade against a futures contract.

premium bond A bond that is valued at more than its face amount. A bond may trade at a premium because interest rates have fallen since it was issued.

premium income Money received by the writer (the creator) of a put or call option. By selling a put or call option, the writer hopes that the option won't be exercised and he or she will be able to collect the premium income.

prenuptial contract A legal agreement, made between two people before they are married, that spells out how their property and assets will be split in the event that they are divorced. Prenuptials are individualized and may include whatever details the couple agrees on, including how financial or other responsibilities are to be shared during the marriage.

prepackaged bankruptcy A bankruptcy proceeding used by corporations in which the major terms of the bankruptcy are resolved before the court is petitioned to begin the proceeding. Often, prepackaged bankruptcies result in more favorable terms for both the creditors and debtors. They also can cut down the amount of time needed to complete a bankruptcy proceedings, and thus save costs.

prepaid expenses Expenses such as prepaid legal expenses, rent, or insurance that a company has paid in advance. These are listed on a company's balance sheet under assets.

prepaid interest An account listed on a company's balance sheet that shows how much money it has prepaid in interest. Prepaid interest is an asset. When it actually comes due, it is moved from the prepaid interest asset account to interest expense.

prerefunding When a corporation plans to redeem a callable bond on the first date the bond can be called, and uses income from a second bond to do so. The process occurs when interest rates have fallen and a company wants to take advantage of the lower cost of money. The company puts the income it receives from the second bond in a safe investment, such as U.S. Treasury bonds, that match the maturity of the first bond. When the first issue reaches the first call date, the funds are available to pay it off. The first bond is called a *prerefunded bond,* which is also called a *pre-re.*

present value   The current value of one or more future cash payments that is discounted at an appropriate, market-based interest rate. Present value is a calculation that is used to value businesses or to measure the return on a capital investment. In the case of an investment, two techniques are used: present value of dividends (DDM) and present value of free cash flow to equity (FCFE). Another method used is present value of free cash flow to the firm (FCFF). Present value tables are widely published and help in the calculation of present value. Also called *time value of money.*

presold issue   A new security issue that has been completely sold before all of the details, such as pricing, have been announced. Often this occurs with government or municipal bond issues. The same phenomenon doesn't happen with corporate bonds, which must be registered with the Securities and Exchange Commission (SEC) before they can be offered for sale.

pre-tax contribution   Money that is subtracted from an employee's gross pay before taxes have been deducted. Pre-tax contributions are often used to fund 401(k) retirement savings plans and Flexible Spending Accounts (FSAs), which can be used to pay for day care expenses or unreimbursed health care expenses.

The benefit of a pre-tax contribution plan is that the entire $1 of salary can be applied to the 401(k) retirement account or Flexible Spending Account. In contrast, employees don't receive their full $1 of salary in their paycheck. Instead, taxes have been deducted; someone in the 25 percent tax bracket will receive only 75 cents of the dollar that he or she earned.

price discovery   The act of finding the price for a stock or commodity in a market environment. Price discovery can occur in open-outcry trading on an exchange floor, or it can be determined through electronic trading systems.

price gap   In technical analysis, a chart pattern of the price movement of a commodity or stock in which the low price of one bar on a chart is higher than the high price of the previous bar. The inverse for lower prices also is true. A price gap also indicates a price range where no trades take place.

price limits   Limits below which a trade cannot be executed that are set by futures exchanges. Price limits are intended to minimize sharp downward price movements. Each contract and exchange has its own rules governing when price limits come into effect and when they should be removed. There are no price limits for U.S. stocks or for equity options. See also *trading halt.*

price range   The highest and lowest prices that a stock, or any other financial instrument, has traded at during a particular time frame. Price ranges are usually stated for each day on Internet sites or in a newspaper's financial section. In the case of stocks, the 52-week high and low prices are frequently stated.

price spread   An options strategy in which one option covering a stock or futures contract is bought while another option covering the same stock or futures contract and with the same expiration month, but with a different exercise price, is sold. For instance a price spread occurs when an S&P 500 September call with a strike price of 850 is bought while an S&P 500 September call with a strike price of 800 is sold. Also called *vertical spread.*

price value of a basis point (PVBP)   The dollar value of 0.01, which is a measure of the change in the price of the bond if the required yield changes by one basis point.

price/book value ratio The price of a stock divided by the estimated year-end book value per share. This ratio has gained in popularity in recent years in the banking industry. Most bank assets, such as commercial accounts and loans, are valued equal to book value.

price/cash flow ratio The price of a stock divided by the expected cash flow per share. The cash flow per share is typically calculated using *EBITDA* (earnings before interest, taxes, depreciation, and amortization), but free cash flow and operating cash flow are also used. This relative valuation technique focuses on a company's cash flow instead of earnings. Cash flow is typically less easily manipulated than earnings.

price/sales ratio The price of a stock divided by expected sales per share. The ratio is useful because strong sales growth is an important requirement for a growth company. It also is used because often there is less room for accounting gimmickry with sales than earnings. What constitutes a good ratio varies significantly between industries, so comparisons must be made between companies in similar industries.

priced into A future event that the market has already anticipated in the price of an investment. Traders say that the event has been *priced into* the market or the prices of a stock. For instance, the stock market may trade lower on the anticipation that an unemployment report will show strong growth and make the Federal Reserve raise interest rates. When the report is released, there will be limited reaction in the market because the report has been priced into the market already.

price-earnings ratio One of the most popular measures for comparing stocks, measured by taking the price per share and dividing it by the amount of earnings per share. If this number is large, particularly against other companies in the industry, the stock is considered overvalued; similarly, low PE ratios may indicate that a company is undervalued. Many times technology companies have very high PE ratios, because of the expectations that their earnings will grow rapidly. Even after the technology market corrected from 2000 to 2002, many PE ratios still remain at relatively high levels.

price-to-growth flow (P/GF) A method of stock evaluation that measures how much money a company spends on research and development expenses and considers that expenditure to be an important factor in assessing a technology company's likelihood of future growth. One opinion is that a company's potential for growth through research and development will compensate for low earnings per share because research expenditures will lead to more innovative products and thus greater profits. To calculate price-to-growth flow, the current stock price is divided by the per share amount of research and development (R&D) spending and earnings per share.

price-weighted index A stock index in which each stock affects the index in proportion to its price per share. Stocks that have a higher price will have a larger impact on the index than lower-priced stocks.

primary dealers Banks that purchase bills, notes, and bonds issued by the U.S. Treasury and then resell them to their customers or retail some of them in their own accounts. There are 22 primary dealers: AMRO Bank, N.V., New York Branch; BNP Paribas Securities Corp.; Banc of America Securities LLC; Banc One Capital Markets, Inc.; Barclays Capital Inc.; Bear, Stearns & Co., Inc.; CIBC World Markets Corp.; Credit Suisse First Boston Corp.; Daiwa Securities America Inc.; Deutsche Bank Securities Inc.; Dresdner Kleinwort Wasserstein Securities LLC; Goldman, Sachs & Co.; Greenwich Capital Markets, Inc.; HSBC Securities (USA) Inc.; J. P. Morgan Securities, Inc.; Lehman Brothers, Inc.; Merrill Lynch Government Securities Inc.; Mizuho Securities USA Inc.; Morgan Stanley & Co. Inc; Nomura Securities International, Inc.; Salomon Smith Barney Inc.; and UBS Warburg LLC.

primary market The market for new issues of stocks or bonds, when the proceeds from the sale go to the company. Once a stock or bond issue is in the marketplace and traded among investors, it is in the *secondary market*.

prime paper Highly-rated commercial paper that is considered investment grade. *Commercial paper* is an unsecured promissory note sold by a corporation. It has a fixed maturity of 1 to 270 days and is usually sold at a discount from face value.

prime rate The interest rate charged by a bank to its best, or *prime,* customers. Each bank has its own rate. An average of prime rates is listed in the *Wall Street Journal*. Consumers often are charged an interest rate on their credit cards that is based on the prime rate with a certain percentage added to it.

principal

1. The amount of money that is borrowed, excluding the interest charge, that remains unpaid. Principal also may be part of a monthly payment that reduces the outstanding balance of a loan. For instance, mortgage payments consist of principal and interest payments.

2. The person or company who is the main party to a transaction.

3. The role that a broker or dealer plays when selling or buying securities for his or her own account.

4. A company executive, typically one with an ownership interest in the company.

principal-protection fund A type of mutual fund that guarantees investors that they will get their money back after a set period of time. Principal-protection mutual funds are marketed to individuals who have had losses in their stock mutual funds. However, the National Association of Securities Dealers has warned that these types of funds may have higher than average expenses and perhaps lower long-term capital gains, which would increase income taxes that must be paid. If the fund is too heavily invested in bonds, then the investor could end up missing out on gains produced by the rising stock market.

priority claim An *unsecured claim* (one that is not backed by collateral) that is entitled to receive priority over other unsecured claims in a bankruptcy proceeding. Priority claims may include administrative expenses; claims arising in the ordinary course of the debtor's business after the filing of an involuntary petition and before the entry of the order for relief; certain wage, salary, or commission claims; certain contributions to an employee benefit plan; certain claims of farmers and fishermen; certain consumer claims of up to $900; and certain unsecured tax claims.

privacy policy A written policy that spells out the details of a company's policy about selling or sharing customers' names, addresses, phone numbers, and e-mail addresses with third parties. A privacy policy also may outline whether the company will sell or share financial information. If a consumer objects to having personal information shared, the law puts the onus on the consumer to object in writing. Privacy policies are often on Web pages, with visitors having to click a button to acknowledge that they have read and agreed to the terms.

private client A wealthy individual who typically has at least $1 million in assets invested with a brokerage or investment management company, though the minimum amount of assets may vary. Competition for private clients has increased as money management firms pursue the lucrative fees they can earn from these clients in order to compensate for decreasing commissions generated by other individual investors who have directed their business to discount stock brokers on the Internet.

private letter ruling A letter written by the Internal Revenue Service (IRS) that explains its position on a tax question related to a specific issue. A letter is requested by an accountant. The private letter ruling gives a taxpayer's accountant an idea of how the IRS will view an issue. However, the letter doesn't have the force of law, so the letter could later be superseded by another IRS ruling or a tax court ruling.

private mortgage insurance (PMI) An insurance policy that a home buyer must buy if the down payment is less than 20 percent of the purchase price. The mortgage insurance is payable to the mortgage lender in the event that the buyer defaults on the mortgage, and is paid monthly as part of the mortgage payment. The purchaser has no option to decline the insurance. However, new federal legislation compels mortgage lenders to cancel the PMI after two years if the equity in the house rises above 20 percent, or in some cases 25 percent, and if payments have been made on time. PMI payments aren't deductible from income tax.

private placement A group of people or institutions providing equity or debt capital to a company. Private placements are privately offered and are restricted to qualified individuals, which typically means individuals with a net worth of at least $1 million. Those investing in the private placement consist of a relatively small group of people or companies, in contrast with public offerings that are sold to thousands of investors. Private placements don't have to be registered by the Securities and Exchange Commission. One advantage of the private placement market is that it offers confidentiality.

private placement memorandum A legal document used in the private placement industry that gives investors details about a company's business plan, investment information, and other pertinent details. Private placements are offerings of stocks or bonds that institutions or accredited, wealthy individuals may participate in, but which the public at large is excluded from.

Private Securities Litigation Reform Act of 1995 A law that was passed with the purpose of reducing the number of lawsuits by disgruntled investors. The law raised the standards that had to be met before a securities lawsuit could be started. The law also allowed companies the leeway of adding disclaimers to its statements as a way to protect against lawsuits in the event of unintentional errors. The law did have the effect of initially reducing the number of lawsuits filed for securities law violations, but those numbers have since increased.

privatization The process of converting a government-operated business to one that is privately owned. Privatization occurs by selling shares in the government-owned business to private shareholders such as individuals and institutional investors. During the 1980s and 1990s, governments throughout the world raised billions of dollars by privatizing companies.

probate The process of presenting a deceased person's will to a court to validate it. An administrator, or *executor,* is appointed to carry out the will's instructions.

producer price index (PPI) A monthly statistical report produced by the Bureau of Labor Statistics (BLS) during the second full week of the month at 8:30 A.M. ET. The PPI tracks changes in prices of components used to create finished goods in industries such as agriculture, electricity, natural gas, forestry, fisheries, manufacturing, and mining. An index is also produced excluding energy and food prices, which are typically the most volatile elements of PPI. Prices for PPI are broken down into three categories: crude materials, intermediate goods, and finished goods. Price increases in finished goods indicate a likely increase in inflation relatively soon. Price increases in crude and intermediate goods indicate future inflationary pressure.

production method of depreciation
A depreciation method that calculates depreciation based on the usage of the asset, not the passage of time. The production method often is used to calculate depreciation for delivery vehicles by using mileage: The cost of the asset, minus its resale value, is divided by the estimated units of useful mileage to arrive at a cost per mile. The cost per mile is multiplied by the actual miles that the vehicle was driven during the year to arrive at a depreciation cost.

productive asset investment ratio (PAIR) Capital expenditures divided by depreciation expense. This ratio is used to measure a company's willingness to maintain its current level of investment in capital assets. Investors watch the ratio because if PAIR decreases, the company may find that its outdated equipment affects its future ability to successfully compete. Companies with a ratio over 1.0 have higher quality earnings because they aren't delaying capital expenditures in order to boost their earnings. Such a delay may reduce future earnings as companies struggle to make capital expenditures to catch up with their competitors.

productivity and cost data Data such as output per hour, unit labor costs, hours worked, and compensation per hour that are reported one month after the end of each quarter by the Bureau of Labor Statistics (BLS). The data provides information about potential wage pressures and thus indicates whether inflation may become a problem. If inflation is a concern in the financial markets, this report will be widely watched.

profit Income minus expenses, if income is greater than expenses. Profit also may be called net income in an informal sense. When looking at trading activity, profit occurs when the sale price of an investment is greater than the purchase price.

profit and loss statement (P&L) A financial statement that lists the different types of revenues that a company has earned and the expenses that it has incurred. It is also referred to as an *income statement*. Typical categories include: revenue, cost of goods sold, gross profit, net income, and net income per share. However, each company has its own categories of expenses, so each P&L will be somewhat unique. Publicly traded companies produce quarterly and yearly P&L statements. In a more informal usage, the term may be used to refer to profit and loss responsibility that a department or project has.

profit center A part of a business organization that produces profits. A business may be broken down into profit centers to give managers of the various profit centers more accountability about making money.

profit forecast An estimate of the future profits of a company. Companies create profit forecasts for themselves, although the number may be disseminated only internally. Generally company executives give guidance to Wall Street analysts about their expectations about profits or other financial measures, without being too specific. Profit forecasts also are created by stock analysts for the companies that they follow.

profit margin A ratio that shows the percentage of profits that are earned on sales. When the term "profit margin" is used, it usually refers to a gross profit margin. See also *gross profit margin, operating profit margin,* and *net profit margin.*

profit taking Selling an investment whose price has appreciated in order to capitalize on the difference between the price at which the investment was bought and the investment's appreciated value. It often is used to explain why a market has moved lower after a sustained period of moving higher.

profit-sharing plan A financial arrangement between a corporation and its employees in which the corporation agrees to share some of its profits with the employees, based upon a pre-determined formula. The company makes annual contributions to the plan, if the company has profits. Employees are given statements showing how much funds are invested in their account. The money accumulates on a tax-deferred basis until the employee leaves the company.

pro forma Earnings that have been adjusted by the company to exclude expenses that are not representative of the company's true business. During the height of the Internet boom during the late 1990s, many companies excluded the cost of employees' stock options. Other items that often are excluded from companies regular earnings are charges for extraordinary items, charges for discontinued operations, and one-time charges. Pro-forma earnings are in contrast to GAAP earnings, which follow set rules developed by accountants. Also called *normalized earnings*. See also *GAAP.*

program trading A computer program that automatically executes trades when certain price levels or other milestones are reached. Typically program trading is used to trade large amounts of stocks, which can produce volatility in the market. Stock exchanges have regulations that restrict program trading during volatile periods.

Project A An electronic trading system for futures and options that is operated by the Chicago Board of Trade (CBT).

project finance The arrangement of debt, equity, or credit that is used to construct or refinance a particular building or other capital-intensive facility. Project lenders form their credit decisions based on projected revenues from the facility, rather than from current income, which is usually non-existent. The buildings that are constructed serve as collateral for the debt.

promissory note An unconditional promise to pay a definite amount of money at a future date. Individuals or businesses can sign a promissory note.

property tax A tax that is assessed on property such as real estate and in some cases personal property such as cars or boats. The assessed valuation of property tax often is based on a rate called *mils* (also spelled *mills*), which is the dollar amount of tax that is paid on $1,000 of assessed value. Each governmental unit, such as a city or county government or a school district, receives the payments from a certain number of mils. Property taxes are assessed by city and county governments, not by the federal government.

proportional voting A form of voting for members on a board of directors in which each shareholder can give multiple votes to the same candidate. The most well-known form of proportional voting is *cumulative voting,* which allows a shareholder to multiply his or her number of shares of stock by the number of board vacancies to get the total number of votes he or she has. All of those votes can be given to one candidate.

prospectus A document that provides financial and other fundamental information about a proposed public stock or bond. A prospectus provides details about the offering, the company's business, management, and financial performance as well as information on how it intends to use the funds raised through the offering. Typically prospectuses are issued for initial public offerings and bond offerings. Mutual funds also issue prospectuses before selling shares to the public, as do limited partnerships seeking investors for real estate, oil, or gas investments. The information in the prospectus comes from the registration statement, which the company has to file with the Securities and Exchange Commission before it can sell stock or bonds to the public. The company may issue a preliminary prospectus, or a *red herring,* while the SEC is reviewing the registration statement. The final prospectus may be called an *offering circular.* The term *red herring* is used because of the red letters that appeared on the cover of the offering, warning that the SEC had not yet approved the security for sale.

protectionism Restricting foreign goods from coming into a country by applying difficult import processes, putting quotas on the number of goods that can be imported, or charging a duty (a tax) on imported goods that makes foreign goods more expensive than domestic goods. Protectionism can lead to trade wars, which have the potential to seriously damage the global economy. The World Trade Organization (WTO) works to reduce such barriers to trade.

protective provisions Requirements specified in financing arrangements such as venture capital that limit what actions management can take without obtaining the prior approval of the investors.

proxy A ballot that allows shareholders to cast their vote at an annual or special meeting without attending the actual meeting. Typically the proxy can be mailed or cast through an automated telephone voting service or on the Internet. Proxies also can be given to someone, who then votes on behalf of the shareholder. This right may be given to an attorney, to the corporation (which will vote the shares in line with its wishes), or to another person the shareholder authorizes.

proxy fight A fight led by dissenting shareholders who are opposed to a company taking a certain action, often a merger. If it is used in a hostile takeover, a proxy fight may allow the potential acquirer to purchase the company without paying a premium. Also may be called a *proxy contest,* where a company attempts to gain control of a firm by persuading enough shareholders to vote to replace existing management.

proxy solicitation The process of obtaining shareholders' agreement for proposals. Proxy solicitation materials are issued to give shareholders information that enables them to vote in an informed manner. The materials presented to shareholders must be filed with the Securities and Exchange Commission (SEC) before they are given to shareholders. The SEC makes certain that the materials comply with disclosure rules, including disclosing all

appropriate facts about the issues that shareholders will be voting on.

prudent-man rule A legal securities standard that asks the question "What would a prudent man do?" in order to determine whether an action was reasonable or whether it violated fiduciary duties. The legal standard originated in 1830 when Judge Samuel Putnum wrote, "Those with responsibility to invest money for others should act with prudence, discretion, intelligence and regard for the safety of capital as well as income."

PSA *Public Securities Association,* the former name of the Bond Market Association.

PSA prepayment speed A measure developed by the Bond Market Association that studies the rate of prepayment of mortgage loans. The model represents an assumed rate of prepayment each month of the then-unpaid principal balance of a pool of mortgages. The PSA prepayment speed model is used primarily to derive an implied prepayment speed of new production loans. A 100% PSA assumes prepayment rates of 0.2% annually of the then-unpaid principal balance of mortgage loans in the first month after origination. An additional 0.2% annually is added in each month thereafter until the 30th month. Beginning in the 30th month and in each month thereafter, 100% PSA assumes a constant annual prepayment rate of 6%. Multiples are calculated from this prepayment rate; for example, a 150% PSA assumes annual prepayment rates will be 0.3% in month one, 0.6% in month two, and 9% from month 30 until the repayment is complete. A 0% PSA assumes no prepayments. The term PSA comes from the Public Securities Association, which was the previous name of the Bond Market Association.

psychological resistance The tendency for a market to not move above certain round numbers. For instance, psychological resistance in the crude oil market exists at

$40 a barrel, which was the highest level it traded to in 1990, ahead of the Persian Gulf War. Less substantial psychological resistance may be found at $35 if crude oil is presently at $30.

psychological support The tendency for a market to not move below certain round numbers. For instance, psychological support for gold can be said to exist at $300. Less substantial psychological support may be found at $320, if gold is presently at $335.

Public Company Accounting Oversight Board An accounting board, created under the 2002 Sarbanes-Oxley legislation, that is charged with overhauling the rules pertaining to the accounting profession, including proposing new standards on how independent auditors should report on their public-company clients' internal financial controls. It was created in the wake of the collapse of Arthur Andersen after its involvement with Enron Corporation came to light. Arthur Andersen was Enron's auditor; it was convicted of wrongdoing and forced out of business.

public finance A sub-industry of investment banking concerned with advising and raising money for public entities such as local, state, or federal governments. Public finance includes any debt offerings that are issued with the intention of raising funds for the government.

public float The last price at which a stock was sold multiplied by the number of outstanding shares of voting and non-voting stocks that are held by public investors, not company directors or executives. Depending upon whether the float is in conjunction with a stock offering, regulators may specify a certain time frame within which the calculation must be made, such as 60 days within the date a registration statement is filed. Stock exchanges typically use public float figures to determine whether companies meet minimum listing standards, rather than looking at market capitalization, which includes the figures from both public shareholder and company directors and executives.

public offering See *initial public offering.*

Public Securities Association (PSA) The former name of the Bond Market Association.

Public Utility Holding Company Act of 1935 A law that requires public utilities to submit reports outlining the company's organization, financial structure, and operations of its holding companies and subsidiaries. As part of the law, the Securities and Exchange Commission (SEC) has jurisdiction over utilities' mergers and acquisitions, the issue and sale of securities and other financing transactions, the structure of their utility systems, and transactions among companies that are part of the holding company utility system. States can't effectively control utilities because their activities cross many state lines. The federal government is able to step in and be involved because utilities are involved in interstate commerce because they sell and transport gas and electricity across state lines, in addition to using the U.S. Postal Service to sell securities or to provide sales and services.

publicly held Refers to a company whose outstanding shares are not held by private owners, but rather by *public investors,* who may buy and sell shares on the open securities markets.

publicly traded Refers to a company whose shares are traded on an organized stock exchange, in contrast with a private company, whose shares can be bought only with the agreement of the owners.

pula The currency unit of Botswana, comprised of 100 thebe.

pullback A term used to indicate that prices have stopped their upward movement after rising for a period of time.

pump-and-dump A scam in which a trader, broker, or other self-interested party promotes shares in a stock as a good purchase. While the person is heavily encouraging others to buy shares, he is secretly selling them on the market. The pump-and-dump practice is illegal.

purchase accounting An accounting method used in mergers in which the purchasing company adds the acquired company's assets to its balance sheet using a fair market value. The acquired company is treated as an investment. Any premium paid above the fair market value is attributed to goodwill on the purchasing company's balance sheet. As of 2001, the Financial Accounting Standards Board (FASB) required the purchase method to be used for all mergers and disallowed the *tax-free pooling-of interest accounting method,* in which the companies' assets and liabilities were added together.

purchase and sale statement A statement mailed by a futures commission merchant to a customer when a futures or options position has been sold or offset. The details of the statement include the number of contracts bought or sold and the prices that were received, the gross profit or loss, commission charges, and the net profit or loss on the transaction. Also called *confirmation statement.*

purchase order A written authorization that tells a vendor what goods or services will be bought. The document typically includes the description, the quantity, and the agreed-upon price.

purchase order financing A financing method that enables a corporation to purchase raw materials or finished goods that will be turned into products and sold in a very short period of time. Purchase order financing is short term in duration and is usually retired within 30 to 60 days of issuance.

purchasing power

1. The amount of goods or services that a defined amount of money can buy. Purchasing power can be used as a proxy for measuring inflation. As inflation rises, purchasing power erodes.

2. How much money someone can invest in a stock or financial market by using the maximum *margin* (amount of money that can be loaned) that the brokerage firm makes available.

purchasing power parity (PPP) The theory that exchange rates will adjust to equalize the relative purchasing power among currencies. The theory is based on the *law of one price,* which says that in competitive markets, identical goods will sell for identical prices when valued in the same currency.

PPP says that in the absence of costs, such as transportation or other costs, markets that have competition will equalize the price of identical goods in two countries when the prices are in the same currency. For example, a stereo that sells for 750 Canadian dollars in Canada should cost $500 in the United States, when the exchange rate between Canada and the U.S. is 1.50 CAD/USD.

While PPP is a useful theory, it has its shortcomings. It assumes that all goods are identical, tradable, and have no taxes or transportation costs that affect the relative value. It also assumes that exchange rates are influenced only by inflation rates, which is incorrect.

pure play A company whose business is restricted to one activity or sector. In contrast, a *conglomerate* is a business that has many different types of business activities.

put An option that gives the holder the right to sell the underlying security at a specified price during a set time period.

put guarantee letter A letter from a bank or other financial institution that says that the writer of the put option has sufficient funds on deposit at the bank to be able to buy the securities that the put has been written on. See also *put.*

put swaption A swaption is an option to enter into an interest rate swap at a specified future date with the put giving the purchaser the right, but not the obligation, to pay a fixed interest rate. *Swaption* is short for *swap option,* which is an over-the-counter option on an interest rate swap.

put to seller A phrase used to indicate that a put option has been exercised. A put entitles the holder to sell the underlying securities to the put writer at the agreed-upon price. If the put holder required the put writer to purchase shares of a stock for $65 a share, the put writer would have to purchase them at that price, even if they were only trading at $55 in the market currently. See also *put.*

put-call parity The concept that the prices for a stock's put or call options with the same expiration date will remain in equilibrium. This occurs because any price discrepancies would be eliminated by *arbitrage,* which is the practice of taking advantage of minute price differences to make a profit.

put-call ratio The volume of puts that traded on a given day divided by the volume of calls. The ratio can be calculated for the overall volume of options trade or for a certain futures, stock, or stock index. The ratio is used as an indicator of investor sentiment. When the ratio is too high, or near the top of the chart, it can signal a time to buy, and vice versa. Technical traders believe that the ratio is a good contrarian indicator. The reasoning assumes that most options investors will be wrong.

PVBP See *price value of a basis point.*

pyramid scheme An illegal scheme that creates investments that end up having no value. Instead, they are fraudulent. One of the more famous pyramid schemes was the one named after Charles Ponzi: In the late 1920s, it paid investors out of the earnings received from new investors. However, there were no earnings, only new investors; the scheme soon collapsed, but not before many people lost money.

pyramiding Using paper profits from one investment as collateral to buy further positions while using a margin loan from a broker. This is a risky strategy because of the potential for prices to fall. Pyramiding also may occur if unrealized profits on existing futures positions are used as a margin to increase the size of the positions in successively larger increments.

Qardhul Hasan The term for an interest-free loan in the Islamic religion, which forbids loaning or borrowing money to earn interest. Thus, the borrower repays only the amount borrowed.

QIB

1. See *qualified institutional buyer.*

2. See *Qualified Investment Buyer.*

QQQ The trading symbol for the NASDAQ 100 Index tracking stock that is traded on the American Stock Exchange. It is pronounced *cubes* but is often spelled *qubes*. An exchange-traded fund (ETF), QQQ allows investors to purchase or sell an investment vehicle that mimics the movement of the underlying price index. The NASDAQ 100 tracks 100 of the top non-financial services companies listed on the NASDAQ Stock Market.

Q-TIP Trust Short for *qualified terminal interest property trust,* a Q-TIP Trust is created through a will and allows some or all of the estate to be left for the benefit of the surviving spouse. The will spells out precisely who will receive or benefit from the trust assets upon the surviving spouse's death. The Q-TIP Trust allows the will maker to ensure that his or her children or stepchildren will benefit from the trust assets when the spouse dies because the surviving spouse is prevented from making changes to the will, such as cutting beneficiaries out of the will or reducing beneficiaries' proceeds.

qualification period A period of time during which an insurance company will not reimburse a new policyholder for a claim. This delay allows the insurance company time to discover any deception or fraud in the policyholder's application. The length of a qualification period varies between several weeks or several months, and often is associated with health or life insurance.

qualified institutional buyer (QIB) An investor who is allowed under Security and Exchange Commission (SEC) rules to trade privately-placed securities with other qualified institutional investors. These sales don't have to be registered with the SEC. A qualified institutional investor must have at least $100 million under management.

qualified investment buyer (QIB) An investor who is judged to be sophisticated and is able to purchase securities that are not offered to the public under U.S. Regulation 144A. QIBs also include insurance companies, licensed small business investment companies, employee benefit plans, business trusts, most corporations, registered investment advisors and individuals who are worth at least $5 million.

qualified opinion An opinion issued by an auditor that expresses reservations about a company's financial statements. The reasons for a qualified opinion are varied, but whatever the source, a qualified opinion is likely to send shock waves through the ranks of the company's investors, and result in a significantly lower stock price. Qualified opinions may be based on concerns about inventory issues, a pending lawsuit that could result in a significant judgment that would produce financial strain on the business, or the possibility of a tax liability from a tax shelter or investment.

qualified plan A retirement plan set up by businesses that allows the company to make tax-deductible contributions either through a profit-sharing plan or a pension plan. Employees also may be able to make their own contributions. The amount paid into a qualified plan is returned to the employee when he or she leaves the company or retires. For a small business, qualified plans are more complex than simplified employee pension (SEP) plans or Savings Incentive Match Plan for Employees of Small Employers (SIMPLE) plans; however, these plans allow more flexibility in the plan design. Employers can deduct their contributions from taxes and employees are not taxed on their funds until they are withdrawn. See also *SIMPLE IRA* and *simplified employee pension plan*.

qualitative analysis A type of analysis that looks at a variety of factors to determine whether an investment should be made. Credit and securities analysts use qualitative analysis to examine general industry trends, analyze the effectiveness of management, determine whether new products or services are being adopted by the market, and determine how the behavior of the overall economy is likely to affect a company's financial performance. Qualitative analysis contrasts with *quantitative analysis*, which uses mathematical analysis of numbers to make investment recommendations.

quality control The system by which goods are checked at different points in the production process in order to make certain that there are no defects and that the goods meet all necessary specifications. Quality control also involves inspecting the finished products. Companies often have quality control departments. Total quality management, which is one specific theory of quality management, recommends that all employees be monitors for quality in their everyday tasks.

quant Derived from the word *quantitative*, a quant is a person who possesses strong quantitative, or mathematical, skills. Quantitative analysts are employed by financial services businesses, such as life insurance companies, pension funds, money

management, and other Wall Street firms. Quants may focus on sales projections, risk management, and the cost of capital.

quantitative analysis The process of analyzing information and making decisions based on numerical data. This is different from *qualitative analysis*, which analyzes fundamental factors such as supply and demand, or competitors' strengths and weaknesses. Quantitative analysts are employed by financial services businesses such as life insurance companies, pension funds, money management companies, and other Wall Street firms.

quarterly Four times a year; every three months. There are four quarters in a year. Financial statements that report revenues and expenses are broken down into quarters by U.S. corporations. At the end of the year, annual financial statements are produced. Typically, dividends are paid quarterly.

quasi-public corporation A corporation whose stock is publicly traded that was started or is backed by the government. Even though the company has close connections to the government, it is run independently of the government. An example of a quasi-public company is Fannie Mae, which was started by a congressional charter in order to encourage home ownership among low- to middle-income Americans. Other examples of quasi-public corporations are the Student Loan Marketing Association (Sallie Mae), which packages student loans and resells them in the secondary market. The U.S. Postal Service and the Tennessee Valley Authority (TVA) are other quasi-public corporations.

Quattrone, Frank P. The former head of Credit Suisse First Boston's (CSFB) technology banking practice and research group; renowned for his dominant industry position during the Internet boom of the late 1990s, during which he was said to earn $200 million personally. When the technology boom went bust, Quattrone was at the center of investigations by federal and regulatory authorities, which also focused on other banks and star employees. He resigned from CSFB in March 2003.

Qubes   See QQQ.

quetzal   The currency unit of Guatemala, comprised of 100 centavos.

quick assets   Cash on hand and assets that can quickly be turned into cash, such as marketable securities and accounts receivable.

quick ratio   A financial ratio that measures a company's ability to meet current liabilities. It is calculated by adding up cash, marketable securities, and receivables and dividing the total by current liabilities. Also called *quick assets.*

quick turn   Trading jargon for buying a security and then selling it right away, or vice versa. Day traders attempt to make a profit by quick turning several small trades. Futures traders also attempt to make a quick profit from small changes in price by doing quick turns. Such traders are called *scalpers.*

quid   A British term that is used as a nickname to its primary currency unit, the pound. It is the equivalent of the dollar and is used in the same way that "buck" is used to refer to the U.S. dollar.

quid pro quo   A Latin term that means "something for something." The term has found much usage in the securities industry and among lawyers. Its use has grown in the stock market context after the stock market bubble burst in 2000. Regulators began investigating conflicts of interest between a bank's allocation of hot initial public offerings and its selection to lead other lucrative investment banking business.

In return for receiving issues in highly sought after IPOs, many companies and corporate executives were expected to give banks other investment banking business or direct trades through the bank, often at inflated commission rates.

quiet period   A period of time that begins when a company files a registration statement with the Securities and Exchange Commission (SEC). The quiet period lasts until the SEC's staff declares the registration statement "effective," or approves it. During this period, federal securities laws limit the information the company and related parties can release to the public.

Despite some corporate executives' claims to the contrary, there is no such thing as a quiet period or period of silence before a company announces its quarterly or year-end financial results. Also called *blackout period.*

quorum   The smallest number of people that must vote (either in person or by proxy) in shareholder meetings, boards of directors meetings, legislative meetings, or other committee and organization meetings. If a quorum isn't reached, then the results of the voting are not valid.

quote   A firm offer to buy or sell a certain security at a specific time. Quotes are given for the price at which the market maker is willing to buy or sell the security. The quote may be given in the form "$45 to $45.10," which means that the best bid price is $45 (the highest price that buyer is willing to pay is $45) while the best offer price (the lowest price that a seller will sell for) is $45.10.

R&D See *research and development*.

Racketeer Influenced and Corrupt Organization Act (RICO) A federal law, passed in 1970, that was designed to eliminate the infiltration of organized crime and racketeering into legitimate businesses involved in interstate commerce. RICO allows civil as well as criminal penalties to be brought against individuals and companies that are allegedly involved in organized crime.

raider An individual or corporation that plans to take control of a company and fire management. A raider buys shares to obtain a controlling interest in the target company. The term was frequently heard in the late 1980s, but its usage has dropped off. To alert companies of potential raiders, anyone who holds 5 percent or more of the outstanding shares in a company must report this fact to the Securities and Exchange Commission (SEC).

rainbow option An option whose payoff is linked to the performance of two or more instruments or indices.

rally An upward movement in a stock market.

RAM Short for *random access memory*, short-term memory used in a personal computer. The computer's processor can access any part of the memory or data storage directly, which makes saving and accessing files faster. See also *DRAM*.

rand The currency unit of South Africa, comprised of 100 cents.

Randolph, A. Philip An advocate for equal rights for black people in labor unions, he organized the Brotherhood of Sleeping Car Porters in 1925 and pursued a contract with the Pullman Co. for 12 years before achieving success. His actions led the United States to create wartime fair-employment commissions to reduce discrimination in the defense industry.

random walk theory The theory that the price of stocks, futures, and other investments move randomly up or down, and that they can't be predicted. Adherents to the random walk theory think that conventional investment techniques such as examining historical price movements, technical analysis, and fundamental analysis are not useful in predicting future price movements.

Random walk theory had its beginnings in research conducted in 1900 by French mathematician Louis Bachelier for his doctoral thesis, *Théorie de la Spéculatio*. He developed a sophisticated model for testing randomness in the French government's bond market. Much of his work didn't catch on for several decades and further significant studies had to await the introduction of the computer.

In 1965, Paul Samuelson wrote a very influential article that further propelled random walk theory, "Proof that Properly Anticipated Prices Fluctuate Randomly." According to Samuelson, in an information-efficient market, price changes can't be forecast if they fully incorporate expectations and information of all market participants.

ratio hedge A comparison between the number of options that are purchased and the number of futures contracts that are held. The ratio hedge describes what both numbers need to be in order to establish a risk-neutral hedge.

ratio spread An options trading strategy. It involves buying options and then selling a different quantity of options. The options that are sold have different strike prices but have the same expiration dates. They can be either puts or calls.

RBOC *Regional Bell Operating Companies,* which were created when the AT&T Corp. telephone monopoly was broken up in 1983. After a series of mergers following the break up of AT&T, four RBOCs remain: BellSouth Corp., Qwest Communications International Inc., SBC Communications Inc., and Verizon Communications Inc.

Reaganomics An economic theory espoused by President Ronald Reagan. Reaganomics follows the school of *supply-side economics*, which believes that the government should cut taxes, especially for the wealthy and businesses. With more funds available, more money will be invested and jobs and economic growth will be created for everyone. Reaganomics says that rising government debt levels are acceptable.

real The currency unit of Brazil, comprised of 100 centavos.

real estate A piece of land, and the buildings that are on it. Natural resources, such as water, that are on the land also are part of real estate.

real estate agent A professional sales person who sells houses, condominiums, and cooperative apartments (co-ops) for a living. The real estate agent legally represents sellers, even if he or she is working with buyers to show them properties. Real estate agents are paid on a commission basis calculated on the selling price of the house, which may be as high as 7 percent. The seller pays the commission. However, buyers can contractually hire their own agent to advise them on the buying process. In that case a fee, which might be a commission based on a purchase price, is paid by the buyer.

Real Estate Investment Trust (REIT) A financial instrument that invests primarily in real estate such as offices, apartments, shopping centers, hotels, or warehouses. REITs tend to pay high returns (often as high as 10 percent), making them attractive investment opportunities, especially when the stock market is falling. Returns on REITs are high because the Internal Revenue Service requires them to pay out at least 90 percent of their taxable income each year in order to retain their favorable

tax treatment. REITs are entitled to deduct dividends paid to shareholders from their taxes.

REITs were created by federal law in 1960 to enable small investors to pool their money and invest in real estate while being able to diversify their risk and have professional managers. There are three main types of REITs: *mortgage REITs, equity REITs,* and *hybrid REITs.* A mortgage REIT makes or owns loan obligations that are secured by real estate property; an equity REIT owns real estate, rather than issuing loans; and a hybrid REIT combines both strategies.

real estate mortgage investment conduit See *REMIC.*

real risk-free rate of return An interest rate that assumes no inflation and no uncertainty about future cash flows or repayments. Treasury bills are one example of an investment with a risk-free rate of return, because the U.S. government is perceived to be stable and guarantees payment. This also can be called the *pure time value of money.*

real time Refers to information that is available a fraction of a second after it happens. Financial news and some price quotations are available in real-time.

rebalancing The act of adjusting a portfolio in order to return it to the appropriate asset allocation mix. For example, an investor's asset allocation plan may call for 65 percent of the funds to be invested in stocks, 30 percent in bonds, and 5 percent in cash. If stocks have risen sharply over the last year, they are likely to occupy a greater percentage of the portfolio than desired. Some of those stocks must be sold to get the portfolio back in balance. The same thing happens when an asset class declines. Portfolios should be rebalanced on a regular basis, such as once a year, or perhaps even once a quarter.

recapitalization A method of exchanging some of the debt of a debt-burdened company by exchanging that debt for new debt with a lower interest rate or a longer maturity or for common stock. When a recapitalization occurs, the current creditors lose money because they agree to take less money than what they ordinarily would have taken. However, if they exchange that debt for equity, they have created the possibility that the stock may one day appreciate and eventually provide a profit. Without recapitalization, the company would likely file for bankruptcy.

receipt zeros Zero-coupon bonds that were created and issued by broker/dealers before the U.S. Department of the Treasury started its STRIPS program in 1985. Zero-coupon bonds are sold at a steep discount and do not pay periodic interest. Instead, the entire principal amount is returned to the bond holder upon maturity. The STRIPS program (Separate Trading of Registered Interest and Principal of Securities) that the Treasury has allows broker/dealers to strip Treasury securities into their component parts. The securities that result are called STRIPS.

Each individual broker/dealer gave its receipt zeros a name. CATS (Certificates of Accrual of Treasury Securities) were issued by Salomon Brothers, which is now part of Citigroup Inc. ETRs (Easy-growth Treasury Receipts) are issued by Dean Witter Reynolds Inc., which is now part of Morgan Stanley. TRs (Treasury Receipts) are generic receipt zeros.

receivership An administrative stage in which a company that is in the midst of bankruptcy proceedings attempts to put its affairs in order with the help of a court-appointed trustee. A company is said to be in receivership if it is attempting to avoid liquidation.

recession A period of slow economic growth. Defined by economists as two consecutive quarters of negative gross domestic product.

recognition point The predetermined time when a transaction should be recorded.

A recognition point emanates from a company's revenue recognition policy. For example, revenue from a contract may be recorded each quarter until the due date, or it may be recorded as the terms of the contract are fulfilled.

reconstituted strips The process of reattaching interest payments, or coupons, that have been stripped from a Treasury bond or note. Coupons are the interest-earning part of the Treasury bond. An active stand-alone market exists in the strips.

record date The date by which an investor must hold shares of a company's stock in order to receive a dividend or capital gains distribution. If someone purchases the company's stock after the record date, he or she isn't eligible to receive the dividend or capital gains distribution. The company determines what the record date will be. An investor becomes a *shareholder of record* on the date the stock is purchased, not on the settlement date, which is usually three days later. Record dates also are used to determine which shareholders can vote on initiatives put forth at the annual or special shareholder meetings, such as merger proposals.

recovery An upward movement in prices after a sustained period of downward price movement.

red herring A preliminary prospectus issued by a company that is planning a public securities offering. The term comes from the bright red letters that are printed on the cover and the fact that the prospectus has not been approved by the SEC. See also *prospectus.*

redlining The illegal practice of eliminating certain parts of a community from consideration for loans or mortgages. Areas are redlined because the area is considered to be a poor investment risk.

REFCORPs Bonds that the Resolution Funding Corp. issued to pay for the financial clean-up necessitated by the failure of savings and loans in 1989. REFCORPS are zero-coupon bonds that were issued by the Resolution Funding Corp., which is a U.S. government agency that was created by Congress to finance the government's plan to bail out failed savings and loans. REFCORPs are still actively traded and are relatively liquid. The principal portions of the REFCORPs are secured by Treasury zero-coupon bonds and the interest portions are guaranteed by the U.S. Treasury.

refund   To replace debt before the original maturity date by issuing refunding bonds.

refunding   The redemption of securities, typically debt, by raising more funds through another offering. When a company conducts a refunding operation, it recalls its existing bonds from the market. In exchange, a new bond issue is sold. Refunding may be done because the bonds are nearing maturity or because interest rates have fallen.

regional equity fund   A mutual fund that invests in equity securities of companies based in specific regions, such as Europe, Asia, or Latin America, or specific countries.

registered agent   A person who, following state requirements, maintains a registered office within the state of incorporation for a corporation. A *registered office* may be at an address that is different from the corporation's business address. Often, companies act as their own registered agents, as long as the address provided to the state is in the state of incorporation. An attorney may serve as a registered agent. The main purpose of a registered agent is to give anyone who is suing a company a location where legal documents can be served, or where governments may mail tax or other official documents. Post office boxes cannot be used for a registered agent's address.

registered bond   A bond in which the identity of the holder is known by the company. The company pays the bond's interest and principal directly to the owner on record. To obtain payment, the holder must send the coupon attached to the bond to the company registrar or paying agent.

registered representative   A person employed by a broker/dealer or brokerage firm to assist customers with the buying or selling of securities. A *registered rep,* as the term is often shortened to, must pass certain examinations given by the Securities and Exchange Commission (SEC).

registered stock   A security that has been issued in the name of the owner and recorded as such on the books of the company or company's agent (the *registrar*). Unlike *negotiable securities,* which include *bearer bonds* and most stock certificates, registered securities can be transferred to another person only if the owner authorizes the transfer. Registered stock also is a security that has had its registration statement filed with the Securities and Exchange Commission (SEC) prior to an initial public offering (IPO). Registered stocks often are issued in unregistered, private sales from the issuer, such as private placement offerings, venture capital deals, employee stock benefit plans, and compensation for professional services. Also called a *registered security.*

registrar   A bank or trust company that is responsible for keeping a record of the owners of a company's securities, such as bonds and stocks, and making sure that the authorized amount of stock in circulation is not exceeded. A company's board of directors or its shareholders must approve any increase in the amount of authorized stock shares over the company's authorized limit.

registration   The process by which the Securities and Exchange Commission (SEC) or a state securities authority reviews a potential stock or debt offering that will be sold to the public. The rules that must be followed are outlined in the Securities Exchange Acts that were passed in 1933 and 1934, and their subsequent amendments. The registration statement filed with the SEC lists the purpose of the offering, identifies the underwriter, and contains detailed information about the company's business, such as its management team, products and services, competitive position, and other financial information.

regression analysis A statistical technique used to show how one dependent variable, such as sales, is affected by other variables, which are independent. Regression analysis measures how correlated the dependent and independent variables are. By using the correlation, an analyst can make an educated estimate about future events. For example, an office supply store may want to find out how the rate of sales depends on the unemployment rate or consumer spending.

Regression analysis is easily done in spreadsheet programs, and the results are presented in a *scatter graph*. A line connecting the two average variables is drawn to connect them to form the *regression line*. The regression line signifies a direct correlation between two variables, so if all the dots are connected, there is a direct correlation. The more the dots are dispersed outside the regression line, the less of a direct relationship there is between the two variables. The unexplained variation is called the *coefficient of determination*. Its square root is the *correlation coefficient*. If the coefficient is 1, there is a direct relationship between the variables. Regression analysis is used in risk-return analysis for portfolios and to analyze individual investments.

Regulation D A Federal Reserve rule that outlines how much money banks are required to keep on hand either in cash sitting in their vaults or on deposit with their Federal Reserve Bank.

Regulation DD A regulation in the Truth in Savings Act that requires depository institutions to disclose important information about deposit accounts, such as the amount of interest that will be paid, so that consumers can make meaningful comparisons between different accounts.

Regulation Fair Disclosure (Reg FD) A rule, approved by the Securities and Exchange Commission in August 2000, that prohibits companies from making a selective disclosure of market-moving news to favored analysts or other prominent people. The rule puts individuals who aren't in the loop on a more even playing field with insiders, and was passed under the tenure of former SEC Chairman Arthur Levitt. More than two years later, the first violations were announced when the SEC issued cease-and-desist orders in civil administrative proceedings. Companies that received the orders were Raytheon Co. and its CFO Franklyn A. Caine; Secure Computing Corp. and its Chief Executive John McNulty; and Siebel Systems Inc. The SEC also announced a new type of violation, a *report of investigation* concerning Motorola Inc. and its management, for engaging in a series of individual conversations with analysts and giving them information that wasn't previously made public. Because management relied on the advice of lawyers, which later turned out to be incorrect, it received a lesser admonishment and not an enforcement action.

Regulation G

1. A Federal Reserve rule that implements the Gramm-Leach-Bliley Act. The act requires that written agreements between banks and community groups relating to the fulfillment of the banks' Community Reinvestment Act (CRA) requirements be publicly disclosed. The CRA is intended to encourage banks to lend to businesses and families in their area of operation even if they are low-income or the area is economically depressed.

2. A series of Securities and Exchange Commission rules for companies to follow when issuing earnings that contain *pro forma accounting treatment*. These rules are more stringent than those methods prescribed by Generally Accepted Accounting Practices (GAAP). For example, Regulation G requires companies to include a separate section that also explains earnings in terms of GAAP.

The rules also specify the types of off-balance sheet items that must be revealed.

Regulation S-B   A securities law that outlines the disclosure requirements that small business issuers must follow under the Securities Act of 1933 and the Securities Exchange Act of 1934. *Small business issuers* are companies that have revenues under $25 million (although if the value of their publicly held stock exceeds $25 million, then they are not considered a small business).

Regulation S-T   A regulation that governs the types of documents the Securities and Exchange Commission (SEC) requires to be filed electronically. Regulation S-T outlines rules governing electronic filing.

Regulation SX   A rule established by the Securities and Exchange Commission that governs what the form and content of financial statements of publicly traded securities should look like.

Regulation S-X   A securities law intended to ensure that auditors are qualified, and are independent from their auditing clients. The regulation outlines restrictions on financial, employment, and business relationships between a company's accountant and auditor.

Regulation T   A Federal Reserve board regulation that governs the amount of credit that may be given to the customers of brokers and dealers so they can purchase securities. This type of credit is called *margin*.

Regulation U   A Federal Reserve rule that limits how much credit banks can give their customers for purchasing or carrying margin stocks.

Regulation Z   A Federal Reserve rule that implements the requirements of the Truth in Lending Act, also known as the Consumer Credit Protection Act. Regulation Z outlines a uniform method lenders must use to present the cost of credit, disclose credit terms, and resolve errors on some types of credit accounts.

rehypothecation   Using collateral that secures one loan to secure a second loan. Rehypothecation significantly increases the original lender's risk because the collateral is pledged twice.

reinsurance   Insurance purchased by a primary insurance underwriter in order to reduce some of the insurance company's exposure to risk. Reinsurance coverage is purchased to cover broad categories of risks or to cover a specific risk. Reinsurance companies work by spreading risks throughout underwriting pools. Each pool member receives a percentage of pool revenue as income and accepts responsibility for a percentage of pool losses.

REIT   See *Real Estate Investment Trust*.

REIT Modernization Act of 1999   A federal tax law change that allows a REIT to own up to 100 percent of the stock of a taxable REIT subsidiary that provides services to REIT tenants and others. The legislation also requires REITs to pay out 95 percent of their taxable income, returning the payout level to the one required from 1960 until 1980. From 1980 to 1999, REITs only had to pay out 90 percent of their taxable income.

relative risk   The volatility of an asset's return, measured against the return of a another asset.

relative strength   In technical analysis, the price performance of a stock compared with a market index. Often this relationship is illuminated using a *relative strength index*.

Relative Strength Index (RSI)   A technical analysis procedure, created by J. Welles Wilder, Jr. and presented in 1978 in "New Concepts in Technical Trading Systems," that solves the problem of trying to construct a momentum line when there are erratic price movements. The formula averages the days' up and down closes and helps to smooth out the price movements. The resulting numbers are plotted on a vertical scale of 0 to 100. An RSI rating above 70 is called overbought, while an oversold condition occurs under 30.

REMIC Short for *real estate mortgage investment conduit,* this security is a multiple-class mortgage cash flow security backed by residential mortgage loans which have been grouped together. The REMIC securities group interest and principal payments into separately traded securities. By redirecting the cash flow from the mortgage-backed security, a security can be created that has different classes (also called *tranches*) that may have different interest-rate payments, maturities, and stipulations for prepayment. The variety of investment options enables these securities to meet the needs of different investors.

The REMIC is a type of collateralized mortgage obligation (CMO) and went into effect as part of the Tax Reform Act of 1986. The REMIC has replaced the CMO; however, the terms are used interchangeably. Freddie Mac and Fannie Mae are the largest issuers of REMIC securities. REMICs guaranteed by Ginnie Mae are backed by the full faith and credit of the U.S. government.

Within REMICs, there are several different types of securities. A Z-class REMIC pays no cash to the investor until other classes are paid off or another specified event occurs. The interest earned but not paid increases the principal balance of the class. Once the previous classes have paid off or the specified event occurs, the Z class becomes an interest-paying amortizing class. A sequential class is a security that receives principal payments in a prescribed sequence. A PO *(principal-only)* class does not bear interest and is entitled to receive only payments of principal. Rising interest rates have an adverse effect on POs because the payments remain steady while interest rates rise, resulting in a financial loss. A PAC *(planned-amortization-class)* REMIC is designed to give investors scheduled payments over a range of constant prepayment times. A *fixed-rate class* is a REMIC with an interest rate that does not change over the life of the class. A *floating-rate class* (floater) is a REMIC class that pays interest at a rate that is subject to periodic adjustments at a predetermined amount above a specific index. A *current-pay* class is a REMIC class that is currently paying principal and/or interest.

renegotiable-rate mortgage A variable-rate mortgage that has a renewable short-term balloon note. Generally, the interest rate on this type of loan is fixed during the term of the note. However, when the balloon becomes due, the lender may refinance the mortgage at a higher rate. A balloon note gets its name from the fact that it matures during a short period of time. Because it was so short, there wasn't enough time to pay off the principal and a large payment must be made at the end of the loan, or it must be refinanced.

renminbi The currency unit of China. One RMB is equal to 10 jiao and 100 fen. Also called *RMB* or *yuan.*

rent control State or local government regulations that limit how much rent landlords can charge their tenants. Rent control legislation usually is passed when the supply of housing is limited and demand for existing homes or apartments is quickly rising. The intent of rent control legislation is to prevent consumers from being subjected to sharply higher rents that they can't afford. Critics of rent control say that the government shouldn't be involved in setting prices. They also point out that by limiting the profit that the landlords make, rent control laws restrict the amount of capital that landlords are willing to commit to upgrading their properties. Rent control boards govern how much of an increase can be passed along to tenants each year. Rent control usually occurs in expensive urban areas such as Boston, New York City, and San Francisco. Another lesser-form of rent control is rent stabilization, which is common in New York City.

reopen an issue When the Treasury Department wants to sell additional securities in an existing debt issue, it will reopen it instead of offering a new issue. This is done to increase liquidity in the existing issue.

reopening Refers to the issuance of additional debt on a previously issued debt, such as a bond or note offering. Instead of selling a completely new note or bond issue, the current issue will be reopened and sold to the public.

repatriate To return foreign-earned profits or financial assets back to the company's home country. A multinational company, such as McDonalds Corp., repatriates its profits into U.S. dollars and brings them back to the United States.

repo rate The interest rate that the Bank of England's Monetary Policy Committee uses to set monetary policy. In setting the repo rate, the Bank of England examines the risk of inflation as well as economic activity. In general, other countries and traders have their own version of a repo rate, which is the interest rate set on repurchase agreements in which a securities holder sells the securities to an investor with an agreement to repurchase them at a fixed price on a fixed date.

reportable position In the futures industry, the level of held futures contracts at which the customer must be identified to the exchange and to the Commodity Futures Trading Commission (CFTC). The CFTC produces a bi-weekly report, called the *Commitment of Traders' Report,* for each commodities market; the report shows whether different classes of traders, such as institutions or hedge funds, are net buyers or net sellers of each commodity or financial instrument. The report summarizes all of the reportable positions. Typically, the CFTC is widely watched in futures markets that are relatively dominant to the cash markets, such as grains, cattle, or energy; they are less widely watched for futures with a large cash market such as Treasury bonds or notes that have a large cash market.

reporting level The number of futures contracts held by one trader or broker that require the trader or broker to make daily reports about the size of the position. A large number of contracts must be held for the reporting level to be reached. In the reports, data must be broken down by commodity, delivery month, and whether the commodity is held by a commercial or non-commercial account. The position must be reported to the Commodity Futures Trading Commission (CFTC) and the exchange, which cooperatively set reporting levels.

repurchase agreement Often called a *repo.* An agreement in which a securities holder sells the securities to an investor with an agreement to repurchase them at a fixed price on a fixed date. In effect, the buyer of the securities is lending the seller money. Dealers typically use this arrangement to finance their positions. Used in the context of the Federal Reserve, however, a repo refers to a situation in which the Fed lends money and increases the reserves of banks. Typically, this is done in an overnight transaction, but there are term repos that last for different time periods.

request for proposal (RFP) A document that tells vendors and service providers what type of service or products a company is attempting to purchase. An RFP is a solicitation for potential contractors to submit their bids in a competitive process. RFPs are issued by a variety of businesses in the financial world. For example, a pension fund creates an RFP to spell out the type of asset management services it is attempting to outsource. Asset management companies respond to the RFP and explain how they can meet the needs of the company. Often investment consultants are hired by the pension funds to manage the RFP process and help select the management.

required rate of return The amount of return that a project or investment is required to have before the company agrees to budget the money or investors agree to make the investment. If the expected return doesn't exceed the required rate of return the project or investment won't be made.

Companies do a required rate of return analysis before deciding to fund a new joint venture or to purchase a piece of equipment. The analysis examines what the expected increase in revenue will be and factors in increased costs as well as the interest that will be paid to borrow the money, if applicable.

research and development (R&D) A company's activities to discover new products and improve current products. These efforts also may focus on providing new services or marketing techniques. Many companies have R&D departments. In prosperous times, companies increase their R&D spending and often reduce their spending when economic conditions turn poor. R&D efforts usually are listed as a separate expense item on a company's income statement. Some companies, such as those in the pharmaceutical industry, spend a large amount of money on R&D in order to always have new, leading-edge products and drugs coming to market. Other companies, such as technology companies, may spend a minimum amount on R&D efforts and instead focus on acquiring start-up companies that have new, innovative technology applications.

reserve requirements Requirements that regulate the amount of reserves that banks and other depository institutions must hold against customer deposits. A lower reserve requirement allows more deposit and loan expansion, and a higher reserve ratio permits less expansion. The Federal Reserve sets reserve requirements, within limits specified by law. Different legal requirements exist for different depository institutions, such as commercial banks, savings banks, savings and loan associations, credit unions, some industrial loan banks, U.S. agencies, and branches of foreign banks that have transaction accounts or non-personal time deposits.

reserves Money set aside by depository institutions to meet reserve requirements. A bank may hold cash reserves in its vault or have reserves on deposit with the local Federal Reserve Bank. Reserve requirements are the minimum amount of money that a bank is required to have available to meet investors' needs to withdraw funds. Other depository institutions that are not members of the Federal Reserve System may hold their reserves in their vaults or put them on deposit with a correspondent institution to the Federal Reserve banks.

residual fuel oil A heavy fuel oil produced from the residue of the fractional distillation process.

residual value The estimated salvage or trade-in value of a tangible asset using an estimated disposal date. Residual value is an important calculation for depreciation expense. Also called *salvage value* or *disposal value.*

resistance In technical analysis, a price point or points that a futures contract or other financial instrument will have difficulty rising above. Resistance is a price level where selling pressure overcomes buying pressure and a price advance is turned back. The opposite is *support,* which is a technical analysis term. It indicates a price point that prices will have difficulty moving below. Technical analysts look at resistance in order to determine the market's next likely move. For instance, if gold prices have been attempting to move higher but each day's gain stops at $335 per ounce of gold or $336, then those two price points are where resistance occurs.

Resolution Funding Corp. (RFC) A government agency created by Congress in 1989 to fund the financial cleanup of failed savings and loans institutions. The agency issues bonds, called REFCORPs, which are zero-coupon bonds that were sold to private investors in order to reimburse the government for its costs of paying depositors of the failed savings and loans. The Resolution Funding Corp. worked in conjunction with the Resolution Trust Corp., which was the government agency created to merge or close failed savings and loans from 1989 until 1992.

Resolution Trust Corp. (RTC) The government agency that was responsible for bailing out the U.S. savings and loan institutions that had become insolvent during the 1980s. The Resolution Trust Corp. either merged failed savings and loans with healthier competitors or closed them and paid off account holders. The RTC replaced the Federal Savings and Loan Insurance Corp. (FSLIC), which was shut down after the savings and loan crisis.

The RTC's charter ended in 1996 and its duties were given to the Savings Association Insurance Fund (SAIF), which is part of the Federal Deposit Insurance Corp.

resting order An order whose price is away from the market and is waiting to be executed. For example, if an investor has placed an order to sell a stock at $70, but the price is at $60, it is away from the market.

restraint of trade Actions taken by a company or individual to restrain or limit trade. Restraint of trade is prohibited by federal antitrust laws. Both the Federal Trade Commission (FTC) and the Department of Justice (DOJ) investigate situations in which companies allegedly have tried to restrain trade. An example of restraint of trade is a restaurant supply company that offers inexpensive prices but requires its customers to purchase all of their supplies exclusively from that company.

restricted A stock or other investment that is off limits. Restricted investments are those that employees of an investment bank are not allowed to trade because the company that made the investment is involved in other non-public transactions that are being handled by the bank. For example, merger deals, stock offerings, or bond offerings that are being planned but haven't yet been announced put the company on the restricted list. Typically, a bank requires its employees to trade only through an account provided by the bank. Restricted transactions are prohibited and the employees' trading activities can be monitored. The bank itself can't trade the company's stock

for its own account, either. However, it can do transactions as a broker for its clients.

restructure To comprehensively reorganize a business with the intention of putting it back on solid, profitable ground. Companies that go through a restructuring process typically work with creditors to change debt terms. For example, creditors may exchange some of the debt for equity or extend the maturity date. Companies also reorganize their product offerings or sales forces by eliminating unprofitable products and reassigning sales people. When workforces are restructured, layoffs of general staff and top management may occur. The company incurs a large expense to pay severance to laid off employees and therefore usually takes a restructuring charge against earnings for one or two quarters after the restructuring is announced.

retail banking Banking services that are offered to consumers and small businesses. If a bank targets only large corporations and institutions, then it is said to offer *wholesale banking* services. A full-service commercial bank offers both retail and wholesale banking services.

retail house A brokerage firm whose primary clientele is *retail investors,* meaning individuals, instead of institutions. A retail house has a large number of brokers and a large research department that caters its efforts to individuals, instead of institutional investors.

retail investor A private investor who typically trades securities in relatively small quantities for his or her own account. Retail investors contrast with businesses or institutional accounts that trade millions of dollars at one time.

retail sales A monthly economic indicator that measures the level of all retail sales in the United States. The data is collected and released during the second week of the month for the preceding month by the U.S. Commerce Department's Bureau of the Census. Retail sales data is not adjusted for inflation, but is adjusted for holiday and seasonal differences. Retail sales figures are widely watched economic indicators because individual spending is a major driver of the U.S. economy, contributing about two-thirds to gross domestic product.

retail sales report Data compiled by the U.S. Bureau of the Census that measures consumer spending at retail establishments. The data is timely, as it covers the previous month. However, the data also can be volatile and is subject to revision because of sampling errors. The data takes on increased importance around major shopping holidays, such as Christmas. The survey also is referred to as the Monthly Advance Retail Trade Survey (MARTS).

retail trade An industry that sells primarily to individuals, not corporations. Usually, retail refers to retail outlets, where customers shop. With the Internet boom, many retail stores also sell products on their Web sites. Retail trade is conducted in grocery, department, specialty, and apparel stores, among other venues.

retained earnings Corporate earnings that are not paid out as dividends. Retained earnings are accounted for on a company's balance sheet as *owners' equity,* and are distinguished from *paid-in capital,* which is the difference between the *par value of equity* and the amount of funds raised from a stock issue. Also called *undistributed profits* or *surplus.*

return on assets Net income divided by average total assets; the resulting number shows how much net income was earned for each dollar of assets. The formula is a combination of the formulas used to calculate profit margin and asset turnover.

return on owner's equity (ROE) A ratio calculated by dividing net income by average total stockholders' equity. It shows what type of return management has earned on capital.

return on total capital A financial measurement that is calculated by totaling net

income and interest expenses and dividing the resulting figure by average total capital. The ratio is expressed as a percentage and shows what the company's return is on all of its capital. Also called *return on capital.*

Reuters/CRB Index An index owned by Reuters Plc, the U.K.-based data and news provider. The index is calculated by the Commodity Research Bureau Inc. (CRB) and was first published in 1957. The index comprises 17 commodities that are averaged using specific months for the futures contracts. The 17 commodities are corn, soybeans, wheat, live cattle, lean hogs, gold, silver, copper, cocoa, coffee, sugar, cotton, orange juice, platinum, crude oil, heating oil, and natural gas.

Reuther, Walter A labor organizer for the United Auto Workers (UAW) who built it up into a powerhouse in the auto industry. He was the UAW president for 24 years and also led the Congress of Industrial Organizations (CIO). He died in 1970.

revenue Money that a company takes in from the sale of goods and services. On the balance sheet, revenues increase assets and stockholders' equity. The cost of expenses is subtracted from total revenue to calculate *net income.* The term *sales* may be used interchangeably on a company's net income statement as another word for revenue.

revenue bond A bond that is paid back by revenues from the project the proceeds from the bond sale went to fund. Often, revenue bonds are used in conjunction with a public utility, a toll bridge, or road.

revenue recognition The process and policy that is used to record revenues. Although revenue recognition is a very straightforward process for a business such as a retail store, it is more complicated for other companies that sell large, expensive contracts or services that last over a several-year period. In this situation, management discretion is involved.

Revenues per average user See *RevPAR.*

reversal A change in direction of a market that is identified by technical analysis. For instance, a rising market that reaches a peak and then begins to move lower is a reversal.

reverse auction An auction process in which buyers announce their need for a product or service, and suppliers bid to fulfill that need. Reverse auctions are used to award new business to the supplier with the lowest bid. Unlike a typical auction, prices in a reverse auction decrease as the bidding process continues. Internet-based industry consortiums have created online marketplaces to run reverse auctions, as have independent, Internet-based companies. A car manufacturer may announce its intention to purchase tires and a reverse auction would be set to find tire sellers willing to sell their product to the car manufacturer. Contrasts with a regular auction where the seller is attempting to sell many products to many purchasers.

reverse conversion The creation of an options position by purchasing a call option, selling a put option, and selling the underlying futures contract. It also is referred to as a *reversal*.

reverse convertible A security linked to a share of stock that gives the bearer the right to cash a dividend coupon whose yield is higher than the market rate. The bearer also receives either the face value of the convertible or a number of shares that were guaranteed at the time when the original investment was purchased. Reverse convertibles typically mature within six months to one year.

reverse crush spread A futures trading strategy whereby soybean futures are sold while the simultaneous purchase of soybean oil and meal futures occurs, or vice-versa. Crush strategies can be profitable to take advantage of price differences between the underlying product and those products that are derived from it. See also *crush spread*.

reverse Dutch auction An auction that has one buyer and many sellers; the auctioneer raises the price from a low starting point until a bidder agrees to sell at the stated price. For example, a reverse Dutch auction could be used to find someone willing to delay travel plans on an overbooked flight. The airline raises the compensatory price until someone raises his or her hand and ends the auction. A passenger unwilling to give up his or her seat for $50 may be more likely to relinquish it for $100, $200, or higher. See *Dutch auction*.

reverse English auction An auction that has one buyer and many sellers. Bidders offer decreasing prices to be able to sell their product to the buyer. The price of bids decreases until an item can be sold. This technique is used on Internet-based auctions.

reverse hedge See *Chinese hedge*.

reverse leveraged buyout The process of turning a privately owned company, or former division of a company, that previously had been a publicly traded company back into a publicly traded company. The leveraged buyouts of the 1980s turned many publicly owned companies into private companies that were saddled with a large debt to pay for the buyout. Once those debts were repaid, the owners of the company were able to increase returns by taking the company public again.

reverse merger A technique used by private companies to go public without registering an initial public offering (IPO). A reverse merger occurs when a private company acquires or merges with a public company that is little more than a *shell*. That is, although the public company is listed on a stock exchange, such as the NASDAQ, or trades in the over-the-counter (OTC) market, its primary business has failed and it has sold off most of its assets and discontinued operations. Reverse mergers became popular after the stock market bubble burst in 2000 and the initial public offering market virtually shut down. Also called a *back-door listing*.

reverse mortgage   A mortgage whose proceeds are made available to the homeowner against the equity that is built up in the house. The homeowner is paid a monthly sum until the monthly payments have equaled the value of the mortgage. Reverse mortgages typically are used by older, cash-poor but equity-rich homeowners who need to access some of the cash value of their house in order to supplement their monthly income. Although the mortgage can be paid back, typically the bank takes ownership of the house when the owners die.

reverse price auction   An auction where the seller sets a minimum price that he or she will accept but does not disclose this price. Bidders must meet or exceed the minimum (reverse) price and have the highest bid to win. If the reverse price is not met, then the seller is not under any obligation to complete the transaction. This is sometimes used by homeowners to sell their homes.

reverse stock split   A process by which a company reduces the total number of shares outstanding while ensuring that the total market value of the company remains the same. For instance, in a *1-for-3 reverse split,* a company with a share price of $2 and 12 million shares outstanding will end up with 4 million shares outstanding that are worth $6 each. The strategy is often used by companies with low stock prices that face being removed, or *delisted,* from major stock exchanges. Companies are subject to being delisted from the New York Stock Exchange (NYSE) or NASDAQ if they do not meet a minimum closing price (typically $1 per share), and their stock remains depressed for a certain period of time, often 30 consecutive days.

Because pension funds and other large investment firms are often restricted from purchasing stocks whose share price is below a certain level, such as $5, reverse stock splits may be used by companies to draw those types of investors. News that a company is planning a reverse stock split is usually not looked upon favorably by investors.

revocable trust   See *inter vivos trust.*

revolver   Short for *revolving line of credit.* A line of credit is given to a corporation in return for a commitment fee; the company can withdraw any or all of the credit line. Typically, revolving credit agreements are good for 364 days. If the company remains in good financial health, the revolving credit line is renegotiated. Banks consider revolvers risky because they have little profit incentive and limit the amount that can be loaned to other customers. Consequently, in tough economic times or when it is difficult to access the capital markets to sell stocks or bonds, banks are more conservative about issuing credit lines, or extend credit lines to only their best clients.

revolving line of credit   A consumer loan account that requires monthly payments that are less than the full amount owed and can vary. The line of credit has a limit. The lender charges a fee for agreeing to make the funds available, in addition to interest charges on the outstanding balance. A revolving line of credit often is issued in the form of a home equity loan. For corporations, a revolving line of credit is more commonly referred to as a revolver. Also may be called *open-ended credit.* See also *revolver.*

revolving-loan fund   A fund that is structured so that repayments can be used to make more loans. The term is used interchangeably with a Community Development Loan Fund, which is a non-profit loan fund that receives public money and gives loans for housing and small business needs. However, revolving-loan funds have a much wider scope than the Community Development Loan Fund, and may fund larger-scale community development projects. A revolving-loan fund can be administered by a non-profit organization or a public agency, and is not overseen by any regulatory agency.

RevPAR *Revenues per average user.* A frequently-used abbreviation by Wall Street analysts, RevPAR is used to measure such things as revenues produced by each hotel customer, telecom customer, and so on.

RFP See *request for proposals.*

rho A measurement of the change in the premium of an option, or its sales price, in relation to a percentage-point change in the interest rate. Rho measures the sensitivity of the option's value to interest rates.

rial The currency unit of Iran, comprised of 100 dinars. Yemen uses it as well, but its version is comprised of 100 fils. Oman uses the sul rial; its unit is comprised of 1000 baisa.

riba A contract under Islamic religious law that calls for interest to be paid. However, because most interpretations of Islamic law don't allow interest to be charged, it often is unenforceable.

Richmond Fed Manufacturing Survey An economic survey of about 190 manufacturing plants within the Richmond Federal Reserve Bank region that examines conditions in the manufacturing industry. The Richmond region is the Fifth Federal Reserve District, which includes Washington, D.C., Maryland, North Carolina, South Carolina, Virginia, and most of West Virginia. The report is released about one week after the beginning of a new month and after the national Institute for Supply Management (ISM) Index is released. The index's changes in shipments are indicators of current conditions. Changes in the prices of raw or finished goods give an indication of pricing trends. Expected shipments, backlogs, and new orders are indicators of future conditions. Because the report is published a short time after the data is collected, it is very useful for getting a quick snapshot of economic conditions. However, the long-term effect of the Richmond Fed Manufacturing Survey on financial markets is usually limited.

There are four indexes that comprise the Richmond Fed Manufacturing Survey. Those are: shipments, new orders, backlog of new orders, and six-month shipment outlook. The indexes can range from +100 to −100 and indicate the general direction of the indicators by showing how the number of plants with improving conditions offset those with worsening conditions. Index values greater than zero suggest expansion, while values less than zero indicate a contraction. Data values are seasonally adjusted.

RICO See *Racketeer Influenced and Corrupt Organization Act.*

riel The currency unit of Cambodia, comprised of 100 sen.

Rigas, John The former chairman and founder of Adelphia Communications, who resigned under pressure after he was charged, along with his two sons who also were company employees, with stealing $1 billion from the company. Rigas pled not guilty to federal charges of bank and wire fraud, securities fraud, and conspiracy. However, James R. Brown, the former vice president of finance for the company, pleaded guilty to fraud and conspiracy charges, thereby implicating the three Rigases.

right of first refusal A right that allows a person or a business to have the first chance to purchase a property before the property is offered to the public for sale. This may occur with a business tenant that is leasing office space. The right of first refusal also occurs with condominium association boards. They are allowed to deny a potential buyer's application to purchase an apartment in the building. However, although the condominium association can keep a potential homeowner out, it can only do so if it is willing to purchase the unit itself.

right of survivorship See *joint tenancy with right of survivorship.*

rights offering The sale of shares of stock to existing shareholders at a discounted price from what the general public will have to pay. Seen more frequently in the U.K. than in the U.S.

right-to-work law A law that prohibits unions from requiring employees of unionized companies to join the union. States were given the right to pass right-to-work laws under the Taft-Hartley Act of 1947.

ringgit The currency unit of Malaysia, comprised of 100 sen.

rising bottom A technical chart pattern that is characterized by low prices that are rising in what is becoming an upward trend. A rising bottom indicates a price area where prices can be expected to find strong support.

risk The possibility that a negative event will occur, such as the value of investments declining below what was paid for them or investments losing all value. Investors attempt to minimize risk through diversification.

risk analysis The process of determining whether an investment or business decision is worth the financial risk involved. Risk analysis for securities portfolios involves using a variety of statistical techniques and other methods to judge how steep losses could be if certain events occur. Companies conduct risk analysis of their information technology systems, building in safety, employee safety, and data safety costs. Numerous systems are used to conduct risk analysis.

risk averse The investing style of someone who is afraid of losing money, and who therefore makes only conservative investments. A risk-averse investor is someone who is willing to put up with less return on his or her investment in order to sleep easier at night.

risk premium The amount of return that buyers demand above a theoretical risk-free return. The risk premium explains the difference in the expected return among similar securities. For example, investors will be willing to buy an A-rated bond that pays a lower interest rate because it has less risk than a B-rated bond, which is riskier. The issuer of a B-rated bond has to pay a higher interest rate in order to attract buyers to make up for the greater risk.

risk tolerance An investor's willingness to accept high risk in the hopes the investments will increase in value. A *risk-averse* investor has investments whose values are relatively stable — they will neither increase greatly nor decrease greatly. An investor with a high risk tolerance has investments whose value might increase dramatically or fall dramatically. An individual's risk tolerance varies by personality and other factors, such as life stage. A retired person is typically less willing to pursue high-risk investments than a younger person, for example.

risk/reward tradeoff An investment principle that says an investment must deliver a higher potential return as compensation for increased risk.

risk-free return A theoretical investment that is free of risk. Usually the three-month U.S. Treasury bill is used as a benchmark for a risk-free return. Although no financial investment is completely risk-free, U.S. Treasuries are considered to come the closest because they are backed by the full-faith and credit of the U.S. Government.

riyal The currency unit of Qatar, comprised of 100 dirhams, and Saudi Arabia, comprised of 100 halalas.

RLEC *Rural Local Exchange Carriers* are rural telecom companies that provide telephone service for defined areas.

road show The process before an initial public offering, or in some cases a debt issuance or follow-on equity offering, in which senior company officials spend anywhere from two days to several weeks traveling to different cities to meet with large investors. The purpose of a road show is to build enthusiasm about the company, answer questions, and encourage the purchase of shares of the company's offering.

Rockefeller, John D. A turn-of-the-century industrialist who started his career making $4 a week as a clerk in Cleveland. He made his fortune by turning oil into products that people needed, such as kerosene. In 1890, he controlled 90 percent of the U.S. oil industry with his Standard Oil Trust, which was broken up by the Sherman Antitrust Act. However, 15 years later he had recreated his monopoly, which the Supreme Court broke up in 1911. He gave $10 million to the General Education Board and his money started the University of Chicago and the Rockefeller Foundation.

ROE   See *return on owner's equity.*

roll down   To move from one option position to another one that has a lower strike price. The first option position is liquidated before the new one is taken. Roll downs occur because the option is going to expire and the trader wants to retain the position.

roll down and forward   To move from one option position into another one that has a later expiration date with a new, lower strike price. If the strike price increases, it is called a *roll forward.* Roll downs occur because the option is going to expire and the trader wants to retain the position.

roll forward   To move from one option position into another one that has a later expiration date. If the new option position has a higher strike price, it is called a *roll up and forward.* Similarly, a lower strike price is a *roll down and forward.* Roll forwards occur because the option is going to expire and the trader wants to retain the position.

roll over   To move funds or an investment from one position or investment to another. In the case of retirement funds specifically, an investor may roll over those funds from one account to another. This often occurs in the case of a 401(k) retirement plans when an employee leaves the company. Another common use is with certificates of deposits (CDs). CDs may be rolled over into another CD when they mature; the new CD will have a different interest rate. Another common use is with debt: Debtors or banks may allow their clients to roll over their debt into a new issue.

roll up   To move from one option position to another one that has a higher strike price. The old option position is liquidated before the new one is taken. Roll ups occur because the option is going to expire and the trader wants to retain the position.

rolling hedge   A hedge carried over for successive periods in order to keep it in place. This is done because even though the underlying contract might be expiring, the trader still wants to keep the hedge in place. The position in the soon-to-expire contract is sold and the equivalent position is bought in a contract in a future month.

rollover   In the futures industry, shift-selling a futures contract, such as a September contract, while immediately buying another contract in the future, such as December. A rollover maintains the original trading strategy.

roll-up merger   A process of acquiring, or "rolling up," smaller companies within an industry in order to create economies of scale and form a larger company. The roll-up may be done by investors who are seeking investment opportunities or by a larger company in the industry. Companies that are purchased often are small, independently-owned businesses whose owners believe that they would be better able to compete if they were larger and could have a national presence. Often roll-ups happen in service industries. They were a popular consolidation tool in the late 1990s in once-stagnant industries, such as waste management, that suddenly had strong financial growth. Other industries where this technique was popular included temporary services agencies, computer services, and advertising.

In the late 1990s, as the initial public offering market boomed, roll-up IPOs became popular. This technique was used by a holding company simultaneously acquiring five to ten privately held companies in an industry, which immediately created a major player. The owners of the companies received cash and shares in the holding company. In order for the new company to get capital, it launched an IPO, which was done at the same time as the acquisitions. The cash was then dispersed to the owners, with the company's coffers funded as well. Stock from the IPO also was given to the owners as part of their payment.

Roth IRA An individual retirement account (IRA) that was introduced in 1998 and provides an alternative to a traditional IRA. With a Roth IRA, deductions can only be made with after-tax money. However, earnings are not taxed when the distribution is taken at 59½ years of age after holding the account for at least 5 years.

Money for certain eligible expenses can be withdrawn before age 59½ without paying tax or penalties, provided that the account has been active for five years. Those expenses include higher education, $10,000 for a first-time home purchase, and payment of health insurance for unemployed people.

A contribution of $3,000 a year can be made for a single person who earns up to $95,000, with ineligibility starting to occur at $110,000. Married couples can contribute $6,000 if they earn up to $150,000, with eligibility phasing out at $160,000.

round lot In the stock market, an order of at least 100 shares, or one that is in 100-share increments. In contrast, an odd lot is an order for some amount that is not divisible by 100 shares. In the money market industry, a round lot is the minimum amount that bond's prices are quoted in. This amount may range from $100,000 to $50 million, depending on the issue, its size, and liquidity.

round trip The opening purchase or sale of a stock or futures contract and the subsequent opposite and closing transaction in the same contract. Transaction costs are usually quoted on a round-trip basis.

round turn The purchase and subsequent sale of a stock, futures contract, or another investment.

rounded bottom A chart pattern in technical analysis that shows prices declining in a moderate fashion and then increasing slightly. This pattern looks like the bottom half of a circle.

royalty A payment made for the right to use an asset, invention, or creation calculated as a percentage of the sale price. For example, the holder of a valuable natural resource may receive a royalty from a company that extracts the resource; the amount of the royalty payment depends on the amount of the resource that the company is able to extract. An author may receive a royalty each time one of his or her books sells.

RPM *Revenue per minute,* calculated by dividing monthly or quarterly revenue by the number of minutes billed. It is a common measurement used in the wireless industry. See also *ARPU.*

RSI See *Relative Strength Index.*

RTC *Resolution Trust Corporation,* which was created to clean up the savings and loan crisis in the U.S. in 1989. RTC replaced the Federal Savings and Loan Insurance Corp. (FSLIC). In 1995, the FSLIC's deposit insurance functions were transferred to the Federal Deposition Insurance Corp. (FDIC). The RTC's responsibilities also were handed over to the FDIC in January 1996.

Rubin, Robert The chairman of Citigroup's Executive Committee and a member of its Office of the Chairman. From January 1995 to July 1999, he was the U.S. Treasury Secretary under President Bill

Clinton. From 1993 to 1995, he directed Clinton's National Economic Council. Before going into government service, Rubin spent 26 years at Goldman Sachs & Co., where, from 1990 to 1992, he was co-chairman and co-senior partner.

ruble   The currency unit of Russia, comprised of 100 kopeks; Tajikistan, comprised of 100 tanga; and Belarus, comprised of 100 kapeikas.

rufiyaa   The currency unit of Maldives, comprised of 100 laari.

Rule 144   A Securities and Exchange Commission (SEC) rule that allows certain holders of unregistered securities to sell them to the public without filing a registration with the SEC beforehand. The rule lets executives who hold very large blocks of their company's stock sell a portion of that stock twice a year without registering with the SEC, if the executives have held the stock for one year. The holding period was reduced from two years in 1997.

Rule 144A   A rule that exempts private security offerings from going through the Security and Exchange Commission's (SEC) registration process that is required under the 1933 Securities Act. The objective of Rule 144A is to increase the liquidity and efficiency of the U.S. equity and debt markets for securities issued in private placements. Thus, large institutional investors are able to trade restricted securities more freely with other institutional investors without subjecting the companies issuing the securities to the SEC registration and disclosure process. However, the buyer of any securities must be a *qualified institutional buyer* (QIB), an institution that owns and manages $100 million or more in qualifying securities. The amount may be dropped down to $10 million for registered broker/dealers.

Rule 27-11   A rule passed by the New York Stock Exchange (NYSE) and the National Association of Securities Dealers (NASD) to handle some of the conflicts of interest between research analysts and investment banking. As a result of Rule 27-11, research reports must say whether the analyst or any member of his or her family owns the stock being discussed, and whether the analyst's firm has or intends to obtain an investment banking relationship with the company.

Also, according to Rule 27-11, banks must divide all their research recommendations into three categories (buy, neutral, and sell), and disclose what percentage of companies fall into each category. The percentage of companies in each category also must be broken out for investment banking clients. In addition, research analysts are prohibited from letting a research report be previewed by investment bankers or by the company.

rule of 72   A formula that calculates the number of years it will take to double your money at various interest rates. To use the rule of 72, divide 72 by the interest the investment returns. The answer will be the number of years before the money doubles.

run on a bank   The simultaneous rush by many depositors to reclaim their deposits. Runs on a bank occur when investors are afraid that the bank is insolvent and that their funds will be lost. This occurred during the Great Depression. Fortunately, in the United States, runs on a bank are rare phenomena. Also called *bank run*.

runaway gap   A chart pattern in technical analysis that shows a strong upward price movement.

runner   A person employed by a futures trading company who delivers price orders to the floor broker in the pit and then returns the completed order to the desk where the order completion is verbally confirmed and entered into the computer system.

rupee The currency unit of Pakistan, Mauritius, Seychelles, and Sri Lanka, comprised of 100 cents. Nepal also uses the rupee; its unit is comprised of 100 paisa.

rupiah The currency unit of Indonesia, comprised of 100 sen.

Russell 2000 Index The Russell 2000 Index is comprised of the 2,000 lowest capitalization stocks in the Russell 3000, which make up the 3,000 largest capitalization stocks in the U.S. stock market. It provides a barometer of how small-cap companies are performing. It is maintained by the Frank Russell Co., in Tacoma, Washington. Its trading symbol is RUT.X.

Rust Belt An area of the United States that once was strong in manufacturing and steel production but has declined in the last 30 years; the region includes states in or near the Great Lakes region, such as Pennsylvania, Ohio, Michigan, and other states. The exact states that comprise the Rust Belt vary depending on who is using the term. Others that may show up on lists include Illinois, Indiana, Wisconsin, parts of upstate New York, and New Jersey.

S

S&P 100 Index This Standard & Poor's Index measures the stock market performance of large U.S. companies. The 100 Index is a weighted index of 100 blue-chip stocks across diverse industry sectors. OEX is the ticker symbol.

S&P 400 MidCap Index This Standard & Poor's Index measures the stock performance of mid-sized companies in the U.S. stock market. The index includes 400 companies spread across many industries. Its ticker symbol is MID.X.

S&P 500 Index This Standard & Poor's Index is a capitalization-weighted index of 500 stocks. It is a popular index and is used to measure the performance of the large cap U.S. stock market. The 500 stocks of this index are selected to be a representative sample of leading companies. Money managers often index their portfolios to match or beat the S&P 500. GSPC is the ticker symbol.

S.A de C.V. A designation used in Mexico to indicate a corporation. It stands for *Sociedad Anonima de Capital Variable,* which is the most formal business structure in Mexico. An S.A de C.V. must consist of at least two shareholders, with no limit on the maximum number, and a minimum capital contribution.

S-1 A registration form required by the 1933 Securities Act that an issuer of securities must file with the Securities and Exchange Commission (SEC) before selling securities to the public.

S-4 A form required by the 1933 Securities Act that is used to register the sale of securities in conjunction with business combinations, such as mergers, or exchange offers. It must be filed with the Securities and Exchange Commission.

SA A French term that is short for *société anonyme* and is used in France, Belgium, and other former French-speaking countries to designate a corporation.

safe harbor statement A statement typically found in the fine print at the end of a corporation's press release that says that the "forward-looking statements" are based on a number of events and assumptions. It cautions investors not to put too much reliance on these statements because they are subject to a number of uncertainties that the company can't control and that may cause the results to differ from the statements. The readers of the release are referred to the company's filings with the SEC for further information.

The safe harbor statement received a large push from the Private Securities Litigation Reform Act of 1995. That law protects issuers of publicly-traded securities from liability for certain financial projections and related facts and figures. The SEC's rules require companies to say that their projections are forward-looking and to include cautionary statements advising investors about key risk factors that might affect the statements' accuracy.

safe haven An investment that people transfer money into in times of turmoil and market uncertainty. Gold, U.S. Treasury bills, notes or bonds, and the Swiss franc are some safe havens for money fleeing trouble.

Sage, Russell A major financier who was a contemporary of Jay Gould and J.P. Morgan in the late 1880s. He promoted investments, loans, and investments that were considered to be little more than manipulations. His efforts created a fortune of $70 million. After his death his widow, Olivia, created the Russell Sage Foundation to promote social issues such as education, religious causes, and women's interests. Before entering finance he was a wholesale grocer and a member of Congress from New York.

salary freeze A company-wide policy in which salaries are frozen at their present level and no raises are allowed. Salary freezes are enacted in bad economic times in order to limit cost increases, and they are lifted when business conditions improve.

salary reduction plan A plan that lets employees put pre-tax wages into a tax-deferred retirement plan. A prime example of this type of plan is a 401(k) plan that allows employees to defer part of their salary into a tax-deferred plan to fund their retirement. Employees are then taxed at the lower salary level.

sale and leaseback An arrangement in which a company sells an asset to a buyer and the buyer immediately leases the property back to the seller. The seller has the use of the asset, but does not need to have capital tied up in the asset and does not have to list the debt it owes on its lease on its balance sheet.

sales discount A custom in some industries of giving customers a discount for paying their bills early. Although the percentage discount may vary, 2 percent is often a standard discount. The invoice may say "2/10, n30," which means that the buyer receives a 2 percent discount for paying the bill within 10 days and must pay the entire amount within 30 days.

sales load A commission charged on an investment product. An example of a sales load is a front-end load assessed on a mutual fund.

sales tax A tax that is assessed on products and services purchased by the end user. Sales taxes are assessed by city, county, or state governments and used to fund the activities of the government. Usually the sales tax rate ranges from 4 percent to 8 percent and is added onto the listed price. In Europe, sales tax takes the form of a value-added tax (VAT), which often ranges from 18 percent to 22 percent. It is usually included in the sales price of the good listed on the price tag.

Sallie Mae A nickname for the *Student Loan Marketing Association* (SLMA), which buys student loans from lenders such as colleges or financial institutions. Sallie Mae pools the loans, packages them, then resells them to investors. This frees up the institutions to issue more loans, because the debts are removed from their balance sheets. Sallie Mae is a federally-chartered corporation that is publicly traded.

salvage value The value of an asset that is estimated to remain after the asset is fully depreciated. Salvage value is subtracted from the acquisition cost of the asset before depreciation is calculated. Also called *residual value*.

Samurai bonds Bonds that are denominated in Japanese yen and are issued by non-Japanese companies. They are primarily sold in Japan.

sanction

1. Any of various penalties that may be imposed against an entity or an individual who has violated federal securities laws.

2. Any of various penalties that may be imposed against a government, typically by using trade sanctions. In addition, international organizations such as the United Nations may issue sanctions against countries as a deterrent to undesirable activities.

Santa Claus rally A loosely defined term that is applied to pre-Christmas trading that has upward momentum. It refers to optimism that Christmas sales will be strong and increase corporate profits.

São Paulo Bovespa A total return index weighted by traded volume comprised of the most frequently traded stocks on the São Paulo Stock Exchange. It has been divided 10 times by a factor of 10 since January 1, 1985, with the last division occurring on March 3, 1997.

Sarbanes–Oxley Act Federal legislation signed into law on July 30, 2002, that tightens financial rules governing corporations. It was passed in response to corporate debacles such as those involving Enron Corp. and WorldCom Group Inc. The wide-ranging legislation covers many topics: It requires companies to have audit committees that are made up of independent members, not corporate employees. It limits an auditor's ability to provide consulting services.

Companies also are required to provide more detailed financial information to investors. In addition, chief executive officers and chief financial officers must attest to the accuracy of their financial reports and their internal control systems. If these rules are violated, executives can be subjected to fines and/or jail terms. The legislation was named for Sen. Paul S. Sarbanes, D-Maryland, chairman of the Senate Banking Committee, and Michael G. Oxley, R-Ohio, chairman of the House Financial Services Committee.

saturation   A point in a product's life cycle when it is widely distributed. In order to sell more units, a company has to come up with a new, innovative marketing strategy to make the product appear fresh. Saturation likely is accompanied by widespread competition and pricing pressure.

Saturday Night Special   A surprise takeover bid for a company. It draws its name from the fact that the takeover announcement is often made over the weekend. The term is less widely used now.

savings account   An account at a bank or other savings institution in which individuals can keep money that is readily accessible, but on which a relatively small interest rate is paid. Savings accounts are insured by the U.S. government up to $100,000 per account through the Federal Deposit Insurance Corp. (FDIC). Banks, credit unions, and savings and loan institutions offer savings accounts. The interest earned on the accounts is taxable.

savings and loan (S&L) association   A federal or state-chartered financial institution that accepts deposits primarily from individuals and then loans money out in mortgages, car loans, or other debt. Savings and loans in the United States went through a period of turmoil in the late 1980s as rising interest rates and deregulation led to the failure of many S&Ls. The Federal Savings and Loan Insurance Corporation (FSLIC) was disbanded and the Office of Thrift Supervision, which is part of the U.S. Treasury Department, took its place. The Resolution Trust Corporation

and the Resolution Funding Corporation were created to close down failed S&Ls and reimburse account holders.

savings bond   A contract representing a loan that an individual makes to the U.S. government. The government repays the loan after a set period of time with a set interest rate. Because savings bonds are backed by the full faith and credit of the U.S. government, they are a safe way of saving. There are two types of savings bonds: Series EE bonds are issued for 30 years and a bond's value increases as the interest earned is added to the principal; Series HH bonds are current income securities issues for 20 years, which includes a 10-year original maturity period and a 10-year extension.

savings deposit   Money on deposit at a bank, savings and loan, or credit union that can be withdrawn without any notice. Types of savings deposits include passbook savings or money market accounts.

savings rate   The amount of money that citizens of a country save divided by the citizens' total disposable income, stated in percentage terms. U.S. citizens have long been criticized for their low savings rate, which amounts to just several percentage points a year. Savings rate details are published in gross domestic product statistics produced monthly by the U.S. government. Other countries, such as Japan, have a much higher savings rate.

SBIC   See *Small Business Investment Company*.

scale-down buying   Scale-down buying tends to match up with scale-up selling, which is buying low and trying to pick a bottom but diversifying the position in time. The lower the price goes, the more you want to buy. For instance, if a trader bought all the way down to $12 for a barrel of oil in 1998 and then sold as the market rallied and kept on selling to $39, one would believe he or she would be rich. However, all of the margin calls to deposit more money into his or her brokerage account would put a different spin on the profit picture. Producers of oil-related products such as gasoline or airlines tend to be scale-down buyers of jet fuel in order to lower their average cost of fuel. With their large credit line they can cope with the margin calls. This term is typically used in the futures market.

scale-down selling Selling into a market that is going down. For instance, crude oil may be sold at $35 a barrel, then more is sold at $34, and additional amounts are sold at $33. The trader is riding the trend lower and is only committing more to the trade as the market confirms and reinforces the bearish point of view. Producers, such as crude oil companies, can easily sell on this basis. Commodity funds more often sell on this basis, as they tend to be trend followers. This term is typically used in the futures market.

scale-up buying Buying into strength and adding onto that position as prices in the market continues to rise. Scale-up buying involves trading with the trend, using the market's money to expand the position because there is a smaller risk of a margin call. For example, if a trader buys crude oil at $35 a barrel and the market goes to $36, $1 in profit has been made. The $1 profit is used to purchase more oil. If oil goes up to $37, the trader uses the larger profit to purchase more oil. If the average price now goes to $38, the trader has a $2 profit on a larger position. However, if the market falls, then the trader risks losing money. This term is typically used in the futures market.

scale-up selling Selling into a market that is going up. For instance, if crude oil is at $37 a barrel, you would sell some crude at $37, then at $38, and then at $39. Often producers of oil, who own the actual commodity, employ this strategy. They know what their costs are and they are locking in a rate of return on their investment. However, at some point the market may continue trending upward, which may produce a margin call at $45. It can be a risky trading strategy, unless the trader has a good sense of what ranges prices will remain in. This term is typically used in the futures market.

scalp

1. In the futures industry, trading for small gains. It normally involves establishing and selling a position very quickly, often within minutes or hours on the same day.

2. In the securities industry, the undisclosed selling of a security by a person or entity such as an investment adviser, securities research analyst, or financial newsletter writer who is simultaneously recommending that the security be bought.

3. The actions of market maker who adds an excessive markup to a trade transaction, in violation of the Rules of Fair Practice of the National Association of Securities Dealers (NASD).

scalper A speculator in the futures market who trades in order to make a small profit from small upticks and downticks in prices. Often local traders, who are those who trade for their own accounts, are scalpers.

Schedule 13D A Securities and Exchange Commission (SEC) form that must be filed when an individual or corporation acquires more than 5 percent of a company's stock. Ownership of greater than 5 percent is considered a *beneficial interest* and may indicate that a takeover of the company is being planned. The 13D filing alerts regulators and other investors to the possibility of a takeover. A Schedule 13D must be filed ten days after the acquisition.

Schedule A An income tax form used by individuals and married couples who itemize their tax deductions. Expenses deducted on this form include mortgage interest and points paid, charitable contributions, investment expenses, and medical and dental expenses.

Schedule B An income tax form used by individuals and married couples to account for income from interest and dividends.

Schedule C An income tax form for individuals and married couples who have business income. The form lists income and expenses and arrives at a net figure that is included on Form 1040.

Schedule C-EZ   A federal income tax form that is used to report net profit from businesses that are owned by a sole proprietorship. A Schedule C-EZ can be used only by taxpayers who have a simplified tax filing situation.

Schedule D   An income tax form used by individuals and married couples to report capital gains and losses.

Schedule SE   A federal income tax form that is used to pay self-employment tax.

Schwab, Charles M.   Not the discount brokerage firm founder, but a powerful figure in the steel industry around the end of the 19th century. He started out at 17 as a laborer earning $1 a day, but by 35 he was the president of Andrew Carnegie's steel mills. Those companies would later be combined with J.P. Morgan's steel mills, which included most of the steel producers in the United States, creating U.S. Steel. After three years as president of the company, he left and began focusing on building up one of his small steel companies, Bethlehem Steel Corp. Although he created enormous wealth, he also was a big spender and his fortune shrunk. He died penniless in New York in 1939.

scorched earth policy   A method of dealing with an unwanted takeover attempt in which the target company sells its valuable assets and takes on debt in order to make itself appear unattractive to the company planning the takeover.

SCORE   See *Service Corps of Retired Executives.*

S-Corporation   A company that has a small number of shareholders and that files with the Internal Revenue Service (IRS) to have its profits taxed to each individual, instead of having the corporation pay income tax on the profits. The advantage is that the owners avoid double taxation of their profits, once at the corporate level and again as individuals. In order to become an S-Corporation and take the special tax election allowed under sub-chapter S of the IRS code, a company must file IRS Form 2553 and the IRS must approve the application. Companies that file as S-Corporations can have a maximum of 75 individual shareholders, although some types of trusts or estates also may qualify. Shareholders must be U.S. citizens or have residency status. Companies can have only one class of stock.

scripophily   A hobby that involves collecting antique stock and bond certificates. Although these certificates don't have any value as securities, they have value due to their antique status. The prestige of the company and the beauty of the certificates determine their value.

SDR   See *Special Drawing Rights.*

seasonality   A market characteristic in which a product or service becomes very popular for a period of a few months each year and then drops off considerably. An example of seasonality would be Valentine's Day candy, swimming suits, summer clothes, or Halloween costumes.

seat   A membership on a stock or futures exchange that traders can buy and sell. The prices of seats are determined by market forces. The term *seat* derives its name from the New York Stock Exchange (NYSE), where, in the early years of its existence, members sat in assigned seats during the roll call of stocks. However, that literal meaning became moot when continuous trading began in 1971. As of this printing, the record sale for a seat on the NYSE is $2.65 million in August 1999.

second mortgage   A mortgage on real estate that already has a first mortgage on it. In the event that the borrower defaults on payment, the original mortgage will be paid first out of any liquidation proceeds. A second mortgage may be an equity line of credit.

second round   The round of venture capital financing after the first round, which is seed funding. After the second round there may be several other rounds of funding before the company is purchased or an initial public offering (IPO) is done. Later-stage funding is called *mezzanine financing.*

secondary distribution The sale of corporate stock, bonds, or other securities that previously have already been issued, either through an initial public offering, in the case of stocks, or a bond offering. This is in contrast with a *primary distribution,* in which the securities are being sold for the first time.

secondary mortgage market The buying and selling of mortgages and mortgage-backed securities. Some of the agencies creating and participating in this industry are Fannie Mae and Freddie Mac. They create mortgage pools that are repackaged and sold as participation certificates or pass-through securities. Anything beyond the primary mortgage market is called the secondary mortgage market.

secondary offering The sale of additional shares of stock to the public after a company's initial public offering. All successive offerings are termed secondary. Also called *follow-on offering.*

Section 8 A rental program for low-income individuals, run by the Federal Housing Administration, that allows renters to rent an apartment that they otherwise could not afford. The FHA then sends Section 8 payments to the landlord with the renter paying only a small portion of the fair-market rent.

sector A group of companies that are in the same industry. For instance, there is a technology sector and a health care sector.

sector equity fund A mutual fund that invests in companies in a specific industry, such as biotechnology, utilities, precious metals, or technology.

sector rotation Moving money from one sector of the stock market to another.

For instance, if it appears the economy is improving, then funds may be moved into companies in the consumer durables sector.

secured bond A bond that is backed by a legal claim on a specified asset or property. A mortgage bond, which is secured by the underlying property, is an example. In the event of a default or a bankruptcy proceeding, a secured bondholder is given preference over other bondholders and shareholders. Secured bonds contrast with *debentures,* which are unsecured bonds. Also called *senior bond.*

secured credit card A credit card that is linked to a savings account, which allows the credit company to accept customers with riskier credit histories. The funds contained in the savings account may be used if the cardholder doesn't make the required payments.

secured debt Debt backed by collateral that can be tapped in the event that the debt holder doesn't make interest payments and defaults on the debt. An example of secured debt is a mortgage that is secured by the actual real estate. Loans to corporations might be backed by securities, such as stock.

Secured Investor Trust A pool of collateralized mortgage obligations that provide the cash flow for kitchen sink bonds. Collateralized mortgage obligations are mortgages that are backed by the underlying security that gives investors protection in the event that the mortgage payments stops. See also *kitchen sink bond.*

securities Financial instruments such as stocks, bonds, futures, or options contracts. Securities may be traded on organized exchanges or on over-the-counter exchanges.

Securities Act of 1933 One of the cornerstones upon which the current financial regulatory system is based, often referred to as *the truth in securities law.* It requires that investors receive any significant or financial information about corporations' securities offerings. It prohibits misrepresentations and fraud in the sale of securities. The law also requires issuers to file a registration statement with the Securities and Exchange Commission (SEC) that outlines the securities offering. Each registration statement has a prospectus, which contains information about the securities being offered. The registration statement also contains information about the cost of doing the offering, a description of current business initiatives, and an indemnification of directors and officers.

Securities Exchange Act of 1934 The law that created the Securities and Exchange Commission (SEC) and gives it broad authority over the securities industry. The SEC can register and regulate brokerage firms, transfer agents, clearing agencies, and self-regulatory organizations (SROs) such as the New York Stock Exchange (NYSE), the American Stock Exchange (AMEX), and the National Association of Securities Dealers (NASD), which operates the NASDAQ stock market. The law prohibits certain conduct and gives the commission disciplinary powers over individuals and companies. The SEC also requires publicly traded companies to periodically report financial information if they have more than $10 million in assets or more than 500 shareholders.

Securities Industry Association (SIA) A trade group for broker/dealers. The SIA represents the industry's interests before Congress and the Securities and Exchange Commission (SEC). It keeps statistics on the industry, including profitability data. The association also educates the members about a variety of issues related to securities.

Securities Investor Protection Corp. (SIPC) A nonprofit corporation that insures investors against the failure of brokerage houses. SIPC (pronounced sip-ic) limits coverage to a maximum of $500,000 per account, but only up to $100,000 in cash. It does not insure against market risk.

securitization The process of packaging debt instruments into one group and then issuing new debt securities that are backed by the pool of assets that the debt is issued on. Investors receive the cash flow from the underlying debt. This process redistributes risk among a wider group of investors. A typical securitization is asset-backed securities where the debt issued is backed by the underlying assets.

security A type of investment instrument that represents either an ownership interest in a company or evidence of debt. Stocks, bonds, mutual funds, variable annuities, and investment contracts all are types of securities. A few other types of securities include debentures, futures, puts, calls, warrants, and mineral rights. Insurance policies and fixed annuities typically are not securities. The term *security* is precisely defined in the Securities Act of 1933 and the Securities Exchange Act of 1934, as well as through case law.

security deposit An amount of money that is put forth as a guarantee or protection that property will be protected or a contract fulfilled. For instance, security deposits often are made when renting property. A security deposit also may be made in order to assure that a buyer will fulfill the contract.

security interest A claim on assets or funds taken by a creditor to insure that a loan or debt will be repaid. The security interest may be a portion of a property or asset for which a loan was issued. If the borrower defaults, the pledged security interest is the property of the buyer.

security market line The relationship between systemic risk and the expected return of an investment, depicted graphically. On the horizontal axis are the betas of the companies in the market and on the vertical axis are the required rates of return listed as a percentage. The return on the security market line says that the return on a security is equal to the risk-free rate of return plus the excess return on the market portfolio times the beta of the security.

seed financing The first financing that a start-up company receives from a venture capital firm or from an *angel investor* (a wealthy individual who provides capital to very small start-up companies or entrepreneurs). Usually the amount of funds are under $10 million. Seed financing typically goes to very young companies that have a product under development or an idea that they want to create, but are a long way away from having an actual product to sell and being able to earn revenues in the market. Also called *first round* or *initial financing.*

seed money See *seed financing.*

selective disclosure The practice of a corporation selectively disclosing information to certain Wall Street analysts or favored investors. Selective disclosure was declared illegal in 2000 when the Securities and Exchange Commission (SEC) passed Regulation FD. Selective disclosure used to be a common practice.

self-directed account A retirement account whose owner makes his or her own investment decisions.

self-employed income Income that is earned by an individual who is employed by a variety of individuals or companies that contract with the individual. Self-employment income is reported on Schedule C of the Internal Revenue Service's 1040 form. Self-employed people pay their own Social Security taxes.

self-employment tax A tax that self-employed people have to pay to cover their Social Security taxes. When people are employed, their employer pays half of the Social Security tax; if a person is self-employed, he or she has to pay the entire amount. The self-employment tax is currently around 15 percent, but is usually adjusted every year.

self-regulatory organization A stock exchange such as the New York Stock Exchange (NYSE), the American Stock Exchange (AMEX), and the National Association of Securities Dealers (NASD), which runs the NASDAQ trading system. An SRO has the ability to make its own rules to govern its practices and membership, and can administer fines and other punishments to its members.

seller financing Financing that is extended by a seller to a buyer in order to complete the sales transaction. In real estate seller financing, the seller likely would keep a lien, or legal right, to the property in the event that the buyer discontinues payments. Seller financing also is provided by large corporations such as telecom equipment companies or computer companies, which extend credit to their customers in order to boost sales.

seller's market A market situation in which a scarcity of goods or services available for sale makes competition among buyers fierce. Selling prices are driven upwards and sellers reap strong profits. It contrasts with a *buyer's market,* in which there are many products or services to choose from and prices are driven down, which potentially can depress profits.

seller's points A lump sum that the seller of a house pays to the buyer's lender in order to reduce the cost of the loan to the buyer. The creditor may require the seller to pay some of the points. Also, the seller may do it voluntarily in order to make certain the buyer can purchase the property by reducing some of the closing costs and thus the amount of money that a buyer has to have upfront. One point equals 1 percent of the loan amount. Seller's points typically are paid only if the seller is anxious to sell the house.

selling climax A sudden, sharp price drop on heavy trading activity that is accompanied by a large decrease in open interest. Selling climaxes occur after a long period of declining prices. This term is primarily used in *technical analysis,* which attempts to determine future price movements by looking at price charts.

selling hedge See *short hedge.*

selling on the good news The practice of selling a stock or other investment after good news is received. The thought behind this tactic is that the good news has already been priced into the stock and the next direction of the stock is likely to be lower. Selling on the good news may also tie in with "buy the rumor, sell the fact," which describes the phenomenon of stocks or futures contracts that trade lower soon after the good news that was expected has been received.

selling short against the box Taking a short position in a security even though the trader already owns it. The *box* comes from the safe deposit box where the security is held. A trader may sell short against the box because he or she doesn't want to disclose ownership of the shares or because retrieving the actual shares is too cumbersome. This technique was formerly used to defer a long-term gain into another tax year, but this was curtailed by the Taxpayer Relief Act of 1997.

sell-off A term used to describe a dramatic fall in the stock, bond, futures, or other financial market.

sell-side The sector of the finance industry that comprises broker/dealers, such as Merrill Lynch & Co. and Citigroup/Salomon Smith Barney, that typically sell products such as stocks, bonds, and mutual funds to investors. The sell-side contrasts with the *buy-side,* on which mutual funds and pension funds buy securities in order to create substantial returns for their clients.

sell-side analyst A research analyst who works for a sell-side company, which is a company that makes its money from selling investments such as stocks, bonds, or mutual funds to investors. A sell-side analyst contrasts with a *buy-side analyst,* whose mutual fund or pension fund employer buys investments with the intention of maximizing its returns for its clients.

sell-side trader An employee of a retail or institutional broker and trader who trades stocks on behalf of his or her firm's clients.

Semiconductor Sector Index (SOX) A benchmark index, used to track the fortunes of the semiconductor industry, that was created by and is traded on the Philadelphia Stock Exchange. The SOX is a price-weighted index composed of 17 U.S. companies primarily involved in the design, distribution, manufacture, and sale of semiconductors. The index was set to an initial value of 200 on December 1, 1993 and was split two-for-one on July 24, 1995. Options began trading on September 7, 1994.

senior debt Debt that is first in line to be paid if the borrower defaults and goes into bankruptcy.

senior loan officer opinion survey A quarterly survey of banks' senior loan officers, conducted by the Federal Reserve Board, that measures lending practices of banks throughout the United States. The survey focuses on whether it is harder or easier for companies to obtain credit and distinguishes between large corporations, the middle-market, and small corporations. It also measures whether lending standards for individuals to obtain credit, such as mortgages or credit cards, are tightening or loosening. How easily corporations or individuals can obtain credit has a direct bearing on how vibrant growth is likely to be.

senior refunding Replacing securities that have been issued many years earlier with the objective of reducing the bond issuer's interest costs, assuming interest rates have fallen. Another reason the senior, or older, debt may be refunded is to consolidate several debt issues into one or to extend the maturity dates of its debt in order to lock in favorable interest rates.

senior security See *senior debt.*

sentiment indicators Indicators that focus on sentiment among investors, rather than fundamental factors. A contrarian investor uses these indicators to assess the price expectations of investors. If the majority feels strongly that the prices will rise, contrarian investors will sell on the expectation that most people will be wrong. Sentiment indicators include Market Vane's

Bullish Consensus, Investors Intelligence, Consensus Inc., and the American Association of Individual Investors.

SEP plan See *simplified employee pension plan.*

sequential comparison A comparison of financial results from a period, usually a quarter, with the results from the period immediately before it. For instance, third quarter results would be compared to second quarter results in a sequential comparison. Sequential comparisons contrast with the more typically used quarter-over-quarter comparisons, where the third quarter 2003 results would be compared with the third quarter 2002. Sequential comparisons often are made with companies that are growing rapidly or in times when business conditions are deteriorating rapidly.

serial bonds Bonds that have a series of maturity dates, perhaps as many as 25. Each maturity date is actually its own small bond issue with different coupons, even though it is part of the overall bond issue. Most serial bonds are issued by cities.

Series 3 A securities license that commodities traders are required to hold. The license is issued by the National Association of Securities Dealers (NASD) after the applicant passes the appropriate test. Continuing education requirements must also be met.

Series 6 A general securities license that allows the licensee to sell mutual funds, closed-end funds, and unit investment trusts. The National Association of Securities Dealers (NASD) issues the license after the applicant passes the appropriate test. Continuing education requirements also must be met. This license is much more narrow than the Series 7 license, and thus it is easier to obtain.

Series 63 The states' securities licensing exams. The test for this license is taken after the applicant passes the Series 6 or Series 7 exam. Series 63 tests vary by state.

Series 65 A test, also known as the *Investment Advisor Examination,* that must be passed in order to obtain a general securities license. This test focuses on knowledge of the Securities and Exchange Commission (SEC) rules that financial planners need to know, not on actual financial knowledge. This license is less well-known than Series 6 (mutual funds), Series 7 (general securities), and Series 63 (Blue Sky Law). However, financial planners must be registered with the SEC, so they have all taken the Series 65 exam. The license is issued by the National Association of Securities Dealers (NASD) after the applicant passes the test. There are no continuing education requirements for this license.

Series 7 A general securities license that allows the holder to execute transactions involving stocks, corporate bonds, government bonds, mutual funds, closed-end funds, limited partnerships, and options. A separate license, Series 3, is required to trade commodities. The license is issued by the National Association of Securities Dealers (NASD) after the applicant passes the appropriate test. Continuing education requirements also must be met.

Series EE Bond A savings bond issued by the U.S. government that doesn't mature for 30 years. Its value increases as the interest earned is added to the principal. A savings bond is a contract that represents a loan that an individual makes to the U.S. government. Savings bonds are risk-free because they are backed by the full faith and credit of the U.S. government.

Series HH Bond A savings bond issued by the U.S. government that provides current income for 20 years. That time frame includes a 10-year original maturity period and a 10-year extension. A savings bond is a contract that represents a loan that an individual makes to the U.S. government. Savings bonds are risk-free because they are backed by the full faith and credit of the U.S. government.

service charge A finance charge that is triggered by a specific event. For example, a service charge may be assessed on checks issued by credit card companies that allow the card holder to use them for purchases or to pay off other credit cards. A service charge also may be assessed when an overdraft protection on a credit card is triggered.

Service Corps of Retired Executives (SCORE) A nonprofit association, with 389 chapters throughout the United States and its territories, that is dedicated to helping and educating entrepreneurs. SCORE consists of retired business executives who provide counseling and mentoring to small business owners, working in conjunction with the Small Business Administration.

service mark A word, name, symbol, or device that is used when selling goods to indicate the source of the goods and to distinguish them from the goods of others. A service mark gives protection to the owner of a service, while a *trademark* gives protection to the owner of a product. Occasionally *trademark* is used interchangeably with *service mark*. The value of a service mark must be amortized over its reasonable life, which can't be more than 40 years.

set-aside A federal contract that only small businesses or minority-owned firms may bid on.

settlement The final and unconditional payment for a trading transaction.

settlement price The price established by the futures exchange's settlement committee at the close of each trading session. The settlement price is determined by calculating the weighted average of prices during the closing period, which typically ranges from five to ten minutes. This is the official price used to determine margin requirements and price limits for the next day. It is also used by trading companies to determine net gains or losses. Also called *closing price*.

settlement process A wide-ranging term for the process of completing a trade or a sale. In real estate, settlement is the formal process of transferring the title of the real estate from the seller to the buyer. Also

during the settlement process, a lien is applied against the property for the benefit of the mortgage lender. The real estate settlement process is governed by the Real Estate Settlement Procedures Act of 1974, which requires that the lender thoroughly explain the settlement process. In a brokerage firm, settlement involves matching buyers' and sellers' transactions and transferring the funds and securities to the appropriate party.

settlement risk The risk that one party of a transaction won't be able to fulfill its part of the transaction between the time the agreement is struck and when it is settled.

severally but not jointly A legal term that is typically used in underwriting agreements which obligate individual members of the agreement to purchase a certain percentage of the issue for resale to their clients. However, they aren't responsible for the percentage of the issue that isn't sold by other members of the underwriting group.

severance A payment made by a corporation to an employee who has been laid off. A typical severance package is 2 weeks of pay for each year a person has worked at the company, although severance packages vary substantially from company to company. Severance payments usually are voluntary payments and are not required by law. Some exceptions occur if a union contract guarantees a certain amount of severance or if other requirements are spelled out in a contract. Severance payments may be made in a lump sum or may be paid out in the regular payroll process.

SG&A Short for *selling, general, and administrative expenses,* which often are referred to as *overhead.* These expenses are lumped together on a company's income statement under the expenses heading, with an SG&A sub-heading, or they may be listed individually.

Shad-Johnson Agreement An agreement, formalized by legislation in 1982, reached by the chairmen of the Securities and Exchange Commission (SEC) and the Commodity Futures Trading Corp. (CFTC) to split jurisdiction over options and futures that are traded in the United States. Under the agreement, the CFTC gained regulatory jurisdiction over futures trading while the SEC was given regulatory authority over options trading.

shadow calendar The backlog of initial public offerings (IPOs) that have been filed with the Securities and Exchange Commission (SEC) to obtain its approval. No date has been set for the actual IPO.

shadow stock plan See *phantom stock plan* and *unit stock plan*.

sham

1. A transaction that is designed to trick or defraud investors.

2. A means to avoid taxes fraudulently.

Shanghai Stock Price Index A capitalization-weighted index of stocks on China's Shanghai Stock Exchange. It tracks the daily price movement of all shares on the exchange, including A-shares, which are available only to local investors, and B-shares, which are available only to foreign investors. It began on December 19, 1990, with a base value of 100.

share A unit of ownership in a corporation, mutual fund, or, less commonly, some other type of financial investment.

shark repellent A measure designed to repel an unwanted takeover attempt. A *supermajority provision,* which requires a two-thirds majority instead of a simple majority to approve a takeover, is an example of one tactic. The company also might stagger the terms of the board members in order to make it more difficult for a potential raider to put his or her own slate of contacts in. Shark-repellent tactics might include poison pills and a scorched earth policy. See also *poison pill* and *scorched earth policy.*

Sharpe Portfolio Performance Ratio The value of the average rate of return for a portfolio during a specific time period minus the average rate of return on risk-free assets during the same time, then divided by the standard deviation of the rate of return for the portfolio during the time period. This performance ratio uses the standard deviation of returns as the measure of risk. The Sharpe measure evaluates the portfolio manager on the basis of rate of return and diversification.

shekel The currency unit of Israel, comprising 100 agora.

shelf registration The process of a company registering with the Securities and Exchange Commission (SEC) to sell shares or debt to the public at an undetermined time during the next two years. Shelf registrations are allowed under SEC Rule 415, which was passed initially in March 1982 and approved on a permanent basis in November 1983. A shelf registration gives a company a maximum amount of flexibility to be able to tap the capital markets whenever conditions are most favorable. Shelf registrations have gained in popularity in recent years with diminishing fears that a shelf registration will create an overhang on the market price of a company's stock. *Overhangs* exist when investors are concerned that additional stock shares coming onto the market will depress the price of the shares of stock that they own.

shell corporation A company that has legal status but provides no service or products and has few, if any, assets. Shell companies may be set up for illegal purposes, such as tax evasion, or formed in anticipation of attracting funding. A shell corporation may also come into existence when a company has failed and operations have ceased, but the "shell" of the company remains.

Shenzhen Composite Index An actual market-capitalization weighted index of stocks on China's Shenzhen Stock Exchange that tracks the daily price movement of all the shares on the exchange, including A-shares, which are available only to local investors, and B-shares, which are available only to foreign investors. The index began April 3, 1991, with a base price of 100.

Sherman Act   One of the laws in the United States that contribute to the body of laws that are called *antitrust laws*. The Sherman Act outlaws every contract, combination, or conspiracy that restrains trade. However, since the law was passed, the Supreme Court has said that the Sherman Act prohibits only the contracts or agreements that unreasonably restrain trade. The courts determine what constitutes unreasonable.

shilling   The currency unit of Kenya, Somalia, Tanzania, and Uganda, comprised of 100 cents.

Shiokawa, Masajuro   The Finance Minister of Japan, as of this printing. Shiokawa was Prime Minister Junichiro Koizumi's campaign chief during the 2001 leadership race for the Liberal Democratic Party, which is Japan's ruling party. Shiokawa belongs to the Mori faction within the LDP. He lost his seat in the Lower House election in October 1996 but made a comeback in 2000 at age 78. Shiokawa has served 11 terms in the Japanese Diet. He was chief cabinet secretary under Takeo Fukuda, transport minister under Zenko Suzuki, education minister in the cabinet of Yasuhiro Nakasone, chief cabinet secretary under Sousuke Uno, and home affairs minister under Kiichi Miyazawa.

shogun bond   A bond issued in Japan by nonresident companies using a currency other than the Japanese yen. Also called *geisha bond*.

short   A synonym for sell, in contrast to *long*, in which a security has been purchased. It also may be used as a noun to refer to a trader who has sold financial instruments or contracts and thereby has a short (position).

short covering   A situation in which traders have sold securities that they didn't own, expecting prices to continue falling. When the trend reverses, they must "cover their shorts" by purchasing back what they sold, often at a loss. Because many traders are buying, prices rise, resulting in a short-covering rally.

short hedge   The sale of futures contracts to protect against possible future falling prices. Also called *selling hedge*.

short interest   A measure of the number of short-selling positions on a stock or futures exchange. The number of short interest positions is a barometer for the bearishness of the market. If the number of short interest positions rises, more people are expecting a downturn. The New York Stock Exchange (NYSE) publishes a monthly report on short interest, while futures positions are reported bi-weekly by the Commodity Futures Trading Commission (CFTC).

short seller   An investor who sells a stock, futures contract, or other security without owning it. A short seller makes a significant profit if the price of the security declines and he or she can buy it at a lower cost than what he or she sold it for, and thereby close out his or her position with a profit.

short squeeze   The situation that occurs when an investment's price begins to rise rapidly, and short sellers of that investment (those that have sold stock on the expectation that it will go lower) scramble to purchase it in an attempt to cover their positions and reduce their losses. The increased buying activity of the short sellers leads to higher prices, causing other short sellers to scramble to cover their positions, thus driving prices still higher. These actions also increase the losses incurred by short sellers who have not yet covered their positions. A short squeeze is not exclusive to stock traders, but commonly is seen in the futures market, as well as other markets.

short the basis   Purchasing futures as a hedge against a commitment to sell in the cash markets. It is the opposite of being *long the basis*.

short-sale rule A rule of the Securities and Exchange Commission (SEC) that says that all short sales have to be made in a rising market. In other words, a short sale can occur only if the last transaction was at a higher price than the previous sale (uptick or plus-tick). If the last sale price is unchanged but still higher than the last preceding different transaction (zero-plus tick), then a short sale can still occur. The short-sale rule also is called the *plus-tick rule*.

short-swing stock trade A trade made by corporate insiders who buy or sell a company's stock within a six-month period. Under Securities and Exchange Commission (SEC) rules, a corporation can seize any short-swing profits made by corporate insiders.

short-term debt Debt that will come due within one year. On a balance sheet, short-term debt is separated out from long-term debt, which is debt that matures in one year or longer.

short-term gain A gain on an investment or on the purchase of an asset that occurs within one year from the investment date. Short-term gains are taxed at ordinary income tax rates, making this type of gain less lucrative than gains on investments held for over one year, which are taxed at the lower, capital gains tax rate.

short-term loss A loss that occurs on an investment or on the purchase of an asset that occurs within one year from the investment date.

shrinkage The difference between inventory that a company believes it has on hand and what the actual physical count reveals the company has. Shrinkage may occur due to theft, loss, or damage. Record-keeping errors also can produce shrinkage.

SIC Code See *Standard Industrial Classification Code*.

sideways market A market with prices that are neither steadily climbing nor steadily falling. If the prices are plotted on a price chart, the main movement is sideways.

signature loan A loan for which no assets or collateral are pledged. Signature loans are relatively rare but may be extended if there is a long-standing relationship between the borrower and the bank and if the borrower's credit is excellent.

silent partner A partner in a business or investment who provides capital but does not actively participate in the management of the business or operations. A silent partner may want to remain anonymous for any of a number of reasons.

silver A white-colored, soft, shiny metal typically used in jewelry making as well as in industrial processes, such as photography and electronics manufacturing. Silver also is an investment vehicle and silver futures trade on futures exchanges. In the United States, the primary futures exchange for silver is the New York Mercantile Exchange. One contract equals 5,000 troy ounces and prices are quoted in cents per troy ounce. For example, 526.5 cents per troy ounce translates into a cost of $5.26 per ounce, thereby making one contract wroth $26,300. Silver futures are traded through open outcry on NYMEX. When the regular trading session isn't open, the futures also can be traded on NYMEX's electronic trading system, ACCESS.

Silver has had an important role in the U.S.'s monetary system. In 1792, Congress based the U.S. currency on the silver dollar and fixed, or set, silver's value to gold. Silver was used to make coins until 1965.

Silver is available in different levels of purity. Fine silver is 99.9 percent silver; sterling silver is 92.5 percent silver, with other metals, typically copper, making up the difference, and coin silver is 90 percent silver with 10 percent copper. Nickel silver, despite its name, is an alloy of 65 percent copper with nickel and zinc, and has no silver at all. Mexico, the United States, and Peru are the primary producers of silver.

Silver Bubble An artificially created spike followed by a rapid decline in silver prices in the late 1970s and 1980. The Silver Bubble was created by the Hunt Brothers, Nelson Bunker and William Herbert, who began buying silver in 1973 when it was $1.95 an ounce. The price hit $5 in early 1979, when the Hunt's and their associates had amassed more than 200 million ounces of silver, which was estimated to be as much as half the world's deliverable supply. By early 1980, the prices had peaked at $54 an ounce. Action by the Federal Reserve and a change in trading rules on Comex, the New York futures market where silver traded, stopped the Hunt brothers' trading strategy. By March 1980, the Hunts were unable to meet a margin call on their futures contracts, sparking a panic on commodity and futures exchanges. A consortium of banks gave the Hunts a $1.1 billion line of credit; despite this, the Hunts lost hundreds of millions of dollars from their speculation. In August 1988, they were convicted of conspiring to manipulate the silver market.

silver fixing A method through which the price of silver is set daily on the London Bullion Market. Three market-making members set the price of silver each day at noon. Clients place their orders with the fixing members, who group all orders before telling the other representatives at the fixing where their price interest lies. Then the price of silver is adjusted up or down until demand and supply are balanced. Customers may change their orders during the fixing process and when that happens the fixing member raises a flag to indicate the change. The price can't be fixed while a flag is raised. Many financial instruments are priced off the fixing, including options and cash-settled swaps.

The three market making members are the Bank of Nova Scotia-ScotiaMocatta, which chairs the group; Deutsche Bank AG; and HSBC Bank USA. The silver fixing began in 1897.

simple interest Interest that is paid only on the original principal or on the amount originally borrowed. Interest earned or interest charges are not included in future calculations. Because of this, the amount of interest earned, or owed, in the case of a loan, will be less than with a calculation that uses compound interest. See also *compound interest.*

SIMPLE IRA and SIMPLE 401(k) Retirement plans that employers who have 100 or fewer employees can offer their employees. SIMPLE stands for *Savings Incentive Match Plan for Employees,* and these plans allow employees who received at least $5,000 in compensation from the employer in the preceding calendar year and who meet other requirements to allocate part of their salary to either a SIMPLE IRA or a SIMPLE 401(k) plan. The employer may match the contribution up to three percent of the employee's compensation below $170,000 or up to two percent of an employee's fixed non-elective contributions. Employee contributions are tax-deductible in the year they are made; employer contributions are taxed upon withdrawal.

An employee was allowed to allocate up to $6,500 in 2001. That increased to $7,000 beginning in 2002 and increases by $1,000 each tax year until it reaches $10,000 in 2005. After then, the maximum is adjusted according to cost-of-living increases.

simplified employee pension plan (SEP) A plan that allows a business to make contributions to a retirement plan for employees. A SEP agreement is adopted by the company and contributions are made directly to a traditional individual retirement account (IRA) or a traditional individual retirement annuity (SEP-IRA) set up for each employee. Employers can deduct the amount of contributions made on behalf of employees from their taxes. Sole proprietors can deduct the amount of a contribution on their tax returns. The maximum contribution is $35,000 or 15 percent of a participant's compensation, which generally is limited to $170,000.

sin tax A slang term for taxes on items considered to be harmful, such as cigarettes or liquor.

Sinclair, Upton A socialist who wrote books and wanted to end poverty. In an attempt to garner sympathy for the working class, he wrote *The Jungle,* a novel published in 1906 about conditions in the Chicago stockyards. The book brought him fame and outraged politicians who were appalled by the poor sanitary conditions in the slaughterhouses. The book prompted Congress to pass the Pure Food and Drug Act.

Singapore Exchange (SGX) The SGX began on December 1, 1999 after the merger of two established exchanges, the Stock Exchange of Singapore (SES) and the Singapore International Monetary Exchange (SIMEX). The exchange electronically trades securities on equities and equity options, warrants and covered warrants, bonds, debentures and loan stock, depository receipts, and exchange-traded funds. Also traded are derivatives, through open outcry and electronic methods. Instruments traded are interest rate futures and options on futures, equity index futures and options on futures, and single stock futures.

Singapore Straits Times Index The benchmark index of the Singapore Exchange (SGX). The purpose of the Straits Times Index is to reflect the daily trading activity of stocks on the SGX. On August 31, 1998, the Straits Times Index replaced the Straits Times Industrials Index (STII) and began trading where the STII ended, at 885.26. When stocks were reclassified on the SGX, the industrials category was eliminated.

single stock futures (SSF) An investment product that has characteristics of both securities and futures. SSFs are futures contracts that, for the first time in the United States, permit futures to be traded on single stocks or on narrow indices. Because these are hybrid products, both the Securities and Exchange Commission (SEC) and the Commodity Futures Trading Commission (CFTC) regulate them.

single-premium deferred annuity A tax-deferred annuity purchased by an investor who makes a lump sum payment to the insurance company or mutual fund that sells the annuity. A single-premium annuity is an investment used to fund retirement. If the funds are withdrawn before age 59 1/2, a 10 percent penalty is assessed. The annuity earns interest, while income tax is deferred. The company issuing the annuity promises to pay back the principal on the maturity date as well as make regular interest payments. See also *annuity.*

single-premium life insurance A whole life insurance policy that is paid for in one payment instead of a monthly or yearly payment frequency. One benefit of this type of policy is that the policy will begin accumulating its cash value at a faster rate than will a policy for which payments are made monthly. See also *whole life insurance.*

sinking fund A fund set up to repay a bond when it matures. Regular payments are made into the sinking fund so that when the bond matures, the bond issuer will have the money on hand to redeem the bonds. Depending on the specific terms of a sinking fund, the expected maturity of the bond may change slightly. For example, a sinking fund may require that a percentage of the bond issue be redeemed beginning in a certain year. In that case, the issuer would negotiate individually with bondholders to buy back bonds at an earlier date with the payment of a small premium.

SIPC See *Securities Investor Protection Corp.*

Six Sigma A management philosophy that the Motorola company developed to eliminate errors in their production process. Six Sigma calls for setting very high objectives, collecting data, and analyzing results to reduce errors. The theory behind Six Sigma is that if the number of defects in a process can be measured, a system can be devised to remove them. In order to achieve Six Sigma standards, there can't be more the 3.4 defects per million. The Greek letter sigma can be used to indicate a variation from a standard.

Skilling, Jeffrey K. Enron Corporation's former chief executive, who replaced

Ken Lay after he resigned in early 2001, before resigning himself as the investigation into Enron continued.

SLGS Short for *State and Local Government Series Securities;* securities sold by the U.S. Treasury to state and local governments to allow them to invest their funds in a way that complies with the regulations of the Internal Revenue Service. These securities are purchased only by state and local governments.

Sloan Jr., Alfred P. The creator of the organization chart and the hierarchical management structure that groups similar jobs and puts an executive in charge of each group while working at General Motors. In 1923, he became president of GM, taking over from its founder, William Durant.

small business An independently owned and operated business, whose owner(s) exercises close control over operations and decisions. The equity is not publicly traded and business financing is personally guaranteed by the owner(s). Typically, a small business employs fewer than 100 workers and has revenues of less than $25 million. It also isn't dominant in its field. However, the definition of small business tends to vary. Federal securities law define small business as a company in the United States or Canada that has less than $25 million in annual revenues and whose outstanding publicly-traded stock is worth less than $25 million.

Small Business Investment Company (SBIC) A private investment company that has been licensed by the Small Business Administration (SBA) to provide debt and equity financing to small businesses.

small business issuer A small business that issues stocks or bonds. Federal securities laws define a small business as a company in the U.S. or Canada that had less than $25 million in revenues in the last fiscal year and whose outstanding publicly-held stock is worth no more than $25 million. A company that fits those requirements is a small

business issuer and has its own set of regulatory disclosures and rules to follow when issuing stocks or bonds.

small cap Short for *small capitalization stocks,* which are stocks with a small total market value. Small cap companies are small compared to other public companies. The market value of a small-cap company ranges from $300 million to $1 billion, although that definition can vary widely depending on who is using the term. Companies with a market capitalization under $300 million are called *micro cap* companies.

Small Order Execution System (SOES) An automated trading system used on the NASDAQ stock market for executing trades. The system bypasses brokers by grouping stock orders under 1,000 shares together before executing them, in order to obtain a better price for the investor.

smart money Investors whose decisions about what products or sectors to invest in turn out to be correct. Everyone wants to invest where the smart money is.

Smith, Frederick W. The founder of FedEx, who almost single-handedly created the overnight air-express delivery business. After writing an economics paper as a Yale undergraduate that received a grade of C, in 1973 he decided to start a company called Federal Express, at the age of 28. He started the company with $4 million from an inheritance and $80 million in venture capital funding. Today FedEx is the dominant overnight air delivery service.

Smithsonian Agreement An agreement, announced in December, 1971, that created a new dollar standard whereby the major currencies of the mostly-highly industrialized nations were pegged to the dollar at central rates, with the currencies being allowed to fluctuate by 2.25 percent. The Smithsonian Agreement by the Group of Ten (G-10) nations (Belgium, Canada, France, Germany, Italy, Japan, the Netherlands, Sweden, the United Kingdom, and the United States) raised the price of gold to $38, up from $35, which was the price at which the U.S. government promised to redeem dollars for gold. In effect, the changing gold price devalued the dollar by 7.9 percent.

Several months after the agreement was announced, it began to unravel, as the dollar and some European currencies were hit by traders and speculators. Fifteen months after the Smithsonian Agreement was negotiated, the price of the dollar again was devalued by 10 percent to $42.22 per troy ounce of gold. In March 1973, the G-10 nations announced that they would let their currencies float.

smoothing A process used in pension fund accounting by which unusually high returns in a given year are spread over a multi-year period. The logic behind smoothing is that it lowers the volatility of the profit and loss credit from pension fund returns. During the bull market of the late 1990s, smoothing helped companies boost up their earnings by including gains from pension fund returns.

Snow, John W. As of this printing, the U.S. Treasury Secretary, appointed by President George W. Bush and sworn into office on February 3, 2003. Before his appointment, he was chairman and chief executive officer of transportation company CSX Corporation. His previous governmental experience includes several senior management positions at the Department of Transportation, including the National Highway Traffic Safety Administration.

He also was chairman of the Business Roundtable, a business policy group comprising 250 chief executive officers of the nation's largest companies. He graduated from the University of Toledo in 1962. He received a Ph.D. in economics from the University of Virginia and he received a law degree from George Washington University in 1967. He replaced Bush's first Treasury secretary, Paul O'Neill, who resigned.

Social Security A federal program, created under the Social Security Act of 1935, that is designed to provide some financial support to retirees. The program is paid for from a Social Security tax that is deducted from employees' paychecks as well as from contributions made by employers. The paycheck deductions show up as FICA, which stands for the *Federal Insurance Contributors Act.*

Social Security Disability Income Insurance An insurance program, financed and administered by the Social Security Administration, that makes disability payments to people who can't work because of an injury or illness or to children whose parents have died. The program is paid for from Social Security taxes that are withheld from employees' paychecks.

Social Security payroll tax A tax paid in equal amounts by companies and employees, whose contributions are deducted from their paychecks. Self-employed workers can deduct one-half of their Social Security payment from their taxes. In 2002, the Social Security tax was 12.4 percent of a worker's wages, up to $84,900. The Social Security payroll tax started in 1937 at a rate of 2 percent.

Social Security tax A tax that pays for retirement benefits, disability benefits, and survivor's benefits that are paid to retired workers, disabled people, widows, and orphaned children. Half of this tax is deducted from employees' paychecks, the other half paid by the employer. Self-employed individuals have to pay the entire amount. Typically the tax rate, as well as the amount of wages that are subject to the tax, varies each year. Also referred to as *FICA (Federal Insurance Contribution Act) tax.*

socialism A political system that believes in society as a whole sharing ownership of property and the means of production, rather than allowing private individuals to acquire them. The government is heavily involved in providing for citizens' needs, such as medical care. Socialism contrasts with *capitalism*, which is based on competition and little government involvement. In capitalism, individuals must provide for their own needs.

socially responsible fund A mutual fund that invests only in companies that meet pre-determined ethical or moral standards. For instance, a socially responsible fund may not invest in cigarette manufacturers or companies that sell alcoholic beverages. *Green funds* may invest only in companies that are deemed to be environmentally friendly. Socially responsible funds have become popular during the last decade.

Society for Worldwide Interbank Financial Telecommunications See *SWIFT.*

SOES See *Small Order Execution System.*

soft dollars A form of payment that mutual funds, pension funds, and other institutional customers can use to pay for goods and services such as news subscriptions or research. When an institution gives its business to a brokerage firm, the brokerage firm in return agrees to use some of its commission dollars to pay for trading-related services, such as independent research or subscriptions to news services or publications. The usage of soft dollars has increased in recent years, as many brokerage firms have dropped their opposition to the practice due to strong demand from their clients.

soft landing A term applied to an economy that begins to slow after a long period of strong growth. A soft landing is characterized by only moderate decreases in growth, employment, and consumer and corporate spending as opposed to experiencing a drastic worsening of economic conditions. The term became popular after the U.S. economy began to slow after its rapid growth in the later half of the 1990s. A soft landing, rather than a recession, is the desired outcome after a period of strong economic growth.

soft market A market in which there is little demand and an excess of supply, creating downward pressure on prices. In a financial market, a soft market consists of low volumes and wide differences between the selling price and the purchase price (called the *bid-ask spread*). Also called a *buyer's market.*

softs The commodities markets for coffee, cocoa, sugar, and orange juice.

sol The currency unit of Peru, comprised of 100 centavos.

sold-out market The situation when nearly all of the remaining investors have finally sold their position. Few traders are left to be able to sell anything and the market is said to be "sold out." The term is typically applied to the futures industry.

sole proprietorship A business that is not incorporated but instead is owned by one individual, the *sole proprietor,* who is entitled to all of the profits of the business. Those profits are taxed at the sole proprietor's individual income tax rate. The sole proprietor is personally liable for all debts of the company.

solvency The ability to pay debts, specifically interest payments on debt, when they are due. *Insolvency* is the opposite of solvency.

som The currency unit of Kyrgyzstan, comprised of 100 tyiyn.

Soros, George One of the world's richest men and the president and chairman of his own hedge fund, Soros Fund Management. In December, 2002, he was convicted of insider trading by a French court and fined $2.3 million, which prosecutors said was the amount of his profit. His conviction stemmed from a plan to takeover Société Générale during 1987 when it was being privatized. The court ruled that Soros had access to inside information, though Soros said he would appeal his conviction.

Soros is well known for selling the British pound in the early 1990s when it became clear that it was overvalued. He is also notable for his philanthropy, which includes donating money to various educational and charitable enterprises, many of which are in Eastern Europe.

South Sea Company Bubble Established in 1711 by Harley, Earl of Oxford, the South Sea Company was formed to take on nearly £10 million of the British Government's debt in exchange for a monopoly on trade to the South Seas and £600,000 from the British government each year. Permanent duties upon wines, vinegar, India goods, wrought silks, tobacco, whale-finds and other articles were approved. Rumors abounded about the immense riches of the lands in the South Seas, including the gold and silver mines of Peru and Mexico. Investors lined up to buy shares in the company, which they saw as a path to great wealth. However, the reality failed to live up to expectations, and the company turned to accounting and stock fraud. The company, which had turned into little more than a con game, collapsed as these frauds and other problems were revealed. The perpetrators were tossed into jail; some investors and perpetrators possibly committed suicide, and the bank accounts of directors were confiscated as the government attempted to restore order.

sovereign risk A legal or political risk that an investment in another country will become worthless because of political turmoil that causes the business environment to collapse or prompts another government to take over and seize foreign assets. A lack of a strong and fair judicial system to enforce contracts and the risk that a government might prevent or limit money from being transferred out of the country to the businesses' home country are other examples of sovereign risks. Another type of sovereign risk occurs when a foreign government defaults on debt that it owes to foreign banks or governmental-sponsored agencies such as the International Monetary Fund.

SOX See *Semiconductor Sector Index.*

soy meal See *soybeans.*

soy oil See *soybeans.*

soybeans An agricultural product grown throughout the United States and other countries. Futures and options on soybeans have been traded on the Chicago Board of Trade (CBOT) since 1936. The soybean can be broken down into soy oil and soy meal. Futures and options contracts for these component parts also are traded on the CBOT, as well as other futures exchanges throughout the world. Trading of soy meal contracts began in 1951 while trading on soy oil contracts began in 1950. Monthly crop reports produced by the U.S. Department of Agriculture are closely watched by soybean traders because they give information about expected supply, which will directly affect prices.

Soy meal, the solid part of the bean, is used to create a variety of food products, such as tofu, soy milk, flour, cheese, and soy burgers. Soy oil is low in saturated fats and thus is helpful for reducing heart disease. It is believed that the isoflavones in soybeans may help reduce the chances of contracting certain types of cancer.

SpA An Italian term that is short for *società per azioni,* used to designate a limited share company in Italy.

spam Unsolicited, unwanted junk e-mail that is sent to thousands, or even millions, of people at the same time.

spark spread The difference between the market price of electricity or natural gas and its production costs. To calculate the spread, the heat rate of a generating unit or power system is multiplied by the cost of energy measured in dollars per BTUs (British thermal units). If the spread is small, production may be stopped until more profit is possible. The spread takes into account the market price of power and whether it makes economic sense for power to be produced. It doesn't measure how efficiently the power can be produced.

SPDRs Short for *Standard & Poor's 500 Depositary Receipts.* A SPDR is an investment vehicle that tracks the return of the S&P 500 index or one of its subgroups. A SPDR is an exchange-traded fund (ETF), which essentially is a mutual fund-like instrument that is traded on stock exchanges. SPDRs make it easy for pension funds and other large institutions to gain exposure to the U.S. equity market without having to buy all 500 individual stocks in the S&P 500. They also are targeted at individual investors. SPDRs were introduced by the American Stock Exchange and are among its most popular ETFs. Other ETFs are Diamonds, Ishares, and Quebes (QQQ). See also *Diamonds* and *Quebes*.

special dividend   A dividend that isn't part of a company's regular dividend payment schedule. For example, a special dividend may be made to give investors a higher return because the company did exceedingly well. Those special dividends usually are paid at the end of the company's fiscal year. A company also may pay a special dividend when it spins off one of its businesses into a separate concern.

Special Drawing Rights (SDR)   An international reserve asset that can be used to supplements members' reserve assets such as gold, foreign currencies, and reserves on account with the International Monetary Fund (IMF). SDR was created in 1969 by the IMF. The value of the SDR is based on a basket of four currencies (U.S. dollar, British pound, Japanese yen, and the euro) and can be used to pay dues or kept in accounts with the IMF.

The SDR was created because the world was quickly outgrowing the Bretton Woods fixed exchange rate system, which came under pressure in the 1960s. The fixed exchange rate system was not able to regulate the growth of countries reserves in order to expand world trade. Gold and the U.S. dollar were the two most common reserve tools, but gold production was becoming inadequate and unreliable. The continuing use of the U.S. dollar as a reserve created a constant deficit in the United States, which threatened to undermine the dollar's stability. To alleviate those problems, the SDR was created to be a new international reserve asset that the IMF administers.

However, the SDR is not a currency or a claim on the IMF. Instead, it is a potential claim on the currencies of IMF members. Holders of SDRs can exchange their SDRs

for these currencies, and an SDR's value as a reserve asset comes from the IMF members' commitments to hold and accept SDRs.

Today the role of the SDR is limited, and it makes up only around 1 percent of IMF members' non-gold reserves. The adoption of SDRs by private financial institutions has been limited. It is used primarily in transactions between the IMF and its members.

specialist   A member of a stock exchange whose purpose is to maintain an orderly market in the securities that are assigned to him. To accomplish this task, the specialist may need to buy or sell for his own account when either buyers or sellers are scarce. The specialist also will act as the broker for other brokers. If a broker has an order to buy 100 shares of a stock at $52, but it is trading at $50, then the order is left with the specialist, who will execute it, if it trades up to $52.

specially targeted issue   A debt issue that has interesting twists to entice potential buyers. Companies try to raise funds through specially targeted issues when there already is a large amount of the company's debt outstanding in the market. For instance, a European telecom company with a large amount of debt may target its debt issue to Asian investment funds because those investors only hold a small percentage of the telecom company's debt. The debt issuer and its underwriters will claim that the group suffers from poor allocations in deals that are targeted at institutional investors. Because these investor groups tend to be smaller, they may not receive as large of an allocation as they might want. A specially-targeted issue resolves this problem. However, others in the market may cast doubts on that rationale for a specially-targeted issue.

special-purpose vehicle (SPV)   A subsidiary or an affiliated business that conducts a specific activity that is crucial to the parent's business. The SPV is designed to protect the parent corporation from the accounting, tax, or regulatory consequences of the SPV's activities. Often, SPVs are used for financial transactions, such as keeping debt or risky business ventures away from the parent company. Also called a *special-purpose entity.*

specific gravity   The ratio of the density of a substance at 60 degrees Fahrenheit to the density of water at the same temperature. Often used in conjunction with minerals such as gold.

specifications   The specific terms of a futures contract that is set up by the futures exchange. Specifications include the size of the contract, the grades of the commodity that can be sold, and the settlement and notice dates.

speculative bubble   A rapid but often short-lived run-up in prices that is caused by irrational exuberance, rather than the basic underlying fundamentals of the market. As the speculative bubble increases, more investors are likely to buy, until it appears that "everyone" believes prices will rise further. When the bubble finally bursts, prices fall even faster than they rose, with everyone rushing to sell at the same time, which produces widespread and severe losses. Tulipmania in Europe during the 1630s and the run-up in Internet stocks in the late 1990s are examples of speculative bubbles.

speculative position limit   The maximum long or short position that a futures or options exchange allows a trader to hold. An exemption is made for hedge funds that comply with rules set up by the exchange or the Commodity Futures Trading Commission.

speculative-grade debt   Lower quality debt held by a company, as reflected by its credit rating. A speculative credit rating indicates that the company is less likely to be able to pay back its creditors than a company with an investment-grade rating. Companies rated BB, B, CC, and C are considered speculative by Standard and Poor's. Moody's Investors Service considers companies with Ba1, Ba2, Ba3, B1, B2, B3, and C ratings to be speculative. Ratings at Fitch from BB to D are considered to be speculative.

speculator   A trader who attempts to gain a profit for himself, his fund, or his firm from buying and selling futures and options contracts, in contrast to a broker who executes orders on behalf of someone else. Speculators add liquidity and capital to the futures market.

spinning   The act of allocating shares in hot initial public offerings to corporate executives and their boards of directors to induce them to award future lucrative investment banking work to the bank giving out the shares. The term came into public consciousness after the stock market and the initial public offering markets collapsed in the early 2000s.

Spitzer, Eliot   The Attorney General of the state of New York who began investigating conflicts of interest between Wall Street's research analysts and investment bankers after the stock market began erasing its record gains in 2000. For 18 months, Spitzer subpoenaed Wall Street executives and their records, including e-mail. In December, 2002, he, along with the Securities and Exchange Commission, National Association of Securities Dealers, the New York Stock Exchange, and a group of state securities regulators, reached an agreement with ten of the largest Wall Street firms to settle conflict-of-interest charges. The ten firms were fined a total of $1.435 billion, which was comprised of $900 million in fines, $450 million in independent research initiatives, and $85 million in investor education.

split coupon bond   A bond that acts as a *zero-coupon bond* (a bond which is sold at a deep discount and pays no interest until maturity when the principal is repaid) at the beginning of its term, but which begins paying interest at a specific date. It combines the advantage of appreciation with regular income received later.

split order   A large order that is broken into smaller pieces to be executed one at a time, in order to lessen the effect on pricing.

sponsor   See *general partner.*

spoofing A fraudulent trading practice that occurs when a trader who owns a particular stock places a large buy order through electronic trading systems and then cancels it within seconds. The order causes the market to shoot higher, which makes it appear that there is high demand for the stock. Spoofers exploit the SEC's Limit Order Display Rule, which requires that market makers display the full size of their customer's limit orders and the desired prices. Customers place *limit orders* with brokers in order to specify the acceptable price ranges for buying or selling a stock.

spot commodity A physical commodity that is traded in the cash market, in contrast to the futures market. A spot commodity that is bought or sold likely will be delivered to the counter-party on the other side of the transaction. A spot commodity contrasts with a *futures contract,* with which there is little expectation that the underlying commodity actually will be delivered to the buyer; futures contracts are used for hedging purposes, in order to protect the purchaser against price risk. Futures contracts are usually sold before expiration so the hedger doesn't need to be involved in the transfer or delivery of the underlying contract.

spot market Throughout different securities and commodities markets, a price that is good only at a particular moment in time. In the foreign exchange market, the spot market involves a straightforward transaction in which one currency is directly exchanged for another. A spot market is in contrast to the *futures market* or *forward market,* in which the price refers to a certain time in the future. References to the spot market are often found in the foreign exchange market. The terms *cash market* and spot market are generally interchangeable.

spot rate The price of a foreign currency that is the current rate at which a currency is trading. It reflects what one currency is worth in terms of another currency within two business days from the trade date, which is the normal settlement period for a spot

transaction. In contrast to spot rates, there are *forward rates*, which is what one currency is worth in terms of another at a specified point in the future.

spot trade An agreement to exchange currency immediately. Spot is used as a synonym for cash. Still, the transaction will take several days to settle. The term typically is used in the foreign exchange market.

spousal IRA An *Individual Retirement Account* that can be opened by a non-working spouse who has an annual income of less than $2,000. Couples using a spousal IRA must file their tax return jointly.

spread The difference between a security's purchase price and its selling price. The term is used in many different contexts. For underwriters of bond or stock offerings, the spread is the difference between what underwriters pay for the security and what they sell it for; the spread provides the basic compensation to the underwriters. In futures trading, the spread is called a *bid/ask spread*. It is the difference between what a futures contract can be purchased at and what it can be sold at. The *ask price*, or the price at which something is sold, nearly always will be higher than the bid price. Market makers make their profit on the spread.

SPV See *special-purpose vehicle.*

SRO See *self-regulatory organization.*

SSF See *single stock futures.*

Stability and Growth Pact The agreement that forms the basis for the euro and outlines the monetary policies followed by the European Central Bank (ECB) in managing interest rates for the European Union (EU). The pact requires EU nations to keep deficits below three percent of gross domestic product and to work to balance them. The pact also requires the ECB to give priority to keeping inflation under control over encouraging growth and employment.

stable value fund A mutual fund whose holdings include high-quality bonds, as well as interest-bearing contracts bought from banks and insurance companies. Those contracts have a guarantee, which is called a *wrapper*, that the principal and interest payments will remain steady. The wrapper guarantees that the net asset value will remain stable for a certain amount of time, regardless of market conditions. Stable value funds often are offered as an option on 401(k) retirement plans.

stagflation An economic condition characterized by slow growth, measured by gross domestic product (GDP), with inflation.

staggered board of directors A board of directors whose members have terms that expire at different times. Staggered boards are one tactic used to prevent hostile takeovers, because any potential acquirer would have to wait longer to take control of the board. Staggered boards have become the norm in recent years.

stagnation A period of several years of near zero or negative economic growth, measured in gross domestic product (GDP).

stake An ownership interest that one company acquires in another that represents less than 100 percent ownership. A company takes a stake in another company in order to obtain the rights to a product or territory that will strategically help it. Companies are willing to sell stakes in themselves for a cash infusion or to partner with a larger competitor and thus improve their relative standing in the market. Often, stakes are popular ways to expand overseas and give both companies an opportunity to work together before considering whether a merger would be appropriate. However, just because a company takes a stake in another one doesn't mean that a merger will be the next step.

Standard & Poor's 500 Depositary Receipts See *SPDRs*.

standard deduction The amount of money that individuals or married couples who do not itemize their deductions are allowed to deduct from their income for purposes of calculating income taxes. For 2002, the standard deduction for those under 65 were: single, $4,700; head of household, $6,900; married filing jointly or a qualified widower, $7,850; and married filing separately, $3,925.

standard deviation The degree that a single value in a group of values varies from the mean (average) of the distribution. Standard deviation is a statistical measure that uses past performance of an investment or portfolio to determine the potential range of future performance and assess the probability of that performance. Standard deviations can be calculated for an individual security or for the entire portfolio.

Standard Industrial Classification Code (SIC Code) A statistical classification system that is used to group companies by industry and sub-industry groups. The purpose is to make industry and governmental statistics comparable to each other. The SIC system is in the process of being replaced by a new system, the North American Industry Classification System (NAICS). The new system was developed jointly by the United States, Canada, and Mexico.

standard of living A measurement of how well off a group of people or an individual perceive themselves to be. Standard of living takes into account the quality of housing, medical care, education, transportation, and entertainment opportunities. There is no objective, single measure of standard of living; rather, it is a value judgment made by individuals. However, to inject a degree of objectivity, sometimes annual per capita income figures are used to compare different standards of living.

stand-by arrangement A funding arrangement in which the International Monetary Fund (IMF) agrees to provide emergency funding to one of its member countries. However, in order to obtain the funding, the country has to agree to follow the IMF's economic plan, which may involve promises to lower inflation, decrease budget deficits, and reduce government spending.

standby commitment See *standby underwriting.*

standby underwriting An underwriting agreement in which the underwriter agrees to purchase any unsold shares of a stock offering being made to current shareholders. The underwriter earns a standby fee, as well as other fees. However, the underwriter also assumes risk if investors don't exercise their rights or if the market price of the stock falls during the underwriting period. Often used in conjunction with a rights offering.

standstill agreement An agreement used by a firm that is the target of a takeover to limit, for a certain period of time, the number of shares that the potential acquirer can purchase. Both firms must agree to a standstill, which allows them to work out the details before proceeding with any share purchase.

Stark, Jürgen Vice president of Germany's central bank, the Bundesbank, as of this printing.

start-up A company that has just begun operations. A start-up has the potential to make the owner a significant amount of money but it also can be a risky investment. Venture capital funds typically invest in start-ups. *Angel investors*, wealthy investors who are willing to give a small amount of initial or seed money, also may fund start-ups.

state bank A bank that is organized under state laws, not federal laws. State banks have their deposits guaranteed by the Federal Deposit Insurance Corporation (FDIC), and have the option of joining the Federal Reserve System. If they don't use that option, they still can purchase services from the Fed, such as check processing and clearing. For a consumer, there is little detectable difference between a state-chartered bank and a federally chartered bank.

state municipal bond fund A mutual fund that invests mainly in municipal bonds of a single state and has an average maturity of either more than five years or no stated

average maturity. The funds are exempt from federal and state income taxes for residents of that state. State municipal bond funds also may invest in short-term securities.

state tax-exempt money market fund A money market fund that invests predominately in short-term municipal obligations of a single state. Such investments are exempt from federal and state income taxes for residents of that state.

state unemployment insurance A benefit paid by states to workers who have lost their jobs. Money to pay for state unemployment insurance comes from taxes paid by the employers.

statement of affairs Pleadings that the debtor files with the Bankruptcy Court Clerk that contains information about his or her financial transactions and status.

statement of assets and liabilities A financial statement used by mutual funds that outlines the fund's assets and liabilities. Assets include such items as investments at market value, interest receivable, and prepaid expenses. Liabilities include dividends to shareholders, accrued expenses, investment adviser and administrator fees, and transfer agent and shareholder service fees. The statement of assets and liabilities sometimes includes the fund's *net assets,* which is assets minus liabilities.

statement of cash flows A financial statement that explains why the amount of cash on hand at a company has changed. It outlines the operating, financing, and investment activities that have produced the change in the company's cash level. The report is made quarterly and annually as part of the company's earnings reporting process.

Statement of Changes in Beneficial Ownership See *Form 4.*

statement of changes in net assets A financial statement that shows how a mutual fund's net assets have changed over the past two reporting periods. Adding to net assets are net investment income and net realized gains, which come from operations. Shares sold and reinvested also add to net assets. The items that subtract from net assets include dividends paid and shares redeemed.

statement of operations A financial report prepared by a mutual fund that reveals how a mutual fund's net assets have changed during the reporting period due to the fund's operations. It shows whether the fund made or lost money from dividend payments, interest income, fees, expenses, and investment gains or losses.

statement of retained earnings A financial statement that shows the changes in retained earnings over a set period of time. Retained earnings is one type of financial report that corporations generate. Retained earnings are not paid out as dividends. Instead, they are retained and reinvested in the corporation.

statute of limitations

1. A legal time limit, after which certain types of lawsuits may not be filed.

2. A time limit, after which a government agency may not pursue certain regulatory actions. For example, the Internal Revenue Service (IRS) has three years to audit tax returns and assess back taxes if mistakes are found; however, that statute of limitations doesn't apply in cases of fraud.

statutory voting A shareholder voting method whereby a shareholder must vote for a different candidate for each available seat. It is in contrast to *cumulative voting*, in which a shareholder can place all of his votes for one candidate.

step-lock option See *ladder option*.

stepping in front See *penny jumping*.

step-up notes A note that is callable. The note has one interest rate that is applicable

for a specified period of time. A second, higher interest rate becomes effective after the first period of time ends, and so on.

sterling Another term for the U.K. currency, the British pound. The symbol for sterling is £.

stochastics A tool used in technical analysis that was created by George Lane, who was the president of Investment Educators Inc., in Des Plaines, Illinois. Stochastics, which are used to predict future price movements, are based on the fact that as prices increase, closing prices tend to be closer to the upper end of the price range. However, in downtrends the closing price tends to be near the lower end of the range. To apply the theory, examine the most recent closing prices for the chosen time period, such as five days. *Oscillators,* which are momentum indicators that measure how strong a price movement is, measure on a percentage basis (0 to 100) where the closing price is in relation to the total price range for a certain number of days. If the percentage is over 70, then the closing price is near the top of the range. If the percentage is under 30, it is near the bottom of the range.

stock dividend Giving shareholders additional shares of stock. A stock dividend doesn't involve assets being distributed as a cash dividend does. Total stockholders' equity is not affected by a stock dividend. Instead, a stock dividend transfers equity from the retained-earnings section to the contributed-capital section of the stockholders' equity section on the company's balance sheet. One reason companies do a stock dividend is to give shareholders a financial reward without paying out cash. Also, a stock dividend spares shareholders from paying tax on a dividend.

stock exchange A business that is organized to trade stocks, bonds, or options, along with other financial instruments. Stock exchanges have membership requirements that listed companies must meet in order to have their stock traded on the exchange. Brokers who trade stocks that are listed on the exchange also must meet certain requirements and comply with exchange rules. The New York Stock Exchange (NYSE), NASDAQ, and the American Stock Exchange (AMEX) are examples of stock exchanges.

stock index   An index whose value represents the combined values of an assortment of underlying stocks, which may number from a few dozen stocks to thousands of stocks. A well-known stock index is the Dow Jones Industrial Average (DJIA), which comprises the stocks of 30 large and well-established U.S. companies. There are hundreds of stock indices for the United States and foreign markets. Some of the popular foreign stock indices are France's CAC 40 and the U.K.'s FTSE 100.

Stock indices include a specified number of stocks. A base period is selected and the index is given a value for the period, such as 100. Future movements up and down in the prices of the stocks push the index number up or down. Guidelines for establishing the stock index are selected by the exchange.

stock market crash   A sudden, severe drop in the prices of most stocks traded on a stock market. During the stock market crash of 1929, the Dow Jones Industrial Average (DJIA) fell by 34 percent from its peak in September to the end of 1929. In the crash of 1987, the DJIA fell 31 percent from its peak in August to the end of 1987. A stock market crash may refer to a specific day when prices drop precipitously or to several days or months of substantial losses.

Stock Market Crash of October, 1929   A period of several days over which the Dow Jones Industrial Average (DJIA) fell by 12.82 percent, which was a strong percentage decline for the relatively low level of the DJIA. From its peak in September to the end of 1929, the DJIA fell by about 34 percent. Black Thursday, Oct. 25, 1929, was one of the days the DJIA fell sharply during this period.

Stock Market Crash of October, 1987   A stock market crash that began at the end of the day on Friday, October 16, 1987, when the S&P 500 cash index fell to its lowest level. Investors worried over the weekend and on Monday, October 19, sell orders lined up and flooded the market, sending prices sharply lower for a second day.

stock option plan   An agreement to issue stock to employees according to specific terms. Typically, upper management obtains the bulk of the benefits of stock options. Employees receiving a stock option have to pay income tax on the difference between the value of the stock options on the date they are issued and the market price of the stock.

stock purchase plan   A benefit plan for employees that allows them to purchase shares of the employers' stock, often at a discount. Money to purchase the stock can be withheld from the employee's paycheck. Dividends also may be reinvested. A stock purchase plan differs from an employee's stock ownership plan (ESOP), which is a qualified retirement plan.

stock split   A situation in which a corporation increases the number of its stock shares that are outstanding and reduces the *par,* or stated value, of the stock proportionally. A stock split doesn't alter the value of a shareholder's earnings. A company may do a stock split when it feels that the share price of its stock is getting too high and it wants to lower it. For example, a 2-for-1 stock split of a stock price that is $20 a share gives a shareholder who has 100 shares worth $2,000 a total of 200 shares that are worth $10 a share and still are valued at $2,000.

stock symbol   A unique identifying symbol assigned to publicly traded companies that makes it easy to identify the company on stock tickers and online services. The symbol also prevents confusion when entering trade orders into an electronic trading system. Typically, New York Stock Exchange companies have two- or three-letter symbols and NASDAQ companies have four- or five-letter symbols. The fifth letter typically is added if the company is traded on the over-the-counter market.

stockholders' equity The amount of owners' capital of a corporation. The stockholders' equity section is located on a company's balance sheet. It has two parts: retained earnings, which come from net income, and contributed or paid-in capital. Stockholders' equity is typically the name of the account for public corporations; a sole proprietorship likely uses the term *owner's equity*; and for a partnership, *partners' equity* is used.

stop order An order to trade that is placed with instructions to execute the trade only if a certain price level is reached. For a *sell stop order,* the trade isn't done unless the commodity or stock reaches or falls below a certain price level. A *buy stop order* is triggered if the price reaches or exceeds a certain level. These orders may be in effect for one day, another specified time frame, or in effect until cancelled.

stop–limit order An order to trade to be executed only at or below a certain price. A stop-limit order means that a contract or stock is not sold below a minimum level. In contrast, a *buy-stop order* ensures that the contract or stock is bought at a certain level or lower.

stopped out An investment that has been sold because its price reached a level where the holder had a stop-loss order placed. For instance, if a stock had a stop-loss order to sell at $50, and the price subsequently fell to $50, the position would be sold and the investor would have been stopped out of his stock position.

straddle A trading strategy that involves the simultaneous purchase and sale of options. A long straddle is the simultaneous purchase of a put and a call. A short straddle is the sale of a put and a call. A straddle is used by a speculator who thinks that asset prices will move significantly in one direction or another. However, if an investor expects prices to remain stable, he can sell a straddle.

straight-line depreciation method A depreciation method where the depreciable cost of the asset is spread evenly over the estimated useful life of the asset. The logic for this method of depreciation comes from the assumption that an asset's depreciation is caused by the passage of time. To calculate the amount of depreciation that should be charged against the asset each year, the cost of the asset, minus its salvage value, is divided by the estimated life of the asset. The resulting amount is the amount of depreciation that should be deducted from the value of the asset each year. See also *double-declining balance method of depreciation* and *sum-of-the years' digit depreciation method.*

straight-through processing (STP) Processing trades automatically without requiring people to be involved in the process. The purpose of STP is to create efficiencies, eliminate mistakes, and reduce costs having machines process trades instead of people. As technology has improved, and as financial services companies struggle to reduce costs, the popularity of STPs has increased substantially.

stranded costs Costs incurred by a utility company, such as an electric company, in building new generation plants and increasing capacity, which the company is not able to recoup because of changes in regulations. For example, a power plant may have been built when prices were regulated and the utility was able to accurately predict the amount of money it would earn. However, if the market is deregulated shortly after a plant is built, and competition comes into the market, the rates that the company can charge will fall. As a result, future revenues won't be enough to pay for the plant thereby *stranding* the costs.

strangle A trading strategy that involves the simultaneous purchase and sale of options (called a *straddle*), in which the two parts of the trade do not have a common strike price. A long strangle strategy is used to profit from a volatile price scenario, while a short strangle strategy is used when the investor believes prices will be stable. Typically, short strangles are more popular than long strangles, because the short strangle is used to take advantage of the declining time value of options in markets where asset prices are expected to be constant.

strategic income fund   A mutual fund that invests in a combination of domestic fixed-income securities in order to provide high current income.

strategic partner   A participant in a joint venture or long-term business relationship. Typically, a company that is larger and more established will join forces with a smaller, less established company for their mutual benefit. Although the larger company may have strong name recognition, more distribution power, or more financial resources, the smaller company may have a new product or technology that will benefit the larger company. Strategic partners have an agreement with a narrow purpose, however they don't get involved in either other's overall business.

Strategic Petroleum Reserve (SPR)   An emergency supply of oil that can be borrowed against in the event that oil supplies are disrupted due to a war, a strike in oil producing countries, or restrictions in production by an oil cartel. SPR is administered by the U.S. Department of Energy and was begun after oil prices rose sharply in 1973–1974 driving up the price of oil and its derivatives, such as gasoline. The rise in energy prices caused inflation and helped to weaken the U.S. economy. In December 2002, the SPR had a 598-million-barrel reserve.

street name   Securities that are held by a brokerage firm on behalf of a customer; the securities are *in the name* of the brokerage firm. Securities held by a brokerage firm are easier to sell, because they can be transferred to another broker without having to deliver the physical certificates that list the customer's name.

stress testing   A scenario-forecasting technique applied to a portfolio or asset that evaluates how the portfolio would respond if different adverse market conditions occurred. Stress testing is one of the techniques done in risk management to evaluate how badly the owner of the portfolio might be affected if certain unexpected events occurred.

strike price   The price at which an option can be exercised. Also referred to as *exercise price.*

STRIPS   Stands for *Separate Trading of Registered Interest and Principal of Securities,* which lets investors hold or trade the interest and principal components of Treasury notes and bonds separately. The program was first introduced in January 1985.

STRIPS often are used by state lotteries, which invest the present value of large lottery prizes in Treasury notes or bonds in order to ensure that funds are available to meet payment obligations. STRIPS are popular for tax-advantage plans such as individual retirement accounts and 401(k) savings plans. Pension funds may buy STRIPS in order to match the income from them to their liabilities.

For example, with a ten-year note that is STRIPPED, the principal payment becomes a separate zero-coupon security that will be paid when it matures in ten years. Then, the 20 interest payments that are made semiannually remain and the principal and the interest become separately traded securities.

strong dollar   A situation in which the U.S. dollar can be exchanged for a relatively large amount of another currency. A strong dollar makes exports relatively expensive because foreign purchasers have to pay more, in their currency, for the goods. Imports are relatively inexpensive because the dollar can purchase a relatively high amount of a foreign currency in order to pay for the goods. A strong dollar occurs when people want to invest in the United States because the financial markets are seen as favorable and providing good returns.

A strong dollar contrasts with a *weak dollar,* which is characterized by a reluctance to invest in the United States and creates a situation where exports are relatively cheap and imports are expensive.

strong dollar policy A policy of the U.S. Treasury that seeks to avoid a weakly valued dollar compared with other currencies. A strong dollar makes the price of U.S. exports more expensive overseas and hurts the profits of corporations that sell to a lot of foreign markets, such as car manufacturers. Even though the strong dollar policy was articulated, it didn't involve intervention in the foreign exchange market to buy dollars and drive the price up. The strong dollar policy was first articulated by U.S. Treasury Secretary Robert Rubin during the latter half of the 1990s, under President Bill Clinton. As of this printing, the administration of George W. Bush appeared to be backing away from the strong dollar policy.

structural unemployment Unemployment that persists even when economic growth is strong. People who have been welfare recipients for a long time or who have limited education or language skills account for much of structural unemployment.

structured note A bond that includes an embedded derivative (a futures contract or feature) that is designed to create a payoff that fits the requirements of a specific investor. A note may be structured to pay interest to the noteholder in the event that gold prices fall or some other situation occurs. A structured note also might involve a series of swap agreements in which one note is exchanged for another after a certain period of time or when a particular circumstance occurs.

subcontract A contract between the primary contractor and a subcontractor for the subcontractor to do some of the contractor's work or provide supplies.

subordinate bond A bond whose claim on income and assets of the issuer in the event of default or if the issuer files for bankruptcy is ranked below the claims of other bondholders. A subordinate bond is paid after other bonds are paid off in the event of a default. Also called *subordinate debenture.*

subordinate debenture See *subordinate bond.*

subordinated Refers to debt a company will pay after other higher-ranking debt in the event that the company files for bankruptcy. Subordinated debt is debt ranked lower than other debt.

sub-prime lender A bank or financial institution that specializes in issuing loans to individuals or businesses with poor credit ratings. Typically those people receiving sub-prime loans are required to pay higher interest rates than those paid by people with good credit ratings.

subrogation A legal process in which an insurance company pays for a loss and then seeks to recover the money from another party who is legally responsible. The responsible party may be the person who caused the damage or that person's insurance company. The person who is owed the money assigns his or her rights to insurance benefits to the insurance company that has paid the claim.

subsidiary A company that is owned by another larger company. A subsidiary is controlled by its parent company.

sugar A popular agricultural product that is derived from sugar cane. Futures and options on sugar are traded on the Coffee, Cocoa, and Sugar Exchange (CSCE), which became a subsidiary of the New York Board of Trade in 1998. To meet delivery terms of the contract, U.S. cane sugars and other foreign-produced sugars can be transmitted.

suitability rules Rules that must be followed by financial advisors when selling investments to the public, which say that brokers have to make certain that the investments they sell are suitable to the buyer. For instance, an 80-year old retiree shouldn't be sold a risky stock; Treasury securities would be more suitable for this person. If suitability rules are not followed and the investment loses money, then the broker and his firm may be liable to the investor for damages.

Sullivan, Scott The former chief financial officer of WorldCom Inc., whose accounting machinations plunged the company into bankruptcy and resulted in his being indicted, in April 2003, on federal charges of defrauding banks out of billions of dollars that were given as loans. He was accused of lying to the banks when he attested to the accuracy of financial statements that the government has alleged were fraudulent.

sum-of-the-parts valuation A calculation showing whether the value of a company would be increased if it were split into separate business units and shares of stocks of the separate units were sold to the public. Conglomerates that buy diverse businesses may decide that the best strategy is to spin-off the separate units because the sum-of-the parts valuation shows that the overall value to the shareholder is increased by spinning off separate units.

sum-of-the-years' digits depreciation method An accelerated depreciation schedule that totals up the digits for the years of the useful life. An asset with four years of life would be added up to produce 10 (4 + 3 + 2 + 1 = 10). A depreciation schedule follows for a $10,000 asset, assuming no resale value.

	Per year	Cumulative
Year 1	$ 4,000	$ 4,000
Year 2	$ 3,000	$ 7,000
Year 3	$ 2,000	$ 9,000
Year 4	$ 1,000	$10,000
	$10,000	

sunk costs Costs that have been incurred in a project or investment that can't be recovered if the project is stopped or altered. For example, sunk costs occur in drilling for new oil reserves. If no oil reserves are found, the amount of money that has been spent to put people and equipment in place can't be recovered, so the costs are *sunk*.

sunset law A law that is passed with a specified date upon which it will expire. Sunset laws are favored by people who disapprove of government intervention and regulation and believe it is a good idea to periodically review whether laws and regulations are still needed. Sunset provisions gained in popularity in the 1970s and 1980s.

sunshine law Laws that require meetings of legislative bodies or regulatory agencies to be open to the public and thus allow "the sunshine to come in." These laws were passed at the state and federal level after Watergate, in order to prevent similar abuses of power.

Super Bowl indicator A theory that if a team from the pre-1970 American Football League wins the Super Bowl, the stock market will decline during the coming year, and that if a team from the pre-merger National Football League wins the Super Bowl, the stock market will be higher by the end of the year. The prominence of the Super Bowl Indicator has declined in recent years as expansion teams that didn't exist during those periods become more prominent.

SuperDOT See *Designated Order Turnaround System*.

SuperMontage System An automated trading system introduced October 14, 2002, by the NASDAQ stock market to make automated trading easier and more transparent. Traders are able to view more orders on their screen, instead of just a "best price" quote. The SuperMontage system processes quotes and orders through one computer system, which adds speed and efficiency to the trading process.

supervisory analyst A financial analyst who has passed a New York Stock Exchange exam that qualifies him or her to supervise other analysts. A supervisory analyst must approve research reports and notes before they are distributed to the firm's clients or the public.

supply chain All of the vendors who sell components that are needed to create a finished good that can be sold to customers. A complicated product with many components has a large supply chain. Research departments of brokerage firms conduct surveys of supply chains, especially in the technology area, because each component of the supply chain is critical to the prospects of the company that uses the supply chain.

supply shock A sharp price reaction, often upward, caused by an event that forewarns that a much smaller quantity of product or goods will be available in the future. The market's perception of supply, rather than actual supply levels, is the crucial element in determining supply shocks. For example, the energy industry experienced supply shock in 1990 when Iraq invaded Kuwait. Traders predicted that the supply of crude oil from Iraq would be impacted by the turmoil and by the anticipated invasion of Kuwait by the United States. Oil prices more than doubled during the following several months. However, those price increases were soon erased in future months when it became apparent that the war would be short-lived and would not disrupt prices. The opposite is *demand shock,* which is a surprise development that impacts buyers' decisions to purchase goods.

supply-side economics A theory that holds that reducing taxes is the key to stimulating the economy, especially taxes for businesses and wealthy individuals. As people have more money to spend, they will make investments that benefit everyone. Savings also can be expected to rise. Supply-side economics was popularized in the early 1980s by President Ronald Reagan and often is referred to as *Reaganomics.* See also *trickle down economics.*

support A technical analysis term that indicates a level that prices will have difficulty moving below. Support is said to help stop prices from declining.

surety bond A bond issued by a company on behalf of a person that guarantees the person will fulfill an obligation to a third party. If the person does not perform those duties, the third party is reimbursed through the bond for losses it suffers. Surety bonds may be used in cases where employees manage money or perform some other sensitive duties.

survivorship bias A situation in which failed companies are excluded from performance studies because they no longer exist. The results of a research study that uses survivorship bias may be skewed because only companies that were successful enough to survive are included in the study. In particular, this bias may occur with mutual fund performance if a poorly performing fund is combined into another fund in the same group.

suspended trading A halt in trading of a stock or security to correct a major imbalance between sell and buy orders. The imbalance may result from a major news announcement, such as a report that a company's earnings will be worse than expected or that a merger announcement is expected. The exchange decides when to halt trading, although the company can request that trading be halted.

sustainable development An economic development theory that calls for raising living standards without destroying the earth's ecosystems or causing environmental problems such as climate changes, water scarcity, or species extinction. Some say sustainable development means that the rich will have to reduce their standard of living in order to share more with poor people; others argue that is not the case.

swap A custom-made and negotiated transaction designed to manage financial risk over a period of 1 to 12 years. Two individuals can create a swap, or a swap may be made through a third party such as a brokerage firm or a bank. Swaps are used to manage risk and often settlements occur in cash, not in delivery of the actual product or financial instruments. Examples of swap transactions include currency swaps, interest rate swaps, and price swaps for a variety of commodities. An example of a currency swap is an agreement to sell $1 million of Japanese yen three months in the future at ¥116.50.

swap curve A yield curve that is created to show the interest rates that are charged at various maturities for swap agreements. A swap curve is based on the zero-coupon yield curve. See also *yield curve* and *swap.*

swap spread A measure of the risk premium for an interest rate swap. The swap spread is calculated as the difference between the swap agreement's fixed interest rate and the yield earned on a Treasury bond with the same maturity.

swaption Common slang for *swap options.* A swaption is an over-the-counter option on an *interest rate swap,* which allows one party to swap an interest-paying investment at a certain price and time in the future with another party. Just as in the case of ordinary options, this contract gives the holder the right, but not the obligation, to enter into an interest rate or currency swap on prearranged terms.

SWIFT Stands for the *Society for Worldwide Interbank Financial Telecommunications,* a bank-owned network for processing securities trades and transferring international messages. Corporations have limited access to the system through their banks.

Swiss franc The currency of Switzerland, which is known as a safe haven for investors. Switzerland is a politically neutral country that has not adopted the euro. If political or financial turmoil affects the United States or Europe, traders and investors often sell the U.S. dollar or euro and buy Swiss francs. Its trading symbol is CHF. Liechtenstein also uses the Swiss franc.

Swiss Market Index A capitalization-weighted index of the largest and most frequently traded stock of Swiss companies on the Swiss stock market. It was developed with a base value of 1,500 as of June 30, 1988.

Swissy Market jargon used in the foreign exchange market to refer to the Swiss franc. The Swiss franc is perceived to be a safe currency because of Switzerland's neutrality in foreign affairs as well as monetary affairs. Switzerland is one of the few European countries that has not adopted the euro. In times of economic or political turmoil, the Swiss franc rises as investors shift funds into Swiss francs.

switching The act of liquidating an existing futures or options position while simultaneously buying another position in the same futures or options contract that has a different expiration month.

SWOT analysis The analysis of a firm's *strengths, weaknesses, opportunities, and threats.* A SWOT analysis helps evaluate how a company will perform in a competitive environment.

syndicate manager A bank that works with a company to bring a new stock or debt issue to market and files the necessary paperwork with the Securities and Exchange

Commission. The manager also creates a group of other banks that will take some of the new issue in order to spread the risk.

syndicated loans   Corporate loans that are purchased or traded by a group, or syndicate, of institutional investors or banks from the corporate debt issuer. Because these loans can total billions of dollars, each bank or institutional investor agrees to purchase only a portion of the loan amount in order to limit its risk that it might not be able to resell the loan. If the debt issuer later defaults, the bank's risk of loss increases significantly.

synergy   The positive gain associated with the benefits of a merger or acquisition. Synergies may be either in the form of selling opportunities (because greater product offerings are available) or in the form of costs savings.

synthetic call   The purchase of an underlying security while a put option is simultaneously purchased on that security. If the investor thinks that the price of the underlying security will rise but still wants insurance against it moving lower, then a synthetic call is one way to accomplish that goal. The investor has effectively purchased a call option on the security that also includes income-related benefits such as dividends or interest that come from owning the underlying securities. The higher the put's strike price is, the greater the insurance that is provided.

synthetic futures   A trading position created by combining two option positions so that the payoff is the nearly the same as what would be achieved by purchasing the outright futures. The options have the effect of creating what resembles a futures position.

synthetic put   The selling short of an underlying security while a call option is simultaneously purchased on that security. The investor does this if he believes that the underlying security will fall in value but wants some insurance in case this doesn't happen. The investor effectively has purchased a put option on the underlying security. Thus, the investor is protected against unlimited loss on the short position by owning the call option. The most that an investor can lose by employing this strategy is the difference between the sale price of the underlying security and the strike price on the call option, plus the cost to buy the call option.

systematic risk   A widespread risk that can't be avoided by diversifying investments. Examples of systematic risk are wars, rising inflation, and turbulent political events. Some effects of systematic risk can be minimized through asset allocation techniques and diversification because different portions of the market tend to underperform at different times. Also called *market risk*.

T+1 Refers to the settlement date after the purchase of a security; T+1 is the trade date plus one day. The securities industry has a goal to reach T+1 by 2004. T+0, T+2, and T+3 are other common references.

T+3 Three days after a security has been purchased and the trade settles. Thus T+3 is the trade date plus 3 days and is the typical time it takes for both parties to receive their respective money or securities. The securities industry has a goal to reach T+1 (trade date plus 1 day) by 2004. T+0 indicates settlement at the end of the day.

Taft–Hartley Act A law passed in 1947 that tilted the balance of power a little more toward business and away from unions following the pro-union laws passed in the first half of the 1900s. The legislation authorized the U.S. president to obtain an injunction to postpone a strike if it would hurt the economic interests of the country. This right has been invoked or threatened in recent years for strikes against airlines. The legislation also gives states the right to enact *right-to-work laws,* which prohibit unions from requiring union membership as a condition of employment. The law also contains disclosure requirements to regulate union business dealings and to discover fraud and racketeering and places a variety of other restrictions on unions.

tail

1. In Treasury auctions, the difference between the lowest competitive bid that was accepted and the average bid by all of those offering to buy the particular Treasury security.

2. In the insurance industry, the time between when premiums are received and benefits need to be paid. For example, a *reinsurance company,* which provides coverage to other insurance companies, has a long tail because their coverage is called on only if the insurance company incurred certain amounts of losses.

Taiwan Weighted Index A capitalization-weighted index of all of the common shares listed on the Taiwan Stock Exchange. The index's base is 1966.

taka The currency unit of Bangladesh, comprised of 100 poisha.

take-down Discount from the offering price that is given to a member of an underwriting group that is selling the securities.

take-or-pay contracts A contract whereby one or more purchasers agree to accept the products produced from the project at a fixed or predictable price. Many project financings are based on long-term, take-or-pay contracts. If the purchaser's credit is sufficient and the project goes well, there is a market for the produce and cash flow occurs. However, competition, changes in technology, or changes in demand might decrease the value of the take-or-pay contracts.

Take-or-pay contracts in the utility industry often are used in conjunction with bonds to finance new facilities. A take-or-pay contract says the purchaser of the power will take it from the bond issuer. If construction isn't completed, the bond issuer will pay back bondholders their investment. The best known instance of utility take-or-pay contract was the contract signed by the Washington Public Power Supply System (WPPSS) to build nuclear plants. The Washington State Supreme Court voided the take-or-pay contracts that many utilities had signed to support the construction. That caused WPPSS to default on some of its bonds.

takeover The acquisition of one company by another, either through friendly or unfriendly means. If the attempt is unfriendly, then the takeover candidate may attempt to mount a defense against the takeover attempt, such as seeking the help of a *white knight,* who is a preferable acquirer to the original acquirer.

tala The currency unit of Western Samoa, comprised of 100 sene.

talking one's book A statement made by a trader or hedge fund manager expressing his or her opinion that a stock or other investment is a good buy. The statement is made without expressly stating that the trader him- or herself owns the stock and stands to profit if the stock price goes up. *Book* is another term for a trader's portfolio of investments.

TAN See *tax anticipation note.*

tangible asset An asset that can be seen and has a physical existence, such as machinery or inventory. An *intangible asset,* on the other hand, is one that doesn't have a physical presence, such as a trademark, copyright, license, or lease.

tankan A survey of business sentiment in Japan conducted by the Bank of Japan. The survey is done quarterly, and its results often influence bond, foreign exchange, and stock market trading activity. Japan is the world's second largest economy and traders evaluate economic conditions in Japan when deciding whether to buy the Japanese yen or to buy Japanese equities or bonds.

target company A company that another company is attempting to take over, in either a hostile or friendly transaction. Once the acquiring company has acquired five percent of the outstanding shares of the company, the acquiring company must report this fact to the Securities and Exchange Commission on a 13D schedule.

tariff

1. A federal tax on exports and imports. Tariffs are imposed to protect domestic markets and give an advantage to domestic producers, or for their financial benefit. Money collected from a tariff is called a *duty.*

2. A list of prices for different types of services, such as moving or shipping services.

tax abatement A temporary suspension of property taxation, generally for a specific period of time. Governments use abatements as an economic development tool. For example, a tax abatement may be given to a developer or building owner who builds or makes improvements to buildings in certain areas. Abatements also may be used to encourage companies to locate in a specific area, or offered as an incentive to stop businesses from moving out of a specific area. Abatements up to 100 percent are offered by governments to certain companies for a limited time.

tax anticipation note (TAN) A note that is a short-term obligation of a state or municipal government that is issued to pay for expenditures until expected tax or other payments are received.

tax audit An audit that is conducted by the Internal Revenue Service (IRS) or a state tax authority. An audit may be done randomly, or may be undertaken because the tax authority believes that there is a problem with the taxpayer's return. If an audit finds an error or a misstatement on the tax return, the taxpayer may have to pay back taxes as well as interest and penalties. Taxpayers can appeal any judgments by the IRS through the IRS's appeals process and the U.S. Tax Court.

tax avoidance Legally lessening the amount of taxes that a person pays. Tax avoidance strategies include making charitable deductions, investing in tax-exempt municipal bonds, and making a variety of retirement-related investments such as contributions to Individual Retirement Accounts (within income limits), salary reduction plans, or 401(k) plans. Using illegal methods to avoid paying taxes is called *tax evasion.*

tax base The total area, including all property, assets, and income that can be taxed by a city or state. If population growth slows in one city or suburb and shifts to another area, the tax bases of the different areas also change. The area people are leaving will see its tax base shrink. The newly popular area will see its tax base grow. If businesses leave an area that also shrinks the tax base.

tax credit A credit against tax owed. Tax credits are subtracted from the tax owed, unlike *tax deductions,* which are subtracted from taxable income. Tax credits allow the government to encourage certain behaviors. Examples of tax credits are those that are allowed for people with disabilities, child care expenses, and the costs of adopting a child.

tax deductible Refers to an expense that can be deducted from income on which a person pays taxes. Individuals can deduct expenses such as mortgage interest payments and charitable contributions. Medical expenses can be deducted if they exceed 7.5 percent of the taxpayer's adjusted gross income for the year. Contributions to Individual Retirement Accounts can be deducted from taxes by people earning below a certain amount of money. Businesses can deduct virtually all of their operating expenses from the income that they earned in order to reduce their tax bill. Tax deductions reduce taxes owed only by the amount of the taxpayer's tax bracket. For example, a taxpayer in the 28 percent bracket could receive a 28 cent benefit for each $1 of a tax deduction.

tax deduction An expense deducted against taxable income that reduces tax liability. Deducting expenses from income reduces taxable income, and thus decreases the amount of tax owed. Tax deductions allow the government to encourage certain behaviors.

tax deferral The postponement of tax payments from the current year into the next year or future years. The Internal Revenue Service (IRS) allows tax deferral under the terms of retirement accounts such as 401(k)s and Individual Retirement Accounts (IRAs).

tax deferred A situation in which taxes will have to be paid at some point in the future, but they are not paid now. An example of a tax-deferred investment is an Individual Retirement Account (IRA), whose earnings accumulate tax free. When the funds are withdrawn after the IRA owner reaches age 59½, taxes have to be paid on the withdrawn funds.

tax evasion Illegally evading paying taxes. Tax evasion differs from *tax avoidance,* which is the legal avoidance of taxes. By evading taxes, taxpayers may hide income or overstate deductions or expenses. Tax evaders risk significant fines, the payment of back taxes, and potential criminal penalties, which can include jail time.

tax haven A country that imposes little or no income taxes. Because of this, businesses in high tax countries find that operating in a tax haven saves a significant amount of money. The Cayman Islands and Bermuda are two countries that are tax havens. Generally businesses operating in tax havens also enjoy a great deal of privacy.

tax liability A bill that is owed to a government for taxes. The taxes may be income, property, or a variety of other taxes. If tax liabilities are not paid, a lien can be placed on the assets until payment is received.

tax lien A lien that is placed on assets, such as real property, that prevent its sale until a tax bill is paid.

tax refund The amount of money that has been overpaid to the U.S. government and is returned to a taxpayer. The taxpayer's Form 1040 indicates the amount, if any, of tax refund that is due. After the tax return is filed, the Internal Revenue Services issues a check or an electronic payment to the taxpayer for the amount of overpayment.

tax schedules Tax forms that are used in addition to Form 1040 in order to complete a tax return. There are dozens of tax schedules, however the more well-known forms include: Schedule A, which reports itemized deductions such as medical expenses, mortgage interest, and charitable contributions, Schedule B, which reports dividend and interest income, Schedule C, which reports business expenses, and Schedule D, which reports capital gains and losses.

tax shelter An investment or accounting technique that is designed to minimize the amount of tax that must be paid on income or profits. Although tax shelters typically start out as legal techniques, the Internal Revenue Service may investigate a shelter and argue that it is in fact breaking the tax laws. Thus, tax shelters often operate in a gray area and eventually may be declared illegal.

taxable money market government fund A mutual fund that invests primarily in short-term U.S. Treasury debt and other short-term financial instruments that are issued or guaranteed by the U.S. government or its agencies.

taxable money market non-government fund A fund that invests in a variety of money market instruments, including certificates of deposit of large banks, commercial paper, and banker's acceptances.

tax-equivalent yield The pre-tax yield that a taxable bond would have to pay in order to produce the same yield as a tax-exempt investment, such as a municipal bond. To calculate the tax-equivalent yield, first subtract the income tax rate from 100, then divide the result by the yield of the tax-exempt investment, and multiply by 100. For example, if the tax rate is 28 percent and a tax-free bond pays 8 percent, then $100 - 28 = 72; 72/8 = .111; .111(100) = 11.1$ percent. Under these circumstances, a taxable bond has to pay 11.1 percent in order to earn as much as the tax-free investment.

tax-exempt security An investment that is not subject to tax at the federal, state, or local level. Typically, the only tax-exempt security is a municipal bond, which is offered by a local government to fund municipal needs. Mutual funds may be tax-exempt if they invest in tax-exempt securities.

Taylor Rule An economic rule that outlines a method to set interest rates. The rule is named for John B. Taylor, an economist who was named by President George W. Bush to be an under secretary for international affairs in the U.S. Treasury Department. Previously, Taylor was an economist at Stanford University.

Taylor designed the rule in 1993 after observing how the Federal Reserve Open Market Committee actually set interest rates. Taylor's rule aims to provide guidelines for a central bank, such as the Federal Reserve, to set short-term interest rates during changing economic conditions in order to achieve both short-term goals for stabilizing the economy and the long-term goal of managing inflation. According to Taylor, the *real short-term interest rate,* which is the interest rate adjusted for inflation, should be determined by three factors: where actual inflation is relative to the targeted level that the Federal Reserve wishes to achieve; how far economic activity is above or below its full-employment level; and the short-term interest rate consistent with full employment. Taylor deduced his rule in 1993. If inflation is above its target, or if employment is above full employment and interest rates are relatively low, relatively high interest rates are justified. However, if the goals are in conflict, such as when the economy is below full employment and inflation is above its target, the rule provides guidance to policy makers on balancing the competing considerations.

Taylor, Frederick W. The creator of scientific management theories that use time-and-motion studies to increase efficiency. His study about how much time it took a laborer to shovel coal saved Bethlehem Steel Corporation millions of dollars in material-handling costs in the 1890s. He was pushed into the national limelight when attorney Louis Brandeis used Taylor's scientific management theories in a highly publicized lawsuit that kept railroads from increasing freight rates. Taylor described his theories in his book, *The Principles of Scientific Management*.

T-bills See *Treasury bills*.

TDMA Stands for *time-division multiple access*, which is a technology used in wireless communication. It divides each cellular channel into three time slots, thereby increasing the amount of data that can be carried.

technical analysis A method of forecasting market movements in the commodities, equities, or futures markets that analyzes price movement, trading volume, open interest, and other numerical and chart-based data. Technical analysis doesn't consider fundamental factors such as supply and demand.

technical rally An upward price movement based on the continuation of a price pattern. Or, in a case in which price has reached a certain low level, an upward movement in price indicates a technical rally. When the market moves up for no explainable reason, traders sometimes call it a technical rally or say that the market is "technically strong."

technical trader A trader who places trades based on the technical analysis of price charts. Technical traders analyze price charts to develop theories about what direction the market is likely to move. Some chart patterns that traders try to identify include head and shoulders, triangles, and price gaps. A technical trader ignores fundamental factors such as the change in supply and demand. Technical traders typically trade with the trend, not against it. In contrast, fundamental traders often trade against the market in a contrarian trading style.

technology bubble See *Internet bubble*.

TED spread The difference between the rate for Treasury bills and the rate for Eurodollar bills. The acronym stands for *Treasuries/Eurodollar spread*. The TED spread is created by taking simultaneous but opposite positions in both Eurodollar and T-bill futures contracts that have the same maturity. Traders create this spread to bet on the general direction of interest rates. The difference in price is an indicator of credit risk. If the TED spread increases, it indicates increasing credit risk, and if it decreases, it indicates falling credit risk.

Telecommunications Act of 1996 A significant piece of legislation that created the current U.S. telecom market. This legislation was the first major regulatory revision to the industry in 62 years. It was signed by President Bill Clinton on February 1996. In addition to its significant changes to the telecom industry, it deregulated the rates that cable service providers can charge and created more competition among Internet service providers. The act allowed small companies to begin to compete against the former regional Bell operating companies. The former Bells also were allowed to begin selling long distance service, but only after they proved that they had sufficiently opened up their infrastructure to competitors.

tenancy at will A situation in which a person occupies real estate with the permission of the owner for an unspecified term. Tenancy at will could occur through a verbal lease or during the time a lease is being negotiated. The laws governing landlords and tenants apply in this circumstances.

tenancy by the entirety A form of property co-ownership in which ownership passes at the death of one co-owner to the surviving co-owner. Tenancy by the entirety is similar to joint tenancy with right of survivorship. However, tenancy by ownership interests are limited to ownership by two persons who are married when the property is acquired. If the couple divorces, then the ownership automatically changes to tenancy in common.

tenancy in common A property ownership situation in which real or personal property is owned by two or more people. If one person dies, the property becomes part of the deceased co-owner's estate. The ownership of the property doesn't transfer to the surviving owner. Tenancy in common owners don't need to be married to each other. This differs from joint tenancy ownership, which confers ownership to the surviving co-owners.

tender offer An offer to purchase shares in a company with the objective of taking over the company. A tender offer is made whether the deal is friendly or hostile. The tender offer outlines the purchase price for the shares and states whether cash or shares of the acquiring company are being offered. A tender offer also includes other relevant details.

tenge The currency unit of Kazakhstan, comprised of 100 tiyin.

Term B loan A loan that costs more than traditional bank debt but costs less than a typical *mezzanine loan*, which may cost as much as 20 percent. In the event of default, Term B lenders are paid back before mezzanine lenders but after bank lenders.

term life insurance A life insurance policy that provides protection for a certain period of time. If death occurs during that time, the benefits are paid to the beneficiary. Term insurance is the least expensive type of life insurance because the policy generates no cash value. *Universal life insurance,* in comparison, has an investment component and allows cash value to build over the life of the policy.

term sheet A document that outlines the terms of an investment that investors plan to make in a company. The term sheet includes the amount of money that will be invested, the schedule of payments, and the value that the investment places on each share of stocks. Typically, a term sheet is used in the venture capital industry and is prepared by the lead investor.

The Mississippi Bubble A market bubble that derives its name from the Mississippi Company, a French trading company. The Mississippi Bubble occurred from August 1719 to May 1720, growing out of France's terrible economic situation in the early 18th century. When Louis XIV died in 1715, the French Treasury was a disaster, with the price of metal coins fluctuating wildly.

The French regent turned to a Scotsman, John Law, for assistance. Law was a gambler who had exiled himself to France in order to avoid a duel. He suggested that the Banque Royale take deposits and issue bank-notes that would be payable in the value of the currency when the notes were issued. His ideas helped France make the transition from metal-based currency to paper currency, which resulted in a brief period of financial stability.

In August 1717, Law formed the Companie des Indes (commonly called the Mississippi Company), which received a monopoly on trading rights with the French colonies in the Americas (the Louisiana territory). By August 1719, Law had created a scheme that would let the Mississippi Company take on the entire French national debt. Portions of the debt would be exchanged for shares in the company. Law promised a 120 percent profit for shareholders. Not surprisingly, 300,000 would-be shareholders vied for the 50,000 shares that were being offered. As demand for the shares soared, the French government, which was effectively controlled by

Law, continued to print paper banknotes, which caused inflation to skyrocket.

The euphoria was short-lived. The bubble burst in May 1720 when a run on the Banque Royale forced the government to admit that the amount of metal-based currency in France wasn't equal to half the amount of paper currency that was circulating. The government issued an order that would gradually depreciate Mississippi Company shares, so that by the end of the year they would be valued at half of their nominal worth. That order was reversed a week later due to extreme public outcry, but the Banque Royale closed. It reopened in June, and the bank runs continued. By November 1720, the Mississippi Company shares were worthless and Law was forced to flee the country.

theoretical value The hypothetical value of an option calculated by the Black-Scholes option pricing model. See also *Black-Scholes option pricing model.*

theoretical value of rights The mathematically calculated value of a *subscription right* (a right to buy stock) after the offering is announced but before the right expires. The theoretical value of a stock option is affected by the underlying stock price, strike price, volatility, interest rate, dividend and time to expiration.

To calculate the theoretical value of rights, start with the market value of common stock, subtract subscription price per share, and divide the result by the number of rights needed to buy one share plus 1. For example, if the stock price of a share is $75 and the subscription price is $65, and five rights are needed to buy one share, one right would be worth $1.66 ($75 - $65 = $10/$6 = $1.66).

therm 100,000 British thermal units (BTUs). One million BTUs is a *dekatherm.*

theta Measures the change in the premium of an option and compares it to a one-day change in time-to-maturity. The longer an option's time to expiration, the more valuable an option is. High theta options are favored by option sellers because options have a high rate of time decay.

thin trade A condition in which there is little trading activity in a market because of a lack of buy or sell orders to drive up the volume. Thin trading usually occurs around holidays and sometimes in the doldrums of August. Thin trading conditions make it difficult for large buyers or sellers to execute orders because their trading activity may move prices. An individual stock, future, or option contract also may be thinly traded.

third market The over-the-counter trading of securities that are listed on an exchange.

Third World A name given to the least developed countries in the world. Typically these countries are located in Africa and parts of Asia and South America.

three-months copper The benchmark copper contract traded on the London Metal Exchange. It gets its name from the time it took to ship copper mined in Chile to London when copper trading first began on the LME in 1877.

thrift Another name for a savings and loan association, which is a depositary institution that issues mortgages and holds deposits for individuals. See also *savings and loan.*

thrift institution A financial organization that accepts primarily savings account deposits and then invests most of the proceeds in mortgages. Savings banks, savings and loan associations, and credit unions are thrift institutions.

tick The minimum price movement on a futures contract. If the tick is up, it is called an *uptick;* if it is down, it is called a *downtick.*

ticker tape A system that displays stock symbols, prices, and volume information in a scrolling manner and is displayed in brokerage offices or in other public places. It derives its name from the loud ticking noise that these machines made when they printed the price and volume information for the stocks in the days before computers.

tie-in sale The sale of one product to a customer on the expressly stated condition that a second product must be purchased. The customer may not want the second product, or may be able to purchase it elsewhere at a lower price. Tie-in agreements are illegal if they restrict competition.

Tier-1 Internet backbone A system for connecting users to the Internet. A Tier-1 Internet backbone has multiple direct connections to other Internet backbones that are geographically dispersed. These connections allow Tier-1 Internet backbones to transfer data much faster and more reliably that other methods.

tight credit Monetary policy that is characterized by high or increasing interest rates. The Federal Reserve Board uses a tight monetary policy in order to contain inflation, which can be very damaging to an economy. Approximately every six weeks, the Federal Reserve's Open Market Committee (FOMC) meets to determine interest rate policy. The FOMC implements its interest rates policy by setting a target rate for the federal funds rate, which is the rate that it charges its member banks for short-term loans. Then the Federal Reserve conducts open market operations by selling or buying Treasury securities, which has the effect of increasing or reducing funds from banks and thus influencing the price, or interest rates, of loans. The inverse of tight credit is *loose credit,* or an *easy monetary policy,* that is characterized by low interest rates intended to stimulate economic growth in a slowing economy.

time deposit A deposit account that has a set time until it matures, at which time the funds can be accessed. Exceptions do exist that allow the funds to be accessed before the account matures, typically with the payment of a penalty.

time series analysis An examination of a firm's performance over a period of time.

time stamp A time-logging machine which records the exact time trading orders are received and the time they're executed. In the instance of computer-driven trading programs, time stamps are applied by the software.

time value In the options market, what the option buyer is willing to pay for an option by anticipating price changes prior to expiration. Options tend to decrease in value as the expiration date nears. The value of an option's *premium,* or price, is comprised of time value, which reflects the length of time that an option has before expiration. It also is comprised of *intrinsic value,* which is the difference between the exercise price of the option and the market value of the underlying security. Time value is also called *extrinsic value.*

time value of money The concept that a dollar in hand today will be worth more than a dollar in the future. The time value of money is typically thought of in terms of the amount of interest that could have been earned had money been invested in an interest-bearing account instead of not investing it.

timeshare A method of owning property that has become popular with people who want to own vacation property but don't want to bear the entire expense by themselves and don't need the property for the entire year. Some publicly traded property-management companies specialize in vacation properties and sell timeshares in property that they are constructing. Timeshare arrangements also occur in many other situations.

TIPS See *Treasury Inflation Protected Security.*

title insurance Insurance that protects a mortgage lender in the event that a problem is found with the title to a property. The insurance is written by a title insurance company, which conducts a thorough search of the title to find any liens, duplicate ownership claims, or any other problems before issuing title insurance. The title insurance remains effective until the property is resold.

TMT *Technology, media, and telecom.* In the 1990s, because there was a great deal of overlap in the products and services performed by TMT companies, investment banks often grouped their capital raising and research efforts under this heading.

TOCOM See *Tokyo Commodity Exchange.*

toehold purchase The acquisition of less than five percent of the shares of a company that is a target for a takeover. Once the five percent level is reached, the acquirer has to file Schedule 13D with the Securities and Exchange Commission to outline its plans and intentions under the requirements of the Williams Act.

Tokyo Commodity Exchange (TOCOM) A Japanese exchange on which a variety of commodity contracts are traded. Materials on which contracts are traded include aluminum, crude oil, gasoline, gold, kerosene, palladium, platinum, rubber, and silver. TOCOM is a non-profit membership organization, as defined under the Commodity Exchange Law that was passed in 1950, which regulates all commodities futures and options trading in Japan. TOCOM was established on Nov. 1, 1984 when the Tokyo Textile Exchange, the Tokyo Rubber Exchange, and the Tokyo Gold Exchange merged. TOCOM is regulated by the Ministry of Economy, Trade and Industry.

Tokyo Stock Exchange Inc. Japan's stock exchange, which comprises five regional stock exchanges. Its most prominent market indicator is the Nikkei 225. On April 1, 1949, three stock exchanges were established in Tokyo, Osaka, and Nagoya. Trading on these exchanges began on May 16. In July of that same year, five additional stock exchanges were established in Kyoto (merged into Osaka Securities Exchange in March 2001), Kobe (dissolved in October 1967), Hiroshima (merged into Tokyo Stock Exchange in March 2000), Fukuoka, and Niigata (merged with Tokyo Stock Exchange in March 2000). In addition, the Sapporo Securities Exchange was established in April 1950.

A variety of financial products are traded on the exchange in addition to stocks such as bonds and Real Estate Investment Trusts (REITs). The Tokyo Stock Exchange was demutualized in November 2001.

Tokyo Topix Index A capitalization-weighted index of all the companies listed on the *First Section* (the most secure stocks) of the Tokyo Stock Exchange. It began January 4, 1968 with a based value of 100. It excludes temporary issues and preferred stocks.

tolar The currency unit of Slovenia, comprised of 100 stotins.

tombstone An advertisement placed by underwriters as part of a securities offering. The tombstone includes basic details about the offering, such as the amount of securities being sold, the name of the selling company, and the names of the investment banks that are selling the offering.

too-big-to-fail A policy that may be followed by governmental regulators, which says that a bank or business is so big that its failure would have a catastrophic effect on the country or the global economy. For example, in the 1970s in the United States, the government bailed out Chrysler Corporation; in the 1980s, it bailed out Continental Illinois, a Chicago-based bank. In 1998, a hedge fund, Long-Term Capital Management, which had made bad investment decisions, was on the verge of collapse when it was saved by a group of banks led by the New York Federal Reserve.

top-down investment approach An investment strategy that identifies stocks and bonds by first deciding what sectors will perform the best. The investor using this approach then seeks out the best companies within those sectors by analyzing the fundamentals of the offered securities.

top-line A frequently used way of saying sales or revenues. It draws its name from the fact that revenue is the top line on an income statement.

top-line growth Common market jargon that refers to an increase in a company's sales or revenues. It comes from the fact that the sales figure is the top line of an income statement.

Toronto Stock Exchange Canada's largest stock exchange, where more than 1,300 senior equities are traded. In 2001, the Toronto Stock Exchange acquired the Canadian Venture Exchange Inc. (CDNX), which lists emerging companies. In April 2002, the TSX brand was launched. TSX includes the Toronto Stock Exchange, TSX Venture Group (formerly CDNX), TSX Markets, and TSX Datalinx. The benchmark index is the S&P/TSE Composite Index, which replaced the TSE 300. Companies included in it are reviewed on a quarterly basis instead of an annual basis. It celebrated its 150-year anniversary in 2002. TSX is the third most active stock exchange in North America after the New York Stock Exchange and the NASDAQ Stock Market, and ranks seventh in the world for domestic market capitalization.

total asset turnover Net sales divided by average total net assets. The resulting number shows how often assets turn over, which can indicate how effectively a company is managing all of its assets. The number by itself isn't informative, it must be compared to other companies in the industry, as well as to the company's historical data. If the asset turnover is high relative to other companies in the industry, it may indicate that too few assets for potential sales are being used or suggest that the company is using too many old and fully depreciated assets. A low asset turnover can indicate that capital is tied up in too many assets relative to what is needed.

Total Information Awareness See *Initiative Terrorist Information Awareness.*

Total Quality Management (TQM) A management philosophy that seeks to improve the quality of products and services by improving work processes in response to feedback from employees and customers. Early adopters of the TQM practices were Japanese corporations that were struggling to rebuild their manufacturing capabilities after World War II. The Japanese were early adherents to the teachings of W. Edwards Deming, a TQM consultant and pioneer. In the 1980s, TQM began to catch on in other countries, such as the U.S. TQM also places emphasis on detecting problems in the system or process, instead of leveling blame at an individual or department. See also *ISO 9000.*

TQM See *Total Quality Management.*

tracking stock A type of common stock that represents a claim on a unit of a larger company. A tracking stock pays dividends, and its price changes based upon the underlying performance of the unit, but a holder of a tracking stock has equity in the parent company, not the unit. Tracking stock is traded in addition to the regular shares in the company. Tracking stocks became popular in the stock market boom of the late 1990s.

trade balance The difference between the volume of a country's exports and its imports. An excess of exports means that a country has a *trade surplus.* An excess of imports means that the country has a *trade deficit.* The balance of trade measures goods and services. The balance of trade is part of the *balance of payments,* a measurement that isn't given much scrutiny by the financial markets. The balance of payments is much more comprehensive than the balance of trade because it includes investment income flows and transfer payments. The U.S. Department of Commerce releases monthly data on the United States' trade balance.

trade credit Credit that is granted to customers by wholesale or retail businesses.

trade data See *international trade data.*

trade house In the futures industry, a firm that deals in physical commodities. For example, a trade house in the silver industry would buy, sell and store actual silver.

trade sanctions A penalty, applied by one country against another, that restricts trading activity. Trade sanctions may involve goods that are prohibited from being imported. A country also may assess excise duties on particular goods in retaliation for another country's trade sanctions.

trademark A symbol or name that identifies a product, business, or service and that can be used legally only by its owner. The value of the trademark is amortized over its reasonable life, which can't exceed 40 years.

trader

1. A person who buys or sells securities with the intention of making a profit. A trader may be employed by a trading firm, or may be an individual who trades for his or her own account. An individual trader's strategy may be to trade for quick profits, such as a day trading, or it may be to take a long-term view of the market and do little actual buying and selling.

2. A person who buys and sells goods with the intention of making a profit.

trading halt A halt in the trading of a particular stock due to excess volatility. A trading halt may occur when bad news, such as the announcement of regulatory investigations, imminent bankruptcy proceedings, or sharp earnings shortfalls seep into the market. Expectations of a merger transaction also may produce volatile situations and halt trading. The company may ask the exchange to halt trading or the exchange may do so of its own accord. Trading halts are temporary and last only until sell and buy orders begin to rebalance. Also called *suspended trading.*

trading limit The maximum daily price movements for stocks, futures contracts, or other securities that are allowed by an exchange. When trading limits are reached, there is a trading halt.

trailing P/E ratio The current price of a stock divided by the past four quarters' earnings per share.

trailing stop loss A stop-loss order placed at the time a stock is purchased that requires the stock to be sold if the price falls below a specified price level. The stop-loss price is set at a fixed percentage point below the market price. If the price increases, the stop-loss price rises proportionately. If the stock price falls, the stop-loss price doesn't change. A stop-loss order allows investors to set a limit on the maximum possible loss without limiting potential gains or requiring a constant monitoring of the investment's performance.

tranche A separate section of an overall bond or investment offering. For example, a $4 billion bond offering may have four tranches, each sold in a different currency, such as the U.S. dollar, Japanese yen, euro, and British pound. Each currency offering represents one tranche of the overall issue.

transaction costs Costs associated with the purchase or sale of securities. Typically, the biggest transaction cost is a brokerage commission. Other transaction costs are taxes or regulatory fees, such as transfer fees.

transfer agent A bank or trust company that keeps a record of the shareholders of a corporation. The transfer agent issues and transfers stock certificates as they are bought and sold.

transfer payments Money that is paid to individuals from government benefit programs such as Social Security, unemployment, and welfare benefits. Transfer payments are identified separately when calculating gross domestic product and gross national product.

transfer tax

1. A local or state tax that is paid on the transfer of official documents such as deeds to property or securities. Often they are paid by purchasing a stamp.

2. A federal tax on gifts and estates.

transparency Describes the situation that occurs when companies openly communicate important information to investors and shareholders.

travel and entertainment expense A business expense that can be deducted from revenues that a business or sole proprietor earns for the purpose of calculating income tax. Unlike other business expenses, only 50 percent of travel and entertainment expenditures can be deducted from income taxes.

Treasury benchmark The primary Treasury debt contract that the market refers to when discussing how Treasuries are performing. The 10-year Treasury note is the current benchmark; as the benchmark, it is the most frequently used instrument for hedging purposes. The 30-year bond used to be the benchmark, but after the U.S. government debt was virtually erased at the end of the 1990s, the Department of the Treasury announced that it would no longer issue 30-year bonds. Because the government simply didn't need the money generated by 30-year bonds, the benchmark shifted to the most liquid, most heavily traded bond, the 10-year note.

Treasury bills (T-bills) Short-term debt obligations issued by the U.S. Treasury that matures in 3 to 12 months. Common maturities for T-bills include 13-, 26-, and 52-weeks. Typically, they are sold weekly to institutions, but individuals also can buy T-bills through the Bureau of Public Debt. Because they are obligations of the U.S. government, T-bills are considered to be risk free. The minimum purchase amount is $1,000, with bids made in multiples of $1,000. Generally, noncompetitive bids from one person may not exceed $1 million for Treasury bills or $5 million for a Treasury note or bond offering.

Treasury bonds Debt obligations issued by the U.S. Treasury that mature in 30-years. The schedule for issuing debt is announced quarterly. Typically, Treasury bonds are sold to institutions; however individuals also can buy them, through the Treasury Direct program. Because they are obligations of the U.S. government, Treasury bonds are considered to be risk free.

Treasury Borrowing Advisory Committee A committee of The Bond Market Association that meets on a quarterly basis with U.S. Treasury officials. The committee represents bond underwriters and dealers, and puts forward the opinions of the industry about whether the frequency of Treasury securities sales should be increased or decreased. The committee also offers opinions about the size of securities sales and recommends the types of securities that should be offered, including maturities, and offers opinions about the buyback of U.S. Treasuries. Often, Treasury officials use meetings with this committee to announce pending changes in policy, such as the elimination of the 30-year bond, so that the private sector has time to prepare.

Treasury budget A monthly report on the U.S. government budget by the Treasury Department. It includes the amount of receipts and disbursements made during the previous month. The data is typically released on the 15th of the month for the prior month at 2 P.M. ET. The data gives the fiscal year-to-date budget surplus or deficit and it gives the year-over-year growth in fiscal year-to-date revenues and expenditures. Its influence on the financial markets is very small; however, the overall trend of the government's deficit or surplus is important.

Treasury Direct A program directed primarily at individual investors who want to purchase bills, notes, and bonds from the U.S. Treasury. These investors want to purchase Treasury securities when they are first issued by the government and plan on holding them until they mature. Treasury Direct's focus contrasts with the Treasury's Commercial Book-Entry System, which is directed toward large institutional investors.

Treasury Inflation Protected Security (TIPS) A treasury note or bond that is issued at a fixed rate of interest. The principal is adjusted every six months based on changes in the consumer price index. TIPS are a form of an inflation-indexed securities. The popularity of TIPS has been limited since they were introduced by the U.S. Treasury Department in the late 1990s because inflation has been very modest.

Treasury notes Debt obligations issued by the U.S. Treasury that mature in 2, 3, 5, or 10 years. In May 2003, the U.S. Treasury reintroduced the 3-year note. The schedule for issuing debt is announced quarterly. Typically, Treasury notes are sold to institutions; however individuals also can buy them, through the Treasury Direct program. Because they are obligations of the U.S. government, Treasury notes are considered to be risk free.

Treasury securities Fixed-income debt securities issued by the U.S. government. Treasury securities have no default risk because they are backed by the U.S. government. *Treasury bills* are securities that mature in less than two years, such as the three- and six-month notes. *Treasury notes* are securities that mature anywhere from two years to ten years, which includes the two-, three-, five-, and ten-year Treasury notes. The *Treasury bond* is a security that matures in 30 years.

Treasury stock Stock that is authorized and issued by a company and is later bought back. Dividends are not paid on Treasury stock, and no voting rights are associated with them. A corporation can hold Treasury stock indefinitely, reissue the shares, or cancel them. Treasury stock is not related to U.S. Treasury debt.

Treasury yield curve A graphical representation of the relationship between the different maturities of Treasury securities and their yield to maturity. Those securities range from three-month Treasury bills up to 30-year bonds. The other points included on the Treasury yield curve include: 3- and 6-month Treasury bills, 52-week bills, and 2-, 3-, 5-, and 10-year Treasury notes. Often short-term interest rate targets set by the Federal Reserve for overnight loans to banks are included on the Treasury yield curve.

Tremonti, Giulio The Minister of Economy and Finance for Italy, as of this printing.

trend The general direction of a market. Traders often say, "the trend is your friend" or "never buck the trend."

trend line The simplest type of technical analysis. A trend line is developed by connecting a series of price points in one line. The line shows the direction the market is heading.

triangle A technical chart pattern in which the price range becomes increasingly narrow over time with lower daily prices or higher daily prices. An ascending triangle occurs when the highest prices on the chart pattern rise more while a descending triangle occurs when the lowest prices on the bottom of the chart pattern increase more.

triangular flags A term in technical analysis that refers to a chart pattern in which prices move sideways, indicating that the market is consolidating. Flags indicate a change in a trend.

Trichet, Jean-Claude As of this printing, the Governor (president) of the Bank of France. He has been the chairman of the Monetary Policy Council of the Bank of France since 1994, was a member of the board of the European Monetary Institute from 1994 to 1998, and member of the Governing Council of the European Central Bank since 1998.

trickle down economics A theory that economic growth is promoted by letting businesses flourish and passing tax laws that reduce the taxes of the wealthy. The theory says that businesses and individuals will make investments that fuel economic growth and the benefits will "trickle down" to the masses. Critics deride this idea as a bad justification for helping wealthy people and businesses at the expense of middle- and low-income people.

triple bottom A pattern on a price chart that is characterized by three moves down, each of which is followed by a move up that roughly equals the move down. It looks like a mountain range with three valleys. The triple-bottom pattern is complete only when both peaks have been broken on heavier volume and the price rises sharply. The price rise will typically equal the distance on the price chart between the triple bottom and the trough.

triple top A pattern on a price chart that is characterized by three moves upward, each of which is followed by a move down that roughly equals the move up. It looks like a mountain range with three peaks. The triple-top pattern is complete only when both troughs have been broken on heavier volume and the price falls sharply. The price fall will typically equal the distance on the price chart between the triple top and the trough.

triple witching hour The simultaneous expiration of stock, index, and futures options. The event often creates market volatility, both on the day it occurs and on the days preceding it. A triple witching hour occurs on the third Friday of March, June, September, and December. See also *double witching hour.*

trough The period when a bear market is ending and prices begin to rise. On a price chart, a trough looks like the bottom half of the letter "o."

troy ounce A unit of weight used for precious metals, specifically for gold and silver. A troy ounce is equal to about 1.1 avoirdupois ounces, 480 grains, or 31.04 grams. The term is believed to be named after a weight used at the annual fair held at Troyes, France during the Middle Ages.

TruPS See *Trust Preferred Stock Units.*

trust

1. An arrangement in which property (either real or monetary) is put under the management and control of a trustee who is responsible for administering it for the trust beneficiary. A trust created by a will is called a *testamentary trust.* A

trust created while the writer is still living is called an *inter vivos,* or *living trust.*

2. A type of a corporate monopoly that was powerful during the late 19th and early 20th centuries that exerted strong influence over prices. Antitrust laws passed in the early 1900s destroyed the power of trusts. The name *trust* comes from a voting trust in which a small number of trustees controlled a majority of a company's shares.

3. A group or board of people who have been appointed to manage the affairs of an institution, such as a university.

trust company A financial organization, which may be part of a commercial bank, that acts as a trustee, fiduciary, or agent for corporations or individuals. Typical work done for individuals by a trust company includes administering trust funds or estates. Work done for corporations by a trust company includes acting as a stock transfer and registration agent and managing custodial relationships.

Trust Indenture Act of 1939 Legislation that applies to bonds, notes, and debentures that are sold to the public. The law requires that the formal agreement between the bonds' issuer and the bondholder, called the *trust indenture,* complies with the requirements of the law. Adherence to the law is required even if the securities are registered under the provisions of other securities laws.

Trust Preferred Stock Units (TruPS) Company-issued bonds that have been repackaged by an underwriter into $25 pieces that are sold to individual investors. These securities possess characteristics of both equity and debt securities. Brokerage firms create this product and give them their own name and acronym, such as CorTS, CTBCSs, and SATURNS. TruPS receive their dividends before common and preferred stockholders; however, many have a clause that allows interest payments to be deferred up to five years.

trustee

1. A person who has been appointed by a court to handle the issues outlined in a legal action. For example, in a bankruptcy proceeding, the judge appoints a trustee who is responsible for such things as liquidating assets and disbursing the proceeds to the creditor.

2. A person who administers a trust. See also *trust*.

3. A group or board of people who have been appointed to manage the affiars of an institution, such as a university.

Truth in Lending Act The popular name for the Consumer Credit Protection Act of 1988. See *Consumer Credit Protection Act of 1988*.

tugrik The currency unit of Mongolia, comprised of 100 mongo.

tulipmania A large speculative bubble that occurred in Europe in the 17th century when the value of tulips skyrocketed, especially in Holland and Britain. By 1634, the Dutch economy focused almost exclusively on tulips to the exclusion of other business activities. The value of special breeds of tulips soared to as much as thousands of florins. In contrast, 12 fat sheep sold for 120 florins. In 1636, the demand for rare tulip species increased so much that tulip exchanges were established on the Stock Exchange of Amsterdam as well as on the London Exchange. By the end of the year, sense returned and people began to sell their tulip interests for just a small profit. Soon, confidence plummeted and the floor in the market gave way. Tulips once again were just pretty flowers and the entire episode was derided as "tulipmania."

Turner, Ted The founder of cable television's first news station, Cable News Network (CNN). He also founded Turner Network Television (TNT). His holding company, Turner Broadcasting System Inc. (TBS), was acquired by Time Warner Inc., which merged with America Online Inc., in 2000.

turnkey A business, such as a franchise, that is created by the seller and sold to the buyer who can "turn the key" and begin work without any other preparation. Often project construction or computer installation are services provided by turnkey businesses.

turnover A ratio that shows how often an asset is replaced, which indicates how vibrant business activity is. Some common turnovers are accounts receivable turnover and inventory turnover.

Turnover also may be used to refer to a company's annual sales or revenues, which is a common use of the term in the United Kingdom.

two-pillar strategy The European Central Bank's strategy for managing monetary policy. On one pillar, the ECB scrutinizes the growth in monetary supply (called aggregate M3) over the medium to longer-term horizons; the ECB believes that looking at monetary supply helps the central bank look beyond short-term effects caused by temporary shocks to the financial system. On the other pillar, the ECB monitors inflation.

UCC See *Uniform Commercial Code.*

umbrella personal liability insurance
An insurance policy that protects against a catastrophic lawsuit or an adverse judgment. An umbrella insurance policy provides expanded insurance coverage and offers more liability protection than standard homeowner, renter, or auto insurance policies. The umbrella policy pays for the part of the claim in excess of the limits of the basic liability coverage not covered by personal liability insurance. An umbrella policy is additional insurance that works in conjunction with auto insurance, homeowner's insurance, and so on.

Unbundled Network Element-Platform (UNE-P) A type of phone service, created by the Telecommunications Act of 1996, in which phone service providers use the local switching and transmission platform of the Bell networks. The former regional Bell operating companies were forced to allow competitors to use the Bell network to increase competition. UNE-P lets emerging telecom providers offer services without owning or building their own network infrastructure or making large capital investments. Regulatory battles over UNE-P service and fees are common between the former Bells and new competitors. The former Bell companies don't want to share their networks because doing so directly takes away from profits. Telecommunications is a high-margin business, and profit margins are reduced because much of the Bell's costs are largely fixed.

Unbundled Network Elements (UNE)
The individual parts of a network that the local, dominant telecom companies are required to share with their competitors. The sharing requirement was made in the 1996 Telecom Act, which said that the local, dominant telecom companies are required to offer the individual parts of their network to competitors to resell if the failure to provide access would impair the ability of a startup telecom carrier to offer services.

uncollected funds Money on deposit in a bank account that hasn't yet been paid out by the bank upon which the check was written. Banks won't let account holders access uncollected funds until the other bank has transferred the funds.

uncovered option An option position in which the writer doesn't own the underlying securities. If the option is exercised, the writer has to purchase the underlying securities in the market, which may result in a loss. Also called *naked option.*

undercapitalization A situation in which a business doesn't have enough capital to successfully operate. Undercapitalized companies have too much debt. Undercapitalized companies need to be recapitalized, meaning that they need to have some of their debt obligations forgiven and get new injections of equity. If they aren't recapitalized, they face bankruptcy.

underfunded pension plan A pension plan whose projected payouts are larger than the value of the plan's assets. Underfunded pension plans must have funds transferred into them by the corporation; the transfer payment shows up as an expense on the company's income statement. In periods of declining stock or fixed-income markets, a company's pension plan often may be underfunded due to stock market losses. Analysts typically predict that when a plan's assets fall below 85 percent of the projected benefit obligations, the Pension Benefit Guarantee Corp. will ask the affected company to fund the pension plan with cash.

underground economy Part of an economy in which illegal transactions take place. Underground transactions are not reported as income and thus are not taxed. The presence of the underground economy results in an undercounting of economic activity.

underlying debt A term that is used in the municipal bond market to refer to the debt of a government agency within the jurisdiction of the larger government unit that has partial credit responsibility for repayment. The larger government unit considers the debt of the smaller agency to be underlying debt. Typically, the larger agency is more creditworthy than the smaller entity and this sharing of credit responsibilities generally acts as a credit enhancement for the issuing authority. For example, a turnpike authority for a state may issue its own debt, but if there is any problem with default, the state government would have some obligation to see that default is avoided.

underpricing Pricing a securities offering too low; typically applied to initial public offerings (IPOs). When the issue begins trading on the stock exchange, the price shoots up, sometimes rising over 100 percent. The price increase indicates that there is strong demand for shares and that they could have been priced higher. If they had been priced higher, the company would have earned more money. When an issue is underpriced, it is said that the company has "left some money on the table." However, those who have bought the shares at the original price benefit from the fact that they can now sell the shares in the *aftermarket,* depending on IPO restrictions, and make a substantial profit.

undervalued Describes a stock or other investment whose price is lower than what is justified by the investment's fundamentals. Often bargain hunters or value investors identify and purchase undervalued stocks, and the price rises until the stock is no longer undervalued.

underwater A call option with a strike price that is higher than the market price of the underlying security or a put option whose strike price is lower than the market price of the underlying security. Until expiration, however, the underwater option still has the time value of money because the price of the underlying instrument can change.

underwater option An out-of-the-money option is often called an underwater option. A call option is underwater if its exercise price is higher than the current price of the underlying contract. An underwater put option occurs when its exercise price is lower than the current price of the underlying contract. An underwater option has no intrinsic value but still has time value.

underweight An investment or a sector that takes up a relatively small percentage of a portfolio. For example, an analyst might tell investors to underweight their holdings of technology stocks, or a person may say that their telecom holdings are underweighted. Underweight contrasts with overweight, which means that there is a disproportionately high amount of funds in a particular stock or sector.

underwriter An investment bank that acts as an intermediary between a company that wants to sell bonds or stocks and the public. *Firm-commitment underwriting,* which is done only for an underwriter's best clients, occurs when the underwriter buys the issue and guarantees to sell a certain number of shares to investors. In order to spread the risk of purchasing the issue, the underwriter forms a *syndicate,* or underwriting group, made up of other investment banks. In insurance, an underwriter assumes the risks for a variety of problems such as car accidents, health problems, or death, in return for receiving premiums.

underwriting

1. The process of selling stocks or debt offerings to the public. Investment bankers provide underwriting services and in return charge a fee, which is a small percentage amount of the amount of funds raised. Underwriters form a syndicate group comprised of other investment banks in order to jointly share in the underwriting risk and sales effort of distributing a new debt or equity issue.

2. In the insurance industry, agreeing to undertake a risk in exchange for earning a fee.

underwriting spread

1. The difference between money paid to a company that issues securities by the underwriter and the amount of money that is raised once the issues are sold. The underwriter keeps the difference.

2. A fee paid by the securities issuer that may range from 1 percent to 2 percent for a bond offering. The underwriting spread sometimes went up to 7 percent for initial public offerings during the technology boom.

undistributed profits Another name for retained earnings. See *retained earnings.*

UNE See *Unbundled Network Elements.*

unemployment rate See *non-farm payrolls report.*

unencumbered Used to describe an asset that doesn't have a corresponding debt. For example, a car whose loan has been paid off or an investment bought with cash, not a margin loan from the broker, is unencumbered.

UNE-P See *Unbundled Network Element-Platform.*

unified credit trust See *bypass trust.*

Uniform Commercial Code (UCC) A coordinated code of laws governing the legal aspects of business and financial transactions in the United States, excluding Louisiana. The UCC regulates the sale of goods, and also regulates financial transactions, such as bank deposits and collections, letters of credit, bulk transfers, and the delivery of title documents. It defines the rights and responsibilities of each party in a commercial transaction and provides a statutory definition of commonly used business practices. The National Conference of Commissions of Uniform State Laws wrote the UCC.

union scale A standard wage that is paid to union members for a particular type of work. For example, a union scale wage for a plumber might be $22.50 an hour.

unissued stock Corporate stock that has been authorized to be issued by the board but has not yet been issued. This stock is listed on a company's balance sheet. Unissued stocks are available to be given as needed to employees for stock options, rights, or warrants. Dividends are not paid on unissued stock and don't have voting rights.

unit investment trust An investment that often is the underlying, legal structure for some exchange-traded funds. A unit investment trust purchases a fixed, unmanaged portfolio of investments according to the objectives of the trust. The trust sells shares to investors and periodically passes capital gains, dividends, and interest onto shareholders. Unit investment trusts are similar to mutual funds, however they differ because the trust doesn't actively manage the investments but a mutual fund does. Unit investment trusts have to register with the Securities and Exchange Commission under the provision of the Investment Company Act of 1940.

unit stock plan See *phantom stock plan.*

universal life insurance A type of life insurance that pays a death benefit and also accumulates a cash value, thus acting as an investment. Some policies offer flexible premium payment plans, in which the amount and timing of the premium can vary based on the insured's needs.

University of Michigan consumer sentiment survey A telephone survey conducted by the University of Michigan Consumer Research Center, which phones 500 consumers to ask their opinion on personal finances and business conditions. Consumers are asked five questions concerning household financial conditions and their expectations for household financial conditions in one year; their expectations for business conditions in one year as well as expectations for the economy in five years, and their buying plans. This release provides an early indication of consumer expectations that are a leading indicator for the business cycle. The monthly survey has a moderate impact on the financial markets because if consumer confidence declines, then consumer spending is likely to weaken. The data is seasonally adjusted. With consumer spending making up two-thirds of gross domestic product, consumer behavior is closely watched.

unlisted security A security that is traded in the over-the-counter market. It is not listed on an organized exchange such as the New York Stock Exchange, American Stock Exchange, or the NASDAQ stock market.

unpaid dividend A dividend that has been declared by a corporation's board of directors but has not yet been paid out. There is typically a lag time between a declaration date and the payment date.

unqualified opinion An independent auditor's opinion that a company's financial statements "present fairly, in all material respects, the financial position of the company." The opinion also says that the financial statements conform to generally accepted accounting principles. An auditor's opinion is included in a letter that is inserted into a company's annual financial report and is filed with the Securities and Exchange Commission.

unrealized gain An economic gain that has not yet been recognized for income tax or reporting purposes. While the gain appears on paper, it remains unrealized until it is recorded. Also may be called a *paper gain*.

unrealized loss An economic loss that has not yet been recognized for income tax or reporting purposes. Also may be called an *embedded loss* or *paper loss.*

unrealized profit or loss A profit or loss that has been incurred in an investment but that hasn't been realized yet because the investment hasn't been sold, which would make it realized. Also called a *paper profit or loss.*

unsecured bond Bonds that are backed only by the issuer's promise to pay interest and repay the principal. There are no assets securing the promise to repay; they are only secured by the overall creditworthiness of the issuer.

unsecured credit Credit that is not backed by *collateral,* or assets that are pledged to make certain the credit is repaid. A credit card is a type of unsecured credit.

unsecured debt Debt that is not backed by collateral, or assets pledged to ensure repayment. An example of unsecured debt is debentures, which are unsecured bonds.

unwind a trade To enact a securities trade that nullifies a previous trade. For example, if five futures contracts were sold short, then five contracts would be bought back.

upgrade An action taken by Wall Street analysts that communicates an increasingly positive outlook for a company's stock or bonds. Typically, analysts upgrade a company's stock if they think the company's earnings, revenues, or share price will improve. Ratings agencies also upgrade credit ratings of corporations, countries, and specialized financial instruments if cash flow improves or if debt levels are reduced.

upside The amount of upward price movement that a stock or investment may be able to reach under optimal conditions. Analysts speak about the upside potential of a stock.

uptick A trade that occurs at a higher price than the previous trade. To indicate that it is an uptick trade, a plus sign is displayed next to the last price where the stock traded. Short sales must be executed on upticks or zero-plus ticks.

uptick rule A rule that attempts to limit short selling in a declining market. Investors are prohibited from selling an exchange-listed stock short unless the stock's last trade was at the same price or higher than the previous trade. For example, if you want to sell a stock short at $40, the previous trade must have been at $40 or higher, such as $40.20. The uptick rule comes from Rule 10a–1 of the Securities Exchange Act. The

New York Stock Exchange (NYSE) also has a similar rule, Rule 440B, that applies to its member brokerage firms and to its specialists. See also *short seller*.

uptrend line A technical analysis charting tool that shows a pattern of upward-moving prices.

USA Patriot Act A law that was passed after the terrorist attacks of Sept. 11. The aspect of the law most relevant to finance is its requirement that banks, mutual funds, brokerage firms, and other financial institutions verify the identity of clients and ensure that accounts aren't being used for money-laundering purposes.

useful life An estimate of how long an asset can be used before it permanently breaks down or before it requires so many repairs that fixing it is not practical. Estimates of useful life are made for purposes of calculating depreciation on fixed assets.

usury Charging interest rates that are higher than the rate allowed under the law.

utility A company that generates, transmits or distributes important services, such as electricity, heating oil, or natural gas that is used to heat homes and businesses. Usually state authorities are involved in regulating utilities, although in recent years there has been a movement to deregulate the electricity market. The natural gas industry is currently deregulated. On a federal level, the Federal Energy Regulatory Commission regulates approximately 200 investor-owned utilities.

utility revenue bond A municipal bond issued to finance the construction of utilities, such as electric generation facilities, water processing facilities, and sewer systems. The bonds are repaid from the revenues of the facility. The bonds typically come with a reserve fund in the event that there is an interruption in cash flow or a delay in cash receipts.

Utility Sector Index (UTY) A benchmark index used in the utilities industry that was created and is traded on the Philadelphia Stock Exchange. Its trading symbol is UTY, and often that name is used. The Utility Sector Index is a capitalization-weighted index composed of 20 geographically diverse public utility stocks listed on the New York Stock Exchange. The UTY was set to an initial value of 200 on May 1, 1987. Options began trading on September 22, 1987.

VA mortgage   A mortgage that is offered to U.S. veterans who have served in the military by the Veterans Administration (VA). Typically VA mortgages require a smaller down payment and have more attractive interest rates than conventional, commercially available mortgages.

valuation   The process of determining the worth, or value, of an asset or business. For example, stock analysts typically give a publicly traded company a valuation. Investment bankers determine a valuation on a company using standard industry comparisons. Real estate has professionals called appraisers who put a valuation on a property.

value at risk   A risk-management technique that measures market risk found in portfolios and decomposes it into individual risk factors that can be quantified and managed. Statistical analysis can be used to estimate the potential loss from adverse price movements. Although value at risk is a useful tool, it only provides an estimate of what losses might be and only gives a probability of events happening.

Value Line Geometric Composite Index   An equally weighted price index of all the stocks covered in The Value Line Investment Survey. Geometric refers to the geometric averaging technique that is used to compute the average, which is the nth root of the product of a set number of terms. For example, if there are 3 terms, then the geometric average of the 3 numbers would be the third root of the product of the 3 numbers. Geometric indices are not commonly used. The index is watched as a proxy for the market's performance and represents the typical retail investor's portfolio. Institutional investors like it because it

is an indicator of how mid-cap stocks are performing.

value-added tax (VAT)   A tax based on consumption that is levied on the price of the goods being sold. VAT is commonly levied in Europe and essentially is a sales tax. However, the VAT is usually included in the price of the item. If something is selling for £35, the VAT is deducted from the £35, not calculated on top of it, in contrast to the way sales tax is calculated in the United States. Businesses also have to pay VAT on goods and services that are sold. VAT charges are criticized as being a regressive tax because they create a greater burden on poor people than wealthy people. VAT is typically larger than U.S. sales tax. In the 1990s, VAT was around 17.5% in the U.K. and 21% in France.

variable annuity   An annuity in which the payment depends on the performance of the underlying investments. An *annuity* is an investment product sold by an insurance company that guarantees a minimum return to the annuitant. A variable annuity contrasts with a *fixed annuity,* in which the insured knows exactly what return he or she will get, and the insurance company bears all the investment risk.

variable cost   A cost that changes based on the level of sales or production. Examples of a variable cost are temporary labor and materials that are used to produce goods. Variable costs contrast with fixed costs, which don't vary with production or sales levels. For example, a manufacturing plant has fixed costs of rent, depreciation, and insurance. These expenses will continue to be incurred even if the plant closes for a two-week holiday.

variable life insurance   A life insurance policy that lets the policyholder choose the underlying investments on which the policy's return will be based. Policyholders can chose from stock, bond, or money market instruments.

variable rate An interest rate, typically one on a loan or credit card agreement, that varies according to whether certain conditions are met. The interest rate is often linked to an index that fluctuates as market conditions change. However, there will be a limit on how high the interest rate can climb.

variance

1. An exception to zoning rules established by a city government. For example, a zoning variance may be granted to allow business activity in an area zoned for residential use.

2. In accounting terms, the difference between the actual costs incurred to purchase materials and the standard costs for material, labor, and overhead. A positive variance occurs when the actual costs turn out to be lower than the standard or anticipated cost.

3. In budgetary terms, the difference between the amount budgeted and the actual expense.

variation margin The funds needed to bring a trading account balance up to required levels. A calculation of profits and losses on open positions is made at the end of each trading day, and the trader is notified if his or her account has fallen below the minimum required in a margin call.

VAT See *value-added tax.*

vatu The currency unit of Vanuatu.

vega A measurement of the sensitivity of an option's value to a change in volatility. Volatility drives price changes in options. Vega measures how much the price of an option will change when volatility increases or decreases. The higher the vega, the more sensitive the price of the option is to volatility and its risk increases. See also *volatility.*

velocity The rate at which a given dollar changes hands during a certain period of time. The faster money turns over, the higher the velocity. A higher velocity is associated with a higher dollar volume of transactions and could lead to inflation. Velocity is calculated by dividing gross domestic product by money supply. Economists who subscribe to monetarism believe that the changes in velocity are fairly predictable, and they study the causes of money growth and changes in velocity to estimate future economic growth.

vendor A person or company that supplies goods or services to a business.

venture capital Money that is given to entrepreneurs to invest in a start-up business or to develop a product. Venture capital is a very risky investment and those investing money may lose their entire investment. However, if a product or business becomes successful, the return can be huge. Venture capital is raised by venture capital firms who solicit investments from institutional investors, such as banks' private equity units, pension funds, or other investment management firms, as well as from wealthy individuals. Venture capital investments are made at different stages, with some venture capitalists focusing only on seed, or initial, investments, others on middle stage firms and others on later stage companies that have a viable product that is producing revenues.

vertical agreement An agreement between a buyer and seller operating at different levels of the production or distribution chain that potentially can violate antitrust laws. An example of a potentially illegal vertical agreement would be a retail store that has an agreement to buy from one manufacturer and is restricted in its ability to buy from others. Price-related agreements are presumed to be violations. However, most non-price agreements are viewed with less suspicion by antitrust authorities because many have valid business purposes. An example of a vertical agreement that may be legal would be a manufacturer that sells goods to a wholesale distributor who in turn sells those goods to a retail store that then sells it to the public.

vertical merger A merger between two companies in the same industry where one company supplies goods to the other company. An example would be an oil company that purchases an oil-equipment manufacturer. Vertical mergers run the risk of violating U.S. antitrust laws.

vertical option spread A trading strategy that involves buying and selling either call or put options that have the same expiration date but different strike prices.

vesting The right that an employee has to receive contributions made by their employers to an employer-contributed pension plan, a 401(k) plan, or a profit-sharing plan. The federal government requires that employees must be fully vested, or be given the right, to own all of their employer's contributions after a certain time period. Usually vesting rights are given on a graduated schedule, with 20 percent of the contribution being vested each year.

Villiger, Kaspar The president of the Swiss Confederation and Finance Minister of Switzerland, as of this printing. He was elected to the Upper House of Parliament in 1989 and headed up the Swiss federal military section from 1989 to 1995.

virtual private network (VPN) A very secure network that is used to transmit sensitive and private data using the Internet as the mode of transportation. The data is encrypted. VPNs are used for a variety of purposes, including electronic commerce.

virus A destructive computer program that typically is passed around unknowingly via infected e-mail messages. Viruses cause problems for corporate networks and individuals' computers.

Voice over-IP (VoIP) Stands for *voice over Internet protocol*. By using this technology, voice information can be sent in digital form over the Internet; as a result, people can use their computers, rather than their telephones, to place phone calls. Because the price of telecom equipment such as switches and circuits has dropped significantly, the cost savings from VoIP isn't as dramatic as it was during the later stages of the telecom boom that ended in 2000. See also *IP*.

vol. See *volatility*.

volatility An extreme fluctuation in price that affects a stock, bond, or other financial instrument and is usually accompanied by unusually high trading volume. Volatility is caused by expectations of poor earnings, unexpected bad news from some other company in the industry, or external events, such as expectations of a war or political turmoil. Poor economic data or bearish comments from Federal Reserve officials also can cause volatility.

Volcker, Paul Former chairman of the board of governors of the Federal Reserve System from 1979 to 1987. While he was chairman, Volcker combated inflation by pursuing a restrictive monetary policy; a high level of unemployment and a stagnant economy made it necessary to increase monetary growth in the mid-1980s. Before serving on the Federal Reserve Board of Governors, Volcker was an undersecretary in the U.S. Treasury from 1969 to 1974 and was president of the New York Federal Reserve Bank from 1975 to 1979. After leaving the Federal Reserve Board, Volcker led a panel in 1999 that investigated the Swiss banks' handling of the accounts held by Holocaust victims. The panel was critical of the banks, but didn't suggest any changes to a settlement that had been reached a year earlier. He wrote, along with Japanese finance official Toyoo Gyohten, *Changing Fortunes: The World's Money and the Threat to American Leadership,* which was published in 1992.

volume The total number of contracts, stock shares, or other investments that are traded in a particular period. Volume figures are compiled by stock and futures exchanges each trading day, both for the overall exchange and for individual stocks and contracts. Technical analysts monitor volume just as much as they monitor price movements. If a particular price movement occurs on a day with a large trading volume, it is said to have a greater intensity than if the same price action had occurred on a day with average trading volume.

voluntary bankruptcy A bankruptcy in which the debtor petitions the court to begin a bankruptcy proceeding. This contrasts with an involuntary bankruptcy, which occurs when creditors petition the court to put the debtor into bankruptcy. Most bankruptcies are voluntary.

voting stock A share of a corporation that entitles the owner to vote on corporate resolutions, elect members of the board of directors, ratify the appointment of auditors, and vote on any other resolutions put before the shareholders. Most stocks have voting rights; however, preferred stock may not have voting rights.

VPN See *virtual private network.*

vulture fund A fund that is started by a group of investors who intend to purchase distressed assets at a fraction of their value. The assets may be businesses, debt, or real estate.

vulture investor A type of investor who obtained notoriety during the late 1980s and early 1990s by investing in businesses that were emerging from Chapter 11 bankruptcy or buying debt that was close to default. Vulture investors paid very low prices for their investment and often made a significant amount of money.

W-2 A federal tax form that is prepared by employers for employees to use in filing an income tax return. It states the total amount of wages paid during the previous year and the total amount of federal, state, and local taxes withheld, including Social Security tax. W-2s must be sent to taxpayers by the end of January. Taxpayers then send the W-2 to the IRS along with their tax return.

W-4 An Internal Revenue Service form that is filled out by employees to instruct their employers on how much tax to withhold from their paychecks. The form helps employees determine how many exemptions the employee is eligible to receive. The form also gives the employee's Social Security number.

WAC See *weighted average coupon.*

WACC See *weighted average cost of capital.*

wage-push inflation A situation where a rapid increase in workers' wages causes the rate of inflation to increase. When workers' incomes rise, they have additional money to spend. As those dollars go into the economy, the competition for goods increase and prices move upward.

Waksal, Samuel D. The former chief executive officer of biotech company ImClone Systems Inc., who pleaded guilty to criminal charges for insider trading violations.

Wall Street Literally, the financial district in downtown New York City. The name is taken from the street on which the New York Stock Exchange is located. The NYSE's address is 11 Wall Street. However, investors typically use the term to refer to the investment community's stock market and capital raising activities overall, even though much of the industry activity takes place at other stock markets and in other cities.

Walton, Sam The creator of Wal-Mart Stores Inc., which revolutionized the discount retailing business. His worldwide empire grew from one store that he opened in Rogers, Arkansas in 1962 to Wal-Mart and Sam's Club stores all over the world with $244 billion in sales in 2002. He took the novel approach of opening his stores in rural, small-town areas. Only in recent years has Wal-Mart opened stores in major metropolitan areas. Wal-Mart has stores in the United States, the United Kingdom, Mexico, Korea, and China among other countries.

WAM See *weighted average maturity.*

war chest Liquid assets set aside by a company that is planning a takeover of another company or planning its defense against an unwanted takeover. Typically, market talk may refer to an acquisition target as having a large war chest, meaning that the company will be expensive to takeover.

warrant A security issued by a company that gives the owner the right to purchase stock shares at a set price within a specific time frame. In contrast, a *perpetual warrant* has no expiration date. Sometimes warrants are given to purchasers of debt or preferred stock as an incentive to buy.

wash-sale rule A tax rule that says if stock or bond is sold and a loss is taken and then the same security is repurchased within 30 days, the sale may be considered a wash and the loss can't be immediately claimed for tax purposes. However, the disallowed amount from the wash sale can be added to the cost of the repurchased securities, which helps reduce the amount of taxable profit from a future sale.

Watson Sr., Thomas J. The founder of International Business Machines (IBM) Corporation, which was created from Computing-Tabulating-Recording Company in the 1920s. IBM built its business on business machines, particularly the keypunch, sorter, and accounting machines. Watson combined an understanding of technology with organization and planning skills. Watson demanded devotion to the business from his employees and preferred his male employees to be married, well groomed, in good physical shape, and teetotalers.

weak dollar A dollar that has relatively little purchasing power abroad and that can be exchanged only for a relatively small amount of foreign currency, such as the Japanese yen, the euro or the Canadian dollar. A weak dollar signifies that imports are increasingly expensive and that exports are inexpensive. Thus, the level of exports tends to rise while imports decline. The dollar may weaken because of government actions, or in response to declining economic conditions, large trade and budget deficits, inflation, or unattractive investment opportunities in the U.S. relative to other countries. A strong dollar, on the other hand, can be used to purchase a larger amount of other currencies and generally makes exporting more difficult.

wealth effect The tendency of consumers to spend more because they believe they are wealthier. This newfound wealth may come from stock gains during a bull market or the rising value of real estate investments. If a wealth effect becomes too pronounced, it can produce inflation. That was a fear of Federal Reserve policy makers who kept watching for signs of inflation from consumers' strong spending habits during the record run-up in the stock market in the late 1990s that peaked in 2000.

wedge A technical formation on a price chart that resembles a triangle in its shape and the amount of time it takes to form. A wedge is created when two converging trend lines come together at an apex. The wedge usually lasts more than a month but not more than three months. Typically, the wedge is slanted either upwards or downwards. The wedge slants against the current trend. A falling wedge (which looks like a flag pointing down) is considered bullish; a rising wedge is considered bearish.

weighted average cost of capital (WACC) The average cost that a firm has to pay for the capital that it borrows. It is calculated by weighting the individual interest rates paid on different amounts of borrowed funds to create an average cost of capital.

weighted average coupon (WAC) The average coupon (interest payment) in a pool of mortgages. WAC is calculated by weighting the coupon rate by the outstanding principal balance of the mortgage at the end of each month.

weighted average maturity (WAM) The average time it takes for securities in a portfolio to mature, weighted in proportion to the dollar amount that is invested in the portfolio. Weighted average maturity measures the sensitivity of fixed-income portfolios to interest rate changes. Portfolios with longer WAMs are more sensitive to changes in interest rates because the longer a bond is held, the greater the opportunity for interest rates to move up or down and affect the performance of the bonds in the portfolio. If interest rates move up, the value of a bond decreases because there are bonds in the market that now pay more interest and therefore are more attractive.

weighted average maturity date An average of the maturity dates of a portfolio's securities, weighted by the dollar amount that is invested in each maturity. The weighted average maturity date is calculated based on the weighted average maturity of the portfolio's investments on a given day. See *weighted average maturity*.

Wells notice A letter issued by the Securities and Exchange Commission to a company advising the company that the SEC is considering possible civil charges against it. The letter outlines the violations that the SEC is contemplating charging the company with and gives the company the opportunity to argue against the potential action. The SEC considers the company's response before any action is taken.

Welteke, Ernst The president of the Deutsche Bundesbank, which is Germany's central bank, as of this printing.

West African Economic and Monetary Union A monetary agreement between eight countries in Western Africa: Benin, Burkina Faso, Cote d'Ivôire, Guinea-Bissau, Mali, Niger, Senegal and Togo. The common currency of the WAEMU is the CFA franc, or *franc de la Communauté Financiére de l'Afrique*. It is issued by the Banque Centrale des Etats de l'Afrique de l'Ouest. The CFA franc has been pegged to the French franc since 1947; when France adopted the euro in 1999, the CFA was pegged to the euro. Only one devaluation has occurred during the history of the currency peg. In January 1994, the CFA was devalued to CFA 100 from CFA 50. The countries using the CFA franc have an arrangement with the French treasury to maintain their currency peg and take the sole responsibility for guaranteeing convertibility of CFA francs into euros.

West Texas Intermediate Crude Oil A popular type of crude oil that is produced in the United States. The New York Mercantile Exchange trades a contract based on West Texas Intermediate (WTI) crude oil delivered in Midland, Texas, which is the U.S. benchmark grade. WTI crude oil is a light, sweet crude oil. Prices for WTI are quoted at Cushing, Oklahoma, which is a major crude oil shipment point that has extensive pipeline connections to oil producing areas and Southwest and Gulf Coast-based refining centers.

wheat An agricultural commodity that is produced throughout the United States, as well as Canada and Australia. Wheat is used in a variety of products such as bread, baked goods, pastas, and cereals. Futures and options on wheat have been traded since 1877 on the Chicago Board of Trade. Futures and options contracts also are traded on many other futures exchanges throughout the world. Traders watch the monthly wheat crop reports produced by the U.S. Department of Agriculture because they give information about expected supply, which will directly affect prices.

when distributed A term used in the fixed-income market that indicates a buy or sell transaction can be transferred to the counter-party only after another one has occurred. See *when-issued*.

when-issued Short for *when issued*, which indicates that a security has been authorized, but not yet issued. It typically is used in the Treasury market, where there is a lag between when the new bond is announced, when it is sold, and when it is issued. The term also is used for new stocks and stocks that have split but haven't started trading yet. During this time period, the security trades with a *wi* next to it.

whisper number Unofficial corporate earnings estimates that are "whispered" among analysts and their favored investors who have private information that they had been told by the company. If the earnings per share amount is below the whisper number, but above the consensus estimate, the stock sells off, which creates volatility. However, since the Securities and Exchange Commission passed Regulation Fair Disclosure in 2000, companies are not supposed to selectively disclose material information to clients or other investors. That rule, along with the bear market that followed the Internet boom in the late 1990s, has restricted the occurrence of whisper numbers.

whistle blower An employee who publicly alleges wrongdoing at his or her company or who reports this information to appropriate government agencies.

white knight A company that comes to the defense of another company that is subject to an unwanted merger attempt. A white knight often will purchase the targeted company in order to prevent its merger with the would-be acquirer.

White, Harry Dexter The designer of the International Monetary Fund and the fixed-exchange rate system that came into existence after the end of World War II that made the dollar the center of the global financial world. White was a bureaucrat who was assigned by U.S. Treasury Secretary Henry Morgenthau to begin planning a system to keep international currencies stable after World War II ended. The fixed currency system remained in place until it was scrapped in 1971. Negotiations were held in 1944 at Bretton Woods, New Hampshire as the war was drawing to a close. A few years later White was accused by journalist Whittaker Chambers of passing secrets to Communists during World War II. The House Un-American Activities Committee, headed by California Representative Richard Nixon, held hearings. White died of a heart attack after being interrogated by the committee.

whitemail A tactic to avoid an unwanted takeover attempt in which the company that is the target sells stock to a friendly company at below-market prices. In order for the potential acquirer to prevail, the company will have to the buy additional shares of stock in order to take over the company. This will cause the purchase price

to rise. Whitemail thus makes the takeover less attractive.

white-shoe firm A top-ranked investment bank that participates only in the best capital-raising and merger deals. The term suggests an elite, upper-class firm. The term comes from the white buck shoes that were popular at Ivy League schools during the 1950s. The people typically hired by the elite investment banks were presumed to have Ivy League backgrounds.

whole life insurance A life insurance policy that combines a death benefit payment to the policyholders' beneficiary along with a savings vehicle that accumulates the policy's cash value. The cash value is determined by the return that the insurance company earns on its investments. The cash accumulates on a tax-deferred basis. Other types of whole life insurance that give the insured more options for selecting the underlying investment options are *universal life policies,* which typically invest in fixed-income securities and *variable life insurance,* which includes the options of investment in stock, bond, and money market accounts. Also called *permanent life insurance.*

wholesale banking Providing banking services to large corporations and institutions. Services are not provided to individuals or small businesses.

wholesale trade A monthly statistical report produced by the Bureau of the Census that measures companies' inventory levels, which is an indicator of the health of business conditions and future manufacturing orders. The survey is conducted by mail and is sent to about 7,100 wholesale firms. The companies report the dollar values of merchant wholesale sales, end-of-month inventories, and how they value their inventories. The data is released six weeks after the end of the month referenced. Firms are grouped by merchant wholesale sales, inventories, and their primary type of business. The data also measures any changes in the inventories-to-sales ratio.

wholly-owned subsidiary A subsidiary whose stock is owned by its parent company or another of the parent's wholly-owned subsidiaries.

widget A generic, often theoretical, item, synonymous with *product*. The term often is used in hypothetical business examples, for example, "Say a company makes widgets."

widow–and–orphan stock Very safe, conservative stock that pays a high dividend. Historically, utility companies were considered widow-and-orphan stocks. However, since the electricity market deregulated in the mid-1990s and utilities began trading electricity capacity, those companies aren't necessarily safe any longer.

Wi-Fi See *wireless fidelity*.

wildcat drilling An exploratory drilling program to locate natural gas or crude oil reserves in an area where no other reserves are known to exist. Wildcat drilling is risky and may result in a significant cost with no oil being found. A less risky drilling program is a *development drilling* program, which occurs in an area where reserves are known to exist.

will A legal document that carries out the last wishes of a deceased person. The will outlines how the deceased person's assets should be distributed and appoints *executors* to carry out those wishes. Wills must be signed and witnessed. See also *estate* and *estate planning*.

Williams Act Legislation passed in 1968 in response to a wave of unannounced takeovers that required companies planning a merger to file documents with the Securities and Exchange Commission. The documents outline the offer's terms, and give information about the bidder, as well as

detailing the plans it has for the company. The documents must be filed within 10 days of any company or person acquiring 5 percent or more of another company. This information is filed using a variety SEC forms. *Schedule 13-D* is a general statement of acquisition of beneficial ownership; *Schedule 13E-3* lists transactions that are planned that will turn a public company into a private company by certain issuers; and *Schedule TO-I* is the tender offer statement by the issuer. There also are a variety of other schedules that may be appropriate to file with the SEC.

Wilshire 5000 Equity Index A market capitalization weighted index that includes all U.S.-headquartered companies, which number about 6,800 as of this printing. It measures the performance of all U.S.-headquartered equity securities with readily available price data.

Wilson, Joseph C. The power behind the development of the copier and Xerox Corporation. Wilson was looking for a product to ensure the success of Haloid Company of Rochester, New York, which made sensitized paper used in photography and copying. An employee saw an article written by Chester Carlson that described the photoelectric copying process. Wilson invested $10,000 and negotiated for limited commercial rights to develop the new copying process. Haloid later raised $3.5 million to make the first-generation copying machines better. The Model 914 was created in 1959, and later Haloid became known as Xerox Corporation.

windfall profit A profit that occurs through no action of a company but is produced by an external event. For instance, oil companies reap windfall profits when oil prices rise due to a system-wide shortage. Electric utilities and traders that have spare generating capacity to sell also may reap windfall profits if prices rise substantially because higher-than-normal temperatures lead to a higher demand for air conditioning, for example.

windfall profits tax   A tax passed by Congress on sudden profit windfalls. The windfall tax was directed at energy companies that had benefited from the sharp rise in oil prices during the OPEC oil embargo of the early 1970s.

window dressing   A portfolio that looks better than it is. For instance, a trader may sell his or her losing positions at the end of the quarter or fiscal year to make the portfolio look more positive and thus impress investors. Positions with a profit also may be sold in order to record a profit.

Winnipeg Commodity Exchange Inc. Canada's only agricultural futures and options exchange, in operation since 1887. It trades futures and options contracts on canola, canola meal, flaxseed, domestic feed wheat, and domestic feed barley. Canola is its most actively traded commodity and the exchange operates the only futures market for flaxseed.

wire house   A brokerage house whose offices are linked by a communication network to enable prices, information, orders and research to be distributed to all the offices. The term is relatively out of date now, but before computers became widely used, only the largest firms had access to the state-of-the-art equipment that interconnected their offices. As used today, wire house generally means one of the biggest brokerage firms.

wire transfer   The process of electronically transferring money. Typically, the term suggests transfers of large amounts of money. However, wire transfer has evolved to include electronic funds transfer (EFT), which is the transfer of money using any method that is not paper based. EFT includes ATM transactions or any transaction that using the telephone or other electronic means.

wireless fidelity   A wireless data Internet technology that lets people connect to the Internet at high speeds through their personal or hand-held devices without needing to use cables. Wi-Fi also is known by its technical name *802.11b*. A newer version of Wi-Fi is called 54G, which gets its name because it can transfer data at speeds up to 54 megabits per second, which is almost five times the speed that the first Wi-Fi operated at. Another competing system that provides similar features is Bluetooth, but it does not work as well at long distances.

wireline   Telephone service that is delivered through telephone lines. Wireline service contrasts with wireless service, which doesn't require that the phone be connected to a telephone line.

Wolfensohn, James D.   President of the World Bank, as of this printing. Wolfensohn is the World Bank Group's ninth president since 1946 and became president on June 1, 1995. He was reappointed to a second, five-year term. Before becoming president, he was an investment banker.

won   The currency unit of South Korea, comprised of 100 chon, and North Korea, comprised of 100 chon.

Woolworth, F.W.   The original retail discounter, F.W. Woolworth started five- and ten-cent stores bearing his name. He introduced fixed-price merchandise, which ushered out the era of customers haggling over prices with the store clerks. He opened up identical stores around the country, which created chain-store retailing.

Workers' Compensation Insurance   A federally run insurance program that pays benefits to injured workers hurt on the job.

Benefits are paid for disability, injury, or death that results from a workplace injury.

working capital The amount by which current assets exceed current liabilities. Working capital is used to fund the operations of the company and pays for inventory purchases, as well as for goods used in the production process; working capital also provides money to expand sales. A shortage of working capital can lead to a company's bankruptcy. Working capital is a good measure of liquidity because it looks at debts that must be paid within one year or less.

working control The possession of 51 percent or more of a company's voting stock. Control of a large corporation can occur when there is less than 50 percent ownership, which is called *effective control.*

work-in-process An interim account that is used in calculating inventory levels. Works-in-process accounts include goods that are in the middle of being produced for sale.

workout A solution for a situation in which a company has a loan it can't pay or is about to file for bankruptcy. Experts in workouts, such as bankruptcy attorneys and restructuring companies, attempt to come up with a solution in a workout.

World Bank A non-profit group, owned by its member countries, that provides loans, technical assistance, and policy advice to more than 100 developing countries. Aid from the World Bank helps these countries improve their living standards by fighting poverty, improving health care and education, and protecting the environment. During its fiscal year 2002, more than $19.5 billion dollars in loans was provided to countries. The World Bank was founded in 1944 and is owned by more than 184 member countries that are represented by a

Board of Governors and a Washington-based Board of Directors. The president of the bank is typically a citizen of the largest shareholder, the United States. The president is elected for a five-year renewable term. The president runs meetings of the Board of Executive Directors and is responsible for the overall management of the World Bank.

The World Bank is actually comprised of five distinct institutions.

The International Development Association helps the world's poorest countries reduce poverty by giving them *credits,* which are loans at zero interest that have a 10-year grace period and maturities of 35 to 40 years.

The International Bank for Reconstruction and Development (IBRD) provides loans and development assistance to middle-income countries and poorer countries that are creditworthy. Typically, IBRD is the name that is most commonly used in Europe, instead of saying *World Bank.*

The International Finance Corporation (IFC) promotes private sector investment, either foreign or domestic, in developing member countries. Its investment and advisory activities are intended to reduce poverty and improve people's lives in an environmentally and socially responsible manner.

The Multilateral Investment Guarantee Agency (MIGA) promotes growth in emerging economies by promoting foreign direct investment. To do this, it offers guarantees to investors and lenders in order to protect them against political risk.

The International Centre for Settlement of Investment Disputes (ICSID) provides methods to resolve investment disputes between foreign investors and their host countries through arbitration or conciliation.

In 1996, the World Bank and the International Monetary Fund (IMF) launched the Heavily Indebted Poor Countries

(HIPC) Initiative to create a framework for all creditors, including multilateral creditors, to provide debt relief to the world's poorest and most heavily indebted countries, and thereby reduce the constraint on economic growth and poverty reduction imposed by the debt build-up in these countries.

The World Bank holds its annual meeting during the fall, at the same time the International Monetary Fund holds its annual meeting. Traditionally, the annual meetings are held in Washington, D.C. during two years out of three. In the third year the meeting is held in a different country. About 10,000 people attend the meetings, including about 3,500 members of delegations from the member countries of the Bank and the IMF, roughly 1,000 representatives of the media, and more than 5,000 visitors and special guests drawn primarily from private business, the banking community and non-governmental organizations (NGOs). A similar, but smaller meeting also is held in the spring.

World Trade Organization (WTO) A global international organization that establishes trade rules and resolves trade disputes. The WTO's rules have been developed through negotiations with member countries. The formation of the WTO came from the Uruguay Round of negotiations held from 1986 to 1994. That round made a major revision to the General Agreement on Tariffs and Trade (GATT), which was created in 1947 to promote trade by reducing trade barriers.

The WTO's agreements form the basis of the multilateral trading system and provide the legal ground rules for international trade. Those rules are legal contracts and bind governments to adhering to agreed-upon trade policies. The WTO also has a dispute resolution process that countries can use to resolve problems, instead of entering into a political or military conflict.

The WTO is headquartered in Geneva, Switzerland and has over 500 employees. It has more than 140 member countries, whose trade accounts for 97% of world trade volume. About 30 other countries are negotiating to become members. The WTO's top-level decision-making body is the Ministerial Conference, which meets at least once every two years. Decisions are made by the entire membership by consensus. Although a majority vote is also possible, it has never been used in the WTO and was rarely used under GATT. The WTO's agreements are ratified by each country's parliament or congress.

Wozniak, Steven The creator of the Apple Computer, along with Steve Jobs. See also *Jobs, Steven.*

wrap account A type of investment account that was created in the early 1980s that offers private investment management at a lower cost. Wrap accounts combine individual account holders' money into one account, thus lowering the total fee paid. Typically, the minimum amount required to obtain a wrap account is $100,000. Wrap accounts were created as a way to get around conflicts of interest. With private accounts, the account holder's broker would rely on a professional money manager to place trades. The broker earned about 3 percent on the funds managed per year as did the money manager. That meant that returns had to be 6 percent for the account just to break even.

wrap fee A comprehensive fee, including all commissions, charged to manage all of a client's investments, even if they are placed with different money managers. A wrap fee is based upon the amount of assets under management. Accounts with wrap fees typically are available only to people with at least $100,000 to invest.

wraparound A financing device that allows an existing loan to be refinanced and new money to be loaned at an interest rate that falls between the old interest rate and current market rates. The lender *wraps* (or combines) the remainder of the old loan with the new loan at the new interest rate.

wraparound loan A financing device that permits an existing loan to be refinanced and new money to be advanced at an interest rate that is between the rate charged on the old loan and the current market interest rate. The creditor combines, or *wraps,* the remainder of the old loan with the new loan at the intermediate rate. A wraparound loan also may be called a *wraparound mortgage*, if a new mortgage is placed in a secondary position to the original mortgage with the new mortgage including the unpaid balance of the first mortgage. The buyer of the property assumes the remaining debt of the seller's current mortgage.

wraparound mortgage See *wraparound loan*.

Wright, Wilbur and Orville Pioneers in the aviation industry, they constructed the first airplane, which remained aloft for less than a minute in Kitty Hawk, North Carolina in 1903. They patented their invention, built improved planes, and continued studying flight techniques. Prior to entering aviation, they owned a bicycle shop in Dayton, Ohio.

write-off To charge an expense or a loss against an asset, thereby reducing its value as listed on the company's balance sheet. Write-offs are taken for the depreciation of a physical asset or the amortization of a non-physical asset. A common write-off is for accounts receivable to reflect the fact that some customers aren't likely to pay their bills. Write-offs are charged against net income during the period they are incurred.

write-up The act of an investment holder increasing the value of an investment in response to its rising market value. It contrasts with a *write-down,* in which the value of an investment is decreased to reflect worsening market conditions or another reasons for decreasing value.

WTO See *World Trade Organization*.

Xbox A gaming console introduced by Microsoft Corporation in November 2002. Xbox lets players talk to each other over the Internet.

Y2K Shorthand for the year 2000, it came to mean specifically the potential difficulty that corporate, governmental, and financial computer systems might have encountered if programming changes were not made. Before 2000, many computer programs allocated space for only two digits in the year instead of four (98 meant 1998, 99 meant 1999, and so on). Once Jan. 1, 2000 arrived, computers would have read the year as 1900 and potentially wiped out data or locked-up computer systems.

Yankee Bank A foreign bank with operations in the U.S. Bonds issued by these banks are called *Yankee bonds.*

Yankee Bond A bond issued in dollars in the U.S. by a non-U.S. company or bank. A Yankee bond is payable in dollars and is registered with the Securities and Exchange Commission.

Yankee CD A dollar certificate of deposit that is issued in the U.S. by a branch of a bank that is headquartered outside of the U.S.

yard In the foreign exchange market, one billion currency units.

year-end dividend An additional dividend beyond the regular, quarterly dividend that is given to stockholders based on the company's profit level at year end. In good years, the dividend may be large, and in bad years, no year-end dividend is paid out. The year-end dividend is discretionary, and many companies don't pay it.

year-over-year A comparison between the current period's performance and the performance of the same period a year earlier.

yen The currency of the Japanese government. While prices fluctuate, as of this printing it takes about 110 to 130 yen to purchase one U.S. dollar. The symbol is ¥, or is written as JPY.

yield The return that is earned on an investment. For example, a bond that pays 7 percent interest yields 7 percent, which also may be called the *nominal yield. Current yield,* however, gives the actual interest rate that will be earned. To obtain current yield, divide the amount of interest earned annually, using the bond's interest rate, by the purchase price. In contrast, the *yield to maturity* is the effective interest rate that is earned if the bond is held until it matures.

yield chaser A person who buys financial investments only because they offer high yields or interest rates. A yield chaser often doesn't determine whether the investment is a safe or prudent one, which may prove to be a costly mistake in the long run, as the yield may drop drastically.

yield curve The visual representation of interest rates on a graph, shown for various points in time. For instance, the Treasury yield curve begins with 3-month bills and has points representing 6-month bills, 52-week bills, 2-, 3-, 5-, 10-year notes, and the 30-year bond. The yield curve often refers to the spread between the 3-month Treasury bill and the 30-year Treasury bond. Typically short-term interest rates are lower than long-term interest rates, creating a positive yield curve that is upwardly sloping. However, if short-term rates are higher, that creates an inverted, or negative, yield curve. By looking at the yield curve, it is possible to see what direction interest rates are heading.

yield spread The difference in the yield between different issues of securities. There is a yield spread between the U.S. Treasury's 2-year notes and the 30-year bond. Yield spread also exists between corporate and

Treasury debt. For instance, the yield spread between a 10-year corporate bond and the 10-year Treasury note could be 75 basis points. This means that the corporate bond pays 0.75 percent more than the Treasury note.

yield spread analysis   An analysis that compares the liquidity, creditworthiness, and maturity of a fixed-income security to a benchmark, which is typically U.S. Treasury securities. The difference in the yield between the two is expressed as a *yield spread*.

yield-to-call   The return that a bond-holder will receive if the bond is redeemed at the first possible call date. In a yield-to-call situation, an investor may earn several year's interest payments instead of the antic-ipated 5- or 10-year's interest. The lower interest earned is divided by the par value of the bond, which typically causes the yield to be much lower than if the bond was held to maturity. The yield-to-call cal-culation represents the worst-case scenario for a bond holder. Also called *yield-to-worst*.

yield-to-maturity   The effective interest rate that a bondholder will earn if the bond is held until maturity. Yield-to-maturity takes into account the bond's purchase price, its current market price, the *coupon rate,* which is the interest rate that the bond pays, and the amount of time remaining until the bond matures. Yield-to-maturity is the most accurate representation of how much a bond will actually receive if the bond is held until maturity.

yield-to-worst   A comparison of yields on a bond that would be earned using the yield-to-maturity and the yield-to-call dates. The lowest of those two yields is the *yield-to-worst* scenario. If a bond is called early, its yield will fall substantially, because the bondholder missed out on interest pay-ments that ordinarily would have been received.

YoY   See *year-over-year.*

yo-yo stock   A stock whose price goes up and down, much in the manner of a yo-yo, in other words, a very volatile stock.

yuan   The currency unit of China, com-prised of 10 jiao. Also called *renminbi.*

zero-based budgeting A budgeting system that sets all budgets to zero and makes departments or government agencies justify all of their expenditures. Money is then allocated to the various departments or agencies based on what is currently needed, not the previous year's budget.

zero-beta portfolio A portfolio created to mimic a risk-free asset. Thus it has a *beta* (risk) of zero. The Standard & Poor's 500 Stock Index has a beta coefficient of 1. A beta above 1 is more volatile than the market while a beta below 1 is less volatile.

zero-coupon bond A bond that pays no interest until it matures. It is priced at a deep discount to make up for the lack of income. These bonds are commonly called *zeros*.

zero-downtick A security sale that occurs at the same time as another sale of the same security but at a lower price. For instance, if a stock sells at $35 and then $34.50 and the next sale is still $34.50, it is considered to be made at a zero-downtick. Short sales can't occur on zero-downticks. Also called *zero-minus tick*.

zero-plus tick A Securities and Exchange Commission rule that says that a short sale (a sale of stock that the trader doesn't own) can occur only if the last transaction price was unchanged from the transaction price directly before it, but higher than the last different sale price.

zeros See *zero-coupon bond*.

zero-sum game A trading situation in which profits are limited and wealth is merely shifted around. The futures and options markets are zero-sum games because for every trader who makes money, another trader loses money.

zero-uptick A security purchase that occurs at the same time as a previous sale but at a higher price. For example, if a stock sells at $40 and then $40.50 and the next sale is still at $40.50, it is considered to be made at a zero-uptick. Short sales must occur on zero-upticks due to Security and Exchange Commission rules that allow investors to sell short only on a zero-uptick. The purpose of the rule is to prevent a group of linked traders from driving down a stock by heavy short selling and then buying back the shares to reap a large profit. Also called *zero-plus tick*.

zeta A pricing model for derivatives that measures what effect volatility has on a portfolio. *Derivatives* are investments whose value is based on the performance of an underlying asset. Examples of derivatives are futures or options contracts.

zloty The currency unit of Poland, comprised of 100 groszy.

Zoellick, Robert B. The U.S. Trade Representative, as of spring 2003, appointed by President George W. Bush in 2001.

zoning laws Local laws that govern what property owners can do with their buildings and lands. A city, town, or municipality deems specific areas for residential, industrial, commercial, recreational, or agricultural use, or sometimes a combination of uses through zoning regulations. While *zoning variances,* which allow the land to be used for another purpose than what the law specifies, can be obtained, the process can be difficult and may not be successful.

Z-score model A model that is used to predict the likelihood of a company going into bankruptcy. The model was developed in 1968 by Edward Altman. A score below 2.675 signals bankruptcy. He developed a more refined model in 1977 that he called the ZETA model, whose characteristics are proprietary.

Chart Shapes

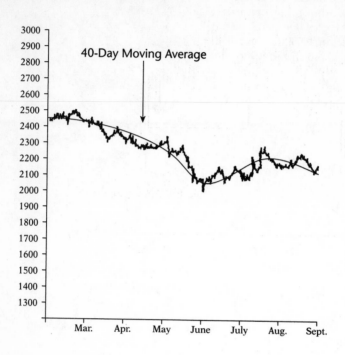

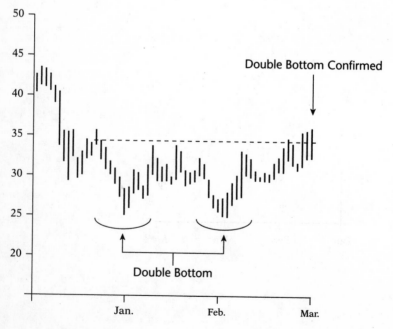

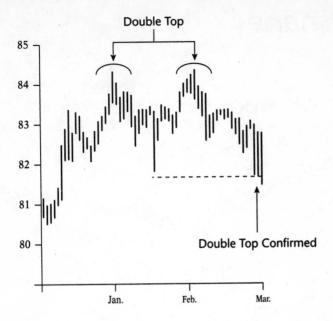

Double Top

Double Top Confirmed

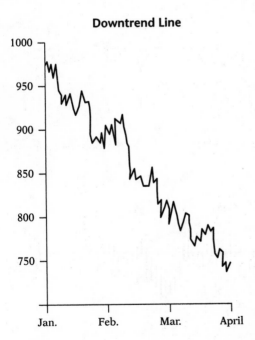

Downtrend Line

Flag

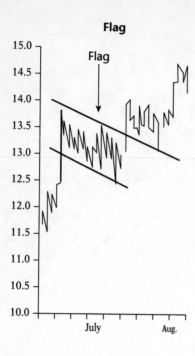

Gaps

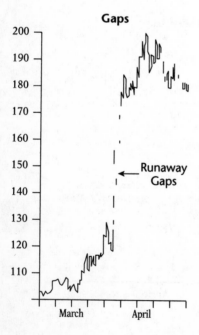

Gaps

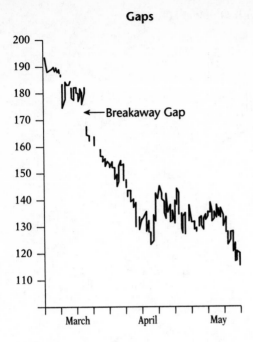

Breakaway Gap

Head & Shoulders (Bottom)

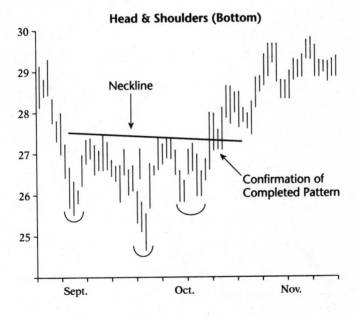

Neckline

Confirmation of
Completed Pattern

Head & Shoulders (Top)

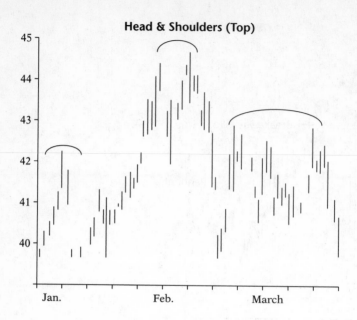

Inverted Yield Curve

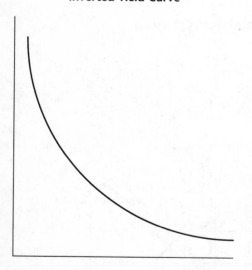

Pennant

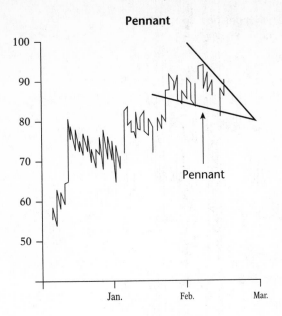

Point-and-Figure Chart

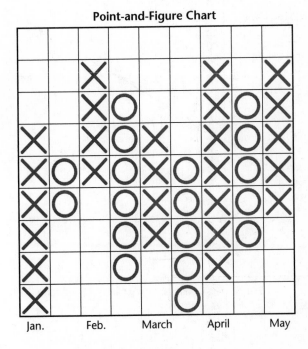

Positive Yield Curve

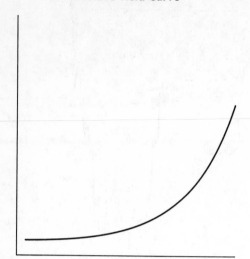

Regression Analysis

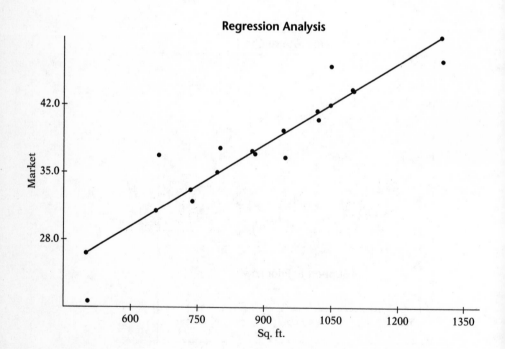

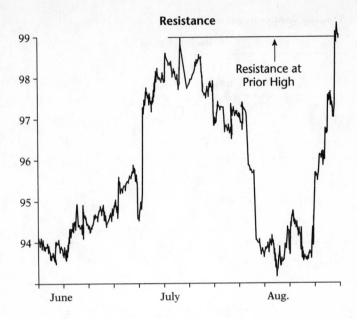

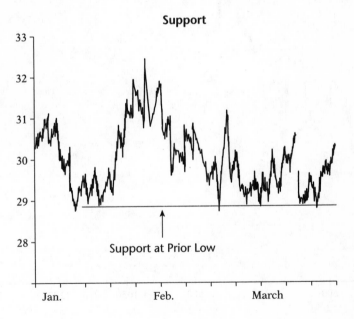

Trading Range Breakout

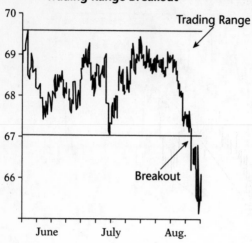

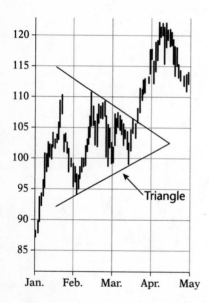

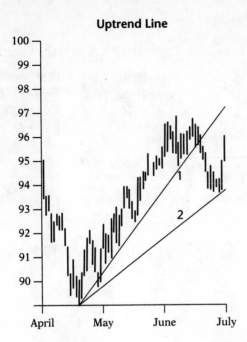

We define your world™

Webster's New World® Dictionaries and Thesauri

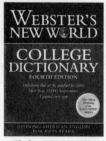

Cloth • 0-02-863118-8
$24.99 US/$35.99 CAN

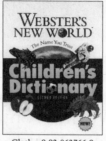

Cloth • 0-02-862766-0
$17.95 US/$25.95 CAN

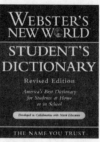

Cloth • 0-02-861319-8
$19.95 US/$29.95 CAN

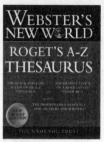

Cloth • 0-02-863122-6
$21.99 US/$31.00 CAN

Paper • 0-02-862381-9
$12.99 US/$18.95 CAN

Paper • 0-7645-6338-6
$9.99 US/$14.99 CAN

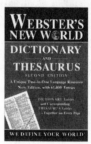

Cloth • 0-7645-6339-4
$19.99 US/$29.99 CAN

Webster's New World® Pocket Editions

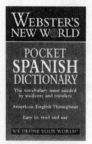

Paper • 0-7645-6543-5
$6.99 US/$10.99 CAN

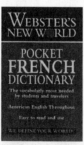

Paper • 0-7645-6544-3
$6.99 US/$10.99 CAN

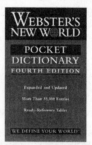

Paper • 0-7645-6147-2
$5.99 US/$8.99 CAN

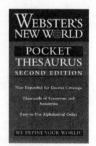

Paper • 0-7645-6148-0
$5.99 US/$8.99 CAN

Paper • 0-02-863486-1
$6.99 US/$10.95 CAN

Paper • 0-02-862157-3
$6.99 US/$7.95 CAN

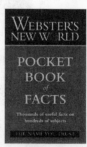

Paper • 0-02-862750-4
$6.95 US/$7.95 CAN

Webster's New World® Handbook Editions

LETTER WRITING HANDBOOK

Paper • 0-7645-2524-7
5.99 US/$25.99 CAN

AMERICAN IDIOMS HANDBOOK

Paper • 0-7645-2477-1
$16.99 US/$24.99 CAN

BUSINESS WRITING HANDBOOK

Paper • 0-7645-6403-X
$19.99 US/$29.99 CAN

ENGLISH GRAMMAR HANDBOOK
The Ultimate Desk Reference

Paper • 0-7645-6488-9
$16.99 US/$25.99 CAN

STUDENT WRITING HANDBOOK

Paper • 0-7645-6125-1
$16.99 US/$25.99 CAN

Webster's New World® Topic and General Reference Dictionaries

DICTIONARY of MUSIC

Paper • 0-02-862747-4
$16.95 US/$23.95 CAN

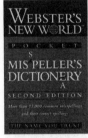

POCKET MISSPELLER'S DICTIONARY
SECOND EDITION

Paper • 0-02-861720-7
$5.99 US/$7.95 CAN

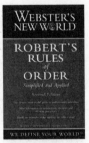

ROBERT'S RULES of ORDER
Simplified and Applied

Paper • 0-7645-6399-8
$10.99 US/$16.99 CAN

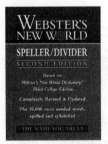

SPELLER/DIVIDER
SECOND EDITION

Paper • 0-13-953654-X
$8.99 US/$12.00 CAN

COMPACT DESK DICTIONARY AND STYLE GUIDE
Second Edition

Paper • 0-7645-6337-8
$12.99 US/$19.99 CAN

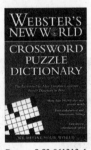

CROSSWORD PUZZLE DICTIONARY

Paper • 0-02-861212-4
$12.95 US/$17.95 CAN

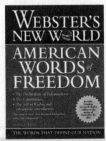

AMERICAN WORDS of FREEDOM

Paper • 0-7645-6638-5
$9.99 US/$14.99 CAN

VOCABULARY of SUCCESS

Paper • 0-02-862328-2
$9.99 US/$12.95 CAN

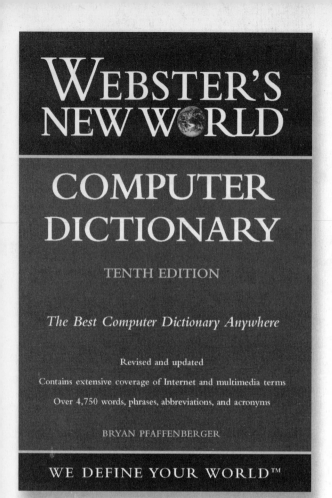

WEBSTER'S NEW WORLD™

COMPUTER DICTIONARY

TENTH EDITION

The Best Computer Dictionary Anywhere

Revised and updated

Contains extensive coverage of Internet and multimedia terms

Over 4,750 words, phrases, abbreviations, and acronyms

BRYAN PFAFFENBERGER

WE DEFINE YOUR WORLD™

- Totally revised and update
- User-friendly and comprehensive
- Ideal for experienced user and novices alike
- With detailed background information for more complete understanding

For professionals and novices alike, *Webster's New World Computer Dictionary, 10th Edition* is one of the most useful computer references money can buy. With clear and concise definitions for more than 4,750 up-to-date terms, you'll find current coverage of the latest standards and protocols in storage, memory, peripherals, and more—plus updated and expanded information on computer security, legislation, and computer and Internet technology. Cross-referencing throughout directs you effortlessly t related terms and concepts that help you understand more about a given subject and put it into a larger context. From using e-mail and going on the Internet to buying or upgrading a computer to boning up on terminology fc a computer industry job, this invaluable resource gives you instant flip-and find access to the information you need—from A (applet) to Z (zip drive).

Paper • 0-7645-2478-X • $16.99 US/$25.99 CAN

- **Information on diseases, treatments, and medicines**
- **Appendices on vitamins and frequently used anatomical terms**
- **Listings of abbreviations used on prescriptions**
- **Listings of health and medical organizations, groups, and associations**
- **Coverage of topics ranging from pediatrics to pathology**

bster's New World Medical Dictionary, 2nd Edition will help you
ke sense of confusing medical jargon, prepare for a doctor visit, or
arch treatment options. This fully up-to-date reference was created
ugh a unique partnership with MedicineNet.com and draws on the
ertise of more than 70 physicians at this popular and reliable health
b site. With over 500 medical terms new to this edition and expanded
erage of new developments in technology and pharmaceuticals, it's
re comprehensive than ever.

er with CD-ROM • 0-7645-2461-5 • $14.99 US/$22.99 CAN

EBSTER'S NEW WORLD™
An Imprint of ⊛**WILEY**
Now you know.